# FRANÇOIS BOUCHER

# FRANÇOIS

The Metropolitan Museum of Art, New York
February 17–May 4, 1986

The Detroit Institute of Arts, Detroit
May 27–August 17, 1986

Réunion des Musées Nationaux, Grand Palais, Paris
September 19, 1986–January 5, 1987

# BOUCHER

## 1703 - 1770

The Metropolitan Museum of Art, New York

The exhibition has been made possible, in part, by the National Endowment for the Arts. In Detroit support was received from the Founders Society Detroit Institute of Arts, the City of Detroit, and the State of Michigan. In New York the exhibition was sponsored by The Real Estate Council of The Metropolitan Museum of Art.

This publication was issued in connection with the exhibition *François Boucher* held at The Metropolitan Museum of Art, New York, February 17, 1986, to May 4, 1986; The Detroit Institute of Arts, May 27, 1986, to August 17, 1986; and the Réunion des Musées Nationaux, Grand Palais, Paris, September 19, 1986, to January 5, 1987.

Published by The Metropolitan Museum of Art, New York
Bradford D. Kelleher, Publisher
John P. O'Neill, Editor in Chief
Katharine Baetjer, Project Coordinator
Margaret Aspinwall, Editor, with the assistance of
Zachary R. Leonard, Ann Lucke, and Jean Wagner
Bruce Campbell, Designer

Translation of "The Mysterious Beginnings of the Young Boucher" from the French by John Shepley; translation of "The Influence of Boucher's Art on the Production of the Vincennes-Sèvres Porcelain Manufactory" from the French by Richard Miller.

Type set by Trufont, Hicksville, New York.
Printed in France by Imprimerie Blanchard, Le Plessis-Robinson.

Library of Congress Cataloging-in-Publication Data
Boucher, François, 1703-1770.
    François, Boucher, 1703-1770: the Metropolitan Museum of Art, New York, February 17, 1986–May 4, 1986, the Detroit Institute of Arts, May 27, 1986–August 17, 1986, Réunion des musées nationaux, Paris, September 19, 1986–January 5, 1987.

    Exhibition catalog.
    Bibliography
    1. Boucher, François, 1703-1770–Exhibitions. I. Metropolitan Museum of Art (New York, N.Y.) II. Detroit Institute of Arts. III. Reunion des musées nationaux (France) IV. Title.
N6853.B58A4 1986     709'.2'4     85-25956
ISBN 0-8109-0743-7 (Abrams)

Front cover/jacket: François Boucher, *The Toilet of Venus* (cat. 60), detail.
Title page: François Boucher, *The Sacrifice of Noah* (cat. 11).

All photography provided by the institutions cited, with the exception of the following:
Jörg P. Anders, fig. 7; Archives Nationales, Paris, cat. 30, 31, fig. 129; Art Resource, cat. 8, 25, 29, 32, 47, 63, figs. 53, 102, 206; Bibliothèque Nationale, Paris, figs. 10, 14, 22, 23, 31, 36, 42, 46, 75, 78, 80, 105, 107, 109, 115, 130, 135, 136, 141, 181; British Museum, London, figs. 100, 106, 125, 167; Maciej Bronarski/ Zamek Krolewski, figs. 65, 66; Caisse Nationale des Monuments et des Sites, Paris, cat. 77; Mr. Choffet, cat. 7; Prudence Cuming Association, Ltd., London, figs. 40, 47, 48; Ursula Edelmann, fig. 166; Marc Jeanneteau, fig. 28; Bruce C. Jones, fig. 77; Sidney Liswood, cat. 2; Newberry, fig. 43; Photo, Inc., cat. 69; Photographie Bulloz, cat. 18, 25, 36, 49, 81, figs. 12, 13, 29, 112, 128, 139; Photographie Giraudon, cat. 8, 21, 32, 47, 63, figs. 53, 93, 102, 172, 174, 187; Eric Pollitzer, figs. 2, 3; Elton Schnellbacher, fig. 120; Walter Steinkopf, fig. 16; Studio André Gray, cat. 37; Studio Zoom, cat. 19; Malcolm Varon, cat. 60 (cover); Robert Wallace, cat. 73; Dorothea Zwicker, fig. 86.

# Contents

Scientific Committee For The Exhibition

Philippe de Montebello
Director, The Metropolitan Museum of Art, New York

Alastair Laing

Pierre Rosenberg
Conservateur en chef, Département des Peintures,
Musée du Louvre, Paris

J. Patrice Marandel
Curator, European Paintings,
The Detroit Institute of Arts, Detroit

# Foreword

It is not by coincidence that, for the past decade, the achievements of the great French painters of the eighteenth century have been the subject of monographic exhibitions and of broader surveys on both sides of the Atlantic. A concerted effort on the part of our museums has allowed an ever-growing public to consider in depth the careers of a Largillierre or a Watteau, of a Chardin or an Oudry, to grasp the variety of genres and styles of the painters of the Age of Louis XIV and of Louis XV or to witness the radical changes which affected the artists in the later part of the century, with David as their most genial leader.

The exhibition we are presenting is of particular importance in that François Boucher, more than any other artist of his time, has epitomized *le goût français*. Longevity of career and industry made him the most diverse and productive artist of his generation. The reproductions or interpretations of his work in other media, tapestries and porcelain in particular—an aspect of his activity we have found essential to represent— have contributed to the spreading of a style which, until the neoclassic upheaval, was the norm throughout Europe.

To fully understand the fortune of the artist, it is necessary to consider his later years: First Painter to the King, in control of Royal manufactories, unmoved by the criticisms of a Diderot, the aging artist may have represented to many not only the ultimate stronghold of establishment but also the exponent of an archaic, even despised, style from which, insensitive perhaps to the novelty of a younger generation, he never departed. Yet that style forced the admiration of the staunchest of the radicals and made David, his one-time pupil, exclaim: "N'est pas Boucher qui veut!"

It is paradoxical that the painterly qualities of his work, his sheer enjoyment and mastery of the material texture of paint, and the brilliance of his colors were not "rediscovered" by those nineteenth-century artists who sought a greater freedom of expression. Perhaps Boucher's choice of subject matter, the immaterial world of gods and shepherds, stood between them and the paintings. Boucher's view of nature was subtle and he was one of the finest landscape painters of the century, both in the early landscapes executed during or shortly after his trip to Italy and in the background of many of his mythological compositions. Yet neither the Romantics nor the Impressionists were able to look at Boucher with an unprejudiced eye. Among the latter, only Berthe Morisot is known to have copied his work at the Louvre. Boucher's true rehabilitation began with the brothers Goncourt. Their studies of the French painters of the eighteenth century justly led them to rank Boucher among the greatest. Although their judgment made a strong imprint upon later scholarly research, it generally failed to change the opinion of the larger public toward a painter who, by then widely stereotyped as the inventor of saccharine images, was seldom considered for his real contribution to art.

Our exhibition proposes to be a true rehabilitation: that of a painter who in his time and country was considered to be the greatest, and that of critics, like the Goncourt who, counter to prevalent taste, nonetheless recognized his genius.

This exhibition is the occasion for our three museums to cooperate once again. Initiated by J. Patrice Marandel, Curator of European Painting at the Detroit Institute of Arts, the exhibition was brought into existence by the indefatigable support of the staffs of the three museums, in particular of the Metropolitan Museum and the Réunion des Musées Nationaux. Mr. Alastair Laing was contracted by the participating institutions to research the works in the exhibition and to write the major part of the catalogue.

It is always a pleasure to thank those who have made the exhibition possible. Its presentation is made possible by grants from the National Endowment for the Arts, a Federal Agency, and the Founders Society Detroit Institute of Arts, the State of Michigan, and the City of Detroit. We are extremely grateful to all collectors and custodians of public collections who have consented to part with works that grace their homes or are a vital part of their galleries.

Philippe de Montebello, *Director*
*The Metropolitan Museum of Art*

Samuel Sachs II, *Director*
*The Detroit Institute of Arts*

Hubert Landais
*Directeur des Musées de France*

8

# Preface and Acknowledgments

For an artist of his importance, Boucher has been curiously ill served by posterity. There is still no catalogue raisonné of his work as either a painter or a draftsman, and there has been no properly representative exhibition devoted to him.

The monographs of André Michel and Pierre de Nolhac follow the tradition set by the Goncourt brothers' pioneering essay (itself still admirable), in yoking catalogues of the artist's work (in the cases of Michel and de Nolhac, the labors of other hands, and drawn primarily from the catalogues of past sales) to unrelated texts. The two volumes produced by Alexandre Ananoff in collaboration with Daniel Wildenstein in 1976, though invaluable as a compilation of documents, illustrations, and cullings from the available literature and sales and museum catalogues, are virtually innocent of authorial comment that might justify either the corpus of works presented or the chronology adopted for them.

The exhibition catalogued in 1932 by Charles Sterling on behalf of the Fondation Foch, while assembling more works by Boucher in all the media that he worked in or was translated into than any before or since, was as unsystematic as the organization of its catalogue into division by subject matter would suggest. What is more—and of crucial disservice to us now—the catalogue is virtually devoid of illustrations. The exhibition mounted by the Galerie Cailleux in 1964 was choice in its selection and a remarkable display by any standards for a private institution to have put on, but it was necessarily composed almost exclusively of loans from French collectors and institutions. The bicentenary of Boucher's death in 1970—nowadays normally the almost ritual pretext for a commemorative exhibition—was saluted by nothing more extensive than exhibitions by the Louvre and the Russian museums of their own holdings. In 1973 there was a pioneering attempt to mount a systematic display of Boucher's drawings, by Regina Shoolman Slatkin in Washington and Chicago, but again, as the title makes clear, it was drawn exclusively from North American collections. Finally, in 1980, Wildenstein in New York mounted an exhibition devoted to Boucher of which a remarkable proportion of the contents was drawn from stock or from the collections of its clients in the United States, as the prelude to a much larger exhibition (swollen by loans from, above all, French museums) held in 1982 in Tokyo and Kumamoto. The catalogue is admirably bilingual in Japanese and English, and almost every exhibit is well illustrated in color, but Japan is regrettably remote from both the country in which Boucher was born and worked and from the one in which perhaps the majority of his works is now to be found, few of whose inhabitants consequently saw it.

Such a preamble might suggest that we regard the exhibition now presented as making up for the limited scope or deficiencies of all its predecessors. We are fully aware that it does not—and cannot—do any such thing. Rather the reverse, since serious study of Boucher has yet to begin, with a few notable exceptions in specific areas, such as the work of Maurice Fenaille and Edith Standen on the tapestries, of Pierrette Jean-Richard on the engravings, and of Hermann Voss on the early works.

None of us is an authority on Boucher (can anyone claim to be so?), so that the object of this exhibition is to explore and propose, rather than to aspire to some definitive or even wholly comprehensive presentation. What is more, although we are showing tapestries and porcelain designed or inspired by Boucher, we have regretfully renounced exhibiting any drawings or engravings. This is partly because a very proper concern for conservation means that it is no longer possible to show drawings adjacent to the paintings to which they may relate, or even to show them in three locations, or to move around at all works in one central but neglected medium in which Boucher worked—pastel. Partly also, and more crucially, because Boucher's graphic output was not only so vast but also so various (and so much of it an entirely autonomous activity) that to do it justice would require an exhibition of its own—and a large one at that. May we even be permitted the hope that the tricentenary of Boucher's birth may be more gloriously celebrated than the bicentenary of his death—and how better than by a comprehensive exhibition of his drawings?

The second and main reason for the present exhibition not being as representative as we should ideally have liked is one that will, sadly, prevent there ever being such a thing. It is a curious quirk of fate that the kind of institutional collection in which several of the most important paintings by Boucher are to be found is often debarred by its statutes from lending. Such collections mostly have a considerable *dix-huitième* component and contain both the major and the minor arts of eighteenth-century France, which they aim to display together to recapture something of the flavor of the period that produced them. It is therefore understandable that provision should have been made against any disruption of such unity. But it would also appear that a kind of snobbery has been at work, as each successive collector—already often motivated by some desire to exist by proxy among the elite of the Ancien Régime—has emulated his predecessors in the ban upon loans incorporated into the gift or bequest of his collection. This restriction appears to have originated in the fear of the former regimental tailor John Jones that the bequest of his collection to the Victoria and Albert Museum (1882) would be dispersed through the building as the Sheepshanks gift of paintings had been. It was then given virtually canonical status for collections of eighteenth-century French art by the interpretation put by the Law Officers of the Crown on the terms of Lady Wallace's bequest of her late husband's collection to the British Nation (1897)—overcompensating for their failure to build "a special museum to contain the said collection" by prohibiting either lending or borrowing, in a way that flew in the face of the quite opposite policy pursued by Sir Richard Wallace during his lifetime.

It is because of these and similar restrictions that neither we nor anyone else can borrow the two pairs of masterpieces of Boucher's early and late maturity—the *Rape of Europa* and *Mercury Confiding the Infant Bacchus to the Nymphs*, and the *Lever* and *Coucher du Soleil*—and neither the seated nor the standing *Portrait of Mme de Pompadour in a Garden*. Nor indeed, since they seem to have been especially favored in this kind of collection, so many of the pictures painted for Mme de Pompadour. Neither—to remain in the field that Boucher so rarely yet so tellingly graced, that of portraiture—can the unique *Portrait of Mme Boucher* in the Frick Collection, nor Boucher's only portrait of a child, the young *Philippe Egalité* at Waddesdon, be borrowed.

Size and fragility prevented the borrowing of other masterpieces: the great pair of *Marches* painted for P-J-O. Bergeret in the Boston Museum of Fine Arts, the enigmatic *Pygmalion* presented by Falconet on behalf of Boucher to the Academy of Saint Petersburg, the enchanting picture at Angers of *Les Génies des Arts* (painted, like the *Lever* and *Coucher du Soleil*, as the model for a tapestry intended for Mme de Pompadour), or more than one of the two large decorative *Village Pastorals* (see cat. 27) on extended loan from the Bayerische Landesbank to the Alte Pinakothek.

Other pictures we were precluded from showing by the policy adopted by the Réunion des Musées Nationaux of not borrowing works of art on the market. Others again were locked away in private collections so discreet that we could not even get a sight of them. Yet there were also refusals—often at the last minute, and curiously, more often from museums than from private collectors, who might be thought to feel the temporary absence of their pictures more—that we felt less justified, above all because, by preventing us from showing the very best of Boucher together, they make it more difficult to rectify the injustice that the painter has so long suffered, of being judged by his inferior productions, when not simply by pictures that have no right to carry his name, and by outright fakes and pastiches. We know that Boucher was an early victim of the picture cooks of the Pont Notre-Dame, and there can be few other painters who have been so imitated that their name has become simply a generic description, rather than a seriously intended ascription.

But enough of regrets and explanations for what we cannot and do not have—there is more than enough to celebrate in what we do. It would be invidious to single out particular pictures or objects, and anyway it is part of our hopes that the exhibition will above all make visitors exclaim at Boucher as Gainsborough did at Reynolds: "Damn him, how various he is!" It is only fair to admit, however, that our choice has particularly gone to the works of Boucher's youth; not, we hope, simply from an unthinking acceptance of the prejudice against his late works—we have tried to show that, in the best of these Boucher can still give considerable pleasure—but because it is from his earlier years (which in Boucher's case means until he was almost thirty) that there are so many rediscovered things to show—and so many potential rediscoveries still to make, which may be aided by the widest possible showing of the protean productions of his youth (yet even here, we must regret that it has not been possible to show any of the small early mythologies).

We have also tried to exhibit—without being excessive—a fair number of sketches, to show Boucher the *peintre-né*; and also some of the best of his pastorals, in the hope that, by at the same time explaining them in terms of the kind of theater that inspired them, we can dispel some of the prejudices against this now despised genre. Above all, we intend the tapestries and porcelain as far more than a sideshow—even though they are a mere fraction of what might be shown, in that we have restricted our borrowing to the works of the leading French royal or quasi-royal manufactories alone. They are to be seen not only as superb or enchanting things in their own right, but also as embodiments of Boucher's enormous and prodigal fecundity (nor should we forget that whole tracts of his activity, such as his work for the stage, have disappeared virtually without trace). We hope that even this limited showing will help to convey how the felicity and fertility of Boucher's imagination contributed to set his stamp —arguably to a greater degree than that of any other artist—indelibly upon the image of his century.

It would not be possible to mount an exhibition such as this without calling upon the help of numerous other people for information and advice and assistance. The institutional and private lenders, without whose cooperation such an exhibition as this could never even be attempted, have already been thanked in the Foreword. We should like to thank here so many others whose generosity with their time and information has been of cardinal importance in running to earth items for exhibition and in the preparation of this catalogue: Colin Anson, Monika Bachtler, Colin Bailey, Madeleine Barbin, Joanna Barnes, Christian Baulez, Reinhold Baumstark, Charles Beddington, A. Bezançon, Fiona Bissett, Anne J. Blankert, Nicole de Blic, Edgar Peters Bowron, Georges Brunel, Julius Bryant, Hélène Bucaille, Frances Buckland, Duncan Bull, André Cariou, J. de Chaignon, John Chesshyre, the Earl of Chichester, Andrew Ciechanowiecki, Isabelle Compin, Félix Davoine, Cara D. Denison, Marie-Anne Dupuy, Judy Egerton, Martin Eidelberg, Jane Farrington, Christine Fournier, Anne French, Monique Fuchs, Peter Fuhring, Thomas Gaehtgens, Kate Ganz, Donald Garstang, George Gordon, Luigi Grassi, Marco Grassi, Richard Green, Rosamund Griffin, Simone Guillaume, Jan Heidner, Christoph Heilmann, François Heim, Werner Helmberger, Ann Hoffmann, Viviane Huchard, Peter Hughes, Beverly Schreiber Jacoby, Christophe Janet, Pierrette Jean-Richard, Christopher Kingzett, David M. Koetser, Günter Kowa, J.H. Kraan, Ch. Lassalle, Alain Latreille, Roger Le Coq, Clare Le Corbeiller, Catherine Legrand, Elizabeth Llewellyn, Annette Lloyd-Morgan, Richard Lockett, Gérard Mabille, Suzanne Folds McCullagh, Stefanie Maison, Philip Mansell, Jonathan Marsden, Jean-François Méjanès, James Miller, William P. Miller Jr., P. Minns, Christopher Monkhouse, Monique Mosser, Edgar Munhall, Albrecht Neuhaus, Philippe Nusbaumer, Jaap Nystaad, R. Pardo, Nicole Parmantier, Nicholas Penny, Ann Percy, Bruno Pons, Elisabeth A. Powis, Alexandre Pradère, Christian Prevost-Marcilhacy, Françoise Pruner, Simon de Pury, Robert Raines, John Rogister, Marianne Roland-Michel, the Earl and Countess of Rosebery, Kate de Rothschild, A. Rottermund, Vincent Rousseau, Francis Russell, Jean-Pierre Sainte-Marie, Guy Sainty, Birgitta Sandström, Rosalind Savill, Maria-Christina Prinzessin Sayn-Wittgenstein, Diana Scarisbrick, Johann-Karl Schmidt, Katie Scott, David Scrase, Lorenz Seelig, Maurice Segoura, Claude Seillier, Regina Shoolman Slatkin, Stephen Somerville, Françoise Soulier-François, Claude Souviron, Timothy James Standring, Marion C. Stewart, Julien Stock, Wolfgang Stolte, Alain Tapié, Gérard Tisserand, Eric Turquin, Horst Vey, Dominique Viéville, Jacques Vilain, David Wakefield, Roger Ward, the late Sir Ellis Waterhouse, Selby Whittingham, Susan Wise, Gretchen Wold, Richard Wrigley, Walford Wynn-Jones, Eric M. Zafran.

The staffs of the following libraries have also assisted us: the Rijksbureau voor Kunsthistorische Documentatie, The Hague; the British Library, the Courtauld Institute, the London Library, the National Art Library (Victoria and Albert Museum), the Warburg Institute, and the

Witt Library, London; the Zentralinstitute für Kunstgeschichte, Munich; the Thomas J. Watson Library of the Metropolitan Museum and the Frick Art Reference Library, New York; the Bibliothèque Nationale and the Bibliothèque d'Art et d'Archéologie, Paris; the Getty Center for the History of Art and the Humanities, Santa Monica; and the Royal Library, Stockholm.

Alastair Laing
J. Patrice Marandel
Pierre Rosenberg

## Additional Acknowledgments

I should especially like to thank, in the first place, Patrice Marandel and Pierre Rosenberg for the immensely challenging invitation to become their collaborator on this exhibition, and for the confidence and support they have manifested toward me throughout. I should then like to thank all those whose generosity with information, particularly when it was the fruit of their own research, and patience with my enquiries have put me in the possession of much knowledge that I could never have acquired through unaided efforts. Several are cited individually in the catalogue, and it is only fair to them to make it clear that the responsibility for any errors of fact or interpretation is mine alone. Others are thanked above (and I crave forgiveness for any inadvertent omissions).

I am also most grateful to Celia de la Haye and Kay Hubble for their success in reducing the palimpsestic confusion of my manuscript to typed order.

I should further like to give special thanks to Mme Beaumont, Conservateur en chef du Cabinet des Estampes de la Bibliothèque Nationale, and Mlle Gazier, Directeur de l'Institut d'Art et d'Archéologie, for according me the inestimable privilege of working directly in the book stacks of their respective institutions, without which I could never have accomplished the self-imposed task of consulting (guided by the near-infallible Lugt) all the catalogues that I could of sales of works of art in Paris in the eighteenth century.

With great sadness I should like to remember Lucienne Didier and Colin McMordie, for the shelter and encouragement that they gave me when I was working in Paris; the loss of each of them is keenly felt.

Finally, it is also usual to thank one's wife for her support and forbearance. In my case the gratitude goes far beyond the conventional, since I am aware that my enthusiasm for the artist, and the need to do so much in so short a time, have kept me from her in a way reminiscent, not so much of Boucher himself (though we know from Desboulmiers that he habitually worked for more than twelve hours a day), as of another painter, Uccello, of whom Vasari relates that he would remain in his study long into the night, working on his diagrams, answering all his wife's pleas to break off and come to bed only with the exclamation: "Oh what a sweet thing is this perspective!"

Alastair Laing

# Lenders to the Exhibition

Amiens, Musée de Picardie

Barnard Castle, The Bowes Museum

Besançon, Musée des Beaux-Arts et d'Archéologie

Bielefeld, private collection

Blois, Musée des Beaux-Arts du Château de Blois

Boulogne-sur-Mer, Musée des Beaux-Arts et d'Archéologie

Chicago, The Art Institute of Chicago

Columbia, South Carolina, The Columbia Museum

Columbus, Ohio, Columbus Museum of Art

Detroit, The Detroit Institute of Arts

Edinburgh, National Galleries of Scotland

Fort Worth, Kimbell Art Museum

Fort Worth, private collection

France, private collection

Gray, Musée Baron Martin

Hallandale, Florida, Mr. and Mrs. Jeffrey E. Horvitz

Hartford, Wadsworth Atheneum

Indianapolis Museum of Art

Kansas City, The Nelson-Atkins Museum of Art

Karlsruhe, Staatliche Kunsthalle

Le Mans, Musée du Mans

Leningrad, The Hermitage Museum

London, private collection

Los Angeles County Museum of Art

Lugano, Thyssen-Bornemisza Collection

Lyon, Musée des Beaux-Arts

Manchester City Art Galleries

Minneapolis, The Minneapolis Institute of Arts

Moscow, Pushkin Museum

Munich, Bayerische Hypotheken- und Wechsel-Bank (on deposit in the Alte Pinakothek)

Munich, Bayerische Landesbank (on deposit in the Alte Pinakothek)

Nancy, Musée des Beaux-Arts

New Orleans Museum of Art

New York, The Metropolitan Museum of Art

Nîmes, Musée des Beaux Arts

Paris, Archives Nationales

Paris, Musée des Arts Décoratifs

Paris, Banque de France

Paris, Musée Cognacq-Jay

Paris, Musée du Louvre

Paris, Mobilier National

Princeton, The Art Museum, Princeton University

Providence, Museum of Art, Rhode Island School of Design

Quimper, Musée des Beaux-Arts

Sainte-Adresse, Dr. Feray

Saint-Jean-Cap Ferrat, Académie des Beaux-Arts, Institute de France, Musée Ephrussi de Rothschild Jardins et Villa "Ile-de-France"

Saint-Omer, Musée Sandelin

Santa Monica, Jean-Luc Bordeaux

Sèvres, Musée National de Céramique

South Queensferry, Scotland, Earl and Countess of Rosebery

Springfield, Massachusetts, Museum of Fine Arts

Stockholm, Nationalmuseum

Strasbourg, Musée des Beaux-Arts

Toledo, The Toledo Museum of Art

Tours, Musée des Beaux-Arts

Troyes, Musée des Beaux-Arts

Versailles, Cathédrale Saint-Louis

Washington, D.C., National Gallery of Art

Williamstown, Sterling and Francine Clark Art Institute

# *Chronology*

ALASTAIR LAING

| | | |
|---|---|---|
| **1698** | February 20 | Marriage in the church of Saint-Gervais, Paris, between Nicolas Bouché, aged 25, "dessignateur," living in the rue Saint-Martin, and Elisabeth Lemesle, aged 20. |

This is the only document in which Boucher's father is referred to as a *dessinateur* (draftsman, provider of designs). In every subsequent document he is called a *maître peintre* (master painter), meaning that he had by then been accepted as a craft painter into the Académie (really the guild) de Saint-Luc. The later attempts (from Papillon de La Ferté onward) to identify him as a *dessinateur des broderies* rest on a confusion between him and Antoine-Claude Boucher (active 1742–56), successively described as a *marchand d'estampes*, selling, inter alia, "toutes sortes de Desseins des plus à la mode, pour Meubles & Broderies"; as a *Maître-brodeur*; and as a *brodeur de Roi*. It appears to have been the latter's son Antoine-François (d. 1787), who had formed a partnership with his father in 1750 (A & W doc. 415), who was the "Boucher fils" responsible for a plethora of designs for furniture and interiors published in *cahiers* from c. 1770 onwards. It was certainly not François Boucher's son, Juste-Nathan. Further confusion is introduced by the existence of an engraver and "peintre du Roy en mignature" living in the Gobelins, called Claude-André Boucher, who was associated with *ornemanistes* such as Pineau, Huquier, and Lajoue.

Elisabeth Lemesle's brother had a daughter, Jeanne-Marguérite, who was grandmother of the painter Jacques-Louis David, hence the interest that François Boucher took in the beginnings of latter.

| | | |
|---|---|---|
| **1703** | September 29 | Birth of François Boucher, in a house in the rue de la Verrerie. |
| **c.1717–c.1720** | | Probable apprenticeship to his father. |

| | | |
|---|---|---|
| **1720/21** | | Painted a *Judgment of Susannah* that encouraged François Lemoine to predict a glowing future for him (*Galerie Françoise*, 1771, p. 1) It is doubtful whether this was the painting measuring 40 *pouces* by 50 *pouces* in the [Le Bas] sale of 26 April, postponed to 10 May ff. 1793, since this was, to judge from its placing and ascription, by a living artist: "BOUCHER, *Artiste moderne.*" |

| | | |
|---|---|---|
| **between 1721 and 1723** | | Pupilage to François Lemoine—for a very short time, according to what Boucher told Mariette. He will nonetheless have been required to be registered as the pupil of some member of the Academy, in order to compete for the *Grand Prix*: the possible candidates are Lemoine's teacher, Louis Galloche, of whom both Natoire and he are described as having been pupils in the *Description Historique des Tableaux de l'Eglise de Paris* (1781, p. 7); or Jean-Baptiste de Troy, who is named as his teacher à propos his copy of the latter's sketch of *Armide visitant Renaud pendant son sommeil dans la forêt* in the de Sireul sale (3 Dec. ff. 1781, lot 28). |

| | | |
|---|---|---|
| **1723** | August 28 | First prize for a painting on the theme set by the Académie Royale de Peinture et de Sculpture for that year, *Evilmerodach, fils et successeur de Nabucodonosor, qui délivre des chaînes Joachin que son père avoit tenu captif depuis dix sept ans* [not recorded in the Academy at its dissolution in 1793; probably one of the 88 already unrecognizable pictures recorded in the *garde-meuble* in 1775]. Though winning the first prize normally entitled the prizewinner to a scholarship of three or more years in Rome, Boucher was |

| | | |
|---|---|---|
| | | denied this because of the prolongation by the *surintendant des Bâtiments*, then the duc d'Antin, of his favorites' stay there, leaving no place vacant for a newcomer (Cochin, 1880, p. 100). |
| c.1723–1728 | | Chiefly employed in making designs for engraving as thesis plates for Jean-François Cars, who gave him bed, board, and 60 livres a month [this probably meant making drawings for the engravers, not only after old masters, but also after paintings of his own, such as the *Jacob Uncovering the Well for Rachel* (A & W 32), the *Bethuel Welcoming the Servant of Abraham* (cat. 4), and the *Martyrdom of the Japanese Jesuits* (A & W 119)]; also apparently for Robert Hecquet—including the *Separation of Jacob and Laban* (?; A & W 35), and *Jacob Deceitfully Obtaining Isaac's Blessing* (engraved by Daullé); and then in making etchings after Watteau for Jean de Jullienne. |
| 1725 | Corpus Christi | Exhibited "several small pictures" in the annual exhibition in the Place Dauphine. |
| 1726 | | Engravings by Valleé, Aubert, Brion, Jacob, Haussard, and Jeaurat, published by the last named, after a set of small pictures of *Christ*, the *Virgin*, and the *Apostles*, probably painted some years before (A & W 13–27; cf. cat. 1). |
| | November | Publication by de Jullienne of the first book of *Figures de différents caractères, de Paysages, et d'Etudes dessinées d'après nature par Antoine Watteau . . .*, with 55 of the 132 plates etched by Boucher (J-R 34–87). |
| ?1726 | | Carle Vanloo's *Mars et Vénus* [according to Dandré-Bardon, 1765; although Fontaine-Malherbe, 1768, less plausibly, says 1735]; apparently painted, as it was published one of the two times that it was engraved (by Jean-Ch. Levasseur) and thrice sold (20 Mar. ff. 1773, lots 21 and 22; [Verrier sale], 14, deferred to 18, Nov. ff. 1776, lots 97 and 98; 14–16 April 1784, lot 74), as the pendant to Boucher's upright *Death of Adonis* (A & W 87; private collection, Saint-Jean-Cap-Ferrat), which thus presumably dates from the same epoch. |
| 1727 | December | Publication of Boucher's etching of Watteau's *Self-Portrait*, intended as a frontispiece for the first book of the *Figures de différents caractères* (J-R 33), and of his engravings after five of the paintings of Watteau, subsequently gathered into *L'Oeuvre d'Antoine Watteau* (J-R 151–158). |
| 1727–28 | | 25 drawings for the third edition of P. Gabriel Daniel's *Histoire de France*, for which a prospectus was issued by Denys Mariette and Jacques Rollin in 1727, and which they published in 1729 (Ruch, 1964 [misdated]). |
| 1728 | February | Publication of the second book of *Figures de différents caractères*, with 64 of the 218 plates etched by Boucher (J-R 88–150). |
| | end March/early April | Sets off for Rome, traveling at his own expense with Carle, Louis-Michel, and François Vanloo, and arriving at the end of May. The director of the French Academy, Nicolas Vleughels, lodges him in a kind of outbuilding. He announces the intention of the new arrivals to compete for the prizes for drawing announced by the Accademia di San Luca, in which two of the classes were won in December by Carle Vanloo and his nephew François. It is possible that Boucher was prevented from competing by the state of illness mentioned by Papillon de La Ferté (1776, II) and the *Discours sur l'origine et l'état actuel de la peinture* (1785). |
| | | Papillon de La Ferté also maintained, however, that Boucher had executed "several exquisite pictures in the Flemish manner" while in Rome, and |

drawings show him to have studied in the Pamphilj gallery, the Piazza Navona, and elsewhere.

A journey to Venice, via Ferrara (cf. J-R 1231), is highly probable, but unproven.

| | | |
|---|---|---|
| **1729** | Easter | His presence in Rome recorded by the *stati d'anime* (information from M. Olivier Michel). |
| **1731, if not before** | | Returns to Paris in time to execute the second book of a dozen etchings of *Diverses Figures Chinoises Peintes Par Watteau . . . au Chateau de la Muette* (J-R 164–175), the whole set of thirty of which, by Boucher, Jeaurat, and Aubert, was announced as forthcoming in July, and as published in November. |
| | August | Announcement of a projected new edition of the *Oeuvres de Molière*, with illustrations to be drawn and engraved by "les meilleurs Maîtres," to be published at the end of 1732 [ultimately brought out, by a different publisher, in 1734/35]. |
| | November 24 | *Agréé* by the Academy as a *peintre d'histoire*. |
| **1732** | | First dated picture, the *Venus Requesting Vulcan for Arms for Aeneas* (cat. 17), one of a whole group of large paintings executed for François Derbais, the son of the marble mason Jérôme Derbais, in order to get himself known. |
| **1733** | April | Advertisement for the publication of the engravings by Scotin (J-R 1585) and Aubert (J-R 191) after *La naissance* and *La mort d'Adonis* [the pictures themselves evidently having been painted before the journey to Italy]. |
| | April 21 | Living in rue Saint-Thomas-du-Louvre [adjacent to the Hôtel de Longueville]; marries, in the church of Saint-Roch, Marie-Jeanne Buseau (1716–after 1786), daughter of Jean-Baptiste Buseau, *bourgeois de Paris*. |
| | | Designs three vignettes engraved by Laurent Cars for the *Satyres et autres Oeuvres de Regnier*, published by Jacob Tonson in London (A & W figs. 9–11). Date on *Aurora and Cephalus* (cat. 18), the pendant to *Venus Requesting Vulcan for Arms for Aeneas*. |
| **1734** | January 30 | *Reçu* by the Academy on presentation of his *Renaud et Armide dans les plaisirs* (cat. 26), the same day as his friend Tocqué. |
| | June 26 | Bernard Lépicié *agréé* by the Academy on presentation of several engravings, including *L'Amour moissonneur* and *L'Amour oiseleur* (J-R 1378, 1377) after two pictures by Boucher belonging to Derbais (see August 1741). |
| | September | Announcement of Boucher's own etching of his *Andromède*, subsequently gone over with the burin by Pierre Aveline (J-R 203); and of Edmé Jeaurat's engraving after the lost painting of the *Paisane des Environs de Ferrare* (J-R 1231), one of a set of six engravings of *Costumes de Femmes du peuple de Rome et des environs*, of which the other five were after Vleughels. |
| | | Date on the *Capriccio View of the Farnese Gardens* (cat. 23). |
| | | Date on *La dame allant au bal* (art market, London and New York; A & W 113). |
| **1734–35** | | Publication of Jolly's edition of the *Oeuvres de Molière* [despite the *1734* on the title pages, the set was only announced as appearing "aujourd'hui" in May |

1735], including 33 illustrations by Boucher, engraved by Cars and Chedel (J-R 402–452). Earliest designs for the tapestries called the *Fêtes Italiennes* (cat. 86–89) for Beauvais, for the new director Oudry, who was appointed on 23 March 1734. The first weaving was in 1736.

| | | |
|---|---|---|
| **1735** | March 24 | Birth of his eldest daughter, Jeanne-Elisabeth-Victoire, subsequently the wife of his pupil Jean-Baptiste Deshays. |
| | April | Announcement of Aveline's engraving after *La belle cuisinière* (cat. 21), which had been borne off to London, and of Aubert's engraving (J-R 192), of the lost picture of *Venus Endormie*, which was then in the collection of the chevalier de la Roque, the editor of the *Mercure de France*. |
| | May | Announcement by Jolly of a projected duodecimo edition of Racine, with title pages by Boucher, to be published before the end of the year [never realized]. |
| | June | Announcement of Boucher's set of twelve etchings, the *Livre d'Etude d'après les Desseins Originaux de Blomart* (J-R 176–186), combining motifs from his copies of a number of drawings by Abraham Bloemaert, from a group of studies, others of which were copied by some of Boucher's fellow students at the French Academy in Rome. The faintly etched inscription *Tonton Boucher* on one of them suggests a student prank. |
| | July 2 | Elected *adjoint à professeur* at the Academy, along with L-M. Vanloo and Natoire, after showing "four little pieces depicting the four Seasons, with little women and children" [probably the set of pictures engraved by Aveline, announced in December 1737 (J-R 208–215)]. |
| | | Publication of volumes II and III of [the abbé Pluche's] *Le Spectacle de la Nature* (1732–51), each with a frontispiece engraved by Cochin after Boucher: *La Vigne plantée dans les Gaules* (A & W fig. 91) and *La jonction de l'Océan et de la Mediterranée*. |
| | | First commission for the Crown: the four grisaille *Virtues* in the ceiling of the *chambre de la Reine* at Versailles. |
| **1736** | January | Rocaille still life engraved by Duflos after Boucher (A & W fig. 42) as the frontispiece to Gersaint's *Catalogue raisonné de Coquilles et autres Curiosités Naturelles*, for a sale held on 30 January ff. [reused, with adjustments to the wording, for Gersaint's miscellaneous sale of 2 Dec. ff. 1737, and his Bonnier de la Mosson sale of 8 Mar. ff. 1745]. |
| | | Announcement of Huquier's engraving after Boucher's *Berger et bergère en conversation* (A & W 54) in an ornamental surround, readvertised in April as *Pastorale* (J-R 1089). |
| | April | Announcement of Huquier's *Recueil de Fontaines* after Boucher (J-R 1090–1097). |
| | May | Birth of his only son, Juste-Nathan (d. 1782); godparents were Meissonnier and his future wife, Françoise Petit [a relation of Boucher's early engraver Gilles-Edmé Petit?]. Though subsequently trained and styling himself as "architecte," Juste-Nathan never practiced as such (other than as an *inspecteur des Bâtiments du Roi*, thanks to his brother-in-law, the *premier commis de Bâtiments du Roi*, Cuvillier) but specialized in drawings and watercolors of architectural capricci. |
| | | *Chasse au tigre* [recte *léopard*] (cat. 29) for the *galerie des petits appartements du Roi* at Versailles (paid in full 7 Jan. 1737). |

Eight sacred scenes, together with frontispieces of three *Theological Virtues* and *Religion* over four locations in Paris, engraved by Le Bas after Boucher for the *Bréviaire de Paris* (J-R 1323–1333).

First order for three of the set of tapestries known as the *Fêtes de village à l'italienne* from Beauvais (cat. 86, 87).

Date on drawing of *La Courtisanne Amoureuse* (Waddesdon Manor; A & W fig. 861), the first of four *Contes* by La Fontaine engraved by de Larmessin after Boucher [professedly after paintings].

| | | |
|---|---|---|
| 1736/37 | | Publication in Paris of the *Tombeaux des Princes, des Grands Capitaines et autres Hommes Illustres . . .,* which included engravings by Aubert, Beauvais, Cars, Cochin, Dorigny, Duflos, de Larmessin, Surugue, and Tardieu, after eight large drawings by Boucher, two by Carle Vanloo, and one by Joseph Perrot, as half titles (J-R 194, 280, 453–454, 511–512, 869–871, 1249, 1590, 1593). Owen MacSwiny had announced his publication of the first 8 engravings of tombs alone, from the intended set of 24 allegorical tombs and titles, in a prospectus reasonably datable to c.1729. Jombert says that the whole work was published toward the end of 1736, but while that is the year found on the first state of Cochin's headpiece for the *Eloge* of the Earl of Dorset, and on Nicolas Dorigny's engraving of Carle Vanloo's half title for the Earl of Cadogan, Dorigny's engraving of Vanloo's half title for George I is dated 1737 [since the tombs of these last two figures were never engraved, the Dorigny/Vanloo plates were omitted from the London edition of 1741]. |
| 1737 | January | Ravenet and Dupuis's announcement of their intention to engrave and publish a group of scenes from *Don Quichotte* after Parrocel, Boucher, Trémolières, and others, and of the publication of the first two, after Coypel. |
| | February | Cochin's engraving after Boucher's *Retour du marché* (cf. cat. 27) as the central motif in an ornamental design for the leaf of a folding screen, entitled *Triomphe de Pomone* (J-R 517–518). |
| | April | Announcement of four scenes from *Don Quichotte,* including Aveline's engraving after Boucher's *Sancho poursuivi par les Marmitons* (J-R 207). |
| | May | Announcement of Le Bas and Ravenet's set of a dozen *Cris de Paris* after Boucher (J-R 1334–1338, 1516–1521), rapidly imitated by Fessard's three sets of *Cris,* elaborated from the comte de Caylus's etchings after Bouchardon (1737–38). |
| | June | Publication by Jacob of Fessard's engraving of *Cérès endormie* (J-R 273) after a lost painting by Boucher, and of Aveline's *Le Printems* (J-R 208), the first of a set of four engravings of the *Seasons* [probably after the lost pictures that Boucher showed to the Academy in 1735], of which the remainder were announced in December (J-R 210–215). |
| | July 6 | On his election as full *professeur,* Boucher shows at the Academy "three fancy pictures, of *Figures,* of *Landscapes,* and of *Animals,* done for the King" [the wording is confusing, but these were most probably two of the four pictures—referred to as *"paysages"* but centered on groups of figures— executed this year for Fontainebleau, together with the *Chasse au léopard,* whose installation at Versailles had probably been delayed by changes to the *petite galerie*]. |
| | August 18– September 1 | First of the revived Salons, in which Boucher exhibited: <br>—A pair of small oval paintings of *Les quatres saisons* [lost]. |

—Four round-headed pictures of *divers sujets champêtres*. [These last are described in the *Mercure de France* as having been painted for the king. They are thus probably to be identified with the four lost pictures painted for the *petits appartements* at Fontainebleau in 1737: two in the *petite salle à manger du Roi*—*Un concert de deux figures* (?drawing engraved by Aveline, J-R 229; ?various copies, including in the Musée Cognacq-Jay) and *Une femme qui tient un pannier, une autre tient du poisson*, and two in the *cabinet du Roi*—*Une femme coëffée d'un chapeau de paille, un enfant sur ses genoux, un jeune homme s'amusant à prendre des oiseaux aux filets* and *Des petites filles qui entourent des moutons avec des guirlandes de fleurs*.]
—De la Tour exhibited a pastel of *Mme Boucher*.

| | | |
|---|---|---|
| | November 25 | Decision to weave a set of six tapestries of the *Story of Psyche* at Beauvais, for which it was understood that Oudry would invite Boucher to make the preparatory paintings. |
| | December | *Le Printems*, *l'Eté*, *l'Automne*, and *l'Hyver* (J-R 208–215) included among the titles of a whole group of engravings after Boucher, Lemoine, N-N. Coypel, etc., advertised by the print publisher Jacob. |
| **1737ff.** | | Following the suicide of Lemoine, Boucher was one of those apparently turned to by J-B. Massé to carry on the task of making his drawings for the engravers of Le Brun's ceilings in Versailles more painterly. |
| **1737–39** | | Supplied designs for the Académie Royale de Musique (l'Opéra) [but see below, under 1743]. |
| **1738** | April | Announcement of Aveline's engravings after Boucher of *La bonne aventure* (J-R 223; numerous copies), *La Fontaine d'Amour* (A & W fig. 493; original drawing in private coll., England), and the *Jeux d'Enfants: La balançoire* (J-R 225; copy of lost painting sold Christie's, 11 July 1975, lot 149), *Pescheurs* (J-R 226), *Le retour de chasse* (J-R 227), *Fête de Baccus* (J-R 228) [two of these may have been after the paintings executed this year for the *cabinet de la Reine* at Versailles]. |
| | June | Announcement of Soubeyran's engraving after Boucher's lost painting of *La belle villageoise* (J-R 1589; variant in the Norton Simon Collection, A & W 78). |
| | August 18– September 10 | Exhibition in the Salon of three of Boucher's curvilinear overdoors for the Hôtel de Soubise: |

—*Venus, qui descend de son Char soutenüe de l'Amour pour entrer au Bain* (A & W 163).
—*Les trois Grâces qui enchaînent l'Amour* (A & W 162).
—*L'education de l'Amour par Mercure* (A & W 164).
   An ovoid replica of *Les trois Grâces*, also dated 1738, is in the Calouste Gulbenkian Museum, Lisbon (A & W 154). A quite different depiction of *L'Education de l'Amour*, also dated 1738, in all probability painted as an overdoor for the Hôtel de Mazarin in the rue de Varenne (exh. cat. 1981, Paris, note by Bruno Pons inadvertently omitted from printed catalogue), is in the Los Angeles County Museum of Art (A & W 151).
   A fourth overdoor in the Hôtel de Soubise (A & W 158) may have been the *Païsage* exhibited ex-catalogue (L.C.D.N., 1738; A & W doc. 107).

Two lost paintings of *Jeux d'Enfans* for the *cabinet de la Reine* at Versailles (possibly two of the compositions engraved by Aveline, published in April).

Frontispiece, *Qui fecit utraque unum*, engraved by Lépicié (J-R 1379), and four vignettes engraved by Cochin (two illustrated as A & W figs. 43, 44) after Boucher, for the second edition of Père Berruyer's *Histoire du Peuple de Dieu*.

Earliest certain weaving of all four of the first set of the *Fêtes de village à l'italienne* at Beauvais: *L'opérateur, La bohémienne, Les chasseurs, La pêcheuse* (cat. 86, 87).

| | | |
|---|---|---|
| 1738–39 | | *La chasse au crocodile* (cat. 32) painted for the *galerie des petits appartements du Roi* at Versailles [paid in full 8 Apr. 1739, as having been executed the previous year, but dated 1739]. |
| 1739 | August 3 | Lundberg takes Carl Gustaf, Count Tessin, to visit Boucher in his studio, only five days after Tessin's arrival in Paris as Swedish envoy. |

September 6–30     Exhibits in the Salon:
—A full-scale painting for Beauvais of *Psiché conduite par Zéphire dans le Palais de l'Amour* (lost; first woven from in 1741).
—*L'Aurore et Céphale, dessus de porte pour l'Hôtel de Soubise* (A & W 161).
—*Un Paysage où paroît un Moulin* [possibly the picture engraved by Le Bas in 1747 as *Premiere veue de Charenton*: in other words *Le Moulin de Quiquengrogne*, A & W 167, which appears to bear this date].
—Oudry's tondo of *A Rabbit and a Partridge* on a white ground, belonging to Boucher.

Date on painting of *Le déjeuner* (cat. 33).

*From this point on Boucher almost invariably appends a date to his signature on paintings, so their chronology is self-explanatory. Listing of them hereafter will accordingly be selective, as will that of datable engravings after his works.*

| | | |
|---|---|---|
| 1740 | April 27 | Birth of Boucher's second daughter, Marie-Emilie (d. 1784), in his house in the rue Saint-Thomas-du-Louvre; successively the wife of his pupil Pierre-Antoine Baudouin (d. 1769), and of Charles-Etienne-Gabriel Cuvillier, *premier commis des Bâtiments du Roi*. |

May 18     Signs receipt of 600 livres from président Crozat de Thugny for a landscape, and for "a little ceiling that he is to do for him in his library" [neither has been identified, since not in Crozat de Thugny's posthumous sale in June 1751, nor subsequently in the collection of his brother, Crozat de Thiers, despite his having inherited de Thugny's *hôtel* in the Place Vendôme and amalgamating it with his own].

July     Announcement by Huquier of P. Aveline's set of six chinoiserie engravings after Boucher's drawings of the *Five Senses*.

July 22     Tessin writes ecstatically to Hårleman to say that Boucher is painting "une naissence de Venus" for him.

August 22–     Exhibits in the Salon:
September 11     —*La naissance de Venus* (Nationalmuseum, Stockholm; A & W 177).
—*Une Forêt* (cat. 35)
—*Un Païsage, où l'on voit un Moulin* (cat. 34).
—P. Aveline's engravings after Boucher's chinoiserie drawings *L'Eau* (J-R 233) and *Le Feu* (J-R 234), from a set of the *Four Elements*.

Cochin's engraving for the *marchand-tapissier* Blangy of the *Foire de Campagne* (J-R 519–522), after his improved drawing of a copy by Francisque of a sketch by Boucher [which was doubtless his *première pensée* for the Beauvais tapestry *L'opérateur*].

The comte de Caylus's etching after Boucher of Gersaint's trade card, *A la Pagode*.

| | | |
|---|---|---|
| **1740/41** | | Engravings by Chedel (J-R 468–478), Cochin, and Duflos after Boucher's illustrations and ornaments for Tessin's fairy tale, *Faunillane, ou l'Infante jaune* (1741), around which Duclos subsequently composed his *Acajou et Zirphile* (1744). |
| **1741** | August 1 | Tessin's first shipment of pictures back to Sweden, including the *Triomphe/Naissance de Venus*, the *Vue de Tivoli* (cf. cat. 16), and a pastel portrait of *Mme Boucher*. |
| | August | Publication of the engravings by Fessard (J-R 962) and Sornique (J-R 1588) after Boucher's *L'Amour vendangeur* and *L'Amour nageur*, the second pair of the set of four putto paintings in the collection of Derbais (see June 1734). |
| | September | Exhibits nothing in the Salon. |
| | November | Publication of Elisabeth Lépicié's engraving after *La vie champêtre* (cat. 9). |
| | | The Cabinet des Médailles transported from Versailles to Paris and installed in the Bibliothèque du Roi, in a room created by Robert de Cotte. Paintings to a program (the Muses and their protectors) devised by Jules-Robert de Cotte commissioned from Carle Vanloo and Natoire (three each for the walls), and Boucher (four overdoors), and the first of the latter painted *(Melpomene/La Tragédie)* (A & W 246). |
| | | Shipment of 139 overdoor and overmantel pictures commissioned by Wasserschlebe, the secretary of the Danish Embassy in Paris, for Christiansborg Castle in Copenhagen, including Boucher's four *Poésies*, engraved by Duflos (J-R 925–928). |
| | | Painted the first three of some fifteen pictures for Choisy, the château acquired by Louis XV from the princesse de Conti in 1739. |
| | | First weaving of three of the Beauvais tapestries of the *Story of Psyche*. |
| **1742** | February 3 | Gustaf Lundberg presents the Academy with his portraits of Boucher and Natoire as his *morceaux de réception* (Cabinet des Dessins, Louvre). |
| | April 15 | Boucher accorded a pension from the Crown of 400 livres per annum, made available through the death of Martin (raised to 600 livres p.a. in 1744). |
| | July 20 | Departure of Count Tessin from Paris, having sent ahead a second consignment of pictures in June, including the *Leda* (cat. 40) and the *Woman Fastening Her Garter, with Her Maid* (cat. 38). |
| | August 25– September 21 | Exhibits in the Salon: <br>—*Un Repos de Diane, sortant du Bain avec une de ses Compagnes* (cat. 39). <br>—*Paysage d'après nature, des environs de Beauvais*, same size (?Hermitage, Leningrad; A & W 220, engraved by Le Bas in 1744 as *Vüe des Environs de Beauvais*). |

—*Esquisse de Paysage, représentant le Hameau d'Issé, qui doit être executé en grand pour l'Opera* (?Alte Pinakothek, Munich; A & W 181) [the opera had actually already been revived in Nov. 1741].
—*8 Esquisses de différens sujets Chinois, pour être executez en Tapisseries à la Manufacture de Beauvais* (including cat. 41–44).
—*Leda* (art market, New York; autograph replica, cat. 40).
—*Un Paysage de la Fable de Frere Luce* (Pushkin Museum, Moscow; cat. 45).
—De Larmessin's engraving (J-R 1250) after Boucher's sketch *en camaïeu brun* of a scene from La Fontaine's tale *Le Calendrier des Vieillards* (art market, Paris; A & W 293).

| | | |
|---|---|---|
| | November 29 | Received payment for five overdoors and a chimney board painted for Choisy that year. |
| | December | Publication by Huquier of Laurent's engravings after Boucher's overdoors in the Hôtel de Soubise, *Le pasteur complaisant* and *Le pasteur galant* (cat. 31, 30), and of his own *Livre de cartouches*, largely consisting of reductions of the half titles of the *Tombeaux des Princes* (J-R 1098–1123), and two *Pastorales* (almost certainly J-R 197, 1124). |
| | | Publication of [Dezallier d'Argenville], *L'Histoire Naturelle eclaircie dans deux de ses parties principales, la Lithologie et la Conchyliologie*, with a frontispiece of rocaille engraved by Chedel after Boucher (J-R 500: second state, for 1757 edition). |
| **1742–43** | | Le Bas's engraving after Boucher of a frontispiece to the *Mémoires de l'Académie Royale de Chirurgie* (1743), promoted by Caylus in place of one previously obtained from Cochin; preference finally given to the latter after all, because Louis XV found his own likeness in it superior. |
| | | Moves to the rue de Grenelle-Saint-Honoré, opposite the rue des Deux Ecus. |
| **1743** | May 26 | Death of Boucher's father, aged 72, in his lodgings in the rue et place du vieux Louvre. |
| | August 5–31 | Exhibits in the Salon: |

—Pair of ovals of *La naissance de Venus* and *Venus à sa Toilette sortant du bain* (art market, New York; A & W 243, 245).
—*La Muse Clio* [dated 1742] and *La Muse Melpomene* [dated 1741] (overdoors for the Cabinet des Médailles).
—*Un Païsage, où paroît un Moulin à eau; & une Femme donnant à manger à des Poules* [lost; probably the picture engraved by Le Bas in 1744 as the *Seconde vue de Beauvais*, J-R 1341; possibly identifiable with a painting, dated 1743, formerly in the J. Lasalle collection, sold Paris, 16 Dec. 1901, lot 1].
—*Son Pendant représent[ant] une vieille Tour, & sur le devant des Blanchisseuses* [lost; probably based on the drawing in the Rijksmuseum engraved (erroneously?) by Chedel as *Veüe d'une Tour près de Blois*, J-R 494].
—*Autre petit Païsage de forme chantournée, représentant un vieux Colombier, & un espece de Pont ruiné, sur lequel est une Femme & son Enfant qui regarde un Pescheur* [probably the picture, dated 1743, last recorded in the collection of John Schiff, New York].
—De Larmessin's engraving after Boucher's illustration of the La Fontaine tale *Le Fleuve Scamandre* (J-R 1254).
—Surugue's engraving (J-R 1591; dated 1742 on plate) after *La mort d'Adonis* [probably painted in 1726—q.v.].
—Gustaf Lundberg's pastel portraits of *Boucher* and *Mme Boucher*.

| | August 31 | Premiere of *L'ambigu de la Folie, ou Le Ballet des Dindons* (Favart's parody of *Les Indes Galantes*) at the Foire Saint-Laurent, with sets and costumes designed by Boucher. |
|---|---|---|
| | | *Presumed Portrait of Mme Boucher* (Frick Collection, New York; A & W 263). |
| | | Three oval *Pastorales* for the marquis de Beringhen, one rectangular (Louvre; A & W 260), and a pair untraced, engraved by Daullé in 1754 as *La Musique Pastorale* (J-R 554) and *Les Amusemens de la Campagne* (J-R 555–557). |
| | | Earliest version of the *Dark-Haired Odalisque* (cf. cat. 48), engraved by Lévesque in 1765 as *Le Reveil* (J-R 1397, 1398). |
| | | Lépicié's engraving of Boucher's grisaille after J-B. Lemoyne's tomb of Pierre Mignard (Marandel, 1975, no. 3). |
| | | Cochin's engraving after Boucher of the frontispiece to the *Réglement pour l'Opéra* [this, and the stage design for *Issé* in 1741, suggest that Boucher's employment by the Opéra may actually have gone on without a break between 1739 and 1744]. |
| | | Publication of Boffrand's *Description de . . . la figure équestre de Louis XIV élevée par la Ville de Paris . . .*, with a headpiece engraved by Cochin after a drawing by Boucher (J-R 509, second state, from reuse for Patte's *Monuments érigés en France à la gloire de Louis XV,* 1765). |
| **1744** | January 11 | Boucher presents Ingram's two suites of engravings after his drawings of *Pastoral* (J-R 1201–1207) and *Chinese* (J-R 1208–1215) *Figures* to the Academy to secure their copyright. |
| | March 24 | Commissioned to paint three pictures for the *appartement des bains* at Choisy: *L'Amour qui caresse sa mère* and *Vénus qui désarme son fils* (art market, New York; A & W 242, 241), and *Vénus qui regarde dormir l'Amour* (lost). |
| | August | Between now and July 1748 Boucher was paid 5000 livres for designs for the Opéra (but see above under 1743). This employment coincides with the extravagant management of Lemoine's former patron, François Berger (Mar. 1744–May 1748). |
| | November | Arrival in Paris of Carl Hårleman to acquire furnishings for the Royal Palace in Stockholm. Commissions six overdoors from Boucher, the last of which were paid for in April 1746 (exh. cat. 1984, Manchester, nos. P4, P5). |
| | | Publication of two works by Alexis Piron, with frontispieces engraved by Duflos after Boucher: the *Bâtiment de Saint-Sulpice* (J-R 876) and the *Deux tonneaux, poème allégorique* (J-R 877). |
| | | First weaving at Beauvais of *La danse,* from the second group of *Fêtes Italiennes.* |
| **1744–45** | | Executed two overdoors for the *bibliothèque du Roi* at Choisy. |
| **1745** | May | Hårleman returns to Sweden. |
| | August 25–September 24 | Exhibits in the Salon:<br>—*Un tableau chantourné, représentant un sujet Pastoral* [unidentified]. |

—*Une Esquisse à gouasse, représentant Venus sur les Eaux* (lost; engraved by Daullé in 1750; J-R 550–552).
—*Plusieurs dessins sous le même numéro* [?the plumbago drawings on vellum for the *Moeurs et Usages des Turcs*, later included in the sale of J-D. Lempereur, 24 May ff. 1773, lots 543–48].
—Tardieu's engraving after Boucher of the armorial headpiece (J-R 1594) for Boffrand's *Livre d'Architecture*, published in 1745.
—Le Bas's engravings after the *Vüe des environs de Beauvais* and the *Seconde vue de Beauvais* (J-R 1340, 1341; see above, Salons of 1742 and 1743).

| | August 28 | Premiere of Favart's *Les vendanges de Tempé* at the Foire Saint-Laurent; this was the inspiration for several pictures by Boucher, including *Pensent-ils au raisin?* (cat. 53). |
|---|---|---|
| | October | Commission from Crown Princess Lovisa Ulrica of Sweden for four pictures depicting the Times of Day, of which only Morning, *The Milliner* (cat. 51), was ever painted, in 1746. |
| **1746** | March | Alexis Piron's poetic petition to Lenormant de Tournehem on behalf of Boucher, for the lodgings in the Louvre rendered vacant by the death of Coustou in February (*Epitres*, 1767, VI). |
| | first half of year | *Venus demandant à Vulcain forger des armes pour Enée* and *L'Apothéose d'Enée* commissioned from Boucher for the redecorated apartments of the Dauphin at Versailles. Cast out by the latter, they were claimed by the king for his *chambre à coucher* at Marly instead. See below, Salons of 1746 and 1747, and 21 February 1748. |
| | August 25–September 2 | Exhibits in the Salon:<br>—*L'Eloquence* [generally called *Erato*, through transposition with the Muse of *La Poësie amoureuse* painted by Carle Vanloo, but properly, *Polymnia*] and *L'Astronomie [Urania]*, for the Cabinet des Médailles (A & W 248, 249).<br>—[An oval picture of *Venus qui ordonne à Vulcain des Armes pour Enée* was listed in the *livret*, but not actually shown until the next Salon]. |
| | November 15 | Revival of Quinault and Lully's *Persée* at the Opéra, with five sets by Boucher.<br><br>Publication of J-A. Guer's *Moeurs et Usages des Turcs*, with a dozen vignettes engraved by Duflos after Boucher (J-R 878–898), and the rest after Hallé. |
| **1746–47** | | The vogue for jointed cutout dolls, called *pantins*, in Paris, some painted by Boucher for individuals such as the duchesse de Chartres, others engraved by Poilly and Cochin, after bodies designed by him, and heads designed by Natoire. |
| **1747** | January 17 | Lenormant de Tournehem announces a *concours* for selected Academicians, including Boucher. |
| | February 26 | Four pictures commissioned from Boucher for the *grand cabinet des Jeux* at Choisy, because of the illness of Parrocel. Only two executed (subjects unknown). |
| | Spring | Boucher paints Easter eggs for Louis XV. |
| | August 25–September 24 | Exhibits in the Salon:<br>—*L'Enlèvement d'Europe* (cat. 54). |

—*Les Forges de Vulcain*, oval, now announced as for the *chambre à coucher du Roi* at Marly [see under 1746] (Louvre; A & W 302/306).
—Two oval *Pastorales* (?cat. 53 and pendant).
—Grisaille sketch for an allegorical thesis plate dedicated to the Dauphin [*not* A & W 308, which is considerably earlier, a variant of it having been engraved by Huquier in his *Livre de Cartouches* (1742; J-R 1122), and for a different purpose; but for the thesis maintained by the abbé Léopold-Charles de Choiseul-Stainville on 1 Feb. 1747, for which the plate was engraved by Laurent Cars].

In response to the unprecedented publication of criticisms of his own and other artists' exhibits in the Salon, Boucher designs and Le Bas engraves a frontispiece to the [abbé Le Blanc's] *Lettre sur l'Exposition des Ouvrages de Peinture, Sculpture &c. de l'Année 1747*, showing the figure of Painting sitting gagged before a picture on an easel, which is derided by figures emblematic of Ignorance, Envy, and Folly (A & W fig. 77).

| | |
|---|---|
| November 7 | Designed set for the first act of a revived production of Quinault and Lully's opera *Atys*, showing Sangar's palace. |
| December | Reported to be working on two sketches of scenes from the ballet *Les Fêtes Vénitiennes*, *L'amour Saltimbanque* and *Les Bohémiennes*, for the queen of Poland [see under 1748]. |
| **1748**   February 21 | Received final payment for *Vénus qui prie Vulcain à forger des armes pour Enée* (Louvre) and *L'Apothéose d'Enée* (National Museum, Manila) for the *chambre à coucher du Roi* at Marly (see under 1746 and 1747). |
| March 11 | Letter from Mme Boucher to Favart in Brussels announcing that her husband had begun making the designs [?for the frontispieces and vignettes of *Les Nymphes de Diane* (which had to be redrawn by Cochin) and *Cythère assiégée* (J-R 524) that Favart was staging for the maréchal de Saxe] and had found a good engraver (?Chedel). |
| July | Replaced by Perronet as stage designer at the Opéra [no doubt because of the appointment of Tréfontaine as director, in place of the deceased Berger]. |
| August 25– September 24 | Exhibits in the Salon: |

—An oval painting of *Un Berger, qui montre à joüer de la Flûte à sa Bergère* (A & W 311; National Gallery of Victoria, Melbourne).
—A small square painting of *La Nativité* [lost].
—De Larmessin's engraving after the *Portrait du maréchal de Woldemar de Lowendal* (J-R 1256), which had already been advertised in May.

Received payment for a curvilinear picture of *Deux Nymphes de Diane au retour de la chasse* for the *salle à manger du Roi* at Fontainebleau [possibly the picture in the ninth catalogue of the Sedelmeyer Gallery, Paris, 1905, no. 61, last recorded in the collection of Dr. Henry Barton Jacobs, Baltimore].

Reported as having shown sketches, and to have begun working on pictures, of the two scenes inspired by the ballet (see December 1747), now said to be taken from the *Fêtes de Thalie* and the *Fêtes Vénitiennes*, and to be intended as the models for a pair of tapestries for La Muette, in a room with two overdoors also to be painted by him (see cat. 55, 56).

Publication of J-C. François's *Nouveau livre de Principes de Dessein recueilli des études des meilleurs Maîtres, tant anciens que modernes*, including the

*Head of a Woman* (J-R 1019) after Boucher's study for *Venus and Vulcan* (cat. 17).

It was probably in this year that Boucher, like Carle Vanloo before him, refused Boyer d'Argens's offer to become first painter to the king of Prussia (Boyer d'Argens, 1768, p. 160).

| | | |
|---|---|---|
| **1749** | August 23 | Date on a drawing by Boucher for *Le petit jardinier* (Savill, 1982, fig. 1), modeled by Blondeau as *Le jeune suppliant*: the first evidence of Boucher's designs for porcelain figures produced by Vincennes. |
| | September 3 | Invoice for *Arion* and *Vertumnus and Pomona* (cat. 55, 56), the first two of four intended pictures representing the Elements for La Muette. |
| | November | Invoice for a picture of *Apollo and Issé* (cat. 58), painted at the behest of the *directeur général des Bâtiments*, but bypassing the *premier Peintre*. |
| | | *Ariane et Bacchus*, the first and most popular of the new tapestries after Boucher to be woven at Beauvais, known collectively as *Les Amours des Dieux*, the first sets of which were woven in 1750. |
| **1750** | March 1 | Mme de Pompadour writes to her brother in Italy, promising to send a copy of a portrait of her by Boucher then in progress (cf. cat. 59), which she does on 26 April, while sending the original itself on 15 June. |
| | August 25– September 24 | Exhibits in the Salon:<br>—*Une Nativité, ou Adoration des Bergers* for the chapel of the Château de Bellevue (cat. 57).<br>—Four oval *Pastorales: Le Sommeil d'une Bergere, à laquelle un Rustaud apporte des Fleurs de la part de son Berger* and *Un Berger qui montre à joüer de la Flûte à sa Bergère* (A & W 320, 311; National Gallery of Victoria, Melbourne, both dated 1748), *Un Berger accordant sa Musette près de sa Bergere* (A & W 319; Major John Mills, Hampshire; dated 1748), and *Deux Amans surpris dans les Bleds* (A & W 341; lost) [the first two were inspired by Favart's *Les vendanges de Tempé*].<br>—A pair of *Paysages, ornés de Figures sur le devant*, approximately 2½ feet [high], belonging to M. Langlois [lost].<br>—Daullé's engravings after Boucher's sketch of *Naissance et triomphe de Vénus* (J-R 550) and *Les Amours en gayeté* (J-R 553). |
| **1750/51** | | Moves to the rue de Richelieu, "la sixième porte cochère après le Palais Royal" [underneath the Cabinet de Médailles in the former Hôtel de Nevers?]. |
| **1751** | February | Announcement of Duflos's engravings after *La toillette pastorale* and *Les confidences pastorales* (cat. 50). |
| | February–July | Wasserschlebe's correspondence with Bernstorff about obtaining overdoors from Boucher and other artists for Moltke's palace in Copenhagen, later the Amalienborg, which were not finally dispatched until 1755. |
| | May | Announcement of Duflos's engravings after *Erigone vaincue* and the *Retour de chasse de Diane* (cat. 49). |
| | August 25– September 24 | Exhibits nothing in the Salon himself. De Larmessin exhibits a *Frontispice allégorique* after Boucher. |
| | October | Boucher proposes eight subjects to the Gobelins for a set of tapestries of the *Aventures de Renaud et Armide*; his suggestion is not taken up, and he |

instead supplies a design of the *Sommeil de Renaud* to Beauvais, which is woven the next year as the first of a set of *Fragments d'Opéra*.

Designs coverings for a set of seat furniture ordered from the Gobelins for Mme de Pompadour, which depicted children (probably the *Amours nus*, representing the Arts).

| | | |
|---|---|---|
| **1752** | March | Following the death of J.-F. de Troy, the director of the French Academy in Rome, his pension of 1000 livres per annum is awarded to Boucher, while Natoire succeeds him in the directorship. |
| | June | Following the death of Charles-Antoine Coypel, *premier peintre du Roi*, Boucher obtains his lodgings in the Louvre, but (for reasons of economy) no successor is appointed. |
| | June 30 | Revival of the Opéra-Comique at the Foire Saint-Laurent, in a theater built for Jean Monnet in 37 days, with an interior and sets designed entirely by Boucher. |
| | July 29 | Elected *adjoint à recteur* by the Academy. |
| | December | Announcement of Duflos's engraving (J-R 923) after *L'Enlèvement d'Europe* (cat. 54). |
| | | The earliest weaving of the first pair of the *Fragments d'Opéra* at Beauvais: *Renaud endormi* and *Vénus et les Amours*. |
| **1753** | April 2 | Blondeau was paid 384 livres for eight models of *Enfants* for Vincennes, after drawings by Boucher. |
| | May 1 | Commissioned to execute paintings for the ceiling of the *cabinet du Conseil* at Fontainebleau: *Le Soleil qui commence son cours et chasse la Nuit*, surrounded by four pictures of the *Saisons figurés par des enfants* (A & W 417–421). Reported as "working without respite" on them in July; the four smaller pictures were exhibited in the Salon at the end of August, and the whole ceiling completed by September. |
| | July | Guillaume Coustou II and Louis-Claude Vassé selected to execute the remaining two of the first four *pierre de Tonnerre* statues of *Enfants* to drawings by Boucher for Mme de Pompadour's dairy at Crécy (the first two sculptors chosen were Allegrain and Falconet). Boucher made seven such designs in all, which were also modeled by de Fernex and Suzanne in porcelain for Vincennes. |
| | August | Announcement of Chedel's engraving after *Le dévot hermite* (*Frère Luce*, cat. 45). |
| | August 25–September 25 | Exhibits in the Salon: <br>—*Le Lever du Soleil* and *Le Coucher du Soleil* (A & W 422, 423; Wallace Collection), intended as models for a pair of tapestries to be woven at the Gobelins [for Mme de Pompadour, like the pictures themselves]. <br>—Four pictures of the *Saisons, figurées par des Enfans*, for the ceiling of the *salle [cabinet] du Conseil* at Fontainebleau. <br>—Two *Pastorales*, as overdoors for Bellevue [oblong variants of two upright pictures of 1750, A & W 363, 364, to judge by their late inclusion, Laugier's descriptions, and the sketches by Saint-Aubin of the pair of drawings in the marquis de Calvière's sale]. |

—Roslin's *Portrait de Mme Boucher en habit de bal* [untraced].

—Aveline's engravings after the *Naissance de Bacchus* and *Enlèvement d'Europe* (J-R 247, 248), [already advertised in June 1748].

| | | |
|---|---|---|
| | December | Announcement of Duflos's engravings after four infant compositions by Boucher: *Le Berger, Le Pêcheur, Le Souffleur,* and *Le Poëte* (J-R 933–937). The latter two recur as inserts in the set of decorative panels reputedly from Crécy [but if done for Mme de Pompadour at all, then more probably from Bellevue] made into a room in the Frick Collection, New York (A & W 365–372). |
| **1754** | April 7 | De Fernex paid by the porcelain manufactory at Vincennes for four models after Boucher. |
| | April 27 | De La Rue paid by Vincennes for two models of groups of three children after Boucher. |
| | June | Premiere of Noverre's ballet *Les Fêtes Chinoises* at the Foire Saint-Laurent, with sets designed by Boucher. |
| | July 2 | De Fernex paid by Vincennes for two further models after Boucher. |
| | July 21 | De Fernex paid for two additional models. |
| | September 4 | De La Rue paid by Vincennes for two further models of groups of three children after Boucher. |
| | December | Announcement of Daullé's engravings after Boucher's pair of lost paintings of 1743 for the marquis de Beringhen, *La Musique Pastorale* and *Les Amusemens de la Campagne* (J-R 554, 555). |
| | December 31 | Received payment of 300 livres by Vincennes, for all the designs that he had supplied up until that date. |
| | | Date on Le Bas's engraving after Boucher of the frontispiece to Favart's *Le Caprice Amoureux ou Ninette à la Cour* (J-R 1349), whose premiere was not until 12 February 1755 [the depiction of Ninette leaning on her rake is identified as a portrayal of Mme Favart in the role she created by a note added to a copy of the engraving in the Collection Edmond de Rothschild in the Louvre]. |
| | | Date on La Live de Jully's etchings of *Ninette* and *La quêteuse du grand chemin* (J-R 1242, 1243). |
| **1755** | February 11 | De Fernex paid for supplying to Vincennes two further models after drawings by Boucher. |
| | March | Boucher accuses Duflos in the *Mercure de France* of using drawings surreptitiously made from his paintings by his least competent pupils as the basis for a recent set of engravings, thus damaging his reputation [these can only have been the infant compositions, published in Dec. 1753 and Aug. 1754]. Duflos does not engrave anything further after Boucher. |
| | May | Announcement of René Gaillard's first engraving after Boucher, *La marchande de modes* (cf. cat. 51), to which he added an engraving after Hubert Gravelot's *Le lecteur*, which was owned by Boucher, as a pendant in January 1756. |

| | | |
|---|---|---|
| | May 27 | Appointed *inspecteur sur les ouvrages de la Manufacture des Gobelins* in succession to the deceased Oudry. Boucher agreed to sever all connection with the rival manufactory at Beauvais, which began this year to weave from the last set of cartoons designed by him, *La Noble Pastorale*. |
| | August–September | Does not exhibit in the Salon, reportedly from pique at the pamphlets reviewing the Salon the previous years. Other exhibits include:<br>—Laurent Cars's engraving after Cochin's medallion drawing of *Boucher* [already advertised in April].<br>—Daullé's engravings after *La Musique Pastorale* and *Les Amusemens de la Campagne* (J-R 554, 555).<br>—J.-J. Flipart's six *petits Morceaux* after Boucher and Cochin. |
| | November | Boucher commissioned to produce seven pictures as models for Gobelins tapestries for the king's new apartment at Compiègne [never executed]. |
| | December 31 | Suzanne paid for supplying seventeen models after drawings by Boucher to Vincennes. |
| | | First weavings from Boucher's last set of tapestries for Beauvais, *La Noble Pastorale*. |
| 1756 | April 8 | Boucher received payment of 485 livres for the drawings that he had supplied to Vincennes in 1755. |
| | April 22 | Boucher commissioned to produce four overdoors of *Landscapes*, measuring approximately 2 feet by 4, for the *petit cabinet* of the Dauphin at Versailles, with instructions to start working on them immediately. It would appear that he only painted two, for which payment was still outstanding at the Dauphin's death in 1765, and that they were never installed, since one of them, described as "un tableau de paysage représentant des pêcheurs," was stored in the Hôtel de la Surintendance in 1760 (Engerand, 1900, p. 637). This was evidently the landscape etched by Saint-Non in 1777 with the (by that date impossible) location "dans l'appartement de Monsieur le Dauphin à Versailles" (J-R 1581). The other might have been *The Mill of Quiquengrogne at Charenton* (cat. 69), painted as a cabinet picture rather than an overdoor, to deduce from a pairing of copies of these two subjects (S. T. Fee sale, Christie's, New York, 9 May 1985, lots 15A, 15B), and the mention of a *Vue d'un moulin de Charenton*, sequestered from Choisy in 1792 (Engerand, 1900, p. 45). |
| | October | Announcement of Daullé's engravings after two pictures belonging to Mme de Pompadour, *La Muse Clio* and *La Muse Erato* [J-R 558, 560, wrongly correcting these designations to *Terpsichore* and *Polymnia* because of the two pictures with these latter titles in Mme de Pompadour's posthumous sale. The pictures in the sale either must have been misidentified or were two further pictures from a set of *Muses*, of which others still are known]. |
| | December | Announcement of Ryland's engraving of Boucher's drawing of *Les Grâces au Bain* (J-R 1549) under the direct supervision of the artist. |
| 1756/57 | | Seven putti pictures emblematic of the Arts (five overdoors and two overmantels) commissioned from Boucher on behalf of Count Adam Gottlob von Moltke and installed in his palace in Copenhagen, now the Amalienborg (A & W 467–473). |
| 1757 | May 15 | Louis XV authorizes Marigny to commission a picture each from Boucher, |

Carle Vanloo, Pierre, and Vien for a set of Gobelins tapestries that were to be known as *Les Amours des Dieux* (cf. cat. 65–67).

| | |
|---|---|
| August–September | Exhibits in the Salon:<br>—*Les Forges de Vulcain*, the model for a Gobelins tapestry (cat. 67).<br>—*Portrait de Mme de Pompadour* (cat. 64).<br>—*Le Repos sur la Fuite en Egypte* (cat. 68).<br>—Fessard's engraving of *Les Bergers à la fontaine* (J-R 995; already advertised in Nov. 1756).<br>—Daullé's engraving of *Les charmes de la vie champêtre* (J-R 571). |
| November | Delafosse and Magny's first engraving *en manière de crayon*, after a drawing of the *Head of an Old Oriental* by Boucher belonging to the sculptor Cayeux. |
| | Further designs for statuettes of children supplied by Boucher to what was now the porcelain manufactory of Sèvres (moved from Vincennes in 1756), as recorded in two books of engravings by Tardieu after drawings of them made by Falconet *fils* and published by Joullain in 1761 (J-R 1233–1236, 1597; exh. cat. 1984, Manchester, no. E24). Some of the designs appear in fact to have been supplied earlier than 1757. |
| | Date on François's pioneering engraving *en manière de crayon* after a drawing by Boucher of 1753 of *Two Cupids Asleep on a Sheaf of Corn* (J-R 1023). |
| **1758** March | Date on François's pioneering engraving *en manière de lavis* after a drawing for an overdoor by Boucher (J-R 1021). |
| April 8 | Double wedding of Boucher's daughters to two of his pupils: of the elder, Jeanne-Elisabeth-Victoire, to Jean-Baptiste Deshays; and of the younger, Marie-Emilie, to Pierre-Antoine Baudouin. |
| July 29 | Maurice Jacques paid by the Gobelins for two oil sketches of ornamental surrounds, containing medallions inserted by Boucher and his studio (cf. cat. 92). |
| August | Announcement of Ryland's engraving of *Jupiter et Léda* (J-R 1535–1539), after the painting belonging to Aranc de Presle (art market, New York; cf. cat. 40). |
| | Boucher paid by the Gobelins for a painting of *Les Jeux de l'Amour* (Louvre; A & W 480) intended to be woven as an accompaniment to *Les Forges de Vulcain*. |
| | Date on Blondel d'Azaincourt's engravings *en manière de crayon* after Boucher's drawings of *La bonne mère villageoise* and *La villageoise* (J-R 305, 307); Papillon de La Ferté's set of 46 etchings of *Divers Paysages*, of which 14 purport to be after paintings by Boucher (J-R 956–961, plus A & W figs. 1145, 1148, 772, and 1150–1154); Le Vasseur's engravings after Boucher's sketches of *Les Differents Genies de la Sculpture* and *L'Amour sur les Eaux* (J-R 1388, 1389); and Saint-Non's etching after Boucher's drawing of a farmyard (J-R 1574). |
| | Publication of F-M. Didier's *Tableaux Anatomiques*, with a frontispiece engraved by Etienne Charpentier after Boucher (J-R 464). |
| | Earliest weaving of the second pair of *Fragments d'Opéra* at Beauvais: *Vertumne et Pomone* and *Le Sommeil d'Issé*. |

| | | |
|---|---|---|
| 1759 | August–September | Exhibits in the Salon:<br>—*Le Silence* [very plausibly a picture painted for Mme de Pompadour and now in the Pushkin Museum, Moscow; A & W 498]. |
| | October | Gilles Demarteau's engraving after Boucher's drawing of a farmyard (J-R 597). This is number 11 of Demarteau's numbered series of engravings *en manière de crayon*, which only commenced after the perfection of the technique in the sixth *Livre de Leçon d'Ornement*, published earlier in the year. The fruitful collaboration between the painter and the engraver, 266 of whose 560 plates were after Boucher, began with number 3, of the head of an old man (J-R 590). Number 11 is dedicated to Blondel d'Azaincourt, who, like his brother-in-law Charles-Marin de la Haye, was to lend Demarteau quantities of drawings by Boucher from his collection to be engraved, and who this same year himself engraved a different farmyard scene *en manière de crayon* after a Boucher drawing (J-R 308), as well as another engraving after virtually the same composition as Daullé's *L'Oiseau Chéri* (J-R 310). |
| | November/December | Boucher completes a pair of pastel heads for Caroline Luise, Margravine of Baden, and offers to paint a pair of *Pastorales* for her (cat. 71, 72).<br><br>This year also found as the date on Henriquez's pair of engravings after Boucher drawings of *La Bergère, ou L'Image du Bonheur* and *Flore, ou Le Doux Loisir* (J-R, 504, 505); Fessard's engraving after Boucher's *Etude* of a female nude done in 1755 belonging to M. de Sireul (J-R 996); Hoüel's etchings after two Boucher landscape drawings, dedicated to Blondel d'Azaincourt and his wife (J-R 1078, 1081), the first from Blondel d'Azaincourt's collection; and G. F. Schmidt's engraving *en manière de crayon*, done in Saint Petersburg, after Boucher's drawing of the head of a child (J-R 1583).<br><br>Publication of Dumurtous's *Histoire des Conquêtes de Louis XV*, with a frontispiece engraved by L-S. Lempereur after a Boucher drawing (J-R 1364).<br><br>Date of Boucher's drawing of act 5, scene 4 in Corneille's *Rodogune*, which was etched by Mme de Pompadour with unacknowledged assistance from Boucher, retouched by Cochin, and used as the frontispiece to the edition of the play printed the next year on a press temporarily installed "Au Nord" [i.e., in her apartments in the north wing of the palace of Versailles] (J-R 1514). |
| 1760 | April | Completion and dispatch of the first of Boucher's pair of *Pastorales* for Caroline Luise of Baden (cat. 71), along with two more pastel heads. |
| | June | Completion and dispatch of its pendant (cat. 72), together with two prints. |
| | August | Announcement of Gaillard's engraving (J-R 1052) after the *Jupiter et Calisto* (cat. 70). |
| | December | Mme de Pompadour obtains a set of tapestries of *Enfants Jardiniers* [for seat furniture, cf. the set woven for the Earl of Jersey at Osterley], in exchange for returning those of the *Lever* and *Coucher du Soleil* to the Gobelins.<br><br>Publication of Poullain de Saint-Foix's *Catalogue des Chevaliers, Commandeurs et Officiers de l'Ordre du Saint-Esprit*, with a frontispiece engraved by Laurent Cars (J-R 460) after a grisaille by Boucher (Musée des Beaux-Arts, Lille; A & W 359). |

| | | |
|---|---|---|
| **1761** | April | Fessard publishes and obtains copyright protection from the Academy for engravings after two paintings by Boucher belonging to Mme de Pompadour, *La Lumière du Monde* (cat. 57) and *L'Amour désarmé* (J-R 999; oval picture last recorded in the Randolph Hearst collection, New York, A & W 375). |
| | first half-year | Executes *Les Génies des Arts* (Musées d'Angers; A & W 545) as the model for a tapestry woven for Mme de Pompadour. |
| | August | Appointed Rector of the Academy. |
| | August–September | Exhibits in the Salon:<br>—An unspecified number of *Pastorales* and *Paysages*, including a *Jupiter and Callisto* and *Sleeping Bacchantes Observed by Satyrs* that belonged to the duc de Deux-Ponts (A & W 533, 534; MacDonald Collection, on loan to the City of Birmingham Museum and Art Gallery, and Feather collection, Woking), a *Shepherd and Shepherdess Gathering Roses* (A & W 543; Wallace Collection; cf. cat. 71), the *Rest of the Voyagers* in its original form (A & W 660; Museum of Fine Arts, Boston), and two smaller *Landscapes* (unidentified).<br>—Roslin's portraits of *Boucher* and *Mme Boucher* (A & W figs. 130, 131; Musée de Versailles, and present whereabouts unknown).<br>—Cars's engraving of the frontispiece of the *Catalogue . . . de l'Ordre du Saint-Esprit* (see under 1760).<br>—Moitte's engraving of the *Vénus sur les eaux* painted for Tessin [already advertised in June 1760]. |
| | October 3 | Emmanuel-Salvador Carmona received by the Academy on the strength of his engravings of portraits of Boucher (after Roslin; Slatkin, 1971[a], fig. 5) and Collin de Vermont. |
| | October | Announcement of the publication by Joullain of the two sets of Tardieu's engravings after Falconet *fils*'s drawings of the children designed by Boucher for Sèvres (see under 1757). |
| | November 3 | Revival of Quinault and Lully's *Armide et Renaud* with the backdrop of the Salvator Rosa-like wilderness in the third act designed by Boucher and with the set for the fifth act, showing the enchanted palace of Armida, designed by him and his son. |
| | | Publication of volume 2 of Savérien's *Histoire des Philosophes modernes*, containing an *Allégorie de Shaftesbury* engraved by François after a drawing by Boucher (J-R 1022). |
| **1762** | August | Announcement of two engravings by Floding after Boucher in a new *manière de lavis: Apollo and Daphne* and a *Guardroom*, dedicated to the brothers Carl Fredrik and Ulrik Scheffer, past and serving Swedish ambassadors to France. |
| | October | Announcement of Gaillard's engraving of *Sylvie Delivré par Aminte* (cat. 62). |
| **1763** | August–September | Exhibits in the Salon:<br>—*Le Sommeil de l'Enfant Jésus* [lost].<br>—*La bergere prévoyante* [lost; but engraved by Aliamet (J-R 187)].<br>—"*Une partie de Paysage*" [unidentified].<br>—Pajou's life-size *pierre de Tonnerre* statue of *Un Amour [mangeant des raisins]*, from Boucher's collection. |

| | | |
|---|---|---|
| **1764** | January 24 | Revival of Gentil Bernard and Rameau's *Castor et Pollux*, with sets designed by Boucher. |
| | April 15 | Death of Boucher's most influential patron, Mme de Pompadour. |
| | August | Boucher's son, Juste-Nathan, sets off for three years at the French Academy in Rome, where Marigny had to create a special place for him by suppressing the architectural students' fourth year, since Juste-Nathan never won the first prize for architecture at the Academy (which would have entitled him to go automatically), but only the second (in 1761 and 1763). |
| | October | Boucher selected as one of the four artists invited to paint the Generous Actions of Rulers in the gallery of Choisy. Reputedly too busy to participate, he was replaced by Hallé or Lagrenée, but when the king ejected the completed pictures two years later, Boucher was chosen to paint all four replacements, with a brush "conducted by the Graces." Since no funds were ever advanced to him, he never embarked on the project, which was finally undertaken by Pierre, his successor as *premier Peintre*, who did not need the money. |
| | December 1 | Elected to occupy the post of *dessinateur du Cabinet du Roi* by the Academy, but declined the honor because of his health. |
| **1765–66** | | Johann Christian [von] Mannlich placed in Boucher's studio by Duke Christian IV of Zweibrücken (the duc de Deux-Ponts). |
| **1765** | February 10 | Death of Boucher's son-in-law J-B. Deshays. |
| | May | Presents Charles Rogers with a drawing of *The Trinity* for his *Collection of Prints in Imitation of Drawings* (1778, vol. II). |
| | August 8 | Appointed *premier peintre du Roi* in place of the deceased Carle Vanloo. |
| | August 23 | Elected Director of the Academy in place of Vanloo. |
| | August–September | Despite illness earlier in the year, exhibits eleven pictures in the Salon, some of which, however, had been painted before the previous Salon in 1763:<br>—Two *Pastorales* (dated 1761 and 1762, from a set of three painted for Marchal de Syncy; Showering collection, England; A & W 554, 555).<br>—*Jupiter and Callisto* and *Angelica and Medoro*, from the collection of [Nicolas-Joseph] Bergeret de Grancourt [uncle of the more celebrated collector of this name] (Linsky Collection, Metropolitan Museum, New York; A & W 575, 576).<br>—Two oval and two rectangular *Pastorales* [for Mme Geoffrin] (cf. cat. 78).<br>—*Pastorale* [lost oval picture of a *Shepherdess Crowning a Shepherd*].<br>—*Une jeune femme attachant une lettre au col d'un Pigeon* [lost].<br>—*Un Paysage ou l'on voit un Moulin à eau* (Ed. Jonas collection, Paris; A & W 600). |
| | December 10 | Record of reception by the Gobelins of four pictures that were to be employed as oval medallions in the *Tentures de Boucher*:<br>—*Vertumne et Pomone* (1763) and *L'Aurore et Céphale* (1764), both now in the Louvre.<br>—*Les Amours de Neptune et d'Amymone* (1764) and *Vénus aux forges de Vulcain* (undated), both now in the *salon des nobles de la Reine* at Versailles. |

| | |
|---|---|
| December 13 | Revival of Quinault and Lully's *Thésée* at the Opéra, with sets designed by Boucher in the second and third acts (Medea's artificial desert, and smiling countryside). |
| | Date on Lévesque's engraving after a lost version of *The Dark-Haired Odalisque* (cat. 48), entitled *Le reveil* (J-R 1397); and on Augustin de Saint-Aubin's engravings after *Vertumnus and Pomona* (cat. 56) and *Arion* (cat. 55), though the latter was only finished by Pasquier in 1766 (J-R 1443–1446). |
| 1765/66 | Boucher's grisaille sketch in oils on paper (Metropolitan Museum, New York; A & W 614) for the masonic Loge d'Amitié in Bordeaux [made at the behest of the duc de Richelieu?], done in 1765, according to the engraving by Choffard dated 1766 (J-R 507). |
| 1766 | Journey to the Low Countries with the *receveur général des Finances* and great collector of his works, Randon de Boisset [this is the year given for the journey by de Sireul in the memoir that he contributed to the catalogue of Randon de Boisset's posthumous sale; but since in 1766 Boucher was not only *premier Peintre* but also Director of the Academy and seems never to have been absent from Paris for more than a month, one should perhaps lend greater credence to de Sireul's original assertion, as communicated for use in the *Almanach Historique* in 1777, that the two went to Flanders only a little time after Randon de Boisset's return from Italy in 1763/64]. |
| January | Mme Geoffrin commissions a picture of *The Continence of Scipio* on behalf of King Stanislas Augustus of Poland. Still only *ébauché* at the end of 1767, it was finally abandoned by Boucher the next year, because of Mme Geoffrin's constant interference. |
| April 28 | Beginning of the partial sale of Mme de Pompadour's pictures, including ten paintings by Boucher. |
| November 18 | Revival of Laujon's ballet *Sylvie*, with new music by Berton and Trial, and sets designed by Boucher for the prologue (Vulcan's cave) and the second act (rocks, hills, and mountains). |
| | Received payment for a further picture used in the *Tentures de Boucher*, an oval *Vénus sortant des eaux* (North Carolina Museum of Art, Raleigh; A & W 637/638). |
| | Date on Saint-Non's etchings after Boucher's drawings of *A Country Child Being Taught to Read*, *Bacchantes at Rest*, and *A Group of Nereids and Tritons* (J-R 1576–1579), the first of which is additionally inscribed with the location "Hénonville," the property of Roslin d'Ivry (cf. cat. 79, 80). |
| | Publication of the abbé Millot's *Histoire philosophique de l'Homme*, with a frontispiece of *Adam and Eve*, illustrating Lucretius's *De Natura Rerum* 5.937–38, engraved by Moreau *le jeune* after Boucher (A & W fig. 170). |
| 1767 May 18 | Announcement of Bonnet's first engraving *aux trois crayons*, the *Bust of a Young Girl* after a drawing by Boucher in the collection of M. de Selle (J-R 339). The original printing in three colors was expanded to five in October, when it was announced as the first engraving *au pastel*. |
| May 25 | Announcement of Demarteau's first engraving *à plusieurs crayons*, after Boucher's drawing of *Head of an Old Man* in the collection of Mme [Blondel] d'Azaincourt (J-R 719), along with four other heads in the like imitation of |

red and black chalk (J-R 720–723), three of them from the same collection, one of which was a study for the old woman in *La Lumière du Monde* (cat. 57).

| | |
|---|---|
| August–September | Exhibits nothing in the Salon. |

The beginning of the publication of Le Mire and Basan's edition of the abbé Banier's translation of Ovid's *Metamorphoses*, whose illustrations include four engravings by Le Mire himself after drawings by Boucher (J-R 1362; A & W figs. 422, 719), five by Augustin de Saint-Aubin and his collaborator Le Veau (J-R 1556–1567), and one by Massard (cf. exh. cat. 1973–74, Washington, no. 92).

**1768**  July — Resigns as Director of the Academy, where he is replaced by J-B. Lemoyne.

August — Boucher and Vien forced to write a letter, published in the *Année Littéraire* and the *Mercure*, retracting certificates that they had written for certain old-master paintings.

The year printed on Pasquier's engravings after Boucher's paintings *De trois choses en ferez-vous une?* (cf. cat. 19) and *Elle mord à la grappe* (J-R 1449).

Grisaille [lost] painted for Désormeaux's *Histoire de la Maison de Bourbon*, engraved by Augustin de Saint-Aubin in 1772 (J-R 1568).

Painting of an unknown subject commissioned by Prince Galitzin from Boucher on behalf of the Czarina Catherine II [not executed; see Diderot's letter to Falconet of 6 Sept. 1768].

**1769**  July — Announcement of Bonnet's engraving of a *Tête de Flore* after a pastel by Boucher of 1757, traditionally supposed to represent his daughter Mme Baudouin (J-R 380).

August 25–
September 25 — Exhibits in the Salon:
—*Une Marche de Bohémiens, ou Caravanne dans le goût de Benedetto di Castiglione* (from the collection of P-J-O. Bergeret; now Museum of Fine Arts, Boston; A & W 661).
—Beauvarlet's preparatory drawings for his engravings of two *Pastorales* after paintings by Boucher [*Le départ du courier* (cat. 78) and *L'arrivée du courier*].

November — Chosen by the Academy to fulfill the place of corresponding member of the Academy of Saint Petersburg [in acknowledgment of which he may have sent the huge uneven picture of *Pygmalion*, A & W 240, which was patently begun much earlier, and over the exact date of whose presentation by Falconet on his behalf confusion reigns].

December 15 — Death of his son-in-law Pierre-Antoine Baudouin.

Publication of Meusnier de Querlon's *Les Grâces*, illustrated with an engraving by Simonet (J-R 1587) after Boucher [it is probable that the neither signed nor dated sketch in the Louvre is a derivative of the lost original, which was not necessarily a painting].

**1770**  January 10 — Received payment for an oval painting of *Jupiter et Calypso* [no doubt really *Calisto*] by the prince de Condé, who apparently used it as a model for one of the medallions in the *Tentures de Boucher* that he commissioned for the winter hanging of the bedchamber in the Palais Bourbon.

| | | |
|---|---|---|
| | Spring | Made designs for the decoration of the staircase of L'Archevéché (the palace of the archbishop of Paris, next to Notre-Dame), which was altered by Pierre Desmaisons in 1770. Two drawings for this, of *Hope* and *Religion*, were described as the last that Boucher undertook in his final illness, when they were included in the [Duquesne] sale of 19 December 1771. Other drawings for which a similar claim was made include two of a *Standing Shepherd* in Boucher's posthumous sale (one of which may have reappeared in Eugène Féral's sale in 1901), and the drawing of *Mausolée* engraved by Demarteau (J-R 793). He left his last painting, which was of an unspecified subject and unfinished, to his doctor and friend M. Poissonnier *l'aîné*. |
| | May 30 | Death of François Boucher in his apartment in the Louvre. |
| | May 31 | Burial in Saint-Germain l'Auxerrois in the presence of his son Juste-Nathan, and Charles-Etienne-Gabriel Cuvillier, *premier commis des Bâtiments du Roi*, the future husband of his widowed daughter, Mme Baudouin, with as additional witnesses Pierre (his successor as *premier peintre du Roi*), the painters Vien and [L-M.] Vanloo, Montucla (also *premier commis*), and the curé Chapeau. |
| | July 25 | Pension of 1,200 livres accorded to his widow. |
| | September | Obituary by Desboulmiers [J-A. Jullien des Boulmiers] in the *Mercure de France*. |
| 1771 | February 18 | Beginning of the sale of Boucher's collections, which realized the considerable sum of 120,844 livres 17 sous. |
| | December 23 | Beginning of a sale of drawings held by the painter-turned-dealer J-B-P. Le Brun, including 73 (mostly multiple) lots with drawings by Boucher and Deshays. [Le Brun was a former pupil of Deshays, and it seems very likely that this was largely a resale of drawings either acquired in their posthumous sales (and Baudouin's), or directly from their estates.] |
| 1772 | November 9 | Beginning of the posthumous sale of the engraver-publisher Gabriel Huquier *l'aîné*, containing 55 (mostly multiple) lots of drawings by Boucher. Huquier had already started to hold sales from his collections, including a considerable number of Bouchers, in his own lifetime, in Amsterdam on 14 September ff. 1761, and in Paris on 1 July ff. 1771. |
| 1773 | April 24 | P-J-O. Bergeret constitutes an annuity of 3000 livres in favor of Mme Boucher. |
| | October 19 | Beginning of the sale of the jeweler and *échevin* J-D. Lempereur, containing 43 (mostly multiple) lots of drawings by Boucher, including the *Annonce aux Bergers* (J-R 1363) and *Le Puits* etched by his son, J-B-D. Lempereur. |
| 1777 | February 27 | Beginning of the posthumous sale of the *receveur général des Finances*, Randon de Boisset, with whom Boucher had made his journey to the Low Countries in 1766. The catalogue, which was prefaced with a memoir of the collector by de Sireul, contains 18 paintings by Boucher, a pastel of the *Bust of a Boy Holding a Parsnip* (cf. cat. 28), and 41 lots of framed and 16 lots of unframed drawings by the artist. |
| 1779 | March 29 | Beginning of the anonymous sale of the *fermier général* Vassal de Saint-Hubert, containing 39 lots of framed and 7 lots of unframed drawings by Boucher (the sale must have represented a change of taste or commercial calculation on the part of the owner, since his posthumous sale on 24 April ff. 1783 contained virtually nothing by the artist). |

| | | |
|---|---|---|
| 1781 | December 3 | Beginning of the sale of Boucher's friend M. de Sireul, who is related to have spent hours watching the artist at work, and after his death collected anything he could by him, particularly drawings, so that his collection was known as "le porte-feuille de M. Boucher." The catalogue contains 16 paintings, 4 pastels, and no less than 173 lots of drawings by Boucher. |
| 1782 | January 17 | Death of Juste-Nathan Boucher. |
| | March 3 | Beginning of the posthumous sale of Mme de Pompadour's brother, by this time known as the marquis de Ménars. Most of the items in it had been inherited from his sister, and it is in the catalogue of this sale, rather than in that of her own exiguous posthumous sale, that most of her Bouchers are to be found. It includes 16 paintings, 3 pastels, and 13 lots of drawings— significantly, virtually all colored—by Boucher. |
| 1783 | February 10 | Beginning of the most extensive of the sales held anonymously by B-A. Blondel d'Azaincourt (1719–1794) in his own lifetime, containing 11 paintings, 2 pastels, and 107 (often multiple) lots of drawings by Boucher. Though numerous, there were considerably less than the 500 or so estimated by Hébert in 1766. Son of the noted collector Blondel de Gagny, d'Azaincourt had inherited many of the items in the sale from him; but not the contemporary paintings, sketches, and drawings, which he had collected to demonstrate his own taste. Brother-in-law of Charles-Marin de la Haye and J-Fr. Bergeret de Frouville, and himself an early exponent of engraving *à la manière de crayon*, d'Azaincourt, like de la Haye, had lent quantities of his Boucher drawings to be engraved in this manner by Demarteau. |
| 1786 | April 24 | Beginning of the posthumous sale of one of Boucher's two most considerable patrons toward the end of his life, Fragonard's former employer as recorder of his travels, Pierre-Jacques-Onésyme Bergeret (de Grancourt). This included 47 paintings, 3 pastels, and 45 lots of drawings by Boucher. Among the paintings were all ten of Boucher's sketches for the chinoiserie tapestries woven by Beauvais (cf. cat. 41-44), the two enormous *Marches* in the Boston Museum of Fine Arts (A & W 660, 661), and the *Arion* and *Vertumnus and Pomona* (cat. 55, 56). |
| 1789 | April 29 | Beginning of the last auction in the eighteenth century to contain a significant number of Bouchers, the posthumous sale of the discreet collector and *économe général du Clergé*, Marchal de Syncy/Saincy. The 17 paintings by Boucher included the *Lever* and *Coucher du Soleil* from Mme de Pompadour's sale, now in the Wallace Collection. |

# Boucher's Prize-Winning Pupils

In the present state of research, it is impossible to draw up a complete list of Boucher's pupils. This table therefore restricts itself to those of whom we can be most certain, who won one of the Grand Prix awarded annually by the Académie Royale de Peinture et de Sculpture. Certain of Boucher's foreign pupils are named in J. Patrice Marandel's essay "Boucher and Europe." Some of the indigenous ones achieved celebrity even without winning a prize, e.g., Jean-Baptiste Le Prince (whose own pupil, Jean-Baptiste Huet, became one of Boucher's closest imitators), his son-in-law Pierre-Antoine Baudouin, and Nicolas-Guy Brenet.

Charles-Michel-Ange CHALLE (2e prix 1738 and 1740; 1er prix 1741)
Pierre-Charles LE METTAY (1er prix 1748—held over from 1747)
Jean-Baptiste HUTIN (1er prix 1748)
Charles-François de LA TRAVERSE (shared 2e prix 1748)
Joseph MELLING (2e prix 1749; 1er prix 1750)
Jean-Baptiste DESHAYS (2e prix 1750; 1er prix 1751)
Jean-Honoré FRAGONARD (1er prix 1752)
Gabriel-Jacques de SAINT-AUBIN (2e prix 1753)
Jacques-Philippe-Joseph de SAINT-QUENTIN (1er prix 1762)
François-Guillaume MÉNAGEOT (2e prix 1765; 1er prix 1766)

# The Mysterious Beginnings of the Young Boucher

PIERRE ROSENBERG

To the memory of Hermann Voss (1884–1969), who was the first to dwell on the works of Boucher's youth.

*"J'avais bien aimé, dans votre* Coup de barre *cette phrase: 'Tout ce que l'on peut dire sur une barre c'est que c'est une barre.'"*
*"Ah! oui."*
*"Je trouve que c'est une bonne façon de tordre le cou aux critiques d'art."*

(Bernard Frank, *Les Rats* [1953], 1985, p. 392: "I really liked this sentence in your *Coup de barre:* 'All you can say about a bar is that it's a bar.'"
"Right!"
"I think it's a good way of wringing the necks of art critics.")

There are artists whose careers end in obscurity. Fragonard, for instance. We know next to nothing, not so much of his official activities, but about the paintings he did during the last twenty years of his life. There are artists whose beginnings still remain shrouded in mystery. François Boucher, born in 1703, is one of them. And this despite a series of articles devoted to the question, following in the wake of those by Voss (1953 and 1954).

Let us marshal the facts: "Born in poverty" (according to a letter of Pierre, Boucher's successor as *premier peintre du Roi*, written in 1788),[1] of a father "who designed for embroiderers,"[2] who was "a mediocre draftsman scarcely favored by fortune" (according to the author of the entry on Boucher in the *Galerie Françoise*, published in 1771),[3] and who was a master painter belonging to the Académie de Saint-Luc,[4] François Boucher is nowhere mentioned before 1723. On 28 August, his painting *Evilmerodach Releasing Jehoiachin from Prison*, unfortunately still untraced (see cat. 5), "won first prize."[5]

We know, however, that before 1723 Nicolas Boucher had placed his son in the studio of François Lemoine, a fact confirmed by all eighteenth-century biographers. At what date? Let us go back to the text of the *Galerie Françoise:* "A painting representing *The Judgment of Susannah* [the painting is likewise untraced], which he did at the age of seventeen [i.e., in 1720/21], won praise from le Moine, who thought he could foresee a great future for him."[6] How long was he there? If we consult Mariette: "M. Boucher assures me that he stayed no more than three months with M. Le Moyne." Mariette added the ironic observation, since for him the imprint of Lemoine's style on Boucher's was flagrant: "Whose disciple is he then? Boucher . . . told me in 1767 [i.e., three years before his death] . . . that although it was true that he had studied under Le Moyne, he had not profited much from a teacher who paid little attention to his pupils and with whom he had not stayed for very long."[7] This sentence is contradicted by Caylus in his biography of Lemoine, read

1. Furcy-Raynaud, 1906[a], p. 236 (the letter is dated 25 May 1788).
2. Papillon de La Ferté, 1776, pp. 657–62 [but see Chronology for the possible unreliability of this information].
3. *Galerie Françoise*, 1771. The author of the life of Boucher remains mysterious. It cannot in any case have been Jean-Bernard Restout, who merely supervised the engravers of the portraits of the "famous men."
   For his part, Papillon de La Ferté [see note 2] wrote that Nicolas Boucher "placed him [his son François], when he was scarcely out of his childhood, in the school of the famous François Lemoine."
4. Georges Wildenstein, 1926, p. 60.
5. *Procès-verbaux*, IV, 1881, pp. 360–62.
6. *Galerie Françoise*, 1771.
7. Mariette, I, 1851–53, pp. 165–66. Mariette's text was written between 1767 and 1770.

Fig. 1. François Lemoine, *The Rape of Europa* (1725). Pushkin Museum, Moscow.

before the Académie Royale on 6 July 1748: "Nevertheless . . . he was kind to his pupils, liked them, corrected them in a friendly manner, and showed them affection and an interest that he truly felt; I have no fear that the pupils he left behind and who today make up a part of your Academy would deny it."[8] True, Caylus added another touch to his apology for Lemoine, in specifying that he was of a "satirical and perhaps envious" nature. Do we have here the explanation for Boucher's abrupt departure? In any case, his stay with Lemoine—which was decisive, as we shall see— came before the latter's trip to Italy (1723–24), at a time when Paris was playing host to more peripatetic foreign painters than ever before, particularly Venetians.

There may have been a more material explanation for Boucher's having spent only a few months in Lemoine's studio: he had to make a living. Boucher was to do so by devoting himself to making drawings to be engraved and reproductive engravings. The artist's activity in these fields, before his departure for Italy, was immense and merits further research. Let us sum up what we know today. Mariette wrote that Boucher "went to live with the father of Cars, the engraver [i.e., Jean-François (1661–1730), father of Laurent (1699–1771)], who dealt in theses and who employed him in producing designs for plates that he then had engraved. He gave him board, lodging, and 60 livres a month, which to Boucher at the time seemed like a fortune."[9] Mariette then mentioned "26 illustrations and vignettes" for the *Histoire de France* by Father Gabriel Daniel, which were engraved by Maurice Baquoy (c. 1675–1747) and C. Mathey. He dated them to 1721, and maintained that the book appeared the following year. It is well known that these drawings, bound in an album belonging to the Cabinet des Dessins in the Louvre, were published in the *Inventaire Général* under the name of Pierre-Jacques Cazes (1676–1754), Chardin's teacher, until John Ruch restored them to Boucher in 1964.[10] Alastair Laing presents below (see cat. 8) the reasons that lead him to doubt the date put forward by Mariette, whose uncle had been responsible for publishing editions of the work in both 1722 and 1729. Let us content ourselves with reproducing here two unpublished studies for these vignettes sheltering under an attribution to Fragonard in the Ian Woodner

Fig. 2. François Boucher, here attributed, *Alarme dans le camp de Chilperic*. Ian Woodner Family Collection.

Fig. 3. François Boucher, here attributed, *L'archiduc fit son hommage entre les mains du Chancelier de France*. Ian Woodner Family Collection.

8. Caylus, 1910, p. 46.

9. Mariette, I, 1851–53, pp. 165–66.

10. Ruch, 1964, pp. 496–500.

11. Exhibited at the Este Gallery, New York, as by Boucher in 1953, when their reattri-bution to Fragonard was suggested anony-mously in *Connoisseur,* August 1953, p. 69.

12. Mariette, I, 1851–53, pp. 165–66.

13. J-R, p. 33. See also Hérold & Vuaflart, 1929, I, pp. 177–78 (who ascribe only 105 pieces from the *Figures de différents carac-tères* to Boucher).

14. For another version of this drawing, see exh. cat. 1985, Paris, no. 2, illus.

15. Campardon, 1880, pp. 19–20.

16. Hérold & Vuaflart, 1929, I, pp. 91–92. See also J-R, p. 74; and Dussieux, 1876, p. 312, which states that Nicolas Dorigny "returned to France in 1724. In 1725, he was commissioned by the English to have a rather considerable series of allegorical compositions designed by French painters in honor of the great men of England. These drawings . . . were executed by Carle Vanloo and Boucher." It is not clear, however, where Dussieux got his informa-tion about the role played by Dorigny and the date. Dorigny only engraved the two half titles designed by Carle Vanloo (which indeed only appear in the French edition of c.1736/37). When MacSwiny issued a prospectus for the *Tombeaux,* at a point datable to c.1729/30 thanks to the dates of completion of the paintings of the tombs, he claimed only that eight of the tombs themselves had been engraved; the half titles (by Boucher and Vanloo) had yet to be commissioned or engraved, and such as are datable, stem only from 1736/37, which is what their style would also suggest.

collection, which show Boucher's stylistic freedom as a young draftsman and that inventiveness and feeling for composition that were to serve him so well throughout his career (figs. 2, 3).[11]

To return to Mariette: "He was not long in making the acquaintance of M. de Julienne, who, wishing to have the drawings of Watteau engraved, distributed several of them to Boucher, who acquitted himself perfectly. His deft, agile manipulation of the needle seemed made for such work. M. de Julienne gave him 24 livres a day, and both were satisfied, since Boucher worked very quickly, etching being child's play for him."[12] It is worth remembering that of all the artists hired by de Jullienne for the *Figures de différents caractères* (two volumes, published in 1726 and 1728), it was Boucher who engraved the largest number of Watteau's drawings, no less than 119, according to Pierrette Jean-Richard, out of a total of 351.[13] It is likewise worth noting that it is an etching by Boucher, *The Graces at the Tomb of Watteau,* based on one of his own drawings (Windsor),[14] that opens the second volume of the work. Finally, it should be mentioned that before his departure for Rome, Boucher undertook a number of engravings for the *Recueil Jullienne* (twenty-one in all, although some of them were only published after his return in 1731).

But the list of works by Boucher the draftsman and engraver does not end here. He assisted in some unspecified way in the splendid set of engravings by Jean-Baptiste Massé reproducing the decoration painted by Le Brun in the *grande galerie* "and the two Salons that adjoin it" at Versailles, which was finally published in 1753. "I owe part of the success [of this volume]," wrote Massé, "to the obliging efforts of MM. Galoche, Boucher, Natoire, and Bouchardon, and especially of the late M. Le Moyne."[15] It was also then that he was supposed to have supplied drawings for the French edition, purportedly due to Nicolas Dorigny, of MacSwiny's compilation, the *Tombeaux des Princes, des Grands Capitaines et autres Hommes Illustres qui ont fleuri dans la Grande-Bretagne.*[16] Lastly, he drew—probably drew a lot—and painted. He participated in the Corpus Christi exhibition in the Place Dauphine in 1725 ("It was a great pleasure to see several small paintings by M.ʳ Bouchet [*sic*], pupil of M.ʳ Lemoine, painted with an excellent sense of color, which make one

Fig. 4. François Boucher, here attributed, *Biblical Scene.* Museum of Fine Arts, Budapest.

Fig. 5. François Boucher, here attributed, *Biblical Scene.* Private collection, Paris.

Fig. 6. François Boucher, here attributed, *David Threatened by Saul while Playing the Harp*. Private collection, Paris.

Fig. 7. François Boucher, here attributed, *St. John the Baptist Preaching*. Staatliche Museen Preussischer Kulturbesitz, Kupferstichkabinett, Berlin.

hope that this young man will be capable of excelling in his Art"[17]). He painted to a moderate degree. But let us leave it to Alastair Laing to comment on this point (cat. I–II).

In 1728, Boucher went to Italy. His Grand Prix of 1723 was supposed to open the doors of the Académie de France in Rome to him. But it did nothing of the kind. How and thanks to whom was he able to go?

Alexandre Ananoff, in the Classici dell'arte volume devoted to Boucher, suggests that he made the journey "thanks to the generosity of some collector, perhaps the duc d'Antin" (Ananoff & Wildenstein, 1980, p. 83). But it was most certainly not the *surintendant des Bâtiments du Roi* who supplied the young artist with the funds necessary for his trip and for his stay in Rome. Cochin ruled this out when he wrote: "M. le duc d'Antin dispensed much patronage, and as frequently happens with the great, even his valets dispensed patronage around him. Excellent pupils, such as

Fig. 8. François Boucher, here attributed, *Christ Healing the Man Blind from Birth*. Private collection, Paris.

Fig. 9. François Boucher, here attributed, *Christ before Caiaphas*. Musée du Louvre, Cabinet des Dessins, Paris.

Fig. 10. François Boucher, here attributed, *Shepherd Driving His Flock*. Bibliothèque Nationale, Paris.

17. *Mercure de France*, June 1725, p. 1402.
18. Cochin, 1880, p. 100.
19. Papillon de La Ferté, 1776.
20. Dandré-Bardon, 1765, pp. 13–14, added: "He thus procures the means to travel comfortably to Rome and to maintain himself there for a few years in order to study"; see also *Correspondance*, VII, 1897, pp. 408, 409.
21. Dandré-Bardon, 1765, pp. 13–14.
22. *Correspondance*, VII, 1897, pp. 420, 423. See also Lapauze, 1924, I, pp. 201–02.
23. This statement can now be qualified, since M. Olivier Michel kindly informs me that Boucher's name occurs in the Roman registers of Easter communicants in 1729 (the *Liber stati animarum*).

Vanloo, Boucher, and others, were left without being sent to Rome, while scholarships were given to untalented pupils recommended by those who approached the great man."[18]

I prefer to go along with Papillon de La Ferté,[19] who maintained that Boucher went to Italy "at his own expense." Very likely he was able to make the journey with the savings accumulated by his extensive work as a draftsman and engraver. He left Paris at the end of March or the beginning of April 1728 in the company, Dandré-Bardon and the *Correspondance des Directeurs* tell us, of the three Vanloo, Carle (1705–1765) and his nephews the brothers Louis-Michel (1707–1765) and François (1708–1732).[20] Carle Vanloo had won the Grand Prix in 1724 (one year before Louis-Michel) and had been able to put a little money aside thanks to his "portrait drawings." "These works, which he did with surprising facility, earned him good takings."[21]

Two letters of 27 May and 3 June 1728 from the painter Nicolas Vleughels (1668–1737), director of the Académie de France in Rome, to the duc d'Antin, the *surintendant*, confirm Boucher's arrival at the Palazzo Mancini.[22] They have often been quoted: "With Messrs. *Vanloo* comes . . . a young man who has plenty of talent; since he is French and very promising, it will be my pleasure to try to serve him as I shall do the others . . ."; and again: "There is also someone named *Boucher*, a simple boy and with a good deal of ability; in a virtual outbuilding there is a little hole of a room, and I have stuck him in there. . . ." In the days that followed, Vleughels presented the new students to Cardinal de Polignac, the French ambassador to the pope, and set them to work. But Boucher's name does not appear again in the *Correspondance* exchanged by the director of the Académie and the *surintendant*, copious as it is, until 14 August 1732, a date by which Boucher was back in France. During these few years his name does not appear anywhere, so far as we know, either in the Italian archives or in writings of the period.[23]

What happened to him? Again, according to Mariette: "He made the Italian journey but it was rather to satisfy his curiosity than to derive any

24. Mariette, I, 1851–53, pp. 165–66.
25. Ingrams, 1970, p. 26.
26. This illness is confirmed by a passage in the *Discours sur l'origine, les progrès, et l'état actuel de la peinture*, Paris, 1785, p. 7: Boucher stayed only "a few months in Italy, in a permanent state of illness that did not allow him to apply himself to anything."
27. Papillon de La Ferté, 1776, pp. 657–62.
28. Dandré-Bardon, 1765, pp. 15–16. Natoire had won the same prize in 1725.
29. Papillon de La Ferté, 1776, pp. 657–62.
30. But he was not in Rome over Easter, since his name does not appear in the register of Easter communicants for that year, M. Olivier Michel kindly informs me.
31. Papillon de La Ferté, 1776, pp. 657–62.
32. Boucher's drawings after Italian old masters can help us to follow the young artist's movements in Italy. An example is the drawing that was in Mariette's posthumous sale, lot 1154: "The Virgin holding the Christ Child, and at her feet several saints in the act of worship: this drawing, done in pen and bister wash with all possible art, is not of Boucher's own composition but after Cavedone's painting in Bologna." It is interesting to note that Trémolières made a red-chalk drawing after the same work (fig. 11; exh. cat. 1973, Cholet, drawing no. 12, pp. 97–98, and pl. XVIII).

Fig. 11. Pierre-Charles Trémolières, after Giacomo Cavedone, *St. Alò and St. Petronio Adoring the Virgin and Child*. Private collection, Paris.

advantage from it. Therefore he did not stay in that country very long."[24] But Bachaumont in 1750 claimed that he spent "a long time in Italy."[25] This is an apparent contradiction, on which a seldom cited yet quite important passage from Papillon de La Ferté (1776) sheds new light: "During the time he [Boucher] spent there [in Italy], the poor state of his health prevented him from pursuing all the studies that he wished to do."[26] "He was not even able to work on the subject that had been assigned to the young artists competing for the grand prize awarded by the pope at the Capitol."[27] This prize, "despite the large number of very skillful rivals, most of them Italian," was carried off by Carle Vanloo in the autumn of their arrival in Rome "crowned by a unanimous voice" and "to the sound of the acclamations of all."[28]

"After staying eighteen months in that superb metropolis of the Arts, he [Boucher] returned to Paris in 1731 . . ." (Papillon de La Ferté).[29] That would mean that Boucher, having arrived in Rome in May 1728, would have left the city in November 1729. Yet two drawings of Tivoli, now in the respective print rooms of the Städel and the Rijksmuseum, signed and dated *Roma 1730*, reveal that Boucher was still in Rome at that date.[30] Was it really in Rome that he painted those "exquisite small pictures in the Flemish style" of which Papillon de La Ferté spoke?[31] How far are we to believe the assertions of eighteenth-century sale catalogues declaring that this or that painting had been "done in Italy" or "done in Rome"? Did he travel? Did he stop along the way to Rome or on the return trip—as is sometimes stated without proof—in Florence, Parma, Ferrara, Genoa, Bologna?[32] Did he go to Naples? Did he follow the advice of Vleughels, who recommended his students (the letter is of 13 February 1727) to stop over in Venice on their return?: "There is a quite skillful painter named *Sebastien Richi*, who volunteers to look after pupils."[33] We do not know.

In any case, Boucher roughed out an overdoor in the Palazzo Mancini; it, too, has disappeared, and we do not even know the subject.[34] We know that he kept the drawings from this period of his career, since on 13 September 1757, Cochin was to suggest to Marigny that he ask Boucher, along with other artists (Bouchardon, Slodtz, Pierre, and Vien), if he would agree "to lend what [he has] kept of the fine studies he [did] in Italy," so that they could be engraved.[35] Was it at this juncture that Jean-Baptiste Hutin (1726–1786) published his *Recueil de différents caractères de têtes tirés de la colonne Trajane?*

It seems certain that Boucher (because of his illness?) did not retain a fond memory of the time spent in Italy. In 1766, he advised the German painter Christian Mannlich (1740–1822) " 'not to spend a lot of time in Rome and to study above all Albani[36] and Guido Reni. Raphael, despite his great reputation, is a very depressing painter, and Michelangelo is frightening,' he told me. 'Believe in them, but don't attempt to imitate them, or you will become as chilling as ice.' "[37]

Boucher nevertheless made a great impression on Vleughels. On 14 August 1732, he placed him, along with the Vanloo, Natoire, Adam, and Bouchardon, among the "subjects with much promise."[38]

On 24 November 1731,[39] Boucher was *agréé* by the Académie. In 1732, he painted his *Venus Requesting Vulcan for Arms for Aeneas* (cat. 17; Louvre), his first masterpiece. He presented his reception piece, *Rinaldo and Armida* (cat. 26; Louvre), on 30 January 1734[40] and entered the

33. *Correspondance*, VII, 1897, p. 311.
34. *Correspondance*, XVI, 1907, p. 442, listing among the objects noted in the inventory of the Palazzo Mancini taken at the Revolution, in a bedchamber: "two overdoors: one only roughed out by M. *Bouché* [sic] the other by *Louis Vanloo*—Both with their frames."
35. Furcy-Raynaud, 1903, p. 131.
36. In the memoir of Boucher in the *Galerie Française* in 1771 [see note 3], the author cites Albani as a comparison. He also mentions "Pierre de Cortonne" [sic] and Lanfranco: "As a general rule, the first pictures that he painted on returning from Italy show the effects of the time he spent there, and are filled with the vigorous and manly beauties of the great masters. Their color is true, *local*, and harmonious, but always striking; the heads and figures have all the expressiveness that it is possible to register on canvas."
37. Mannlich, 1948, pp. 285–86.
38. *Correspondance*, VIII, 1898, p. 360. Alastair Laing kindly points out that there is a further reference, which can only refer to Boucher, in a previous letter from Vleughels to d'Antin (p. 306): "I can assure you that *C. Vanloo* is an able man, and that no one more gifted has passed through this Academy, with the possible exception of a poor lad who, with your indulgence, spent some time at the Academy and has since returned to Paris very able."
39. *Procès-verbaux* V, 1883, pp. 95, 136.
40. *Procès-verbaux*, V, 1883, pp. 95, 136.

Académie as a history painter. Meanwhile he had gotten married. From now on the painter's career was to unfold in broad daylight.

But it would still take time for him to emerge as the leading artist of his generation. What had he retained of the art of his French and Italian seniors? How did he carve out a place for himself among his contemporaries? How did he acquire that "style," at first so admired and later just as violently decried?

Put like this, Boucher's rise might seem both rapid and irresistible. Actually it was nothing of the kind. It was slow and for a long time uncertain.

To begin with, here are two observations out of many that one might make, of widely differing weight, which will nonetheless help to identify the issue. Boucher's earliest paintings, the first in the chronological order adopted in this exhibition, have often borne—until quite recently—the most varied assortment of names. Today their attribution to Boucher can no longer be questioned, both for the documentary reasons set out in the entries and on stylistic grounds. It is nevertheless interesting to recall that these paintings have been variously sold or published over the last ten years as works by Sebastiano Ricci, Pellegrini, Subleyras, Dumont le Romain, Dandré-Bardon, and even Lemoine or Carle Vanloo. The same is true of the drawings of Boucher's youth, which have in their turn been attributed to Cazes; to Gaspare Diziani; to Gian Antonio Guardi; to Carle, Jean-Baptiste, or François Vanloo; to Cellony; and even to Fragonard.

One can see from this that the works of Boucher's youth are easily confused (or were easily confused until the present exhibition), both with those of older masters and also with those of his contemporaries belonging to the "generation of 1700."

For those who visit the Hôtel de Rohan, the present Archives Nationales—and this is the second observation—comparison between Boucher's overdoors and those of Restout, Trémolières, Carle Vanloo, or Natoire by no means always results in a judgment in our painter's favor. We know that this ensemble, among the finest to be seen in Paris, was

Fig. 12. Pierre-Charles Trémolières, *Minerva Teaching a Nymph to Weave Tapestry* (1737). Archives Nationales, Paris.

Fig. 13. François Lemoine, *The Continence of Scipio* (1727). Musée des Beaux-Arts, Nancy.

Fig. 14. *Paisane des Environs de Ferrare*, engraved by Edmé Jeaurat after Boucher (1734).

Fig. 15. Nicolas Vleughels, *Rebecca and Eliezer*. Private collection, Paris.

41. Bordeaux, 1985.
42. Hercenberg, 1975.
43. Nor did the works of Lemoine's rival, Jean-François de Troy, born in 1679, leave Boucher indifferent. Their brio and bold use of color were to attract him, as were the genre scenes that he imitated and whose subjects he repeated. Alastair Laing informs me that the de Sireul sale of 3 Dec. ff. 1781 even contained (lot 28): "Armida visiting Rinaldo asleep in the forest. This picture is a sketch copied by M. Boucher from M. Detroy, during the time that he was in his school." There exist two sketches of this subject, both attributed to J-F. de Troy (figs. 17, 18). One, recently acquired by the Musée de Lille, was published by Jacques Vilain (1971, pp. 353–56); the other is in an English private collection (exh. cat. 1980, Albuquerque, no. 63). Could one of these be by Boucher? It is difficult to decide, but I would rather incline toward the one in Lille.

executed between 1735 and 1740. At that epoch, the game was not yet won for Boucher; but, as we shall see, he held a winning hand. If we are to understand the reasons for this triumph—a fleeting triumph and perhaps less obvious to the eyes of his contemporaries than to ours—we must reconsider the early struggles of the young Boucher.

In the first part of this essay I have listed the names of a certain number of older artists admired by Boucher. From Lemoine, he was to retain, to repeat what has been said by others before me, the striking, light tonality; the noble, elegantly articulated figures; the fluency of effortless, natural-seeming compositions.[41] But are these qualities present in Boucher's early works, or are they not rather to be found in the works painted after 1737? That was the year in which Lemoine, by then *premier peintre du Roi*, committed suicide, after executing that uniquely grandiose work in the history of eighteenth-century French painting, against which Boucher surely dreamed of measuring himself, but either never dared to or never had the opportunity—the ceiling of the Salon d'Hercule at Versailles. The

Fig. 16. Jean-François de Troy, *Le déjeûner* (1723). Staatliche Museen Preussischer Kulturbesitz, Gemäldegalerie, Berlin.

Fig. 17. Jean-François de Troy or François Boucher(?), *Armida Struck with Love for Rinaldo when about to Kill Him*. Musée des Beaux-Arts, Lille.

Fig. 18. Jean-François de Troy or François Boucher(?), *Armida Struck with Love for Rinaldo when about to Kill Him*. A. S. Ciechanowiecki collection, on extended loan to the University of New Mexico Art Museum, Albuquerque.

Fig. 19. François Boucher, *The Graces at the Tomb of Watteau*, etching. Musée du Louvre, Collection Edmond de Rothschild, Paris.

Fig. 20. Antoine Watteau, *Pittoni a Parigi Broccantor da Quadri*. . . . Fondazione Cini, Venice.

44. Jacoby, 1979, pp. 261–72.
45. Other artists, such as Cazes, or Jean-Baptiste and François Vanloo (the last died prematurely in 1732 at the age of twenty-four, but some of his drawings are known), ought likewise to be mentioned here.
46. Exh. cat. 1969, Venice.
47. *Revue de l'Art*, no. 9, 1970, p. 92, fig. 2.
48. Zava Boccazzi, 1977, p. 104.

death of Lemoine, Boucher's senior by fifteen years, while it did not leave him absolute master of the field, rid him of a formidable rival.

The same year—but in Rome—Vleughels died.[42] There is no question but that the two artists had known each other in Italy (Boucher had contributed one of the six small pictures representing women from the environs of Rome to the set painted by Vleughels, engraved in 1734 by Edmé Jeaurat), and we have already noted that the director of the Académie de France in Rome considered Boucher one of the most promising students of his generation. But I am convinced that the two artists had met before Vleughels's departure for Rome (1724). Not only did Vleughels contribute two illustrations to the 1722 edition of Father Daniel's *Histoire de France;* not only did he handle themes—the *Fortune-Teller,* La Fontaine's *Contes,* and numerous mythological subjects—dear to Boucher; but also and above all the first works of Boucher attest his admiration for the complex compositions, meticulous yet delectable handling, and studied chromatic effects practiced by Vleughels.[43]

Vleughels's name evokes that of Watteau, whose friend he was, and with whose landscape drawings Boucher's have so long and so often been confused. We do not know if Boucher ever knew Watteau. The portrait he drew of Watteau shows him as young and handsome, but Watteau was never—alas!—old, and passed for handsome in the eyes of his admirers. Boucher was one of those who eagerly engraved so many of his drawings. The aims of the two artists had nothing in common, Watteau being the very example of the introverted painter, and Boucher the extrovert par excellence. Nor is there much that is comparable in their works (though Boucher was also in his youth to depict a *Fortune-Teller*); and yet Boucher learned something from the older artist: not simply that he would never paint the *Enseigne de Gersaint,* but a technique and a certain way of approaching painting. He could not or did not want to imitate Watteau, but he knew his secrets and testified to his admiration for the draftsman, to the point that certain drawings by Boucher—I am thinking of the *Landscape* in the Fitzwilliam Museum in Cambridge, the subject of a recent article by Beverly Schreiber Jacoby[44]—were quite recently being exhibited under Watteau's name.[45]

Even before his departure for Italy, Boucher was sensitive to the examples of Venetian painting that he had before his eyes in Paris: the visits of Sebastiano Ricci and Rosalba Carriera, the ceiling of the Hôtel Law (alias the Banque Royale, or Banque de Mississipi) by G. A. Pellegrini, could not leave indifferent an ambitious young artist who aspired to be utterly up-to-date. There is nothing particularly new about this last observation—I simply wish to dwell for a moment on a suggestion that has perhaps not received sufficient attention. The Fondazione Cini in Venice owns a now-dismantled album of drawings, which is attributed to Anton Maria Zanetti (1680–1767).[46] I have previously reattributed one of the drawings in this album to Watteau, an attribution that now seems to be unanimously accepted (fig. 20).[47] Now this drawing bears an inscription in ink identifying its subject as: *Pittoni a Parigi Broccantor da Quadri Pittore, ed Amico del Zanetti.* Franca Zava Boccazzi,[48] the leading specialist on G. B. Pittoni (1687–1767), is aware of this drawing but discards the notion of a visit to Paris by her artist. Yet it seems to me that Boucher's early works display such affinities with those of Pittoni—mouvementées, "*déjetées*," willfully complex compositions, executed with small, saturated brushstrokes, and enlivened by judiciously distributed highlights—that contact between the two men in Paris before Boucher's Italian journey seems difficult to exclude.[49]

To return for a moment to Boucher's visit to Italy: his illness would not have prevented him from looking at works of art in that country, even if he did not greatly admire them. What is interesting is that his own work shows so little influence of them, and that it is difficult—once one has cited the names of Castiglione (less often mentioned in connection with Boucher in the eighteenth century than it is today) and Albani (which by contrast recurs constantly in the writings of his contemporaries)[50]—to pinpoint that influence. To be sure, the names of certain Italian artists are mentioned in eighteenth-century sale catalogues; Boucher himself, a discerning collector, owned—as the catalogue of his posthumous sale demonstrates—a fine selection of Italian drawings; and Boucher's biographers never fail to allude to a certain number of Italian painters and to evoke their influence,[51] but up until now no one has tried to define this more precisely or analyze the specific traces of it. That may be because this influence is hard to pinpoint exactly, but it may also be because it is not easy to define.

I would not go so far as to claim that Boucher left for Italy perfectly formed, nor even that he was not sensitive to Italian models (or northern ones in some cases, as will be seen below in relation to Subleyras), still less that his style did not undergo a succession of developments, transformations, and mutations (although this process is a tricky thing to follow and has yet to be grasped in all its complexity), but I do not think it is necessary to go searching at all costs through the works of Boucher's youth for what—as he himself admitted as we learned from Mariette at the beginning of this essay—he made no attempt to assimilate. We are accustomed to study dead artists by trying to discern the influences of their predecessors in their paintings. But the work of some painters—

Fig. 21. Michel-François Dandré-Bardon, here attributed, *Sepelire mortuos* (before 1725). Musée du Louvre, Cabinet des Dessins, Paris.

Fig. 22. *Sepelire mortuos*, engraved by Laurent Cars after M-F. Dandré-Bardon. Bibliothèque Nationale, Paris.

Fig. 23. Jacques Dumont, called Le Romain, *Hagar Visited by the Angel* (1726). Bibliothèque Nationale, Paris.

Fig. 24. Jacques Dumont, called Le Romain, *Hercules in Thrall to Omphale* (1728). Musée des Beaux-Arts, Tours.

Fig. 25. François Vanloo, *Moses*. Musée Paul Arbaud, Aix-en-Provence.

Fig. 26. François Vanloo, *St. John the Evangelist*. Musée Paul Arbaud, Aix-en-Provence.

49. For Zava Boccazzi, the person in Watteau's drawing is too old to be G. B. Pittoni. Besides, the latter seems to have been in Venice in August 1720. According to her, the drawing may show Pittoni's uncle, Francesco, who was also a painter and an art dealer. Might it not be in that case, that Francesco Pittoni had introduced his nephew's works to Paris and that they had made a powerful impression on the young Boucher?

50. The abbé de Fontenai in his *Dictionnaire des Artistes,* published in 1776, calls Boucher "the Albani of France."

51. The best perspective on Boucher and Italy is to be found in Slatkin, 1971[b], p. 402, nn. 1–3. See also Jacoby, 1979, p. 269.

52. Preface by Pierre Rosenberg. The major portion of the catalogue is by Jean-François Méjanès.

53. Catalogue by Isabelle Julia, Lise Duclaux, Georges Brunel, Patrick Violette, and Pierre Rosenberg.

54. Preface by Pierre Rosenberg. Catalogue by Marie-Catherine Sahut.

and Boucher is one of them—does not lend itself to this favorite and now all-too-automatic tactic of the art historian. Do we not run the risk of seeing influence where there is only fortuitous resemblance, thereby forcing and falsifying reality?

Let us now turn to the "generation of 1700." But first a reminder of the birth dates of this group of artists, whose achievement was to establish the dominance of French art in Europe: Bouchardon (1698); Chardin, Subleyras, and Etienne Jeaurat (1699); Dandré-Bardon, Natoire, and Adam (1700); Frontier, Louis-Gabriel Blanchet, and Dumont le Romain (1701); Aved (1702); Boucher and Trémolières (1703); La Tour (1704); Carle Vanloo and Michel-Ange Slodtz (1705). Some of the more important of them follow on one another's heels in winning the accolade of the Grand Prix bestowed by the Académie: Natoire was awarded it in 1721, the following year it was Bouchardon's turn (as a sculptor, of course), Boucher (beating Quillard, the ape of Watteau) in 1723, Carle Vanloo the next year (and Slodtz for sculpture), Louis-Michel Vanloo in 1725 (beating Dandré-Bardon), Subleyras in 1727 (beating Blanchet; in 1726, Trémolières had only won second prize), and Frontier in 1728. Despite the intervals between their awards, the times of a number of them in Rome were to coincide: if Boucher's stay there only overlapped that of Natoire, Etienne Jeaurat, and Nicolas Delobel, not only were his traveling companions, the three Vanloo, there the whole time that he must have been, but so also were the painters Dandré-Bardon, Pierre Bernard, Trémolières, Subleyras, and Louis-Gabriel Blanchet, the sculptors Michel-Ange Slodtz, Edmé Bouchardon, and Lambert-Sigisbert Adam, and the architects Etienne Le Bon and Etienne Dérizet.

Beginning with the Trémolières exhibition at Cholet in 1973,[52] which was the first of its kind to draw attention to this ambitious and triumphant generation, its leading members have successively been the object of serious study. Natoire received his due from an exhibition held in Troyes, Nîmes, and Rome in 1977,[53] as did Carle Vanloo from one held the same year in Nice, Clermont-Ferrand, and Nancy.[54] Soon Subleyras, who is shortly to be the object of an exhibition at the Villa Medici in Rome and the Musée du Luxembourg in Paris, which will be followed up by a

Fig. 27. Jean-Baptiste Vanloo, *The Raising of Lazarus*. Private collection, United States.

Fig. 28. Jean-Baptiste Vanloo, *The Raising of Lazarus*. Private collection, Paris.

55. This catalogue and book are being written by Pierre Rosenberg and Olivier Michel.

56. By Pierre Rosenberg and Elisabeth Foucart Walter.

57. It should be noted, however, that Chardin's posthumous inventory contained "A Boucher landscape, by Le Bas"—no doubt the very engraving of the *Seconde vue de Beauvais* dedicated to him by the owner of its pendant, Le Noir (J-R 1341). The absence from this inventory (see G. Wildenstein, 1933, pp. 144–50) of any of the pictures or drawings by Boucher found in Chardin's posthumous sale promotes the suspicion that these were introduced by the auctioneers.

58. No. 4 in exh. cat. 1977, Troyes.

59. Rosenberg, 1970, pp. 133–38.

60. Slatkin, 1976, pp. 247–60. Boucher was not alone in copying Bloemaert's drawings; today we know of seven similar copies bearing the old inscription in pen: *P. Subleyras*. Alastair Laing thinks it not impossible that at least one of these, with studies of two seated women, from the d'Orsay collection in the Louvre (exh. cat. 1983, Paris, no. 99), may actually be by Natoire.

61. A & W 171. The painting is today in the Louvre (Rosenberg, in the catalogue *Musée du Louvre. Nouvelles acquisitions du Département des Peintures* [*1980–1982*], pp. 53–55).

62. We still do not know what role the instruction given by the Académie played in the development of this style. It should be noted that no painter of the "generation of 1700" was asked to participate in the 1727 competition.

63. Rosenberg, 1977, pp. 29–42.

monograph,[55] and Dandré-Bardon[56] will in their turn be better known.

These surveys, copiously illustrated with the artists' works, have greatly facilitated the tasks of distinguishing these figures from one another and of attempting to define their styles. They have been of special help in the study of their beginnings, which were sometimes brilliant (as in the case of Carle Vanloo), and sometimes awkward (as with Chardin—whose only connection with Boucher, however, is that Fragonard was passed as a pupil from one to the other, and we cannot even be sure of that).[57] Have these investigations given us a better idea of Boucher's place among the artists of this generation and made it easier to understand his exact role and define his character as an artist?

We might begin by noting that Boucher was personally acquainted with all the artists of this generation. He had already collaborated with some of them in Paris and for a few years was in the company of others in Rome. But we do not know which ones were his friends, which ones he envied, or which ones were jealous of him. At the deaths of Natoire and Dandré-

Fig. 29. Charles-Joseph Natoire, *Christ Expelling the Money Changers from the Temple* (1727–28). Saint-Médard, Paris.

Fig. 30. Carle Vanloo, *The Apotheosis of St. Isidore* (1729). Kunsthalle, Hamburg.

Bardon, which occurred well after Boucher's own (1770), some of his works appear in their posthumous sales. But there has never been any proof that one of these artists dominated or set the tone for the rest.

The question is nevertheless of some importance. It is generally agreed, as we have noted, that there is an air of kinship among the juvenilia of the artists of this generation. A picture such as *Christ Expelling the Money Changers from the Temple* (fig. 29), painted in Rome by Natoire in 1727–28 for Cardinal de Polignac (today in the church of Saint-Médard in Paris), and which I have written about elsewhere,[58] or Carle Vanloo's sketches for the *Good Samaritan* (1723, Musée Fabre, Montpellier) or the *Apotheosis of St. Isidore* (fig. 30; 1729, Kunsthalle, Hamburg),[59] or even the earliest works of Trémolières, Dumont le Romain, and Dandré-Bardon—how did they strike the young Boucher?

To take another example: Subleyras and Boucher must have known each other. They copied—but was it in Rome or while both were still in Paris?—drawings by Bloemaert (figs. 32, 112, 114);[60] they treated the same subjects (La Fontaine's *Contes*); and one of the finest portraits by Subleyras (fig. 33), of which the Louvre is now the fortunate possessor, was until recently catalogued under the name of Boucher,[61] while number 1 in the present catalogue was once thought to be by Subleyras. Both of them, in their early works, like most of the artists we have mentioned, were fond of over-elongated figures with tiny heads, skinny bodies enveloped in large cloaks and ample drapery, and long hands with knobbly fingers. But who evolved these mannerisms, which Boucher was to adopt, only to abandon such exaggerations and distortions not long after his return to France? We still have no certain answers.[62]

Finally, we need to ask why it should have been Boucher who ultimately triumphed. Chance played its part: the deaths of François Vanloo in 1732, Noël-Nicolas Coypel in 1734 (connoisseurs had considered him the real winner of the competition of 1727),[63] and Trémolières in 1739, together with the fact that Subleyras and Blanchet chose to settle in Rome, to which Jean-François de Troy and Natoire were successively sent as directors of the French Academy in 1738 and 1750 respectively, removed

Fig. 31. *Mars and Venus*, engraved by Simon-François Ravenet after Carle Vanloo. Bibliothèque Nationale, Paris.

Fig. 32. Pierre Subleyras, *Study of a Seated Cowherd*. Private collection, Paris.

Fig. 33. Pierre Subleyras, *Presumed Portrait of Giuseppe Baretti*. Musée du Louvre, Paris.

64. "Your idea, my dear niece [Mme de Fontaine], of having copies of the beautiful nudes of Natoire and Boucher painted to enliven my old age shows a tender spirit" (Voltaire, XXXIX, 1880, p. 221. The names of Boucher and Natoire are also associated in a letter from Mariette to Gabburri of 28 January 1732 (Bottari & Ticozzi, 1822, II, p. 331).

65. *Mercure de France*, September 1770, pp. 181–89.

66. Mannlich, 1948, p. 216.

67. Diderot, 1983, p. 238.

68. Diderot, 1975, p. 205.

some formidable rivals. There remained a few older artists, such as Jean Restout, who was to specialize in ecclesiastical paintings, or Charles-Antoine Coypel (1694–1752), without an equal for paintings inspired by the theater, but otherwise notoriously unproductive. More seriously, there were Carle Vanloo, who was younger than Boucher yet his senior in the Academy and who was to be preferred over him for the post of *premier peintre du Roi* in 1760; or (while he remained in Paris) Natoire, whom Voltaire ranked equally with Boucher in 1757.[64] The standing of both Vanloo and Natoire in the eyes of their contemporaries was by no means negligible, and they were rated among the great painters of their time. But even if Boucher's triumph was less absolute than we see it as nowadays, the fact nevertheless remains that from around 1740 Boucher occupied the limelight, and symbolized in his own person a new and original style that had broken with the past, rather as Simon Vouet had done in the previous century.

Boucher owed this position above all to his extraordinary capacity for work, which impressed his contemporaries and ought to scotch the still prevalent image of a frivolous and sybaritic man. "Constant work for more than twelve hours a day, from the moment in his childhood when he first took up his pencils to the very end of his life, did not cause his imagination to run dry."[65] "M. Boucher hardly ever went out, and his sorties were limited to Versailles, to the Gobelins, of which he was the director, to the Opéra, where he was likewise head of the department of sets and costumes, and to visit naturalists and lovers of natural history. . . . He placed himself in front of his easel in his studio, where he painted even the meanest utensils from nature. . . ."[66]

He also owed this position to the experiments of his youth, to the technique and tricks he had mastered during his apprenticeship: he engraved more quickly and skillfully than the professional engravers; he drew from life as from imagination as though for enjoyment; he painted with disconcerting abundance and facility. For more than ten years,

Fig. 34. Noël-Nicolas Coypel, *The Rape of Europa*. Philadelphia Museum of Art.

Boucher had been obliged to copy, recopy, imitate, and engrave; he had cast himself in the mold of a new manner of painting that fitted him easily, the better to be able to manipulate this to his advantage and gain acceptance as the master of this new idiom.

We often forget that Diderot was at first an unconditional admirer of this early manner. "The Boucher whom I have just relegated to fashionable levées and the company of courtesans, painted on his return from Rome some pictures that ought to be seen. . . ."[67] "This man, when he had just returned from Italy, did some very fine things; his coloring was vigorous but true; his composition was well planned, yet full of fire; his handling was broad and bold. I am familiar with some of his earliest pieces, which he now calls *daubs* and would buy back if he could in order to burn them. He has old portfolios stuffed with admirable things. . . ."[68]

Diderot, waving the standard of the return to nature and of truth (but what exactly did he mean by these two expressions?), was one of the mature Boucher's fiercest critics. He upbraided him, perhaps justly, for his excessive facility; he also scolded him for his lack of naturalness and for his artificiality. And yet it was this very artificiality that he so much admired in the works painted immediately after the artist's return from Rome. Indeed, what Diderot criticized in Boucher is what constitutes the very essence of his genius—his inventiveness, his verve, and his endlessly fertile imagination.

Scorned and swiftly forgotten, then once again adulated and popular, Boucher, like Renoir, currently seems to suffer from his excessive celebrity. His deliberately make-believe world, those goddesses, nymphs, and shepherdesses so far removed from everyday reality, and yet so delightfully and carnally present, need to be looked at with fresh eyes.

# Boucher: The Search for an Idiom

ALASTAIR LAING

*Ce n'étoit point un peintre, mais la peinture elle-même.*
(*Journal Encyclopédique*, 1 October 1757, p. 101: He was not a painter, but painting itself.)

*Cet homme a tout—excepté la vérité.*
(Diderot, *Salon de 1761:* That man is capable of everything—except the truth.)

*N'est pas Boucher qui veut.*
(David, before going to Italy, as quoted in *Le Pausanias Français*, 1806, p. 147: Wishing does not make a Boucher.)

1. Mariette, I, 1851–53, p. 166. Thesis plates are the engravings published to celebrate the successful maintenance of a doctoral thesis, generally in theology. They consist of a lower part giving the text of the arguments maintained and the details of the occasion, and an oblong upper plate illustrating some scriptural—generally Old Testament—episode embodying the theme, which would normally have been supplied from stock.

Fig. 35. Thesis plate incorporating *Jephthah Bewailing the Sight of His Daughter*, engraved by P-F. Basan after a lost painting by Boucher. Employed here on a thesis sustained by J-P. Ravette in 1789, but previously employed on another sustained by Henri Agasse in 1769, and very probably upon others before that. Published by Robert Hecquet.

Boucher is inseparable from his reputation. Adulated by his contemporaries, excoriated by immediately succeeding generations, the idol of collectors of eighteenth-century French art in the nineteenth century, and now mostly the object of grudging or apologetic admiration, the artist has consistently been praised or denounced as much for what he stood for, as for what he actually did. In this respect he presents a contrast to an artist such as his former master, Lemoine, whose ceilings in Saint-Sulpice, Saint-Thomas d'Aquin (the "Jacobins"), or the Salon d'Hercule were inseparable from any serious assessment of him, or to his contemporaries Natoire and Carle Vanloo, whose decoration of the Chapelle des Enfants-Trouvés and cycle of paintings in the church of Notre-Dame-des-Victoires (the "Petits Augustins") respectively never failed to be cited in any extended consideration of these artists and their oeuvres.

This celebration of Boucher as a phenomenon began in his own lifetime, a few years after his return from Italy, and it would almost appear that it was something that he consciously set out to achieve. Rather than seeking a major commission that would have occupied him for several years, in the hope that it might make his fame overnight upon its unveiling, he seems to have been determined to demonstrate his diversity and fecundity all at once. In a way, he may have been compelled to, since—after the false beginnings of the *Judgment of Susannah*, painted at the age of seventeen, which so impressed Lemoine, and the *Evilmerodach Releasing Jehoiachin from Prison*, which won him the first prize at the Academy in 1723—he was a late starter. The denial of the journey to Rome that should have accompanied the prize meant that he had to earn his living by engraving Watteau's drawings for de Jullienne, and by providing what the Augsburg artists called *Delineations-Sachen*—compositions for engraver-publishers to have thesis plates scraped from:[1] no basis for a reputation as a painter. Having probably made enough money by this means to finance the journey to Rome himself, he appears to have been unmoved by what he saw there, and also possibly prevented by illness from either succeeding in the Concorso Clementino or working on anything to be sent back to France.[2]

Fig. 36. *The Encounter of Jacob and Rachel,* thesis plate after a lost painting by Boucher, published by Laurent Cars.

Thus, when Boucher arrived back in Paris in 1731, he was already twenty-eight, and with very little to show for it. This helps to illuminate Mariette's statement that the *Rape of Europa* now in the Wallace Collection (which he significantly regarded as having been painted by Boucher "dans sa jeunesse," showing how late in Boucher's career his so-called juvenilia persisted) "was one of a number of large pictures that he had painted for a marble mason called Dorbay, who had furnished his whole house with them, which was perfectly easy for him to do, since Boucher, not seeking to do anything but make a name for himself at that period, would, I believe, have done them for nothing rather than pass up the opportunity."[3]

Thanks to Georges Brunel's discovery of the posthumous inventory of the lawyer François Derbais (who was actually the *son* of the marble mason Jérôme Derbais, who had died around 1715—too early to have himself been the client in question), which I am exceedingly grateful to him for having communicated to me, we now have a much fuller idea of what these pictures may have been (the absence of artists' names makes certain identification impossible). In addition to the four large putti pictures—*L'Amour nageur, L'Amour vendangeur, L'Amour moissonneur,* and *L'Amour oiseleur* (see cat. 15)—proclaimed as belonging to Derbais by the engravings after them, and the *Rape of Europa* (see cat. 25) and its pendant, *Mercury Confiding the Infant Bacchus to the Nymphs of Nysa* (fig. 39), which could be assumed to have belonged to him on the strength of Mariette's statement in the *Abecedario,* he also evidently owned the *Venus and Vulcan* of 1732 (cat. 17) and the *Aurora and Cephalus* of 1733 (cat. 18), as well as, in all probability, another overdoor of *Amours*[4] and a large *Birth of Venus,*[5] both of which were in the same *salle de billard* as the four last. The four putti pictures were on the stairs, and it is very possible that there were other pictures by Boucher scattered about the house, including *Moses before the Burning Bush* (cat. 14) in the *salle à manger.* Did he also paint a large room in another house with episodes from Ovid's *Metamorphoses,*[6] as stated by Papillon de La Ferté, or is this a confused reference to the miscellany of pictures in Derbais's *salle de billard?*

The pictures that Boucher did for Derbais reveal a new ambitiousness: on the one hand, he painted the same kind of mythologies that he had

2. Papillon de La Ferté, 1776, II, p. 657; A & W doc. 1140. The "plusieurs tableaux précieux, à la maniére des Flamands" that Papillon de La Ferté says he did produce in Rome were presumably for a local clientele, since there is not much trace of any such pictures in French collections.

3. Mariette, I, 1851–53, p. 165: "faisoit partie du nombre de grands tableaux qu'il avoit fait pour un sculpteur marbrier nommé Dorbay qui en avoit garni toute sa maison, ce qui lui avoit été très-facile, car Boucher, ne cherchant alors qu'à se faire connoître, les auroit, je crois, faits pour rien, plus tost que d'en laisser manquer l'occasion."

4. Possibly the *Bacchanal* formerly in the Cl. Riche collection, Voss, 1953, fig. 57.

5. Almost certainly the picture last recorded in the collection of the comtesse de Béhague, Fenaille, 1925, p. 55 and pl. p. 51.

6. Could the house have been that of Crozat de Thiers, for whose cabinet the memoir published in the *Galerie Francoise* (1771, no. V, p. 1) says Boucher painted a number of pictures before he went to Rome? We have no further knowledge of them in either case.

Fig. 37. *Studies of Two Women* (after the Bassanos' *Return of the Prodigal* in the Galleria Doria-Pamphilj, Rome). Albertina, Vienna.

Fig. 38. *Study of Bernini's Fontana del Moro.* Formerly in Huquier's sale, Amsterdam, September 1761, and subsequently with Pardo, Paris.

Fig. 39. *Mercury Confiding the Infant Bacchus to the Nymphs of Nysa*. Wallace Collection, London.

done before going to Italy,[7] but on a monumental scale and with a new mastery of anatomy; and on the other, he created a new kind of putto picture on the same large scale. In all of them, there is also a roughness of facture and coloring—taken to extremes in *Moses before the Burning Bush* —underlining an overt virtuosity in the handling of paint, that broke entirely with the smooth handling, warm Italianate palette, and delicate glazes of the tradition embodied by Galloche, Lemoine, and J-F. de Troy. Not that this radical break, both with the then exemplars of the French School and with his own past, was not also indebted to Italian models, but this indebtedness bespoke a novel choice of paradigms: Sebastiano Ricci and—above all—Castiglione.

Significantly, Derbais's collection itself included two pairs of *Caravanes* —the archetypal Castiglione subject. Were these by Benedetto himself or an imitator—or were they pastiches by Boucher? Obituaries and sale catalogue entries about Boucher and his works frequently refer to Castiglione as a yardstick of comparison, but generally only on this rather superficial level of subject matter. It is, as usual, Mariette who goes beyond this to the manner, rather than the matter, of the artist's works; not in the entry on Boucher himself, where he implicitly confesses himself somewhat baffled by the homegrown sources of the artist's style, but in the entry on his son-in-law Deshays. Contrary to the critical consensus, he did not see Deshays as having really assimilated anything from Italy into his style: "he seems only to have been affected by that of Castiglione; and in any case this very free kind of handling is sufficiently evident in that of Mr. Boucher, of which Deshays was full, and never attempted to rid himself."[8]

The influence of Castiglione—or "le Benedette," as he was most commonly known—on French eighteenth-century painted and graphic art is a chapter in the history of art that cries out to be written. There is no room to do so here (but I should like to acknowledge the benefit of conversations and correspondence with Ann Percy and Timothy J.

7. E.g., the *Birth* and *Death of Adonis*, only now engraved by Scotin and Aubert, A & W 38, 39; the *Death of Adonis* (private coll., Saint-Jean-Cap-Ferrat), apparently painted as a pendant to Carle Vanloo's *Mars and Venus* of 1726(?) and engraved by Surugue and Le Vasseur; and the *Selene and Endymion* from the prince de Conti's collection, exh. cat. 1982, New York, no. 5.

8. Mariette, II, 1853–54, p. 95: "c'étoit seulement celle du Benedette dont il avoit paru affecté; aussi cette manière libertine rentre-t-il assez dans celle de M. Boucher, dont s'étoit rempli Deshays, et dont il ne chercha jamais à se défaire."

9. Mariette, II, 1853–54, p. 132.

10. The listings in D. Wildenstein, 1982, p. 20, are by no means complete—*teste* the omission of the [Viallis] sales of 28 Dec. 1781 et seq., which contained no less than eleven.

11. Dezallier, 1752, pp. 22, 77, 211, 302; and 1757, pp. 130, 131.

12. Lorck, 1967.

13. A & W 35; drawing recently acquired by the Cabinet des Dessins of the Louvre; exh. cat. 1984, Paris, Cabinet des Dessins, no. 78.

14. In a letter of 13 Feb. 1727, Vleughels reported that Ricci had offered his services as a mentor to students from the French Academy in Rome sojourning in Venice (Hercenberg, 1975, p. 16). Although Vleughels recommended against acceptance, he probably still gave his charges introductions to Ricci.

15. Haskell, 1971, pp. 266–67, 312.

16. J-R 1454.

Fig. 40. *The Genius of the Artist Torn between Nature and the Antique*, wash drawing. Whereabouts unknown.

Standring on the topic, in expanding my ideas as to what works by the artist might have been accessible to Boucher in Italy). In a curious lapse, Mariette[9] even claims that that least painterly of artists, Dumont le Romain, actually studied in Rome under Benedetto Castiglione (d. 1665 in Mantua! Presumably he intended to say Benedetto Luti). Boucher's indebtedness to Castiglione was twofold: to his subject matter, in opening his eyes to nature, and to his technique, in liberating his facility with the brush.

It is clear from their frequent occurrence in French sales[10] and from those cited in Paris collections by Dezallier d'Argenville,[11] that there must have been a number of paintings by Castiglione to be seen in France in the eighteenth-century—though how many of them were already present in the first quarter of the century is less easy to establish. Nevertheless, it is probable that, since Boucher's original response was to the subject matter rather than to the manner of Castiglione's paintings, his initial exposure to them was in the form of prints. There is an intriguing and little-known wash drawing by Boucher, which is not only indebted to one of Castiglione's most celebrated etchings, *The Genius of Castiglione*, but also uses it to express his own artistic credo (fig. 40).[12] Where Castiglione's slouching, dandified, and epicene youth is at the center of a Testa-like dream-confusion of nature and symbol, Boucher's less bizarre figure in the same pose is confronted with the choice—like a kind of artistic *Hercules at the Crossroads*—between the Antique and Nature: the latter being symbolized by sunrise over a Castiglionesque *Marche* to which cupids beckon him away.

From its style and subject, this drawing would appear to date from just before Boucher went to Rome, or from his first few months there; the absence of any identifiable piece of Antique sculpture rather suggests the former. Whichever is the case, at this point Castiglione seems to have represented for Boucher essentially the resort to nature for subject matter, as embodied in the caravans of people and animals that he had already introduced into the *Separation of Laban from Jacob*,[13] *La vie champêtre* (cat. 9), or the two pictures of Noah painted for de Jullienne (cat. 10, 11). It was only with extensive exposure to Castiglione's paintings themselves—aided, perhaps, by advice from Sebastiano Ricci in Venice[14]—that Boucher transformed the actual way in which he painted. There would certainly have been some paintings by Castiglione to be seen in Rome, including in the Pamphilj collection, where we know that Boucher studied, from the evidence of his drawings (fig. 37). It would, however, probably have needed more than an isolated picture here or there to have made an impression on him. Thanks above all to the final dissolution of the Mantuan ducal collections, considerable quantities of both paintings and drawings by Castiglione were to be found in Venice,[15] and it was surely there that he studied them. Their impact is particularly overwhelming in the pictures that would appear to have been painted for Derbais immediately after Boucher's return to Paris, and in other pictures evidently from this epoch, such as *Putti Playing with Birds* (cat. 15), or *Le repos de Diane* (see cat. 14),[16] which survives in mutilated form at Montluçon.

What makes Boucher's development hard to establish even at this stage, however—before he had gotten into the habit of dating his works—is that he was prepared to try his hand at anything, before finding his winning veins. As Mariette said of him: "Boucher was born a painter; there are few who surpass him in facility. One could say that he was born with a brush in his hand."[17]

After mythologies and putti pictures of the kind that he painted for Derbais, the field that beckoned most obviously was landscape. It was one in which there were no distinguished practitioners, only uninspired exponents of the fag end of the Claudian and Poussinian traditions, such as Domenchin de Chavannes and the third "Francisque" (Joseph-François Millet), or history painters who made only the most occasional forays into the genre, such as de Largillière or Lemoine. Even a decade later Mariette could complain of the dearth of practitioners of landscape throughout Europe: "Our best Masters rarely devote themselves to this kind of study: they regard the pieces of Landscape that they deign to chance to spend a few moments on, as an amusement and distraction. . . ."[18] By that time, Boucher himself must have been—somewhat unjustly—in Mariette's mind as one of these negligent "best Masters," while Oudry, despite Mariette's admiration of him, was evidently simply left out of account, as by avocation a practitioner of the inferior branch of animal painting. Nonetheless, Oudry had been keeping a sketchbook of landscape studies since 1714[19] and had been painting landscapes from the 1720s, including his earliest-known in 1722 and a whole set for the marquis de Beringhen in 1727.[20]

It is very possible that it was Oudry—who was certainly the leader of the sketching expeditions to Arcueil, and who procured the services of Boucher as a designer of tapestries for Beauvais—who encouraged Boucher to employ French motifs in his landscapes (see cat. 34, 35). Yet one should not forget either the likely lead that Boucher had been given in Rome by Vleughels, who had himself previously sketched motifs in France,[21] or Watteau's advice to Lancret[22] and the stimulus afforded by his studies of the stream of the Gobelins, the Bièvre, some of which Boucher had engraved,[23] and which inspired both Lemoine[24] and Boucher himself[25] to use the same motif in paintings.

Nevertheless, it was not landscapes based upon picturesque locations around Paris that Boucher began to paint after his return, but idealized depictions of Italy. The earliest of these appear to have been "arranged" views of celebrated sites in Rome and its environs (e.g., cat. 16, 23); but these gave way to scenes that were entirely the product of Boucher's imagination, combining the classical ruins of Rome with distant views of the Veneto, inspired (via Watteau) by the woodcuts of Campagnola (e.g., *Le moineau apprivoisé*, fig. 100,[26] and *Le pont de bois*, fig. 41[27]). One of the most distinctive features of both these kinds of idealized landscape was the contrastingly rustic character of the figures with which Boucher peopled them—variously employing reminiscences of Castiglionesque *Marches* (cat. 16), the figure studies by Abraham Bloemaert that he himself etched (cat. 23), and his own drawings from life. This combination of idealized landscape and rustic protagonists was one that he was to take over into his large decorative compositions of the second half of the 1730s—both in such large, ornamental paintings as those purported to have come from the Hôtel de Richelieu (see cat. 27) and in his first set of tapestries for Beauvais, the so-called *Fêtes Italiennes* (see cat. 86–89).

17. Mariette, I, 1851–53, p. 165: "Boucher est né peintre; il en est peu qui le surpassent en facilité. On peut dire qu'il est né le pinceau à la main."

18. Gersaint, 1744, p. 198: "Rarement nos meilleurs Maîtres s'appliquent-ils à cette étude: ils ne regardent que comme un amusement, & un délaissement, les morceaux de Paysage, auxquels ils veulent bien par hazard passer quelques momens. . . ."

19. Exh. cat. 1982–83, Paris, nos. 22–25.

20. Opperman, 1977, I, pp. 65–66, and cat. nos. P583–89.

21. Hercenberg, 1975, cat. no. 324, pp. 152–53, and fig. 174; exh. cat. 1984, New York, P.M.L., no. 34.

22. Ballot de Sovot, 1873, p. 18.

23. See J-R 43.

24. Bordeaux, 1985, pp. 56, 132.

25. [Trouard] sale, 22 Feb. ff. 1779, lot 33—probably the oval version of *Les villageois à la pêche* that reappears in the [Morel] sale, 3 May ff. 1786, lot 154 (AA 627); and the Choiseul-Praslin sale, 18 Jan. ff. 1793, lot 168.

26. J-R 1033–1035.

27. A & W 52.

28. A & W doc. 224; see Watelet & Lévesque, *sub voce*.

29. Papillon de La Ferté, 1776, II, p. 657.

30. Sotheby's, London, 5 July 1984, lot 369; now in a private collection in Germany.

31. Cayeux sale, 8 Jan. ff. 1770, lot 50.

32. [Dujarry] sale, 4–5 July 1783, lot 34.

33. A & W 78.

34. See also A & W 76.

35. Exh. cat. 1979, Paris, pp. 187ff.

36. A & W 90, recently acquired by the Wadsworth Atheneum, Hartford.

37. J-R 542–549.

Fig. 41. *Le pont de bois* (oblong version).
Hermitage Museum, Leningrad.

Fig. 42. *La Marchande d'Oeufs*, engraved by
Jean Daullé after a lost painting by Boucher.

This use of peasants as staffage in his landscapes dovetailed quite
naturally with pictures in which they were the focus of interest—what
Boucher's contemporaries referred to as *bambochades*.[28] This was a kind
of subject that he had painted before going to Italy and possibly while he
was there, if Papillon de La Ferté's reference to the "plusieurs tableaux
precieux, à la manière des Flamands"[29] that he did in Rome can be
believed (see cat. 9, and *Le repas champêtre*[30]). But when he returned,
such subjects were given a new scale and amplitude, thanks to the wide
Italianate landscapes in which they were set and the studies that he must
have made for each individual figure (e.g., cat. 23).

A related field with which Boucher experimented was that of genre
scenes in domestic interiors, in the Dutch tradition. However, although he
did make what sound like straight pastiches of Dutch pictures, such as
*L'estaminet*, in the "goût de Teniers,"[31] or *Le cabaret*,[32] Boucher's few
surviving pictures of the kind dwell with more involvement on their
protagonists, whether the setting be a kitchen (*La belle cuisinière*, cat. 21;
and *La belle villageoise*[33]) or an artist's studio (cat. 22).[34] It was not a genre
in which Boucher persisted, and the reason for this may have been that
Chardin was extending his range into the same kind of subject matter in
these very years,[35] and that the latter could accommodate himself more
easily to the degree of finish expected by the potential Dutch-oriented
collectors of such works.

Despite the attention lavished on the details of the kitchen in *La belle
cuisinière*, the focus of the scene is the amorous encounter. This was the
vein that Boucher also began to exploit in a series of half-length pictures
with more or less life-size protagonists (e.g., cat. 28), many of them oval
(e.g., the adult version of *La marchande d'oeufs*;[36] *De trois choses en ferez-
vous une?*, cat. 19; and the four slightly later pictures engraved by
Daullé,[37] including one with the same title as the Hartford picture, fig.
42). In these lay the germ of one of Boucher's most successful specialties,
the pastoral—but of that anon.

Fig. 43. *Woman Applying a Mouche*. Formerly in the collection of Count Carl Gustaf Tessin(?), currently on the London art market.

In the same kind of format, he also painted three pictures of single women of the leisured class in occupations characteristic of the Times of Day.[38] One of these is apparently dated 1734;[39] another may only have existed in the form of a grisaille that Count Tessin sent back to Sweden in 1741, which has since disappeared,[40] although a related oval picture exists[41] that may also have belonged to Tessin (fig. 43);[42] while the third is known only from Petit's engraving.[43] These herald more elaborate pictures of similar subjects, for which the obvious paragons are the paintings of socially more elevated protagonists by J-F. de Troy: *Le déjeuner* (cat. 33) of 1739, *Woman Fastening Her Garter, with Her Maid* (cat. 38) of 1742, and *The Milliner* (cat. 51) of 1746, the only picture to be executed from another projected set of the Times of Day for Crown Princess Lovisa Ulrica of Sweden. The exquisite quality of all three pictures sometimes makes it seem as if Boucher, in failing to complete the set or to paint any further pictures of the kind, betrayed his own gifts, but from the new evidence of Scheffer's letters (see cat. 51) it would appear instead that it was around this epoch that the deficiencies in his eyesight first began to manifest themselves, and that these consisted not only of a loss of discrimination toward the red end of the spectrum,[44] but of a blurring of vision that made minute finishing difficult as well. A possible explanation for this is that Boucher may have suffered from a progressive cataract.[45]

The remarkable versatility evident in Boucher's ability to master these diverse branches of painting, not to mention all the other expertises that he deployed in an ancillary capacity, is suggested by the enumeration of his gifts, additional to those of a history painter, set out in the list of Academicians prepared for the Direction des Bâtiments in 1745: "he excels likewise in landscape, in *bambochades*, and in grotesques and ornament in the style of Watteau. He is equally competent in doing flowers, fruit, animals, architecture, little *galant* and society subjects, etc."[46] This makes his initial failure to tackle two of the major and most profitable branches of his art, altarpieces and portraiture, all the more conspicuous. The avoidance of portraiture may be accounted for by his acknowledged difficulty in capturing a likeness,[47] and by the fact that there was no dearth of specialists in the field. What is more, as the career of a Nattier or a J-B. Vanloo tended to demonstrate, once designated as a portrait painter, one became chained to that specialty. The failure to paint altarpieces, or any of the other large paintings required by religious institutions, is more difficult to account for, particularly in view of Boucher's professed search for opportunities to paint on a large scale.[48]

The problem may partly have been artistic, in that another of Boucher's acknowledged difficulties was in creating plausible male physiognomies and in making them emotionally convincing. Yet the two *Exotic Hunts* (cat. 29, 32) surely demonstrate that he could—even if with a certain sense of strain—rise to the occasion. It needs to be considered whether factors of personality and attitude were not also involved (we know, for instance, from Mannlich[49] that Boucher was a Freemason)—which raises the elusive question: what kind of a man was Boucher?

For a painter who achieved such eminence, we have extraordinarily little evidence of Boucher's nonartistic life and character. The obituaries and brief biographies written about him say very little about the man (his life could not even supply any matter to the *Anecdotes des Beaux-Arts*

38. J-R 1456–1458.
39. A & W 113.
40. Sander, 1872, p. 57, no. 88 and p. 63.
41. London art market; exh. cat. 1980, London, Agnew's, no. 28.
42. See Granberg, II, 1930, p. 238; Sander, 1872, p. 66. Tessin's posthumous inventory and sale contain a picture, which does not appear in the bills of lading of 1741/42, showing: "The bust of a woman, sitting in a chair, fastening her eyes on the portrait of a man that she holds in her hands, painted by Boucher." But for the exact direction of her gaze, this corresponds with the picture exhibited in 1980.
43. J-R 1456.
44. *Galerie Françoise*, 1771, p. 5.
45. Trevor-Roper, 1970, pp. 86–91.
46. A & W doc. 244: "il excelle aussi au Païsage, aux Bambochades, aux grotesques et ornemens dans le goût de Vateau. Il fait également bien les fleurs, les fruits, les animaux, l'architecture, les petits sujets galants et de mode &c."
47. Pompadour, 1878, p. 50; Cochin, 1880, p. 81.
48. Mariette, I, 1851–53, p. 165.
49. Stollreither, 1910, p. 232.

50. Houssaye, 1845, pp. 414–26; put into verse by Dobson, 1873. See below in text and note 56 for evidence of the politically inspired vilification of Boucher's name that occurred in the Revolution.

51. Diderot, *Salon de 1765*, II, 1979, p. 75: "Et que peut avoir dans l'imagination un homme qui passe sa vie avec les prostituées du plus bas étage?"

52. Marmontel, 1972, I, p. 168: "il n'avoit pas vu les grâces en bon lieu; il peignoit Vénus et la Vierge d'après les nymphes de coulisses; et son langage se ressentoit, ainsi que ses tableaux, des moeurs de ses modèles et du ton de son atelier."

53. Soyer, 1834: "François Boucher offre, comme homme et comme peintre, l'image de son siècle. La dépravation de ses moeurs, la décadence de son goût, la factice de sa couleur, le prétentieux de ses compositions, la mignardise de ses caractères de tête, son dessin, ses expressions, ont suivi pas à pas la marche licencieuse et dévergondée de la société sous la régence et le régne de Louis XV."

54. Houssaye, 1845, p. 429—who even makes his wife Marie Perdrigeon, the *Mme Boucher* painted as a vestal by Raoux, and kills her off at twenty-four.

55. Mariette, II, 1853–54, p. 96; and I, 1851–53, p. 85.

56. Méré, 1806, I, pp. 73–78. This bizarre tale presents Boucher as the man who, overcome by the duchess's near nudity when posing for him as Hebe, first set her on the path of infidelity to her husband. This is typical of the stories, invented to discredit the Ancien Régime (or, in this case, the house of Orléans), rather than Boucher himself in the first instance, that circulated during the Revolution. A much viler story depicting "Le barbare *Boucher*" as a pimp for Louis XV employed by Mme de Pompadour, "un des *proxenètes* en sous-ordre qui peuploient le Parc-aux-Cerfs," is to be found in Fantin-Desodoards, 1796, II, pp. 214–16; whence it was picked up and given wider circulation by Fiorillo, III, 1805, pp. 369–70.

57. Blanc, 1851, p. 10.

58. Fontenai, 1776, II, pp. 639, 640.

59. Mantz, 1852–53, p. 289: "Et Boucher e[s]t-il bien raisonnable?"

compiled by Nougaret and Leprince); we have barely any letters by him; and the references to him in the letters and memoirs of others are few and ambiguous. It is scarcely surprising that the nineteenth century fell back on sheer invention—most preposterously in "The Story of Rosina," which Arsène Houssaye related as if it were attested fact, but appears simply to have made up[50]—or that invention should have taken its cue from the subject matter of Boucher's art.

The simplistic attempts of moralists to deduce Boucher's character from his works, which began in the eighteenth century with Diderot: "And what can a man who spends his life among prostitutes of the lowest sort have in his imagination?";[51] and Marmontel: "he had seen the Graces in no good place; he painted Venus and the Virgin from the nymphs of the boards; and his language, just like his pictures, smacked of the morals of his models and the tone of his studio"[52]—by which they in fact intended nothing worse than consorting with actresses and singers (many of whom did, of course, have more conspicuous careers as courtesans)—plumbed virulent depths in the early years of the nineteenth century: "As a man, and as a painter, François Boucher is the very image of his century. The depravity of his morals, the decadence of his taste, the artificiality of his palette, the speciousness of his compositions, the affected character of his heads, his draftsmanship, and his expressions, all followed step by step the licentious and degenerate course of society under the Régence and the reign of Louis XV."[53]

The picture is palpably overdrawn. Boucher remained married to his wife, without any *séparation des biens,* or any scandal such as afflicted the ménage of the unfortunate Greuze (nor can I find an authentic source for his supposed statement when getting married, that he was doing so despite the fact that "le mariage ne fût pas dans ses habitudes"[54]). The letters to Favart in 1748 suggest that the couple worked in close harmony with one another. They brought up their son and two daughters without any of them turning to the bad, and married each of the latter to one of his pupils, rather than to any of the rich *partis* apparently proffered by Mme de Pompadour. Mariette specifically says of his two sons-in-law that Deshays was "sincerely attached to him," while Baudouin "adored" him.[55] No specific scandal or liaison ever attached itself to his name, other than the patently fabricated story of his seduction of the nymphomaniac duchesse de Chartres.[56] Even the account of his having compromised himself to the extent of having painted a set of erotic pictures to stimulate the jaded sensibilities of Louis XV seems to have been another nineteenth-century fabrication (the story is supposed originally to have been set down by Thoré, according to Charles Blanc,[57] but I have failed to find where).

That Boucher was pleasure loving, on the other hand, there can be little doubt. There is first of all the evidence of the spirited pastel by his friend Lundberg (fig. 53), which, since it was one of the pastel painter's *morceaux de réception* presented to the Academy, must surely reflect an image of himself that Boucher was happy to have projected. Then there are the little indications to be gleaned from the comments of others: his friendship with the pleasure-loving Tocqué,[58] and Natoire's ironic enquiry after his friends and acquaintances from Rome in 1754: "And Boucher, is he behaving himself?"[59] Or there is Carl Fredrik Scheffer, failing to account for yet a further delay in Boucher's production of *The Milliner* since: "I have no supporting evidence to allege but Boucher's libertinage [the word did not then necessarily carry the freight of moral condemnation that it does today], which has to be seen to be believed. . . . Boucher never renounces his pleasures for one [client] or the next."[60] In support of this, there is Mme de Pompadour's droll letter to the comte d'Argenson, of about 1750, depicting Boucher's despair at having his entrées to the Opéra withdrawn, and fearing that the consequence would be crippled, one-eyed nymphs in the pictures that he was painting for Bellevue.[61]

There is also the implied complicity in carnal pleasures, in Petit de Bachaumont's aside upon his recommendation for the eighth picture in the set of tapestries of the *Story of Psyche*, Psyche whipped by the Nymphs in the presence of Venus: "Quelle croupe &c &c."[62] The same document is one of a number to suggest that Mme Boucher was far from being a stranger to her husband's pleasures, or to his fellow sybarites: "Happy Apelles, to have a living Psyche at home, out of whom you can make a Venus when you please, etc., etc. . . . The best thing to do is to read and reread La Fontaine's *Psyche*, but above all to look long at Mme Boucher." ("*Heureux Apelle, qui avés une Psiché vivante chés vous, de laquelle vous pouvés faire une Vénus quand il vous plaira, et Cetera, et Cetera. . . . Ce qu'il y a de mieux à faire, c'est de lire et relire la Psiché de la Fontaine, et surtout bien regarder Mad<sup>e</sup>. Boucher.*") The fact that de Bachaumont could write like this to Boucher about his wife suggests that the painter took pleasure in the effect of her attractions upon his friends, while possessing such complete confidence in her as not to be aroused to jealousy. The same attitude is suggested in one of the only two at all lengthy letters emanating from Boucher himself, to Favart in Brussels in 1748, about their mutual friend, the abbé de la Garde, which is all the more piquant in that he was apparently using his wife as his scribe: "He is now a courtier . . . he has left off his abbé's habit and now wears a wig, has a full purse, and is quite the gay dog. The ladies will lose their heads over him, and I am not without some anxiety for Mme Boucher."[63] We can be sure that he looked on Count Tessin's evident susceptibility to his wife's charms with the same amused eye. That he was justified in his confidence in her is borne out by the testimony of Christian IV of Zweibrücken, who, seeing his protégé Mannlich struck by her enduring beauty at the age of forty, told him: "You should have seen her twenty years ago, my dear Mannlich: she was then not just the most beautiful woman in Paris, but in the whole of France . . . but she was as virtuous as she was beautiful, and she made herself generally loved and esteemed."[64]

Mannlich was not slow to spin a lubricious story if there was one to tell, but he has nothing to say of any amorous escapades on Boucher's part, not even with his favorite model (whom Mannlich himself claims to have seduced). It is true that Boucher was by then in his sixties, but there is not even a hint that he was a reformed rake. Indeed, what Mannlich says of him is that he was "full of imagination, wit, gaiety, and of utter probity."[65] Elsewhere he refers to him as "cet homme aimable," with the affection that all his pupils seem to have felt, and not only they, since Cochin wrote to an unknown correspondent at Blois in 1769: "You are like Mr. Boucher, who has effortlessly performed fine actions throughout his life: such are the truly great masters."[66]

Boucher was apparently convivial then, but with whom? In the latter

60. Scheffer, 1982, pp. 124–25: "[je] n'ai d'autres pieces justificatives à produire que le libertinage de Boucher, dont il faut etre temoin pour le croire. . . . Boucher ne cede jamais ni aux uns ni aux autres ses plaisirs."

61. Argenson, 1922, p. 287; I am indebted to John Rogister for this reference.

62. A & W doc. 130.

63. Exh. cat. 1964, Paris, Cailleux, no. 88A; A & W doc. 343: "C'est un homme de cour à présent . . . il a quitté [l'habit] d'abée, il est actuellement en peruque, en bourse, et en cavalier fort leste. Les femmes en vont perdre la tete, et je ne suis pas sans inquietudes pour madame Boucher." This portion of the letter was reproduced in the *Isographie* in 1828–30, when it was still in the possession of Favart's descendant. It and two other letters written by Mme Boucher on her husband's behalf were later in the collections of Benjamin Fillon (Charavay, 1879, II, p. 223) and Alfred Morrison (Thibaudeau, 1883, I, pp. 104–05) before being ultimately acquired by Frits Lugt and placed in the Institut Néerlandais in Paris.

64. Mannlich, 1948, p. 73.

65. Mannlich, 1948, p. 215: "plein de génie, d'esprit, de gaiété, et d'une probité à toute épreuve."

66. Furcy-Raynaud, 1904, p. 176: "Vous êtes comme M. Boucher, qui à toute sa vie fait des belles choses sans peine; tels sont les grands maîtres."

67. Jean-Augustin Jullien des Boulmiers, himself significantly a historian of the theater, has a brief allusion to Boucher's moving in literary circles in his obituary in the *Mercure*. After noting that he possessed "natural wit and a penchant for gaiety," he goes on to say "he was fond of literature, and enjoyed the company of those who cultivate it" ("*Il avoit de l'esprit natural & du penchant à la gaieté . . . il aimoit les lettres, se plaisoit avec ceux qui les cultivent . . .*" [Desboulmiers, 1770, pp. 188–89] ).

68. Laujon, 1811, IV, p. 226–27.

69. Stollreither, 1910, p. 232.

70. Piron, 1776, I, pp. 77–82.

71. Saurin, 1783, II, pp. 193–98.

part of his life it was apparently with his clients and the collectors of his work, the majority of whom were from the class of *financiers* and *fermiers-généraux*, including Mme de Pompadour herself. What effect their patronage and hers had on the evolution of the subject matter of his art is a topic well worth more widely ranging consideration than that based on Boucher's works alone, and does not belong here.

Were one to judge from Marmontel's disapproving comments on the tone of Boucher's conversation at Mme Geoffrin's (see above), Boucher had spent his life up until then in the company of his fellow artists and of the actresses, singers, and dancers that he took as his models. The truth is potentially more interesting, in that he may have acquired a frank and uninhibited way of speaking in company, from the more intellectually stimulating circles in which it is possible that he moved in his younger days.[67]

What is potentially the key passage occurs in a short piece of reminiscence by Pierre Laujon, exploring the origin, dissolution, and successors of the "dîners du Caveau."[68] These took their name from their location, the cellar of the cabaret run by the *traiteur* Landelle, in the rue de Buci (significantly, this also housed the first Masonic lodge in Paris; as we have seen from Mannlich's *Mémoires*,[69] Boucher was a Freemason). In this met every Sunday from the early 1730s to around 1739, at their common expense, a group, composed chiefly of writers. The distinguishing note of these gatherings was lively and uninhibited conversation, seasoned with songs and epigrammatic duels, and stimulated by copious drafts of wine. Bores and merely social figures were—until the pressures that contributed to the dissolution of the institution—excluded. The founder-members were three, or possibly four: Piron, Collé, Gallet, and Crébillon *fils*. Laujon lists as other occasional or regular participants (though he extends the life of Le Caveau some years beyond 1739): Fuselier, Saurin *père* and *fils*, Sallé, Crébillon *père*, Duclos, La Bruère, Gentil Bernard, Moncrif, Helvétius, Rameau, and Boucher. He goes on to claim that Boucher frequently brought his drawings to these gatherings, which sometimes sparked off the idea for a song, and which on one occasion, when he brought his designs for Count Tessin's self-suppressed conte called *Faunillane*, supplied Duclos with the basis for his novella called *Acajou et Zirphile*.

The problem with this engaging picture is that Laujon appears to be alone in making Boucher a member of the circle. He is not mentioned in either the more authoritative-sounding account in Rigoley de Juvigny's *Vie d'Alexis Piron*,[70] or in Saurin's poetic reminiscence of it in his *Epitre à mon vieil ami, M. Collé*,[71] which concur in the inclusion of Piron himself, Collé, Crébillon *fils*, Gentil Bernard, and La Bruère, and in the addition of the singer Jélyotte, but otherwise diverge both from one another and from the list of participants given by Laujon. Such is in the nature of things with so shifting an institution as a dining club. What gives greater pause for thought is that the list in the *Vie d'Alexis Piron*, which uses sobriquets to list the participants in the text, only identifying the bearers of them in footnotes, uses one for the poet Gentil Bernard that suggests what it might have been that prompted Laujon to suppose that Boucher had been a member of these gatherings (it is true that Laujon claimed to derive his information from word of mouth, from attendance at successor

Figs. 44 and 45. Plates facing pages 60 and 82, etched by P-Q. Chedel after drawings by Boucher for Count Tessin's *Faunillane* (1741). Reproduced from a copy of Duclos's *Acajou et Zirphile* (1744) in the Metropolitan Museum of Art, New York.

72. We know that Boucher in his youth belonged to "a *conversazione* of painters, in which each is bound to pay his way by contributing a drawing," from a letter of Mariette's to Gabburri of 1 Dec. 1732 (Bottari, II, 1757, p. 300).
73. Piron, 1776, *Epitres*, VI.
74. J-R 876, 877.
75. Montaiglon, 1858–60.
76. Duclos, 1806, I, p. 4.
77. Duclos, 1806, X, p. 360; unfortunately, he does not name the subject, and no Boucher appears in Du Tartre's posthumous sale on 19 Mar. ff. 1804.
78. Honour, 1961, pl. 34. Tessin had this trade card blown up into part of a trompe l'oeil decoration painted by O. Fridsberg in his wife's cabinet at Åkerö, and there is a charming watercolor by the artist showing her sitting there (Leijonhufvud, II, 1933, p. 53 and frontis.). It was also adapted to form the title pages to Duvaux, 1873.
79. Chennevières, 1887.
80. Cochin, 1880, p. 81.
81. Lespinasse, 1929, p. 9.
82. See Thibaudeau, I, 1883, pp. 104–05; A & W doc. 343; the letter from a "chevalier Boucher" to Favart, Thibaudeau, I, 1883, pp. 104–05, and A & W doc. 784, is clearly from an altogether different correspondent.
83. Favart, 1808, II, p. 387, 396.
84. *Manuscrit trouvé à la Bastille*, 1868.

dining clubs to Le Caveau, but garbled memories of other accounts, seasoned with fantasy, may also have been involved).

Piron gives Gentil Bernard a sobriquet that he bore elsewhere as well—and it may indeed well have been that it was later transferred from the word-painting poet to the artist: "the painter of Love and the Graces" (*"le Peintre de l'Amour et des Grâces"*). Although Laujon includes Gentil Bernard as well as Boucher as members of the Caveau, it would have been all too easy for him to have at some point assumed that the sobriquet referred to the painter rather than the poet, and thus to have added the former. Reminiscences of the *dîners de Vaudeville,* at which Vincent drew his fellow guests, and of a dining club of artists themselves, at which they set to, to make drawings on a given theme, may have done the rest.[72]

Piron himself would appear to have been a friend of Boucher's, on the evidence of the poetic petition that he drew up on behalf of Boucher for lodgings in the Louvre in 1746[73] and the two frontispieces designed by the latter for his works in 1744.[74] Otherwise, the only part of Laujon's account for which we have corroboration is that concerning Duclos and the composition of *Acajou et Zirphile*. Well known is the story, inserted into a copy of the book from Voyer de Paulmy's library in the Bibliothèque d'Arsenal, that Count Tessin invited Boucher to illustrate his original fairy tale, *Faunillane, ou L'Infante Jaune* (1741), as a pretext for frequently seeing Boucher's wife.[75] According to Laujon's account, Tessin originally wrote it in order to shine in the salon of Mme de Tencin, and was on the point of having it handsomely published by Prault when he was recalled to Sweden. Thinking its publication might give him a reputation for frivolity at home, he had no more than two copies printed, took them and the manuscript back to Sweden, but left the plates with Prault, who got Duclos to write a new story around them. The version given in L. S. Auger's *Notice sur Duclos* involves Boucher more directly, since this says that Tessin left the artist both his drawings and the plates, and that the latter turned to Duclos for advice over what to do with them.[76] Duclos showed them to his regular dining companions, who included the comte de Caylus, de Surgères, and Voisenon, and they each set to find some story that would make sense of the bizarre illustrations. Duclos's was voted the best, and it was his that was then published with Boucher's illustrations as *Acajou et Zirphile* (1744).

This story has the merit of connecting Boucher with another convivial society of litterateurs, the Société du Bout du Banc (for which, see also Voisenon's *Anecdotes Littéraires*), with which Boucher is associated by other evidence. Duclos himself owned a picture by Boucher that evidently had some special significance for him, since he singled it out alone for mention when leaving his pictures and prints to Du Tartre de Bourdonné.[77] Caylus was associated with Boucher in a number of ways, even though his antiquarianism can scarcely have found an echoing chord in the artist. Boucher designed, and Caylus etched, Gersaint's new trade card, *A la Pagode*, in 1740 (fig. 46);[78] Caylus is thought to have been the anonymous correspondent to whom Lenormant de Tournehem turned for advice about Boucher's sketches for the two overdoors for the *chambre du Roi* at Marly;[79] and that Boucher took care to cultivate him precisely because of his influence as an artistic adviser we know from Boucher's advice to Cochin to do the same,[80] and from his presentation of Roslin to the count.[81]

Duclos's *Acajou* was turned into a very successful *opéra comique* by Charles-Simon Favart in the same year as the conte was published (1744). With Favart we arrive not only at one of the few people of whose friendship with Boucher we can be certain, but also at one whose influence upon him is palpable. The evidence for Boucher's friendship with Favart resides in a handful of letters—not only in a group of them (now in the Institut Néerlandais in Paris) written by his wife to Favart on his behalf in 1748,[82] but also in the mentions of him as "notre ami Boucher" in two letters to Favart from the partial subject of his own, the abbé de la Garde.[83] All these letters concern the theater. The first reference, in a letter from the abbé de la Garde of 3 June 1746, is to Boucher's intention of going to see the *spectacle* at Versailles, where the abbé was to be appointed costume designer in 1748, and ultimately *organisateur des fêtes particulières* to the king. The reference in the abbé's other letter, of 3 April 1748, is to the main topic of the letters from Boucher and his wife of the same year. These were all addressed to Favart in Brussels, where—after the closure of the Théâtre de la Foire in Paris in 1745—his troupe was playing under the protection of the maréchal de Saxe, "protection" that ultimately turned into the opposite when the *maréchal*, infatuated with Mme Favart, abducted her and incarcerated her husband.[84] At this stage, although the *maréchal*'s inclinations had evidently already become apparent, relations between the Favart and himself were still good, and the Favart had commissioned Boucher to design and have engraved frontispieces for the plays that they were putting on before the *maréchal* and his troops for presentation to their patron.

Fig. 46. *A la Pagode,* trade card of Edmé-François Gersaint (1740), etched by the comte de Caylus after Boucher.

Fig. 47. *Rinaldo and Armida*, engraved by Ingram and Cochin after Boucher, as a frontispiece to C-S. Favart's *Cythère assiégée* (1748).

The plays in question were the *Nymphes de Diane*, for which Boucher's design was so free that it had to be redrawn by Cochin before it could be engraved by Chedel,[85] and *Cythère assiégée*, for which Boucher designed a frontispiece depicting *Rinaldo and Armida*, alluding to the *maréchal's* infatuation (fig. 47).[86]

The chief topic of the three letters from Boucher to Favart concerns the designs and engravings for these plays, but it is in the last of them, of 17 August 1748,[87] that the badinage about the abbé de la Garde and Mme Boucher also occurs. Further evidence of the friendly relations between Boucher and the Favart is the landscape, described in the de Sireul sale as "une de ses plus brillantes productions,"[88] that Boucher apparently painted for Mme Favart this same year (1748), and two further frontispieces for Favart's plays, engraved by Le Bas and published in 1755, both depicting Mme Favart in the title roles: of *Le Caprice Amoureux ou Ninette à la Cour*[89] and *La Bohémienne* (fig. 48).[90]

The evidence of Boucher's close association with Favart in supplying illustrations for his plays is particularly valuable, because it provides additional underpinning—if any were needed—for the indebtedness of Boucher's pictures to the innovations that Favart made upon the stage. For Boucher's single most influential contribution to French eighteenth-century painting was the painted pastoral—"un genre, dont M. Boucher est le créateur"[91]—for which his inspiration was drawn, above all, from the Théâtre de la Foire.[92] This, in turn, had been transformed by Favart, as Voltaire acknowledged,[93] since it was he who refined the coarse popular entertainments generally given there by his introduction of pieces revolving around the naïve emotions of country folk: "From the first

Fig. 48. Left, *Mme Favart in the Title Role of "La Bohémienne,"* frontispiece engraved by J-P. Le Bas after Boucher (1755); right, *Mme Favart in the Title Role of "Le Caprice Amoureux ou Ninette à la Cour,"* frontispiece engraved by J-P. Le Bas after Boucher (1754).

85. Jombert, 1770, p. 67, no. 173.

86. Jombert, 1770, no. 174; J-R 524–527.

87. A & W doc. 343; last page reproduced in facsimile, *Isographie*, I, 1828–30 (see note 63).

88. 3 Dec. ff. 1781, lot 23; A & W 317.

89. J-R 1349–1350.

90. J-R 1351.

91. Le Blanc, 1753, p. 18.

92. The only person who ever appears to have seized this vital point, before Gisela Zick's seminal article (1965), is Henry Lemonnier (1912).

93. Albert, 1900, p. 178.

94. Favart, 1763, I, p. ix: "Les premières Pièces de M. Favart décéloient déjà son goût pour *le Sentiment*, & c'est là proprement le genre qu'il a introduit dans un Spectacle où l'on n'en voyoit presque aucune trace." The abbé Le Blanc (1753, p. 18), while crediting Fontenelle with introducing "a new species of Shepherds, notable for the gallantry and delicacy of their sentiments" into the literary pastoral, praised Boucher for adding "that precious simplicity and naïveté not always possessed by those of M. de Fontenelle." By 1791, however (Watelet & Lévesque, II, p. 138), they were being dismissed as "lovers . . . who are incapable of declaring their love."

95. Kettering, 1983, p. 85, fig. 108.

96. Although one of his early *bambochades*, A & W 54, already has the sentimental overtones of the true pastoral, and the engraving after it was published with that title by Huquier in 1736 (J-R 1089). A yet earlier painting with many of the characteristics of the pastoral is the *Shepherd and the Grape Picker Exchanging Toasts* in the Hermitage (Ermitazh, 1976, no. 1275, p. 187, fig. 14).

97. See exh. cat. 1984, Paris, esp. pp. 523–24.

98. See exh. cat. 1978, Braunschweig, nos. 23, 37.

99. J-R 544.

100. 23 Mar. 1984, lot 136; see A & W 88.

101. J-R 571–572; probably cut down to make a pendant to *Le nid* (fig. 50), and identifiable with the painting now in the Louvre, A & W 147, 148.

M. Favart's pieces revealed his penchant for *Feeling*—and that is really the kind of thing that he introduced onto a stage where previously virtually no manifestation of it had been shown."[94]

The painted pastoral was not a new invention; it already had a long history in Holland; Boucher's frequent exemplar, Abraham Bloemaert, was even the first Utrecht artist to paint a full-length shepherd piece in a landscape setting.[95] Nor was the painted pastoral unrepresented in France—Jacques Stella, for instance, painted a number of idealized depictions of the simplicity of rural life that were engraved by his neice. Most painted pastorals in France, however, were indebted to the mainstream tradition of the literary pastoral—to Guarini's *Il Pastor Fido*, to the rustic passages of Ariosto's *Orlando Furioso*, or to Honoré d'Urfé's *Astrée*—and, whatever their source, dressed their protagonists in the elaborate costumes of the stage or the fête galante. Such was the practice of Boucher's closest predecessor in the genre, Lancret, and of Boucher himself in his earliest essays of the kind.[96] These were *Le pasteur galant* and *Le pasteur complaisant* (cat. 30, 31), which he painted as overdoors for the Hôtel de Soubise around 1738/39.

In these two pictures Boucher for the first time reduced his protagonists to the amorous shepherd couple of the classic tradition (with a peeping tom in *Le pasteur galant*) from the more miscellaneous participants and detail of his previous, merely rustic scenes, such as *La vie champêtre* or the large, decorative pictures purportedly from the Hôtel de Richelieu (see cat. 27). Their dress, however, still represents a compromise, with the barefoot shepherdess in *Le pasteur complaisant* in a loose approximation of rustic attire, whereas the other figures are bedecked with rich stuffs, cloaks, sashes, scarves, and silk stockings, more appropriate to the fête galante, or to the "habits de paysan" of the stage.[97]

The action of *Le pasteur complaisant* belongs to the old tradition of equivocal play with the notions of birds and cages as not very veiled allusions to sexual organs and virginity,[98] and it was employed by Boucher in two of his oval half-lengths of the 1730s: in *Le Marchand d'Oiseaux* engraved by Daullé,[99] and in another picture of which there is a photograph, without any details, in the Witt Library (fig. 103), and of which a rectangular copy was sold at Christie's East, New York, in 1984.[100] *Le pasteur galant* is, by contrast, a true pastoral, with both delicate sentiment and rural simplicity suggested by the shepherd encircling his shepherdess with wild flowers beside a fountain. The presence of the peeping tom, however, suggests the intrusion of some narrative element, a triangular situation akin to that in Favart's *Vallée de Montmorency*. This had not yet been written by the time of *Le pasteur galant*, but it remains possible that the situation derives from one of the early pieces that Favart wrote for the Théâtre de la Foire between 1734 and *La chercheuse d'esprit* in 1741, before which he neither acknowledged his authorship of them nor had them printed. What it does not suggest is any connection with Fontenelle, with whose name Boucher's was constantly to be linked after his establishment of the pastoral as a settled genre. In view of the fact that Boucher does not seem to have painted anything further of the kind until 1743, with the probable exception of the uncertainly datable *Les charmes de la vie champêtre* (fig. 49),[101] which has a more rustic equivalent in the composition engraved by F. A. Aveline and published by

Fig. 49. *Les charmes de la vie champêtre.*
Musée du Louvre, Paris.

Huquier in December 1742,[102] it would seem possible that the choice of
theme was dictated by prince Hercule-Mériadec or his advisers, rather
than chosen by Boucher himself, just as the subjects of the mythological
overdoors would have been. That Boucher's innovation with this pair of
pastorals met with an immediate and enduring response is suggested not
only by the engravings after them by André Laurent that Huquier
published in 1742, but also by the numerous copies that these in turn gave
rise to, particularly in porcelain (cat. 30, 31, 97).

The pastorals that Boucher painted in 1743—a pair of ovals engraved by
Daullé as *La Musique Pastorale* and *Les Amusemens de la Campagne*[103]
and an oblong picture of *La bergère endormie*[104]—may also have been
painted at the behest of the client, the marquis de Beringhen, who would
appear, from his patronage of Oudry, not only to have had clear ideas as
to his requirements, but also to have favored rural subjects.[105] It is
certainly significant that he also commissioned three overdoors of *Sujets
champêtres* from Lancret.[106] The dress of the protagonists in the Bouchers
is still something of a compromise, in that although all the protagonists are
now barefoot and in loose dress without hoops or stays (so loose in *La
Musique Pastorale*, indeed, that the drapery and pose of the shepherdess
make her almost indistinguishable from the Callisto in the *Jupiter and
Callisto* in the Pushkin Museum[107]), the stuffs are of an impossible cut and
richness for real peasants. The action of netting birds in the latter
introduces echoes of the equivocal meaning of *La Marchande d'Oiseaux*,
and it could be argued that the flutes in *La Musique Pastorale* carry the
same kind of association.[108] There is even a pair of versions (private coll.,
New York) in which, in *La Musique Pastorale*, the shepherd is holding
two flutes: one must belong to the shepherdess, and he is either trying it
out or giving her a lesson. A flute lesson was one of the most popular
scenes of Favart's *Vallée de Montmorency*, with the shepherd doing the
fingering while the shepherdess blows, but even the first redaction of this,
as *Les vendanges de Tempé*, was not to be performed until 1745.[109]

Both the brothers Parfaict in their *Dictionnaire des Théâtres de Paris*[110]
and A-P-C. Favart in his memoir of his grandfather[111] agree that Boucher

Fig. 50. *Le nid*. Musée du Louvre, Paris.

102. J-R 197.
103. J-R 554–557; various replicas known.
104. A & W 260; Louvre, Paris.
105. See Opperman, 1977, p. 43; exh. cat. 1982–83, Paris, pp. 75, 110.
106. Georges Wildenstein, 1924, p. 42.
107. A & W 267.
108. See exh. cat. 1978, Braunschweig, nos. 3, 7.
109. See Parfaict, 1756, VI, p. 69; Zick, 1965.
110. Parfaict, 1756, VI, p. 70.
111. Favart, 1808, I, p. xxi.
112. Favart, 1808, I, p. lxxvii: "Ce fut elle qui, la première, observa le costume; elle osa sacrifier les agrémens de la figure à la vérité des caracteres. Avant elle, les actrices qui représentoient des soubrettes, des paysannes, paroissoient avec de grands panniers, la tête surchargée de diamans, et gantées jusqu'au coude. Dans *Bastienne* elle mit un habit de laine, tel que les villageoises le porte; une chevelure plate, une simple croix d'or, les bras nus et des sabots."
113. Exh. cat. 1977, Nice, no. 297.

derived the inspiration for a number of his pictures from the *Valleé de Montmorency,* or from its original redaction as *Les vendanges de Tempé;* what does not seem to have been given consideration is that, since Favart and Boucher were friends, the inspiration may have been in part reciprocal (particularly when one considers that this piece began life as a wordless pantomime). After the enormous success of *Les vendanges de Tempé* in 1745, however, it was clearly Boucher who was the debtor. Not only did he pluck the subjects of a number of pictures, including *Pensent-ils au raisin?* (cat. 53), from the pantomime, but it also seems probable that he derived from these performances in the Théâtre de la Foire a further impulse toward greater naturalism in the dress of his shepherds and shepherdesses. This was never to be completely realistic, any more than it was on the stage, but it is surely significant that in his obituary of his wife in 1772 Favart wrote: "She was the first to dress in character; she took the bold step of putting truth to life before personal adornment. Prior to this, actresses playing maidservants or rustics appeared in great hooped skirts, their heads sparkling with diamonds, and gloved up to the elbow. In *Bastienne* she wore a woolen dress such as countryfolk do, straight hair, a plain gold cross, bare arms, and clogs."[112] So she appears in Daullé's engraving after the lost picture of her in the role by Carle Vanloo.[113] None of the shepherdesses in Boucher's paintings is quite so realistic, and *Bastien et Bastienne* was anyway not put on until 1753, but the transition to this kind of realism on the stage was no doubt a gradual one— interestingly, it was one being pursued at a more exalted theatrical level by their mutual friend, the abbé de la Garde—and Boucher was hardly going to want to hobble himself with clogs when he could with equal legitimacy depict bare feet.

The fact that Boucher was not aiming at a depiction of actual rustics, as he was to a greater degree in his youth, but at a reflection of the protagonists of the sentimental dramas of the Théâtre de la Foire, helps to account both for the popularity of his pastorals in his own day, and for the discredit into which they have fallen since. Nothing can command such popularity as the performing arts, and nothing can seem so dated and incomprehensible to subsequent generations, once the echoes of actual performance have died away. We no longer perform or read the vaudevilles, ballet-pantomimes, and opéra comiques of Piron, Panard, Favart, Vadé, and the like, nor does a revival seem likely. The whole literary tradition of the pastoral has been superseded by the taste for different kinds of fiction. Boucher's pastorals will thus always lack a dimension, not to make them credible, but to encourage the suspension of disbelief necessary to enjoy them fully. In compensation, however, we can enjoy the artifice and the sheer artistry more, as Théophile Gautier did when he celebrated with perfect clarity of vision: "that idyllic world invented by Boucher for the use of the eighteenth century—the least rural of centuries, in spite of its bosky pretenses. The sheep are shampooed, the shepherdesses are tight-laced with rows of ribbons, and their complexions quite without that weather-beaten country look, while the shepherds look like ballet dancers. But it is all irresistibly seductive, and the lie is much more agreeable than the truth."[114]

114. Gautier, 1867, pp. 404–05: "ce monde idyllique inventé par Boucher à l'usage du 18ᵉ siècle, le moins champêtre des siècles, en dépit de ses prétentions bocagères. Les moutons sont savonnés, les bergères ont des corsets à echelles de rubans et des teints qui ne sentent pas du hâle campagnard, et les bergers ressemblent à des danseurs d'opéra. Mais tout cela est d'une séduction irrésistible, et d'un mensonge plus aimable que la vérité."

# Boucher and Europe

J. PATRICE MARANDEL

On 29 April 1750, François Boucher wrote an embarrassed letter to Carl Fredrik Scheffer, the Swedish minister in Paris. Excusing himself for not having delivered a painting he owed Count Tessin, Boucher's patron who had occupied Scheffer's position in Paris between 1739 and 1742, he went on to explain: "I would long ago have had the honor of sending it to him if my occupations for the king had allowed me to do so. Furthermore, I am still in charge of part of the works at Bellevue for the marquise de Pompadour. These are things one cannot refuse or neglect; it would be depriving oneself of all means to obtain favors. . . ."[1] This clear statement of the artist's priorities may account for Boucher's limited success outside France during his lifetime. Although his compositions were well known throughout Europe—perhaps more through their reproductions and interpretations as engravings and tapestries—the particular circumstances of his career did not allow him to enjoy the European fame of Ricci, Pellegrini, Tiepolo, or, because of the many foreigners who sat for him, Batoni. In this respect, the opinion of the Goncourt that "Boucher est une gloire parisienne" acquires an added significance.[2]

It would be erroneous, however, to consider Boucher an artist who had hardly any contact with the rest of Europe. The impact of this artist who, in the eyes of many, exemplified French taste at its best could not be ignored at a time when the enlightened world had its eyes set on Paris. In fact, the accounts of Boucher's contacts with Europe provide many insights into the mechanisms of the Parisian art world, as well as into the history of patronage and collecting.

Patrons and collectors of Boucher's paintings during the eighteenth century were limited almost exclusively to northern countries: Sweden, Denmark, Germany, Poland, and, to a lesser extent, Russia. His contacts with Italy were nonexistent following his poorly documented stay in that country some time after he obtained the Prix de Rome in 1723. Although what he saw in Italy—in particular the works of Ricci and Castiglione—did have some impact upon his own development, his lukewarm interest in the arts of the peninsula is well known. In spite of the rhetorical language in which various elegies pronounced or written after his death stressed his debt to Pietro da Cortona, or established a parallel between Maratta or Albani and him,[3] the reality lies closer to Mariette's judgment that "he undertook the Italian journey . . . but it was rather to satisfy his curiosity than to draw any profit from it."[4] J.C. Mannlich, Boucher's pupil, related in his memoirs how on the eve of his departure for Italy, he was warned by his master to limit himself to the study of Albani and Reni and to shun Raphael, "un peintre bien triste," and Michelangelo, who "fait peur,"[5] opinions echoed by the—perhaps apocryphal—similar recommendations made by Boucher to Fragonard before the latter's departure for Rome.[6] Boucher's own coterie in Paris seems to have included few artists or connoisseurs from Mediterranean countries. The list of foreign engravers after Boucher, rich in Germans, Swedes, and Britons, includes only one

1. Scheffer, 1982, pp. 253–54: "Il i a lontems que j'aurois eu l'honneur de lui envoyer si mes occupations pour le roy ne l'avoient permis. De plus je suis encore chargé d'une partie des ouvrages de Bellevue pour madame la marquise de Pompadour. Ce sont des choses qu'on ne peut refuser ni négliger, ce seroit s'ôter tous les moyens d'obtenir des grâces. . . ."
2. E. & J. de Goncourt, 1880, p. 136.
3. A & W doc. 1082, quoted from *Nécrologe des hommes celebres*, VI, Nécrologe de Boucher.
4. Mariette, I, 1851–53, pp. 165–66: "Il fit le voyage d'Italie . . . mais ce fut plustot pour satisfaire sa curiosité que pour en tirer du profit."
5. Roland, 1959, p. 95.
6. A & W doc. 655.

Fig. 51. Giuseppe Baldrighi, *The Family of Filippo Borbone*. Galleria Nazionale, Parma.

Fig. 52. François Boucher, *Study for a Group Portrait*. Museo Glauco Lombardi, Parma.

Spaniard, Pascual Pedro Moles (1741–1797), and no Italian. If the scarcity of Italians among Boucher's pupils is notable, it should make the presence of Giuseppe Baldrighi (1723–1802) from Parma in Boucher's studio between 1752 and 1756 all the more remarkable. Baldrighi played a particularly important role in recommending Petitot to Claude Bonnet, the man entrusted with the task of finding a suitable architect for the court of Parma. Baldrighi's suggestion was approved by Boucher himself.[7] The relationship between master and pupil must have been cordial, for shortly after his return to Parma, Baldrighi seems to have sought his old teacher's advice on the group portrait commissioned from him of the family of Filippo Borbone (fig. 51; 1757, Galleria Nazionale, Parma). Its composition leans directly on a drawing by Boucher sent to Parma, presumably to Baldrighi himself (fig. 52; Museo Glauco Lombardi, Parma).[8]

## SWEDEN

Boucher's lack of success with Italy was largely compensated for by the wealth of influential patrons elsewhere. For instance, various circumstances made his relationship with the Scandinavian countries particularly noteworthy, not the least the presence of Carl Gustaf Tessin, the Swedish envoy to France, in Paris between 1739 and 1742. Through Tessin's personal patronage and continuing interest in Boucher even after his return to Sweden, some of Boucher's finest works found their way to Stockholm. Tessin, however, was not the first Swede Boucher counted among his acquaintances. During his grand tour, between 1721 and 1725, the young architect Carl Hårleman (1700–1753) visited France. In 1732, he returned to Paris with the mission of recruiting artists to work on the decoration of the Royal Palace in Stockholm.[9] Boucher was not among the artists directly contacted by Hårleman for this task; those who were included Pater and Oudry. Hårleman, who knew Boucher personally, may already have been discouraged by the prices charged by the artist. His mission to France was marred by strict economic considerations, which led to his final selection of secondary artists, headed by Taraval.[10]

Fig. 53. Gustaf Lundberg, *Portrait of François Boucher*. Musée du Louvre, Cabinet des Dessins, Paris.

7. Briganti, 1969, p. 18.
8. Briganti, 1969, p. 48.
9. Lespinasse, 1910, pp. 276–98.
10. In 1736, Tessin passing through Italy was also looking for artists to work in Stockholm. His choice of Tiepolo and the negotiations he began with the Venetian artist did not result in a commission because of Tiepolo's previous commitments and high fees. See Lespinasse, 1910, pp. 288–90.
11. Tessin's diary written at Åkerö is kept at the Kungliga Bibliotek, Stockholm (31 volumes, unpublished). I am grateful to Jan Heidner and Birgitta Sandström for having brought it to my attention. The same library also keeps nine volumes of documents pertaining to Tessin's acquisitions.
12. Proschwitz, 1983, pp. 70–71: "Boucher me fait une naissance de Vénus: Cospetto che bella Cosa! Il n'y a des yeux que comme les vôtres qui en soient dignes. . . ."
13. Lundberg, 1972, pp. 126–33: "1) Fruntimmer vid sin spis, som knyter på sig strumpebandet, medan kammarpigan städar nattduken, 2) 1 st. på ryggen liggande såfvande naken kvinnobild på en Couleur de Lilas säng, 3) 1 st. såfvande, halft på sidan liggande naken kvinnobild, under ett rött sparlakan, 4) 1 st. Bild af ett halft Fruntimmer gör sin Toilette med en papegoja på stolskarmen, original maladt i grisaille eller grått i grått, 5) Et Fruntimmers bröstbild, sittande på en stol med et portrait i händerna, 6) 1 st. Quinnohufvud med rögula hår, lutande åt vänster."

Nevertheless, Hårleman returned to Paris in November of 1744 and commissioned six overdoors for the Royal Palace in Stockholm. Boucher delivered one, *Venus at Her Toilet,* in 1746 and was paid five hundred livres for it.

Tessin's relationship with Boucher began immediately upon the envoy's arrival in Paris. In his diary, Tessin related his first visit to Boucher's studio, which took place on 3 August 1739, only a few days after his arrival.[11] Tessin was introduced to Boucher by another Swede, the pastelist Gustaf Lundberg, a prominent figure in Paris and a close friend of Boucher, of whom he executed a portrait (fig. 53; Cabinet des Dessins, Louvre). Tessin's purchases of works by Boucher for his own collection began that day, and culminated a year later with that of *The Birth of Venus* (fig. 54; Nationalmuseum, Stockholm), of which he wrote to Hårleman in July 1740: "Boucher is doing for me a Birth of Venus: Cospetto che bella Cosa! Only eyes such as yours are worthy of it. . . ."[12] After the sale of his most important Bouchers to Queen Lovisa Ulrica in 1751, several works by the artist still remained in Tessin's collection. The inventory after his death lists several works that can be partially traced:

1) A woman near a fireplace who ties her garter while her chambermaid arranges her nightcap, 2) a large picture of a naked woman lying on her back upon a bed *Couleur de Lilas,* 3) a large picture of a naked woman, half-reclining on her side under a red bed-curtain, 4) a large bust picture of a woman at her toilet with a parrot on the arm of her chair, original painting in grisaille or gray-on-gray, 5) a bust picture of a woman sitting in a chair with a portrait in her hands, 6) a large picture of a woman with reddish hair, leaning out of a window.[13]

To the above, the portrait *aux trois crayons* of the countess Fersen, "smaller than nature, with red dress, black hood, and a coffee cup in hand," is to be added. The first of the paintings described in the inventory is evidently the picture entitled *Woman Fastening Her Garter, with Her*

Fig. 54. François Boucher, *The Birth of Venus.* Nationalmuseum, Stockholm.

Fig. 55. *Le matin*, engraved by Gilles-Edmé Petit after François Boucher. The Metropolitan Museum of Art, New York.

Figs. 56–58. Frontispiece and plates facing pages 51 and 57, etched by Pierre-Quentin Chedel after drawings by Boucher for *Faunillane* (1741). Reproduced from a copy of Duclos's *Acajou et Zirphile* (1744) in the Metropolitan Museum of Art, New York.

*Maid* in the Thyssen-Bornemisza Collection (see cat. 38). The fourth painting is known through the engraving of Gilles-Edmé Petit, published as *Le matin La Dame à sa Toilete* (fig. 55),[14] while the description of the fifth corresponds to a picture *(Woman Applying a Mouche,* fig. 43) presented in Agnew's winter exhibition of 1980.[15] Boucher's gratitude toward his Swedish patron, and the link that united them—exemplified in their collaboration on the publication of *Faunillane,* a libertine novelette by Tessin for which Boucher provided ten illustrations[16] (figs. 44, 45, 56–58)—were, however, not sufficient to override the priority Boucher had established for himself to first serve the French Crown. In October 1745, Tessin informed his successor, Carl Fredrik Scheffer, that Lovisa Ulrica wished to purchase four paintings by Boucher and two by Chardin. The subjects of the four paintings are clearly described in a letter from Carl Reinhold Berch to Tessin.[17] They were to be Morning, Noon, Evening, and Night—the four Times of Day representing also the Four Seasons. Boucher promised the four paintings for March 1746. Only one was ever delivered, *The Milliner (Morning)* (cat. 51; Nationalmuseum, Stockholm), seven months after the promised date. In spite of Scheffer's continuing requests, Boucher was unable to finish the commission.[18] Reporting on the lack of progress with the paintings, Scheffer wrote in June 1746 that the reasons for the delay included Boucher's incredible "libertinage" and the commissions the painter was receiving from M. de Tournehem. Boucher's inability to produce his paintings did not deter Tessin from ordering other works from him, such as a fan that Boucher delivered after much delay due, according to the artist, to his poor eyesight and lack of experience in this technique. (Scheffer, displeased with the result, refused to pay the price that had been set, but nonetheless sent the fan to Tessin on 23 June 1747). Shortly after being entrusted with the Swedish commission, Boucher was made member of a committee (which

included Berch and Gersaint) whose purpose was to acquire works of art for Lovisa Ulrica at the sale of the cabinet of M. de la Roque.[19]

The popularity of Boucher among Swedes is also confirmed by the fact that in 1741 Gustaf Lundberg (1695–1780) was received at the Academy with his portrait of Boucher, and by Boucher's close relationship to the portrait painter Alexander Roslin (1718–1793), whom he asked to execute a portrait of Mme Boucher (exhibited at the Salon of 1753). Upon his arrival in Paris in 1752, Roslin depended upon Boucher to be introduced to enlightened collectors. Obligingly Boucher facilitated his first meetings with the comte de Caylus. Another occurrence exemplifies the rapport between the two painters: in 1755, Boucher asked Roslin to help him with the execution of the dress in the portrait of the marquise de Pompadour he was doing at the time.[20] Is it possible, however, that Boucher reserved his treatment of equal-to-equal to well-qualified painters but discouraged others? How otherwise to explain that Roslin, so close to Boucher, directed young Swedish artists who came to Paris and sought his advice to other studios? Such was the case with Johan Säfvenbom whom he sent to J. Vernet, Jonas Hoffman who was sent to Vien, and Lorenz Pasch who, although briefly trained by Boucher from whose teachings he obviously profited, studied above all with Pierre. Swedish pupils of Boucher included, however, the docile Mandelberg, who brought into Sweden Boucher's style with little change, and Per Hilleström, whose apprenticeship with Boucher was motivated by his interest in tapestry.

Swedish engravers of compositions by Boucher included Gustav Floding (1731–1791) and Jacob Gillberg (1742–1793). It was, however, Johann Heinrich Eberts—a man important for the diffusion of Boucher's work in Germany (see below)—who engraved a design by Boucher for a memorial monument to Fräulein von Sandow from Berlin, commissioned by Fredrik Ulric Friesendorff, a Swedish diplomat serving in Paris in 1762.[21] A year earlier, Friesendorff had purchased from Tessin—then in disgrace and financial need—the diamonds of his North Star decoration, so one can surmise that it was Tessin who, once again, directed the newly posted envoy toward Boucher.[22]

## DENMARK

In neighboring Denmark, the interest in Boucher was no less than in Sweden. Again, Boucher's contacts with that country were through diplomatic channels and the support of three men whose roles can be compared to Tessin's, even though their efforts did not bring to Copenhagen as many fine paintings. These three men were the ministers Bernstorff and Moltke, and the *secrétaire de légation* in Paris, Joachim Wasserschlebe, who was the *cheville ouvrière* of the operation.[23]

In 1731 Wasserschlebe arrived in Paris, to remain until 1752. As he was a friend of many artists, his role was particularly crucial in executing Christian VI's wish to obtain paintings by the most representative artists of the time to decorate his residence of Christiansborg. Until destroyed by fire in 1794, Christiansborg represented an anthology of French eighteenth-century art. By 1741 Wasserschlebe was able to organize the shipment of about one hundred and forty pieces, for the most part overdoors or trumeaux by, among others, Lancret, J.-F. de Troy, Charles Parrocel, Oudry, Natoire, Restout, and Dandré-Bardon.[24] Four paintings

14. J-R 1456.
15. Exh. cat. 1980, London, Agnew's, no. 28.
16. Three copies, and possibly more, were printed in 1741 by Prault *fils*; Boucher's drawings were engraved by Pierre-Quentin Chedel.
17. 27 Oct. 1745; see Scheffer, 1982, p. 104, no. 9.
18. Scheffer, 1982, p. 146, n. 4.
19. Scheffer, 1982, p. 80.
20. Lespinasse, 1929, ser. 1, pt. 2, II, p. 9.
21. J-R 952. The original drawing for the composition was, in 1973, in the collection of Arthur L. Liebman; see exh. cat. 1973–74, Washington, p. 115, no. 87.
22. Lundberg, 1972, p. 132.
23. Réau, 1931, pp. 26–27.
24. Réau, 1931, p. 25.

Figs. 59–62. *Allegories of Heroic, Lyrical, Satirical, and Pastoral Poetry,* etched by Claude-Augustin-Pierre Duflos (Duflos *le jeune*) after François Boucher. The Metropolitan Museum of Art, New York.

by Boucher were part of the shipment. According to an inventory of 1765, they represented *La* [sic] *poëme héroïque, lirique, satirique, et pastorale,*[25] and are known today only through their engravings by Duflos (figs. 59–62).[26] Following Wasserschlebe's orders, Boucher discreetly clothed the children in order not to offend the prudish court of Denmark.

In 1751, shortly before his departure from Paris, Wasserschlebe wrote Bernstorff about his commission to find suitable painters to execute overdoors. Rejecting both Jeaurat for the poor quality of his work, and Vanloo for the unsuitability of his style to such work, he proposed the name of Boucher.[27] It is somewhat unclear if these overdoors were ordered for Bernstorff himself or for Moltke, in which case they would be those still in situ at Amalienborg, Moltke's sumptuous residence in Copenhagen. Whatever the situation, Boucher's Danish patron would have experienced delays on the part of the artist as long as those suffered by Tessin: these allegories of Sculpture, Painting, Architecture, Music, Poetry, Geography, and Astronomy were delivered only in 1756. A letter from Massé to Wasserschlebe stresses the difficulties encountered in executing these overdoors.[28]

Like Tessin, Wasserschlebe, besides acting as an agent between Boucher and his Danish patrons, collected works by Boucher for himself after his return to Copenhagen, albeit not on the same scale as the former Swedish

25. Krohn, 1922, p. 20.
26. J-R 925–928.
27. A & W doc. 442.
28. A & W doc. 644. This source does not give the location of the manuscript. In this letter, Massé declares himself satisfied to know that Bernstorff was pleased with the paintings but does not mention Moltke's opinion. Could this letter—and Wasserschlebe's letter of 1751—refer to a set of lost overdoors executed for Bernstorff himself?
29. A & W doc. 1026.
30. Dussieux, 1876, p. 215; Oesterreich, 1774, pp. 44, 45. Oesterreich lists specifically: "Dans le cabinet, 384–386, De Paris, Sur la cheminée, qui est admirablement travaillée de jaune antique, nommé Giallo Antico, sont posés trois vases d'une très belle forme & d'une éspèce d'agate, ornés richement et avec beaucoup de goût de bronze doré, d'après le dessin et l'invention de M. François Boucher . . ." and "Dans la salle à manger, 389–93, De Paris, Boucher. Cinq vases d'une très belle forme, dont trois de porphyre vert d'Egypte et deux de crystal de roche, noblement ornés de bronze doré; d'après le dessin de M. Boucher. Le corps de ces pièces destinées pour Mme. de Pompadour, est antique; on a seulement voulu les orner plus richement, pour qu'ils puissent accompagner les autres vases déjà indiqués."
31. Eisler, 1977, p. 318, n. 11.
32. The original manuscript of Johann Christian Mannlich's memoirs, kept in his family until the 20th century, seems to have vanished in Berlin during the Second World War. In 1913, Stollreither published large parts of it, translated into German from the original French under the title *Rokoko und Revolution* (Berlin, 1913). A partial French edition by Joseph Delage was published in Paris by Calman-Lévy in 1948. Three copies of the original manuscript still exist: one in a private collection in Zweibrücken, one in the manuscript section of the Staatsbibliothek, Munich, and one in the collections of the Wittelsbach family; see Weber, 1970, p. 18.
33. Roland, 1959, p. 95.

envoy. A letter of 14 April 1769, addressed to Wasserschlebe by his successor in Paris, Gottfried Schutze, informs us that six drawings and a small painting were on their way to him.[29]

There are records of only a couple of Danes associated with Boucher's studio, unlike the case with the more numerous Swedes. More prominent of the two was Anton Müller, who was in the studio between 1752 and 1754 before moving to Rome, but one should also name Isak Henningsen, who engraved after Boucher.

## GERMANY

Boucher's impact upon Germany, both in terms of collecting and of his influence upon younger painters, was strongest in the part of that country adjacent to France. In Baden or Pfalz-Zweibrücken, Boucher found a clientele of enlightened sovereigns eager to bring to their capitals the latest development in French culture or art, and obviously anxious to secure fine works by one of France's most renowned exponents. Although the same can be said of Frederick II in Berlin, his choices of individual artists led him in a different direction, and he never bought works by Boucher, instead focusing his attention on Watteau and Lancret. In fact, the only work by Boucher that has occasionally been connected with his collection, *L'Education de L'Amour*, appeared in inventories of Potsdam only in 1864, and it is now generally agreed that it was not one of Frederick's purchases. Frederick II was, however, aware of Boucher's accomplishments, for he had asked one of his agents in Paris, Mettra (also active for Catherine II), to purchase precious vases executed after designs by Boucher.[30] Just as linking Frederick II with *L'Education de l'Amour* becomes untenable on closer inspection, so the two allegories of Music and Painting by Boucher (Kress Collection, National Gallery, Washington), traditionally credited to the patronage of Maximilian III of Bavaria, may have originated elsewhere. As noted by Colin Eisler,[31] there is no mention of them in the Staatsarchiv für Oberbayern, and there is no evidence that Joseph von Dufresne, the duke's agent in Paris, commissioned them from Boucher.

Christian IV of Pfalz-Zweibrücken, or duc de Deux-Ponts, as he was known in Paris where he mostly resided, was an ardent collector. A large part of his painting collection contributed to the formation of the Munich Pinakothek. His sale, held in Paris on 6 April 1778, included no less than seven paintings by Boucher, of variable quality, apart from which he owned the version of the *Odalisque* (cat. 61), today in Munich. Zweibrücken's name is linked, however, even more with that of Mannlich, the young man he selected as his court painter and had trained in Boucher's studio. Today Mannlich's fame relies less on his paintings than on his memoirs in which he drew a vivid—and sometimes devastating—account of the practices in Boucher's studio.[32] By the time he wrote his memoirs, Mannlich had embraced the Mengsian aesthetic, which he had discovered in Rome after his years with Boucher, and renounced Boucher's Rococo style, which he had assimilated to the point of plagiarism—on his own account—having had to execute paintings in the style of the master that Boucher then approved and signed. In any case, through his copies, paintings in the manner of, and reinterpretation of subjects typical of Boucher, Mannlich was responsible for spreading his teacher's style throughout Germany.[33]

The same can be said of Joseph Melling, a pupil of Boucher's as well as an engraver of compositions after him. Hired as a court painter in Karlsruhe, he apparently played an instrumental role in convincing Caroline Luise, Margravine of Baden, to commission paintings directly from Boucher.[34] The enlightened margravine, herself an artist and friend of Liotard who had executed her portrait at the easel, decided in 1759 to systematically build a picture gallery. Drawing up lists of pictures and artists to be included in it, she also visited neighboring galleries at Mayence, Mannheim, and Zweibrücken. Jean-Henri Eberts, already mentioned in connection with the engraving after Boucher he executed for Friesendorff, Tessin's acquaintance, a banker and engraver established in Strasbourg, acted as an agent for the margravine. He arranged in particular the various commissions Caroline Luise gave Boucher. Shortly after the inception of the gallery, Boucher delivered two pastel heads. In 1760, two more followed, including one of a girl reading a letter. In 1762, a portrait of the marquise de Pompadour and one of a dancer were added to the collection. Only two paintings among those commissioned by the margravine can be traced today: *The School of Love* and *The School of Friendship,* now at the Kunsthalle, Karlsruhe (see cat. 71, 72). These pictures, in fact, did not hang in her picture cabinet. They were instead sold by the margravine to her husband to be used as decoration at the Schloss at Karlsruhe. In spite of their rejection from the picture cabinet, these two paintings were well thought of: in 1772, Melling executed two vertical copies of them for the Sickingen Palast in Freiburg.

Boucher's influence in Baden is reflected also directly upon the artistic production of the margravine herself. Caroline Luise, who occasionally copied the works she purchased, sent in 1763 to Count Hermann Woldemann Schnettow, for the Fine Arts Academy of Copenhagen of which she was a member, several works, including a sanguine drawing of a *Woman Reading* (fig. 63; Kunstakademiets Bibliotek, Copenhagen), which shows her debt to the figures in the two Karlsruhe pastorals, and presumably to the lost pastel of the same subject that she owned.

The *registres d'inscription* at the Académie Royale de Peinture indicate that besides Mannlich, Martin Ferdinand Quadal was registered there in 1767 under the protection of "Monsieur le Prince de Lorraine et Monsieur Boucher."[35] Boucher also lent his protection to the engraver Antoine Dunker (1746–1807), who was in his studio in 1765. One of Boucher's most famous German pupils was Januarius Zick (1732–1797), who was in Paris around 1757.[36] But deeply rooted in the South German tradition, Zick's art bears little evidence of Boucher's direct influence, except for some idyllic peasant scenes which are a distant echo of Boucher's pastorals and an obvious delight in the tactile quality of paint, which his apprenticeship under Boucher may have reinforced. In Paris, Zick was friendly with J. G. Wille (1715–1808), the engraver and author of memoirs which stress his part as an art entrepreneur, often establishing bridges between French artists such as Boucher and German collectors.[37]

Boucher's influence is traceable in many German artists established in Paris in the second part of the eighteenth century, whether they were apprenticed to him or not. Active in Paris from 1756 after an initial visit in 1744, Johann Anton de Peters (1725–1795) engraved after Boucher, and his own compositions often reflect Boucher's manner. Peters owned a version

Fig. 63. Caroline Luise, Margravine of Baden, after François Boucher, *A Woman Reading.* Kunstakademiets Bibliotek, Copenhagen.

of the *Odalisque*, which he sold in 1779 following some financial difficulties, as well as several other paintings by Boucher that were sold after his wife's death in 1787.[38] Johann Heinrich Tischbein (1722–1789), Georg Melchior Krause (1737–1800), and the Swiss Sigmund Freudenberger (1745–1801) are only a few names that can be added to the list of German artists who responded to Boucher's style.[39] The list of German engravers after Boucher includes Johann Georg Hertel, Johann Georg Merz, and August Hermann Degmair from Augsburg, Georg Friedrich Schmidt (1712–1775) from Berlin, Johann Heinrich Wiese (1748–1803) from Leipzig, and an engraver named Halbauer, who executed single figures after Boucher's frontispiece for the *Tomb of Charles Sackville, Count of Dorset*.[40]

POLAND

The correspondence between King Stanislas Augustus Poniatowski (1732–1798) and Mme Geoffrin shows the monarch's desire to secure works by the two artists who, in his eyes, were the leading French painters of his time, Carle Vanloo and Boucher. Stanislas Augustus's intention to commission these artists was linked to the projects of renovation of the Royal Castle in Warsaw, for which the architect Victor Louis (1731–1802) had provided designs during his stay in Warsaw in 1765. The death of Carle Vanloo in 1765 brought an end to his part of the project, and Mme Geoffrin suggested transferring the commission to Vien. The king's exacting instructions for the paintings he commissioned were not always welcome to his mentor, Mme Geoffrin, who wrote to him on 29 January 1766:

but I request as the ultimate favor from Your Majesty to give me entire discretion in regard to the two paintings that will be executed by Boucher and Vien. They are two men I love and esteem with all my heart, as much for the decency of their minds as for their talent. Trust me for the execution of these two paintings; it is a sacrifice I request Your Majesty to make in the name of the old friendship with which He has honored me. I beg Your Majesty to find it acceptable that they do not send preliminary drawings, as one must leave their imagination free. If they felt constrained to follow exactly the projects they had sent Your Majesty, they would believe they were executing copies: I beg you, as they do, to let them have a free hand. These two men are friends, a rare thing among artists: they will agree to make their compositions look well together.[41]

Yielding to Mme Geoffrin's plea, the king replied on 22 February 1766:

In order to show you how I wish to please you in everything, I agree not to demand these preliminary drawings by Boucher and Vien, since such is your pleasure; but you should know that you are perhaps the only person in the world for whom I would be so complaisant, for one has never commissioned large painted compositions (when one cares and believes that he knows something about it) without sketches. I know these sketches are not totally binding for the artists, but there may be something in the composition or the costume completely different from what the person who commissioned those works had in mind. These are to me far from being indifferent. I would like it, if

34. Exh. cat. 1983, Karlsruhe, Schloss.
35. Réau, 1924[a], pp. 113–46.
36. Feulner, 1920, pp. 6–15.
37. Wille, 1857.
38. Exh. cat. 1981, Cologne.
39. Becker, 1971, pp. 22–24.
40. J-R 194.
41. Moüy, 1875, p. 208: "mais je demande pour dernière grâce à Votre Majesté de me laisser la disposition en entier des deux tableaux qui seront faits par Boucher et par Vien. Ce sont deux hommes que j'aime et estime de tout mon coeur, autant pour l'honnêteté de leur âme que par leur talent. Fiez-vous à moi pour l'éxécution de ces deux tableaux, c'est un sacrifice que je demande à Votre Majesté en faveur de l'ancienne amitié dont Elle m'a honorée. Je supplie Votre Majesté de trouver bon qu'ils ne vous envoient pas des dessins de leur idée, il faut laisser leur imagination à l'aise; s'ils étaient obligés de suivre exactement les dessins qu'ils auraient envoyé a Votre Majesté, ils croiraient faire une copie: je me joins à eux pour supplier Votre Majesté de leur laisser la bride sur le cou. Ces deux hommes sont amis, ce qui est rare à trouver chez les artistes, ils seront d'accord pour que leurs compositions aillent bien ensemble."

I would like to thank Dr. A. Rottermund for his considerable help with the Polish section of this essay.

Fig. 64. François Boucher, *Project of a Design for the Coat of Arms of the Polish Commonwealth and King Stanislas*. Warsaw University, Print Room.

Fig. 65. Jan Chrystian Kamsetzer, *Royal Throne of Poland*. Royal Castle, Warsaw.

42. Moüy, 1875, p. 216: "Pour vous marquer combien je désire de vous contenter en tout, je veux bien ne plus exiger de dessins de Boucher et de Vien, puisque cela vous fait plaisir, mais comptez que vous êtes peut être le seule au monde pour qui j'aurais cette complaisance, car jamais on n'a commandé de grandes compositions de peinture (quand on s'en soucie et qu'on croit s'y connaitre un peu) sans esquisses. Ces esquisses ne font pas, je le sais, une loi rigoureuse aux artistes, mais il y a quelquefois des choses dans la composition ou dans le costume qui peuvent s'éloigner éxtrêmement de la pensée de celui qui demande les tableaux. Ceux-ci ne me sont rien moins qu'indifférents. Je voudrais, s'il était possible, qu'au premier coup d'oeil le spectateur fût frappé des idées de justice, d'émulation, de magnanimité et de con-

possible, if the viewer were at once struck by the ideas of justice, achievement, magnanimity, and harmony that these compositions are meant to suggest. But since you want it that way, Boucher and Vien do not have to provide sketches. My faith is blind and I will receive the paintings from your hand, no matter what they are. I beg you to understand that I am making a big sacrifice for you.[42]

Boucher's reluctance to provide a drawing or oil sketch is further confirmed in Mme Geoffrin's letter to the king, dated 13 March 1766:

My dear son, I cannot but admire your complaisance in the matter of your paintings; I sense the magnitude of your sacrifice inasmuch as it would be the greatest I could make myself, but I mustn't abuse your kindness toward me. I will bring you a small colored sketch by Vien, and I will try to obtain a drawing from Boucher. . . . Everything you said on the subject is very reasonable, but our painters cannot be ordered around as one would like: I became their friend because I see them often, make them work a lot, flatter them, praise them, and pay them very well. I promise to do the impossible so that your faith in me will prove to be not entirely blind.[43]

The last mention of the commission in the correspondence between the king and Mme Geoffrin appears on 27 December 1767: "Three of Your Majesty's paintings are executed; it will be possible to ship them only in the spring. Boucher's painting is only sketched so far. Boucher is old and ill; he goes slowly but he is still all right."[44] In fact, Boucher never delivered his painting, but the king received works by Vien, Noël Hallé, and Louis Lagrenée.[45]

Boucher, however, produced at least one drawing of significance for King Stanislas Augustus. The drawing[46] represents the coat of arms of the Commonwealth and King Stanislas and was doubtless also executed in connection with the new decoration of the Royal Castle (fig. 64). The two allegorical figures of Peace and Justice flanking the coat of arms were

corde que ces tableaux sont destinés à faire naître. Mais soit, vous le voulez ainsi, eh bien, Boucher et Vien seront dispensés de l'esquisse. Ma foi est aveugle, et je recevrai les tableaux de votre main tels qu'ils soient. Je vous prie de croire que c'est un sacrifice très pénible que je vous fais."

43. Moüy, 1875, pp. 218–19: "Mon cher fils, je suis dans l'admiration de votre complaisance au sujet de vos tableaux; je sens la grandeur du sacrifice, d'autant mieux que ce serait pour moi le plus grand que je pourrais faire; mais il ne faut pas abuser de votre douceur pour moi; je vous porterai une petite esquisse de Vien coloriée et je tâcherai d'obtenir de Boucher un dessin. . . . Tout ce que vous dites là-dessus est très-raisonnable, mais nos peintres ne se gouvernent pas comme on voudrait: je suis devenue leur amie parce que je les vois souvent, les fais beaucoup travailler, les caresse et les loue, et les paye très bien. Je vous promets de faire l'impossible pour que votre confiance en moi ne soit pas tout à fait aveugle."

44. Moüy, 1875, p. 319: "Il y a trois tableaux de Votre Majesté de faits; ils ne pourront partir qu'au printemps. Celui de Boucher n'est qu'ébauché. Boucher est vieux et infirme; il va doucement mais il va encore bien."

45. Budzińska, 1971, pp. 154–57.

46. Pen and brush in grayish ink (and wash), white laid paper, 264 × 372 mm. Inscribed in pen at the bottom: *Dessiné par Boucher. Cartouche aux armes du Roi*, Print Room of Warsaw University Library; inv. vol. 140, no. 52/1. See exh. cat. 1980, London, Heim, no. 9 and illus. on cover.

47. Krol, 1926, pls. 65, 66.

48. Mańkowski, 1932.

49. Réau, 1932, pp. 225–48.

50. Mańkowski, 1932, p. 40: "Nous n'en ferions l'acquisition qu'en présence de Mr. Cochin ou d'un autre artiste célèbre, afin de n'avoir aucun doutte sur le mérite de ce tableau que le propriétaire estime être un des meilleurs ouvrages de Mr. Boucher."

51. Mańkowski, 1932, pp. 291, 341.

52. Mańkowski, 1932, pp. 288, 292; Réau, 1932, p. 238, nos. 628, 673.

53. Mańkowski, 1932, pp. 466, 469; also Réau, 1932, p. 246, nos. 29, 65.

54. Bernoulli, 1780.

55. Exh. cat. 1973, Poznan, p. 18.

56. A & W 63. The dimensions of this painting are almost identical to those of the composition of the same subject, *L'Amour moissonneur*, shown at the Galerie Cailleux, Paris, in 1985 (no. 3). Could it indeed be the same painting?

57. Only one copy of the catalogue of Vincent Potocki's collection seems to have survived. It is kept today in the Rijksbureau voor Kunsthistorische Documentatie in The Hague.

copied by other artists in various decorative schemes: J. Monaldi used them to flank a marble medallion portrait of the king by André Le Brun in an overdoor in the ballroom,[47] and the architect Jan Chrystian Kamsetzer adapted the design for the finial of the throne that has been recently reinstalled in the throne room of the Royal Castle (fig. 65).

Louis Réau had not been able to consult the inventories of the royal collection published by T. Mańkowski in 1932[48] before he published his catalogue of French works in the collection that same year.[49] These inventories give a much fuller account of the king's collections and of their holdings in works by Boucher.

Like many other European monarchs, Stanislas Augustus wished to establish in his capital a painting gallery and used diplomatic channels to obtain works of art by Boucher, among others. Feliks Loyko, Stanislas's envoy at the court of Louis XV, wrote, for instance, how he was offered a painting by the artist: "We would acquire it only in the presence of Mr. Cochin or of another famous artist so that we could not have any doubt concerning the merit of the painting its owner believes to be one of Mr. Boucher's best works."[50] Although none of the works by Boucher that once belonged to Stanislas Augustus has yet been located, descriptions in the inventories give a clear idea of what each was: a *Landscape* of 1744, measuring about 73.5 by 64.5 centimeters, a *Sleeping Shepherdess*, measuring 52 by 43.5 centimeters,[51] two copies after Boucher, one of the *Odalisque* by Anna Rajecka and the other an oval pastel of *Vénus instruisant l'Amour*,[52] and two miniatures based on Boucher's compositions, a *Vénus à demi couchée et l'Amour*, and *Les Trois Grâces*.[53] The most important work by Boucher in the Polish Royal Collection was, however, a gift from Ignacy Krasicki, Bishop of Warmia. This large painting (112 × 87 cm) was noted by Johann Bernoulli when he visited the Royal Castle in 1778. In his *Reisen durch Brandenburg . . . Pohlen*, Bernoulli wrote:

> In leaving a large oval room we came upon one end of the castle, namely to the study, which was hung with paintings favored by the King, paintings which bear true witness to his refined taste in art. Found here are the following paintings: . . . *Children Playing* by Boucher, an agreeable gift of the present Bishop of Warmia, who has transferred many paintings from his collection to the King, either as gifts or having sold them to him.[54]

Further described in the inventories as "Enfants faisant la moisson, dont un chatouille avec un épi les lèvres de celui qui est endormi," it was sold in 1810 to Wojciech Boguslawski. In Boguslawski's posthumous inventory there was, indeed, reference to a painting of this subject bearing the monogram S. A. Bought by his widow at his estate's sale,[55] the painting has vanished, but was evidently a version of the *Amour moissonneur*, executed by Boucher in 1731.[56] Stanislas Augustus was not the only Poniatowski to collect Boucher: Bernoulli mentions several drawings in the collection of his nephew Stanislas, the sitter for David's equestrian portrait, and more important yet was the collection of Vincent Potocki (see Appendix),[57] which included no less than thirty-eight works by or after Boucher.

Izabella Lubomirska, born Czartoryska, owned a considerable collection of paintings, which numbered between fifteen hundred and two

Figs. 66, 67. J-P. Norblin de la Gourdaine, after François Boucher, *Pygmalion and Galatea* and *Hercules and Omphale*. Private collection.

thousand items. Two Frenchmen traveling through Poland in 1790–92 saw in the Lubomirski Palace (destroyed in 1899), "in small chambers, paintings of Boucher, whose style has today very much declined."[58] Later moved to Lancut, these paintings may have been part of the three hundred and fifty works that were inventoried there in 1802 and 1805 as "large oval paintings in gilt frames of French workmanship."[59] As recently as 1944, three canvases considered to be original paintings by Boucher were in the Lubomirski residence at Lancut: a *Sleeping Diana*, *The Toilet of Venus*,[60] and a *Bacchanale*, while two studio pieces were recorded: *Diana with Shepherd* and *The Bath of Diana*.

Earlier in the century, Boucher may also have provided works for the Czartoryski family. Juste-Aurèle Meissonnier's etchings of a "projet de Sallon de la Princesse Sartoriski" refer to the Golden Salon in the family residence at Pulawy. Although it was demolished in 1840–43, the existence of this superb example of French Rococo decoration is confirmed not only by Meissonnier's engravings, but also by the inventory of the palace kept at the Hermitage in Leningrad.[61] Decorations by Boucher, now lost, were part of the decorative scheme.[62] The Czartoryski's taste for Boucher was also exemplified by the decoration of the Ecole des Chevaliers founded by Stanislas Poniatowski in Warsaw, for which Adam Casimir Czartoryski commissioned a series of decorations from Jean-Pierre Norblin de la Gourdaine in 1772. This French painter established in Poland adapted quite literally for this project the engravings after Boucher published between 1767 and 1771 by Basan and Lemire as illustrations for the translation by the abbé Banier of Ovid's *Metamorphoses*. The decoration was dismantled in the early part of this century, but at least two bozzetti by Norblin have survived (figs. 66, 67).[63]

Meissonnier also organized the decoration of the study in the Bielinski Palace in Warsaw. The ensemble was executed entirely in Paris and exhibited at the Tuileries before being shipped to Warsaw around 1736.[64] The ceiling painting representing *Apollo in His Chariot* may have been, according to Stanislaw Lorentz, the work of Boucher, who was perhaps also the author of the *Venus and Adonis* and *Zephyr and Flore* that adorned the room. Dismantled at the end of the nineteenth century, the decoration has left no tangible trace that allows proof of that assumption.

RUSSIA

In spite of an honorary membership bestowed upon him in 1766 by the Saint Petersburg Academy—a distinction which Boucher reciprocated with the dispatch through Falconet of his large *Pygmalion and Galatea* (Hermitage, Leningrad)—Boucher did not fare as well in Russia as he did in neighboring Poland. His main advocate in Russia was Falconet, but the disfavor in which Falconet rapidly found himself while working on his equestrian monument of Peter the Great did not help promote Boucher's cause with Catherine II. The empress's own taste, guided by Grimm and Diderot, who both disliked Boucher, led her toward other choices. If the acquisition of such fine paintings as *Frère Luce* (cat. 45) and perhaps the *Paysage à l'Etang* were due only to her massive purchase of the Crozat de Thiers collection in 1772, her individual purchase sometime between 1766 and 1774 of *The Rest on the Flight into Egypt* (cat. 68), originally commissioned by Mme de Pompadour, nevertheless indicates discriminating taste in one of the genres for which Boucher was least appreciated.

Russian commissions of Boucher are practically nonexistent. In July 1771, two compositions that Boucher had executed "for a fan of the late Czarina" (Elzvieta) figured in the Huquier sale; and the correspondence of Diderot with Falconet indicates that in 1768 Prince Galitzin asked for five paintings from the most renowned French painters, Michel Vanloo, Vernet, Vien, Casanova, and Boucher, presumably to offer Catherine II. In his letter of 6 September, Diderot commented: "One should not expect anything from Vernet. He is too busy and he owes, out of gratitude, his entire time to M. de Laborde who pays for his pictures in advance. Nothing either from Boucher, who is fickle, old-fashioned, and lazy."[65] The Galitzin collection included, presumably already in the later part of the eighteenth century, Boucher's *Hercules and Omphale* (cat. 13), which was sold in 1820 to the Yusupovs. Prince Nikolai Yusupov (1751–1831) arrived in Paris shortly after Boucher's death and started to collect French paintings. This great patron of the arts, who commissioned fifty paintings from Hubert Robert (today at the Hermitage), acquired the *Jupiter and Callisto*,[66] the *Baigneuse surprise*,[67] a set—perhaps good studio pieces—of the *Naissance* and the *Toilette de Vénus* (Hermitage), and, of course, in later years the *Hercules and Omphale* already mentioned.

A systematic review of eighteenth-century sales catalogues, inventories after death, and correspondence of *marchands-amateurs* would certainly reveal that beyond the official patronage of foreign monarchs and purchases by a European elite of works by Boucher, an active market linked his studio to all corners of Europe. Already by looking at the English sales of the period, Alastair Laing has been able to remark that most of Boucher's paintings traded in eighteenth-century London are "different in character from the sentimental pastorals or nude mythologies . . . sought after by . . . English collectors in the nineteenth century" (see cat. 9). But such a pattern of collecting may well be particular to England only, or may only be traceable in a country where trading was important and has remained well documented. For the rest of Europe, we are so far limited to scant information, whether it is a notation in Wille's journal telling us that on 20 December 1764 he had sent to the Baron de Rautenfeld in Riga the engravings the latter had requested from Boucher; or the indication in the catalogue of Herr Gottfried Winkler's collection published in Leipzig in 1768[68] of a painting by Boucher among the few works of the French school he owned; or again, the indication of several drawings and occasionally fairly large collections of engravings after Boucher assembled by some German collectors.[69]

The international career of Boucher may, after these notes, seem rather limited. If compared, for instance, to his exact contemporary Giambattista Tiepolo, who decorated gigantic ensembles in Venice, Würzburg, and Madrid, was courted by everyone in Europe, and responded vigorously to the demands of his patrons, Boucher does not fare well. The duties of the French artist, expressed in the letter to Scheffer quoted at the beginning of this essay, were, indeed, restrictive and prevented him from experiencing the boundless freedom of the Venetian artist. But had he been given this freedom, would he have used it to respond to the expectations of a large cosmopolitan clientele? Probably not. Obviously little interested in the

58. Piles & Kerdu, 1796, V, p. 56: "Dans les petits appartements, tableaux de Boucher, dont le genre est bien tombé aujourd'hui."
59. Majewska-Maszkowska, 1976, p. 316.
60. A & W 174, now on the London art market.
61. Lorentz, 1958, pp. 186–98; 1962, pp. 42–46.
62. Dembowski, 1898, I, pp. 130–31.
63. Michalowski, 1972, pp. 74–80; exh. cat. 1985, Paris, nos. 27, 28, illus.
64. Réau, 1924[b], p. 11.
65. A & W doc. 1016, quoted from Diderot, 1876, p. 301: "Il ne faut rien attendre de Vernet, il est trop occupé, et il doit, de reconnaissance, tout son temps à M. de Laborde qui lui paye la vente du prix de ses tableaux d'avance. Rien non plus de Boucher, qui est léger, caduc et paresseux."
66. A & W 267.
67. A & W 205.
68. *Historische Erklaerungen*, 1768, p. 603, no. 602: "Francois Boucher, Auf Leinwand, 1 Fuss 11½ zoll hoch, 2 Fuss 3 zoll breit: Vier reizende Liebesgötter wälzen sich, am niedern Gebüsche im frischen Grase, auf ihren bunten Gewändern. Der zur linken sitzende Liebkoset dem in der Mitte hingestreckten, welcher sich zum andern Paare wendet, und lächelnd nach dem kleinen Vogel blicket, der an den Faden gebunden, aus der Hand des zur Rechten hinten im scherzenden Gespielen flattert." The picture may have been another version of the *Amour oiseleur*, A & W 62.
69. Tenner, 1966. The following collectors of works by Boucher are mentioned: Georg Franz Ignaz Leopold von Stengel (1775–1824), whose drawing by Boucher is now in the Staatliche Graphische Sammlung, Munich (inv. 9006); Emmerich Joseph von Dalberg (1773–1833), who owned eleven drawings by Boucher, now in the Hessisches Landesmuseum, Darmstadt; and Johann Carl Piton (1746–1825).

world outside Paris, an infrequent traveler who left Paris twice in his whole life, once to go to Italy and once to Holland, Boucher felt more comfortable with a limited Parisian audience who appreciated his work and used it appropriately in newly conceived interiors which excluded all Baroque grandeur. Curiously, denounced in his old age as the last exponent of a dated style, Boucher had understood a very modern concept: that in order to be known all over the world, his style might as well be transmitted by the reproductive processes resulting in prints, or in models executed after his designs in Sèvres, Bow, Chelsea, Derby, and many other types of porcelain; and that the superb tapestries woven at Beauvais would, better than his pictures, carry the inventiveness of his compositions from Stockholm to Parma and beyond Europe to China,[70] where until 1860 his *Tenture chinoise* was kept in the Yuen-Min-Yuen Palace in Peking.

70. Bernard-Maître, n.d. One of these tapestries is now in the Cleveland Museum of Art, the others of the series in a French private collection.

## Appendix

Because of the rarity of the catalogue of the Vincent Potocki collection (see note 57), we are reproducing below the pages of this publication that concern Boucher. The works described in this catalogue have, thus far, not been traced. We hope that this document will help establish the provenance of yet undiscovered paintings and drawings by the artist.

Vincent Potocki (d. 1825) first married Ursule Zamoyska, whose mother, Louise Poniatowska, was the sister of Stanislas Augustus, King of Poland. He divorced her in 1781. Their son, François Potocki (1778–1853), married Sidonie de Ligne (1786–1823) in 1807. It is likely that the collection of paintings of Vincent Potocki was eventually inherited by members of the Ligne family in Vienna. Vincent Potocki's third marriage was in fact to Princess Helene Massalska, whose first marriage had been to Charles-Joseph de Ligne.

Following are works by or after Boucher in the collection of Vincent Potocki listed in the *CATALOGUE DES DESSINS, TABLEAUX, MINIATURES, ESTAMPES &c. . . . CONTENUES Dans le Cabinet de S.E. Mr. le Comte VINCENT POTOCKI, Duc de Zbaraz . . . &c. Mis en ordre par Henri Amiet,* Warsaw, 1780.

### DRAWINGS

205 Un Dessein representant une Femme, beau morceau, d'une touche hardie, à la sanguine. Haut 9 pouces, 6 lignes, large 7 pouces 10 lignes.

206 Un Groupe de trois hommes supérieurement bien dessiné à la sanguine. Il porte 9 pouces 6 lignes de haut, sur 8 pouces 1 ligne de large.

207 Une belle étude d'une Tête d'Enfant à la sanguine. Haut 4 pouces 11 lignes, large 4 pouces 6 lignes.

208 Etude d'une Minerve, d'un grand effet, au crayon noir. Il porte 7 pouces 10 lignes de haut, sur 6 pouces 8 lignes de large.

209 Etude de Chinois au crayon noir. Haut 6 pouces 7 lignes, large 5 pouces 2 lignes.

210 à 216 Sept études diverses, parmis se voyent, Venus à sa toilette & deux petits enfans, plein d'expression et de légérete, la plus grande partie au crayon noir.

217 Superbe Dessin représentant une femme coeffée en cheveux nattés, autour de la tête & mêlés de perles, à la sanguine.

218  Une femme échevélée, regardant en haut contre la gauche, représentant une Magdeleine, à la sanguine.

219  Un Dessein contenant deux tête d'enfans, bien exprimé au crayon noir et rouge, sur papier de couleur.

220  Un ditte, contenant une tête de Diane, sur la droite, et de jeune Femme contre la gauche, dessiné aux trois crayons sur papier gris.


ENAMELS

30  La Voluptueuse, par F. *Bourgoin*, d'après F. *Bouché*. Une belle tête exprimant la Passion, un beau Corps, une belle Gorge, de beaux Bras, une belle Draperie, enfin une situation digne de son sujet se voient dans ce morceau rond, et peint sur émail. Il porte 2 pouces 3 lignes, en tout sens.


PAINTINGS

184  Vénus donnant une couronne de fleurs à l'Amour. Esquisse peinte sur toile: haut 15 pouces 2 lignes, large 12 pouces.

185  Une Baigneuse. Esquisse terminée ceintrée du haut, peint sur toile d'après *Bouché* par *Briagard*: haut 15 pouces, large 12 pouces.

186  La toilette de Vénus, l'Amour devant elle tenant un ruban bleu, au bout deux Colombes sont attachées. Esquisse peinte sur toile: haut 15 pouces, large 12 pouces.

187  Angélique et son Amant, devant eux deux Brébis et un Bouc, l'homme écrivant, sur le pied d'un arbre Angélique. Esquisse peinte sur toile, même grandeur.

188  Le trait dangereux. Vénus tenant de la main droite une flêche et de la gauche un carquois rempli de flêches, l'Amour appuyé contre sa mere, la prie instament les mains jointes de lui rendre ces armes. Esquisse peinte sur toile: haut 14 pouces, large 11 pouces 8 lignes.

189 & 190  Deux Paysages, sur l'un à droite un jeune Homme assis, jouant de la Clarinette, devant lui une Femme appuyée sur son genou de la main gauche, et de la droite reçoit une corbeille de fleurs d'un autre jeune Homme qui se voit sur la gauche, sur l'autre une jeune Femme reçoit une poire d'un jeune Homme assis à son côté, à gauche se voit un panier remplis de fruits &c. Tableaux peints sur toile d'après *Bouché*: haut 15 pouces 4 lignes, large 18 pouces 4 lignes chaque.

191 & 192  Une Vénus et une Léda d'après *Bouché*. Tableaux peints sur toile: ils portent chacun 24 pouces de haut, sur 26 de large.

193  Un Cupidon en l'air, tenant d'une main une flêche, & de l'autre un flambeau, au dessus de lui se voient deux Colombes. Tableau peint sur toile, d'aprés *Bouché*: haut 17 pouces, large 14 pouces.

194  L'Amour aiguisant ces flêches pendant du précédent et même grandeur.

195  Vénus sur les eaux. Tableau peint sur toile: d'après *Bouché*: haut 19 pouces 4 lignes, large 23 pouces 6 lignes.

196  Alliance de Bacchus et de l'Amour, d'après *Bouché*, même grandeur.

197  Un Enfant jouant du hautbois, plusieurs livres et instruments de Musique se voyent devant lui. Esquisse sur toile: haut 24 pouces large 26 pouces.

198  Diane et Endimion, à droite se voient la Lune sur un nuage, ses deux mains allongées sous la tête d'Endimion dormant, sur les genoux d'un Vieillard qui est le symbole du tems. Belle esquisse bien terminée, peint sur toile: haut 11 pouces 3 lignes, large 8 pouces 10 lignes.

199  Les Nymphes de Psyche volent les flêches et le carquois de Cupidon endormi.

200  Pendant du précédent, où se voit Vénus à sa toilette, faite par les trois Graces et servie par une quantité de Cupidons. Ce tableau et le précédent sont peints sur toile: ils portent chacun 24 pouces de haut, sur 30 pouces de large.

201    Paysage, où se voit un Homme, un bâton à la main et une besace sur le dos, qui mène devant lui un Cheval et un troupeau de Moutons, allant de la droite du Tableau sur la gauche, à son côté son Chien, et plus loin un Rocher qui remplit toute la gauche, peint sur bois: haut 6 pouces 6 lignes.

202    Idem, où se voit à droite un Homme à cheval, tenant un autre tout sellé à l'abreuvoir, à gauche un Homme et une Femme assis, et derrière eux un Chien, au fond de la droite est un grand Rocher. Tableau peint sur bois: haut 6 pouces 2 lignes, large 5 pouces.

203    Idem, où se voit une quantité de grands Rochers, à droite un Homme à cheval mène plusieurs autres Chevaux chargés, au milieu un Chien qui passe l'eau, à gauche un Homme à cheval qui en mène aussi un chargé, parlant à une Femme qui a un panier à son bras gauche, et une verge à sa main droite, trois Moutons et une Chèvre autour d'elle, en haut de la gauche, sur un Rocher une Femme assise et un Homme appuyé sur le derrière du Boeuf, qui est à côté d'eux, ainsi qu'une Chèvre et un Mouton.

204    Idem, pendant, au milieu une Femme assise derrière trois Moutons, et devant elle une Chèvre regardant deux Hommes, un à cheval, avec qui elle semble faire conversation, l'autre arrange la selle du sien, la gauche est terminée par deux arbres. Tableaux capitaux et d'un beau coloris, peints sur toile, ils ont chacun 28 pouces de haut, sur 43 pouces de largeur.

# Explanatory Notes to the Catalogues

**Titles**  English titles have been used for the works exhibited except when translation would result in absurdity. Elsewhere, English has been used unless there is a French title hallowed by long usage, such as the title to an engraving.

**Abbreviations**  S & M
SOULLIÉ, L. & MASSON, Ch. "Catalogue raisonné de l'oeuvre peint et dessiné de François Boucher." In *François Boucher*, by André Michel. Paris, 1906.

A & W
ANANOFF, Alexandre, & WILDENSTEIN, Daniel. *François Boucher*. 2 vols. Lausanne and Paris, 1976.

J-R
JEAN-RICHARD, Pierrette. *Musée du Louvre, Cabinet des Dessins . . . Ecole française*. Vol. I, *L'oeuvre gravé de François Boucher dans la Collection Edmond de Rothschild*. Paris, 1978.

The references to S & M and A & W numbers at the head of each entry are in parentheses when the picture exhibited is described as lost since the original record(s) of it, or when its identity or status is otherwise called into question.

**Loans**  *New York*: exhibited only at The Metropolitan Museum of Art
*Detroit*: exhibited only at The Detroit Institute of Arts
*Paris*: exhibited only at the Grand Palais

**Provenances**  Owners and sales are in Paris, unless otherwise stated.

**References**  Throughout the essays and catalogue entries, references are abbreviated. For full references, see References Cited. Publications are listed in alphabetical order except for exhibition catalogues, which are arranged by date.

I

# 1 | St. Bartholomew

Oil on paper laid down on panel
11¾ × 8 in. (29.5 × 20 cm)
Inscribed bottom left: *S. barthelemi*
Collection of Jean-Luc Bordeaux,
Santa Monica
(S & M 833)      (A & W 24)

PROVENANCE
Paris art market, c.1980.

ENGRAVING
*S. Barthélemy*, engraving by Etienne Brion
dated 1726, published by Jeaurat (J-R 396);
inscribed with John 1:47, which reports
Christ's words at the calling of Nathaniel
(traditionally identified with Bartholomew):
*Voici un vrai Israëlite sans déguisement et sans
artifice.*

Fig. 69. *St. Andrew*. Private collection, Paris.

Fig. 70. *Dream of St. Joseph*. Art market,
Paris.

The rediscovery and recognition of this painting and its former companion, a *St. Andrew* (fig. 69), by Pierre Rosenberg a few years ago has for the first time given us some secure knowledge of Boucher's earliest style as a painter. The absence of the *Judgment of Susannah* that he is supposed to have impressed Lemoine with at the age of seventeen (*Galerie Françoise*, 1771, p. 1), and the realization that the picture now in the Columbia Museum of Art (cat. 5) does not represent Evilmerodach, and so cannot be the composition with which he won the first prize at the Academy in 1723, leave us with no other painting that is datable with certainty to his tyro years in Paris. These two *Saints* must indeed be the earliest surviving pictures by Boucher.

The two pictures can be identified thanks to their having been engraved as two of a set of depictions of Christ, the Virgin Mary, and the Twelve Apostles plus St. Paul, published by Edmé Jeaurat, all of which are dated 1726. The *St. Bartholomew* was engraved by Etienne Brion (J-R 396), who also engraved *St. James the Greater, St. Jude,* and *St. Simon;* the *St. Andrew* was engraved by Louis Jacob (J-R 1216), who was also responsible for the *St. Matthew* and *St. Thomas.* None of the originals of the other engravings has as yet come to light—no doubt in some cases because their authorship has not been recognized (although a drawing of *St. Peter* by J-B. Deshays, which takes Haussard's engraving after Boucher as its point of departure, has recently been exhibited [1984, London, no. 9]). The engravings all say "F. Boucher inv." rather than "pinx.," which suggests that their originals might not all have been painted, but some of them drawn instead, and the "inv." employed to cover the two cases throughout.

The date 1726 is only a terminus ante quem for the originals: the stylistic differences between these two not very distinctive little pictures, and others that one is led to ascribe to Boucher's pre-Rome years, suggest a more precocious dating, despite the fact that one might otherwise have been tempted to see in them precisely the kind of painting referred to in passing as "plusieurs petits tableaux" in the review of the "Exposition de la Fête-Dieu" in the *Mercure de France* (June [II] 1725, p. 1402). In fact, they are almost more suggestive of the kind of mass-produced saints' images that Watteau was reduced to a part in producing for a devotional picture seller on the Pont Notre-Dame in his earliest years in Paris.

Thanks above all to the head of the present *St. Bartholomew*, one is also enabled to recognize as Boucher's a *Dream of St. Joseph* (fig. 70) that has recently appeared on the art market in Paris (Bordeaux, 1985, p. 31). Its awkwardness of composition and woodenness of gesture can likewise only indicate a work of Boucher's extreme youth. Stylistically, the *St. Bartholomew* (and the *St. Andrew*) scarcely suggest any very exalted precedents; they are rooted in the guild routine to which Boucher's father belonged, and they clearly antedate his son's contact with the academic tradition, in the shape of Lemoine.

As is the nature of such essentially devotional images, the saints are all clearly denoted by their attributes—generally by the respective instruments of their martyrdoms. Here, St. Bartholomew holds out the knife with which he was flayed. The presence of the Castel S. Angelo-like rotunda in the background is hard to explain, since St. Bartholomew's apostolate and death are supposed to have occurred in India and Armenia.

# 2 | *The Surprise*

Oil on canvas
32 × 25¾ in. (81.5 × 65.6 cm)
New Orleans Museum of Art
(S & M 1170)          (A & W 79)

PROVENANCE
[The ownerships claimed by 18th-century sale catalogues, and the division into versions suggested here, are both subject to caution.] *Catalogue des Tableaux des Trois Ecoles . . . &c. du Cabinet de MM.* *** [Sorbet & ?], Hôtel d'Aligre (Remy), 1 Apr. ff. 1776, lot 46: "ce Tableau peint par *François Boucher,* est ragoûtant, vigoureux de coloris, & d'un pinceau large; il est peint sur une toile qui porte 2 pieds 6 pouces de haut, sur 2 pieds de large" [in Saint-Aubin's copy of the catalogue in the Wrightsman coll., New York, the picture is illustrated, and the price given as 700 livres]; *Notice des principaux Articles de Tableaux . . . &c., provenans du Cabinet de feu M. CONTANT [D'IVRY], Architecte de Roi . . . &c.,* sa maison, rue de Harlay (Joullain), 27 Nov. ff. 1777, lot 6: "Ce tableau par le même [i.e., the author of lot 5, *Vénus couchée avec l'Amour dans un paysage:* 'peint par *Fr. Boucher* à son retour de Rome'], est peint vers le même tems. Hauteur 30 pouces, largeur 24 pouces. Toile"; *Catalogue de Tableaux Originaux des Grands Maîtres des Trois Ecoles, qui ornoient un des Palais de feu son Altesse Monseigneur Christien, DUC DES DEUX PONTS* [i.e., Zweibrücken], Hôtel d'Aligre (Remy), 6 Apr. ff. 1778, lot 71: "Ce tableau tient beaucoup de la manière de François le Moine; il est peint sur toile qui porte 2 pieds 6 pouces de haut, sur deux pieds de large" [bought by Noyer for 433 livres]; *Notice de Tableaux et Dessins du Cab. de M.* ***, Hôtel de Bullion (Paillet), 3 Apr. ff. 1783, lot 9: "Ce Tableau admirablement touché & d'une très-belle couleur, est

This is the most enigmatic picture in Boucher's oeuvre, both because of its subject, which appears already to have baffled eighteenth-century cataloguers, and because of the problem of locating it within Boucher's output, since it is virtually sui generis in handling as well. There is not even any engraving or documentation to link it incontrovertibly with Boucher; but the repeated ascription of the composition to him in eighteenth-century sales, and the presence of a very similar cat advancing off a woman's lap in the engraving by Joseph de Longueil after Boucher called *Les caresses dangereuses* (fig. 71; J-R 1402), support the attribution. This is despite the fact that the waters are further muddied by this engraving (only inscribed *F. Boucher inv.*) being merely an adaptation—with cat substituted for fan, and library for boudoir—of another untitled print of 1750 by Claire Tournay (J-R 1613; inscribed *Bouché Pinx.*) after a lost painting.

The spelling of Boucher's name on the latter engraving probably points to this painting of the *Woman at Her Dressing Table with a Fan,* presumably so signed or inscribed, having been executed very early in his career before the orthography of his name was settled, though not as early as *The Surprise,* to judge by the woman's features and the treatment of the drapery in the engraving. The closest parallels that are to be found for the Lemoinean features of the woman and young girl in *The Surprise* are those of the wife in *Joseph Presenting His Brethren* (cat. 5). The treatment and coloration of the drapery of the young girl also find echoes in that picture, as does the looped-back curtain. The head of the woman would appear to be further related to those in the engravings after *The Encounter of Jacob and Rachel* and *Bethuel Welcoming the Servant of Abraham.* All these comparisons point to the picture's having been painted in the period before Boucher left for Italy.

2

Fig. 71. *Les caresses dangereuses*, engraved by Joseph de Longueil after Boucher.

In its theme, however, and in the broken handling of paint, and even in its unexpected delight in fabric and pattern (but compare the turkey carpet in *Joseph Presenting His Brethren*), the present painting appears worlds removed from these solemn biblical representations and other pictures painted around the same epoch. The contrasting patterns of chintz cushion and striped mattress ticking anticipate similar juxtapositions in Liotard's *Sultana Reading* (Loche & Roethlisberger, 1978, color pl. XXVIII); but it should not be forgotten that Liotard may have drawn his inspiration for his depictions of this subject not simply from Duflos's engraving after Boucher in J-A. Guer's *Moeurs et Usages des Turcs* (1746), as Sir Karl Parker was the first to suggest (Parker, 1930), but from an actual colored drawing by Boucher, such as that once owned by Tessin (Sander, 1872, p. 61, no. 126), which is possibly one of those now in the Pierpont Morgan Library.

The broken, flickering touch of the brush in *The Surprise* resembles nothing so much as what we find in Lemoine's *Cleopatra* (Minneapolis

Fig. 72. *La jardinière surprise*. Private collection, Paris.

Institute of Arts; exh. cat. 1983, Atlanta, no. 2), of which the woman here might almost be a blonde transposition in a genre subject. Here lies, surely, the clue to the proper dating of the picture. For Pierre Rosenberg, in attributing the *Cleopatra* to Lemoine (Rosenberg, 1971–73, pp. 54–59), has very plausibly dated it to just before his departure for Italy in 1723, before the transformation of his manner effected by the encounter with the breadth and light of Venetian painting. Boucher's brief passage through Lemoine's studio can only have occurred at this self-same period, when he needed to take instruction from an established master in order to compete for the Grand Prix. Boucher's sojourn in Lemoine's studio was, by his own account, a short one, from which he profited little (Mariette, I, 1851–53, pp. 165–66), which his work generally bears out (but see cat. 4). Now that we can also see that the Lemoine under whom he studied was not the mature artist whose works are so easily recognizable, but the artist of the *Cleopatra*, we can also see why the little that Boucher did paint under Lemoine's influence has passed unrecognized as such. What makes this phase of Boucher's development even harder to grasp is that, having attained such virtuosity in the "manner of Lemoine," he turned his back on it, to forge a highly individual, less painstaking style and handling of his own. One further influence can be detected in the present picture, which is apparent both in the choice of subject and in the features of the man pulling aside the curtain, and that is of Lancret, whose reputation was at its height in these years immediately after the death of Watteau.

Marianne Roland-Michel has suggested that *The Surprise* may have been painted as a pendant to *La jardinière surprise* (fig. 72; A & W 91, fig. 376, but since transformed by the removal of repainting that had added the wall on the left and concealed the vase on the right, very possibly to make the picture balance internally, rather than with a pendant). The suggestion is very tempting—and the two pictures must certainly date from around the same time. The only objection to it is that in none of the sales in which either composition is recorded is it ever with a pendant; but then, as can be seen below, the present picture appears to have had a very changeable history, which cannot even be traced back to Boucher's lifetime.

Two apparently autograph versions of this picture are known. Voss, who knew both of them at first hand, believed that the present one was the "first essay, executed with much greater freshness and immediacy" (*"mit weitaus grösserer Frische und Unmittelbarkeit ausgeführten ersten Wurf"* [Voss, 1959, pp. 353–54, fig. 2]).

l'original de celui que nous venons de vendre, du Cabinet de M. Sprot" [see under Copies]; sale of the comte de Pourtalès-Gorgier, Paris, 6 Feb. 1865, lot 252 (as Deshays); sale of Prince Paul Demidoff, 3 Feb. 1868, lot 21 (as Deshays) [reputedly bought for 5,900 francs by the marquess of Hertford, according to annotation in the copy of the sale catalogue in the Cabinet des Estampes, but not recorded as ever having formed part of his collection]; Bloomingdale sale, Parke-Bernet, New York, 30 Oct. 1942, lot 23 (as Deshays); Paul Drey, New York (exh. cat. 1951, Oberlin, ex catalogue [as by De Troy]; exh. cat. 1958, Munich, no. 21 [as "attributed to François Boucher"]; Voss, 1959, p. 355 and fig. 2 [as by Boucher]); Georg Schäfer, Schweinfurt; Christie's, London, 14 July 1978, lot 150; Galerie Cailleux, Paris; from which acquired by the New Orleans Museum in 1984.

REPLICAS

1. [*Catalogue d'une belle Collection de Tableaux des Trois Ecoles . . . &c., provenans du Cabinet de M. *** [Tronchin (père?) ], Hôtel de Bullion (Dufresne & Le Brun), 12 Jan. ff. 1780, lot 105: "Le fond offre un jardin [not present here]. Hauteur 29 pouces, largeur 23 pouces. Toile" [bought by tronchain (*sic*) for 202 livres]; *Notice de Tableaux . . . &c., après le décès de M. TRONCHAIN* [i.e., Tronchin *fils*], *Trésorier du Marc d'Or*, Hôtel de Bullion (Paillet & Chariot), 10 Feb. ff. 1785, lot 16: "un homme qui paroît à une croisée [rather than the simple opening seen here]. Hauteur 30 pouces, largeur 24. Toile" [If the descriptions were merely loose, possibly identifiable with:]

2. Kraemer sale, 5–6 May 1913, lot 21, 80 × 64 cm (as "Ecole française"); Paul Cailleux, Paris (Voss, 1953, p. 90, fig. 67; 1959, pp. 353–54, fig. 1).

3. Version containing cat with different markings, 32 × 26 in., always attributed to J-F. de Troy: Warren Wright coll., New York; Arnold Seligmann, Rey & Co., New York; Julius Weitzner, Inc., New York (exh. cat. 1936, Dallas, p. 29, no. 9); misc. sale, Parke-Bernet, New York, 24 Feb. 1949, lot 84.

COPIES

1. Misc. sale, Hôtel d'Aligre (Basan), 1 Mar. ff. 1779, lot 11: "dans le genre de Boucher, 2 pieds et demi sur 2 pieds de large"; *Catalogue des Tableaux . . . &c. du Cabinet de M. *** [Sprot], Hôtel de Louvois (Paillet), 6 Mar. ff. 1783, lot 61 [s.m.; sold for 72 livres].

2. Version without the man, c. 68 × 60 cm, Palais Galliera, Paris, 3 Dec. 1969, lot 47; Hôtel Drouot, Paris, 1 Dec. 1977, lot 4.

3. Miniatures by Charlier, sale of L[ainé], "peintre en miniatures," 19 Apr. ff. 1784, lot 154.

# 3 | Bethuel Welcoming the Servant of Abraham

Oil on canvas
18¼ × 14½ in. (46.5 × 37 cm)
Musée du Louvre, Paris (R.F. 1977–15)

# 4 | Bethuel Welcoming the Servant of Abraham

Oil on canvas
39½ × 32 in. (100 × 81 cm)
Musée des Beaux-Arts, Strasbourg
(S & M 715)          (A & W 33)
*New York and Paris*

PROVENANCE OF SKETCH
Le Rouge sale, 12 May ff. 1809, lot. ?; Österby coll., Sweden (as Tiepolo); misc. sale, Bukowski, Stockholm, 29 Mar.–5 Apr. 1976, lot 175 (as Pellegrini); Aldo Poggi, Rome; from whom acquired by the Louvre in 1977.

PROVENANCE OF FINISHED PICTURE
*Catalogue de Tableaux Précieux . . . &c., le Cabinet de feu M. BLONDEL DE GAGNY, Trésorier-Général de la Caisse des Amortissements*, Place de Vendôme (Remi), 10 Dec. ff. 1776, lot 240: "Rebecca qui reçoit les présents du serviteur d'Abraham, composition de douze figures. Ce tableau est du meilleur *faire* de cet Artiste, & d'un coloris vigoureux; il est peint sur toile qui porte 3 pieds 1 pouce de haut, sur 2 pieds 10 pouces de large" [bought by the chevalier Lambert for 1230 livres, according to a copy of cat. in Bibliothèque d'Art et d'Archéologie, Paris, which has an additional note to the effect that he sold it in 1778 to M. Haudry for 1239 livres 10 sous (presumably in the following sale), and that: "Il avait été fait sous les jeux de Lemoine avant que Boucher alla à Rome, il tient beaucoup de ce maître"]; *Catalogue des Tableaux des Trois Ecoles . . . &c.* [assembled by Le Brun], Hôtel d'Aligre (Chariot & Le Rouge), 19 Jan. ff. 1778, lot 102 [width reduced to 2 *pieds 6 pouces*; apparently bought by M. Haudry for 1239 livres 10 sous (see preceding and succeeding sales)]; *Belle Collection de Tableaux Originaux . . . &c., composant le Cabinet de feu le C.en HAUDRY*, à vendre, s'adresser à Orléans, place de la réunion, no. 4 [s.d., but c. 1800, when Haudry died], lot 26 [height reduced to 36 *pouces*, width to 29 *pouces*; sold for 1200 francs]; sale of M.B ***, Paris, 24 Nov. 1831, lot 24; misc. sale, Nouveau Drouot, Paris, 14 June 1985, lot 73.

Both recent rediscoveries (the sketch suggestively lurking under the successive names of Tiepolo and Pellegrini before its acquisition by the Louvre), this sketch and finished picture belong to the series of depictions of the lives of the Old Testament patriarchs that preoccupied Boucher in the years before his stay in Italy. The reason for such a choice of subjects appears to have been twofold: On the one hand, Boucher was responding to the demand of the print publishers Jean-François and Laurent Cars and Hecquet for images to engrave, to be put at the top of their thesis plates (there being a surprising dearth of depictions of the Old Testament in France, in contrast to Italy). On the other hand, by attempting such subjects as autonomous paintings rather than merely as disposable designs for the engravers, Boucher was announcing his ambitions as a history painter. These were the very kind of themes set by the Academy of Painting and Sculpture for the Grand Prix, which he himself had won, but without receiving the usual recompense of a scholarship in Rome, so that he finally had to make his way there at his own expense.

At first sight, the present composition appears to have been intended for just such a thesis plate, but the sequence of events is a little more complicated than that. The engraving by Jean-Baptiste Perronneau after the finished picture is, as are all such plates, oblong, not upright (fig. 73). Moreover, Perronneau was not born until 1715 and could never have engraved this plate before Boucher left for Rome in 1727. Although the very patchy and random survival rate of thesis plates and their long continuance in the stock of the publisher make it hazardous to draw any conclusions from their use in this form, the date of 17 March 1740, on which H-M-B. de Rosset de Fleury de Ceilhes maintained the thesis for which he used the engraving as a headpiece, is likely to be much closer to the date at which it was engraved. What Cars, therefore, appears to have done in the present case was, some time after it was painted, to have borrowed the upright painting and to have had the print scraped in the usual oblong format. In doing so, he appears to have glossed over the fact that the moment of the story depicted was not exactly what he needed, since there is a discrepancy between the subject suggested by the verse

ENGRAVING
Finished picture engraved in horizontal format
in reverse by [J-B.] Perronneau, published by
Laurent Cars, with an inscription in Latin,
taken from Genesis 24:50–51.

ANALOGIES

1. Another painting identified (possibly erroneously) as *Eliezer Offering Jewels to Rebekah*, 26½ × 27½ in., Augustin de Saint-
Aubin's posthumous sale, 4 Apr. ff. 1808, lot 1
[sold with sketch of *Pilgrims of Emmaus* in
same lot, for 63 francs].

2. *Eliézer et Rebecca*, oil on canvas, 155 ×
122 cm, Meffre *aîné*, [comte de Morny] sale, 9
Mar. 1863, lot 5 [bought by Febvre for 276
francs].

3. Framed pen and bister drawing on white
paper, 9 × 13⅔ in., identified (possibly
erroneously) as *Rebekah Receiving Presents
from Eliezer*, with 10 figures, in Bergeret's
posthumous sale, 24 Apr. ff. 1786, lot 148;
possibly the same drawing (no details given),
misc. sale (Regnault), 21 germinal, l'an IV
(10 Apr. 1796), lot 37.

*3*

Fig. 73. *Bethuel Welcoming the Servant of
Abraham*, engraved by J-B. Perronneau after
Boucher.

from Genesis quoted on the plate and the actual subject of the picture (it
must be admitted, however, that since their reappearance, both the sketch
and the finished picture have been similarly mistitled).

Whereas both sketch and finished painting clearly show the moment
when, presented by Rebekah's brother Laban, the servant of Abraham
(traditionally called Eliezer) is made welcome by their father Bethuel,
while Rebekah's maidens admire the jewels that Eliezer had given her at
the well (Genesis 24:24–33), the caption (Genesis 24:50–51) denotes the
moment when the servant of Abraham had finished explaining his mission
and was entrusted with conveying Rebekah back with him to become the
wife of Abraham's only son, Isaac. The finished picture makes the episode
depicted even more clear-cut than the sketch by removing from the
foreground the inappropriate figure of the slave proffering gold plate, who
belongs to a later moment in the story. The title given to the picture in
Blondel de Gagny's sale and subsequently, *Rebekah Receiving Presents
from the Servant of Abraham*, by contrast, refers either to the encounter at
the well, when the servant of Abraham rewarded Rebekah for voluntarily

**4**

Fig. 74. François Lemoine, *The Adoration of the Magi* (1715). Courtesy of Christie's, London.

Fig. 75. *The Death of Adonis,* engraved by Michel Aubert after Boucher (1733).

drawing water for his camels by presenting her with a golden earring and bracelets (Genesis 24:22), which she is seen showing off here, or to the moment after he was entrusted with her, when he heaped her with "jewels of silver, and jewels of gold, and raiment" (Genesis 24:53). Cars had no need of any depiction of *Rebekah at the Well,* however, since, as the catalogue of his stock of thesis plates drawn up by his nephew Babuty in 1771 reveals, number 6 of the Old Testament subjects on Papier Grand Aigle was "*Rebecca destinée à Isaac,* d'après Hallé," which must have been Desplaces's engraving after Claude-Guy Hallé, of *Rebekah at the Well;* number 7 was listed, with evident uncertainty as to its exact subject, as "Une autre *Rebecca,* d'après F. Boucher." It is possibly significant for Boucher's choice of theme that Lemoine had exhibited a small picture of *Rebecca qui reçoit les presents qu'Isaac lui envoit* at the "Exposition de la Fête-Dieu" in 1723.

This confusion over the exact subject of the finished picture strengthens the hypothesis of some interval between painting and engraving. A manuscript note in the copy of the catalogue of Blondel de Gagny's sale in the Bibliothèque d'Art et d'Archéologie in Paris asserts that the finished picture "had been executed under the eyes of Lemoine, before Boucher went to Rome; it has much of that master in it." This, as we can now see better, thanks to Pierre Rosenberg's recognition of a crucial early picture by Lemoine, the *Adoration of the Magi* (fig. 74) that he showed the Académie in 1715 in order to be *agréé* (Bordeaux, 1985, p. 71, no. 5), whose appearance was previously known only from the drawing in the d'Orsay collection in the Cabinet des Dessins of the Louvre (exh. cat. 1983, Paris, no. 81), is the exact truth. It is not simply that the crowded composition, with its wealth of carefully studied figures, their types, and the shimmering treatment of drapery (but also the nervously broken folds of that of the woman in the foreground, see *The Surprise*, cat. 2) are all Lemoinean; but that the figure of the servant of Abraham is clearly indebted to that of the foreground Magus in the *Adoration*. Already, however, Boucher lays on the paint—particularly in the foreground sheep and dog (who is employed in very similar fashion in both the vertical and horizontal versions of the *Death of Adonis* and in the *Martyrdom of the Japanese Jesuits*, see figs. 78, 75, 89)—with an impasto that was foreign to the less declamatory brushwork of Lemoine. There is also a sense of movement, extending even to inanimate things such as the tree, that sets Boucher apart from the more measured Lemoine. Interestingly, this is reduced in Perronneau's engraving after the finished picture, which also gives all the figures greater amplitude and gravitas.

If the finished picture strongly reflects Lemoine, the sketch—and here the former reattribution was by no means unintelligent—has a quick, evanescent quality that suggests Pellegrini. It must have been very shortly before this picture was painted that Pellegrini painted the brief-lived ceiling of the Banque de Mississipi (1720), which Mariette (IV, 1856–58, pp. 92–98) for one admired, and for which Lemoine produced a rival design (Bordeaux, 1985, no. 21). Despite this rivalry, it would appear that Pellegrini's sketches—possibly for this very ceiling—were not without influence on Lemoine's pupil, the young Boucher. Perhaps one can even see the effect of the criticisms made by Lemoine, as Boucher's teacher, in the more substantial air given to all the figures in the finished picture, as in the numerous small adjustments of pose and characterization. The more rustic notes sounded by the additional sheep (some of which were necessitated by the removal of the inappropriate figure of Eliezer's servant displaying plate), on the other hand, may be a shift of emphasis ascribable to Boucher himself. All in all, however, either this picture gives the lie to Boucher's claim to Mariette to have spent only a short time in Lemoine's studio, and to have learned little from him, or—if it was simply painted during or shortly after this brief period of preparation for the Grand Prix—it shows formidably quick powers of assimilation.

# 5 | Joseph Presenting His Father and Brothers to Pharaoh

Oil on canvas
22¾ × 28½ in. (58 × 72.5 cm)
Inscribed lower left: *boucher*
The Columbia Museum; Samuel
H. Kress Collection (K2148)
(S & M 700)      (A & W 9)

PROVENANCE
?*Catalogue raisonné d'Estampes . . . &c. . . .
du Cabinet de Mʳ PREVOST, Dessinateur et
Graveur,* rue des Bons-Enfans no. 30 (Re-
gnault-Delalande), 8 Jan. 1810, lot 277; private
coll., London; sold Sotheby's, London,
20 May 1953, lot 90 (as *The Continence of
Scipio*); H. D. Molesworth, London; Samuel
H. Kress coll., 1956; allocated to Columbia
Museum in 1957.

Ever since the subject of this painting was misidentified in 1954 by Hermann Voss—understandably overjoyed to have found what he thought was the linchpin of his brilliant reconstruction of Boucher's juvenile oeuvre—as *Evilmerodach Releasing Jehoiachin from Prison*, the theme set for the Prix de Rome in the year in which it was won by Boucher (1723), this picture has enjoyed canonical status within the artist's oeuvre. Now that its true subject has been perceived (Pigler's discreet rectification in his *Barockthemen*, 1956, I, p. 89, having apparently passed unnoticed, the present writer, having independently come to the same realization and found confirmation in Pigler, communicated his findings for use in the catalogue of the Kaufmann and Schlageter donation to the Louvre; see Rosenberg, 1984[a], pp. 33–34), we no longer have a certain date for the picture; yet it retains its importance as an undoubtedly early work. The question is: how early—since it is too facile to retain, while overturn-ing the traditional identification, the dating of the work that this carried with it.

But first it is necessary to justify the reidentification of the subject. The theme set by the Académie Royale de Peinture et de Sculpture in 1723 was taken from 2 Kings 25:27–30 (repeated virtually word for word in Jeremiah 52:31–34) and relates how Jehoiachin, the former king of Israel, was released by Evilmerodach on his succession to Nebuchadnezzar as King of Babylon after thirty-seven years' captivity (but still only aged fifty-five) and set upon a "throne above the throne of the kings that were with him in Babylon." In the present picture, the central figure is an aged patriarch, not a middle-aged king; there are no signs of former captivity, and no throne is prepared for him. Instead, a young man in a turban (Joseph) is introducing to a ruler (Pharaoh) his 130-year-old father (Jacob) and his brethren and their wives, whose calling as herdsmen can be recognized from their staffs (the youngest, on the far right, may well be Benjamin), exactly as narrated in Genesis 47:1–10.

The setting of this composition and, in particular, the figure of Pharaoh have something of the character of certain of the drawings for the *Histoire de France*, as Colin Eisler (1977, pp. 315–16) and Eric Zafran (exh. cat. 1983, Atlanta, no. 3) have indicated (fig. 76); but as Eisler also observed, the organization of the picture, with the protagonists disposed upon steps in the front plane, and with a looped curtain and salamonic columns flanking an arch framing a patch of cloud-flecked blue sky forming a backdrop, is essentially Venetian in character. Furthermore, as compared with the *Mutius Scaevola* (cat. 8), the forms of the figures and drapery are

5

Fig. 76. *Homage Paid to Louis XII by the Archduke.* Cabinet des Dessins, Louvre.

less mannered, and the fall of light is more studied, and its effects on flesh and stuffs exploited. The whole painting is on a small scale, and the handling is appropriately delicate, but the overall impression is of scaled-down monumentality. Despite the presence of details that suggest French models—the head of the wife behind Jacob evokes those of Lemoine's women, while that of Jacob himself draws upon a patriarchal type apparently established by Antoine Coypel (see exh. cat. 1983, Karlsruhe, Kunsthalle, no. 10)—the overall impression is as much almost, if not more, Italian.

The French painter with the "miniature monumentality" of whose works the present picture immediately prompts comparison is Nicolas Vleughels, the director of the French Academy in Rome from 1724 to his death in 1737 (see esp. his *Circumcision* of 1726, and his *Christ in the House of Simon the Pharisee* and *Marriage at Cana* of 1727 and 1728; Hercenberg, 1975, cat. nos. 107, 109, 110). Vleughels, with his well-known admiration for the Venetian school, is also the likeliest conduit for its influence upon Boucher, before the latter had had the opportunity of seeing an appreciable number of its works at first hand. This might suggest that the present picture had been painted in Rome, but it does not fit comfortably so late in Boucher's development. In handling the drapery Boucher still employs little squiggles to suggest broken folds, in a way characteristic of the early Lemoine (see *The Surprise*, cat. 2). Many of the heads employ his types, but above all, the eager boy at the far right is evidently studied from the same model as the young servant crouching at the far left of the *Bethuel Welcoming the Servant of Abraham*. The handling of the present picture is both more lively and more idiosyncratic than that of the latter, however, so that it would appear that Vleughels's was simply one of the influences that Boucher drew upon in order to emancipate himself from his former master and forge a style of his own, one less monumental and more miniature. The subject matter of the painting—taken from the lives of the Old Testament patriarchs—is also of the kind that appears to have occupied his brush in the years before and during his sojourn in Rome, and it is early in this group that it probably should be placed, after his Lemoinean pictures for Cars, but before he embarked on his Castiglionesque scenes from the Old Testament and from rural life, or on his small mythologies, in other words, in the period 1723–26.

# 6 | *The Sacrifice of Gideon*

Oil on canvas
49½ × 33 in. (126 × 84 cm)
Othon Kaufmann and François
Schlageter collection, Strasbourg;
donated, subject to life interest, to the
Musée du Louvre, Paris (R.F. 1983–72)
(S & M 721)     (A & W 37)

PROVENANCE
La Live de Jully coll., salon of his house in rue Saint-Honoré (by 1757; see Dezallier, 1757, p. 150) and then (by 1764; see *Catalogue historique*, p. 92: "Ce morceau, d'une très-belle couleur & d'une heureuse composition, rappelle avec plaisir l'Ecole où cet agréable Artiste a perfectionné ses talens naturels") rue de Richelieu [no. 81], salon sur le jardin; his sale, 5 Mar. ff. 1770, lot 93: "Un autre Tableau aussi très ragoûtant . . ." [bought for 758 livres by Métra, who is claimed by a ms. note in copy of cat. in Bibliothèque de l'Art et de l'Archéologie, Paris, to have been acting as agent for the Czarina; if true, she must have declined the purchase]; [de Vassal de Saint-Hubert] sale, rue Vivienne, 17 Jan. ff. 1774, lot 99: "Un tableau d'un bon *faire*, & vigoreux de coloris . . ." [bought for 1400 livres by Boileau, acting for the prince de Conti]; prince de Conti's sale, 8 Apr. ff. 1777, lot 720: "Ce

The most spectacular of all the rediscoveries of a work by Boucher since the *Rape of Europa* and the *Mercury Confiding the Infant Bacchus* now in the Wallace Collection were rescued from their misattribution to Lemoine in 1860, *The Sacrifice of Gideon* was recognized by Pierre Rosenberg when it was offered for sale some years ago masquerading as a Sebastiano Ricci (see Rosenberg, 1984[a], no. 1). This not wholly implausible attribution, together with the for the young Boucher apparently unprecedented scale and character of the work, led Rosenberg to the natural—albeit tentatively advanced—conclusion that the picture was one of the first fruits of Boucher's journey to Italy. In this he was at the time wholeheartedly seconded by the present writer. That would also appear to have been the opinion of so fine a contemporary connoisseur as Mariette, if he was indeed at the elbow of La Live de Jully when the latter drew up the catalogue of his own collection in 1764, in which it is said that the picture: "recalls with pleasure the School where this delightful Artist perfected his natural endowments" ("*rappelle avec plaisir l'Ecole où cet agréable Artiste*

6

tableau ragoûtant de coloris, est d'une touche très savante . . ." [bought for 2012 livres by Paillet]; misc. sale, Hôtel de Bullion (A-J. Paillet), 23 May ff. 1780, lot 23: "Un des chef-d'oeuvres de ce Peintre, tant par le beau ton de couleur que par la touche sçavante & le génie de la composition . . ." [sold for 1700 livres]; [Montaleau] sale, Maison du Mont-de-Piété (Paillet & Delaroche), 19 July ff. 1802, lot 5: "Ce morceau a toujours été distingué dans le nombre des ouvrages de ce Peintre, autant par la richesse de la couleur que par le brillant de son exécution . . ." [bought for 225 francs by Penose (sic);] Cooper Penrose, Waterford, and thence by descent; Somerville & Simpson, London, from whom acquired in 1978.

ENGRAVING

*Sacrifice de Gédéon*, published by Jean-François Cars on Papier au Petit Chapelet (see *Catalogue*, 1771, p. 10, no. 16) [no example traced].

Fig. 77. *Selene and Endymion*. Private collection, France.

Fig. 78. *The Death of Adonis*, engraved by Louis Surugue after Boucher (1742).

*a perfectionné ses talens naturels"* [*Catalogue historique*, 1764, p. 92]). Written with a capital E, and put in this way, "Ecole" could only have been intended to refer to one of the four acknowledged national schools of painting at this epoch (training at the Academy was not yet sufficiently organized for it to have been called an "Ecole," nor would a single master such as Lemoine have been so described). The only two national "Ecoles" that the cataloguer could have had in mind were the French and the Italian. Bearing in mind Mariette's inability to identify any native master by whom Boucher had been formed, it is evident that only the *Ecole italienne* could have been intended.

Nor was this invocation of the Italian school misguided. The error has been to go on to draw the natural conclusion that this influence had to wait until Boucher's journey to Italy to make itself felt. There are in fact several indicators that attach this picture to works painted some time before he finally traveled there in 1728. Some of them have only recently become apparent, with the rediscovery of the finished picture of *Bethuel Welcoming the Servant of Abraham* (cat. 4), the engraving after which has always been somewhat misleading about its style and character. Most readily apparent are the resemblances between figure types. The head of Gideon is patently conceived along the same lines as that of Bethuel (in certain respects, the affinities are even closer with his head as it is painted in the sketch, cat. 3), his hands are similarly articulated, and their manner of gesticulation common to that of both Bethuel and the servant of Abraham (and beyond them, to that of St. Joseph in the yet earlier *Dream of St. Joseph*, fig. 70). The witness to the left of Gideon's sacrifice is clearly studied from the same model as the servant holding a loaf to the right of Bethuel. The female witness in the foreground of the *Sacrifice of Gideon* is a variation upon the similarly posed and placed figure of a maidservant in the foreground of *Bethuel Welcoming the Servant of Abraham*. The latter is even pouring water into a ewer of almost identical form to the one found in the *Sacrifice of Gideon*.

In handling, however, the *Sacrifice of Gideon* is very different from the *Bethuel Welcoming the Servant of Abraham*. Gone are the muted colors and the Lemoinean preoccupation with the fall of light on drapery and flesh; in their place are more vivid coloristic effects, as in the sacrificial fire and Gideon's robe, and a much more pronounced chiaroscuro. At the same time, the handling of paint has become freer and rougher, drawing attention to its own virtuosity in a way that would have been inconceivable in the carefully toned and modulated compositions of Lemoine (at least until he started to react to the innovations of his own former pupil). In this it most resembles the handling of the early group of small mythological paintings, none of which, regrettably, has it proved possible to borrow for this exhibition: *The Birth* and *Death of Adonis*, which, significantly, also once belonged to La Live de Jully (A & W 38, 39; last recorded with the heirs of Matthieu Goudchaux; a pair of replicas of the same size in a private collection in Switzerland; a pair of replicas of larger dimensions, 96 × 128 cm, sold Paris, Palais Galliera, 22 Nov. 1972, lots 23, 24); the *Selene and Endymion* (fig. 77; A & W 36; since rediscovered and exh. 1982, New York, no. 5; now in a private collection in France); and the upright *Death of Adonis* (see fig. 78; A & W 87; sold Sotheby's Monaco, 26 May 1980, lot 553; now in a private collection, Saint-Jean-

Cap-Ferrat), which provides the best chance of dating the whole group, since it appears to have been painted as a pendant to Carle Vanloo's *Mars and Venus* (see fig. 31; exh. cat. 1977, Nice, no. 259; still missing), which Dandré-Bardon (1765, p. 63) dates to 1726. It is with the androgynous, elongated bodies in the last of these mythological paintings by Boucher that the figure of the angel in the *Sacrifice of Gideon* has most affinity. Common to the whole group of pictures is the profusion of frothily rendered, color-flecked clouds and smoke.

The problem with placing the *Sacrifice of Gideon* in relation to these small mythological pictures lies in deciding whether it was painted before, after, or even concurrently with them, and in the fact that there is no other picture that is strictly comparable. It represents an extreme of both size and painterliness to which Boucher did not again aspire until after his return from Italy. Although of an Old Testament subject, it is quite different in character from the paintings of this kind that are currently known. It must fall in time between the *Bethuel Welcoming the Servant of Abraham* (cat. 4) and the *Joseph Presenting His Brethren* (cat. 5), which betray an apprentice indebtedness to Lemoine and Vleughels respectively, and the two paintings of *Noah* (cat. 10, 11), which embody the distinctive miniature manner that Boucher had evolved before leaving for Rome. Although the Sacrifice of Gideon was one of the three subjects set by the Academy for the *concours* of 1721—in which Boucher was probably anyway too young and inexperienced to have competed—and although his composition was engraved for Jean-François Cars's stock of thesis plates, it is of the wrong size and format to have been executed for either contingency. It seems instead to have been a rare example of a commissioned picture, painted after Boucher had emancipated himself from the chore of providing designs for thesis plates, while still in that vein of infrequently depicted Old Testament subjects.

The episode illustrated (which was curiously one much favored by Boucher's Venetian contemporaries) is that of Judges 6:21, in which Gideon, having asked for a sign that he had indeed been chosen by God to deliver Israel from the Midianites, has his sacrifice consumed by fire kindled by the staff held by an angel. Whereas the better-known episode of Gideon and the fleece was sometimes depicted as an antetype of the Virgin birth, the present scene had no such significance, and one can therefore perhaps see it chiefly as a pretext for Boucher to impress potential clients with a novel subject, which gave him the opportunity of displaying his most *ragoûtant* color and bravura *faire* in the flames and smoke of the sacrifice.

What models Boucher looked at to aid him in this emancipation from Lemoine and his other early mentors is not readily apparent. It was surely paintings of the Italian school that provided the inspiration for the *ragoûtant* effects of his brushwork; but to point to a particular painter—if such there was—is more problematic. The obvious figure, Sebastiano Ricci, does not appear to have left much evidence of his passage through France (his *morceau de réception* in the Academy, the *Triumph of Learning over Ignorance*, Daniels, 1976[a], no. 297, is one of his more conventional performances), nor is there any real sign of influence emanating from him or from that other recent bird of passage, his compatriot Pellegrini, in either the types or the brushwork of the present picture. There is also no trace as yet of the bravura color effects or hatched brushstrokes that Boucher was to absorb from his study of Castiglione, which are only evident after his return from Italy. One can only echo Mariette's exasperated question: "Whose follower is he then?" ("*De qui est-il donc le disciple?*" [Mariette, I, 1851–53, p. 165]), and admit that Boucher had a striking ability to transmute whatever influences he did undergo into not one, but a succession of striking personal idioms. It is especially fitting that this key work of Boucher's early development should have found its place in a collection begun under the auspices of the greatest expositor of that development, Hermann Voss.

## 7 | *Les oies de Frère Philippe*

Gouache on taffeta
8¼ × 16½ in. (21 × 42 cm)
Musée des Beaux-Arts et d'Archéologie
de Besançon (inv. 848.7.1)
(S & M 2605)          A & W fig. 8
*Paris*

PROVENANCE
?Collection of Jean de Jullienne; thence by gift or descent to: *Catalogue d'une belle Collection de Tableaux . . . &c, venans du Cab. de M.M[on]t[ullé],* Hôtel de Bullion (Le Brun), 22 Dec. ff. 1783, lot 99 [bought for 29 livres 19 sous by Constantin]; *Catalogue d'une belle Collection de Dessins des Trois Ecoles,* Hôtel de Bullion (Constantin), 2 Apr. ff. 1787, lot 63: "Cette charmante gouache, faite dans la manière de Vateau . . ."; Bruzard sale, 23–26 Apr. 1839, lot 25; acquired by the Musée de Besançon in 1848 for 100 francs.

PREPARATORY DRAWING
De Jullienne sale, 30 Mar. ff. 1767, lot 947: "Les Oyes du Frère Philippe: dessein à la plume & coloré, de 7 pouces 6 lignes de haut, sur 11 pouces 9 lignes de large" [sold for 47 livres]; misc. sale (Le Brun), 11 Dec. ff. 1780, lot 212: "Dessins aquarelles [*sic*] sur papier blanc. Hauteur 9 pouces. Largeur 12 pouces 6 lignes" [sold for 9 livres]; marquis de Sabran sale (Basan), 2–4 Dec. 1782, lot 92; Ch. Drouet coll. (exh. cat. 1901, Paris, no. ).

This gouache is unique in Boucher's surviving oeuvre, not only in its medium, but also in the Watteauesque character of its female protagonists and landscape. It is also rare among his paintings in illustrating a story, although between 1736 and 1747 he was to prepare monochrome oil sketches of four of the *Contes* of La Fontaine for de Larmessin to engrave. If it were to be a fan leaf, which would help to account for some of these singularities, it would also be a unique survival, but it is by no means sure that is what it is, despite its recent inclusion in an exhibition of designs for fan leaves (exh. cat. 1984, Stuttgart, no. 31).

The story is taken from La Fontaine's version of one told in the introduction to the fourth day of Boccaccio's *Decameron*. Frère Philippe was a widower turned hermit who had brought up his only son in the wild to preserve him from the evils of human contact. When finally taken to town, the son was filled with insatiable curiosity about everything they saw. Their encounters included one with a group of finely dressed young women. Never having seen a woman in his life, the son asked his father what kind of thing that was. "It's a bird—called a goose," replied the father. "Oh!" said the son, who had some familiarity with poultry and felt strangely drawn to this new variety of fowl. "Can't we take one home and feed it up?"

The story was illustrated by a number of French artists in the eighteenth century, most notably by Vleughels (a painting, dated 1729, sold 6 June 1805, lot 61), by Subleyras (Louvre), and by Lancret on more than one occasion (see G. Wildenstein, 1924, nos. 658–62). Subleyras's picture has no affinity with Boucher's, which, like Lancret's, somewhat traduces the story (but creates a subtle suggestion of the encounter with a gaggle of birds of exotic plumage) by situating it in the countryside. Why Boucher

7

Fig. 79. *Landscape in the Veneto (after Campagnola).* Fitzwilliam Museum, Cambridge.

should have adopted this uncharacteristic subject is uncertain; however, it is evidently a work of his youth, when he would naturally have been disposed to try his hand at anything.

Yet this versatility never normally seems to have included the execution of fans. When Grimm (*Correspondance littéraire*, II, p. 282) said in 1753 that, "Il y a longtemps qu'on appelle ce peintre un peintre d'éventail," it was because of his garish colors, not because of any such activity. If we come across mentions of fans in connection with Boucher, these generally concern designs supplied for execution by others: e.g., the two depictions of *Amusemens de Campagne* composed for the Czarina Elzvieta (Huquier sale, 1 July ff. 1771, lot 18); the drawings in the Lempereur and Collet sales (24 May ff. 1773, lot 538 [A & W fig. 413], and 14 May ff. 1787, lot 439); or the drawing of *Bacchus and Ariadne* in the National Gallery of Canada (see exh. cat. 1984, Stuttgart, no. 32). The one occasion on which we know Boucher accepted a commission for a fan, for Count Tessin in 1746, he proposed executing it in india ink and watercolor and, having been persuaded to paint it on vellum instead, took almost a year to produce it, because of his unfamiliarity with the difficulties of the task (Scheffer, 1982, pp. 135–66 passim). Most significantly of all, on neither of the two occasions when the present gouache passed through the salerooms in the eighteenth century was it suggested that it was intended as a fan (see Provenance). Closer examination of the object bears this out: there is nothing in the composition to suggest that it was intended to fit into a semicircle (unlike all the other designs by Boucher's contemporaries illustrated in the above-mentioned catalogue), and it is impossible to detect any difference of support or handling in the "added" segments. The presumption is, therefore, that they are not added at all, but evidence of

Fig. 80. *La bonne aventure*, engraved by
Pierre Aveline after Boucher (1738).

Fig. 81. *The Death of Meleager*.
A. S. Ciechanowiecki collection, on extended
loan to the University of New Mexico Art
Museum, Albuquerque.

arrested vandalism, when someone's hand was stayed from cutting this
gouache on silk into the web of a fan.

The medium alone is almost enough to declare this gouache an experiment of Boucher's youth, since references to other gouaches by him
are extraordinarily rare: there was an *écran* with *La belle Bouquetière*,
"drawn in pen and painted in gouache" in Huquier's posthumous sale
(9 Nov. ff. 1772, lot 7); a pair of oval gouaches, *Painting* and *Sculpture*, in
Bergeret's posthumous sale (24 Apr. ff. 1786, lot 114); and the rather
surprising use of gouache, for a sketch, *Vénus sur les eaux*, which was
engraved by Daullé and included in Vennevault's posthumous sale
(26 Mar. ff. 1776, lot 19) and Basan *père*'s sale (1 Dec. ff. 1798, lot 74).
The preparatory watercolor also points to an early date, since this was
a medium that Boucher only employed in his youth.

Details of the composition likewise point to Boucher's early years,
principally its Watteauesque elements, of which the most obvious is the
Campagnola-derived view of a town on the right (fig. 79). There are
parallels for this in a signed drawing by Boucher in the de Boer collection
in Amsterdam (see exh. cat. 1974, Amsterdam, no. 17) and in a drawing
disputed between Watteau and Boucher in the Fitzwilliam Museum,
Cambridge, which seems to sit most comfortably with the drawings of the
latter (see Jacoby, 1979). Watteau's is the very influence that one would
expect to see predominant in the years immediately prior to Boucher's
departure for Italy, when his main occupation must have been making
etchings after Watteau's compositions for de Jullienne's *Recueil*. The
umbrella pine and the cypresses, on the other hand, might almost suggest
firsthand experience of Italy on Boucher's part, were they not also to have
been constant elements of Watteau's landscapes, and hence additional
evidence of his influence.

The figures of the women are modish, and thus perhaps more suggestive
of Lancret than Watteau, but those of Frère Philippe and his son relate
directly to Boucher's own early works, particularly the old man, with face
and beard fusing into one long vertical, who has an extensive kindred in
these years. His closest relative is the fortune-teller in Aveline's *La bonne
aventure* (fig. 80), an engraving that was announced in the *Mercure de
France* in April 1738, but whose strikingly Watteauesque original must
date from at least a decade earlier. Related again is the figure supporting
the body of the hero from behind in the various versions of the sketch of
*The Death of Meleager* (one of which, paired with *The Birth of Meleager*,
was in Dandré-Bardon's posthumous sale [23 June ff. 1783, lot 5]; a pair,
attributed to Dandré-Bardon himself and called *La naissance d'Oedipe* and
*La mort de Méléagre*, in the Musée Bargoin, Clermont-Ferrand; a *Death
of Meleager* with the same attribution in an English collection on loan to
the New Mexico Art Museum [fig. 81; see exh. cat. 1980, Albuquerque,
no. 12]; and another, formerly attributed to Fragonard, called *Antiochus et
Stratonice* [see Portalis, 1889, p. 271], currently on the Paris art market).
The hounds in the two compositions are also visibly from the same ken-
nels. Related, via the figure in *The Death of Meleager*, is also that of the
pontifex in the *Mutius Scaevola* (cat. 8). And finally there is the figure of
Laban in the drawing *The Separation of Laban from Jacob* recently
acquired by the Louvre (see exh. cat. 1984, Paris, Cabinet des Dessins,
no. 78).

*Les oies de Frère Philippe* appears to stand alone in Boucher's oeuvre. One can only speculate at his motives for adopting this medium and kind of subject, and for his soon virtually abandoning them, but it is evident that lack of capability was not among them. We should be grateful that chance has also preserved—in this unaccustomed mode of painting—Boucher at his most Watteauesque. In this feature, at least, we can surely detect the endeavor to cater to the tastes of his client, particularly if—as seems likely—this was Watteau's great propagandist, de Jullienne. Not only did the latter own the preparatory watercolor for this gouache, but its first recorded owner, J-B-F. de Montullé, was his son-in-law.

# 8 | *Mutius Scaevola Putting His Hand in the Fire*

Oil on canvas
23½ × 19 in. (60 × 48.5 cm)
Musée Sandelin, Saint-Omer (inv. D.3)

This vibrantly treated sketch was once demoted—no doubt because of the apparent absence of anything comparable in his oeuvre—to "school of Boucher," and then somewhat willfully ascribed to Dumont le Romain because of his derivative signed and dated oblong picture of 1747 of the same subject in the Musée des Beaux-Arts at Besançon (see Locquin, 1978, pp. 6, 177, and pl. 5).

On the cumulative strength of the evidence, as was tentatively proposed by Philippe-Gérard Chabert in 1980 (exh. cat. 1980, Nord, no. 106), this sketch must, however, be given to Boucher himself. Not only does the style point to the artist, although admittedly to a previously unsuspected phase of his development as a painter, but we also have a closely related drawing by the young Boucher of this composition, and the record of an oil sketch by him of this subject, of the same dimensions, in an eighteenth-century sale.

Most telling, particularly for the prospect that it opens up of recovering a crucial phase in Boucher's development before he went to Rome, is the kinship between the ductus of this oil sketch and that of Boucher's pen-and-wash drawings prepared for the 1729 edition of P. Gabriel Daniel's *Histoire de France,* which are now in the Louvre (for the recognition of these as Boucher's, overturning their old ascription to Cazes, see Ruch, 1964). The affinity is not limited to the handling, to the types of the figures, and to the character of the drapery, with its multiple sausagelike folds; it extends to the almost direct repetition of the figure of the fallen warrior (a device first used for the body of Adonis in the *Venus and Adonis* of about 1726 [private collection, Saint-Jean-Cap-Ferrat; A & W 87, unlocated and misdated]) in *Charles Martel Annihilating the Saracen Army* (fig. 82; Guiffrey & Marcel, III, 1909, no. 2169; see also A & W fig. 2) in that of Porsenna's assassinated secretary in the forefront of *Mutius Scaevola,* and to the repetition of the figure of François II in the

8

Fig. 82. *Charles Martel Annihilating the Saracen Army*. Cabinet des Dessins, Louvre.

Fig. 83. *The Condemnation of the Templars*. Cabinet des Dessins, Louvre.

Fig. 84. *Mutius Scaevola Putting His Hand in the Fire*. Collection of Robert and Bertina Manning.

*Requête des Huguenots* (Guiffrey & Marcel, III, 1909, no. 2185; Ruch, 1964, fig. 22) in that of Porsenna himself. Furthermore, both the *Condemnation of the Templars* (fig. 83) and the *Querelle entre le Comte de Valois et Enguerant de Marigny* employ a repoussoir figure with outstretched hand at the edge of the picture in a similar way to the pontifex (Guiffrey & Marcel, III, 1909, nos. 2181, 2180; Ruch, 1964, figs. 21, 24).

Having established the close kinship of the *Mutius Scaevola* with the drawings for the *Histoire de France*, we need to rectify the common misdating of the latter. Encouraged, no doubt, by a belief that the distortions of these drawings indicate Boucher's stylistic immaturity, most commentators follow P-J. Mariette and imply an association in date between them and the second edition of the *Histoire de France*, dating from 1722. The case is quite otherwise. The 1722 edition published by his uncle Denys Mariette was adorned mostly with woodcuts, and the only illustrations with any artistic pretensions were the two commissioned from Vleughels (see Hercenberg, 1975, nos. 333, 334). Boucher's illustrations appear only in the third edition, published jointly by Denys

Mariette and Jacques Rollin in 1729. The preparation of this edition can hardly have begun much before 1727, the date on the false title page announcing the project, which is bound in with the copy in the Bibliothèque Nationale. The distortions apparent in Boucher's illustrations are thus not the product of artistic immaturity, but the willed pursuit of an individual hand, such as was also to characterize the years after his return from Italy. The disconcerting thing about Boucher, however, is that his development was not linear, and that, having achieved so intensely personal a manner just before his departure for Rome, albeit one that was really suitable only for application on a small scale, he could *reculer pour mieux sauter* and forge a quite different manner in Italy and in the years immediately after his return, one that enabled him to become an artist of quite a different stature.

There is no indication that any large-scale work was ever executed from the present sketch; indeed the drawing (fig. 84; see exh. cat. 1973–74, Washington, no. 2) possibly suggests that none was intended, that the sketch existed in its own right, and that its vibrant qualities were to be disseminated in an etching or engraving. The story of the Roman Mutius Scaevola (Mutius the Left-Handed) relates how, when he had concealed himself in the camp of Porsenna, the king of Etruria, in order to assassinate him and had killed his secretary in error, he thrust his right hand into the sacrificial fire to make his point that, even though he had failed, there were three hundred more young Romans with like courage to renew the attempt—a demonstration that so alarmed Porsenna that he sued for peace. In the painting, Mutius is indeed putting his right hand into the fire, but in the drawing, in which the whole composition has been reversed (so as to produce an image the right way round when engraved) and slightly altered, it is his left. It is intriguing that the picture should first be recorded in the possession of a painter-etcher, Philippe-Louis Parizeau (1740–1801), who also recorded one of Boucher's sketches in an etching, his *Psiché refusant les honneurs divins* (see cat. 34); but Parizeau was not even alive at the time the present picture was painted. Possibly he acquired it from whichever engraver had intended but failed to make a plate from it.

## 9 | *La vie champêtre*

Oil on canvas
24¼ × 19 in. (61 × 48 cm)
Private collection, London
(S & M 1844)      A & W 55

PROVENANCE
Sale held by Andrew Hay, London, [14/15 Feb.] 1744 (O.S.)/1745 (N.S.), 2nd day, lot 33, *A Harvest with Fig.*, *a Man Sleeping* [bought for £15 by Peters]; sale held by Bragge, 1756, 2nd day, lot 32, *A Harvest* [bought for £13 2s. 6d. by Banks; Banks can plausibly be identified with the later Sir Henry Bankes (d. 1774),

This picture is unique in having a virtually unbroken English provenance extending back to a date not long after it was painted. Like almost all the other Bouchers that featured in English sales or collections in the eighteenth century, it is quite different in character from the sentimental pastorals or nude mythologies that were so avidly sought after by a number of English collectors in the nineteenth century. Indeed, as with *La*

9

whose name appears to be decipherable, together with the numbers *N. 13* and *H.R.6*, on
an old label on the back of the picture,
apparently one of those with details of attribution and provenance affixed by Elisabeth Cust
to the pictures at Belton House, since they
correspond with those in the entry on the
picture in the first manuscript catalogue of the
collection drawn up by her in 1805–06 (I am
most grateful to John Chesshyre of the National Trust for supplying me with a transcript
of this); see F(rancis) R(ussell), "The Picture
Collection at Belton," foreword to cat. of
Belton House sale, Christie's, London,
30 Apr.–2 May 1984]; his coll., Wimbledon,
whence inherited by his daughter, Frances,
Lady Cust (from 1776, Lady Brownlow), and
brought to Belton House, Lincs.; thence by
descent, until sold at Christie's, London,
3 May 1929, lot 1 [bought by "Smith"]; Frank
T. Sabin, London (exh. cat. 1935, no. 6); with
Fröhlich, London, in 1946; Dr. E. Sklarz,
London, from whom it passed to the present
owner.

ENGRAVING
*La vie champêtre*, engraved by Elisabeth
Lépicié in 1741 and published by her husband
Bernard Lépicié in the same year, with a verse
by him:
*Le Repos et l'Amour regnent dans ces aziles*
*Et sont la source des plaisirs:*
*Le Tumulte et la haine habitent dans les Villes*
*Et sont la source des soupirs.*
(J-R 1382)

DRAWING
?*La sieste des moissonneurs*, pen and sepia
wash, heightened with carmine, sale of MM.
D____ et P____, Paris, 19 Dec. 1898, lot 9.

COPIES
1. Misc. sale, Versailles, 11 Mar. 1973, lot
93.
2. The boy from the foreground of the
engraving reproduced on a Capodimonte covered jar in the Hispanic Society of America,
New York (see Frothingham, 1955, p. 10 and
fig. 13).

ANALOGY
*Boy Standing behind a Laden Mule* (fig. 87),
black chalk with touches of red, Cabinet des
Dessins, Louvre (R.F. 14751), [a variant in
reverse of the similar detail in the painting].

*belle cuisinière* (cat. 21), it was no doubt because of the genre in which it
was painted, rather than because of Boucher's own reputation, that it was
taken over to England in the first place.

The genre here is Dutch. Into a setting that owes something to the rural
scenes with ruins by the Italianate school of landscapists, Boucher has
inserted figures indebted to his imitations of Abraham Bloemaert's studies
from everyday life (see Slatkin, 1976). The figure of the sleeping harvester,
in particular, is almost a quotation from Bloemaert's *Pastoral Scene with
Tobias and the Angel* in the Staatliche Museen in East Berlin (see
Rosenberg, Slive & ter Kuile, 1977, pl. 193; for Subleyras's copy of
Bloemart's drawing for this figure, see exh. cat. 1983, Paris, no. 100).
From a study identifiably for the latter Boucher directly quoted the figure
of the boy standing with a basket, which he was to employ in his
*Capriccio View of the Farnese Gardens* (cat. 23), and in the tenth etching
of his *Livre d'Etude d'après les Desseins Originaux de Blomart* (J-R 184).

This book of etchings was only published in 1735, to judge from the
advertisement of it in the *Mercure de France* for June of that year (pt. II,
p. 1382). Must we therefore place the painting as late? Although
juxtaposed by Ananoff with the painting that he calls *La tendre pastorale*
(A & W 54; last recorded with David Findlay in New York around 1955,
according to information kindly supplied by David M. Koetser), itself
dated too early (to 1730), in view of the fact that (as the drawings
associated with it bear out) it was probably painted much nearer to the
date at which an engraving incorporating it was published by Huquier, in
1736 (*Mercure de France*, Jan., p. 134), its affinity with this painting is a
fortuitous one of composition, and not at all one of handling (as far as can
be judged from reproductions of *La tendre pastorale*). The brushwork of
the present picture, and the types of the figures in the middle plane in
particular, associate it rather with such paintings as *La fontaine* (fig. 85;
A & W 46; engraved by Jean Pelletier, J-R 1453), or the two depictions of
*Noah* (cat. 10, 11) and, slightly more distantly, with certain of the early
group of pastoral landscapes published by Voss in 1953: *Rustic Scene with
a Mother Spinning* (Voss, p. 82, and fig. 45; A & W 50; last recorded in
the Frey collection in Paris in 1953); the *Landscape with Bathers in a
Moat* (Voss, p. 82, and fig. 37; A & W 72; last recorded in a private
collection in Paris in 1966); and the *Crossing the Ford* (Voss, p. 82, and
fig. 38; exhibited at the Galerie Georges Petit as a Fragonard in 1907). All
but the last of these have the slumped figure of a peasant acting as a
repoussoir in the foreground, and one can well believe that if they were
not derived directly from drawings by Bloemaert, they were at least
inspired by such. In the three last, the landscape predominates over the
figures and is characterized by exaggeratedly plunging effects of perspective recession and by vegetation of almost demented vitality (partially
inspired by Lemoine). In *La fontaine,* as in the present picture, it is the
figures that predominate over the setting, and the distortions of perspective and foliage are less extreme. The brushwork and the treatment of
drapery have also shed the mannerism of Boucher's earliest pictures,
without acquiring the summary quality of those that he painted after his
return from Italy. Despite the fact, therefore, that *La fontaine* was said by
the catalogue of the fourth sale in which it appeared, that of M. Bourlat de
Montredon (16 Mar. ff. 1778, lot 15; which also mistitled it *Bergers à la*

Fig. 85. *La fontaine*. The J. B. Speed Art Museum, Louisville.

Fig. 86. *Le repas champêtre*. Private collection, Germany.

Fig. 87. *Boy Standing behind a Laden Mule*. Cabinet des Dessins, Louvre.

*Fontaine*), to have been painted by Boucher after his return from Rome, it is most probable either that both these pictures just antedate the journey there, or that they are examples of the "tableaux précieux à la maniere des Flamands," that Papillon de La Ferté (1776, II, p. 657) asserts Boucher did in Rome.

Additional support for an earlier dating of the present picture can be obtained from closer consideration of the etchings after Bloemaert. Although these were made as late as 1735, the drawings from which they were done seem to have been available to Boucher for some time before. Not only is there the evidence of their exploitation in other early works, as seen above, but they also appear to have come from a larger group of drawings circulating among Boucher's fellow students in Rome. This would at any rate appear to be the explanation of the two sheets of copies of Bloemaert drawings among the three *fonds d'ateliers* of French artists in Rome acquired by the comte d'Orsay and now in the Louvre, whether one accepts their ascription to Subleyras or not (see exh. cat. 1983, Paris, nos. 99, 100). None of the figures on either of the two sheets was etched by Boucher, but the second contains a study for the sleeping farmhand in the *Pastoral Scene with Tobias*, who is so closely related to the sleeping harvester in the foreground of the present picture. Are these in fact further compilations by Boucher after Bloemaert's drawings that he did not proceed to etch (but the face of the seated young woman has been altered from Bloemaert's original in a way that is more suggestive of Natoire)? Or did a group of students at the French Academy originally think up this idea of compiling etchings after Bloemaert's drawings when Boucher was still in Rome? One of Boucher's rustic scenes in his precious earlier manner, very close to *La vie champêtre*, but with more monumental figures, which strongly suggest that it was one of those painted in Rome , is the *Repas champêtre* formerly in the collection of R. H. Benson (fig. 86; Sotheby's, London, 5 July 1984, lot 369 [bought by Neuhaus]; private collection, Germany; drawing in the National Gallery of Canada, Ottawa [Popham & Fenwick, 1965, no. 225] as J-P. Le Bas). While it is not yet possible to indicate specific models, the figures in this painting give every impression of having been derived from more of these Bloemaert drawings.

An indicator that needs to be accounted for suggesting a later placing of the present picture than the one proposed here is the date of Elizabeth Lépicié's engraving of it: 1741. The date of an engraving after Boucher bears no necessary relation, however, to that of the original painting or drawing, least of all by the 1740s, when his reputation was made and engravers eagerly sought out anything of his to reproduce. The absence either of a dedication or of any indication of ownership on the plate might even suggest that it was simply made to assist the picture's resale. Significantly, the advertisement for the engraving in the *Mercure de France* in November 1741 (p. 2456) says that the picture was "entierement peint dans le goût de *Benedetto Castillon*," which is palpably not the case but which was no doubt intended to associate this picture with Boucher's later paintings, in which the influence of Castiglione is evident. So, too, the verses underneath the engraving, hymning the simple pleasures of rustic society, belong more to the time of the engraving, when Boucher was painting his first sentimental pastorals, than to the epoch of the picture itself, although these implications may well have been latent in it. It is, indeed, the concentration upon a group of rustics without the introduction of any erotic or sentimental note, while not reducing them to mere staffage in a landscape, that sets this painting, *La fontaine,* and one or two transitional later works apart from the themes of Boucher's maturity.

## 10 | *Noah Entering the Ark*

Oil on panel
12¾ × 25½ in. (32.5 × 65 cm)
Private collection, Fort Worth
(S & M 707)      (A & W 29)

## 11 | *The Sacrifice of Noah*

Oil on panel
12½ × 25½ in. (32 × 65 cm)
Private collection, Fort Worth
(S & M 707)      (A & W 30)

PROVENANCE
?Painted for Jean de Jullienne; certainly in his collection by c. 1750–60, when in [J-B-F. de Montullé] ms. *Catalogue des tableaux de M<sup>r</sup>. de Jullienne*, pp. 49–50, nos. 76, 85, as *Entrée dans l'Arche* and *Sortie de l'Arche,* and illustrated in the "2e Cabinet de M<sup>r</sup>: côté en face de l'entrée" (Pierpont Morgan Library, New

The recent rediscovery of this pair of pictures is important, not merely because they were originally in a celebrated collection, that of de Jullienne, but also because they are additions to a still scantily attested phase of Boucher's career. Despite the assertion of the catalogue of the Français sale in 1815 that they were "done in Italy," it seems much more plausible that they were executed before the artist went there, very

## 10

York, 1966.8); *Catalogue Raisonné des Tableaux . . . &c. après le décès de M. de Jullienne* (Remy), 30 Mar. ff. 1767, lot 270 [bought for 1190 livres by the président d'Albertas]; *Catalogue de Tableaux . . . &c. du Cabinet de M<sup>r</sup> [Barré & autres]*, rue des Bons-Enfans (Regnault), 17 prairial, l'an XIII (6 June 1805), lot 8; *Catalogue d'une Collection de Tableaux des Ecoles Italiennes, Flamandes, Hollandaises et Françaises [du comte Français]*, Hôtel de Bullion (Constantin & Chariot), 16 Jan. ff. 1815, lot 12, "faits en Italie" [sold for 75 livres; the *Entry* erroneously identified as the *Exit from the Ark*, and the support as canvas]; misc. sale, Palais des Congrès, Versailles, 24 Oct. 1982; Galerie Pardo, Paris, from which acquired by the present owner in 1983.

REPLICA OR COPY
*Noah Entering the Ark*, sold anonymously, Versailles, 18 Nov. 1962, lot 32; private coll., Paris: canvas, 50 × 60 cm [i.e., extended in height, but not in length, with no compensating adjustments, in such a way as to suggest a copy, rather than a finished version or replica from Boucher's own hand, despite the apparently good quality of the picture as reproduced in A & W fig. 216].

ANALOGIES
1. *The Animals Entering the Ark*, by J-B. Deshays, Mariette sale, 15 Nov. ff. 1775, lot 1221: "grande composition en travers, & peinte sur papier dans le style de Benedette" [sold with Castiglione drawings in lot 357 to Lempereur for 24 livres]; Debuscher sale, 28 [advanced to 18] June 1804, lot 52, "Esquisse

possibly as a present for their original owner, whose steady employment of Boucher to engrave Watteau's works over the previous four or five years had enabled him to accumulate the funds with which to make the journey.

At first blush, this early dating must seem implausible, since the obvious indebtedness of the two pictures to Castiglione's *Marches* suggests exposure to Italy, while the character of such details as the animals and the gleaming copper basins cannot but evoke similar elements in the Dutch-influenced pictures painted after Boucher's return. The handling of these two paintings is, however, quite different from those executed after his return from Italy and associates them backward with such works as the *Mutius Scaevola* (cat. 8) rather than forward with such apparently related pictures as the lost *Départ de Jacob* (engraved by Elisabeth Cousinet Lempereur; J-R 1375) or the *View of Tivoli* (cat. 16). This is evident above all in the brushstrokes, which are small and liquid, and in the color, which is rich and saturated. The folds of drapery still retain some of the mannerism of those in the *Mutius Scaevola*, and the faces of the figures are likewise variations on shorthand formulas, particularly those of the women, with their tilted noses and coiffed hair with escaping strands, and the half-naked children, with their sideswept licks of hair. The perspective diagonals in the *Noah Entering the Ark* have the vertiginous exaggeration characteristic of a group of Boucher's early pastoral landscapes, and the trees and foliage are imbued with the sinuous, bushy vitality also found in those youthful works (see cat. 9), which he seems to have caught from Lemoine.

The most obvious affinities of other details of the present pictures are also with those pastoral scenes: the same drawings (fig. 88; Nationalmuseum, Stockholm; Bjürstrom, 1982, nos. 823, 824) appear to have been adapted for the hen and cock in the *Noah Entering the Ark* as were used directly in *La fontaine*; the hen recurs in a picture painted after Boucher's return from Italy, *Le repos des fermiers* (cat. 20), and the types of the

II

au pinceau et coloriée à l'huile, sur papier . . . d'après *Benedette Castiglione*."

2. *Noah Entering the Ark*, by J-J. Lagrenée, canvas, 18 × 22 in., described as "d'un ton de couleur analogue au sujet" [i.e., Castiglionesque] when in the Dulac and Lachaise sale, 30 Nov. ff. 1778, lot 280; and as "dans le goût de Boucher," when up again in an anonymous sale, 11 Jan. ff. 1779, lot 89.

Fig. 88. *Study of a Strutting Cock*. Nationalmuseum, Stockholm.

Fig. 89. *The Martyrdom of the Japanese Jesuits*, after Boucher, published by Laurent Cars.

Fig. 90. *Jacob Obtaining Isaac's Blessing*, pirated engraving by P. A. Kilian, after Jean Daullé's engraving after Boucher.

women and children are the same as those in *La vie champêtre* (cat. 9). Prophetically for Boucher, men play a somewhat restricted role in the present pictures, with the exception of the patriarch, Noah, himself. He again, rather than looking forward to the vigorous figures of Jacob (cat. 5) or Gideon (cat. 6), has the miniaturized features of the old man remonstrating with one of the victims in *The Martyrdom of the Japanese Jesuits* (fig. 89; engraved by Laurent Cars as a thesis plate; last recorded in Germany before World War II; A & W 119). This last is one of a small group of early religious scenes, the other two being *Jacob Obtaining Isaac's Blessing* (fig. 90; engraved by Daullé, pirated by P. A. Kilian; whereabouts never recorded), and *The Separation of Laban from Jacob*, whose affinity with the present pictures is much more evident in the drawing in the Louvre (exh. cat. 1984, Paris, Cabinet des Dessins, no. 78) than in the thesis-plate engraving after the lost painting of this composition, which was apparently in Bergeret's posthumous sale, whose changes from the drawing amount to the implication of an altogether different subject (*The Separation of Jacob and Esau?*).

Significantly, *The Separation of Laban from Jacob* was engraved by Etienne Brion, who also engraved Boucher's early *St. Bartholomew* (cat. 1) and other *Saints*, but nothing further of his, and published by Hecquet, who issued another thesis plate done after a painting of Boucher's youth (*The Return of Jephthah*, examples on theses maintained 15 July 1767 and 30 Jan. 1789 in the second volume of thesis plates in the Cabinet des Estampes) and Daullé's engraving of *Jacob Obtaining Isaac's Blessing*. Boucher told Mariette that the father of Laurent Cars, whose name is on the known prints of *The Martyrdom of the Japanese Jesuits*, employed him to make designs for thesis plates for his bed and board and 60 livres a month after he had left the studio of Lemoine: all additional indications of the early date of this group of religious paintings.

The present pair of paintings is probably the first in which Boucher adopts the Castiglionesque theme of the *Marche*, but at this point his indebtedness to the Genoese master was purely thematic. Not only are the flocks and herds kept subordinate to the central protagonists of the compositions, which was not the case with his models, but there is also no impact of Castiglione upon his palette or brushwork. Nor did Boucher need to go to Italy to see works by this master: Castigliones (or pseudo-Castigliones) appeared frequently in Paris sales from the moment that we have some record of their contents, from the 1730s onward (see D. Wildenstein, 1982, pp. 20–21; the Viallis sale of 28 Dec. ff. 1781 [not cited there] included no fewer than eleven); the royal collections had at least three by 1753, all now in the Louvre; and Dezallier d'Argenville records half a dozen in the ampler 1757 edition of his *Voyage Pittoresque*. It is, indeed, precisely the fact that in these pictures Boucher has imitated the content but not the facture of Castiglione's paintings that leads one to suppose that he painted them in France—inspired perhaps as much by engravings as by the sight of original paintings—and not in Italy, where he was to respond to the full resonance of Castiglione's brushwork, no doubt because he could see it emulated in the work of contemporary masters, such as Sebastiano Ricci.

When these two pictures were sold in 1805, they were described as "esquisses." There is, however, no record of any finished paintings of these

Fig. 91. Illustration of the end wall of de Jullienne's second cabinet, showing the two paintings of *Noah* hanging bottom left and right, and a pastel *Head of a Woman* by Boucher, center left (from the partially illustrated manuscript catalogue in the Pierpont Morgan Library, New York).

subjects; both the support and the elongated proportions of the sketches speak against any ever having being intended. De Jullienne was not one of those who made a point of collecting sketches, and neither the enchantingly illustrated manuscript catalogue of his collection in the Pierpont Morgan Library (see fig. 91) nor the printed catalogue of his posthumous sale says that they were sketches. The use of the term in 1805 simply reflects the Davidian expectations of finish that then prevailed. What is unexpected is that, despite the great appeal of these pictures, and the close association that Boucher must have had with de Jullienne over the engraving of Watteau, there was only one other painting by Boucher in de Jullienne's posthumous sale (we cannot, of course, know what paintings by Boucher de Jullienne may have owned and traded in earlier, as was the case with his Watteaus; he may have given *Les oies de Frère Philippe* [cat. 7] to his son-in-law, de Montullé). That picture was a grisaille of *Cassandra before the Statue of Minerva* (lot 271; subsequent fate unknown). Evidently, de Jullienne was one of those who preferred a still traditional and Italianate Boucher to Boucher the founder of a new *école française*.

# 12 | *The Encounter on the Road*

Oil on canvas
16⅛ × 12½ in. (41 × 32 cm)
Museum of Fine Arts, Springfield,
Massachusetts; The James Philip Gray
Collection (55.01)
(S & M 1424, 1756)        A & W 53

PROVENANCE
*Catalogue de Tableaux . . . &c. formant le Cabinet de feu SON EXCELLENCE M. LE BAILLI DE BRETEUIL*, Faubourg Saint-Honoré [no. 83] (Le Brun), 16 Jan. ff. 1786, lot 46: "Une Marche d'Animaux. . . . Ce tableau, qui est de la belle maniere de ce maître, doit être recherché des amateurs" [bought for 371 livres by "Cailar" or "Quesnet"]; *Catalogue d'une précieuse Collection de Tableaux, choisis dans toutes les Ecoles Anciennes et Modernes par Mr DIDOT*, Hôtel Bullion, 6 Apr. ff. 1825, lot 96: "La Rencontre sur la Route . . ." [sold for 71 livres]; sale of Dr. Ricord, Hôtel Drouot, Paris, 29 Mar. 1890, lot 5 (attributed to Boucher): "Bergers en Voyage. . . . Ce tableau rappelle les oeuvres de Boucher en Italie imitant Benedetto Castiglione" [sold for 105 francs]; baron Philippe de Rothschild, Paris (exh. cat. 1951, Geneva, no. 4; Voss, 1953, p. 85); Frank T. Sabin, London; David M. Koetser, London and New York; acquired by the Springfield Museum in 1955.

This is one of the most spontaneous pictures in Boucher's oeuvre but nonetheless not immediately easy to situate. There are elements in it, such as the writhing tree, the compressed perspective, the facial types, and the character of the animals, that seem to link it with pictures that Boucher painted before he went to Italy, whereas the hatched brushwork declares it to date from a later epoch, associating it with other pastoral scenes and landscapes painted in the years immediately after his return.

Although the coloring of the present picture appears to be much warmer, the closest parallel to it can probably be found in the *Washerwomen at the Fountain*, on loan since 1967 from the Académie des Sciences, Belles-Lettres et Arts de Clermont-Ferrand to the Musée Bargoin (fig. 92; A & W 56; see Hallopeau, [1980], p. 18, fig. 8), in which there is a tree of similarly tormented form, and women with small, chignoned heads of the same character. Nonetheless, the recession of planes in the *Washerwomen at the Fountain* is more regular, as in all the other landscapes painted after Boucher's return from Italy. The face of the young man is not of a type immediately recognizable as Boucher's (and, indeed, it should be remembered that another version of this picture has

## 12

Fig. 92. *Washerwomen at the Fountain*. Académie des Sciences, Belles-Lettres et Arts de Clermont-Ferrand, on loan to the Musée Bargoin, Clermont-Ferrand.

Fig. 93. Hubert Robert, *The Ruins* (1777). The Metropolitan Museum of Art, New York; Gift of Mrs. William M. Haupt, from the collection of Mrs. James B. Haggin, 1965.

been published as a Fragonard), but then it is, unusually for him, seen en face—and Boucher anyway notoriously had difficulty with men's faces. Curiously, the young man's features have most affinity with those of the young mother in the picture of a *Mother and Children beside a Fountain* (A & W 564; formerly collections of Edmond and Maurice de Rothschild, Paris; sold Sotheby's Monaco, 26 June 1983, lot 487; currently on the Japanese art market), whose apparent date of 1762 is most probably a corruption of 1732.

The catalogue of the Didot sale of 1825 captioned the lot containing the present picture with: "BOUCHER (FRANÇOIS), en Italie," and went on, after describing the picture, to say: "If Boucher had remained in Italy, the bad taste prevalent in France would not have subjugated him on his return home, and he would have left a distinguished reputation as a painter. Nevertheless, in exercising a choice among his works, one could easily encounter several worthy of featuring among the ranks of good painters of the French School. . . ." ("*Si Boucher fût resté en Italie, le mauvais goût qui régnait en France ne l'aurait pas subjugué à son retour dans sa patrie, et il aurait laissé la réputation d'un peintre distingué. Cependant, en faisant un choix dans ses ouvrages, il serait facile d'en rencontrer plusieurs dignes de figurer dans la collection des bons peintres de l'Ecole française. . . .*") This, however, is more interesting as a document in the history of French taste and as an illustration of the way in which attempts to rescue the reputation of Boucher from his critics were made than reliable as evidence proving its date. For even in Boucher's lifetime, sales catalogues made it clear that the value of a picture of his could be increased by claiming that it dated from his years in Italy; and in this case, the claim was not even made in the eighteenth-century sale in which the present painting was sold, but only in the nineteenth century, when there were no longer any connoisseurs of his work to challenge the assertion. Nonetheless, the Didot in whose sale this picture featured, later known as Didot de Saint-Marc, was apparently an experienced *marchand-amateur,* so that the claim, if not adducible as evidence, does provide some support for supposing that this picture was painted, if not in Italy, immediately after Boucher's return. It may be that the first record of the picture, in the posthumous sale of Jacques-Laure Le Tonnelier de Breteuil, known as the bailli de Breteuil (1723–1785), lends support to the idea that the picture was painted—and remained—in Rome, since this collector was ambassador from the Sovereign Order of the Knights of St. John (Malta) to the Holy See (1758–77). It is certainly supported by Hubert Robert's use of the group in a drawing done in Rome (see below, Analogies).

PREPARATORY DRAWING
Red chalk, 258 × 190 mm, R[ouillard] sale, 1–3 Mar. 1869, lot 35; coll. of M. X., Paris; engraved by Claude Briceau (active from 1767) as *Les Voyageurs* (J-R 394); a black chalk variant, 253 × 184 mm, belonging to a private coll. in Virginia, sold Sotheby Parke Bernet, New York, 3 June 1980, lot 60.

VARIANT VERSION
17½ × 14¼ in. (44.5 × 36 cm): Earl of Pembroke sale, Paris, 30 June 1862, lot 33 (as Fragonard) [bought by Michaud]; Michaud posthumous sale, Paris, 11–13 Oct. 1877, lot 61 (as Fragonard); Edouard Michel coll.; Wildenstein, New York (exhibited as Fragonard, 1926, New York, no. 18, and 1929, Hartford, no. 11); private coll., Buenos Aires (exhibited as Fragonard, 1945, Buenos Aires, no. 5); Christie's, London, 7 July 1978, lot 157 as Boucher [see G. Wildenstein, 1960, no. 113; D. Wildenstein & G. Mandel, 1972, no. 123].

ANALOGIES
The group was employed by Hubert Robert in a group of ruin pieces: a drawing done in Rome in 1760, Bourgarel sale, Paris, 15–16 June 1922, lot 199; a circular painting, dated 1777, in the Metropolitan Museum, New York (fig. 93; Baetjer, 1980, I, p. 156, and III, p. 521); a painting, based on the drawing in the Bourgarel sale, in a sale at the Palais Galliera, Paris, 26 Nov. 1975, lot 9.

# 13 | Hercules and Omphale

Oil on canvas
35½ × 29 in. (90 × 74 cm)
Pushkin Museum, Moscow (inv. 2764)
S & M 167        A & W 107
*Paris*

PROVENANCE
*Catalogue des Tableaux & Dessins précieux des Maîtres célebres des trois Ecoles . . . &c., du Cabinet de feu M. RANDON DE BOISSET Receveur Général des Finances*, rue Neuve des Capucines, près la place Vendôme (Remy), 27 Feb. ff. 1777, lot 192: "Ce tableau est dans le style de François le Moine, le coloris & la touche sont admirables" [bought by (Philippe-Guillaume) Boullogne de Préninville for 3,840 livres, but alienated before his death in 1791]; collection of M. de Vaudreuil, rue de la Chaise, no. 7 (Thiéry, 1787, p. 54) [*hôtel* sold in 1787]; *Catalogue d'une très-belle Collection de Tableaux d'Italie, de Flandre, de Hollande et de France . . . &c., provenans du Cabinet de M\*\*\** [de Vaudreuil], grande Salle, rue de Cléry (Le Brun), 26 Nov. ff. 1787: "Ce Tableau, de la plus belle couleur possible, a toujours été regardé comme l'un des plus beaux de ce Maître" [bought by Donjeu(x) for 900 livres]; *Catalogue d'une belle Collection de Tableaux*, Hôtel de Bullion (Paillet), 7 [deferred to 13] Feb. 1792, lot 37: "Un tableau de ton de couleur le plus riche & de la touche la plus savante & la plus gracieuse"; Prince Galitzin, Moscow; Prince Youssoupov, Saint Petersburg (1839 cat., no. 86); preempted from the Youssoupov coll. for the Hermitage in 1925; transferred to the Pushkin Museum in 1930.

COPY BY FRAGONARD
Varanchan sale, 29 Dec. 1777, lot 32 [in the handwritten breakdown of this lot in the copy of the catalogue in the Bibliothèque Nationale are a number of Fragonards, including a "copie d'après boucher, hercule et omphale," which was bought by Boinet(?) for 123 louis 1 sol. The *Avis* to the catalogue states that the (small) collection is chiefly remarkable for "the finest sketches and drawings by one of our first Painters (Boucher), still regretted, and sought after ever more now that he is no longer with us; there will also be pleasure in finding several of the spontaneous compositions of one of his Pupils (Fragonard), who has attained celebrity with a manner of his own" ("*les plus belles esquisses & les plus beaux Dessins d'un de nos premiers Peintres toujours regretté, & recherché davantage depuis qu'il n'est plus: on verra avec plaisir beaucoup des pensées d'un de ses Eleves, devenu célèbre sans lui ressembler*"); de Sireul sale, 3 Dec. ff. 1781, lot 37: "Ce tableau est la copie exacte de celui

Despite his reputation as an erotic artist (for one of the most extreme—and ill-informed—denunciations of which, see Fiorillo, III, 1805, pp. 364–71), Boucher rarely depicted subjects of overt sensuality. It was, indeed, one of the grounds for both Diderot's and Grimm's complaints against his pastorals, that they were not frank enough (Diderot, 1979, p. 81; cf. cat. 78), while his mythological paintings remained well within the conventions of the genre. It was only in the nineteenth century that the improbable story arose of his having painted a set of erotic pictures for Mme de Pompadour with which to stimulate the jaded appetite of Louis XV (Charles Blanc, 1851, p. 10, ascribes the tale to Thoré, but I have not succeeded in finding it among the latter's writings). Rather the reverse, it was in fact she who at one point put herself on a bizarre diet of *ambré* vanilla chocolate, truffles, and celery soup to combat the frigidity that the king found in her (Hausset, 1824, p. 92). Nor does the set of pictures that may have inspired the story (one pair in the Louvre, M.N.R. 117, 118; another pair, location unknown, photographs in the files of H. Roger-Viollet, L.M. 15.684, 15.685 bis; a bowdlerized version of the former, reputedly painted for Louis XV, in Sedelmeyer Gallery, 1898, no. 268) suggest anything closer to Boucher than the hand of a later *pasticheur*.

The *Hercules and Omphale* was probably best characterized when it became known to a wider public through the inclusion of a sepia plate and an analysis of it by Alexandre Benois in the commemorative volume of the great exhibition of European paintings in Russian collections mounted by the magazine *Staryé Gody* in 1909 (see Benois, 1910, p. 115). Benois contrasts the picture with a pair of *Pastorales* painted in the year of Boucher's death (curiously rejuvenated to works of 1760 by the time that they were exhibited in 1932) and goes on to say, "One has difficulty, on the other hand, in believing that it is Boucher who painted the heroic, impetuous scene of Hercules with Omphale, in which everything—from the dash of the lines to the ardent flesh tones—is more evocative of the tendency to excess inherent in the Flemish artistic temperament. This picture is instinct with youth throughout, and it is much closer to Lemoine and even to the brutal frankness of Rubens than to the works of Boucher's own maturity." ("*Par contre on a peine à croire que c'est Boucher qui ait peint l'héroïque et impétueux épisode d'Hercule chez Omphale, où tout—en commençant par la fougue des lignes et finissant par les couleurs ardentes des chairs,—rappelle plutôt le tempérament porté aux excès des Flamands. Ce tableau est tout pénétré de jeunesse, et il s'approche beaucoup plus de Lemoine et même de la sincérité brutale de Rubens que des oeuvres de la maturité de Boucher lui-même.*")

The mention of Lemoine chimes with that in the catalogue of the sale from which we first learn of the picture's existence, that of Boucher's later

13

de M. Boucher, décrit dans le Catalogue de M. de Boisset, sous le No. 192" [bought by Payenne(?) for 23 louis 19 sous. It is worth noting that de Sireul's sale also included an oval pen and wash drawing of *Hercules and Omphale* (lot 92), which was bought by M. Lallié, in whose collection it was engraved (J-R 1645). The engraving, which may have taken some liberties with details and format, reveals the drawing to have been a smaller version of that in the d'Orsay coll. (see p. 123), which is evidently also a work of Boucher's youth].

Fig. 94. *Hercules and Omphale.* Cabinet des Dessins, Louvre.

friend and patron, Randon de Boisset, in 1777: "This picture is in the style of François le Moine, its color and brushwork are admirable." Comparison with Lemoine suggests that this picture should have been painted shortly after Boucher emerged from his pupilage and before he went to Rome. In fact, in the case of other pictures, we find the comparison being much more loosely applied, sometimes even to works painted after Boucher's return from Rome, partly because it was not (and still is not) appreciated to what extent Lemoine's own later manner reflects the influence of his returned former pupils, Boucher and Natoire.

Nothing could in fact be less Lemoinean than the present picture, as a glance at his *Hercules and Omphale* of 1724 in the Louvre is sufficient to demonstrate (Bordeaux, 1985, no. P.47, pp. 93–95, and fig. 43). In contrast to Lemoine's aim of combining, as Bordeaux puts it, "Venetian coloring and decorative brilliance . . . and Parmesan sensuality with the solid form of the Roman school" in a light-bathed picture set in the open air, Boucher presents an indoor picture of hothouse intensity, in which contours are dissolved by the flickering, lambent manipulation of the brush (rather as the extraordinary lion skin held by the cupid on the right is decomposed into a formless monster), and in which color is used to intensify the conveyance of passion rather than to reflect the fall of light. The two pictures even differ widely in their message. Whereas Lemoine underscores the traditional import of this episode in Hercules's career, that he was for a time completely unmanned by his physical and amorous enslavement to Queen Omphale, Boucher places the distaff and spindle in the hands of one of the cupids rather than in those of Hercules himself, leaving the hero (Benois's choice of adjective exhibits a nice sense of irony) free to indulge his ardor to the full. Since Boucher's intentions are not pornographic, however, he uses the convention of the "slung-over leg" to stand in for the actual consummation of their passion.

None of this forecloses the possibility that the picture was in fact painted before Boucher went to Rome—nothing, that is, except the very conspicuousness of the brushwork. Though of a mythological subject, both in this and in its "fougue," or energy, it is worlds away from the various early depictions of Venus and Adonis, and Selene and Endymion (see figs. 78, 77). On the other hand—and despite its not implausible juxtaposition by Ananoff and Wildenstein with the *Rinaldo and Armida* of 1734 (cat. 26), with which it shares such features as the banded column and drapery, and the use to which cupids are put—in scale, handling, and the character of the protagonists, it is also remote from the mythological pictures painted even shortly after Boucher's return from Italy (e.g., cat. 17, 18).

These seemingly conflicting arguments point to the conclusion that the *Hercules and Omphale* was painted in Rome. This is hard to substantiate, since we have no certain knowledge of any picture having been painted in Italy (but see cat. 12). There is, however, one small piece of possible supporting evidence. Among the drawings in the Cabinet des Dessins of the Louvre that bear the stamp identified by Jean-François Méjanès as that of Pierre-Marie-Gaspard Grimod, comte d'Orsay (1748–1809), which were mostly acquired by him from the *fonds d'ateliers* of French artists deceased in Rome, is one that Hercenberg (1975, cat. no. 417, p. 178 and fig. 27) entitled *Les amours de Mars et de Vénus* and calls (without indicating the existence of any original) "after N. Vleughels," but which Méjanès (exh. cat. 1983, Paris, p. 181, Ors. 827) correctly identifies as *Lucrèce et Tarquin*, and tentatively proposes as "a study done by the young F. Boucher in Rome between 1728 and 1730." The attribution is plausible, but hard to substantiate, since the drawing is a black-chalk counterproof gone over in black chalk—and it is very possible that the original was by another hand (perhaps indeed that of Vleughels), making the end result difficult to read as that of a particular artistic personality. The similarities in the character of the scene and of its setting with those of the *Hercules and Omphale* are telling. Most striking of all, however, is the affinity between the head of Tarquin and that of Hercules. The face is a bizarre (and somewhat unappealing) one, whose use in both drawing and painting surely points to an identity of hand. It also indicates Boucher's difficulty in inventing convincing male physiognomies even at this early date. (It is worth noting here that the d'Orsay collection also contains an oval pen and wash drawing of *Hercules and Omphale* by Boucher, which, although in no way related compositionally, is similar in spirit and in date [fig. 94; see under Copy by Fragonard].)

Ultimately, however, it is the verve and intensity manifest throughout the *Hercules and Omphale* that tell over any deficiencies in detail. Benois thought that in enjoying this picture we should regret "that Boucher 'found himself' later, and that he did not remain for the rest of his life the vigorous, full-blooded sensualist that we have here" (*"que Boucher se soit 'retrouvé' plus tard, qu'il ne soit pas resté pendant toute sa vie ce sensuel fort et vigoureux"*). That would be to wish too much undone. Yet might not even Boucher have had his regrets by the 1760s, and even have feared invidious comparisons being drawn between his output then and such brilliant essays of his youth? Such at any rate is the implication behind Diderot's (more maliciously concluded) assessment of Boucher's works immediately after his return from Italy, which could have been applied to the *Hercules and Omphale* equally well: "His color was forthright and true; his composition was sound, yet full of verve; his handling was broad and grand. I know some of his earliest pieces, that he nowadays calls *croûtes*, which he would love to buy back so as to burn them." (*"Il avait une couleur forte et vraie; sa composition était sage, quoique pleine de chaleur; son faire large et grand. Je connais quelques-uns de ses premiers morceaux qu'il appelle aujourd'hui des croûtes et qu'il rachèterait volontiers pour les brûler"* [Diderot, 1975, p. 205].)

## 14 | *Moses before the Burning Bush*

Oil on canvas
46½ × 38¼ in. (118 × 97 cm)
Private collection, France

PROVENANCE
?François Derbais, rue Poissonnière, *salle à manger* (*inventaire après décès* 2 Mar. ff. 1743, no. 4) [I owe the communication of this important document to the kindness of its discoverer, Georges Brunel]; Bragge's Sale of

The coarse vigor of this large painting will come as a shock to many after the delicate little pictures of Boucher's early years, even to those who have been somewhat prepared for it by the new scale and boldness (and the fiery glow of the sacrificial flame) of the *Sacrifice of Gideon* (cat. 6). For

Pictures, London, 1743/44, 3rd day, lot 33: "Moses and the burning bush. Bouchée. £4.17s. 6d. (Houlditch mss. extracts of sales, 1711–59, Victoria and Albert Museum Library, London); posthumous sale of baron Emmanuel Léonino, Galerie Jean Charpentier, Paris, 18–19 Mar. 1937, lot 23, as "Ecole italienne"; private coll., France, whence sold at the Palais Galliera, 24 June 1968, lot 17; private coll., France, and acquired by the present owner.

Fig. 95. *Nymph and Satyr (Jupiter and Antiope?)*. Château de la Louvière, Montluçon.

*Moses before the Burning Bush* represents the furthest extreme to which Boucher ever went in his adoption of a rough facture and the inclusion of patches of violent color (already reduced to his preferred basic palette of red, blue, and yellow), for both of which he drew his inspiration from the paintings of Benedetto Castiglione.

Some might even go so far as to question Boucher's authorship of the picture, but of that there can be no doubt. The rough facture, with its hatched effects; the arbitrary yet wholly convincing folds of the drapery, which are the product of sheer dexterity with the brush rather than the result of laborious imitation; the gnarled and curving forms of the tree, and the seemingly invented form of leaves of the foreground plant: all these have parallels in Boucher's first pictures after his return from Rome—above all in the putti pictures, of which it has regrettably only been possible to show one in this exhibition (cat. 15), but also in *La marchande d'oeufs* (A & W 90), now in the Wadsworth Atheneum, Hartford. There are still echoes of all these things in the *Venus and Vulcan* of 1732 (cat. 17) and its pendant, *Aurora and Cephalus* of 1733 (cat. 18), but in these the brushwork is already less furious, and the *peintre des Grâces* is starting to emerge from these unlikely beginnings.

In detailing these correspondences, it must seem as if the character of the picture's sole protagonist, the young Moses, has been deliberately avoided. Not so; it is merely that the closest parallels for his vibrant form, with its sinewy limbs and knobbly extremities, are to be found in a previously unpublished picture whose state regrettably prevents its being shown here. This is *Le repos de Diane*, which should perhaps more properly be called *Jupiter and Antiope,* but was engraved by Pelletier under the former title (J-R 1454). The engraving was doubtless made after the picture's purchase by the painter-dealer Godefroy at the de Vassal de Saint-Hubert sale of 17 January ff. 1774, when it was sold, without any title, as lot 101, and said to be: "executed with verve and facility, much in the manner of Lemoine" (*"fait facilement & avec esprit, tient beaucoup de la maniere de* le Moine")—words that themselves suggest an early work.

Such is indeed the case, as can be seen from the wreck of this picture among the Troubat le Houx bequest in the Château de la Louvière at Montluçon, where it is awaiting eventual exhibition (fig. 95). Remarkably for this bizarre collection of hopefuls, it is under its proper name; the optimistic attributions of its companions no doubt account for the fact that this one does not seem to have found credit. It is visibly, however, the same picture as that engraved by Pelletier (who modestly reversed the position of the phallic-looking quiver), albeit badly damaged (by fire?), partially repainted, and truncated of its upper half. The bodies of both the nymph (who appears to have been studied from the same model as the exquisite red-chalk drawing of the *Diane endormie* in the Ecole des Beaux-Arts, Paris, exh. cat. 1981–82, no. 88) and the satyr have the same sinewy forms and knobbly extremities as the young Moses. More tellingly still, they, the quiver, and the drapery are all painted, like the present picture, with vigorous parallel strokes—"cette manière de peindre par hachures," as Chaussard described it (*Pausanias français*, 1806, p. 51), albeit miscrediting Carle Vanloo rather than the young Boucher with the technique, which was one of the things that the latter had acquired by studying Castiglione.

It is at first sight surprising that there appears to be no reference to the present striking picture, and that—unlike most of Boucher's ambitious attempts at Italian old-master-like renderings of Old Testament subjects—it was not engraved. There are good reasons for this, however. First of all, it in fact represents a considerable advance over the latter. Boucher is here experimenting with new effects of painterliness, and on a larger scale than anything hitherto save the *Sacrifice of Gideon.* All of these effects would have been lost in engraving; Boucher's ambitions evidently lay in a different direction. We should remember Mariette's statement about: "a number of large pictures that he had painted for a marble mason called Dorbay, who had furnished his whole house with them, which was perfectly easy for him to do, since Boucher, not seeking to do anything but make a name for himself at that period, would, I believe, have done them for nothing rather than pass up the opportunity" ("*nombre de grands tableaux qu'il avoit fait pour un sculpteur marbrier nommé Dorbay qui en avoit garni toute sa maison, ce qui lui avoit été très-facile, car Boucher, ne cherchant alors [dans sa jeunesse] qu'à se faire connoître, les auroit, je crois, faits pour rien, plus tost que d'en laisser manquer l'occasion*" [Mariette, I, 1851–53, p. 165]).

Most of the "Dorbay" pictures that it has been possible to identify with any confidence, thanks to Georges Brunel's discovery of the *inventaire après décès* of the actual commissioner of them, the marble sculptor Jerôme Derbais's lawyer son, François (and in spite of the fact that this gives no artists' names), are mythological and were either on the staircase (cf. cat. 15, Analogy 1) or in the *salle de billard* (cat. 17, 18). Mariette, who may of course have been exaggerating, implies the presence of rather more than these; if his explanation of Boucher's motives was correct, one would certainly expect pictures of Old Testament subjects to have been among them, not least because the *Sacrifice of Gideon* suggests that immediately after Italy Boucher's ambition ran along such conventional lines.

Sure enough, the inventory contains a *Buisson ardent*, in the *salle à manger.* The valuation put upon it is admittedly low—ten livres—but that may do no more than reflect the discredit into which this kind of painting had fallen in a city avid for subjects and palettes more compatible with light Rococo interiors; Derbais had, on the other hand, placed the picture in an important room, along with such things as a large portrait of Louis XIII (itself only valued at twenty livres) and a pair of much more highly valued mythologies. The subject was not a common one in France, despite the distinguished precedents set by Poussin and Le Brun.

Perhaps most telling, however, is the one probable record of this picture in the eighteenth century, in a sale held in London between 1 January and 25 March 1744 (N. S.). This is only a year after the posthumous inventory taken of François Derbais's effects. It is unlikely that his sole heir, his niece Marguérite-Julie Langlois, née Derbais, should have wanted to retain her uncle's very miscellaneous-sounding collection of pictures; and if she was selling them, there was no better outlet for such an old-master-like subject than England, whose "prétendus connoisseurs" would pay absurd sums for what they regarded as old masters, while rejecting anything that looked as if it belonged to the modern French school (see Boyer d'Argens, 1752, p. 20)—something that would not have been thought of this picture in the 1740s, by which time Boucher himself had taken his style in a quite different direction.

*Putti Playing with Birds (Summer)*

Oil on canvas
28 × 28½ in. (71 × 72.5 cm)
Signed bottom center: *f. Boucher*
Museum of Art, Rhode Island
School of Design, Providence;
Anonymous Gift (64.15)
S & M 1455          A & W 61

PROVENANCE
*Catalogue Raisonné de Tableaux . . . &c. après le décès de M. Fortier . . . Doyen des Notaires du Châtelet de Paris,* rue neuve des Petits-Champs, première porte cochère à gauche après la rue de Richelieu (Remy), 2 Apr. ff. 1770, lot 42: "L'Eté, représenté par quatre enfans, dont deux assis sur des épis; ils s'amusent avec des oiseaux . . . [and *L'Automne*]. . . . Ces deux Tableaux, très ragoûtans, sont peints sur toile, chacun porte 26 pouces en quarré"; coll. of M. D ***, 4–5 Feb. 1833, lot 61 (with its pendant); Alfred de Rothschild, 1 Seamore Place, London (acquired subsequent to the privately printed catalogue of his collection, compiled by Charles Davis, 1884); the sale of his legatee, Almina, Countess of Carnarvon, Christie's, London, 22 May 1925, lot 60 (separate from its pendant, lot 61) [bought by Pawsey & Payne for 600 guineas]; Cailleux, Paris (Voss, 1953, p. 89 and fig. 60); Christie's, London, 25 July 1958, lot 61 [bought by Davidge for 1250 guineas]; private coll., New York, from which donated anonymously to the museum in 1964.

ANALOGIES
1. *L'Amour oiseleur,* Derbais coll., Paris (by June 1734, when B. Lépicié presented his engravings after this picture and its pendant, *L'Amour moissonneur,* to the Academy among his *morceaux de réception*): Derbais's pictures never having reappeared as a set (although a pair of *L'Amour oiseleur* and *L'Amour moissonneur* appeared in Ph. Sichel's posthumous sale, 22–28 June 1899, lots 3 and 4, 85 × 113 cm, described as overdoors), it is hard to be certain that any of the surviving versions of individual compositions come from the set, not least because all appear to differ in minor particulars from the engravings, though the engravers may have been at fault; the best version of *L'Amour oiseleur* would appear to be that which resurfaced in the sale of M. H *** in Paris, 7 May 1898, sole lot, with a highly dubious provenance from a supposed sale of effects from the queen's apartments at Fontainebleau in 1794, and which was last seen at Sotheby's, London, 1 Nov. 1978, lot 33.
2. [F. W. Kreuzschauf], *Historische Erklaerungen der Gemaelde welche Herr Gottfried Winkler in Leipzig gesammlet,* Leipzig, 1768, no. 602: "Vier reizende Liebesgötter wälzen sich, am niedern Gebüsche im frischen Grase,

At the same time as, or not long after, extending his range into large mythological compositions, Boucher began to develop another speciality. This was one that would become—after his depictions of nymphs and shepherdesses—most indelibly associated with his name: scenes of little children or cupids at play. For reasons that have never been adequately expounded, depictions of putti have been common since the Renaissance, particularly for decorative and allegorical purposes. Among paintings, Titian's *Worship of Venus* (and Rubens's copy of this), Poussin's *Bacchanals,* and the *Triumph of Cupid* ascribed to Parmigianino are (or were in their day) simply the most celebrated. Significantly, most—if not all—of these were based upon literary or pictorial models from Antiquity. What was novel with Boucher was that he (not unlike his contemporary Jakob de Wit in Holland) made the depiction of putti into a genre in its own right, extending through his painted and graphic oeuvre.

Boucher may have acquired his taste for putti in Italy, since it was in the French Academy in Rome under Vleughels that students acquired practice in drawing them (Hercenberg, 1975, nos. 368–72, figs. 214–18), including very probably Boucher himself (a group of drawings of putti with the mark of the artist Baptistin Rousseau [Lugt, supp., 1956, 403] attributed to Boucher in the Musée de Nîmes, inv. 754, 756–58). After Boucher's return they began to play a conspicuous part in his paintings (see cat. 18, 1733) and in the designs that he supplied for engravers (the vignettes for the *Satyres de Regnier,* 1733; the *Tombeaux des Princes . . . ,* c. 1736).

One of the earliest autonomous compositions of putti from his hand would appear to be the *Putti Playing with a Goat,* since this still adheres most closely to the bacchanalian model established by Antique reliefs and Duquesnoy. This painting exists in two versions: a more complex oblong picture, in which the children are denoted as cupids by little wings, with six playing with the goat and grapes on the ground, and two carrying a basket of grapes in the air (Voss, 1953, p. 89, fig. 57; formerly Ch. E. Riche coll., sold Nouveau Drouot, 30 Mar. 1984, lot 57; Paris art market); and a simpler square version, in which the children have no wings, and there are only five of them on the ground and none in the air (fig. 96; Voss, 1953, fig. 58; formerly H. E. Ten Cate and Thyssen collections; currently on the Swiss art market). Both of these in turn relate—neither exactly, but the Riche picture more closely because it is of cupids and has a group in the air—to an ornamental engraving for the leaf of a screen, scraped by Duflos after Boucher around 1737, entitled the *Triomphe de Priape* (J-R 875).

The Ten Cate picture first came to light in the collection of Alfred de Rothschild, as the pendant of the present picture; the pair of them can in

auf ihren bunten Gewändern. Der zur Linken sitzende liebkoset dem in der Mitte hingestreckten, welcher sich zum andern Paare wendet, und lächelnd nach dem kleinen Vogel blicket, der, an den Faden gebunden, aus der Hand des zur Rechten hinter ihm scherzenden Gespielen flattert," 1 ft. 11½ in. × 2 ft. 3 in. [Saxon measures].

3. *Spielende Kinder*, Stroganoff sale, Lepke, Berlin, 12–13 May 1931, lot 64, signed, 69.5 × 137 cm (pendant to lot 65, *Die Musik*).

4. *L'Air*, one of a set of the *Elements* engraved by Cl. Duflos (J-R 909–916), most probably (with the four *Seasons*) his earliest engravings after Boucher, since he spells his name on them as *Bouché*. The *inv.* probably refers to the engravings having actually been made from drawings after shaped over-doors(?), the offsets of which may have been those from sanguines in Huquier's posthumous sale, 9 Nov. ff. 1772, lot 377. What may be the original painting, much truncated (to reduce it to a regular shape?), is in the W. A. Clark Collection of the Corcoran Gallery of Art, Washington.

5. Painting in a misc. sale, Paris (Monroy & Saubert), 25 Mar. ff. 1793, lot 128: "Un sujet de deux amours, dont un assis ayant les mains appuyées sur un cage. Ce tableau, peint par Boucher, est de son bon temps. Toile."

*15*

Fig. 96. *Putti Playing with a Goat (Autumn)* Art market, Switzerland.

turn be reasonably identified with lot 42 in the posthumous sale of Fortier, the *doyen des notaires du Châtelet*, in 1770. Not only do size and descriptions correspond, but the very word "ragoûtans" used to praise them implies pictures from Boucher's earlier and most painterly period.

Nothing that has been said so far enables us to date these pictures any more precisely than to the 1730s. A probable terminus ante quem is supplied by Cochin's engraving of the fifth of the five ornamental screen-leaf designs, the *Triomphe de Pomone*, which was completed in February 1737 (J-R 517, 518). However, it is possible to push the date of the present painting and its pendant back yet further, because of their evident affinity with a set of four putti pictures originally painted for Derbais (see cat. 17), none unfortunately in the present exhibition: *L'Amour moissonneur* (Voss, 1953, p. 89, figs. C, 56, 61; a cut-down version, formerly in the Contini-Bonacossi collection, Florence; and an intact version now on the Paris art market [fig. 97], exh. cat. 1985, Paris, no. 3); *L'Amour oiseleur* (fig. 98; Voss, 1953, figs. D, 59; see under Analogies); *L'Amour nageur* (Voss, 1953, fig. E; cut-down picture at Waddesdon Manor, England); and *L'Amour vendangeur* (A & W 65, figs. 305 [engraving by Fessard, J-R 962], 302: a painting cut down to an oval, in a private collection, Switzerland). The first two of these compositions were engraved by Lépicié (J-R 1378, 1377) in prints that he included among the *morceaux de réception* with which he presented the Academy in June 1734 and that were advertised in the *Mercure de France* in October 1734 and March 1735.

Fig. 97. *L'Amour moissonneur*. Art market, Paris.

Fig. 98. *L'Amour oiseleur*. Courtesy of Sotheby's, London.

Since I have not seen either version of the Derbais composition of *L'Amour oiseleur* (in both of which the vegetation looks sobered and tamed by comparison with the picture presented in Lépicié's engraving), it is hard for me to establish priority between that composition and the one here, from Rhode Island. The bold simplifications of rock and foliage in the present picture, however, by comparison with the more elaborate landscape setting of the Derbais composition (which has certain parallels with the background of the *Mercury Confiding the Infant Bacchus* in the Wallace Collection), suggest that it is the earlier of the two. So too does the transformation of the four putti in the present picture into the more tightly grouped set of cupids in the Derbais composition—a transformation comparable to that effected upon its pendant of *Autumn* in the Riche picture. Thus if Lépicié's engraving makes 1733/34 the latest possible dating for the Derbais picture, the present painting seems likely to date from 1732/33.

Once embarked on this new genre of putti depictions, Boucher was not only prolific in it, but he also made it clear that he did not regard it as an inferior sideline. For when in 1735 the Academy instituted a small exhibition of freshly completed works by its members to see which of them should be advanced in office, Boucher showed "four little pieces, depicting the four Seasons in the shape of little women and children, which were found very fine, as much for their striking color, modeling, and brushwork, as for their charming conception" *("quatre petits Morceaux, représentans les quatres Saisons, par de petites femmes et des enfans, qu'on trouva très-beaux, tant pour la vive couleur, le relief et le Pinceau, que pour l'aimable invention"* [*Mercure de France*, June [II] 1735, p. 1386]), which earned him an associate professorship. These are probably (given the presence of a "petite femme" at the center of *Le Printems*) the four lost paintings recorded in engravings by Aveline (J-R 208–215), the *Printems* from which was advertised in the *Mercure* in June 1737. These compositions have palpable affinities with a set of *The Four Seasons* etched by Natoire, aided by B. Audran and P. Aveline (see exh. cat. 1977, Troyes, p. 55). Natoire's etchings were published in 1735, after a set of pictures he had painted for the Château de La Chapelle-Godefroy, belonging to the *contrôleur général des Finances*, Philibert Orry, that must have been completed shortly before. If Natoire drew inspiration from Boucher for his *Venus Requesting Vulcan for Arms for Aeneas* (see cat. 17), it is by no means so clear where the priority lay in the present case, since Natoire seems always to have had an independent predilection for putti. Was he inspired by such pictures by Boucher as the present one and its pendant to paint his set of putti *Seasons* for La Chapelle-Godefroy, or was Boucher fired by those to paint the set that he exhibited at the Academy? In either case, it would appear that the two artists consciously measured themselves against one another on the same subjects. Natoire, by three years the elder, at first had the edge over Boucher in the commissions in which they both partook (La Chapelle-Godefroy and the Hôtel de Soubise), but it was Boucher who was thereafter to sweep the field. One of the ways in which he became the darling of collectors was by his prolific output of putti pictures in these years, of which those listed opposite (mostly from sets of the *Elements, Seasons,* and the like) are a mere fraction.

# 16 | Capriccio View of Tivoli

Oil on canvas
25½ × 21¼ in. (65 × 54 cm)
Musée des Beaux-Arts et
d'Archéologie, Boulogne-sur-Mer

PROVENANCE
Left to the museum in 1848 by Pierre Cary
(no. 317, attributed to Rosa di Tivoli).

ANALOGIES
1. Drawing in black chalk, 346 × 221 mm,
Cabinet des Dessins, Louvre (Guiffrey &
Marcel, II, 1908, p. 1408; here fig. 99).
2. Painting, 74 × 95 cm, acquired by Tessin
in Paris and shipped back to Sweden in 1741;
bought for Lovisa Ulrica in 1749; Drottningholm until 1953, when transferred to
the Nationalmuseum, Stockholm (fig. 101).
3. Painting, 60.5 × 73.5 cm, [de Vassal de
Saint-Hubert] sale, Paris (Remy), 17–21 Jan.
1774, lot 100: "Une vue intéressante de
rochers, fabriques & chûtes d'eau; plusieurs
figures, des cheveaux chargés de bagages, une
vache & des moutons se voient dans un chemin
presque sur le devant de ce tableau qui nous
paroît avoir été fait en Italie; il est sur toile de
22 pouces de hauteur sur 26 de largeur"
[bought by Norblin for 501 livres 1 sol];
?anon. sale, Paris (exp. Laneuville), 29 Feb.
1856, lot 7: "Paysage avec cascades"; private
coll., England (since the 19th century); Christie's sale, London, 14 Dec. 1984, lot 92.
4. ?One of a pair of paintings in the
posthumous sale of M. Williot, Hôtel de
Bullion, Paris (Paillet & de Caudin), 26 Feb.
1788, lot 8: "Deux Tableaux de forme en
hauteur, représentans des paysages & chutes
d'eau, ornés de différentes figures touchés avec
l'esprit & l'intelligence connus à cet habile
Artiste. Hauteur, 22 pouces, largeur 15."

The problem of repetitions in Boucher's early career is particularly thorny, as Voss (1959) was the first to recognize. For, whereas in later life he was prosperous enough, and sufficiently well-supplied with able pupils, to have made in his studio repetitions that he barely touched himself, at this stage in his career his involvement was necessarily greater. If he was not always wholly responsible for the repetitions, as Voss implied he was—making a first version that more than redeemed by its spontaneity small faults of drawing and composition, and a second that improved upon the first in detail, but at the price of a certain slickness of execution—he must still have been involved in each stage of the process. The various versions of the *Capriccio View of Tivoli* exemplify this phenomenon.

It must be admitted straightaway that none of the currently known painted versions of this composition would appear to be the prime original. That distinction probably belongs to one of a pair of finished drawings, which are in the Cabinet des Dessins of the Louvre, both of which were drawn on subsequently to create rather different paintings (see Slatkin, 1971[b]). The Louvre drawing (fig. 99) is in turn based upon a drawing, *The Waterfall and the Temple of the Sibyl at Tivoli*, done by Boucher when he was in Rome in 1730 (Rijksprentenkabinett, Amsterdam; exh. cat. 1982, Tokyo, no. 77; two drawings of Tivoli by Boucher, of which this may have been one, were in de Jullienne's posthumous sale, 30 Mar. ff. 1767, lot 938). This was one of the classic views drawn and painted by foreign artists in Italy. Boucher's drawing, which was probably based on a study made on the spot but worked up in the studio afterward, nevertheless succeeds in seizing a novel aspect of the site, one that emphasizes the rocaille, as it were, out of which the temple arises. The Louvre drawing, which adopts a vertical format, makes a more balanced and picturesque composition out of this: reducing the amount of craggy rock, taming the fall of water, introducing a bridge, an umbrella pine, and different buildings on the brow of the hill, and peopling the scene with a shepherd boy following a packhorse, ox, and sheep, and two people leaning over the bridge. The boy was subsequently to be reemployed in another (lost) capriccio Italian landscape, entitled *Le moineau apprivoisé* in the engraving after it by Gaillard (fig. 100; J-R 1033).

The ensuing sequence of pictures is not easy to put into proper order—and it is always possible that there is a missing link in the chain that is unrecorded (it is tempting to speculate, for instance, that the two upright pictures "representing landscapes and waterfalls" in the posthumous sale of M. Williot in 1788 were made from the pair of drawings in the Louvre). What would appear to have happened is that Boucher, with studio assistance, proceeded to make salable paintings of the composition in the more usual oblong format. There are two versions of this: one of larger dimensions (74 × 95 cm), which was shipped back to Sweden by Tessin in

*16*

Fig. 99. *Capriccio View of Tivoli*. Cabinet des Dessins, Louvre.

Fig. 100. *Le moineau apprivoisé*, engraved by René Gaillard after a lost painting by Boucher.

Fig. 101. *Capriccio View of Tivoli* (retouched by Boucher). Nationalmuseum, Stockholm.

August 1741, and already described in his bill of lading as merely "retouched by Boucher" (see Sander, 1872, p. 57, no. 73), which he was forced by his debts to sell to Crown Princess Lovisa Ulrica in 1749 and is now in the Nationalmuseum in Stockholm (fig. 101; A & W 48; exh. cat. 1984, Manchester, no. P1). The other, of smaller dimensions (60.5 × 73.5 cm), which was recently sold from an old English private collection, can from its size almost certainly be identified with a picture bought by Norblin for the healthy price of 501 livres 1 sol in the sale of de Vassal de Saint-Hubert.

In these two paintings the composition was extended to the left by adding a further group of herdsmen and their beasts climbing the track now linked (somewhat contrivedly) with the bridge, and to the right by some more rocks. Boucher obviously no longer had access to the drawing he had made in 1730, since the paintings omit all the terracing that made this part (which is the weakest in both paintings) interesting. In both paintings, indeed, it would appear that it was the landscape that he turned over to his studio assistants, and the figures, at least the more important of them, that he put in himself. It is not possible to say for certain which of the two paintings had the priority, but the apparently higher quality of the figures in the de Vassal de Saint-Hubert picture and the fact that it exhibits a pentimento in the placing of the shepherd boy suggest that it was the earlier.

The present picture reverts to the upright format of the Louvre drawing but changes the vertical relation between foreground and background in order to retain the additional group of herdsmen on the left (it was, after all, these Castiglionesque details that made Boucher's early landscapes popular). At the same time it alters both the detail and the scale of the bridge and ruins and completely does away with the buildings beside the Temple of the Sibyl and with the subsidiary figures on the track and bridge. In this picture, even more than in the other two, the landscape is the least inspired element. The figures, however, appear to be as vigorous as ever (possibly even strengthened in the group on the left, among which the boy behind the second horse is treated less perfunctorily, and to which a sheep has been added at the extreme left) and from Boucher's own hand.

It would thus appear that all three of the known versions of the *Capriccio View of Tivoli* are by Boucher, but with studio assistance. It seemed worth showing the present version (which was recognized by Pierre Rosenberg in 1979 but has remained unpublished) to shed fresh light on the manner in which Boucher made repetitions of his compositions. In the present case, the tight, slightly summary manner of rendering the figures indicates that all three versions were made not long after Boucher's return from Rome. It was not until 1734, however, when his manner was again more liquid, that Boucher painted the *View of the Farnese Gardens* (cat. 23) from the drawing that was made as a pendant to that of the *Capriccio View of Tivoli*.

# 17 | Venus Requesting Vulcan for Arms for Aeneas

Oil on canvas
99 × 69 in. (252 × 175 cm)
Signed bottom right: *f. Boucher 1732*
Musée du Louvre, Paris
(inv. 2709)
(S & M 315, 322, 353)    A & W 85

PROVENANCE
François Derbais, rue Poissonnière, *salle de billard (inventaire après décès*, 2 Mar. 1743, Archives Nationales, Minutier Central, LIX, p. 230); *Catalogue de Tableaux . . . & Le tout provenant du cabinet de feu M. WATELET, Conseiller du Roi, Receveur Général des Finances d'Orléans . . . &c.*, appartement de M.ᵉ Hayot de Long-Pré, Huissier-Priseur, cour du Vieux-Louvre (Paillet & Hayot de Long-Pré), 12 June ff. 1786, lot 11 (with the *Aurora and Cephalus*, miscalled *Venus and Adonis*): "deux morceaux, aussi gracieux qu'il soit possible de les desirer . . . peints dans la grande force de cet Artiste, tant par la beauté de la couleur, que par un empâtement admirable & la touche la plus savante" [bought for the Crown by Paillet for 3,121 livres; Engerand, 1900, p. 594, records their purchase for 3,201 livres (the difference reflecting Paillet's commission?) but garbles the purchase by omitting the title of the present picture and dividing that of the *Aurora and Cephalus* into two separate paintings]; placed in the Louvre in the same year.

PREPARATORY DRAWING
*Tête de femme (Vénus)*, medium unknown, engraved by J-C. François (J-R 1019).

COPY
*Head of Venus*, canvas, 38 × 40 cm, Corrodi sale, Antonina, Rome, 16–23 Jan. 1935, lot 56.

ANALOGY
*Vénus demandant des armes à Vulcain*, 43 × 32 *pouces*, Chardin's posthumous sale, 6 Mar. ff. 1780, lot 11 [the proportions of this are virtually identical to those of the picture in the Louvre, which is the only surviving upright version other than the much narrower picture in the Wallace Collection. The picture owned by Chardin might thus have been a model for, or reduction of, the former]. His sale also included a red-chalk drawing of the same subject, paired with another of *Venus and Mars* (lot 41). What was very possibly the same drawing was on its own in Bergeret's posthumous sale, 24 Apr. ff. 1786, lot 151, measuring 11½ × 7½ *pouces*.

This *Venus and Vulcan* is the first dated, or even securely datable, painting in Boucher's oeuvre. It also announces new ambitions, both in its size and in its treatment of a mythological subject on such a scale and with such boldness and visibility of brushstroke. Boucher was to return to its subject throughout his career. There was thus considerable vision and appropriateness in its acquisition by d'Angiviller for the Muséum, along with its pendant, *Aurora and Cephalus* (cat. 18), at the Watelet sale in 1786.

It is hence all the more extraordinary that we have no certain record of the picture before this date: we do not know for whom it was painted or from whom Watelet acquired it, nor whether it was engraved. It is like a manifesto of Boucher's gifts after his return from Italy that went unpublished. The temptation is therefore strong to see in it one of the "grands tableaux" that Mariette (I, 1851–53, p. 165) says Boucher painted in his youth for the "sculpteur marbrier nommé Dorbay," all the more so in that Mariette identifies the *Rape of Europa* in the Watelet collection as having been painted for the same individual. The pendant to the *Rape of Europa*, *Mercury Confiding the Infant Bacchus* (both now in the Wallace Collection, London), must have had the same origin, and we know from the ascription of ownership on the engravings after the four large putti pictures called *L'Amour moissonneur*, *L'Amour oiseleur*, *L'Amour nageur*, and *L'Amour vendangeur*, that they, too, were in the same collection, there called the "Cabinet de M.ʳ Derbais."

That makes six large pictures—but would that have been enough to justify Mariette in saying that this "Dorbay" had "furnished his whole house" with paintings that "Boucher, not seeking to do anything but make a name for himself, would have done for nothing, rather than pass up the opportunity"? One might think not; in which case it is not unreasonable to suppose that Watelet acquired his *Venus and Vulcan* and *Aurora and Cephalus* from Derbais, just as he did his *Rape of Europa* and *Mercury Confiding the Infant Bacchus*.

Who was this Dorbay or Derbais, and why should Boucher have imagined that by painting large pictures for him he would gain a reputation? The only *sculpteur marbrier* of whom there is any record in the eighteenth century is Jérôme Derbais, who frequently appears in this role in the royal accounts between 1668 and 1715 (see Lami, 1906, pp. 145–46), but who is best known for the bronzes supposedly done from his busts of the *Grand Condé* and *Turenne* (examples of both in the Wallace Collection, and of the latter alone in the Frick Collection, New York). However, 1715 was the year of his death. The natural assumption, since

Fig. 102. C-J. Natoire, *Venus Requesting Vulcan for Arms for Aeneas* (1734). Musée Fabre, Montpellier.

Jérôme Derbais belonged to a kin group of sculptors (his father in-law was Gilles Guérin), was that he had had a son who carried on the same profession, but in greater obscurity. I am deeply indebted to Georges Brunel for pointing out to me that this was not the case, and for communicating to me his discovery of the *inventaire après déces* of François Derbais, the lawyer son of the sculptor, taken on 2 March 1743. It is frustratingly unspecific in not supplying any artists' names, but it does indicate that the son of the *sculpteur marbrier* Derbais did have a substantial collection of pictures, and that this collection included in the *salle de billard* a *Rape of Europa* and a *Birth of Bacchus*, together with a pair of larger pictures of *Aurora and Cephalus* and *Venus Requesting Vulcan for Arms*, and a large *Birth of Venus*, which were the most highly assessed pictures in the whole collection. There can be little doubt that these, and two pairs of depictions of children on the staircase, were the pictures by Boucher that we have been considering.

It is still not wholly apparent how Boucher expected to gain from this connection. Derbais is not cited as a celebrated collector in his own day; his social station and connections were unremarkable; and if he was instrumental in having *L'Amour moissonneur* and *L'Amour oiseleur* engraved in 1734, their fellows were not engraved until 1741, while the *Rape of Europa* and *Mercury Confiding the Infant Bacchus* were not engraved until after his death, in 1748. The *Venus and Vulcan* and the *Aurora and Cephalus* were not engraved at all. One can therefore only suppose that—if Mariette's account of the relationship is to be trusted—Boucher was able to use Derbais's house in the rue Poissonnière as a kind of gallery to display his work to prospective clients.

The *Venus and Vulcan* was indeed a remarkable new departure in French painting for the time. In its strong, acid coloring, reduced to a few striking notes, in the serpentine vitality of its forms (notably of the armor on the ground), and in the broad, highly evident strokes of its brushwork, it broke decisively with the even gradations and delicate glazes and finish of the then leader of the French school, François Lemoine, and his emulators. Its frank sensuality—above all in the pose of Venus (who, one should remember, needed to seduce her alienated husband into forging arms for her illegitimate son) and in the shape of the nymph with her upturned bottom (the first occurrence of this celebrated pose in Boucher's oeuvre)—must also have been startling. So too, even though treating a well-tried theme, Boucher managed to create a composition of such originality and narrative force that it evidently left an indelible impression on his two near-contemporaries and rivals, Natoire and Carle Vanloo, as witness the former's *morceau de réception* of 1734 (fig. 102; Musée Fabre, Montpellier; exh. cat. 1977, Troyes, no. 17) and the latter's painting of 1735 (private collection, France; exh. cat. 1977, Nice, no. 39). Thus, whether the assumption about the presence of Boucher's picture in Derbais's collection is correct or not, it was evidently somewhere that satisfied the young Boucher's requirement of getting himself known.

In view of the fact that this must have been the first picture with which Boucher carved out for himself the leading position within the *école française*, there is particular piquancy in its having been singled out for criticism by the determinedly anti-Gallican Julien de Parme, when he described a visit to Watelet's collection in a letter to André Lens of 9 May

1774—one of a whole series of diatribes against the *école française* (Rosenberg, 1984[b], p. 224):

> Would you believe that such a man had nothing in his collection but Vanloos, Bouchers, Pierres, Viens, Doyens, etc. . . . which he finds very beautiful, and I find detestable? . . . But Mr. Watelet not only owns pictures that are worse than mediocre, he seeks to justify them and get them appreciated, despite one's having had enough of them. Not having been able to prevent my saying that the body of a Vulcan, painted by Boucher, had nothing at all of the beauties of antique forms, he replied that it exhibited many traits of observed nature, and a charged brush. But the truth is that there was nothing there but *la maniere françoise* in its most extreme form. *(Croiroit-on qu'un tel homme n'eut dans son cabinet que des Vanloo, des Bouchers, des Pierre, des Vien, des Doyen, etc. . . . qu'il trouve très beaux, et que je trouve détestables? . . . Mais Mr. Watelet non seulement a des tableaux audessous du mediocre, mais il veut encore les justifier et les faire trouver beaux, malgré qu'on en ait. N'ayant pu m'empêcher de dire que le corps d'un certain Vulcain, peint par Boucher, n'avoit rien du tout des belles formes antiques, il me répondit qu'il y avoit beaucoup de vérités de nature et un pinceau moëlleux. Mais la vérité est qu'il n'y avoit autre chose que la maniere françoise la plus outrée.)*

# 18 | *Aurora and Cephalus*

Oil on canvas
98½ × 69 in. (250 × 175 cm)
Signed bottom center: *boucher/173[3?]*
Musée des Beaux-Arts, Nancy (inv. 143)
S & M 88          A & W 86

PROVENANCE
François Derbais (see cat. 17); Watelet's posthumous sale, 12 June ff. 1786, lot 11 (see cat. 17), as *Vénus et Adonis* [bought with its pendant *Venus and Vulcan* for the Crown by Paillet for 3,121 livres, but Engerand (1900, p. 594) omits the title of *Vénus et Vulcain,* instead dividing the present picture into two, as *Céphale* and *L'Aurore*]; placed in the Louvre in 1786; sent to Lunéville for the negotiations preceding the Treaty of Lunéville, 1801; transferred to the museum of Nancy when the conference was over.

PREPARATORY DRAWINGS
 1. *Female Nude, Seated on Clouds, Holding Drapery (Aurora)*, red chalk heightened with white on buff paper, 370 × 231 mm, signed lower left *f. Boucher*; Peter Jones; Basil Dighton; Hon. Irwin Laughlin; by descent to Rear Adm. and Mrs. Hubert Chanler (exh. cat. 1973–74, Washington, no. 20).

Since it shares the same dimensions, and provenance from the Watelet sale, as the *Venus and Vulcan* (cat. 17), there can be little doubt that this *Aurora and Cephalus* was also originally painted for the same patron, despite the one year's difference of date between them. As has already been suggested, this must have been the *avocat au Parlement* François Derbais. What has been said of the novel technique and effects of the *Venus and Vulcan* is perhaps even more strikingly apparent in this picture. In Nancy this emerges even more vividly, through the painting's juxtaposition with Lemoine's *Continence of Scipio* (fig. 13) and de Troy's *Diana and Her Nymphs in Repose*. Two additional elements in *Aurora and Cephalus*, both prefatory of Boucher's subsequent oeuvre, are the extraordinary freedom of his characteristic fantasy plant in the foreground (now rendered even more unreal by the loss of surface glazes, which has turned it gray-blue) and the gamboling cupids in the air, who introduce a note of festivity that had almost been banished from monumental French history painting through the influence of the Academy. One of the few pictures in which such an uninhibited use of putti is found in the work of Boucher's seniors

2. ?*Head of Cephalus* (medium and dimensions unstated), engraved in reverse under the direction of Deseve, as a representation of the youthful male head, fig. 1 of pl. 23, *Dessin, les Ages*, in the supplementary volume of illustrations (1805) to the two volumes of the *Encyclopédie Méthodique: Beaux Arts* written by Watelet and Lévesque (1788 and 1791).

was Noël-Nicolas Coypel's *Rape of Europa,* which the artist submitted as his entry in the 1727 competition (fig. 34; Philadelphia Museum of Art; see Conisbee, 1981, pp. 78–80). Both Coypel and Boucher, however, were probably encouraged to adopt this Rubensian device by Watteau's depictions of Cythera. What sets Boucher apart is the unidealized, almost grotesque, features and poses of his infants.

This also happens to be the first painting by Boucher for which we possess a nude study of the principal figure, Aurora. It is not exactly an *académie,* for not only is the pose conceived specifically for the painting but also some of the drapery on which the model must have sat is transformed into clouds. Her hair, however, is still her own, under a little kerchief, and awaits its embellishment in the painting by coiffure and pearls. Regina Slatkin (exh. cat. 1973–74, Washington, p. 27) suggests that the model was "undoubtedly" the seventeen-year-old Marie-Jeanne Buseau, whom Boucher married in the year that he painted this picture. This is not only inherently implausible—there is not even any facial resemblance with the accepted depictions of her—it also traduces the deliberate piquancy of the presentation. For this is the body not of a young girl but of a mature woman; in thus pointing up the discrepancy in age between the older woman and the beardless boy, Boucher evokes the legend that Aurora was cursed by Venus with nymphomania for having slept with her lover, Mars. He takes some liberty in suggesting enthusiasm on Cephalus's part, however, since the legend has it that he attempted to remain faithful to his wife, Procris. Despite the error of the Watelet sale catalogue, there is no question (as has generally been recognized, *pace* Levey, 1982) but that the scene represented is that of *Aurora and Cephalus* rather than *Venus and Adonis,* because the chariot, the torch bringing light, and the putto watering the plants with dew denote the woman as Aurora, while the horn, hounds, bow, and arrows denote the male figure as Cephalus, the passionate hunter (whose passion for hunting led to the death of his wife). What is more, the subject of the picture was already correctly identified when it was acquired for the French Crown at the Watelet sale (see also the same elements in the overdoor of *Aurora and Cephalus* of about 1739 in the Hôtel de Soubise).

Regrettably, we only know what appears to have been a study for the head of Cephalus through an ambiguous engraving. His face, with its sharply receding forehead, tilted nose, and high-set eye, is curiously similar to those in the later paintings of Vouet and the early paintings of Le Sueur, and it is possible that the engraving (if it is not simply after a study made by Watelet when the painting was in his possession) records a drawing by Boucher after such a work. The back-tilted pose of the foremost cupid can be paralleled by others—notably in the ex-Watelet *Rape of Europa* in the Wallace Collection—and must also have been studied in a drawing, but none has so far come to light. In general, however, it is the spontaneity of the picture that is most apparent; it is far from being a labored assemblage of separately studied figures, as in the academic tradition, but gives the feeling of having been created at the tip of the artist's brush—Watelet's "pinceau moëlleux" (see cat. 17).

# 19 | De trois choses en ferez-vous une?

Oil on canvas
Oval, 41½ × 33½ in. (105 × 85 cm)
Institut de France,
Musée Ephrussi de Rothschild,
Saint-Jean-Cap-Ferrat
S & M 1439, 1490, 1506
A & W 88 bis

## PROVENANCE

?*A Young Man, & his Mistress*, oval, Andrew Hay sale, [14–15 Feb.] 1744/45, 1st day, lot 30 [bought by Lord Hume (Home) for £16.5s 6d]; [Lecomte & Escudero] sale, exp. Febvre, Paris, 12 Dec. 1854, lot 36; anon. posthumous sale, exp. Haro, Paris, 22 Jan. 1874, lot 1 (with *La Marchande d'Oeufs* as its pendant, lot 2); anon. sale, Hôtel Drouot (Féral), Paris, 14 May 1877, lot 7 (with the same pendant, lot 8); Mme C. Lelong, Paris [not included in her sale of 11–15 May 1903, unlike its pendant]; sale of Mme X [Lelong?], Petit, Paris, 26 June 1924, lot 70; Mme Ephrussi, Saint-Jean-Cap-Ferrat; donated with the foundation established in memory of her parents Alphonse and Eleonora de Rothschild in 1938.

## VARIANT VERSION

?*Catalogue de Tableaux . . . &c. provenant du Cabinet de M\*\*\** [Defeure, brocanteur], Hôtel d'Aligre (Bresse & Joullain), 21 May ff. 1778, lot 23: "Un jeune homme aux genoux d'une jolie femme. Ce tableau, d'une touche franche, a été fait à son retour de Rome. Hauteur 3 pieds 1 pouce largeur 2 pieds 6 pouces. Toile" [bought by Le Febvre for 96 livres]; baron Edmond de Rothschild, Paris; baron Edmond de Rothschild, Château de Prégny, Switzerland.

## ENGRAVING (OF VARIANT VERSION)

Jacques-Jean Pasquier with the title *De Trois Choses en ferez-vous une?*, dated 1768, and inscribed *Gravé d'après François Boucher premier Peintre du Roi, Directeur de son Académie Royale de Peinture et Sculpture* [J-R 1447–1448], with *Elle mord à la grappe* as a pendant.

## COPY

*Lovers in Conversation*, 87 × 66.5 cm, Sotheby's, New York, 13 Mar. 1985, lot 16 [copied from the engraved version].

The riddling title given to this composition in the engraving of it (literally: "Of three things will you make/do one?") has thus far defied elucidation. It is obvious that it contains an element of sexual innuendo, but that is all. There are two autograph versions of this picture, as is not uncommonly the case at this relatively early stage in Boucher's career (see Voss, 1959). The other version, to which it has regrettably been impossible to gain access (baron Edmond de Rothschild collection, Château de Prégny; Voss, 1953, pp. 90–93, fig. 71), simplifies the arrangement of flowers in the girl's hair, places a pearl bracelet on her left forearm, clothes her in a shawl, and substitutes a ribbon with a bow for the scarf around her neck. Although it is this latter version that was engraved by J-J. Pasquier (J-R 1447–1448), it cannot be regarded as any more canonical than the other, because the engraving was not published until 1768, when it is possible that the version shown here had gone to England and was thus no longer available. Voss, indeed, saw the picture here as the earlier one, and the other as a more disciplined and considered revision of it.

Pasquier engraved the composition with *Elle mord à la grappe* as its pendant (J-R 1449–1451); that painting, though lost, can be seen from the engraving to have been later than the present one, however—the version of the picture exhibited in 1860 was dated 1749 (S & M 1566). When the present picture was in the sales presided over by Haro and Féral in 1874 and 1877, and in the collection of Mme C. Lelong, it had another pendant, an adult version of *La Marchande d'Oeufs* (engraved with child protagonists by Daullé, J-R 546; the adult version formerly with Cailleux, 1975, no. 3, and now in the Wadsworth Atheneum, Hartford). But this too neither matched it in date (it must, from its coarser facture, have been a little earlier) nor in the character of the couple portrayed. What is more, the two pictures had separate histories before they were united in the Haro sale (*La Marchande d'Oeufs* first appeared separately in the sale of the Pillot collection, 6–8 Dec. 1858, lot 17). If the present picture were ever to have had a pendant, it is much more likely to have been *The Bird's-Nesters* (fig. 103; photograph in the Witt Library, without any details; a delicious pastel study by Boucher of the girl's head was in the Donald S. Stralem collection, sold Christie's, London, 13 Dec. 1984, lot 158, under the name of J-A. Portail). Between these two pictures, the protagonists are comparable in type and years; and the two compositions balance, while contrasting an indoor and an outdoor scene.

The dating of the present picture is not immediately easy to establish, for although it evidently relates in theme and format to the set of four paintings of *La Souffleuse de Savon*, *Le Marchand d'Oiseaux*, *La*

19

Fig. 103. *The Bird's-Nesters*. Whereabouts unknown.

*Marchande d'Oeufs*, and *La Vendangeuse*, engraved by Daullé and published in 1748 (J-R 542–549), it is evident from the types of the protagonists in these that, even though the paintings themselves are lost and otherwise unrecorded, they dated from another period. The eager, aspiring boy in the present picture, wearing his own flowing locks tied behind with a ribbon, would on first sight appear to find his closest fellow in the lovely pastel of a *Boy Holding a Parsnip* in the Art Institute of Chicago, which is signed and dated 1738 (exh. cat. 1973–74, Washington, no. 32, color pl. p. xiv). Both handling and other elements, however, point to a rather earlier date for *De trois choses en ferez-vous une?* Its brushwork is not very manifest, but the folds of drapery have the narrow pleated form found in pictures painted rather sooner after Boucher's return from Italy, such as *La Pastorale* (Voss, 1954, fig. 22) or *Aurora and Cephalus*, and even in those painted as late as the grisaille *Virtues* in the *chambre de la Reine* at Versailles (1735). The rather broad, small-featured faces of the girl and of Aurora would also appear to have been based on the same model, who may again appear, in profile, in the *Woman at Her Dressing Table* engraved by Claire Tournay (J-R 1613) and in *Les caresses dangereuses* engraved by Joseph de Longueil (fig. 71; J-R 1402), as well as repeatedly in the engraved illustrations to Molière (J-R 402–452).

Since all these features indicate a dating to around 1733/34, it would be very tempting to see in this picture an idealized representation of Boucher making his suit to Marie-Jeanne Buseau, whom he married on 21 April 1733. But if the girl in the present picture could very possibly be, like his new wife, only seventeen, her blond hair and features do not otherwise agree with those of his wife, as we believe them to have been from the presumed portrait in the Frick Collection, while Boucher would have been double the age of the boy. The painting should instead be seen as one of his earliest treatments of the pastoral theme of juvenile love, albeit not yet with rustic protagonists or setting.

# 20 | *Le repos des fermiers*

Oil on canvas
34¼ × 53½ in. (87 × 136 cm)
Collection of Mr. and Mrs. Jeffrey E.
Horvitz, Hallandale, Florida

PROVENANCE
Baron Henri de Rothschild, Paris (exh. cat. 1928, Paris, no. 47); baron James de Rothschild, Paris (exh. cat. 1951, Geneva, no. 3, as *La sérénade villageoise);* private colls., England and U.S.A.; Claus Virch; art market, New York, from which acquired by the present owners in 1985.

DRAWING
*Study of a Hen with Wings Outstretched,* drawing, red, black, and white chalks, 170 × 200 mm, Count Carl Gustaf Tessin (acquired in Paris, 1739–42), Åkerö (1749 ms. cat., IV, p. 20, no. 76); Kongl. Biblioteket, Stockholm (1790 cat., no. 2846); transferred to the Kongl. [now National] Museum in 1863 (inv. NM 2952/1863; Bjurström, 1982, no. 823; here fig. 104).

It is perhaps a reflection of Boucher's inexhaustible fecundity that by the time he died and his obituaries came to be written, one entire phase of his development had been virtually forgotten, and was almost wholly overlooked: that of his early scenes of peasant life, most of them vignettes of rustic domesticity in landscape settings functioning not just as a mere backdrop, but as a participatory element in the rural idyll that is there presented.

There is, however, what appears to be one somewhat cryptic reference to these early scenes of peasant life in the very generalized *Eloge* written by Jullien des Boulmiers, published in the *Mercure de France* in September 1770 (pp. 181–89, esp. pp. 184–85):

But what must seem incredible in this astonishing fecundity is that he only painted nature under its beautiful aspects, that he never portrayed it as anything but cheerful and agreeable; above all, he avoided that absurd juxtaposition of objects that are never to be found together and that are an affront to good taste, in that they require us to suspend our critical faculties: if he sometimes diverted himself with *bambochades,* he knew how to improve without distorting them, and never presented hideous or disgusting objects, because he knew that our eyes find repugnant what we cannot bring our hands to touch. . . . (*Mais ce qui paroît inconcevable dans cette étonnante fécondité, c'est qu'il ne peignit la nature qu'en beau, qu'il ne la montra jamais que sous un aspect*

*aimable & riant; il évita sur-tout ce mélange ridicule d'objets qui ne se sont jamais trouvés ensemble & qui répugnent au goût en mettant le jugement en défaut: s'il s'égaya quelque fois dans le genre de Bamboche, il sçut l'embellir sans le dénaturer & n'offrit jamais des objets odieux ou degoûtans, parce qu'il savoit que les yeux ont horreur des choses que les mains ne voudroient pas toucher. . . .)*

It is perhaps significant that the short biography in the *Galerie Françoise*, which clearly drew on this passage for a similar one of its own (1771, p. 2), omitted the reference to Bamboche altogether—whether because his was not thought a suitable brush to tar Boucher with, or, more probably, because the writer was uncertain as to exactly what works of the artist were being referred to. He knew *Marches de Bohémiens et d'animaux* in the manner of "Le Benedette" (i.e., Castiglione), in which Boucher stuck closer to nature as a model than in the landscapes for which he was celebrated (p. 3), but not apparently this other early group of works.

*Bambochade*—a word seemingly first imported from Italian into French when it was used to describe two of Pierre's exhibits in the Salon of 1743, and applied to certain of Boucher's own productions in the list of painters' specialties drawn up for the Direction des Bâtiments in 1745 (A. Michel, 1906, p. 52; A & W doc. 244), and derived from the nickname of the Dutch painter active in Italy, Pieter van Laer (c. 1592–1642), *Il Bamboccio* —chiefly evokes the scenes of urban lowlife depicted by this artist and his imitators. Boucher—with the possible exception of a pastiche or two of Teniers—never painted exactly this kind of scene, and the application of the term to him must rather be taken to refer to his early depictions of the communal activities of peasants out of doors (see the definition in Watelet & Lévesque, 1788), as opposed to his later pastoral fancies of amorous couples, or the conventionalized depictions of fishermen, drovers, washerwomen, or young mothers and children with which he was to people his later landscapes. Yet, as Desboulmiers perceived, even in the preceding and more naturalistic depictions of rustic domesticity, Boucher was careful to avoid the coarse or grotesque features associated with the Dutch tradition.

Boucher was already painting this kind of scene before he left for Italy. One example is exhibited here, *La vie champêtre* (cat. 9), and others are cited in the entry on it. These pictures were, however, on a small scale, painted with a rich, saturated palette and carefully controlled brush, and visibly inspired by Dutch models. The present painting belongs, by contrast, to a group of pictures painted shortly after his return, as was first observed by Voss (1953, p. 85, fig. 46; his proposed sequence of datings is, however, predicated on the mistaken belief that the painting of *La vie champêtre* just antedates the engraving after it). These are generally larger, looser and freer in handling, their groups of figures are more open and active, and their compositions altogether less homogeneous. Knowing most of them only from reproductions, I offer the list with all due caution, but it would appear to include *La famille de villageois* (first recorded in the posthumous sale of Hubert Robert, 5 Apr. ff. 1809, lot 32 [in the description of the picture, the well is transposed from right to left]; subsequently Mrs. Young, London; Rodolphe Kann, Paris; baron Maurice de Rothschild [Voss, 1954, p. 209, fig. 23; A & W 40]), which, but for its discrepant format, could almost have been the pendant of the present picture; and *L'Abreuvoir* (first recorded in the Penard-Fernandez collection, Buenos Aires, as by Fragonard; Sotheby's sale, London, 14 June 1961, lot 73, retaining this attribution; art market, New York [A & W 51; exh. cat. 1982, Tokyo, no. 2]). There is also what appears to be the sketch for another picture of the kind, although its handling is strange, suggesting that it may not in fact be the original that was drawn by Saint-Aubin when it appeared in Natoire's posthumous sale of 14 December ff. 1778, lot 33 (art market, New York; A & W 69; exh. cat. 1982, Tokyo, no. 4; a closely related composition is recorded in an engraving by Joseph Varin [J-R 1619]). From these cabinet pictures it is but a short step to the set of four large decorative paintings of village pastorals purportedly from the Hôtel de Richelieu (see cat. 27; A & W 41, 42, 82, 83). After that, the vein dried up, replaced by the theater-inspired *Pastorales* for which Boucher was to become famous.

What an early place these pictures take in Boucher's output after his return from Italy can be seen from the landscape in the present example. The distant view on the left still incorporates the castle and concave-thatched farmhouses ultimately derived—via Watteau—from the woodcuts of Campagnola; but the handling of these and of the distant hills now has a broad, painterly application of pigment that is absent from the more tentative landscapes in the earlier pictures. The closest parallels for both sky and landscape in the present picture are to be found in the *Putti*

Fig. 104. *Study of a Hen with Wings Outstretched*. Nationalmuseum, Stockholm.

*Playing with a Goat* (Voss, 1953, p. 89, fig. 58; A & W 60; currently on the Swiss art market), the pendant of *Putti Playing with Birds* in the present exhibition (cat. 15). The foliage of the trees, by contrast, seems somewhat less idiosyncratic and particularized than in these early putti pictures, and already tends to the increased generality and conventionality of the ex-Hôtel de Richelieu village pastorals. Equally striking, perhaps, is the change in the character of the figures from those of Boucher's earlier pictures. Whereas in the earlier works there were fixed types for men, women, and children, and their poses suggest that they were largely composed on the canvas, here each is an individual, and its basis in a figure study can be sensed—very strongly in the case of the droll child submerged under a large hat, which conveys the impression of a cutout stuck down amid the rest. Regrettably, in the case of *Le repos des fermiers* we do not know of any drawings for the figures, whereas for the closely related picture of *La famille de villageois* we know of two (A & W figs. 234, 236). Their draftsmanship and the form of signature on the first of them clearly indicate studies from the early 1730s.

There is, however, one drawing, which has been described as a study not only for the present picture, but also for two other paintings, whose probable dating might seem to call into question that proposed for the picture here. This is a drawing *aux trois crayons* of a *Hen with Wings Outstretched* in the Nationalmuseum, Stockholm (fig. 104; NM 2952/1863; AA no. 618, fig. 108; A & W fig. 251; Bjurström, 1982, no. 823, color pl. p. xvii). Originally described as a study for the present picture, including by Ananoff himself in 1966, after this painting had silently been omitted from the canon the drawing was instead described as a study for *Noah Entering the Ark* (A & W 29) and *La fontaine* (A & W 46). There is nothing to prevent a study being used for more than one composition—particularly in the case of the thrifty Boucher! But can one accept what I am in effect proposing here, that the same drawing should have been used at least twice with an interval of several years between, during which time Boucher had made a journey to Italy and radically transformed his style? I have argued earlier that both the original of *Noah Entering the Ark* (cat. 10) and *La fontaine* (fig. 85) should be regarded as works executed immediately before Boucher went to Italy, whereas the present picture should be seen as dating from not long after his return. I believe that if one looks at the use to which the study of the bird is put in the various pictures, the hypothesis of a hiatus between the first two and the last acquires additional strength.

In both *La fontaine* and *Noah Entering the Ark*, this *Study of a Hen* is employed in conjunction with another of *A Strutting Cock*, also *aux trois crayons* and in the Nationalmuseum in Stockholm (NM 2953/1863; A & W fig. 253; Bjurström, 1982, no. 824). They are not placed in exactly the same relation to one another in the two paintings, and indeed, the *Noah Entering the Ark* takes altogether greater liberties with the two, suggesting that, if anything, they were made as studies for the former rather than for the latter. However, there is no particular motivation for their inclusion, even in *La fontaine*, and the fact that they are—unusually for Boucher's animal studies—elaborately carried out *aux trois crayons* suggests that they were originally executed as studies in their own right, with the ultimate end in view of their disposal to a collector such as Count

Tessin, who acquired them from the artist in Paris between 1739 and 1742. In the present picture the hen is employed alone, without anything, such as the dog in *La fontaine*, to provoke it into an attitude of self-defense (although the original study must surely have been made from a hen defending her chicks). What is perhaps most significant for the suggested disparity in dating between *La fontaine* (and *Noah Entering the Ark*) and *Le repos des fermiers*, however, is the difference in the handling of this hen between the pictures. In the former the birds have many of the qualities of the studies for them; the softness of chalk is translated into the liquidity of paint. In the present picture the handling is much harder; the hen shares the same bold, hatched brushwork of the rest of the composition and stands out sharply from the ground in consequence.

A final note. It was not only drawings that Boucher put to use over an extended span of years, but also studio or household props. The great copper cooking pan features in numerous other paintings, both from before Boucher went to Italy, such as in the *Noah* pictures (cat. 10, 11) and *La vie champêtre* (cat. 9), and from after his return, such as the *View of Tivoli* (cat. 16), *La belle cuisinière* (cat. 21), and *La belle villageoise* (see fig. 105); with such an essential and picturesque object, this is not unexpected. Rather more unexpected is to find the urn beside it cropping up again as the support for the joined hands of the woman in the drawing that served as a study for the old woman in *La Lumière du Monde* (cat. 57)—but this is one of a number of indications that the drawing was originally conceived for some other purpose, some years before.

# 21 | *La belle cuisinière*

Oil on panel
22 × 17 in. (55.5 × 43 cm)
Signed bottom right: *f. Boucher*
Musée Cognacq-Jay, Paris
(S & M 1135)        (A & W 75)
*Paris*

PROVENANCE
Acquired by an Englishman and taken off to London soon after having been painted, according to the advertisement for Aveline's engraving of it in the *Mercure de France,* Apr. 1735, p. 737; no further trace until included in the sales in Paris of the coll. of Sir William Jackson, 25 Feb. 1848, lot 46 [unsold or withdrawn], and 12 Mar. 1849, lot 53; acquired at an unknown date by Ernest Cognacq and his wife Louise Jay, and bequeathed to the city of Paris in 1929.

ENGRAVINGS
1. *La belle cuisinière,* engraved (in reverse) by Aveline, published by Drouais, and subsequently by Jacob and by Basan; advertised in

The theme of amorous dalliance between adolescents was one that Boucher rapidly made his own after his return from Italy, but it was some time before—with the aid of inspiration from the Théâtre de la Foire—he settled upon the social character of his couples and the locus of their activity: shepherds and shepherdesses in the open fields.

The present picture is one of a contemporaneous trio of scenes whose setting is the kitchen. In two of them—this and the *Kitchen Maid and Young Boy* (cat. 28)—the message is explicitly or implicitly erotic, while in the third, *La belle villageoise* (fig. 105; engraved picture lost, last recorded in the sale of the duc de Luynes, 1 frimaire [21 November] 1793, lot 46 [with measurements inverted]; smaller modello, or variant, in the collection of Norton Simon, Pasadena, A & W fig. 341 and color pl.), which was engraved by Soubeyran in 1738 as a pendant to Aveline's earlier

the *Mercure de France* in Apr. 1735, June 1737, and June 1738 (when Soubeyran's engraving after *La belle villageoise* was announced as its pendant); inscribed with the following verses by the writer and engraver Bernard Lépicié:

*Vos oeufs s'échapent Mathurine*
*Ce présage est mauvais pour vous,*
*Ce grivois dans votre cuisine*
*Pouroit bien vous les casser tous.*
(J-R 205–206)

2. *L'infortunée pourvoieuse*, engraved (same direction) by P. Duverbret [possibly a pseudonym adopted because of piracy], no publisher, inscribed with the following anonymous verses:

*Suson, si sur votre Chemin*
*Vous rencontrez encor quelqu'un,*
   *qui vous lutine*
*Je prédis sans etre Devin*
*Que vous ne porterez point d'oeufs*
   *à la Cuisine*
*Fillette doit toujours veiller*
*Sur ses Oeufs en son tablier.*
(J-R 948)

3. Untitled, engraved (in reverse) by P. de Colle, Venice.

4. *The Handsom Cook Maid*, engraved (in reverse) by P. Benazech, published by Fr. Vivares, London.

5. *Eggs in Danger*, glass picture (same direction) by J. Johnson, published by J. Fisher; example in the coll. of Stephen Winkworth, *Connoisseur*, June 1931, p. 349, no. xiii.

Fig. 105. *La belle villageoise*, engraved by Pierre Soubeyran after Boucher (1738).

engraving of the present picture, it is simple domesticity.

It is commonly and rightly said that the inspiration of these paintings was Dutch; while this holds true to the extent that they are indeed genre pictures and thus take their place in a tradition of painting that the Dutch made particularly their own, and that was coming into special favor with Parisian collectors in these years, it should not be taken so far as to imply dependence upon specific Dutch models (unlike, say, Boucher's lost *Estaminet* "in the manner of Teniers," as described in the Cayeux sale, 8 Jan. ff. 1770, lot 50). Not only can one point to no specific source, but also, whereas in Dutch pictures interest focuses upon the interior setting and upon the protagonists as exemplifications of a social type, in Boucher the purely human interest of the scene comes first, carrying with it the implication that in these humble settings uncomplicated happiness is more easily achieved (the moralizing content of the verses appended to the engravings after these pictures is inherent in this kind of engraving, rather than necessarily a reflection of the intentions of the artist). So, too, such commonplaces of Dutch "lowlife" painting as the amorous encounter in the present picture, or the infant being held to piss by its mother in *La belle villageoise*, are treated with a sympathy for the participants absent from most Dutch paintings.

It is in the teeming detail of the setting and the prominence accorded to the still life that these pictures appear most Dutch. In the case of *La belle villageoise*, the expert Pierre Remy actually attributed them to Willem Kalf himself when drawing up the posthumous inventory of the duc de Luynes's collection in 1771 (see exh. cat. 1984, Paris, Musée Rodin, p. 61; Boucher indeed owned a *Kitchen Scene* by Kalf, which was acquired by the Crown at the comte de Vaudreuil's sale, and is now in the Louvre). There are instances of kitchen scenes by Kalf with the original figures painted out and others substituted by Lancret (*Wallace Collection Catalogues*, 1968, p. 378), but this is clearly not the case with Boucher. In his pictures, the main function of the still-life details is to underline the message of rustic simplicity. The obvious symbolic allusions of the present picture—the eggs held in the girl's apron, one of which has been dislodged and broken, standing for virginity and a presage of its loss, and the cat seizing the "bird," betokening the predatory urges beneath the young man's naïve ardor—likewise have Dutch precedents. Thérèse Burollet (1980, p. 43) has compared the symbolism of the eggs in particular, which is taken up in Lépicié's verse under Aveline's engraving, to that of a painting by Frans van Mieris the Elder that was to be directly drawn upon by Greuze in his more moralizing picture in the Metropolitan Museum.

In view of the mastery that Boucher achieved in his genre scenes—and indeed in his episodes of daily life in general—it is at first sight a little puzzling that he should have abandoned them after painting so few. The answer may reside in the fact that his near-contemporary Chardin appears to have diversified from still lifes into a similar kind of subject matter at the very same epoch. In Chardin's case the year would appear to have been 1733 (see exh. cat. 1979, Paris, pp. 187 ff.). We have no means of dating Boucher's pictures precisely, but the fact that Aveline's engraving after the one here was advertised in the *Mercure de France* in April 1735 and that the picture itself had already been borne off to England by that date suggest that it must have been painted no later than 1734.

"Une Etude de femme très-spirituellement
faite pour la composition de la belle
Cuisiniere," sale of the Cabinet de M.***
[Huquier *père*; 1 July] 1771, lot 43 [among
framed drawings, bought by Lavocat for 6
livres]; probably identifiable with a drawing in
the Le Pelletier coll., Paris (A & W 75/4,
fig. 335).

REPLICAS AND COPIES

1. *Catalogue des Tableaux qui composent le
Cabinet de M. le Comte de Merle*, Hôtel de
Bullion (Paillet & Julliot), 1 Mar. ff. 1784, lot
20, on canvas, 20 × 17 *pouces*, with description [bought by Cuvillier, Boucher's son-in-
law, for 125 livres].

2. [Henri] Serrur sale, 15–16 Jan. 1866,
lot 117.

3. *The Declaration*, 29 × 24 in., J. Forbes
Robertson coll. (exh. cat. 1902, London, no.
137, as "French School"; identified as
Boucher's *La belle cuisinière* by Lady Dilke in
her copy of the catalogue in the Victoria and
Albert Museum Library, London).

4. J. E. Galloway, Ayr (photo of 1925 in
Witt Library, London), on panel, 18¾ ×
11¾ in.

5. Brunner Gallery, Paris, sold in 1921, [on
canvas?], 90 × 70 cm, as J-B. Huet.

6. Versailles sale, June 1968 (according to
Thérèse Burollet, 1980, p. 45).

7. Musée Cognacq-Jay, Paris, red-chalk
drawing, 415 × 335 mm (Burollet, 1980,
no. 121).

8. Sotheby's, London, 3 July 1985, lot 171,
73.5 × 61 cm (copied from Aveline's engraving).

ANALOGIES

1. The figure of the kitchen maid re-
employed in a drawing engraved by S-F.
Ravenet as *Des Radix des Raves*, in the set of
*Les Cris de Paris*, advertised in the *Mercure de
France* in May 1737 (J-R 1520).

2. Pose of the couple adopted by J-B.
Le Prince in a sepia drawing, *La Vivandière*,
Masson sale, Hôtel Drouot, Paris, 20 Mar.
1924, lot 92.

3. The head of the kitchen maid, studied at a
slightly different angle and in a more elaborate
kerchief, in a drawing from the cabinet of M.
de la Haye, engraved by Demarteau, no. 25,
and by Huquier *fils* (J-R 1189).

Mariette related that Chardin was encouraged to essay genre painting,
partly by the raillery of Aved (who was, significantly, active as a dealer as
well as a painter) and partly by the fear that he could not compete
successfully with the already established Desportes and Oudry in his
original field. In pitting himself in turn against Chardin, Boucher was not
challenging an established master of genre, but he was up against an
acknowledged expert in its still-life component. Moreover, in undertaking
this kind of subject, one of Boucher's chief strengths—the displayed
virtuosity of his brushwork—probably ran counter to the tastes of the
potential clientele for such pictures: the collectors of actual Dutch
paintings. It is admittedly evidence from much later in his career, but
something of the kind is suggested by the pair of pictures that was
commissioned from him in 1760 by that passionate admirer of Dutch *Fein-
malerei*, Caroline Luise of Baden-Durlach, only to be banished from her
*Malereikabinett* almost immediately after their arrival (see exh. cat. 1983,
Karlsruhe, Schloss, pp. 135, 208). *La belle villageoise*, on the other hand,
did pass as partly from the hand of Kalf and retained its place in the duc
de Luynes's cabinet of Dutch pictures.

It is of some interest that *La belle cuisinière*, like *La vie champêtre*
(cat. 9), was promptly carried off to England—to which, by contrast,
Boucher's mythologies and amorous pastorals scarcely gained access. His
most characteristic productions were not to find favor there in the
eighteenth century, and it was really only as a draftsman that he was to be
appreciated among the narrower circle of connoisseurs, including Charles
Rogers, William Esdaile, and Sir Joshua Reynolds (see Denys Sutton, in
exh. cat. 1984, Manchester, pp. 7–8).

It is the apparently English provenance of the present picture that
reinforces its claim to be the original painting engraved by Aveline, for it
reemerged in the mid-nineteenth century in the collection of an
Englishman, Sir William Jackson, albeit that this was sold in Paris.
Furthermore, it is in reverse of the original engraving by Aveline, as one
would expect, and it is on panel, like the comparable painting of *The
Landscape Painter* in the Louvre (cat. 22). By contrast, the version sold
with the collection of the comte de Merle in 1784, which is commonly
inserted into the provenance of the present picture, was on canvas. Too
few details are given to identify the picture sold in a mixed lot (9) in the
posthumous sale of the collection of M. Davoust on 27 April 1772 with
any certainty, but it could equally well have been the half-length picture
also shown here (cat. 28). The quality of the present picture undoubtedly
denotes it as autograph, although there would appear to be an area of
unsatisfactorily restored damage around the farther eye of the girl. This,
and the out-of-focus photograph by which it has so long been known,
may help to account for its unjustified dismissal by Ananoff and
Wildenstein, who consider the original to be lost.

## 22 | The Landscape Painter

Oil on panel
10½ × 8¾ in. (27 × 22 cm)
Musée du Louvre, Paris (M.I. 1024)
S & M 1063, 1228          A & W 424
*Paris*

PROVENANCE
*Catalogue de Tableaux des Ecoles d'Italie, de
Flandre, et de France . . . &c. formant le
Cabinet de feu M. COLLET . . .*, rue de
Cléry no. 96 (Le Brun), 14 May ff. 1787, lot 99
[with impossible height; bought by François
for 259 livres 19 sous]; Hubert Robert's posthumous sale, 5 Apr. ff. 1809, lot 33; sale of
Col. Devère, Paris, 17 Mar. 1855, lot 7 bis;
coll. of Dr. Louis La Caze, left to the Louvre
in 1869.

PREPARATORY DRAWING
*Painter at His Easel*, red chalk, 355 × 260
mm: ?sale of baron d'Ivry, Paris, 21 May 1884
[not in Lugt, but this drawing not in catalogues of 7 or 12 May]; private coll., Paris; Los
Angeles County Museum of Art (fig. 108).

Since the Renaissance, whenever painters had depicted themselves or their colleagues at work, or had wanted to show artistic activity in general, it had been customary to do so in a way that exalted the artist's calling. This was achieved on one level by presenting the painter (as in the Middle Ages) as *St. Luke Painting the Virgin* or (as in the unique instance of Dosso Dossi) as *Zeus Painting Souls*. On a more mundane level, he might be shown as the head of a studio or academy, or, in greater isolation, as a figure whose dress and demeanor clearly denoted him as the genteel and

*22*

Fig. 106. *Le Berger Napolitain*, engraved by
Jean Daullé after Boucher (1758).

Fig. 107. *La Peinture*, engraved by Marie-Madeleine Igonet after Boucher (1752).

Fig. 108. *The Painter at His Easel*. Los Angeles County Museum of Art.

thoughtful exponent of a free art, rather than as the manual practitioner of a craft (for useful recent surveys of the topic, see the catalogues of the two exhibitions mounted by Pierre Georgel, 1976, Paris, Louvre, and 1982–83, Dijon). Even the more genrelike depictions of Gérard Thomas and Balthasar van den Bossche presented the artist as in charge of a busy workshop, sought out by his clients.

Boucher here broke with these traditions, by showing the artist alone at his easel in a garret. In doing so, he appears to have drawn on rather different kinds of depiction: on the one hand, that of the young pupil drawing from some studio property, as in paintings by Michael Sweerts and Wallerant Vaillant, and on the other, that of the *singe-peintre*, as depicted by Teniers, Watteau, or Chardin (see Feinblatt, 1959). In both these types of portrayal, however, the artist is shown, whether metaphorically or literally, as "the ape of nature," painstakingly imitating what is set before him. Boucher's bold stroke was to show his young artist conjuring a finished landscape out of the air, aided by no more than a rough sketch in the sketchbook beside him. The sketchbook (which is not present in the preparatory drawing for the composition) prevents the message being as stark as in Rembrandt's *Self-Portrait in His Studio* (Museum of Fine Arts, Boston), but it is surely no less implicit: that it is from his imagination that the painter creates—or re-creates—his subject.

The message—and the piquancy of the contrast between the dingy disorder of the studio and the bright vision on the easel—is underlined by this picture within a picture, which is one by Boucher himself: *Le Berger Napolitain* (lost, but known from the engraving, fig. 106, made of it by Daullé in 1758 [A & W fig. 1216], when it was in the collection of the chevalier de Damery). For this, as the title attached to the engraving makes clear, was of a half-remembered, half-imaginary view of Italy, painted after the artist's return, as in the case of the *View of Tivoli* (cat. 16) and the *View of the Farnese Gardens* (cat. 23). We cannot, however, deduce from this that the figure of the artist is a self-portrait, since he is patently a young student, whereas Boucher would have been around thirty at the time this was painted. The boy, indeed, appears to be one who served him as model on other occasions in these years (e.g., in *Le retour du marché*, fig. 119, and *Les bulles de savon*, A & W 96), just as some of the studio props also recur: the suspended candles (see cat. 28) and the bottle stopped with a twist of oiled paper (see cat. 21, fig. 105). The original model for this composition was, however, not this but an older boy, who seems to have been used instead in the first of the two pictures mentioned below.

This was not the only occasion on which Boucher depicted this subject, though the other portrayals were less intimate. About the same period, he painted another picture of a young man at his easel painting a landscape (baron Edmond de Rothschild collection, Château de Prégny, A & W 76; engraved, as *La Peinture*, fig. 107, by Marie-Madeleine Igonet in 1752 [J-R 1193], along with its subsequently painted pendant of *La Sculpture* by Pierre), but this figure is witnessed by a trio of studio assistants. When the picture appeared in the posthumous sale of the architect Pierre-Hippolyte Lemoyne in 1828, the painter was identified as Boucher himself, the woman as his wife, and the young pupil with a portfolio under his arm (who was to spawn a host of similar depictions by Drouais, Lépicié, and others) as Deshays. Not only do the ages of these characters, in view of the evident epoch of the picture, render these identifications wholly fanciful, but they were not even hinted at when the picture was in the posthumous sale of Pierre-Hippolyte's father, the sculptor Jean-Baptiste Lemoyne, in 1778. It belongs instead to the satirical genre of the *peintre-barbouilleur*, as represented by Paulus Fürst's engraving after Ch. Walch, *Ars mendica gemit* (exh. cat. 1982–83, Dijon, pp. 123, 135, and fig. 223).

The other painting by Boucher of a painter in his studio was allegorical: it was an oval oil sketch on paper, reputedly showing Boucher himself receiving an inspirational visit from Venus and several cupids (de Sireul sale, 3 Dec. ff. 1781, lot 30). This sketch is lost, but one may be permitted to doubt whether even that was actually a self-portrait, since a drawing of exactly this subject by Boucher in the Musée des Beaux-Arts, Lille (exh. cat. 1974–75, London, no. 7, pl. 16) must date from the 1760s, yet still shows the artist as a green youth.

Not the least interesting aspect of *The Landscape Painter* is the identity of its earliest recorded owner, the diplomat, playwright, and *censeur Royal*, Louis-Jean-François Collet (1722–1787), since he may also have been the owner of *Le Berger Napolitain*. It is not clear that he was, since it was lot 296 in his posthumous sale, among the addenda. These would for the most part have been additions to the sale collected by the auctioneer (many were not so scrupulous in setting these apart from the collection that they professed to be selling), but could have included accidental omissions from the principal collection (see cat. 2 for the comparable uncertainty over the parts of the Sorbet sale). Since *Le Berger Napolitain* is recorded by Daullé's engraving as having been in the collection of that notable patron of French artists, the chevalier de Damery, it is conceivable that *The Landscape Painter* had been as well.

# 23 | *Capriccio View of the Farnese Gardens*

Oil on canvas
25 × 31⅞ in. (63.5 × 81 cm)
Signed lower left: *boucher · 1734*
The Metropolitan Museum of Art, New York; The Jack and Belle Linsky Collection (1982.60.44)
A & W 101
*New York*

PROVENANCE
Private coll., France (until 1952); Julius Weitzner, London (exh. cat. 1959, Rome, no. 98); the Jack and Belle Linsky Collection, New York (private coll., c. 1960–80; Foundation, 1980–82); given with the collection to the Metropolitan Museum in 1982.

With this picture we reach the first dated landscape in Boucher's oeuvre. The dating of his paintings (which appears to begin with the *Venus and Vulcan* of 1732 [cat. 17], a picture manifestly pioneering in its scale and ambitions) suggests that Boucher was now sufficiently established to wish to mark the stages of his output. Whereas the pleas in the *Mercure de France* (April 1735, p. 736; August 1735, pp. 1818–19) to engravers to date their works went largely unheeded, Boucher henceforward adopted the practice very consistently in his paintings, no doubt partly from

*23*

PREPARATORY DRAWINGS

1 *View of the Farnese Gardens*, black chalk, 255 × 375 mm, Réserve du Cabinet des Estampes, Bibliothèque Nationale, Paris (fig. 109).

2. *View of the Farnese Gardens with Two Cowherds*, black chalk, 346 × 221 mm, Cabinet des Dessins, Musée du Louvre, Paris (Guiffrey & Marcel, II, 1908, no. 1409), acquired before 1827 (fig. 110).

3. Seated cowherd, on a mixed sheet of *Studies after Abraham Bloemaert*, red chalk, Musée des Beaux-Arts, Orléans (fig. 112; the two studies of the seated cowherd on this sheet were etched by Boucher in reverse as plate 8 of his *Livre d'Etude d'après les Desseins Originaux de Blomart* [J-R 182]).

4. *Standing Cow*, red chalk, 215 × 330 mm, Nationalmuseum, Stockholm (NM 2955/1863; Bjurström, 1982, no. 832; brought from France by C. G. Tessin in 1741/42; here fig. 113).

commercial considerations. Ironically, in later years it was his undated early works that were to be the most sought after, with their very lack of dating permitting them to be ascribed to his supposedly best years, as a pupil of Lemoine and in Rome.

Were it not to have been dated, the present picture would no doubt have been similarly ascribed, on account of both its manner and its subject matter. Such occurred with the horizontal version of the *View of Tivoli* in Stockholm (cf. cat. 16), which we know to have been painted later, while certain lost pictures of Rome and its environs were likewise assumed to have been painted there, e.g., the smaller version of *Le Tombeau de l'Âne à Sacchetti* (misc. sale [Chariot & Paillet], 22 Apr. ff. 1776, lot 78, 26 × 21 *pouces*: "Ce tableau a été fait à Rome, dans le temps que Boucher sortoit de l'école de le Moine"; posthumous sale of M. Remond, 6 July ff. 1778, lot 66, 27 × 22 *pouces*); *La Vue du Temple de la Concorde* (de Sireul sale, 3 Dec. ff. 1781, lot 26); and another painting that can be identified from Saint-Aubin's sketch of it as *Le moineau apprivoisé*, which, to judge by the engraving of it by Daullé, is also likely to have dated from after

5. Sheet with *Boy Holding a Basket* (not recorded, but presumed to have been the intermediate stage between Abraham Bloemaert's *Peasant Boy Holding a Basket* in the Frits Lugt Collection, Fondation Custodia, Institut Néerlandais, Paris, and Boucher's etching in the *Livre d'Etude*, no. 10 (fig. 114; J-R 184).

Boucher's return (*Cabinet d'un Artiste* [M. Martin, Peintre], 13 Dec. ff. 1773, lot 173; Saint-Aubin's copy in the collection of Mr. and Mrs. Charles Wrightsman, New York).

We know nothing for certain of Boucher's output in Rome, but as a self-financed student at the Academy without a protector, he is likely neither to have had anyone to send such paintings back to, nor to have been able to afford the materials to paint them and the costs of their transport. He is far more likely to have made drawn studies on the spot, which he would then have been able to exploit after his return home.

In the case of the present picture we have two drawings that would appear to have served as the basis of the composition. The first of these, in the Cabinet des Estampes of the Bibliothèque Nationale in Paris (fig. 109; A & W 101/6, fig. 396), is of the same format and adopts the same viewpoint as the painting, but differs from it in several small particulars, and quite radically in its foreground and staffage. The second drawing, in the Cabinet des Dessins of the Louvre (fig. 110; Guiffrey & Marcel, II, 1908, no. 1409; Slatkin, 1971[b], pp. 399–400, pl. 41), is vertical rather than horizontal, and also differs from the painting in a number of little details, but otherwise faithfully echoes its foreground elements and human and animal staffage. The natural assumption would be that the first is a study from nature and the second, as Regina Slatkin maintained, a "precise design" for the painting. The truth would appear to be a little more complex.

The drawing in the Cabinet des Estampes would indeed appear to belong to a group of three drawings actually done in Rome, the other two both inscribed *Roma 1730*: the *View of Tivoli* in the Rijksprentenkabinett, Amsterdam (exh. cat. 1974, Amsterdam, no. 14) and the *Study of a Waterfall* in the Städelsches Kunstinstitut in Frankfurt (A & W fig. 256). But even these have the appearance of worked-up compositions done back in the studio rather than simple depictions done on the spot: the inscriptions indeed denote them as finished works. Not that Boucher appears to have taken many liberties with his motif in the case of the drawing in the Cabinet des Estampes, to judge from Vasi's engraving of *La Chiesa di S. Maria Liberatrice*, taken from a very similar viewpoint

Fig. 109. *View of the Farnese Gardens*. Cabinet des Estampes, Bibliothèque Nationale.

Fig. 110. *View of the Farnese Gardens with Two Cowherds*. Cabinet des Dessins, Louvre.

Fig. 111. *La Chiesa di S. Maria Liberatrice*, engraved by Giuseppe Vasi.

Fig. 112. *Two Studies of a Seated Cowherd (after Abraham Bloemaert)*. Musée des Beaux-Arts, Orléans.

Fig. 113. *Standing Cow*. Nationalmuseum, Stockholm.

Fig. 114. *Studies of a Boy Holding a Basket and a Seated Girl*, etched by Boucher after Abraham Bloemaert (1735).

(fig. 111). What he did was simply to suppress features in the foreground—the enclosing wall in front, and S. Maria Liberatrice (alias S. Maria Antiqua) to the right—which detracted from the rusticity of the site. This process he took even further in the drawing in the Cabinet des Dessins, and in the present painting, by substituting a tumbledown thatched hut for the bastion between the church and the villa.

Particularly instructive is the difference between the staffage of the two drawings. Whereas the early drawing is enlivened by a small boy with a windswept head, similar in character to those in such early paintings as the pair of *Noah* subjects (cat. 10, 11) and *La fontaine* (fig. 85), the later drawing and the present painting are peopled by two substantial figures of peasant lads that make direct use of Boucher's copies of drawings by Abraham Bloemaert (fig. 112; see Slatkin, 1971[b], and 1976, pls. 1, 2), which he then went on to etch in 1735 (fig. 114; J-R 176–186, esp. nos. 182, 184). There is also a study by Boucher for the foremost cow, in the Nationalmuseum in Stockholm, as Ananoff first noticed (fig. 113; A & W 101/4, fig. 401). What does not seem to have been appreciated is that this is no more a direct study from the life than are the two cowherds: the way in which it is cut off at the legs and shaded indicates that it too must be a study from another work of art—in this case no doubt a Dutch painting that has yet to be identified.

It is this combination of a slightly capriccio view of a romantic Italian site and the rustic (if borrowed) realism of the Dutch staffage that gives this painting its particular charm. Knowledge of the various designs that contributed to its genesis enables us to see, as with almost no other early work by Boucher, the way in which even his most "naturalistic" phase was the product of considerable artistic preparation and manipulation. This may help us to comprehend better the supposedly contrasted "artificiality" of his later landscapes.

Beverly Schreiber Jacoby is cited in the catalogue of the Linsky Collection (Metropolitan Museum, 1984, p. 120) as opining that the drawing in the Cabinet des Dessins and its pendant *View of Tivoli* were done after this painting and the picture in Stockholm respectively. This would have been an unparalleled procedure by Boucher, but while only oblong versions of the two compositions were known, it was a not unreasonable assumption. Now that another version of the *View of Tivoli*, with an upright format, has been discovered in the Musée des Beaux-Arts in Boulogne (cat. 16), however, it is less plausible. Instead, we are faced with the question as to whether there might not also be or have been an upright version of the present painting, forming a pendant to the Boulogne picture, as in the case of the two drawings. There is no record of such a thing (unless such were the two pictures in the Williot sale in 1788; see cat. 16, Analogies 4)—or indeed of any other version of the present picture—while both the inherent quality and the dated signature of this make it unlikely that it is in any way a repetition.

It is worth noting that the buildings of the Farnese Gardens appear, observed from a different viewpoint, in a capriccio *View of a Stone Bridge*, bearing a partial signature, *fran.*, whose decipherment as a fragment of *françois Boucher* is by no means self-evident, to judge by reproductions of the picture (A & W 102; Sotheby's, London, 1 Nov. 1978, lot 34; Galerie Koller, Zurich, 18 Nov. 1983, lot 5065).

# 24 | *Les génies des Beaux-Arts*

Oil on canvas
40 × 51½ in. (102 × 130.5 cm)
Signed bottom right: *Boucher*
Musée des Beaux-Arts, Troyes
(inv. 835.8)
S & M 916    A & W 67

PROVENANCE
Château de La Chapelle-Godefroy; confiscated
in 1793; entered the Troyes museum in 1835.

This is a putto picture of a slightly more conventional kind than *Putti Playing with Birds* (cat. 15) since here the cupids and infants are more clearly allegorical, being emblematic of the fine arts. The presence of a winged child not engaged in the practice of any art himself, with one hand resting on a quiver, who should probably be seen as Cupid, would appear to carry the implication that Love is the motive force of Art (see exh. cat. 1982–83, Dijon, p. 261).

This is the first of several depictions of putti embodying the arts by Boucher, of which the most ambitious and superb is the painting in the Musées d'Angers (A & W 545, wrongly locating it in Amiens), which was painted in 1761 to be translated into tapestry by the Gobelins. The presence of a sketched-in oval painting with a medallion of Louis XV at the center, implies that it is thanks to royal patronage that the arts flourish.

Some such message might well have been anticipated from the present picture, since it was apparently painted for Philibert Orry (1689–1747), *contrôleur général des Finances* from 1730, and *directeur général des Bâtiments du Roi* from 1737 until his disgrace in 1745. It was, however,

24

Fig. 115. *L'Eté*, engraved by P. Aveline, after a destroyed painting by Natoire formerly in the Château de La Chapelle-Godefroy.

painted for his country retreat, the Château de La Chapelle-Godefroy near Nogent-sur-Seine, the iconography of whose decoration appears to have been almost wholly hedonistic but for the unusually precocious cycle of six paintings from French medieval history telling the life of Clovis. The present picture was recorded in the inventory taken when the château was confiscated at the Revolution as "enfants avec les attributs de la peinture," serving as an overdoor in the *antichambre du Roi et de la Reine,* where the sovereign and his consort were received on their visits in 1740 and 1744 (I am most grateful to M. Jean-Pierre Sainte-Marie for communicating this information to me, from the entry in his forthcoming catalogue of pictures in the Musées de Troyes).

Virtually all the pictorial decoration of La Chapelle-Godefroy was by Natoire (see exh. cat. 1977, Troyes, esp. pp. 54–60; Sainte-Marie, 1977, pp. 14–20). It is therefore not immediately apparent why Orry should have commissioned this one picture from his rival. It would be nice to think that it was to celebrate his appointment as *directeur général des Bâtiments,* since one of his first acts in office was to encourage the arts by reviving annual exhibitions in the Salon of the Louvre. This painting can scarcely, however, be datable as late as 1737. It is much more likely to date from the time when Natoire was executing his first paintings for La Chapelle-Godefroy, in 1731, or shortly thereafter. Orry might thus have been trying out the two young artists, both recently returned from Rome, before deciding to give all his patronage to Natoire. The latter painted three pictures devoted to Cupid among the set of nine mythological paintings comprising his first commission, including the *Cupid Scattering Flowers* in the museum in Troyes (Sainte-Marie, 1977, fig. p. 16), and Orry may simply have preferred his more orthodox, light-bathed, Lemoinean manner. There is always the possibility that the present picture was not painted for Orry, but for one of the subsequent owners of the château, the de Boullongne. They, however, only seem to have introduced pictures by their painter forebears, or specially commissioned works, such as the Cl-Fr. Desportes *View of the Grand Avenue with Hounds and Dead Game* (1768). The probable date of the present picture, as well as its subject and the fact that it was fixed as an overdoor, makes it far more likely to have been a commission from Orry.

The bust being sculpted by the putto at the center of the picture is of some interest. In most subsequent depictions of the theme Boucher was to employ the bust known as the *Fillette aux nattes* by Saly, whose recurrent use in Boucher's paintings, particularly those for Mme de Pompadour, has never been satisfactorily explained (see Benisovitch, 1945; Beaulieu, 1955; Levey, 1965).

In the present, earlier, painting Boucher employed the Antique bust known as the *Vestale Zingarella,* now in the Louvre (see Clarac, VI, 1853, p. 193, pl. 1105), which inspired heads in depictions by other artists as various as that in G. M. Crespi's *Charon Ferrying the Dead* and Canova's busts of *Vestals.* The precise significance of this bust in the present context is not wholly clear, but there is an obvious piquancy in the coupling of the god of Love with the bust of a priestess vowed to virginity.

# 25 | The Rape of Europa

Oil on canvas, *en camaïeu brun*
20 × 24 in. (51 × 61 cm)
Musée de Picardie, Amiens
S & M 143        A & W 103

PROVENANCE
*Catalogue d'une petite Collection de Tableaux
. . . &c. provenans du Cabinet de M. V\*\*\**
[Vallet: possibly identifiable with the goldsmith Vallat, the owner of a house at Pierre-
fitte, "lié intimement avec les Artistes les plus
distingués en Architecture, Peinture, & autres
Arts utiles," who designed and executed for
him an additional "sallon spacieux . . . que le
célebre Boucher voulut encore enrichir des
chefs-d'oeuvres de son pinceau" (Piganiol de la
Force, 1765, IX, pp. 328–29) ], Grands-
Augustins (Joullain & Chariot), 7 Apr. ff.
1774, lot 40; one of posthumous Marcille sales,
1857 (S & M 143); Lavalard coll., Amiens;
given to the Musée de Picardie in 1894.

RELATED SKETCH
?Dandré-Bardon's posthumous sale, 23 June
ff. 1783, lot 6, grisaille on paper, 14 × 18½ in.

FINISHED PICTURE
François Derbais, rue Poissonnière, *salle de
billard* (according to his *inventaire après décès*,
2 Mar. 1743); Watelet's posthumous sale, 12
June ff. 1786, lot 12; Bruslé & de Morny sale,
Paris, 16–17 Dec. 1841, lot 61; Paul Périer sale,
16–17 Mar. 1843, lot 56 [bought by Lord
Hertford]; thence, by descent and bequest, to
the Wallace Collection.

ENGRAVINGS OF FINISHED PICTURE
    1. *Enlèvement d'Europe*, by Pierre Aveline
(J-R 248–249; advertised in *Mercure de
France*, June 1748; exhibited in the Salon,
1753; in reverse of painting).
    2. *La Terre*, by Louis Jacob (after Aveline, in
reverse, simplified, and with putto supporting
basket of fruit substituted for the bull and the
three figures on the left).
    3. *Enlèvement d'Europe*, by Edmé Bovinet
(J-R 392; after Aveline, in reverse, A & W
fig. 414).

PREPARATORY DRAWINGS
Oblong drawings of this subject are recorded
in pen and wash (Lempereur sale, 24 May ff.
1773, lot 534; sale of "Un Artiste" [Clisorius],
31 Mar. ff. 1795, 10 × 15 in.); red chalk (de
Sireul sale, 3 Dec. ff. 1781, lot 86, 10 × 15½
in.), and red and black chalk (ibid., lot 87, 12½
× 18 in.), but without sufficient indications to
decide whether they were for the present
picture or for that in the 1747 composition
(cat. 54). Some slight indication that the draw-

It cannot be disguised that at this point, because of the restrictive
interpretation put upon the terms of Lady Wallace's bequest to the British
Nation by the Law Officers of the Crown, there is a gaping hole in this
exhibition. The two major pictures of Boucher's early maturity, *Mercury
Confiding the Infant Bacchus* and the *Rape of Europa* (figs. 39, 116), the
latter of which was the only work of Boucher's to be singled out for
specific mention by Mariette (I, 1851–53, p. 165), cannot be borrowed.
    It is worth quoting in full what Mariette says of these pictures:

One could say that he [Boucher] was born with a brush in his hand.
One only has to look at what he painted in his youth, and in particular
at that Rape of Europa owned by M. Watelet, which was one of a
number of large pictures that he had painted for a marble mason called
Dorbay, who had furnished his whole house with them, which was
perfectly easy for him to do, since Boucher, not seeking to do anything
but make a name for himself at that period, would, I believe, have done
them for nothing rather than pass up the opportunity. I admire that
picture every time that I study it. Everything in it is admirable—above
all a brush manipulated with as much decision as grace. (*On peut dire
qu'il est né le pinceau à la main. Il ne faut que voir ce qu'il a peint dans
sa jeunesse, et en particulier cet enlevement d'Europe qu'a M. Watelet et
qui faisoit partie du nombre de grands tableaux qu'il avoit fait pour un
sculpteur marbrier nommé Dorbay qui en avoit garni toute sa maison, ce
qui lui avoit été très-facile, car Boucher, ne cherchant alors qu'à se faire
connoître, les auroit, je crois, faits pour rien, plus tost que d'en laisser
manquer l'occasion. J'admire ce tableau toutes les fois que je le considère.
Tout y est admirable, et surtout un pinceau aussi ferme qu'il est
gracieux.*)

As has been said earlier, it is hard to see what the advantage of this
arrangement was for Boucher. Were one not to have known the pictures in
question (see cat. 17, 18), one would have taken this account to mean that
Boucher was painting pictures for a patron of inferior social standing, for
virtually nothing, at the very outset of his career. It is evident, however,
that he painted them after his return from Italy, when he was already
almost thirty, with several years' practice as a painter behind him. Only
the four putti pictures were engraved in Derbais's lifetime, so it was not in
this way that Boucher's prowess received publicity. The crucial word in
Mariette is, however, "large."
    It is above all a change in scale that sets off the pictures that Boucher
painted after his return from Italy from those that he had painted before
going there, and with this change in scale came a new breadth and
boldness of treatment. One of the problems for the aspiring painter in

25

ing in the Lempereur sale was for the present composition may be gleaned from the fact that a fan design of this subject by Boucher in the same sale (lot 538; A & W fig. 413, whereabouts unstated) draws upon it rather than upon the other picture. S & M 497 identifies the first of the two Lempereur drawings with one in india ink in the sale of M. E***, 4–5 June 1874, lot 28; this was in a rich ornamental surround, and can therefore be excluded.

France in those years was precisely that the opportunities for large-scale painting were diminishing: as La Font de Saint-Yenne (1747, p. 19) and Caylus (see Rosenberg, 1984[c], p. 61) observed, ceilings painted with pictures had been replaced, first by painted grotesques, and then by their equivalent in gilt stucco on white. At the same time, as père Laugier (1753, pp. 61–62), the abbé Le Blanc (1753, pp. 154–55), and abbé Gougenot (1748, pp. 136–37) decried, hung pictures by contemporary artists were being elbowed out, either by the taste for carved boiseries and large looking glasses, or by the taste for old masters. Even among those few who did set aside galleries for the display of their paintings, small Dutch cabinet pictures had the preference, and it was noted as a singularity in La Live de Jully that he made a point of collecting the contemporary "Ecole Françoise."

In these circumstances, a house in which his new large-scale paintings could be seen—precisely because of their owner's unexalted social standing, visits by interested clients would presumably have been easier to arrange—would have been an asset to Boucher; all the more so in that he

Fig. 116. *The Rape of Europa.* Wallace Collection, London.

Fig. 117. Sketch for *Mercury Confiding the Infant Bacchus.* Private collection.

could demonstrate his ability to adorn a whole room with them, to maintain his own against the new modes of decoration. The room in which they were placed in Derbais's house was the *salle de billard,* according to the *inventaire après décès* of the owner taken on 2 March 1743, generously communicated to me by Georges Brunel. This, to deduce from the subjects of the pictures, was exclusively adorned with paintings by Boucher: the *Rape of Europa* and the *Birth of Bacchus* (the pair of pictures now in the Wallace Collection); large pictures of *Aurora and Cephalus* (cat. 18) and *Venus Requesting Vulcan for Arms* (cat. 17); another large picture of the *Birth of Venus* (almost certainly the picture last recorded in the possession of the comtesse de Béhague: A & W 180, whose true dimensions, 250 × 300 cm, are recorded by Fenaille, 1925, p. 55, and which is clearly contemporaneous with the *Aurora and Cephalus*); and an overdoor of *Cupids.*

It is tantalizing only to be able to allude to the full-scale versions of the present sketch and its pendant (fig. 117). Something of their revolutionary freedom of handling can, however, be imagined both from this sketch and from their former companions (cat. 17, 18). Of the two, the *Rape of Europa* is the more brilliant performance, and it is evidently the picture that most struck Boucher's contemporaries. Not only do we have the remarks of Mariette quoted above, there is also a reference, which seems to have gone unnoticed, to one of the most striking parts of the picture in Bachaumont's advice to Boucher when he came to paint *Psyche Snatched from the Wilderness by Zephyrs:* "You paint Landscape like an Angel. I can hear from here the sound of the waterfall; remember carefully everything that you did at Mr. Derbais's" ("*Vous faite le Paysage comme un Ange. J'entends d'icy le bruit du torrent; souvenés vous bien de tout ce que vous avés fait ché M. d'Herbais*" [A & W doc. 130, quoted from a manuscript in the Bibliothèque de l'Arsenal]). The waterfall can only be that in the background to the left of the Wallace picture, which is already indicated in the present sketch. It is, indeed, the introduction of strikingly picturesque landscape details that distinguishes the two Wallace pictures—above all the *Rape of Europa*—from the *Venus and Vulcan* and *Aurora and Cephalus,* and from the putti pictures, and which suggests an advance over them. The *Europa* is additionally enriched by the inclusion of an astonishing profusion of vivid flowers: a detail that is not only inevitably absent from the present very summary sketch but may also have been an afterthought, since the most significant change between sketch and finished picture is in the position and pose of the cupid holding on to the garland around the bull's neck.

Hermann Voss detected a lapse of several years between the execution of the *Europa* and the *Bacchus* (1953, p. 86), with the former appearing to him richer and warmer in coloring, and more fluid and painterly in execution, making it the earlier—because the more traditional—of the two. Some difference between the two paintings there indeed is, and it is underlined by the differing character of the two sketches for them, but the time lapse should not be exaggerated, nor is it certain that the sequence perceived by Voss is the right one. Whereas the concentration upon the figural group in the *Bacchus* attaches it to the preceding *Venus and Vulcan* and *Aurora and Cephalus,* the landscape elements of the *Europa* look forward to those in the *Leopard Hunt* of 1736 (cat. 29).

The difference in character between the sketches for the two compositions does not simply reside in the fact that the present sketch is monochrome, and the slightly larger sketch for the *Bacchus* polychrome (New York art market; 58.5 × 73.5 cm; exh. cat. 1982, Tokyo, no. 9, color pl.). The *Bacchus* sketch is executed in a technique more reminiscent of the early finished pictures themselves, with emphatic dragging of the brushstrokes in the flesh and drapery, and with startling applications of color, particularly the reds. The present chocolate-brown sketch is not only put on with a more liquid and loaded brush, many of the figures are outlined with the brush in black rather than modeled—an emphatic technique that was to be adopted in coarser form by Boucher's pupil and son-in-law Deshays—with white heightening employed in a similar way to a chalk drawing. Of the two techniques, it was the monochrome sketch *en camaïeu brun* or *en grisaille* that Boucher was to adopt the more frequently, apparently preferring to work in the warmer tonalities of brown when preparing designs for paintings and tapestries, and working in a more precise technique in gray when making designs for the engraver (see the remarks in exh. cat. 1983–84, Rotterdam, no. 57). The present sketch may be only an adumbration of the finished painting in the Wallace Collection, but in boldness yet sureness of touch it is an astonishing performance in its own right.

# 26 | *Rinaldo and Armida*

Oil on canvas
53½ × 67 in. (135.5 × 170.5 cm)
Musée du Louvre, Paris (inv. 2720)
S & M 256      A & W 108

PROVENANCE
Académie Royale de Peinture et de Sculpture, Paris; Musée Napoléon, and thus to its successor, the Musée du Louvre.

PREPARATORY SKETCH
*Notice de Tableaux . . . &c. provenant du Cabinet de M. L[emonnier], Peintre, membre de l'ancienne Académie Royale de Peinture & de Sculpture*, his apartment, rue de Vaugirard no. 9 (Regnault de Lalande), 26 Nov. 1810, lot 2, 12 *pouces* × 16½ *pouces*; *Cabinet d'un amateur*, Paris, 18 Jan. 1860, lot 10.

COPIES
1. Unframed picture brought to the Hôtel de Pompadour (l'Elysée) after Mme de Pompadour's death, and placed in the *antichambre* (Cordey, 1939, p. 84, no. 1163).
2. Sèvres porcelain plaque signed *d'après F. Boucher, Dodin en 1783*, presently let into the front of a *secrétaire à abattant* by Bernard Molitor, in the Henry E. Huntington Library and Art Gallery, San Marino, California (see

This is the obligatory picture that Boucher painted to secure his reception as a full member of the Académie Royale de Peinture et de Sculpture on 30 January 1734. As was not infrequent with such productions, the picture is in some ways more a reflection of the Academy's expectations than of Boucher's particular gifts. The literary subject is not of the kind to which he was often drawn; an architectural setting (here with Rubensian banded columns, such as were also used by Watteau, prominent in the foreground) was not a device that he cared to employ thereafter; and the painting is crammed with so much incident—armor, tiger skin, curtain, mirror, flowers, sculpture, etc.—to display his virtuosity that it appears congested to the point of confusion.

The strengths of the picture are the parts of it that were to be more characteristic of his regular output: the provocative half-draped figure of Armida, and the lively putti seized in striking poses. Interestingly, almost every attitude of the figures is closely echoed in some other painting: that of Armida resembles the pose of Europa in the *Rape of Europa* in the Wallace Collection, inclined to the right rather than to the left; that of Rinaldo employs in reverse the pose of the boy with the parsnips in *Le*

26

Wilson, 1977[b]), but originally set in the center of a *table-guéridon* surrounded by grisaille plaques of other episodes from the romance, given to the Duke of Sachsen-Teschen by Louis XVI in 1786 (see Cohen, 1980, p. 6 no. 2). A copy of the tabletop, giving an idea of the original arrangement, sold at Sotheby's, London, 6 July 1984. (I am most grateful to Miss Rosalind Savill for extensive help with this item.) Boucher's picture was lent to Sèvres by the Académie Royale, evidently for this purpose, on 1 Dec. 1783 (Fontaine, 1910, p. 79 n. 2).

*retour du marché* (fig. 119), with his left hand to his breast rather than outstretched, and is repeated in the pose of the ardent suitor in *Les charmes de la vie champêtre* (fig. 49; Louvre); that of the cupid in the foreground resembles, again in reverse, that of the foremost cupid in *Les génies des Beaux-Arts* (cat. 24); that of the cupid supporting the mirror is echoed in the pose of the bottom putto in the grisaille of *Charity* in the *chambre de la Reine* at Versailles; and that of the half-concealed cupid holding the arrow recurs in *Le sommeil de Vénus* (A & W 173; since sold at Sotheby's Monaco, 26 Oct. 1981, lot 548). The effect of such a concentrated display of contrived attitudes only enhances the feeling of a certain excess.

The theme chosen by Boucher was one of the most frequently depicted episodes in literature. It is taken from Torquato Tasso's *Gerusalemme Liberata*, the romanticized account of the First Crusade, in which the Circe-like Saracen maiden Armida, having fallen in love with the Crusader Rinaldo, keeps him in her enchanted domain. Two other Crusaders, Carlo and Ubaldo, set out to rescue him, and the moment shown is of their coming upon him gazing at his own love-struck reflection in Armida's eyes, while she sees hers reflected in a mirror. The elaborate architecture stands for her enchanted palace, while the cupid holding an arrow that points at Rinaldo underscores the latter's lovelorn state.

In choosing such an oft-depicted episode, Boucher was not simply measuring himself against a long European pictorial tradition, he was choosing a theme depicted by many of his seniors in France: notably the just-deceased *premier Peintre*, Louis de Boullongne (in a recently rediscovered painting of 1704, exh. cat. 1985, New York, no. 7), and Jean-Baptiste Vanloo (Musée des Beaux-Arts d'Angers, from the collection of the marquis de Livois). Louis de Boullongne's painting was used as the basis for a tapestry (Fenaille, III, 1904, p. 124 and pl.), and immediately after Boucher's *morceau de réception*, Charles-Antoine Coypel was likewise to start painting a series of enormous pictures of episodes from the story of Rinaldo and Armida for the *Fragments d'Opéra* woven by the Gobelins (Fenaille, III, 1904, pp. 323–44); while Boucher himself subsequently proposed another series to the Gobelins in 1751 (Fenaille, III, 1904, p. 328) and executed a cartoon of *Rinaldo Asleep* for Beauvais, which was first woven in 1752 (Badin, 1909, p. 62; A & W 384). Much earlier in his career, Boucher had made a copy sketch of J-F. de Troy's depiction of the preceding episode, of *Armida Struck with Love for Rinaldo when about to Kill Him* (de Sireul sale, 3 Dec. ff. 1781, lot 28), which may be identifiable with one or the other of the sketches supposedly for this painting, that in the Musée des Beaux-Arts, Lille (fig. 17; exh. cat. 1975, Brussels, no. 30), or that in an English private collection on loan to the New Mexico Art Museum (fig. 18; see exh. cat. 1980, Albuquerque, no. 63). When in Rome, he also appears to have drawn a hasty sketch of *Carlo and Ubaldo Surprising Rinaldo*, which subsequently remained with Subleyras and passed for his (exh. cat. 1983, Paris, no. 115).

The reasons for the popularity of the story in France were less purely literary than theatrical: *Armide et Renaud* was the most successful of all the operas set to music by Lully. Known as the *opéra des dames*, it was first produced in 1686, but was revived no fewer than eight times up until 1761, as well as being the object of three parodies (Chouquet, 1873, pp. 321–22). Boucher himself collaborated with his son on the sets for the 1761 staging of it (see Dacier, 1920, pp. 14–16, 104), and may have designed sets for the 1746 and 1747 revivals, since these fell within his second period of employment by the Opéra (see E. & J. de Goncourt, 1881, p. 223). In its choice of theme the present picture was thus not merely the gauge of his acceptance by the artistic establishment—it was also a manifesto of his future polymorphic activity as a designer.

# 27 | *Le bonheur au village*

Oil on canvas
96 × 100 in. (243 × 254 cm)
Signed on plank, bottom center:
*f. Boucher*
Bayerische Landesbank, on deposit in the
Alte Pinakothek, Munich (BGM 2)
S & M 1472       A & W 41

PROVENANCE
*Catalogue de Quatre Tableaux, Chefs
d'Oeuvre peints par François Boucher, provenant de l'Hôtel du duc de Richelieu, dont ils
décoraient le salon de réception*, Hôtel des
Ventes, Paris, 18 May 1852, lots 1–4 [bought
for 15,850 francs by M. de Rothschild]; baron
Edmond de Rothschild, Paris; divided between
his heirs:
  *Le retour du marché* and *L'heureux pêcheur*
passed to baron Alphonse de Rothschild;
Robert Lebel, Paris (1954); Walter P. Chrysler
Jr. (by 1956), who sold *L'heureux pêcheur* at
Christie's, London, 26 June 1970, lot 87,
whence it was acquired by the Frick Art
Museum in Pittsburgh, but made *Le retour du
marché* over to the Chrysler Museum in 1971.
  *Le bonheur au village* and *La halte à la
fontaine* passed to baron Edmond de Roth-
schild, from whom acquired, via Colnaghi's,
London, by the Bayerische Landesbank in
1976.

ENGRAVING
*Le retour du marché* engraved as the central
motif in an ornamental design for the leaf of a
folding screen, under the title *Triomphe de
Pomone*, by Cochin *fils*, [completed?] in February 1737, and published by the veuve
Chereau and Huquier (J-R 517–518).

DRAWINGS
For *Le retour du marché*
  1. *Studies for the Head, Legs, and Hands of
the Boy Proffering Parsnips*, red chalk heightened with white on buff paper, 260 × 360
mm, Antoine Vollon coll.; Léon Michel-Lévy's
posthumous sale, Galerie Georges Charpentier, Paris, 17 June 1925, lot 33 [AA 537 and
fig. 99; A & W fig. 360].
  2. *Standing Servant Girl*, red chalk heightened with white on brownish gray paper, 353
× 224 mm, acquired by Count Carl Gustaf
Tessin in Paris, 1739–42; Åkerö (1749 cat.,
livré 14, no. 91); Kongl. Biblioteket, Stockholm (1790 cat. no. 2820); transferred to
Kongl. [now National] Museum, Stockholm,
in 1863 (inv. 2927/1863) [AA 131 and fig. 27;
A & W fig. 359; Bjurström, 1982, no. 836]
(fig. 121).

This picture belongs to a now-scattered set of four that must once have
formed one of the most remarkable decorative ensembles produced by
Boucher in his earlier years. In the event, it has for various reasons proved
possible to borrow only one of these village pastorals, which is all the
more regrettable in that they have never been shown publicly together
since their first emergence at auction in the mid-nineteenth century.
Because confusion reigns over the identity of the four pictures that form
the set, and because they cannot sensibly be discussed in isolation from
one another, all four will be treated in this entry.

The set falls into two pairs of pendants. The larger, almost square pair,
*Le bonheur au village* (cat. 27) and *La halte à la fontaine* (fig. 118), are still
together, on loan from the Bayerische Landesbank to the Alte Pinakothek.
The narrower pair, of the same height but only approximately five and a
half feet (170 cm) wide, was sundered by Walter P. Chrysler, Jr., who
retained *Le retour du marché* (fig. 119) for the Chrysler Museum,
Norfolk, Virginia, but sent *L'heureux pêcheur* (fig. 120) for auction,
whence it was acquired by the Frick Art Museum in Pittsburgh.

The original location of this set of pictures is an enigma. They first
made their appearance, as the only paintings, in a sale held in Paris in
1852, with their dimensions given but no description beyond that implicit
in their titles, and accompanied by the assertion that they had adorned the
*salon de réception* of the duc de Richelieu. Hence, in part, the numerous
confusions as to which pictures had constituted the set after it was broken
up, including Ananoff and Wildenstein's strained attempt to associate
*L'heureux pêcheur* and *Le retour du marché* with the two paintings of a
whole generation later from baron d'Ivry's collection (here cat. 79 and 80),
in support of their equally farfetched yoking together of four other
pictures of disparate origins and date (A & W 70, 681, 682, 683) and their
assertion that these had formed the decoration of another room in the
maréchal-duc de Richelieu's *hôtel* (A & W II, pp. 307–09).

The 1852 sale catalogue itself contained the decidedly fantasizing
statement that the four pictures "were painted expressly by Boucher for
the duc de Richelieu, the joyous companion of his pleasures" ("*ont éte
peints expressément par Boucher pour le duc de Richelieu, le joyeux
compagnon de ses plaisirs*"), which should perhaps caution one against
accepting uncritically the further statement that: "Until this day they were
the principal adornment of the main salon of the Hôtel de Richelieu"
("*Jusqu'à ce jour, ils ont fait l'ornement principal du grand salon de l'hôtel
de Richelieu*")—all the more so in view of the similarly pretentious, but in
the event spurious, provenance from the Folie de Chartres attached to

27

Fig. 118. *Le halte à la fontaine*. Bayerische Landesbank, on deposit in the Alte Pinakothek, Munich.

Fig. 119. *Le retour du marché*. Chrysler Museum, Norfolk, Virginia.

Fig. 120. *L'heureux pêcheur*. The Frick Art Museum, Pittsburgh.

another set of pictures by Boucher in a sale some years before (see cat. 49 and 50).

For, as Denys Sutton has implied (exh. cat. 1980, New York, no. 36; repeated almost verbatim in exh. cat. 1982, Tokyo, no. 6), the supposed provenance from the Hôtel de Richelieu presents problems. The building that most commonly went under that name was the former Hôtel de Travers, or d'Antin, in the rue Louis-le-Grand. But this was only acquired by the *maréchal* in 1756. What is more, it was divided into lodgings in 1824, and demolished in 1839—too long before the sale for the claim of the catalogue that the paintings had "until this day" adorned the Hôtel de Richelieu to be applicable. Prior to acquiring the Hôtel d'Antin, the maréchal de Richelieu had lived in what are now numbers 21 and 23 of the Place des Vosges, but since he sold it when he moved and it had had a succession of proprietors thereafter, it is unlikely to have retained his name in the mid-nineteenth century. He never inhabited the other *hôtel* he owned, on the Quai de Béthune, which came to him from his stepmother-cum-mother-in-law, Marguérite-Thérèse de Rouillé. The *hôtel* in the rue neuve des Mathurins inhabited by the then duc de Richelieu up until the Revolution of 1848, not having been one that had belonged to the *maréchal*, any provenance from there would scarcely substantiate the claim that the fixed decorations in it had belonged to the latter.

Nonetheless, it is with reluctance that one abandons the purported provenance of this set of pictures from the house best known as the Hôtel de Richelieu. Not because of the supposed personal liaison between Boucher and the *maréchal*, who seems to have had neither the leisure nor the resources from his embassies and campaigns to commission extensive decorations until the acquisition of this *hôtel* in the rue Louis-le-Grand, but because of its previous proprietor, the duc d'Antin. Not only were the improvements that he made to the Hôtel de Travers extensive and celebrated, but from 1708 until his death in 1736 he was *directeur général des Bâtiments du Roi*. It is true that, as such, it was he who, through his partiality to his favorites already there, had denied Boucher the funds to take up his scholarship in Rome (Cochin, 1880, p. 100), but there are signs that before his death his attitude had relented, and that he had come to appreciate Boucher's talents. For it was while he was still *directeur général* that Boucher had not only been invited to decorate the *chambre de la Reine* at Versailles with four grisailles of the *Virtues*, but also—since d'Antin did not die until late 1736—that he was asked to contribute the *Leopard Hunt* (cat. 29) to the *galerie des petits appartements du Roi*. It is tempting to wonder whether d'Antin did not himself enjoy the first fruits of Boucher's talents before allowing him to work for the Crown, and whether such a significant commission as that represented by the present set of pictures does not owe its origin to such an important client.

The difficulties with this hypothesis—which is purely speculative at best—do not merely reside in the hiatus between the demolition of the Hôtel d'Antin/de Richelieu and the appearance at auction of the pictures. There is also the fact that, according to Patte (Piganiol de la Force, 1765, III, pp. 484–85), the duc de Richelieu had completely destroyed the grand rooms, in which such decorations as these might have been placed: "on a détruit & refait dans le gout regnant, c'est à dire petit & mesquin, la décoration des pieces, qui étoit grande & majestueuse." Furthermore,

165

For *Le bonheur au village*

1. *Man Embracing Servant Girl*, red chalk heightened with white on brownish-gray paper, 345 × 248 mm, acquired by Count C. G. Tessin in Paris, 1739–42; Åkerö (1749 cat., livré 14, no. 93); Kongl. Biblioteket, Stockholm (1790 cat. no. 2821); transferred to the Kongl. [now National] Museum, Stockholm in 1863 (inv. 2928/1863) [AA 217, fig. 38; A & W fig. 241; Bjurström 1982, no. 829] (fig. 122).

2. *Seated Woman Holding Long Handle*, red chalk counterproof, retouched, 343 × 228 mm, acquired by Count C. G. Tessin in Paris; Åkerö (1749 cat., livré 27, no. 188); Kongl. Biblioteket, Stockholm (1790 cat. no. 2822); transferred to Kongl. [now National] Museum in 1863 (inv. 2929/1863) [A & W fig. 242; Bjurström 1982, no. 831; as Ananoff and Wildenstein suggest, the pose of the woman in this drawing was inspired by another study made by Boucher, on the left half of a sheet now in the Albertina (inv. 12.174). This is not after Bloemaert, as they propose, however, but after a figure in the Bassano painting of *The Return of the Prodigal* in the Doria(-Pamphilj) Gallery in Rome, where Boucher must have studied] (fig. 123).

3. *A Seated and a Sleeping Child*, red and black chalk, 212 × 225 mm, acquired by Count C. G. Tessin in Paris, 1739–42; Åkerö (1749 cat., livré 14, no. 96); Kongl. Biblioteket, Stockholm (1790 cat. no. 2832); transferred to the Kongl. [now National] Museum in 1863 (inv. 2938/1863) [AA 17, fig. 2; A & W fig. 240; Bjurström 1982, no. 830] (fig. 124).

An elaborated version of this was engraved by Gilles-Antoine Demarteau as no. 562 in his deceased uncle's series, and advertised in Mar. 1777 (J-R 859).

For *La halte à la fontaine*

1. *Study of a Goat*, engraved in reverse by Lépicier [Bernard Lépicié] and published by Odieuvre, as *CHEVRE. 30* (fig. 125).

according to Bruno Pons (to whom I am most grateful for communicating to me the results of his research in the archives), there is no trace of any set of pictures such as these in the inventories taken on the deaths of either the duc d'Antin or the maréchal de Richelieu.

Thus, for the time being, unless and until something is found in the inventories taken in houses of the deceased, or of emigrés in the Revolution, we must remain in ignorance of the original destination of these paintings. It happens that in such inventories there is an otherwise untraced set of four paintings that it might have been very tempting to associate with these, the four *Paysages d'architecture et figures* confiscated from the Palais Royal for the Muséum Central in 1796 (Furcy-Raynaud, 1912, p. 314). But, whereas the height of these—7 *pieds* 2 *pouces*—is virtually exactly that of the present set of pictures, the width—4 *pieds*—is too narrow for any of them. Nor can one readily imagine the duc d'Orléans of the epoch when these pictures were painted, the Régent's devout son, Louis (1703–1752), ever having commissioned decorations of the kind (it was he who destroyed or mutilated his father's Correggios because of their eroticism). The pictures in question are thus much more likely to have been later works, commissioned by his son, the pleasure-loving Louis Philippe I, known as le Gros (1725–1785), whose own son Boucher had painted in 1749 (Waddesdon Manor; A & W 332).

That the present commission was an important one for Boucher is suggested not merely by the size of the paintings themselves and the wealth of effects crammed into them, but also by the number of studies for them that survive (see figs. 121–125). The handling of these, together with the early form of signature found on many of them (with a lowercase "b"), agree with the style of the paintings themselves to suggest a date in the first half of the 1730s—to somewhere between *Le repos des fermiers* (cat. 20) and the *Famille de villageois* (A & W 40), which, as I have argued, must have been executed shortly after Boucher's return from Italy, and the *Leopard Hunt* (cat. 29) of 1736. And though the background buildings in *Le bonheur au village* and *La halte à la fontaine*, and the classical ruins and umbrella pine in the latter, are carried over from the kind of capriccio Italian landscape that Boucher was doing in the years immediately after his return from Italy, up to at least 1734 (cat. 23), the broader handling and less intense coloring of these pictures (even allowing for their size and decorative function) suggest that they were painted much closer to the *Leopard Hunt* of 1736—and even, conceivably, between that and the *Crocodile Hunt* (cat. 32) of 1738/39. Their closest affinity—and especially that of *La halte à la fontaine*, with its combination of slightly exotic rustics and an Italianate setting—is with Boucher's earliest tapestry designs for Beauvais, the so-called *Fêtes Italiennes*, which he began supplying around 1735 (cf. cat. 37, 86–89).

A terminus ante quem for one picture in the set, *Le retour du marché*, is supplied by Cochin's *feuille de paravent* titled *Triomphe de Pomone* (J-R 517–518), which places the composition of *Le retour du marché* in an ornamental surround of rocaille and trelliswork. Cochin says that he engraved this in February 1737 (Jombert, 1770, p. 14, no. 38). It is, however, inscribed *Boucher inv.*, not *pinx.*, while Cochin also says that the composition was "dessinée" by Boucher, so that it seems fairly clear (as one would indeed expect) that his engraving was based on a drawing.

Fig. 121. *Standing Servant Girl.*
Nationalmuseum, Stockholm.

Fig. 122. *Man Embracing Servant Girl.*
Nationalmuseum, Stockholm.

Fig. 123. *Seated Woman Holding Long
Handle.* Nationalmuseum, Stockholm.

Fig. 124. *A Seated and a Sleeping Child.*
Nationalmuseum, Stockholm.

Fig. 125. *Study of a Goat*, engraved by
Lépicier (Bernard Lépicié) after Boucher.

However, the drawing cannot have been a preparation for the painting, but
rather an ornamental design based on it. That such was the case is
reinforced by the fact that another screen leaf in the same series, the
*Triomphe de Priape* engraved by Duflos (J-R 875), is partially based on the
earlier painting of *Putti Playing with a Goat*. What is more, the original
drawing for another of the screen leaves engraved by Duflos, *Rocaille*
(J-R 872), is now in the Ecole Nationale des Beaux-Arts (inv. 0.403; I am
most grateful to Peter Fuhring for sending a photocopy of this to me).
Another such drawing (last recorded in the collection of Maurice Fenaille
in 1932), which was engraved by Duflos as *Hommage Champêtre* (J-R
873), was centered around an amorous couple evidently originally
employed in the Beauvais tapestry, *La bohémienne*, which was first woven
in 1736 (cf. the juxtaposition of A & W figs. 462, 464), thus further
underlining the close temporal conjunction between the present pictures
and the set of tapestries known as the *Fêtes Italiennes*, of which *La
bohémienne* was a member.

In view of the time taken to make an engraving, Cochin's *Triomphe de
Pomone* suggests that *Le retour du marché* must have been painted by 1736
at the latest: probably not much before, in view of the affinities of its

central male protagonist with the *Kitchen Maid and Young Boy* (cat. 28), the pastel derived from which is dated 1738. The dating of one picture, however, does not necessarily determine that of the whole set. This was a large undertaking, and there is an evident evolution, not only in handling, but even in conception, within the series. It is difficult to pronounce on this now that the set has been broken up, but it would appear that *Le retour du marché*, which is richer in color, more crowded—especially with still life elements—in composition, and has one of Boucher's fantasy plants in the foreground, is the earliest of the four. This may not have been immediately followed by its more loosely painted pendant, *L'heureux pêcheur*, but rather by *Le bonheur au village*, which shares its kind of setting. Nevertheless, there is more that links the two Munich pictures together in handling than associates them with either of the other two pictures in the series. Of the two—though the repair of past damage may influence one's impression—*La halte à la fontaine* seems the more successfully composed and fluidly painted, indicating perhaps that it is the later. It is, however, *Le bonheur au village* which includes a figure reminiscent of the inspiration behind the earliest of Boucher's depictions of peasant life: the sleeping figure with a water flask, who looks as if he had come straight out of a picture by Abraham Bloemaert. The whole set of paintings marks a transitional moment between what might be called Boucher's *bambochades*, or straightforward peasant pictures, and his later, sentimental *Pastorales*.

# 28 | *Kitchen Maid and Young Boy*

Oil on canvas
34 × 49½ in. (87 × 125.5 cm)
Signed bottom right: *f. Boucher*
Dr. Feray, Sainte-Adresse

PROVENANCE

?*Notice de plusieurs beaux Tableaux . . .* , maison de feu M. Davoust (Basan), 27 Apr. 1772 [the handwritten breakdown of lot 9 in the copy in the Bibliothèque Nationale includes as (e) *Une cuisiniere avec un jeune homme par Boucher* (Boileau 261 livres 19 sous). This could, however, equally well have been the version on canvas of cat. 21]; Ch. E. Riche coll., Paris; Nouveau Drouot, Paris, 30 Mar. 1984, lot 58, acquired by present owner.

ANALOGY

*Bust of a Young Boy Holding a Parsnip* (occasionally described as a carrot), pastel, 306 × 242 mm, signed *f. Boucher 1738*; Dezallier d'Argenville's posthumous sale, 3 Mar. ff. 1766, lot 72 [sold for 14 livres 1 sol]; Randon de Boisset's posthumous sale, 27 Feb. ff. 1777,

In the mid-1730s it is evident that Boucher struck out in a number of different directions, before finding the kind of subject matter that was most congenial both to him and to his public. Thus, in addition to putti pictures and mythologies, we find him trying his hand at pastoral themes (see cat. 27), half-length *galant* subjects (cat. 19), quasi-Dutch interior scenes (cat. 21), and hybrid combinations of the last two, as in the present picture. Interestingly, as with his interiors, this appears to be a field where his experiments overlapped with Chardin's (see, above all, the *Woman Sealing a Letter* [1733?], Schloss Charlottenburg, Rosenberg, 1983 [b], no. 79; *Le Souffleur* [1734], Louvre, Rosenberg, 1983, no. 99; and a series of depictions of children at play, Rosenberg, 1983, nos. 97–112). But whereas Chardin from the first avoided the *galant* bias of Boucher's themes, and went on to minuter pictures with full-length figures, Boucher was to make *galant* themes the focus of his art in his pastorals, while expanding to the full-length treatment of figures still on a large scale.

28

lot 201 [bought with a Greuze pastel by Millon Dainval for 1101 livres]; Bruun-Neergaard sale, 29 Aug. ff. 1814, lot 45 [height misprinted; sold for 25.95 francs]; anon. sale, Palais Galliera, Paris, 7 Dec. 1970, lot 1; Art Institute of Chicago.

The present picture has not been universally accepted as a work of Boucher's since it was first published by Voss (1953, p. 90, fig. 66), despite its perfectly convincing signature, and in spite of the fact that, since Voss wrote, an evidently related pastel study of the *Boy Holding a Parsnip* has come to light (fig. 126; Art Institute of Chicago; see exh. cat. 1973–74, Washington, no. 32, color pl. p. xiv). The chief gainsayers of the picture, Ananoff and Wildenstein (A & W 83/6, p. 217), are indeed driven to assert that the signature and date on the pastel are spurious, and to doubt its authenticity, despite its exceedingly distinguished pedigree, and have come up with an unargued, and scarcely sustainable, attribution of the present painting to Bouys.

That there are weaknesses in the picture is undeniable. There is an area of damage around the play of hands in the center, and past ill-treatment of the paint surface may account for certain rather lifeless details, such as the suspended candles upper right and the pair of onions bottom left. In general, however, the touch of the brush is excitingly broad and free and can be compared with that of other paintings of the mid-1730s. The least satisfactory aspect of the picture is the profile head of the kitchen maid, but profiles were evidently something that could occasion difficulty to Boucher at this stage, as witness that of the *Woman Applying a Mouche* (fig. 43; exh. cat. 1980, London, Agnew's, no. 28). The treatment of half-length figures in general was something that he never resolved entirely satisfactorily—see also *La dame allant au bal* (London art market, A & W 113)—hence, perhaps, his ultimate abandonment of the genre.

It might be thought that the pastel of the *Boy Holding a Parsnip*, which is dated 1738, was a study for the picture, and thus provides a means of dating the latter. The careful signature and date, however, indicate what the finished character of the pastel itself suggests: that it is a composition in its own right. As in other instances in Boucher's oeuvre, it is much more likely that it took the bust of the boy in the painting as its point of departure, rather than the

Fig. 126. *Boy Holding a Parsnip* (1738). Art Institute of Chicago.

other way about. The breadth of handling of the present picture suggests that it should even date from one or two years before, from around the time of the ex-Hôtel de Richelieu village pastorals, with two of which, *Le bonheur au village* (see cat. 27; A & W 41, but unaware of provenance) and *Le retour du marché* (fig. 119; A & W 83), it has an obvious affinity of subject matter as well as of handling.

It is possible that the present picture was conceived with a pendant, for in its protagonists and dimensions (especially if its apparent truncation on top is taken into account) it comes very close to the *Boy and Girl Blowing Bubbles* in the Antenor Patiño collection (A & W 96). However, the fact that in both pictures the girl appears above and to the right of the boy probably militates against their having been hung together. The rapprochement, however, is a fruitful one, because it returns us to the parallel activity of Chardin, whose own composition of *Les bouteilles de savon* (Rosenberg, 1983[b], no. 97) was thought by Mariette to have been his first treatment of the human figure, even though the engraving of it was not made until 1739, and the picture was probably nearer to this date; whatever its exact date, it must have been closely contemporaneous with these experiments of Boucher's.

# 29 | *The Leopard Hunt*

Oil on canvas
68½ × 50¾ in. (174 × 129 cm)
Signed bottom right: *Boucher 1736*
Musée de Picardie, Amiens
S & M 1728          A & W 125

PROVENANCE
*Galerie des petits cabinets*, Versailles (installed 1736, dismounted 1767); ?Hôtel de la Surintendance, Versailles; sent by Napoleon to the Hôtel de Ville of Amiens for the peace negotiations of 1802; transferred to the Musée de Picardie in 1874.

ENGRAVING
*La chasse au tigre*, by Jean-Jacques Flipart, with Carle Vanloo's *Chasse à l'ours* as its pendant, dedicated to the marquis de Marigny, exhibited in the Salon of 1773 (J-R 1007).

SKETCH
?*Chasse au lion*, Pillot sale, Paris, 6 Dec. 1858, lot 15; ?*Chasse au tigre*, sale of comte de M***, 29 Dec. 1860, lot 2; ?*Chasse au lion*, Lefèvre-Soyer sale, Beauvais, 6 June ff. 1864, lot 19; *Chasse au tigre*, Seligmann & Co. sale (part I), Paris, 11 Mar. 1914, lot 374 (74 × 55.5 cm) [these are the measurements of the Cologne picture, to which this, and one or more of the preceding citations, may in fact refer].

In 1735 Boucher received his first commission from the Crown. As part of the modernization of the *chambre de la Reine* at Versailles, undertaken for Marie Leczinska from 1730 onward (Gallet & Bottineau, 1982, pp. 144–48), he was invited to execute grisailles of four *Virtues* in the ceiling, to replace darkened paintings by Gilbert de Sève (Engerand, 1900, pp. 39–40). Although they had only been commissioned the year after Belle, de Troy, and Natoire had executed the overdoors, and for a remoter location, Boucher's delicious grisailles (sadly traduced by the available photographs of them) must have made an impression. For the next year he and de Troy, along with four other artists (but including neither the deceased Belle nor Natoire), were each invited to paint one of the six *Chasses des pays étrangers*, to be set in rich frames and paneling by Jacques Verberckt in the *galerie des petits cabinets* in the newly created interior apartment of Louis XV at Versailles (Engerand, 1900, p. 40; Gallet & Bottineau, 1982, p. 151; Hazlehurst, 1984).

This *Leopard Hunt* must have met with royal approval too, since in 1738/39 Boucher, along with Carle Vanloo and Charles Parrocel, was asked to produce an additional exotic hunt for the series: in his case, the *Crocodile Hunt* (cat. 32, for which see a more general discussion of the set). Boucher's success—which is immediately apparent today, when one views all the paintings in their present home at Amiens—was all the more remarkable in that he was not, unlike Parrocel, a painter given to depicting animals and

## 29

PREPARATORY DRAWINGS
    1. *La chasse au tigre*, plumbago drawing, sale of the marquis de Calvière, 5 May ff. 1779, lot 393.
    2. Offset of *Deux Cavaliers*, "avec quelques changemens," ibid.
    3. *Studies of a Head and Hands* (mostly for huntsman at extreme right, with variant headgear, red, black, and white chalks, 370 × 280 mm, Pierre Dormeuil coll., Paris (A & W fig. 451).

EXHIBITED
Probably the painting of *Animaux,* one of three *tableaux de fantaisies* done for the king, shown at the Academy on 6 July 1737, on the occasion of Boucher's promotion to full *professeur* (see *Mercure de France,* July 1737, p. 1620).

Fig. 127. Anonymous sketch of a *Leopard Hunt*. Private collection, Paris.

riders, nor even, unlike Carle Vanloo, particularly fond of painting dramatic episodes. Indeed, though the drama and poses of the *Exotic Hunts* are tense, it is above all their landscapes that delight and astonish. Although the rocks and gnarled shrubs are recognizably from the same hand as those in *Putti Playing with Birds* (cat. 15), they are painted with a new liquidity and movement that rise to a climax in the exotic distant view, which has all the *fouillis* (literally "jumble")—to use the technical term of the day—that Boucher's contemporaries found so exciting in his early works. Of all Boucher's landscapes, that in the *Leopard Hunt* is the one that gives most delight from the sheer vitality of the paint, and only the landscape in the *Rape of Europa* in the Wallace Collection comes close to rivaling it in this respect.

There is a confusion inherent in the *Leopard Hunt,* in that what Boucher was invited to paint was a *Tiger Hunt*; and that is how the picture was described in the supplement to the inventory of the king's pictures drawn up the year after it was delivered ("Un tableau représentant des *Turcs qui combattent contre des tigres,* dont un paroit très effrayé . . ."), as well as in the engraving after it. Yet the beasts in this picture are clearly leopards. It was Lancret who was asked to paint a *Leopard Hunt,* but the animals in his picture are equally evidently tigers. The switch may well have occurred (and the confusion of title have persisted) because of the fact that in the eighteenth century (and even today, according to *Le Grand Robert*) *tigre* was used for spotted felines as well as striped: Furetière's *Dictionnaire Universel* (1727) defines a tiger simply as an "Animal féroce & cruel qui a des griffes, & la figure d'un chat, mais qui est plus grand, & qui a la peau tachetée," and gives an almost identical definition of a leopard.

This taxonomic confusion has extended to the supposed oil sketch for the present picture, in the Wallraf-Richartz-Museum in Cologne (see Klesse, 1973, pp. 29–30). For although it is there called a *Tiger Hunt,* and cautiously put forward as a sketch for the present picture, and indeed signed *f.Boucher,* all these indications are misleading. What is shown in the sketch is a lioness at bay; there is no compositional relationship with the present painting; and the hand is not Boucher's.

A seemingly more plausible candidate as a sketch for the present picture is an *Exotic Hunt* in a private collection in Paris (fig. 127), bearing an old label as "Carl Vanloo" (a spelling of the christian name that also suggests a German provenance). In this the beasts are leopards, and their poses, together with those of the man defending himself on the ground and of the foreground rider, are related (sometimes in reverse) to their equivalents in the present picture. Disconcertingly, however, not only is the half-naked figure at the left-hand side of the picture repeated verbatim in or from the figure in the same position in the Cologne sketch, but the two sketches (allowing for the better preservation of the Paris one) would appear to be by the same hand. Their kinship with one another, coupled with their remoteness from (or at most dependence on) the finished picture, seemingly concur with stylistic discrepancies in precluding Boucher as their author.

The hand visible in these sketches looks as if it is one that recurs in another composition, two versions of which have been attributed to Boucher, and for which a connection has also been proposed with the decoration of the *salle à manger* adjacent to the *petite galerie* at Versailles. This is the *Repas de chasse,* of which three sketches of different sizes are known, but no finished picture:

one in the Musée Nissim de Camondo (1983, no. 441); another exhibited by Cailleux, Paris, in 1964 (exh. cat. 1964, Paris, no. 13); and a third in the André Meyer sale, Sotheby Parke Bernet, New York, 22 October 1980, lot 11. The same hand would appear to have been the author of a sketch of *A Sultan with Three Ladies in an Interior* (Mrs. Charles Wrightsman's Palm Beach house sale, Sotheby's, New York, 5 May 1984, lot 25, as by Leprince). It would be tempting to see this hand as that of Charles Parrocel, either making sketches for a commission with which he may have been entrusted with overall control (see Hazlehurst, 1984, p. 234), or as the subsequent author of two small rectangular pictures of a *Lion Hunt* and a *Tiger Hunt* that were exhibited in the Salon of 1745, but it is hard to equate their style with that of the two sketches for Parrocel's contributions to the commission, which now hang alongside the finished pictures in Amiens (Hazlehurst, 1984, figs. 2, 22).

Whatever the answer to the conundrum of these sketches, it is clear that Hazlehurst (1984, pp. 227–29) is right in seeing Parrocel as the major influence upon how Boucher depicted this unfamiliar scene. Not only are such details as the pose of foremost horse and rider clearly derived from Parrocel's earlier depiction of this subject for the duc de Mortemart, engraved by Desplaces in 1731 (Hazlehurst, 1984, fig. 11), but so are such technical details as the glass balls on the ground. These, as the caption to Desplaces's engraving elucidates, were designed to distract the attention of the tigers: their own cubs having been taken away, they were supposed to be deceived into playing with the glass balls, which reflected their own diminished images, as if they were their removed young. The charming naïveté of this idea is an unintended indication of how seriously these exotic hunts were to be taken.

## 30 | *Le pasteur galant*

Oil on canvas
58 × 78 in. (147 × 198 cm)
Signed lower right: *f. Boucher*
Archives Nationales (Hôtel de Soubise), Paris
(S & M 1529)     A & W 159

## 31 | *Le pasteur complaisant*

Oil on canvas
56 × 74½ in. (142 × 189 cm)
Signed bottom right: *Boucher*
Archives Nationales (Hôtel de Soubise), Paris
(S & M 1529)     A & W 160

PROVENANCE
*Salle d'audience* of the *appartements du prince*, Hôtel de Soubise, Paris; displaced in the mid-19th century through destruction of the room by the Archives Nationales; now displayed in the *chambre de parade de la princesse*.

In 1732 the sexagenarian prince Hercule-Mériadec, duc de Rohan-Rohan, married for the second time, and to celebrate the event, got Boffrand to transform the *hôtel* that had been built for his father a generation before (see Babelon, 1969, pp. 24–48). Boffrand's chief efforts were devoted to the creation of a pavilion containing two oval salons for the prince and princess,

30

Fig. 128. *Pastoral Landscape*, overdoor in the Hôtel de Soubise, Paris.

Fig. 129. *Venus and Cupid at the Bath* (1738), overdoor in the Hôtel de Soubise, Paris.

one above the other, and to the transformation of the adjoining apartments (see Boffrand, 1745, pls. LXI–LXIX). To paint the *salon de la princesse* and overdoors in the other rooms the services of the foremost members of the new generation of artists were obtained: Natoire, Boucher, Carle Vanloo, Restout, and Trémolières. If Natoire was accorded the single most prestigious room, the *salon ovale de la princesse,* on his own, Boucher was awarded the lion's share of the commissions for overdoors: seven all told, ranging from mythological scenes, through pastorals, to a pure landscape—his very versatility helps to account for his preeminence. Not that he appears to have been an immediate choice, to judge by the fact that, whereas the other artists began to exhibit their contributions in the first of the revived Salons in 1737, he only did so in 1738. The reason for this may partly have been his prior employment by the Crown, but it may also have been due to a prejudice of Boffrand's, who is recorded as disapproving of "les peintres entraînés par un goût dépravé"—by which, one should hasten to add, he meant not their morals, but their use of irrational and asymmetrical ornament; for he ascribed the corruption of architectural taste to the introduction of forms borrowed from painting. Patte records him as specifically singling out Boucher for censure (see Dezallier, 1788, I, pp. 427–28).

Of all the overdoors that Boucher painted for the Hôtel de Soubise, these two were the most novel and (thanks to the engravings after them) the most

*31*

influential. Whereas his other pictures (see figs. 128, 129) were conventional mythological scenes and a landscape (though it should be noted that this landscape may have been his first to abandon capriccio views of Italy for something more suggestive of common nature in France), these two pictures appear to be his first surviving pastorals. "Pastoral" is employed here in the narrower sense that it came to have when used with reference to paintings in France in the eighteenth century, to mean idealized depictions not simply of the life of shepherds, but of their amorous activities in particular. Pictures of country life merely, such as Boucher had painted for the *petits appartements du Roi* at Fontainebleau and exhibited in the Salon in 1737, were referred to as "sujets champêtres," if not simply as "paysages."

It is curious that such novel subject matter should have been introduced without any allusion being made to it at the time. One reason is no doubt that it was done in a private *hôtel*, without the pictures being exhibited, and that by the time they came to be described in guidebooks such as those of Dezallier d'Argenville (1749, pp. 139–43), they had become so commonplace in Boucher's oeuvre that they were not thought worth remarking. A more telling reason at the time they were painted may have been that Boucher's stroke of inspiration was, precisely, not to invent anything utterly new, but to assimilate into painting something that had long been familiar elsewhere—in this case, in poetry and upon the stage. It was no mere figure of speech when

Fig. 130. *Les charmes de la vie champêtre,*
engraved by Jean Daullé after Boucher.

VARIANT

*Le pasteur complaisant,* signed and dated 1742,
dimensions and whereabouts unknown (looted
in World War II? Photograph in the Zentral-
institut für Kunstgeschichte, Munich) [in reverse, with numerous variants, and the types
of the boy and girl updated].

COPIES

*Le pasteur galant*

 1. Christie's, London, 23–24 May 1928, lot
265; Vermeer Galleries, London, 1937 [in
reverse].

 2. Painted on a Sèvres *vase hollandois* of
1762 in the Wallace Collection (Savill, 1982,
p. 167, and fig. 12). A copy of Laurent's print
survives in the Sèvres archives.

 3. Painted by Dodin on a Sèvres pot-pourri
vase of 1763 in the Rothschild Collection at
Waddesdon Manor (Eriksen, 1968, no. 56).

 4. Painted by Chabry *fils,* on the saucer of a
Sèvres *goblet calabre,* Jones Collection, Victoria and Albert Museum, London (778–1882).

 5. By Kändler, as a Meissen group, Victoria
and Albert Museum, London (C.141–1931
and C.50.1962).

 6. Meissen group (exh. cat. 1970, Leningrad, no. 96).

 7. Vincennes group (listed in 1752 inventory); examples in Forsyth Wickes Collection, Museum of Fine Arts, Boston; and in the
Mentmore sale (Sotheby's), 24 May 1977, lot
2010.

Boucher was called the Fontenelle of painting (*Lettre,* 1757), for he had
followed the recommendations of this author in presenting the simplicity of
pastoral love, without the poverty of peasant existence (Fontenelle, 1688).
Those, such as the abbé Le Blanc, who did recognize Boucher's originality in
creating the painted pastoral in France (Le Blanc, 1753, p. 18: "un genre, dont
M. Boucher est le créateur"), while appreciating the affinity with Fontenelle,
nonetheless insisted on the new vein of sentiment tapped by the painter. His
immediate inspiration was nonetheless more probably the stage than poetry,
and, in particular, the early and unacknowledged opéras comiques of his
friend Favart.

These theatrical antecedents are visible in the costumes of the protagonists
in these two pictures, which are still far from the (admittedly laundered)
peasant simplicity of Boucher's mature works, particularly those of the men.
They even suggest the permissive words of Fontenelle, who allowed that the
clothes of peasants in ballets "are of much finer stuff than those of true
peasants, they are even adorned with ribbons and with ornamental stitching
. . ." (Fontenelle, 1688, p. 130). The same overrich dress and overcoiffed hair
can be found in another picture of these years, albeit of uncertain origin, *Les
charmes de la vie champêtre* (fig. 49; Louvre; A & W 147, 148),
subsequently cut down to form a slightly inconsequential pendant to a more
thoroughgoing rustic picture, *Les présents du berger* (A & W 146). By the
time of his next securely datable *Pastorales,* by contrast, the three painted for
the marquis de Beringhen in 1743, the shepherds, though still dressed with
impossible richness, are bare legged and footed (if not wearing Antique
buskins), and wear hair cut short (A & W 260–262).

Boucher's idealization of his shepherds is the more surprising when one
considers the context in which they were originally placed, which accounted
for the choice of subject matter in the first place. For it would appear that
they were originally two overdoors in the *salle d'audience* of the prince on the
ground floor of the Hôtel de Soubise, the walls of which were adorned with
three tapestries from the first set of the *Fêtes de village à l'italienne* woven at
Beauvais (Babelon, 1969, p. 35). This first set of tapestries boasted quite
convincingly rustic protagonists (see cat. 86, 87), but without any emphasis
upon the amorous activities that brought the present pictures within the more
artificial ambit of the eclogue. It is these activities that give the protagonists of
the present pictures more affinity with those of the second set of tapestries
(see Standen, 1977[b]). Nonetheless, it would appear Favart may have stood
godfather to tapestries and pictures alike, since his *Foire de Bezons* (1735)
included "la scene épisodique d'un savoyard montrant la lanterne magique"
(Favart, 1808, I, p. x), precisely the central scene of *La Curiosité,* which was
one of the three Beauvais tapestries in the *salle d'audience* (and is now in the
Philadelphia Museum of Art). When a variant composition of *Le pasteur
galant* was engraved by Duflos after a drawing by Boucher in his set of *Les
amours pastorales* in 1751/52 (J-R 931), it was inscribed with verses written by
Favart commenting upon the triangular situation. This was one such as he
was to describe in *Annette et Lubin* (1762). In this opéra comique the
protagonists have different names from those of the etching, and it was
anyway written later than the compositions in question; nor, of course, can
one safely argue from Duflos's much later print to Boucher's painting here of
about 1738/39. Nonetheless, the verses suggest some earlier redaction of the
theme, and the possibility that Boucher took his inspiration from one of

8. Red-chalk drawing, inside a pen and wash drawing for a frame, 135 × 225 mm, close, but not corresponding exactly, to that in which it is now set, Paris art market, 1985.

*Le pasteur complaisant*
1. Mme Debacker sale, Paris, 1 June 1908, lot 32 [in reverse].
2. Blumerel sale, Bordeaux, 1–5 April 1913, lot 290, shaped overdoor, 100 × 85 cm [in reverse].
3. Ibid., lot 326, panel, 40 × 32 cm [in reverse].
4. Sale, Christie's, London, 6 Mar. 1936, lot 51.

5. Painted by Dodin on a Sèvres pot-pourri vase of 1763 in the Rothschild Collection at Waddesdon Manor (Eriksen, 1968, no. 56). A copy of Laurent's print survives in the Sèvres archives.
6. Painted on lid of Ottweiler terrine, in Museum für Kunst und Gewerbe, Hamburg (*Keramos*, 84, p. 11, fig. 2).

Favart's earlier works for the Théâtre de la Foire, which the latter neither acknowledged nor published, is at least worth entertaining. The general derivation of these, Boucher's earliest pastorals, from the stage seems beyond question.

ANALOGY
Drawing by J. A. Portail of *Le pasteur galant* holding up a (?) sheet of paper, red, black, and white chalks, 133 × 171 mm, Funck-Brentano sale, Paris, 29 Apr. ff. 1921, lot 48 (as 18th-century French School); given to the British Museum in 1926 by Henry Oppenheimer (facsimile published by the Vasari Society, as J-A. Portail).

## 32 | *The Crocodile Hunt*

Oil on canvas
71¼ × 50½ in. (181 × 128 cm)
Signed bottom center: *Boucher 1739*
Musée de Picardie, Amiens
S & M 1728          A & W 126
*Paris*

PROVENANCE
*Galerie des petits cabinets,* Versailles (installed 1739, dismounted 1767); Hôtel de la Surintendance, Versailles; sent by Napoleon to the Hôtel de Ville of Amiens for the peace negotiations of 1802; transferred to the Musée de Picardie in 1874.

ENGRAVING
*La Pesca del Crocodilo,* engraved by P. P. Moles in 1770–74: *Dedicada à la Real Junta Particulár, y Consuládo de Comercio, Fabricas, y Agricultúra del Principádo de Cataluña &a por P. P. Moles su Pensionista en Paris* (J-R 1432; Cochin's letter to de Marigny about Moles's choice of this picture and Vanloo's *Chasse à l'autruche* [which he never executed] to engrave, out of all the pictures in the *cabinet du Roi,* printed in Furcy-Raynaud, 1905, p. 193).

DRAWINGS
1. *Tête d'un Turc dans la Chasse au Crocodile,* sale of the marquis de Calvière 5 May ff. 1779, lot 393.
2. *Académie* used for rear figure with pole, red chalk, 251 × 307 mm, with stamp of Carl Hårleman, Nationalmuseum, Stockholm (Bjurström, 1982, no. 854; here fig. 131).

The original set of six paintings of *Chasses étrangères* commissioned in 1736 for the *galerie des petits cabinets* at Versailles (for whose plan and elevation, see Racinais, 1950, pls. 30, 32, 67) was allocated as follows: Boucher, *Chasse au tigre* [recte *au léopard,* cat. 29]; J-F. de Troy, *Chasse au lion*; Carle Vanloo, *Chasse à l'ours*; Lancret, *Chasse au léopard* [recte *au tigre*]; Pater, *Chasse chinoise*; Charles Parrocel, *Chasse à l'éléphant* (see Hazlehurst, 1984). It is evident from the finished paintings, all of which are now in the Musée de Picardie at Amiens, that the artists must have been given instructions over such matters as their palette and the size of their figures, so that their contributions should harmonize with one another; only Pater seems to have been incapable of adhering to the guidelines. Nonetheless, the pictures by Boucher and Vanloo show that they alone possessed the imagination to go beyond a trivial fascination with the exotic aspects of their allocated hunts to seize their dramatic potential.

It was surely this manifest superiority that led to their being selected to provide two of the additional three hunts required in 1738, along with the other painter much favored by the king (as witness his continuous employment at Choisy), Charles Parrocel (though it should be remembered that Pater had died, while de Troy had gone to take up the post of director of the French Academy in Rome, and that he and Lancret had already been asked to paint the *Déjeuner d'huîtres* and the *Déjeuner de jambon* for the *salle à manger*). At first sight more surprising is the fact that neither of the two outstanding animal painters of the age, Desportes and Oudry, was asked for a contribution to either the first or the second commission. This would appear to indicate that Louis XV (who was a passionate huntsman) commissioned

32

Fig. 131. *Study of a Man Wielding a Pole.* Nationalmuseum, Stockholm.

the series less for the sake of the depiction of the animals involved than as opportunities for the depiction of action and emotion—hence his having chosen a team made up of history painters and painters of *fêtes galantes.*

It is this lack of scientific intent that also accounts for the painters chosen having preferred to go for inspiration to such sources as the engravings after Stradanus of the *Venationes Ferarum* (see Hazlehurst, 1984, passim) rather than to the Jardin des Plantes (in this connection it is worth mentioning that the royal collections included eighteen drawings of often exotic *Hunts* made by Stradanus; see exh. cat. 1977–78, Paris, Orangerie, no. 105). More puzzling as an influence is that of Rubens's *Exotic Hunts,* also alluded to by Hazlehurst, but never demonstrable as a specific source. For if these four hunts, sometimes representing the pursuit of more than one species of exotic beast, which were painted for the elector Maximilian I of Bavaria (see exh. cat. 1980, Munich, nos. 801–03), would seem likely to have inspired both Louis XV's choice of subject matter and Boucher's unwonted display of male anatomy, it is less easy to say in what form these pictures, which were then all in Schleissheim and had never been engraved, were known to king and painter.

The reasons for the commissioning of three additional pictures in 1738 are also not immediately apparent. They may have had something to do with the enlargement of the gallery, since we know that in 1737 its form had already been altered by heightening (Gallet & Bottineau, 1982, p. 151). For his second contribution, Boucher would appear to have drawn even more heavily on Stradanus for specific details, such as the mastiff at the right and the idea of gagging the crocodile with a pole (fig. 131; see Hazlehurst, 1984, pp. 233–34), yet the overall impression of the seething mass of beasts and straining bodies is even more Rubensian than in the *Leopard Hunt*—albeit again without specifically demonstrable borrowings. The palm trees in the middle ground (coexisting with one of Boucher's favorite fir trees in the foreground!) and the small overacute pyramid in the distance were intended by him to locate the scene in the cataracts of the Nile. I am grateful to M. Christian Baulez for having communicated to me an unpublished memorandum from Boucher to the Bâtiments du Roi (Archives Nationales O[1] 1802, *pièce* 729) that contains this statement. It was drawn up to support his claim that he should be paid as much for this picture as for the *Leopard Hunt,* since it cost him much more time.

# 33 | *Le déjeuner*

Oil on canvas
32 × 25¾ in. (81.5 × 65.5 cm)
Signed bottom right: *f. Boucher 1739*
Musée du Louvre, Paris (R.F. 926)
S & M 1157, 1184      A & W 165

PROVENANCE
*Catalogue d'une grande Collection de Tableaux des meilleurs Maistres . . . &c.,* Grands Augustins (Gersaint), 26 Mar. ff. 1749, lot 50:

Confronted with this delightfully detailed but informal scene of a family at breakfast, one cannot but regret Boucher as a genre painter manqué. Perhaps, however, this is to look at this picture and its few fellows in the wrong way:

## 33

Fig. 132. *Study of a Man Serving Coffee*. Art Institute of Chicago.

Fig. 133. Overmantel mirror and painting, plate 67 of J-F. Blondel's *De la distribution des maisons de plaisance*, vol. II (1738).

"Sujet galant & agréable. . . . Il représente deux Dames ausquelles on sert de caffé, avec deux Enfans"; *Catalogue des Tableaux Originaux des Trois Ecoles . . . &c., du Cabinet de M. PROUSTEAU, Capitaine des Gardes de la Ville*, sa maison, rue des Tournelles (Remy), 5 June ff. 1769, lot 51: "Deux femmes, deux enfans, & un garçon Limonadier qui a servi du caffé, dans une chambre à cheminée agréablement ornée: sur ce Tableau est marqué l'année 1763 [*sic*]. Les ouvrages de ce celebre Artiste, M. Boucher, sont si géneralement au goût du public, qu'il n'est pas nécessaire de faire l'éloge du morceau que nous annoncons" [sold for 200 livres]; *Catalogue de Tableaux, Dessins, Miniatures, Estampes . . . &c. du Cabinet de M\*\*\**, Hôtel de Bullion (Paillet), 9 Dec. ff. 1783, lot 3, *F. Boucher, en 1739*: "Un Tableau

rather than asking ourselves why Boucher should have abandoned such subject matter, we ought to be looking for the circumstances that occasioned his few essays in this field. For, as we know from the history of *The Milliner* (cat. 51), it was not for want of urging that Boucher left such pictures unpainted.

Since Tourneux, taking up an identification originally made in the Duclos sale, proposed it with proper diffidence in 1897, *Le déjeuner* has generally been regarded as depicting the painter himself and his young family. There is much that speaks for this: the ages of the father and mother and of the two young children (Boucher had married the then seventeen-year-old Marie-Jeanne Buseau in 1733; their first daughter was born in 1735, and their only son in 1736; their other daughter was not to be born until 1740) do not contradict it, and, since it is the woman drinking coffee who appears to have the features of Mme Boucher, Georges Brunel's discovery (which he has kindly communicated to me) that Boucher had a sister might resolve the identity of the other woman, feeding the child. The main drawback is the figure of the man, for there is a drawing of him by Boucher with the same features as in the painting that by its very character can scarcely be a self-portrait (fig. 132). What is more, he is wearing the apron of a servant, and was called a "garçon Limonadier" when the picture was sold for the second time. It is true that Louis XV took special pleasure in making coffee in the intimacy of the *petits appartements* and Boucher might have worn an apron to do the same, and the placing and attitude of the figure in the picture are scarcely those of a deferential servant or waiter; but on balance it is probably wiser to see this as a genre picture, in which Boucher may have taken his family as convenient models, rather than an actual family portrait.

This way of regarding the picture is reinforced by a previously unnoticed fact about its history. The painter whose works this painting most strongly echoes is Jean-François de Troy, for it was he who made a specialty of depicting gatherings of figures from the higher reaches of society, in minutely descriptive representations of their surroundings. It is therefore of some interest that when this picture, described as a "Sujet galant & agréable," first appeared at auction—only ten years after it was painted, and one of the earliest paintings by Boucher to do so—it was in company with a picture by Raoux of identical dimensions, described as "un autre Sujet galant" of *Deux jeunes Hommes et deux Dames dans un Jardin* (lot 51), and two paintings by de Troy, only one *pouce* shorter, of *Plusieurs personnes qui s'habillent pour le Bal* (lot 48). These lots were grouped together in the catalogue, giving the impression of a set of paintings of polite society commissioned by one person from different hands. Furthermore, the other picture by Boucher in the sale, of *Cupid and Psyche* (lot 49), was of exactly the same dimensions as another picture by de Troy of *Diana at the Bath* (lot 47), suggesting a similar proceeding.

The sale was one of mixed properties, held by Gersaint, and in the event—according to a copy of the catalogue in the Cabinet des Estampes of the Bibliothèque Nationale—the two Bouchers and the Raoux were not on view. Since the de Troys were apparently sold, this might be thought to weaken the argument for some connection between them and the Bouchers. However, twenty years later, the pair of pictures by de Troy, now called *La toilette pour le bal* and *Le retour du bal*, reappear in the same sale as *Le déjeuner*. This was of the "Cabinet de M. Prousteau, Capitaine des Gardes de la Ville,"

bien peint & du meilleur ton de couleur; il représente l'intérieur d'un appartement, dans lequel est une dame assise devant une table, & prenant son déjeuné que lui apporte un jeune garçon: autre dame & 2 enfans ajoutent à l'agrément de cette composition"; *Catalogue d'une Collection intéressante de bons Tableaux des Trois Ecoles*, Hôtel Bullion (Bons & Bonnefons), 22–23 Mar. 1827, lot 18; posthumous sale of Gueting, carrossier de la Cour Impériale de France, 19 Feb. 1848, lot 11; sale of Camille Marcille, 12–13 Jan. 1857, lot 6; relics of the collection of J[ules] Duclos, Hôtel Drouot, 20–21 Nov. 1878, lot 50, as *Intérieur de sa famille (le Déjeuner)*; anon. posthumous sale (exp. George), 13–15 Apr. 1881, lot 1; Dr. Achille Malécot, Paris, by whom left to the Louvre in 1895.

ENGRAVING

*Le déjeuné*, engraved by Bernard Lépicié, with verses by him:
*Caffé charmant ta liqueur agréable*
*De Bacchus calme les accès*
*Ton feu divin dissipe de la table*
*Et les dégoûts et les excès.*
(J-R 1380–1381)
[Engraving (in reverse) and verses copied by an anonymous contemporary print inscribed with the curious assertion that "L'Original est dans le Cabinet du Roy."]

PREPARATORY DRAWINGS
1. *Seated Woman Taking Coffee*, Hermitage, Leningrad (inv. 10632), red, black, and white chalks, 246 × 225 mm, signed *boucher* (exh. cat. 1970, Leningrad, no. 17).
2. *Seated Woman Taking Coffee*, inscribed *Chardin*, red chalk, 392 × 287 mm, formerly Liechtenstein coll., Vaduz (Schönbrunner & Meder, II, 1897, p. 131), sold after the Second World War to an unknown buyer.
3. *Man Serving Coffee*, red, black, and white chalks, 345 × 195 mm, Art Institute of Chicago (exh. cat. 1973–74, Washington, no. 36).

ANALOGY
*Interior with a Woman Taking Coffee*: misc. sale (Le Brun), 19 Jan. 1778, lot 103: "L'intérieur d'une chambre, où l'on voit une femme couverte d'une pélisse, qui prend du chocolat," 18 × 14 in.; misc. sale [Dulac & Lachaise], 30 Nov. ff. 1778, lot 212: "Une Dame assise devant une table, prenant une tasse de chocolat."

COPIES
1. Bourgarel coll., Paris.
2. Mrs. A. James coll.; sold Christie's, London, 15 Oct. 1948, lot 87, 31½ × 25½ in. (in reverse).

according to the catalogue. The research of Bruno Pons (to whom I am most grateful for communicating this information to me) has identified this individual as Salomon-Pierre Prousteau (d. 1781), a *marchand de vins*. It would appear, however, that Prousteau's dealings extended from wine to pictures, on the evidence not only of this sale midway through his life (which might, of course, also have been occasioned by a crisis in his business), but also of the fact that he owned two replicas of Bouchers made for engravers (a *Rape of Europa* possibly identifiable with the picture now in the Museum of North Carolina at Raleigh [cf. cat. 54] and *The Milliner* [cf. cat. 51] now in the Wallace Collection), and that he owned two further pictures by Boucher that were neither in his sale nor recorded in his *inventaire après décès* (*Vénus donnant du nectar à l'Amour* and *L'Amour instruit par Mercure*, engraved by Basan [J-R 263, 262] and Mme Dupont [J-R 944, 945]), which would originally appear to have been overdoors in the Hôtel de Mazarin, according to the drawings for them in the Nationalmuseum in Stockholm (Bjurström, 1982, nos. 850, 849). The engraving of *Le déjeuné*, without the name of any owner or dedicatee, by the Lépicié in 1744 already carries with it a certain suggestion that the picture was on the market then (the de Troys were engraved by Beauvarlet). Whatever the true explanation, it would appear that so apparently spontaneous an exercise in this, for Boucher, unusual genre was in fact a commissioned work, and possibly even a commercial speculation.

None of this detracts from the great qualities of the picture itself. The impression of a family seized at one of the most informal and intimate moments of the day is brought to a point in the gaze of the child being fed, by which we are fixed, almost as if the scene had been caught by the instant eye of the camera, rather than by the laborious hand of the painter. This feeling of a photographic record is enhanced by the myriad details caught by the painter's brush: the *bourlet* worn by the small child on the right to protect it from knocks, its little doll (prophetic of the cutout *pantins* that Boucher himself was to color at the height of their vogue seven years later), the bulbous high-spouted silver coffeepot (so shaped the better to retain the grounds) held by the man, and the teapot and pagod on the étagère behind him—the pagod reminiscent of the kind of Chinese porcelain that we know, from his posthumous sale, Boucher himself owned. But most of all, what this picture conveys is the impression of an up-to-date Rococo interior. In fact, the forms of the chimneypiece and of the overmantel mirror incorporating a picture of the *Ponte Salario* (a less curvilinear version of one of the more modest designs in J.-F. Blondel's *De la distribution des maisons de plaisance*, II, 1738, pl. 67, p. 73; here fig. 133), and of the console table, dated back a decade or more, and are certainly less advanced than the interiors shown in Boucher's illustrations to the *Oeuvres de Molière* (1734/35); only the cartel clock and the sconces manifest real asymmetry and rocaille. Nonetheless, from no other picture do we gain so vivid an idea of life in an up-to-date, if not modish, household in the Paris of the day.

## 34 | View of a Mill with Distant Temple

Oil on canvas
49¾ × 63 in. (126.5 × 160 cm)
Signed on rock, lower right:
*f. Boucher 1740*
The Nelson-Atkins Museum of Art,
Kansas City (59–1)
S & M 1738      A & W 175

## 35 | Forest Scene with Two Roman Soldiers

Oil on canvas
51½ × 64 in. (131 × 163 cm)
Signed on rock, lower right:
*f. Boucher 1740*
Musée du Louvre, Paris (M.N.R. 894)
S & M 1750      A & W 176

PROVENANCE
Exhibited in the Salon of 1740, nos. 10, 11,
with no name of owner; *Catalogue de Tableaux Originaux . . . &c. après le décès de
Madame veuve de M. DE LA HAYE, Fermier-
Général*, Hôtel Lambert (Remy), 1 Dec. ff.
1778, lot 30: "Ces deux tableaux . . . sont
riches & intéressans de composition, d'un *faire
savant* & d'un coloris clair, mais agréable &
bon. *François Boucher* qui en est l'auteur, les a
faits en 1740, dans son bon tems"; *Catalogue
de Tableaux . . . &c. après le décès de Madame
LANCRET, & de M\*\*\**, Hôtel de Bullion
(Remy), 3 [postponed to 5] Apr. ff. 1782, lots
156, 157; coll. of M. Pinard (exh. cat. 1860,
Paris, nos. 85, 86), after which separated:
   *View of a Mill*: private coll., France (exh.
cat. 1932, Paris, no. 74); coll. of the duchesse
d'Harrincourt; sold anonymously, Sotheby's,
London, 2 July 1958, lot 111 (bought by
Leggatt, from whom acquired by the museum
in 1959).
   *Forest Scene*: M. Jacques de Chefdebien
(exh. cat. 1932, Paris, no. 73); third Dubois-
Chefdebien sale, Paris, 13–14 Feb. 1941, lot 17;
recovered after the war, and presented to the
Louvre by the Office des Biens Privés in 1951.

PREPARATORY DRAWINGS
?"Deux sujets de soldats, dans la manière de
S. Rose, au bistre," Mariette's posthumous
sale, 15 Nov. ff. 1775, lot 1158; "deux Desseins
à la plume, sur la même feuille, representans
des groupes de Soldats, dans le genre de
Salvator Roza," Blondel d'Azaincourt sale,
10 Feb. ff. 1783, lot 195.

In 1744, after writing about the oeuvres of Lancret and Pater in the catalogue
of the posthumous sale of Quentin de Lorangère (Gersaint, 1744, pp.
197–98), Mariette digressed to regret the fact that:

> there is a fairly strong feeling in our day, of how much the Landscape
> side of things has been too neglected. In no Country is anyone being
> bred up to this specialty, which is agreeable (in its own right), and very
> often a necessary complement to the other aspects of Painting. Our best
> Masters rarely devote themselves to this kind of study: they regard the
> pieces of Landscape that they deign to chance to spend a few moments
> on, as an amusement and distraction: it is uncommon to see such things
> from their hands, despite the beauties that are appreciated in them, and
> the unanimous approval that such productions generally earn.
> *(On sent assez de nos jours, combien on a trop négligé depuis quelques
> tems la partie du Paysage. Il ne se forme dans aucun Pays, nul élève dans
> ce genre, qui est agréable, & très-souvent nécessaire pour les autres
> parties de la Peinture. Rarement nos meilleurs Maîtres s'appliquent-ils à
> cette étude: ils ne regardent que comme un amusement, & un
> délaissement les morceaux de Paysage, auxquels ils veulent bien par
> hazard passer quelques momens: il n'est pas commun d'en voir sortir de
> leurs mains, malgré les beautés que l'on y reconnoît, & les suffrages
> universels que ces productions leur attirent ordinairement.)*

There was an element of exaggeration in what Mariette said, but it was in
essence true in France at least: none of the leading history painters of the
day—not Coypel, Vanloo, Natoire, or de Troy—painted landscapes or even
allocated a significant role to landscape in their compositions. There was no
figure comparable to Claude or Poussin of the previous century, and there
were barely any minor practitioners of the genre—at most, such peripheral
figures as the primarily architectural painters Lajoue or Lallemand. Yet we
know that Vleughels had encouraged his pupils at the French Academy in
Rome to go out and sketch in the Campagna, and one of them—Natoire—

34

Fig. 134. *The Mill of Quiquengrogne at Charenton*, signed and dated 1739. Private collection, England.

made numerous landscape drawings and watercolors, at least after his own appointment as director of the Academy in Rome. Natoire, while still in France, belonged to a circle of artists that also included Boucher and Portail, and later Pierre and Wille, who followed Oudry's lead in going to sketch in the romantically abandoned grounds of the château of the prince de Guise at Arcueil (see exh. cat. 1982–83, Paris, pp. 231–44). Apart from Boucher, however, only Oudry produced and exhibited any significant quantity of landscape paintings. Mariette not only knew and appreciated Oudry, he owned four of his drawings of Arcueil (see Opperman, 1977, cat. nos. D.1051, 1063–64, 1074); nonetheless it is unlikely that he had that artist in mind when he uttered his lament, since Oudry's devotion to landscape was far from intermittent, and he was not a history painter. It is much more likely that it was Boucher whom Mariette had in his sights.

This was less than wholly fair to Boucher, who, as we have seen (cat. 16, 23), had been painting landscapes since his return from Rome. He had included *tableaux de fantaisies* of landscape among the three pictures that he showed at the Academy on his election as full *professeur* in 1737 (see *Mercure*

35

Fig. 135. *Seconde veue des environs de Charenton*, engraved by J-P. Le Bas after Boucher.

*de France*, July 1737, p. 1620), no doubt from the set of landscape subjects that he had painted for the *petits appartements* of Fontainebleau that year (Engerand, 1900, p. 42), and he had exhibited four *sujets champêtres* in the first of the revived Salons, later in the same year (possibly again the pictures for Fontainebleau).

Boucher's earliest landscapes were, however, all reminiscences of Italy. Opperman ascribes a crucial role to Oudry and to his involvement of Boucher in the design of tapestries for Beauvais, in the latter's switch to painting from actual motifs in the environs of Paris (exh. cat. 1982–83, Paris, no. 90). How true is this? Boucher's earliest datable landscape not of Italian or Italianate sites seems to be the panel painting of *The Mill of Quiquengrogne at Charenton*, formerly in the collection of Mrs. Derek Fitzgerald, and now in an English private collection (fig. 134; A & W 167), apparently signed and dated 1739. This composition was engraved in 1747 by J-P. Le Bas as the *Premiere veue de Charenton* (J-R 1342), with a *Seconde veue des environs de Charenton* as its pendant (fig. 135; J-R 1343; possibly based on the picture paired with *The Mill of Quiquengrogne* in the collections of Mrs. Meyer Sassoon and Mrs. Derek Fitzgerald, and now in the Kunsthalle in Hamburg [A & W 170]; but the difference of support, which is copper rather than panel, and the absence of a date from the signature on the picture in Hamburg, together with the lack of any early record of either picture, enjoin caution over accepting it unconditionally as such). The engraving of the *Premiere veue* is, significantly, dedicated to one of the sketching party at Arcueil, Portail, and that of the *Seconde veue* to the amateur artist and historiographer of the art of the Low Countries [J-B.] Descamps. Perhaps of even greater significance is the fact that there is a drawing by Oudry in the Louvre (Duclaux, 1975, no. 286) of the same mill—which was celebrated for its picturesqueness, since there were also three paintings of it by Lancret (G. Wildenstein, 1924, nos. 41–43), and there are what would appear to be two drawings of it by Vleughels, one in the Pierpont Morgan Library (exh. cat. 1984, New York, no. 34) and another at present untraced (Hercenberg, 1975, no. 324, fig. 174). One cannot prove that Oudry's drawing has the priority and that it was he who had led Boucher to the motif, but this would at least be consistent with his later primacy at Arcueil, where he "primoit comme un professeur au milieu de son école" (Gougenot, 1761 [1854], p. 378).

Even more telling for the hypothesis that it was his association with Oudry at Beauvais that led Boucher away from Italianate views and into deriving his inspiration from local sites is the other pair of landscapes engraved by Le Bas in 1744 (J-R 1340, 1341). These are after paintings of 1742 and 1743 of the environs of Beauvais itself (the fact that both the original painting of 1742, and the engraving after it, were exhibited in the Salons of 1742 and 1745 respectively, as depictions of that locality, and that a third painting, employing the same pointed tower as the first view of Beauvais, but in a slightly altered setting, was shown as a pendant to the second view of Beauvais in the Salon of 1743, suggests that all three pictures at least took motifs from Beauvais as their starting point. This is despite the fact that Chedel appears to have engraved the third picture as *Veüe d'une Tour près de Blois* [J-R 494; see also exh. cat. 1974, Amsterdam, no. 15], which must have been an error or a flight of fancy on his part). What is more, the mill in the *Seconde vue de Beauvais* is precisely the building depicted in the present picture from Kansas City. In this earlier painting, however, Boucher still shows himself reluctant to commit himself entirely to the representation of a rustic local site. Instead, he combines it with a romantic vision of the Temple of the Sibyl at Tivoli in the distance. In exactly the same way, the strikingly naturalistic view of a forest glade in the pendant in the Louvre (not a little reminiscent of the forests seen in Oudry's *Chasses*) is peopled by two soldiers who look as if they have strayed from a painting by Salvator Rosa. A group of three banditti taken from the same source can be seen in the middle distance of the Kansas picture (it is worth recalling here that Boucher even painted a pastiche Salvator Rosa landscape, currently on the Paris art market [A & W 73]).

The present pair of landscapes is first recorded in the collection of Mme de la Haye (d. 1776), widow of the immensely rich *fermier-général* Marin de la Haye (d. 1753), the owner successively of the Hôtel de Bretonvilliers and of the Hôtel Lambert, where her posthumous sale was held. Only an unspecified copy of a Boucher had been mentioned in her husband's posthumous sale; but this pair, of strikingly large dimensions, was no doubt painted for him and retained by his widow. A brother of his, Salomon de la Haye

Desfosses, had one daughter who was married to Bergeret de Frouville (see cat. 84, 85), and another who was married to the most avid collector of Boucher's drawings, Blondel d'Azaincourt. Either Salomon de la Haye or, more probably, his son, Charles-Marin de la Haye, the "Benjamin" and heir of the childless Marin de la Haye, had a notable collection of Boucher's drawings, which we know from the engravings after them by Demarteau and Ouvrier.

The fact that these two landscapes were put on the market only as recently as 1778, however, makes it doubtful that, when they reappeared in the posthumous sale of the painter Lancret's widow in 1782 (see M. R. Michel, 1969), they had really belonged to her. It is much more probable that they were inserted into her sale by the auctioneer Pierre Remy, who had also held the posthumous sale of Mme de la Haye.

## 36 | *Psyche Declining Divine Honors*

Oil on canvas, grisaille
16½ × 21¼ in. (42 × 54 cm)
Musée des Beaux-Arts du Château de Blois
A & W 186

PROVENANCE
Coll. of M. Rosat, by whom left to the museum in 1882.

RELATED WORKS
1. *Psiché refusant les honneurs divins*, etching by Philippe Parizeau (J-R 1441).
2. *Psiché recevant les honneurs divins*, "esquisse très-avancée en grisaille. Cet aimable tableau, par F. Bouchet, a été gravé par N. Pariseau. Il est peint à l'huile sur papier, & porte 16 pouces en tout sens"; *Catalogue de Tableaux . . . &c. provenans du Cabinet de feu M. SALY, &c.*, sa maison, rue du Doyenné (Joullain *fils*), 14 June ff. 1776, lot 9 (sold for 150 livres).
3. *Psichée qui refuse les honneurs de la Divinité*, "Un très-beau Dessein de Fr. Boucher," sale of the abbé Guillaume, 18 May 1769, lot 268 [sold for 90 livres]; *Psiché refusant les honneurs divins*, "riche composition à la plume & au bistre; ce Dessein a été gravé par M. Pariseau," Jacqmin sale, 26 Apr. ff. 1773, lot 843 [sold for 300 livres]; *Psiché refusant les honneurs divins dans le temple de Venus*, "belle et riche composition, connue par l'estampe gravée par M. Parizeau; elle est à la plume, lavée de bistre. Hauteur 16 pouces, largeur 21 pouces," [Bellanger] sale (Le Brun & Constantin), 17 Mar. ff. 1788; Le Brun & Constantin sale, 31 May ff. 1790, lot 144, "dessein très-terminé à la plume, lavé de bistre; il est gravé par Mr. Parizeau. Hauteur 17 pouces, largeur 20 pouces"; *Cab de Ci-*

On 30 September 1737 a memorandum was drawn up recording the Crown's decision to order tapestries from Beauvais that could be used as diplomatic gifts. The existing compositions being regarded as insufficiently "elevated," Oudry was to provide pictures for new sets, beginning with the *Story of Jason and Medea*, and, since history pieces were by definition more demanding, he was only required to produce six every three years instead of his previous contractual obligation of eight (see Fenaille, IV, 1907, pp. 99–100). In transmitting this memorandum to Oudry, however, Fagon as administrator made it clear that he was not expected to produce these pictures himself (his talents scarcely lay in that direction), but to get Boucher to do so (see A & W doc. 89). In the event, somebody else (apparently Dandré-Bardon, who exhibited one in the Salon of 1739) produced a set of five pictures (see Badin, 1909, p. 90), but they were not used, and the *Story of Jason* was ultimately woven at the Gobelins instead, after seven pictures painted by J-F. de Troy in Rome between 1743 and 1746 (see Fenaille, IV, 1907, pp. 101–35).

Two months later, on 25 November, another memorandum was drawn up recording the choice of the *Story of Psyche* for the second set of hangings, and emphasizing that they were to be of "six less hackneyed subjects, affording the greatest scope for richness and charm, and the most apt for exhibiting the skills of the weaver" (see Fenaille, IV, 1907, p. 100). These Boucher did undertake, but not immediately. The first set of the *Fêtes Italiennes* had to be completed beforehand—*La pêcheuse* was not put on the looms until 1738— and it was not until 1739 that he exhibited in the Salon the full-scale painting that was to serve as model for the inaugural tapestry in the new series, *Zephyr Ushering Psyche into Cupid's Palace*, and as late as 1741 when the first three tapestries were woven and 1742 before the set of five was completed.

36

*toyen*\*\*\* sale (Regnault), 25 brumaire, l'an III (15 Nov. ff. 1794), lot 13.

4. *Psichée qui refuse les honneurs de la Divinité,* "un Dessein par S. Quentin, d'après Fr. Boucher . . . dans sa bordure dorée," sale of the abbé Guillaume, 18 May 1769, lot 261 [sold for 42 livres 16 sous].

Faced with the demand for novel and rich episodes from the story, Boucher turned for advice to the writer and journalist Petit de Bachaumont (later to become one of his severest critics). By this point the commission had expanded to nine compositions, and though de Bachaumont calls them "tableaux" (pictures), it is clear from what he says about the ninth and last of them, that it was tapestries that were being envisaged (see A & W doc. 130). Otherwise, one might easily have supposed that Boucher was seeking advice because he was in competition with Natoire for the commission to paint the spandrels of the *salon ovale de la princesse* in the Hôtel de Soubise, which the latter was decorating with eight scenes from the *Story of Psyche* in these very years (1737–39). These paintings by Natoire (and the engravings after Raphael recommended by de Bachaumont) aside, there were few available precedents to follow; most French painters (such as the Coypel) had only depicted *Psyche Examining Cupid by Lamplight* or *Cupid Abandoning Psyche*. There were, however, sets of tapestries telling the story of Psyche, that were woven in Paris before the creation of the Gobelins (Fenaille, I, 1923, pp. 287–92),

Fig. 136. *Psiché refusant les honneurs divins*, etched by Ph. Parizeau after Boucher.

Fig. 137. *The Apotheosis of Psyche*, grisaille sketch. Musée des Arts Décoratifs, Paris.

and in Brussels in the early eighteenth century (Göbel, 1923, I, vol. i, pp. 361, 591).

Neither de Bachaumont's proposals nor Boucher's compositions make any allusion to these paintings by Natoire (despite the fact that Boucher was simultaneously contributing overdoors to the Hôtel de Soubise, see cat. 30, 31); one reason for this was probably that, unlike Natoire, Boucher and de Bachaumont were in search of subjects that afforded the greatest opportunity to bring on rich settings and a tumultuous cast of characters (for a contrary assessment, which also exaggerates the correspondence between the subjects suggested by de Bachaumont and those painted by Natoire, see the otherwise very rewarding article by Kathryn Hiesinger, 1976).

De Bachaumont's garbled recommendations to draw for inspiration on the collaborative *tragédie-ballet* by Molière, Quinault, and Pierre Corneille, and the *tragédie-opéra* variously ascribed to Thomas Corneille or to Fontenelle, both of which had music by Lully, were probably particularly welcome to someone of Boucher's theatrical bent. That just two of the five scenes eventually depicted in Boucher's tapestry designs were suggested by de Bachaumont may reflect not only the fact that the latter had omitted certain central episodes, but also that the set of tapestries as it stands—which in turn omits other key scenes—is incomplete. It was a cycle scarcely ordered by private customers (most went, as intended, to the king or as diplomatic gifts) and for this reason may have been abandoned without intended further scenes having been added.

De Bachaumont had already told Boucher that the story afforded the possibility of depicting many more than the nine episodes for which he had been asked, and had suggested that he make drawings for a set of engravings, which de Bachaumont predicted would outstrip even those for the *Oeuvres de Molière* (1734–35) in popularity. Regrettably, Boucher never took this advice, but he did produce a *Psyche Declining Divine Honors* that was etched by Philippe Parizeau (fig. 136; J-R 1441). This does not correspond exactly to the present picture but is a square composition derived from it. An oil sketch on paper of the same square format as the etching was in the posthumous sale of the sculptor Saly (whose bust of the *Jeune fille aux nattes* Boucher had so often depicted in his putti pictures of the *Arts*), and it was probably this that is recorded by the etching, albeit at one remove. That the present grisaille was an earlier version of the oil sketch on paper is suggested not only by its evident closeness to the etching, but also by the fact that the details in which it differs (e.g., the fanciful head scarf of one of the priestesses) appear to have been improved in the etching (to a more correct mantle). What is more, the final drawing for the composition (often mistakenly held to have been the model for the etching when it appeared in sales in the eighteenth century) was of the same format as the present oil sketch, suggesting that it was in this form that the composition was first elaborated. The change in format was not achieved simply by truncating the sides: the foremost girl making a burnt offering was excised from the center as well, and a prostrate supplicant substituted, an excision that makes the gestures of Psyche's companion hard to comprehend.

It is evident that from the outset Boucher was making this sketch with a print, not a tapestry, in mind. Not only is it a true grisaille, unlike the two sketches *en camaïeu brun* for the tapestries of *La toilette de Psyché* and *Les richesses* (fig. 206; A &W 191, 193, now in a private collection in the United

States; illustrated in color in exh. cat. 1982, Tokyo, nos. 19, 20; knowing the sketch of *Le Vannier* only from an unlocated photograph, I do not know whether it is truly a grisaille, as was said when it was in the posthumous sale of M. de Livry in 1772), but it is also, necessarily, much more precise in execution than sketches that Boucher would himself elaborate into finished compositions. In this it differs from another true grisaille, the *Apotheosis of Psyche* in the Musée des Arts Décoratifs in Paris (fig. 137; A & W 194; exh. cat. 1983–84, Rotterdam, no. 58), which, though commonly regarded as the sketch for a sixth (and unexecuted) tapestry in the set, would appear to be not only in an earlier, bolder manner, but also out of character with the other compositions, and indeed more suited to the decoration of a ceiling (it may even have helped to inspire Pierre's ceiling painting of this subject in the Palais Royal). The present sketch is, in any event, clearly significantly earlier than another grisaille prepared for an engraving, the design for the frontispiece etched by Laurent Cars for Poullain de Saint-Foix's *Catalogue des Chevaliers . . . &c. du Saint-Esprit*, 1760 (J-R 460–461), now in the Musée des Beaux-Arts in Lille (A & W 359).

Even though the present sketch and the final version in the Saly sale were made to be engraved, Parizeau appears to have had recourse to an intermediate drawing, but not the one frequently cited as such in the eighteenth-century sales, since it was of the wrong format—though the mistake is revealing. Not only does the careful hatching of the etching suggest that it was made via a pen drawing, the *F Boucher inv.*, as opposed to *pinx.* or *del.*, also points to the existence of an intermediate stage. It is even possible to point to a probable trace of this missing link. In the abbé Guillaume's sale in 1769 there were two drawings of this subject: one by Boucher himself, which was sold for 90 livres, and the other which, though it went for only half the amount, still fetched a very healthy 42 livres 16 sous and was in a gilt frame; it was by Boucher's faithful pupil J-P-J. de Saint-Quentin (b. 1738) and was probably the intermediate drawing used by Parizeau for his etching.

Nothing was said in this sale about the composition being engraved, but four years later a pen and bister drawing in the Jacqmin sale was said to have been the model for Parizeau's engraving. Since this sold for 300 livres, it was probably the autograph drawing from the abbé Guillaume's sale and the oblong drawing that appeared in subsequent sales, so the assertion must have been mistaken; nevertheless, the two facts indicate that the etching had been made between 1769 and 1773. Parizeau was only born in 1740, so he could not have done such an accomplished etching much earlier than 1760.

None of this is of much help in dating the present grisaille, and indeed, such indications as there are, are contradictory. The style and features of it suggest a date not far removed from that of the sketches for the tapestries, possibly a little later, closer to the *Marriage of Cupid and Psyche* (A & W 196), which shows that Boucher was still preoccupied with the story in 1744. This would be consonant with the ownership of the final finished sketch by Saly, since the sculptor's collection seems to have consisted largely of things acquired from his contemporaries before he left for Copenhagen in 1753. He did not return to France, however, until the summer of 1774. In which case, how could either Saint-Quentin (who was only born in 1738) have made a drawing from his oil sketch, or Parizeau (who was only born in 1740) have made an etching from it by 1773? Either Saly must have acquired the grisaille in the two years between his return to France and his death, or the sketch must have been inserted into the posthumous sale of his effects by the auctioneer, a not uncommon practice.

The subject of this grisaille was not suggested by de Bachaumont, nor was it depicted by Natoire, yet it is in fact crucial to the whole story of Psyche since it shows the tale's beginning (it was, however, included in the set of Brussels tapestries, and in an eighteenth-century expansion of the pre-Gobelins Paris set [see Göbel, 1928, II, vol. i, p. 53]. I am most grateful to Edith Standen for drawing my attention to this). What we see are Psyche's compatriots paying to her beauty the tributes that were due to Venus, so infuriating the latter that she dispatches her son Cupid to make Psyche fall in love with an outcast—only for him to succumb to her charms himself. The episode is not one that was developed by any of the sources recommended by de Bachaumont, but it is to be found in the original recording of the story in Apuleius's *Golden Ass* (as the inscription under the engraving makes clear). This has already—albeit too contrivedly, I believe—been proposed as the source for the tapestry design known as *Le Vannier* (Hussmann, 1977), but in the present case the correspondence is almost entire: "When the young princess went out on her morning walks through the streets, victims were offered in her honour, sacred feasts spread for her, flowers scattered in her path, and rose garlands presented to her by an adoring crowd of suppliants who addressed her by all the titles that really belonged to the great Goddess of Love herself" (translation by Robert Graves). It says much for Boucher's erudition—or for his openness to advice from his friends—that he should thus have gone back to consult the *Urtext* of his story.

## 37 | *The Little Pedlar*

Oil on canvas
63½ × 63½ in. (161 × 161 cm)
Musée Baron Martin, Gray
A & W 132/1 (as *La Curiosité*)

PROVENANCE
?*Catalogue d'une Collection de Tableaux et Dessins composant le fonds de marchandise de M. SAMSON*, Hôtel de Bullion (Chariot & Henri), 27 and 28 Oct. 1812, lot 17 [described but without dimensions; sold for 9.10 francs]; Billardet coll. (as Fragonard), entered the museum at an uncertain date (see Mirimonde, 1955).                                      A.D.L.

TAPESTRIES
1. Combined with *La danse*, a title that was woven twelve times between 1744 and 1753, without its being possible to say when on its own and when in combination (Badin, 1909, p. 60). Some surviving examples of *La danse* do not include *The Little Pedlar*. Those that do (but exclude the figure of the Savoyard) are:
   a. Sale of M. X., Galerie Georges Petit, Paris, 23 May 1927, lot 1 (Standen, 1977[a], fig. 15).

Around 1735 Boucher was entrusted by Oudry, the new director of the tapestry manufactory at Beauvais, with the task of supplying designs to the weavers on a regular basis. This was to be one of the outstandingly successful episodes of his career, making the fortune of this commercial enterprise. As the directors of the rival state-run establishment of the Gobelins wrote when desperately pleading for his services in 1754: "for almost the last twenty years the Beauvais Manufactory has only been sustained by the appealing pictures made for it by Mr. Boucher. . . . Leaving the merits and demerits of these works aside, private individuals without much connoisseurship will always go for novelty and be satisfied with designs exhibiting the composition and manner of the said Mr. Boucher." (*"la Manufacture des Beauvais ne s'est soutenue depuis près de 20 ans que par les tableaux gratieux que luy a fait le Sr Boucher. . . . Que ces ouvrages soient bien ou mal, le particulier peu connaisseur donnera toujours la préférence à la nouveauté et se contentera des sujets traittés de la composition et du goust du dit Sieur Boucher"* [Fenaille, IV, 1907, p. 226].) It is for this reason that, in addition to showing examples of

37

Fig. 138. *La danse*, Beauvais tapestry. Reproduced from the M.X sale catalogue, Galerie Georges Petit, Paris, 23 May 1927, no. 1.

the tapestries themselves, we have sought to include at least one painting with a claim to be considered one of those supplied by Boucher to Beauvais, even though the exact status of such pictures remains open to question.

What format of painting did Boucher supply Beauvais with? Documentation of Boucher's work for the manufactory is wretchedly inadequate (see Badin, 1909, passim), but much sense has been made of what there is by the lucid studies of Edith Standen (see, in addition to the essay and entries in this catalogue, esp. 1977[a] and [b]) and by Hal Opperman's work on Oudry (1977, pp. 87–89, 93–98, and exh. cat. 1982–83, Paris, pp. 109–10, 126, 149–50, 156). When Oudry was appointed official painter to Beauvais in 1726, he was initially required to supply six pictures a year, each three to four feet high, from which full-size *patrons* (cartoons) were to be made at the manufactory's expense. Two years later, to avoid duplication of work and cost, the arrangement was changed: after presenting preliminary sketches to the *contrôleur général des Finances*, Oudry was himself to supply full-scale pictures, at the rate of eight every three years. In the low-warp method of weaving employed at Beauvais, the actual cartoons had to be cut up into

b. Comte Greffulhe sale, Sotheby's, London, 23 July 1937, no. 62.

c. Baron Guy de Rothschild, Paris.

2. Perhaps on its own: woven in 1752 for M. Camusat, as *Le marchand bijoutier* (Standen, 1977[a], p. 113, no. 21), but perhaps part of *La danse* woven for him in that year (Badin, 1909, p. 60).

3. Combined with *La danse*, with the figure of the Savoyard: Gaston Menier sale, Paris, 24 Nov. 1936, lot 115 (A & W 132/2, fig. 470); sold again at Christie's, Geneva, 8 May 1973, lot 116b (Standen, 1977[a], fig. 18), one of three pieces of a single *La danse*.　　E.A.S.

strips about a yard wide, which were placed under the warps upon which an individual weaver worked. Whether what Oudry supplied was treated in this way, or was used by the painters in the regular employ of Beauvais to make copies that were so treated, is not clear; the absence of any surviving full-scale pictures by Oudry suggests that it was these that were used, and that they perished because of being so cut, and through wear and tear.

Boucher never appears to have had a formal contract with Beauvais; he seems rather to have been invited by Oudry to fulfill his obligation, after Oudry had been appointed director in March 1734. Once he had received the more prestigious invitation to supply pictures to the Gobelins in 1733, Oudry had ceased to make fully original designs for Beauvais, drawing on earlier pictures and drawings instead, and it was no doubt dissatisfaction with the chore of making full-scale pictures from these (even with studio assistance), combined with recognition of the commercial failure of his designs (for instance, only one set of the *Metamorphoses* ever appears to have been woven, in 1734), that prompted him to appeal to Boucher, whose ambition was precisely to work on a large scale, as we have seen with the pictures painted for Derbais (cat. 17, 18).

Boucher does not appear to have painted cartoons, but rather full-scale pictures from which cartoons could be copied to be cut into strips for the weavers. What is more, he appears to have seized the essence of tapestry design in a way that few of his predecessors had: that tapestries were bought to furnish particular rooms, that these rooms differed in their dimensions and in the division of their walls, and that what was therefore needed was a supply of groups of figures of similar character that could be put together in differing combinations to yield tapestries of the required dimensions and number. Piquantly, it may have been the insight he acquired into Watteau's method of composing paintings from his drawings, which Boucher acquired when etching the latter for de Jullienne, that gave Boucher this idea.

The evidence for this insight of Boucher's resides in the combinations found in the tapestries from the *Fêtes Italiennes* series themselves, and in what are apparently the four paintings made for the series to survive: the present picture, *La bohémienne*, *La pêcheuse* (New York art market; A & W 129/2, 131/2, figs. 463, 468; exh. cat. 1982, Tokyo, nos. 14, 15), and *La jeune mère et deux enfants* (?H. Winterfeld sale, London, 9 Dec. 1936, lot 86; allocated to the Louvre by the Office des Biens Privés in 1950; on deposit with the Mobilier National since 1960 [M.N.R. 79]; A & W 134/3, fig. 473). All the pictures have suffered, as one would expect from their having been kept in the less than ideal conditions of a manufactory, and have evidently had pieces added and subtracted. The widths of the present picture and *La bohémienne* are, however, the same, while that of *La pêcheuse* (whose height, 260 cm, is identical to that of *La bohémienne*) is very close (152.5 cm). Whereas the present picture and *La jeune mère* (which is of approximately the same height) appear exactly as they occur in the tapestries, except in reverse, the other pair of pictures has undergone much more substantial modifications to make them into self-sufficient compositions. The fact that this is sometimes gratuitous (as in the transformation of the setting and the removal of the supporting girl from *La bohémienne*, and in the substitution of a tree for the temple in the background of *La pêcheuse*) suggests that loss and damage to these must have been more substantial, which would help to account for any apparent defects of quality. An interesting fact, which does not seem to have been observed, is that there is a picture (S & M 1426; exh. cat. 1952, London, no. 1) that appears to have been an example of the kind of combination predicated by Edith Standen: it shows the group of *La bohémienne* in its proper setting (which was derived from a lost painting by Boucher, known from a copy in the Munier-Jolain sale, Paris, 9 Dec. 1910, lot 2, and a circular gouache in a sale at Sotheby Parke Bernet, New York, 5–7 Dec. 1974, lot 575), associated with the group that is combined with it in all the surviving tapestries, a *galant* couple of quite a different social class, in which the boy is holding a crown over the girl; an amusing feature is that the gaze of the boy has been changed and he has been given a rather crude wig, no doubt in an early attempt to repair some damage.

All four pictures appear to be very broadly handled, with none of the subtleties that characterize Boucher's handling of paint at this period. Since Boucher was painting directly for the tapestry manufactory—unlike his work for the Gobelins, to which were lent finished pictures that entered the royal collections in their own right—it is uncertain how much this reflects studio assistance, and how much a deliberate intent to simplify for the sake of the weavers. Seeing that it was stated in the case of the *Chinoiseries* alone that the sketches were by Boucher and the full-scale pictures by the manufactory's own artist, and that is the only instance where we have such sketches (the grisailles for some of the *Psyche* series were stages in Boucher's own resolution of the compositions, lacking the essential element of color that would have guided other artists), whereas in the case of the *Fêtes Italiennes* the full-scale pictures at least purported to be from Boucher's own hand—this early in his career they are likely to have been so to a great extent.

Edith Standen has pointed out that although *The Little Pedlar* was mostly woven with *La danse* into one composition (fig. 138) from what she has identified as the second set of tapestries forming the *Fêtes Italiennes*, which was composed of *galant* depictions of the amusements of higher strata of society than the first, it is to the first set of more huckstering scenes that the present group of a pedlar offering his wares to two country girls and a resting Savoyard belongs in spirit. Nevertheless, the way in which *La danse* is found flanked by the pedlar and his customers on the one side, and by the peasant *Mère et deux enfants* on the other, suggests that in the second set there was a deliberate piquancy in the combination of two spheres, whereas Boucher's first set only had rustic protagonists (and may partly have been designed as a replacement of the set of tapestries after Teniers, which had last been woven in 1725; see Badin, 1909, p. 56). So, just as the early tapestry of *L'opérateur* combined a motif from Dutch genre painting with *souvenirs d'Italie* in the setting (Slatkin, 1977, pp. 130–32), the completed series afforded the possibility of combining actual country people with fashionable folk playing out a game of pastoral love. The number of weavings of each tapestry—a dozen or more in every case but two—testifies to the success of the formula.

## 38 | Woman Fastening Her Garter, with Her Maid

Oil on canvas
20¾ × 26¼ in. (52.5 × 66.5 cm)
Signed bottom left: *f. Boucher 1742*
Thyssen-Bornemisza Collection, Lugano
A & W 208

PROVENANCE
Count Carl Gustaf Tessin, Paris [acquired for 648 livres]; shipped to Stockholm in June 1742; his posthumous sale, Åkerö, 4–16 Feb. 1771; L. Masreliez, Stockholm; Baron E. Cederström, Löfsta; Baron Nathaniel de Rothschild, Vienna (Rothschild, 1903, no. 249); Baron Alphonse de Rothschild, Vienna; Rosenberg & Stiebel, New York; acquired by the present owner in 1967.

PREPARATORY DRAWINGS
1. *Standing Girl Seen from Behind* [employed for the lady's maid, with several variations], red, black, and white chalks, 353 × 199 mm, Institut Néerlandais, Paris (exh. cat. 1964, Paris, no. 86).
2. *Seated Woman Fastening Her Garter*, red, black, and white chalks, 325 × 232 mm, posthumous sale of [Sébastian II] Le Clerc, Hôtel d'Aligre (Joullain *fils*), 17 Dec. ff. 1764, lot 351: "une jolie femme habillée à la Françoise, elle est assise & occupée à remettre sa jarretière" [revealed by notes in the copy in the Bibliothèque d'Art et d'Archéologie, Paris, actually to have belonged to (Blondel) d'Azaincourt, and to have been sold to Le Brun for 9 livres]; Le Brun sale, Hôtel Serpente, 23 Dec. ff. 1771, lot 14: "L'étude d'une femme à sa toilette, mettant sa jarretière, aux crayons rouge & noir" [bought by Bautrüe for 9 livres 19 sous]; Clément sale, Paris, 15 Feb. 1864, lot 3; P. Fourché, by whom donated to the Musée des Beaux-Arts, Orléans, in 1907 (with an attribution to Fragonard; here fig. 139).

RELATED WORK
Painting, 45 × 36 cm, [Bon & others] sale, Hôtel Bullion, 22–23 Mar. 1827, lot 17: "Dans un intérieur d'appartement, une jeune dame assise près du feu met sa jarretière" [sold for 27.50 francs; lot 18 was *Le déjeuner* (cat. 34)]; Col. Devère sale, 17 Mar. 1855, lot 7; Marcille sale, 12–13 Jan. 1857, lot 7?; [Maulaz] sale, 29 Nov. 1875, lot 33; Cailleux, Paris; Jesse I. Strauss coll., New York (1930); Irma N. Strauss coll., New York, Parke-Bernet sale, New York, 22 Oct. 1970, lot 13 (color illus. on cover).

Of all Boucher's clients, the Swedish envoy Count Carl Gustaf Tessin was surely the most congenial to him and thus also the one who extracted the best from him in a variety of modes. One can almost believe it when Hårleman wrote to Tessin from Paris after the latter's return to Sweden, on 28 February 1745: "Poor Boucher, his pretty wife . . . and so many other artists, ask me with tears in their eyes if they cannot go and join your Excellency in Sweden, and it is with great regret that I realize that our resources are too small for such great figures" (see Proschwitz, 1983, p. 34). Tessin appears to have had a special admiration for Boucher, not simply as a painter of women, but of women in their domestic surroundings, to judge from his ownership not only of the present picture but also of a (now lost) grisaille of a *Woman at Her Toilette with a Parrot* (Sander, 1872, pp. 57, 63; probably the original of the engraving by Petit called *Le Matin*, J-R 1456); of a finished oval variant of this, showing her looking at the miniature of a man in her patch box (Sander, 1872, p. 66, and exh. cat. 1980, London, Agnew's, no. 28—if these are, as seems likely, one and the same picture); and of the pen and wash drawing of a *Young Woman Being Dressed by Her Maid* (Bjurström, 1982, no. 946— capriciously reattributed to Durameau). At the same time, he was closely involved with Lovisa Ulrica's commission for a set of four pictures of the Times of the Day, each denoted by a woman at some characteristic occupation of the hour (see cat. 51), possibly inspired by the inclusion of the engraving after his grisaille in just such a set. It is surely also not devoid of significance that the present picture was not among those that Tessin sold to Lovisa Ulrica in 1749, despite her having been thwarted in her desire to have the set of pictures, but was retained by him until his death in 1770. Yet one wonders whether Boucher's failure to complete the commission for Lovisa Ulrica does not indicate that Tessin was inducing Boucher to go against his natural bent in painting such pictures.

This is hard to believe when faced with the present composition, which has every appearance of having been painted by someone who relished detailing the disorder of fashionable bric-a-brac behind the scenes of an elegant lady's toilette. Most conspicuous are the items from the Far East: the stuff of the folding screen (identical to the one in the presumed portrait of Mme Boucher in the Frick Collection in New York; fig. 149) and the fire screen (note also the hand-screen on the floor, of a form for which Boucher had made designs for Huquier), the tea set, and the cassolette on the mantelpiece. There is thus a special aptness in the fact that the playful kitten is repeated in the chinoiserie overdoor *en camaïeu bleu* of *Le thé à la chinoise* of the same year (exh. cat. 1964, Paris, Cailleux; now in the collection of the Earl of Chichester), as well as (in reverse) in Aveline's engraving after a Boucher chinoiserie drawing, *Le*

38

Fig. 139. *Study of a Woman Fastening Her Garter*. Musée des Beaux-Arts, Orléans.

*mérite de tout pais* (J-R 199). Also of interest is the half-concealed painting of the head of a woman on the wall, which Allen Rosenbaum has plausibly suggested might represent a pastel by Rosalba Carriera (exh. cat. 1979–81, Washington, no. 49)—though it should also be remembered that Boucher himself did pastels in the same vein.

Whether the picture is more than a simple genre scene is something that has exercised many commentators. There is no good reason for supposing that it was intended, like *The Milliner* (cat. 51), as one of a set, in this case depicting the occupations of a courtesan, as in Hogarth's *Harlot's Progress*, but without the moralizing sequence of degradation, as suggested by Charles Sterling (see *Sammlung Thyssen-Bornemisza*, 1971, no. 39). Sterling's further suggestion, that Mme Boucher might be the protagonist, is more arresting. It certainly looks as though the woman fastening her stocking is the same as in the *Woman Holding a Pug*, formerly in the collection of Mme Pétin (A & W 268), but there are no good grounds for supposing the latter to have been Mme Boucher. She is much more plausibly identified with the sharp-faced, dark-haired woman in the portrait of a woman on a daybed of 1743 (A & W 263) in the Frick Collection. And although it is evident that Tessin had a tendre for Mme Boucher (Lundberg, 1972, p. 130), the story that he got

Boucher to design the illustrations for his fairy tale, *Faunillane*, in order to create opportunities of têtes-à-têtes with her (Montaiglon, 1858–60) becomes less plausible in view not only of the uxoriousness recently revealed by the publication of Tessin's letters from Paris to his own wife, but also of his addressing the latter as if she were a character in the tale (see Proschwitz, 1983, pp. 33–34, 242, 343). The fact that Tessin's shipments back to Sweden included a pastel of Mme Boucher—perhaps the very pastel peeping over the folding screen—further supports the supposition of his fondness for her; but it would also argue very strongly against the anonymous woman fastening her garter being her, since the identity of the two would have been readily apparent and a shocking affront to Tessin's wife—let alone a singular prostitution of Boucher's wife. Boucher might conceivably have turned a blind eye to his wife's fascination of an important client, but to suppose two such mutually complaisant spouses outruns even the license of the eighteenth-century French novel.

There is one further argument for supposing that the woman portrayed was intended as a portrait, even if that portrait cannot be of Mme Boucher: that is the evident difference between her features and those of the woman in what is apparently the preparatory study for her (though Sterling thought it a copy), a drawing *aux trois crayons* in the Musée des Beaux-Arts in Orléans (fig. 139; A & W fig. 644). Yet what the comparison between the two suggests is that the features of the woman in the painting are a fashionable mask—the depiction of a type rather than an individual, as has been proposed by Denys Sutton (exh. cat. 1982, Tokyo, no. 23). Somewhat disconcerting is the existence of another painting, of the woman alone, much more closely based on the drawing. However, not only does the handling of this appear from reproductions to be uncharacteristic of Boucher, there are also elements of the furnishings—the fire screen in the shape of a hand-screen and its placing, the grotesquely curved overmantel mirror, the form of the chair and its *capitonné* buttoning—that arouse disquiet. Yet the apparent first record of this picture would seem surprisingly early for any pastiche, so that until the painting is subjected to scrutiny, it must remain an enigma—just as must the full story of how Tessin's picture ever came to be painted.

# 39 | *Diana at the Bath*

Oil on canvas
22 × 28¾ in. (56 × 73 cm)
Signed bottom left: *1742 f. Boucher*
Musée du Louvre, Paris (inv. 2712)
S & M 130      A & W 215

For Boucher, 1742 was something of an *annus mirabilis*. He was at the peak of his powers, and he exhibited more pictures in the Salon than he was ever to do again. These pictures included the eight chinoiserie sketches for Beauvais (cat. 41–44), the *Leda* (cf. cat. 40), the *Frère Luce* (cat. 45), a sketch for a stage set for the Opéra, a *Landscape in the Environs of Beauvais*, and the

39

Diane au retour de la chasse; la Déesse est
assise sur une draperie dans un paysage, &
accompagnée de ses Nymphes dont une vient
de lui ôter ses brodequins; on y voit pour
accessoires de la composition, deux chiens et
du gibier mort. Hauteur 26 pouces 6 lignes,
largeur 20 pouces 6 lignes. Toile. Ces deux
morceaux sont agréables de composition, & du
bon tems de M. *Boucher*'' [sold for 409 livres
to Hamont]; ? sale of baron Thibon, 14 May
1821 or 1841 (inscribed on destroyed stretcher);
sale of the comte de N[arbonne], 24 Mar. 1851,
lot 6; M. Van Cuyck, from whom acquired by
the Louvre in 1852.

ENGRAVING
*Diane sortant du bain*, by Edmond Hédouin
in 1864 (J-R 1073).

present picture. Dated works not shown in the Salon included the *Clio* in the
Cabinet des Médailles, the *Toilette de Vénus* in the Rothschild collection, the
*Education of Cupid* at Charlottenburg, and *Woman Fastening Her Garter*
(cat. 38).

Of all these, the present picture is the most celebrated (so much so as to
have aroused the covetousness of Ribbentrop in World War II), and it is
something of a surprise to realize that this was not so in the eighteenth
century. It aroused no special comment at the Salon (but this was because
Salon criticism was not properly launched); it was not engraved in the
eighteenth century; and we do not know who owned it. It would perhaps be
more accurate to say that we are not certain who owned it, any more than we
are certain that it is this picture that was exhibited in the Salon. For if a literal
reading of sales catalogues were to prevent us from identifying this picture
with any in eighteenth-century sale catalogues, consistency requires that we
should be as strict in our reading of the catalogue of the 1742 Salon; in which
case, one would have to note that Diana is not "leaving the bath" in the
present picture, while its dimensions are marginally too small for it to be

PREPARATORY DRAWING

*Seated Nude* (study for Diana), red chalk heightened with white on pinkish paper, 318 × 267 mm; Maurice Delacre coll., Ghent; his posthumous sale, Gutekunst & Klipstein, Berne, 21–22 June 1949, lot 44; Walter Baker coll., New York (Virch, 1962, no. 74); his bequest, Metropolitan Museum, New York, 1971 (exh. cat. 1973–74, Washington, no. 46; here fig. 140).

COPIES

(Purportedly eighteenth-century only)

1. Painting, 71 × 58.5 cm, Evensen sale, Konserthus, Hälsingborg, 13–15 Sept. 1934, lot 16.

2. Painting, oval, Union sale, Berlin, 8 May 1937, lot 158.

3. Painting, 27 × 33½ in., Christie's, London, 27 July 1962, lot 113.

Fig. 140. *Seated Nude.* The Metropolitan Museum of Art, New York; Bequest of Walter C. Baker, 1971.

Fig. 141. *Le fleuve Scamandre*, engraving by Nicolas de Larmessin after Boucher, exhibited at the Salon of 1743.

readily identifiable as the Salon entry. These, however, are obviously quibbles, and to deny that the present picture was the one in the 1742 Salon would not only fly in the face of their common date but would also invite the objection that the composition described in the Salon catalogue is not otherwise known, even in the form of a copy. The same objection obtains if one attempts to deny the identification of the present picture with the one with which it is most natural to connect it, the *Repos de Diane* in the posthumous sale of Blondel d'Azaincourt.

The crucial discrepancy between the present picture and the description of the *Repos de Diane* in the Blondel d'Azaincourt sale is that in the latter Diana is "accompanied by her Nymphs, of whom one has just removed her buskins." The action is the one suggested here, but there is only one nymph. The obvious explanation is that the fault lay with an overhasty redaction of the catalogue, and that what was intended was: "accompanied by one of her Nymphs, who has just removed her buskins." This emendation made, the rest of the description fits perfectly, down to the dimensions, once it is realized that these are inverted (an error that itself makes another error more plausible).

That the dimensions of the painting were inverted we know from its having been sold with a pendant, the *Repos de Vénus*, whose description enables us to identify it with the picture engraved by Duflos (J-R 939) and recently acquired by the Staatliche Museen in Berlin (A & W 217; exh. cat. 1982, Tokyo, no. 24). Perhaps the most significant fact about the two pictures is that, though an attempt was made to sell them as a pair because of their affinity of subject and identity of dimensions, the attempt failed, and they were in fact sold to separate buyers for quite discrepant prices. The *Repos de Vénus* went to Paillet for 680 livres, while the *Repos de Diane* went to Hamont for 409 livres. The lower price may seem surprising, but of the two the *Repos de Vénus* is palpably the earlier picture and the one that would therefore have been regarded in the 1780s as belonging to the "bon tems de M. *Boucher*" (see Provenance), consequently fetching the higher price. The fact that it alone was engraved (evidently before it entered Blondel d'Azaincourt's possession), and that it was not exhibited in the Salon, is additional confirmation that the two pictures were not true pendants.

Today, we can only marvel at the comparative esteem in which the two pictures were once held. The pose of Diana, in particular, is one of Boucher's happiest inventions. It is closely related to that of the girl removing a stocking in the lost picture of *Le fleuve Scamandre*, which may well have been painted in the same year, since de Larmessin's engraving after it (fig. 141; J-R 1254) was shown at the Salon of 1743, and thus also related to a whole group of depictions whose original inspiration may have been a sculpture (see cat. 49, 50). In the present variation, however, it derives from a drawing, whose quickness and delicacy suggest a product of Boucher's imagination rather than the study of any model (fig. 140).

# 40 | *Leda and the Swan*

Oil on canvas
23½ × 29 in. (60 × 74 cm)
Signed: *f. Boucher*
Nationalmuseum, Stockholm
(NM 771)
A & W 222

PROVENANCE
Acquired by Count Carl Gustaf Tessin in Paris
for 372 livres and shipped to Sweden in June
1742; sold to Crown Princess Lovisa Ulrica in
1749; Drottningholm; transferred to the
Nationalmuseum in 1865.

OTHER VERSION
22 *pouces* by 26 *pouces* (59.5 × 70.5 cm),
exhibited in 1742 Salon (21 bis); Harenc de
Presle coll. (engraved by W. W. Ryland in
1758); first Aranc de Presle sale, 16 Apr. 1792,
lot 59 [presumably bought in]; his sale, 11
floréal, l'an III (30 Apr. 1795), lot 67 [bought
for 1,200 livres by Le Brun]; Théodore Patureau coll., Paris; privately sold before 1857
to Dr. Lombard, Liège (d. 1860); posthumous
sale of comte d'Hane de Steenhuyse et de
Leuwerghem of Ghent, Hôtel Drouot, Paris,
27 Mar. 1860, lot 3; Carlton Gates, U.S.A.; his
sale, New York, 21 Dec. 1876, lot 480;
Countess of Pembroke, Rome (this ownership
is recorded for the first time in the catalogue of
the Paolini sale; it is possible that it was taken
from a label and that the Countess of
Pembroke in question was the divorced wife,
née Principessa Octavia Spinelli, of the 12th
Earl, who was a pioneering collector of eighteenth-century French art. She died in 1857, so
would have owned the picture between Harenc
de Presle and Patureau. No other Countess of
Pembroke is known to have lived in Rome.);
Prof. Paolo Paolini sale, American Art Galleries, New York, 11 Dec. 1924, lot 112;
George F. Harding Museum, Chicago; on the
dissolution of this, included in a Sotheby
Parke Bernet sale, New York, 2 Dec. 1976, lot
153 [sale annulled]; reoffered for sale,
Sotheby's, New York, 6 June 1985, lot 147, as
"studio of François Boucher," when acquired
by the present owners (exh. cat. 1985, New
York, no. 15).

COPIES
Ananoff and Wildenstein list a dozen copies
(222/4–222/15), including the Harenc de Presle picture, which should not have been so
described. It has not been possible in the time
available to check which of these were indeed
copies of the present composition. The following copies may be added to that list:
1. 24 *pouces* by 26 *pouces*, Vincent Potocki
coll., Warsaw, 1780, cat. no. 192 (paired with
lot 191, a *Venus*).

The loves of Jupiter were to be numbered among Boucher's favorite themes; were one to be cynical, one might suggest that Jupiter's metamorphoses happily resolved Boucher's apparent difficulties in depicting the adult male physiognomy. Certainly the fact that Jupiter and Callisto was the amour that he chose most frequently to depict must have owed something to the fact that in this Jupiter disguised himself as another deity, Diana. It thus perhaps is a little surprising that Boucher only depicted Leda in one composition, even though, by depicting Leda with a companion, he had resolved the inherent implausibility of the episode by relegating Jupiter, in the form of the swan, to a mere intrusion. There are not even the cupids that, in the drawings engraved by Demarteau (J-R 820) and Léveillé (J-R 1395), allude to the amorous outcome of the episode, from which Castor, Pollux, Clytaemnestra, and Helen were to be born.

Nevertheless, the success of this composition of Leda was such that he painted it twice. One would have expected the first version to have been the one exhibited here, since this was shipped to Sweden by Tessin in June 1742 (Sander, 1872, p. 60, no. 116), whereas the other was exhibited in the Salon in August–September of the same year. It is the Salon version that was engraved by Ryland in 1758 (J-R 1535–1539). The inscription on the engraving reveals that the painting was already in the collection of the banker Hareng, Harenc, or Aranc de Presle (the name is spelled in numerous ways; see Duvaux, 1873, I, p. cclxxvi), in whose sales it appeared at the time of the Revolution. It then disappeared from view, but its reemergence and subsequent history can be traced very fully, from the middle of the nineteenth century down to the present (see exh. cat. 1985, New York, no. 15). X-rays showing that it was originally begun the other way up on the canvas, several pentimenti, and its brushwork all declare it to be the prime version, despite overzealous restoration in some parts.

One of the interesting quirks of Boucher's output was that he seems to have been more prepared to produce and sign a second autograph version of a painting if the first had gone to a foreign client, so that the possibility of invidious comparisons was avoided. In the present case, Tessin must have seen the first *Leda* in Boucher's studio and have ordered a replica for himself, stipulating that it should be the work of the artist's own hands. This is evident not merely from its high quality and the signature, but also from the bill of lading when it was shipped to Sweden. For although its valuation (which was evidently its original price) was only about three-fifths that of the unique and, no doubt, specially commissioned *Woman Fastening Her Garter* (cat. 39), it was over six times that of the *Capriccio View of Tivoli* (cf. cat. 16), which was described as "retouched by Boucher," and over ten times that of a copy of an oval *Venus and Cupid* (Sander, 1872, p. 57).

40

2. No dimensions, sale of the duc de Gramont, 21 nivose, l'an II (11 Jan. 1794), lot 41 (paired with a *Femme couchée*).

3. Large picture, misc. sale, rue Saint-Lazare 76 bis, Paris, 28 Apr. 1819, lot 112 bis (paired with a *Venus and Adonis*): possibly identical with the picture subsequently in the [comte de Morny] sale, Meffre *aîné*, Paris, 25 Feb. 1845, lot 6 [bought by M. d'Herambault]; Dr. Benoist sale, 19 June 1867, lot 19 [according to S & M 189].

4. Painting called "Ecole de Boucher," Adolphe Warneck sale, Paris, 20–21 Aug. 1849, lot 106.

5. Miniature attributed to Charlier, 50 × 72 mm, Wallace Collection, London (*Wallace Collection Catalogues*, 1980, no. 77).

6. Miniature, diam. 77 mm, Wallace Collection (*Wallace Collection Catalogues*, 1980, no. 84).

7. Miniature, Morosini sale, American Art Association–Anderson Galleries, New York, 10–15 Oct. 1932, lot 1583.

Of the gallery pictures that went to Sweden (as opposed to the overdoors painted for the Royal Palace, which were already somewhat unoriginal jugglings with stock motifs, such that the autograph status of one of them, the *Venus, Graces, and Cupids Bathing*, has been doubted despite its documentation; see Chomer, 1981, p. 82), only the *Venus on the Waters* and *Woman Fastening Her Garter* went uncopied, probably because they were both suggested and commissioned by Tessin, whose intense enthusiasm for the former, in particular, gave Boucher no chance to do so before he removed it and dispatched it to Sweden. Curiously, Moitte's later engraving of the *Venus on the Waters* does not appear to have inspired subsequent copies of the picture; Ryland's engraving of the *Leda*, by contrast, seems to have prompted several, although in many cases in early sales, the description is too terse to make it certain that this was the composition in question.

## 41 | *L'audience de l'Empereur chinois*

Oil on canvas
16¼ × 25¼ in. (41.5 × 64.5 cm)
Musée des Beaux-Arts, Besançon
S & M 2474      A & W 225

## 42 | *La foire chinoise*

Oil on canvas
16¼ × 25¼ in. (41.5 × 64.5 cm)
Musée des Beaux-Arts, Besançon
S & M 2474      A & W 226

## 43 | *Le jardin chinois*

Oil on canvas
16 × 19 in. (40.5 × 48 cm)
Musée des Beaux-Arts, Besançon
S & M 2474      A & W 230

## 44 | *La pêche chinoise*

Oil on canvas
16½ × 22 in. (42 × 56 cm)
Musée des Beaux-Arts, Besançon
S & M 2474      A & W 228

PROVENANCE
Exhibited with four of the other sketches in the Salon of 1742; *Catalogue des Tableaux des Trois Ecoles . . . &c. qui composoient le Cabinet de feu M. BERGERET . . . Receveur-Général des Finances*, son hôtel, rue du Temple, 24 Apr. ff. 1786, lots 55 (*La Pêche Chinoise* with *La Danse Chinoise*), 56 (*Le Jardin Chinois* with *La Chasse Chinoise*), 57 (*La Foire Chinoise*), 59 (*L'Audience* with *Le Repas de l'Empereur Chinois*) [all ten sketches bought by Pierre-Adrien Pâris for 270 livres]; bequeathed by Pâris to the Bibliothèque de Besançon in 1819, whence transferred to the museum in 1843, with the exception of *Le jardin chinois*, which did not reappear until it was exhibited in Tokyo in 1982 by MM. Wildenstein, from whom it was acquired in 1983.

Such was Boucher's enthusiasm for depicting things Chinese that in 1748 one of his admirers felt constrained to say: "Those who support him nonetheless fear lest the constant study of the Chinese mode, which appears to be the ruling passion of M. Boucher, will ultimately affect the grace of his contours. They will no longer have the same charm, if he continues to design figures of this kind." ("*Ceux qui s'intéressent à lui, craignent donc que l'étude habituelle du goût chinois, qui paroît être la passion favorite de M. Boucher, n'altère enfin la grace de ses contours. Ils n'auroient plus la même douceur, s'il continuoit à dessiner des figures de ce genre*" [Saint-Yves, 1748, p. 28].) His output in this vein was indeed extraordinary, ranging from paintings through tapestry designs and stage sets to engravings, and would on its own have been enough to sustain the career of a lesser artist, yet it would appear only to have preoccupied him over a relatively limited number of years at the peak of his career, when the fashion was at its height. In these years, however, one could say that he was to "make China into one of the regions of the Rococo" (E. & J. de Goncourt, 1881, I, p. 244).

41

42

43

44

204

Fig. 142. *Le mariage chinois.* Musée des Beaux-Arts, Besançon.

Fig. 143. *La danse chinoise.* Musée des Beaux-Arts, Besançon.

Fig. 144. *La chasse chinoise,* engraved by Huquier *fils* after Boucher.

Fig. 145. *Le chinois galant,* signed and dated 1742. Davids Samling, Copenhagen.

Fig. 146. *Le thé à la chinoise.* Earl of Chichester's Trustees, Little Durnford Manor, Wiltshire.

The taste for chinoiserie in Europe, though fed by items such as silk and porcelain imported from the East, evolved rather into one of the licensed forms of the grotesque, permitting fantasy and the breach of established aesthetic rules, than into any serious attempt to discover and imitate its supposed originals (see Honour, 1961; exh. cat. 1973, Berlin; M. Jarry, 1981). Appropriately, it was thus the Chinese figures contributed by Watteau to grotesque decorations by Claude Audran in the Château de la Muette, and the engravings after these by Boucher, Jeaurat, and Aubert (J-R 164–175), that appear to have given the chief impetus to the genre in France in the eighteenth century. The vogue was not immediate, but the most telling sign of it was the name that Gersaint gave to his shop on the Pont Notre-Dame, *A la Pagode,* for which Boucher designed an appropriately chinoiserie trade card in 1740 (fig. 46). Huquier had already advertised a set of a dozen engraved designs for hand-screens "dans le goût Chinois" in July 1737, which may have been versions of Boucher's *Scènes de la vie chinoise* in ornamental surrounds (J-R 1125–1133, see esp. note on 1131); and in July 1740 he advertised a set of the *Five Senses,* in the form of "différens Amusemens chinois" after Boucher; these were engraved by Pierre Aveline, who also exhibited *L'Eau* and *Le Feu* in the Salon in August, from a chinoiserie set of the *Four Elements* published by Huquier. In January 1744 Boucher himself presented to the Academy the set of six *Figures chinoises* engraved by Ingram after his drawings in order to secure their copyright. None of the numerous other engravings after Boucher's chinoiseries are securely datable, but the character of almost all of them is so similar as to make it evident that their originals were all produced within this relatively short time span. One of them, indeed, *Le mérite de tout pais,* engraved by F. A. Aveline (J-R 199), contains features relating it closely to the rocaille overdoor *Le thé à la chinoise* (fig. 146; Earl of Chichester's collection, Little Durnford Manor, Wiltshire; exh. cat. 1964, Paris, Cailleux, no. 40). Although the date was misread as 1747 when it was exhibited, this is in fact one of a pair of overdoors *en camaïeu bleu* (the other, *Le chinois galant,* is in the Davids Samling in Copenhagen [fig. 145; see Honour, 1961, pl. 40]), both of which are dated 1742. That is the year in which the present sketches for a new set of Beauvais chinoiserie tapestries were exhibited in the Salon.

Beauvais already possessed cartoons for one set of chinoiserie tapestries, the joint product of Guy-Louis Vernansal, Blin de Fontenay, and Jean-Baptiste Monnoyer in the 1690s (see Standen, 1976). Though popular enough

Fig. 147. *La pêche chinoise*, Beauvais tapestry. Philadelphia Museum of Art; Given by Mr. William Fahrenstock.

ENGRAVINGS
All four included in the set of six engravings after the sketches by Huquier *fils* (J-R 1164–1170).

ANALOGIES
*Le jardin chinois*, copy of engraving (Humbert, 1982, fig. p. 28).
*La pêche chinoise*:
1. Offset of a red-chalk drawing after the group in the boat, 450 × 405 mm, National Gallery of Scotland, Edinburgh (A & W 688) [seemingly an adaptation of Boucher's design made with the pirated Aubusson version of the tapestry in view].
2. Autonomous variant of group in boat, oil on canvas, 40 × 29 cm, Ch. Michel coll., Paris, in 1932 (A & W 234).
3. Autonomous variant of group around old fisherman, oil on paper laid down on canvas, 38 × 52 cm, Boymans van Beuningen Museum, Rotterdam (A & W 235).
4. Old man with net and boy, drawing, engraved by Aveline as *L'Eau* in 1740 (J-R 233).
5. Ornamental painting in rocaille frame, 31½ × 46 in., attributed to J. Pillement, sold at Christie's, London, 8 July 1983, lot 83, paired with another chinoiserie scene of musicians [related to pirated Aubusson adaptation of *La pêche*].                    A.D.L.

TAPESTRIES
The only complete set of six pieces appears to be that in the Palazzo Reale, Turin, which was presumably one of those delivered to the king, though it lacks the royal arms. The five pieces in the collection of the Earl of Rosebery may also be a complete set, as one of this size is recorded.

in its day, it does not appear to have been woven after 1727, and a set still remained unsold in 1732 (Badin, 1909, pp. 18, 21, 24, 56). The cartoons were also barely legible by then (M. Jarry, 1981, p. 16). There was thus a clear need for a fresh set that would also escape from the old-fashioned Bérainesque appearance of the previous one. This need Boucher supplied, with ten sketches, eight of which were exhibited in the Salon of 1742 (the remaining two were the pair of small vertical panels, each centered upon the single figure of a woman, which were no doubt thought insufficiently important to exhibit).

This exhibition of sketches for Beauvais tapestries betokens a change of procedure in Boucher's role. Previously, as his exhibition of a large picture of *Zephyr Ushering Psyche into Cupid's Palace* in the 1739 Salon indicated, he had conformed to Oudry's practice of supplying full-scale paintings to the manufactory. In the present case, as we know from the registers of Beauvais, Boucher's sketches were worked up into full-scale pictures by a certain Aumont (Weigert, 1933, p. 232), or Dumont (A & W doc. 581), whose traditional identification with Jean-Joseph Dumons of Tulle presupposes an improbably peripatetic existence between Aubusson and Beauvais, as Edith Standen implies (see cat. 90). However, the fact that this limitation of Boucher's role to the production of sketches was expressly mentioned in this one case alone indicates that it was exceptional; it had more to do with the crescendo of demand for Boucher's services in the 1740s, of which we are only too well informed via Scheffer's despairing letters (see cat. 51), than with some permanent change of working practice at Beauvais.

One of the most intriguing questions about Boucher's chinoiserie tapestries concerns their source. They give so convincing—if inaccurate—a picture of Chinese life that it has been felt that they must be based upon some firsthand visual record of China (but for a more judicious assessment, see the excellent discussion of the problem by Denys Sutton, exh. cat. 1982, Tokyo, pp. 231–32). This has traditionally been believed to have been a group of drawings sent back by the Jesuit artist Brother J-D. Attiret. The suggestion must have had special appeal for the museum in Besançon in that Attiret, who was born in Dôle, was also from the Franche-Comté, although the presence of Boucher's sketches in the museum was of course due to no more than a mere accident of ownership by another Franc-Comtois, the architect P-A. Pâris. That Attiret was furthermore a professionally trained artist (he was also uncle of the sculptor Claude-François Attiret) must also have made some sort of connection with Boucher seem more plausible. However, Brother Attiret was only sent out to China in late 1737. His first extended account of what he found there, a description of the emperor's "Garden of Gardens," was in a letter to M. d'Assaut written in November 1743, which was only published in volume 27 of the *Lettres édifiantes . . . écrites des missions de la Compagnie de Jésus* in 1749, too late to have been of use to Boucher, while Attiret's drawings used for the *Victoires et Conquêtes de l'Empereur de Chine* (1770–74) were only sent back in 1765.

To suggest that Boucher had private channels of communication of his own with the Jesuit mission in China stretches belief too far, particularly when he did not even draw upon the illustrations to the recent 1735 reedition of the *Description . . . de l'Empire de la Chine* by the Jesuit Father Du Halde. What is more, it is unnecessary. For if we look closely at Boucher's sketches, we see that each is an inspired pot-pourri of exoticisms, built up around some

Individual tapestries with the designs of sketches in this exhibition are as follows:

*La foire chinoise*, see cat. 90.

*Le jardin chinois*, see cat. 91.

*L'audience de l'Empereur:*

The title is not in the list of the tapestries of the series (Badin, 1909, p. 61) nor in that of the set in Turin. The design is known only from the sketch in this exhibition and the engraving by Huquier (A & W 225/1, fig. 680).

The tapestry versions of it woven at Aubusson may have been copied from the print: one is in a set in the Museum of Fine Arts, Springfield, Mass., and one in the Musée Nissim de Camondo, Paris (1983, no. 456, paired with *Le jardin chinois*); others were in sales at the Palais Galliera, Paris, 9 June, 1961, no. 105 (A & W 225/2), and at the Palais d'Orsay, Paris, 6 Apr., 1978, no. 79.

*La pêche chinoise:*

Philadelphia Museum of Art, 340 × 335 cm, with the royal arms, very close to the sketch (fig. 147).

Amalienborg, Copenhagen; from the Moltke set made in 1759 (A & W 228/10).

Turin, Palazzo Reale, 370 × 520 cm, with additions to the design of the sketch on left and right, showing the boats in their entirety, with water beyond them and a large basket behind the kneeling boy (Chierici, 1969, pl. 10).

Daniel Wildenstein (A & W 228/6, fig. 687); previously sold at the Palais Galliera, Paris, 10 Dec. 1973, no. 122; less tall than the sketch and with the figures at each side curtailed (exh. cat. 1982, Tokyo, no. 133).

Rosebery coll., Dalmeny House, Scotland (*Mentmore*, 1884, illus. p. 23), inscribed *Besnier et Oudry à Beauvais* (Wingfield Digby, 1950, p. 50); compressed but complete.

E. T. Stotesbury sale, Parke-Bernet, New York, 18 Nov. 1944, nos. 36, 37, two separate tapestries, showing the left and right sides of the sketch; from the Stettiner coll. (exh. cat. 1921, London, p. 7).

American coll. or dealer in 1926 (Hunter, 1926[b], p. 88, illus.; Badin, 1909, pl. facing p. 48), left half only, but not the same as the Stotesbury piece.

Palais Galliera sale, 18 June 1965, no. 238 (A & W 228/7, 228/8), possibly the Stotesbury pieces.

Prince Murat sale, Nouveau Drouot, Paris, 14 June 1983, no. 213, right side only, with the mark of A-C. Charron (1753–1780) and the royal arms; said to be from the set sent to China.

Little Durnford Manor, Wiltshire, England, owned by the Earl of Chichester.

Aubusson partial adaptations: 1. with J. Klausner & Sohn, Berlin (Göbel, 1928, II, vol. ii, pl. 275); 2. sold at the Palais des Congrès, Versailles, 3 Mar. 1968, no. 168B (A & W 228/9 and fig. 60).                    E.A.S.

perfectly western motif. The Chinese elements in them are no more than what he might have seen painted on the porcelain, lacquer, and wallpaper for sale in Gersaint's shop or in his own possession, and in such much-plundered sources as the illustrations to Nieuhoff's *Het Gezantschap . . . aan den Grooten Tartarischen Cham* (1670). In *L'audience de l'Empereur*, for instance, the potentate is surmounted by the kind of baldachin found over a *lit à la polonnaise*, and flanked by two more based on the baldachin in St. Peter's. The guards on the left wear exotic straw hats out of paintings by Bassano, while the incense burner in front of them sits upon a plinth of the purest Antique form. So too, *La foire chinoise* is no more than the Foire de Saint-Germain transformed by the addition of chinoiserie staffage, and such standard indications of exoticism as elephants, camels, and palm trees. More convincing are *Le jardin chinois* and *La pêche chinoise*, perhaps because in these the setting gave more opportunity to depict such things as plants, boats, and garden pavilions that could be imitated from Chinese decorative painting.

In the final analysis, however, what is remarkable about Boucher's chinoiseries for Beauvais is not simply that they create a Chinese never-never land that is perfectly plausible in its own terms, but that they also give the impression of a new "Chinese" style of painting. This is in no sense an imitation of actual Chinese pictures—it must remain doubtful that Boucher would ever have seen such things (but see exh. cat. 1982, Tokyo, p. 231, for instances of their occurrence in France)—it is an invention of Boucher's own. These sketches are unlike any others that Boucher ever painted, in both handling and palette—so much so as sometimes to have occasioned doubts (remembering that the actual paintings that the tapestries were executed from were by Aumont or Dumont) that they are by him at all. It is above all their spiky linearity that is uncharacteristic of Boucher's voluptuously loaded brush; and it is this that has vanished in their translation into tapestry by other hands (in which some of their pullulating detail was also sacrificed). If Saint-Yves had these sketches in mind in 1748, his fears for Boucher's style are indeed understandable.

Perhaps the most piquant aspect of all about these chinoiseries concerns the tapestries that were woven from them. Not only did the second weaving of three of them (*La danse*, *La pêche*, and *La foire*) in 1744 go to the future owner of the sketches, the financier Pierre-Jacques-Onésyme Bergeret, who adorned his salon with them (see G. Wildenstein, 1961, p. 42, corrected by reference to Badin, 1909, p. 61), but a complete set went via the Jesuit mission in China to the emperor. He is reputed to have admired them so much that, after originally intending to place them in a temple, he proposed building a special palace for them instead. He was presumably blissfully unaware—and the Jesuits too tactful to tell him—that he was himself supposed to be represented in them! (For the whole improbable story, see Leroy, 1900, and exh. cat. 1982, Tokyo, pp. 231–32.) Either the whole set, or a single tapestry of *La foire chinoise*, was looted in the sack of the Summer Palace in 1860 and returned to France, a not inappropriate event, since this disgraceful episode epitomizes the predatory new realism in attitudes toward China that thrust aside the gentle fantasies that had given rise to Boucher's chinoiseries.

## 45 | Frère Luce

Oil on copper
26½ × 21½ in. (67 × 55 cm)
Signed bottom right on a stone: *f. Boucher / 1742*
Pushkin Museum, Moscow (inv. 2765)
S & M 1735, 1739, 1788        A & W 223
*Paris*

PROVENANCE
Exhibited in the Salon of 1742, as *Un Paysage de la Fable de Frère Luce* (no. 21 bis), without any owner given; Louis-Antoine Crozat, baron de Thiers, Hôtel Crozat, Place Vendôme, *cabinet à la suite de la Bibliothèque* (La Curne de Sainte Palaye, 1755, p. 59); his posthumous inventory, 1771, no. 370 (Stuffmann, 1968, p. 126, no. 108); acquired with the totality of the collection by Catherine the Great in 1772; the Imperial Palace of Gatchina; removed to the Hermitage, Saint Petersburg, in 1882; transferred to the Pushkin Museum, Moscow, in 1930.

ENGRAVINGS
*Le dévot hermite*, engraved by Chedel, and published by August 1753 (J-R 482), with no owner's name given.

COPY
Gouache, 15¾ × 12½ in.: Earl of Rosebery coll., Dalmeny (formerly in the Blarenberghe Room at Mentmore; see *Mentmore*, 1884, II, p. 15, no. 31, called *Landscape; 2 girls crossing a stream*, not illus.).

Boucher and his contemporaries frequently depicted episodes of La Fontaine's *Contes et Nouvelles en vers* (1664 ff.), and when they did so it was almost invariably the tales with some amorous interest that they chose to illustrate (see cat. 7). Boucher and Vleughels appear to have been alone in depicting the same episode from *L'Ermite*, but Boucher is singular in using it essentially as a pretext for a landscape painting, making the hermit and his hermitage establish the mood for the wilderness that he depicts in the foreground, and contrasting this with the sunbathed river valley in the distance. There is an English parallel that suggests itself (although there, neither of the pictures in question is known to illustrate any particular story or poem), and that is with two of Richard Wilson's most popular compositions, *Solitude* (first exhibited in 1762 as a *Landskip with Hermits*) and *The White Monk*. Comparison is perhaps apter with the latter than with the former, despite the fact that in it the eponymous monk (or pair of monks) is removed to a distant eminence, in that Wilson, like Boucher, there creates an antithesis between the apparent austerities of the hermit's life and setting, and the worldly figures and smiling landscape beyond. In neither Boucher nor Wilson is there any persistence of the element of the grotesque that characterizes previous depictions of hermits, by such artists as Magnasco and the Ricci.

The story as told by La Fontaine (which was not taken, as he advertises, from Boccaccio, but from the *Cent Nouvelles nouvelles*) is, however, far from austere or gloomy in intent—even though the ostentatious devotions of Boucher's friar are enough to have convinced one commentator that the ribald Frère Luce was none other than the self-mortifying Greek anchorite, St. Luke the Younger (exh. cat. 1982, Tokyo, no. 26). It concerns a hypocritical hermit who was taken with the charms of the dowerless virgin daughter of a neighboring widow. To enjoy her, he devised the stratagem of counterfeiting the voice of God, which instructed them to yield the girl to Frère Luce in order that a pope might be born of this union. The girl finally complied and became pregnant, but so enjoyed repeating the experience that she succeeded in disguising her pregnancy from both mother and hermit for seven months. All were undeceived when the child was finally born, however, since the promised future pope was—a girl! What is shown in the painting is the trusting mother encouraging her timid daughter on their first visit to the hermit.

*Frère Luce* is first recorded as having belonged to Louis-Antoine Crozat, baron de Thiers (1699–1770), and it may well have been he who both proposed the subject to Boucher and invited him to treat it as a landscape—having no doubt selected him on account of this aptitude. The picture was certainly the result of a specific commission (even though no

45

owner was named when it was exhibited in the Salon) since only a wealthy client would have insisted on the employment of a costly copper support for a painting on this scale. If that client was indeed Crozat de Thiers, the composition is nonetheless likely to have been elaborated by Boucher in consultation with him rather than simply dictated to the artist, since there is other evidence of long-standing links between the two.

Boucher had designed de Thiers's bookplate (Deroy, 1952, fig. p. 61; graphite drawing, Pereire sale, Paris, 25 Mar. 1921; acquired by the Art Institute of Chicago, 1984.627). This bookplate may even have been engraved by de Thiers himself; he certainly later made a number of etchings after drawings by Boucher (J-R 1598–1610; A & W figs. 321, 1470, 1512), mostly of rustic scenes and figures, but also of landscapes (e.g., Paignon Dijonval, 1810, cat. no. 8534). The catalogue of the posthumous sale of Huquier's stock of engravings (Paris, 4 Nov. ff. 1772, lot 44) includes no less than twenty-four different compositions etched by de Thiers after Boucher. Two of these are of *galant* themes (J-R 1599, 1600)—one of them a version of *La belle cuisinière* (cat. 21), here importuned by a youth of rather higher social standing than in the Boucher original—again suggesting some measure of complicity between the draftsman and his etcher.

We also know that in 1746 Boucher was pressed by de Thiers to sell *The Milliner* (cat. 51) to him for double what it had been commissioned for by Crown Princess Lovisa Ulrica, although in the event the painter was not persuaded to go back on his original undertaking (Scheffer, 1982, p. 144).

What are lacking, however, from the evidence of contacts between Boucher and Crozat de Thiers are pictures painted by the one for the other. The posthumous inventory of de Thiers's pictures drawn up by Tronchin prior to their acquisition by Catherine the Great in 1772 (see Stuffmann, 1968, pp. 115–35, esp. p. 126) only contains a *Landscape* apparently identifiable with one of 1746 now in the Hermitage (A & W 300), the present painting of *Frère Luce*, and two drawings. What is more, only the *Frère Luce* appears earlier in the printed catalogue of de Thiers's collection (see La Curne de Sainte Palaye, 1755, p. 59). It is of course true that in this collection, having inherited and kept the pick of the Italian- and Dutch-oriented picture galleries of his uncle and brothers, Crozat de Thiers devoted only one room to works of the French school, the cabinet adjacent to the library, and that in it his aim appears to have been to represent each major figure by one painting, or at most a pair of pendants, as some connoisseurs recommended.

What is particularly curious about the scarcity of paintings by Boucher in Crozat de Thiers's collection is that, according to the author of the life of Boucher in the *Galerie Française* (1771, p. 1), Crozat de Thiers was one of the artist's earliest patrons, during the very period he was etching Watteau's drawings for de Jullienne, when, indeed, he "painted some pictures for the cabinet of M. de Thiers that did not seem at all out of place in that magnificent collection." Quite what these paintings can have been, and why Crozat de Thiers should have divested himself of them later, is unclear.

There is just one picture that it is tempting to identify with one of those painted by Boucher for Crozat de Thiers in these early years, which would certainly not have seemed "at all out of place in that magnificent collection," because it purports to be a copy of a painting by Watteau, by whom de Thiers owned at least five pictures. This is the painting of a "Sleeping woman lying down, seen from behind, watched by a child holding a curtain from the other side of the bed, with a landscape beyond," which was lot 68 in the baron [Baillet] de Saint J[ulien] sale of 21 June ff. 1784, described as by "Boucher, after Watteau." The picture may well be the one (somewhat cut down) that was in the sale of Mme de V[ermeulez] at the Galeries Georges Petit in Paris on 6 May 1909, lot 1, and subsequently in the Labouret collection (*Burlington Magazine*, Apr. 1966, supp., fig. 3) and the collection of H.L.G. in New York (A & W p. 322). Now no original of this description is known to have been painted by Watteau. There was, however, in the Crozat de Thiers collection *Une femme nue couchée* by Watteau (Stuffmann, 1968, no. 183), which is commonly identified with a composition known in the form of a smaller painting in the Norton Simon collection and a drawing (with the added figure of a maid administering an enema) in a private collection in Paris (exh. cat. 1984–85, Washington, no. 88). There is no certainty that this (in whatever form) was the Crozat de Thiers picture, but if it were to have been, one can well imagine the Boucher having been painted for de Thiers not as a copy of a Watteau whose existence is otherwise unknown, but rather as a nicely counterpointed albeit slightly larger pendant to the *Femme nue couchée* of the same woman, in a closely similar pose, lying in a different direction, and seen from behind (it may also be relevant that there was an oval miniature after the same reputed Watteau, by Boucher's friend Massé, in the Godefroy sale on 25 Apr. ff. 1785, lot 171). It is just the kind of pastiche that one can imagine Boucher having produced in these years of intense study of Watteau necessitated by his etchings and engravings after the latter's drawings and paintings.

It is therefore more than a little curious that another version of the same picture but without the child (thus conceivably a better pendant to the presumed Crozat de Thiers Watteau), which was once in the Fairfax Murray collection (Chiesa sale, American Art Association, New York, 27 Nov. 1925, lot 61), bore Boucher's signature and the date 1746—one of the years of Boucher's later, better-documented contacts with Crozat de Thiers (it is of course possible that the date was misread, or both date and signature spurious, though the latter seems unlikely in view of the obviously Watteauesque characteristics of the picture, which would have been more conducive to the forging of his rather than Boucher's signature); we are thus still left in doubt as to whether Boucher's untraced pictures for Crozat de Thiers were indeed painted in his youth, as the *Galerie Françoise* claims, or in the 1740s, as *Frère Luce* was. That his connection with the nephew of Watteau's most devoted patron did date back to the time of his intense involvement with the artist's *Nachlass* nonetheless seems highly probable.

There is one further link with Crozat de Thiers that deserves scrutiny, since it could provide an alternative provenance for the *Frère Luce*. On 18 May 1740, Boucher signed a note acknowledging the receipt of six hundred livres from "le président de thunis" "for a picture of landscape and a little ceiling that I am to execute in the library" (*"pour un tableau de payissage et un petit plafond que je dois luy faire dans la bibliothec"* [published in facsimile in Charavay, 1887, pp. 548–49, no. 1474]). "Le président de thunis" was none other than one of Crozat de Thiers's elder brothers, Joseph-Antoine, baron de Thugny (1696–1751), *président des enquêtes au Parlement*. When he died without issue, both his collections and his *hôtel* (generally known as the Hôtel d'Evreux), which was adjacent to the one already occupied by Crozat de Thiers in the Place Vendôme, were inherited by the latter, who took his pick of the collection and spread himself over both *hôtels*. Interestingly, the library for which Boucher was to execute his "little ceiling" would appear to have been the one adjacent to the cabinet later used by Crozat de Thiers to display his French pictures, having been converted from a gallery in the course of the extensive alterations carried out by Contant d'Ivry in 1747 (see Blondel, 1904–05, III, pp. 101–02, pls. III, IV, and p. 104, pl. IX). Whether Boucher's ceiling picture was commissioned in anticipation of these changes, or whether it was intended for a previous library (none is shown in the old plans) we do not know—any more than we know whether Boucher even fulfilled the commission (no fixed pictures are included in either Crozat de Thiers's catalogue of 1755 or his posthumous inventory of 1771).

At first reading, the wording of the receipt suggests that Boucher was being paid for an already executed landscape and for a ceiling picture to come. There is, however, no breakdown of the payment into a part in final settlement and a part in advance or on account. It would therefore appear that the loosely worded document in fact contains a promise to execute both works for the sum stated, in which case, it is very possible that the "tableau de payissage" in question was the *Frère Luce*, which is dated two years later—not untypical arrears for Boucher. This identification would have the merit of reducing the total of missing or unidentified pictures executed by Boucher for the Crozat brothers by one—but it would leave us further than ever from knowing what it could have been that was painted specifically for Crozat de Thiers. One thing is sure: the almost unique use by Boucher of copper to paint on (but cf. the *View of the Environs of Charenton* in the Kunsthalle in Hamburg, A & W 168), and the fact of its being a plate of exceptional size, is the kind of gratuitous extravagance that would have befitted either of these sons of Antoine Crozat, "the Rich," and heirs of Pierre Crozat, ironically kown as "the Poor."

# 46 | *Landscape with Watermill and Temple*

Oil on canvas; 36 × 46½ in. (91 × 118 cm)
Signed bottom left: *f. Boucher/1743*
The Bowes Museum, Barnard Castle, England
A & W 254

PROVENANCE
Benjamin Gogué, Paris, from whom acquired by John and Josephine Bowes for 1,600 francs, on 19 Jan. 1863; included in the museum that they created, made public after their deaths, in 1892.

One of Boucher's most striking landscapes, because of its brilliant blue sky and overall bluish tonality, this was no doubt the very kind of picture that Gautier d'Agoty had in mind when he compared the artist unfavorably with Oudry, for his "brillantes couleurs . . . teintes vives indécises & trop

46

prodiguées," in contrast to the latter's scientific study of the fall of light (Gautier [d'Agoty], 1753, p. 77). It was not a criticism that would have caused Boucher concern, since—as the combination of the French mill and the ruined Italian temple makes clear (see cat. 34)—he rejoiced in artifice, in taking elements of reality, but producing them in such a way as to suggest a world of illusion, as in the theater. The abbé Gougenot, indeed, specifically praised his stage sets at this period for their "heureux mélange des vûes de Rome & de Tivoli, avec celles de Sceaux & d'Arcueil" (Gougenot, 1748, p. 52).

Regrettably, we do not know for whom this picture was painted. It cannot, as has been asserted by Ananoff and Wildenstein, be identified with the landscape in lot 26 in the posthumous sale of M. de Sireul, since that was called a *View of the Temple of Concord and of the Road that Leads to the Vatican*, and was described as having been painted in Rome. Not only is the Temple of Concord a very different structure from the temple seen here (its remains consist of a straight row of columns), but the date 1743 on the present picture would have precluded anyone from asserting that Boucher had painted it in Rome.

# 47 | *Sketch for a Stage Set*

Oil on canvas
20½ × 26½ in. (52 × 67 cm)
Musée de Picardie, Amiens
A & W 221

Boucher's activity as a theater designer is one of the most intriguing aspects of his career, since it was so evidently congenial to him; yet it is also one of the most elusive, not only because it was of its very nature ephemeral, but also because the concrete evidence for it is so fragmentary. We have on the one hand the tantalizingly terse information, rescued by the Goncourt from a manuscript history of the Opéra in the Bibliothèque de l'Hôtel de Ville before its destruction in the Commune, that Boucher worked on scenery for the Opéra in 1737–39, and again from August 1744 to 1 July 1748 (E. & J. de Goncourt, 1881, I, p. 223), but the pieces on which he worked are not stated. From Mannlich (1948, pp. 56–58, 216) and from various reviews in the *Mercure de France* we know that he was artistic director there about 1761–66, during the management of Rebel and Francoeur (1757–67). On the other hand, we know from the *Mémoires* of Jean Monnet, the director of the Théâtre de la Foire/Opéra-Comique, that Boucher worked for him on three occasions between 1743 and 1754, quite apart from other contributions that may have gone unmentioned (Monnet, 1909, pp. 85, 166–67, 175–76). The first was when he designed the scenery and costumes for Favart's very successful parody of *Les Indes Galantes, L'Ambigu de la Folie* or *Le Ballet des Dindons,* for the Foire Saint-Laurent in August 1743. The second was when he designed the whole interior decoration, from the ceiling down to the ornament, of the Théâtre de la Foire Saint-Laurent that Monnet rebuilt in an

Fig. 148. *Design for a Stage Set (for the First Act of* Issé?*),* signed and dated 1741. Alte Pinakothek, Munich.

47

astonishing thirty-seven days in 1751. The third was when he designed the sets for Noverre's brilliant ballet, *Les Fêtes Chinoises,* in 1754. Otherwise, we are dependent on stray mentions in reviews and sales catalogues for our knowledge of what plays, ballets, and operas he made designs for. From these we know, for instance, that he created scenery for *Issé* in November 1741 (see below), *Persée* in 1746 (*Mercure de France,* Nov. 1746, p. 123), *Atys* in November 1747 (Gougenot, 1748, pp. 49–50), the *Devin du Village* in 1752/53 (B. de B[oynes] sale, 15 Mar. ff. 1785, lot 192; Ch[ariot] sale, 28 Jan. ff. 1788, lot 54), *Armide et Renaud* in 1761 and possibly before (*Mercure de France,* Dec. 1761, pp. 178–81; Dacier, 1920, pp. 14–15, 104; de Boynes sale, lot 192), *Castor et Pollux* in January 1764 (*Mercure,* Feb. 1764, pp. 189–94), and *Silvie* in 1766 (*Mercure de France,* Dec. 1766, pp. 179–80, 182–83).

For which of all these, if any, was the present sketch produced? It has been almost universally identified as a design for the hamlet in the first act of *Issé* for no better reason than that Boucher exhibited such a sketch in the 1742 Salon, and that the present sketch shows a hamlet. Not only are the measurements of the present sketch thoroughly incompatible with those of the one exhibited (which measured two *pieds* by three), however, but so is its character. For *Issé* was a *pastorale héroïque,* performed at court and at the Académie Royale de Musique (the Opéra), whereas the present scene suggests an altogether more rustic entertainment. What is more, from the few indications of the character of the *hameau* in the first act of *Issé* to be gleaned from the text, it is clear that, as the word properly suggests, it was no more than a settlement in a clearing, surrounded by woods and water. There is every chance, indeed, that the picture exhibited in the Salon is actually the landscape in the Alte Pinakothek in Munich (fig. 148; A & W 181), which is compatible in date (since the revival was for the winter season of 1741/42), measurements, and character. Nowhere in *Issé* is there any call for so urbanized a setting as in the present sketch, in which the most prominent features are a tavern and a table set for drinking under a tree.

It is hazardous, in view of our very patchy knowledge of Boucher's activities as a stage designer, to propose an alternative identification of the scene, but one may perhaps be attempted. The first point to be made is that the very rustic—as opposed to pastoral—character of the scene suggests a set not for the Opéra, but for the Opéra-Comique or Théâtre de la Foire (it also rules out Rousseau's *Devin du Village,* since the *hameau* in that, for which Boucher designed the set, was different in character from the one presented here). Knowing that Boucher was associated with these theaters via Jean Monnet, but perhaps even more through his friendship with their most successful playwright, Charles-Simon Favart (see A & W doc. 343 [doc. 784 is from quite another Boucher], and Favart, 1808, II, pp. 387, 396), the obvious place to look is among Favart's pieces for the Théâtre de la Foire. Not all of these were printed, or even extracted by the brothers Parfaict in their *Dictionnaire des Théâtres de Paris,* but among those that were there is one whose stage directions, even if they do not correspond point by point with the set shown in the present sketch, do suggest the same scene. The piece in question is *Les Amours Grivois,* a one-act *opéra-comique-ballet* first performed in 1744 (Favart, 1763, VII). The stage directions for this run as follows:

> The Theater represents a Flemish Hamlet. One can see a Town in the distance, whose Ramparts are destroyed by Cannon fire; on the other

side a Camp, at the head of which is a Battery of Cannon. The Wings represent Peasants' Houses and Taverns. The center of the Scene is occupied by several Flemings, some of whom are playing various instruments under a large tree, while others, around several tables, drink, smoke, game and dance. *(Le Théâtre représente un Hameau Flamand. On voit dans l'éloignement une Ville, dont les Remparts sont détruits par le Canon; de l'autre côté un Camp, à la tête duquel est une Batterie de Canon. Les Aîles représentent des Maisons de Paysans & des Estaminettes. Le milieu de la Scêne est occupé par plusieurs Flamands, dont les uns jouent de divers instrumens sous un grand arbre, pendant que les autres, autour de plusieurs tables, boivent, fument, jouent & dansent.)*

The main departure from the directions lies in the background, but, if there is not a camp, there is a castle. What is more, these directions have the great merit of providing a plausible explanation for one of the least explicable elements of the present sketch, the buildings on fire in the background on the right: these are surely intended to represent the "Ramparts destroyed by Cannon fire." The piece began with an overture suggesting the rumblings of war, interspersed with cannon fire, and this is the visual equivalent.

One matter remains to be resolved, and that is whether the suggested identification is compatible with the apparent date of the sketch. So long as it was assumed that it was for the *Hameau d'Issé*, no objections were raised to the implied dating of 1741/42. This may partly have been because there is really no landscape sketch of such character with which it can be compared. One can only say that nothing in it appears to militate against the dating to 1744 implied here, and that it has a confident spontaneity and freshness that suggest the mastery of Boucher's maturity.

# 48 | *The Dark-Haired Odalisque*

Oil on canvas
21 × 25½ in. (53.5 × 64.5 cm)
Signed on the bedside table: *f. Boucher 174[5?]*
Musée du Louvre, Paris (R.F. 2140)
A & W 285

PROVENANCE
(There is no certain means of distinguishing among versions in early sales and inventories, so only the known provenance of the present picture is given here. Other mentions are given separately below in order of date, with no attempt to consolidate them; only mentions that can reasonably be identified with this painting, rather than the *Blonde Odalisque,* are listed): comte de Magny, by whom ceded to baron Basile de Schlichting for 3,500 francs; in the de Schlichting bequest to the Louvre, 1914.

OTHER VERSIONS
1. ?Posthumous inventory of A-J-J. Le Riche de la Poupelinière ["l'homme de la che-

It is perhaps not entirely proper to name this coquettish creature an odalisque, since neither was she so called in the eighteenth century, nor is there any definite indication that she is a denizen of a seraglio. Many things, however, suggest that a certain oriental exoticism was intended—the bed composed purely of mattresses and cushions, the unusual little low table supporting a cassolette (for all of which, cf. the *Sultane lisant au harem* engraved by Duflos for the *Moeurs et Usages des Turcs* in 1746 [J-R 879]), the low screen covered with some oriental sprigged material, the feathers in the woman's hair—and the title is hallowed by long use, so it may reasonably be retained. Certainly, the title given to Lévesque's engraving after this composition, *Le Reveil,* seems no more appropriate, since there is scant indication that the bed was ever arranged for sleep.

48

minée"], 4 Feb. 1763: "Tableau representant une femme nue couchée sur le ventre" (D. Wildenstein, 1967, p. 184; there is of course no certainty that this was the present composition, rather than the *Blonde Odalisque*, but Lévesque's engraving of 1765 suggests that a version of it had recently come onto the market).

2. Dated 1743, with a different face, engraved by P-C. Lévesque in 1765, and published by Bligny as *Le Reveil* (J-R 1397–1398; advertised in the *Mercure de France* in Apr. 1773).

3. *Catalogue des Tableaux des Trois Ecoles . . . &c., qui composent le Cabinet de M. [Johann Anton] de P[eters]*, Grands Augustins (Remy & Basan), 9 Mar. ff. 1779, lot 103: "Une femme couchée sur son canapé; ce bon tableau est daté de 1745; il est sur toile, qui prend 18 pouces de haut, sur 23 pouces de large. Lévêque l'a gravé" [sold for 235 livres; see drawing by Saint-Aubin, Dacier, V, no. 9, 1919, pp. 20–21, 31, facsimile]; *Catalogue d'une belle Collection de Tableaux . . . &c. composant le Cabinet du M. Dubois, Marchand Orfèvre Jouaillier, rue des Poulies*, Hôtel de Bullion (Le Brun), 31 Mar. ff. 1784, lot 88: "Une jeune Femme sur son lit de repos

In Paul Frankl's austere interpretation of this picture and its fellows (Frankl, 1961), this picture is no more than an academic exercise worked up into a composition that exploits a pose originally developed for bathing nymphs and naiads. This filiation is perfectly true (cf., for instance, the *Leda* painted only a year before the original version of this composition, in 1742, cat. 40), and Boucher's interest in the pose for these purposes can be pursued back even earlier in his career than was done by Frankl, to the attendant of Venus in *Venus Requesting Vulcan for Arms for Aeneas* (cat. 17). However, it still begs the question as to what or whom Boucher was intending to depict. A completely unmotivated nude, with nothing at least to allow an interpretation as some mythological figure, was after all something exceptional at this epoch (though there were certain precedents, such as Jacob Vanloo's *Coucher à l'italienne*, which was itself an adaptation of Jordaens's *Candaules and Gyges*). What is more, the features of the model are so particularized and also such a departure from Boucher's preferred types that—with her direct gaze—they irresistibly suggest a portrait.

The various versions of this composition have indeed been seen as depictions of specific individuals from very early on; suggestions have ranged from the inevitable Mme de Pompadour (wholly precluded by the date) to Victoire O'Murphy, alias Mlle de Saint-Gratien, the elder sister of the supposed subject of the *Blonde Odalisque* (cat. 61), even though she would only have been ten in 1743! The only proposal with any plausibility is that of

Fig. 149. *Presumed Portrait of Mme Boucher*, signed and dated 1743. Frick Collection, New York.

entouré d'accessoires agréables: le fond est orné d'un grand rideau bleu. Quoiqu'il y ait des répétitions de ce Tableau, nous ne doutons pas de son originalité. Il vient de la Vente de M. Peters. Hauteur 19 pouces, largeur 24 pouces. Toile" [bought by Milliotti for 150 livres, hardly more than for the avowed copy of a *Diane au Bain*, and less than a quarter of the 699 livres 19 sous fetched by the pair of pictures of a *Femme à sa toilette*].

4. M. R. R[ochard] of Brussels sale, Paris, 13–14 Dec. 1858, lot 6.

5. With body draped, signed on the table, *f. Boucher 174[3?]*, 51 × 65 cm, Gustave Rothan coll. (exh. cat. 1874, Paris, no. 29); his sale, Paris, 20–31 May 1890, lot 125 (with suggested identification as Mme de Pompadour); baron Maurice de Rothschild, Paris (exh. cat. 1910, Berlin, no. 146, as *Mlle Victoire O'Murphy*); M. Otto Bemberg, Paris.

6. Signed and dated 1755, anon. sale, Paris, 19 May 1884, lot 6.

7. Signed on the carpet bottom right, *f. Boucher, 1743*, 53 × 65 cm, on the Paris art market in the Second World War; recovered by the Service de la Récupération Artistique in 1945; allocated to the Musée de Reims in 1951 (A & W 264).

8. There are two mid-19th-century photographs of these or other versions in the Cabinet des Estampes: one taken by Courtéhoux and entitled *Mme de Pompadour*, and the other taken by Ch. Barenne and located in the "Cabinet de M. Parmar." H. Roger-Viollet possess the damaged negative of a photograph taken early this century of a good version of this picture, signed *f. Boucher 1745* on the side table, but are unable to supply any information as to where it was taken.

DRAWING

Red, black, and white chalks, 316 × 462 mm, C. F. Greville; Earl of Warwick: H. Michel-Lévy sale, Paris, 12–13 May 1919, lot 45; A. Mayer; Kimbell Art Museum, Fort Worth (fig. 150).

Jean Cailleux, that she is Boucher's wife (Cailleux, 1966). Unfortunately, when making this bold suggestion, he confused the issue by introducing a number of other supposed likenesses whose affinity with this picture is far from apparent, and he failed to muster the full panoply of corroborative evidence.

One point must be made straight away: we have no certain portrait of Mme Boucher until Roslin's of her in 1761 (A&W fig. 131). Neither the pastel of her that Tessin took back to Sweden, nor La Tour's pastel of her wearing fingerless mittens shown in the Salon of 1737, nor Lundberg's pastel shown in the 1743 Salon, nor Roslin's oil of her "en habit de Bal" shown in the 1753 Salon has ever been identified and published, while the inscriptions on the terra-cotta busts of her and her husband supposedly by J-B. Lemoyne in the Sackler Collection (Avery & Laing, 1981, nos. 75, 76) arouse grave doubts about their authenticity. There is, of course, that celebrated picture supposed to be of her reclining on a daybed in the Frick Collection (fig. 149; *Frick Collection*, 1968, pp. 3–7); but it is rarely remembered that there is no record of the existence of this picture before this century, and thus no way in which we can be sure that it is of her. It would, however, be carrying pyrrhonism too far to doubt the traditional identification. Boucher was not a portrait painter, so that the few portraits from his hand all owe their origin to some special connection with the sitter. Her age appears right, and the Chinese bibelots are in keeping with what we know of Boucher's collections; and there is above all the fact that, in addition to the signature, Boucher's name appears on a little note on the étagère—surely a sly indication of the link between sitter and painter.

Arguments for imagined likenesses are always dangerously subjective, but the similarity between the features of the sitter in the Frick portrait and those of the subject of the present picture seems undeniable. Nor does the linkage between the two pictures end there. Their dimensions are almost identical, and the date of the Frick picture and that on the earliest known version of the present composition is the same. What we would thus appear to have here would then be precursors of Goya's *Maja vestida* and *Maja desnuda*, with the difference that their pose and setting are not identical (it is true that there is a draped version of the present picture—see no. 5 under Other Versions—but the draping in it is thought to have been a prudish later camouflage). Goya's pictures are no longer thought to represent his presumed mistress, the duchess of Alba; can the identification of the dark-haired odalisque with Boucher's wife, by contrast, be sustained?

If the idea of Boucher painting his wife in this fashion seems shocking, one of his contemporaries was certainly shocked—or professed to be shocked—by it; it is thanks to his utterance that this otherwise somewhat speculative structure puts on, as it were, some flesh. Though Boucher did not exhibit in the 1767 Salon, Diderot in his review of it nonetheless used the exclusion of Mme Therbouche [Liszewska]'s *Jupiter and Antiope* as a pretext to attack his *bête noire* (Diderot, 1983, p. 252):

> For didn't we see in the Salon seven or eight years ago, a woman, completely nude, stretched out on some pillows, one leg here, another there, presenting the most voluptuous head, the finest back, the most beautiful thighs, an invitation to pleasure, inviting to it with the easiest attitude, the most comfortable—from what they say the most natural even, or at least the most advantageous. . . . No offense to Boucher,

(Again, only those that can reasonably be assumed to be of the *Dark-Haired Odalisque* are listed, in date order):

1. Carpentier sale, 14 Mar. ff. 1774, lot 24: "Deux copies de M. Boucher, l'une représentant Vénus qui dort avec l'Amour; la seconde, une figure de femme couchée sur un lit, vue par le dos, ces deux copies sont très-bien faites: hauteur 19 pouces, largeur 24 pouces" [sold for 120 livres].

2. ?Anon. sale, 17 Feb. ff. 1777, lot 216: "Un grand tableau peint sur toile, d'après Bouché; il représente une femme sur un lit, de repos"; ?[d'Espagnac-Tricot] sale, 22 May ff. 1793, lot 118 (as by Boucher): "Une femme de grandeur naturelle, et vue couchée. Ce tableau, de la couleur la plus belle, est de dessin gracieux et aimable, si justement admiré dans les productions de ce maître; il a passé dans plusieurs collections de choix" [bought by Hamont or Chaumont for 2400 livres]; currently on the art market in New York (43½ × 56⅛ in.).

3. [De Jogues] sale, 23 Sept. ff. 1784, lot 41: "Deux Etudes de Femmes nues & couchées, l'une vue par dévant & l'autre par derrière, bonnes copies d'après le *Titien* & *F. Boucher*; hauteur 17 pouces 6 lignes, largeur 21 pouces 6 lignes: toiles de forme ovale"; misc. sale, Versailles, 3 Mar. 1968, lot 194.

4. With a face resembling that in a print by Lévesque, but with a bunch of flowers in her hair, 50 × 61 cm, formerly Youssoupov coll., Saint Petersburg, in which ascribed to Louise Arnault-Boucher (*Trésors*, VI, 1906, p. 211, pl. 103).

5. With the face of Mme de Pompadour superimposed, 54 × 65 cm, Fairfax Murray coll., London (Pilon, 1909, pl. facing p. 46); Prince Massimo, Rome [reputedly with the dowry of his wife, née Marlborough (itself an impossibility), in 1810, probably through confusion with the *Blonde Odalisque* also owned by Fairfax Murray, which was purportedly acquired from the Duke of Marlborough's collections]; Galerie Charpentier, Paris, 10–11 June 1958, lot 82 (as "atelier de Boucher"); Joseph Sayag sale, Palais Galliera, Paris, 16 June 1961, lot 16 (as "atelier de Boucher").

Fig. 150. *Study of a Nude Young Girl Prone upon Drapery.* Kimbell Art Museum, Fort Worth.

who didn't blush to prostitute his wife, from whom he had painted this voluptuous figure. . . . (*Car enfin n'avons-nous pas vu au Sallon il y a sept à huit ans, une femme toute nue étendue sur des oreillers, jambes deçà, jambes delà, offrant la tête la plus voluptueuse, le plus beau dos, les plus belles fesses, invitant au plaisir, et y invitant par l'attitude la plus facile, la plus commode, à ce qu'on dit même la plus naturelle, ou du moins la plus avantageuse. . . . N'en déplaise à Boucher, qui n'avait pas rougi de prostituer lui-même sa femme, d'après laquelle il avait peint cette figure voluptueuse. . . .*)

Even if Diderot's memory was confused when he wrote this passage—there is no indication that such a picture was ever exhibited in a Salon (it is most likely that Diderot had, in fact, seen some version of the picture in the rather similar context of a sale room; possibly the Le Riche de la Poupelinière version was sold in a sale without a catalogue)—he is clearly recording some piece of inside knowledge, or alternatively mere gossip, that was current at the time he wrote.

There is one further piece of evidence that the identity of the sitter was not thought fit for public consumption, and that is the print of it put out in 1765 by P-C. Lévesque (J-R 1397–1398). The face of this sits very awkwardly upon the head and would appear to have been corrected. It is not the head found in the present version of the picture, nor is it the head on the Fairfax Murray version (Pilon, 1909, pl. facing p. 46), which appears to have been the result of a subsequent alteration designed to buttress the assertion that the subject of the picture was Mme de Pompadour. Nor does it correspond to the head found in any of the extant paintings. It is possible that the adjustment to the plate was simply made in order to present a more "fashionable" head for 1765; but though Mme Boucher's own features would of course have changed considerably in the interval, it would also be legitimate to speculate as to whether the alteration was not made to protect the identity of the sitter. This is unlikely, because it looks as if the print may have been maliciously intended to discredit Boucher, since it was published in the very year that he was appointed *premier peintre du Roi*, a title given full prominence in the title to the engraving. It is certainly significant that not only was Lévesque not otherwise an engraver of Boucher's works, but he was also a protégé of Diderot's, and was subsequently responsible for the first of the outright public assaults on Boucher's reputation (Watelet & Lévesque, II, 1791, p. 138).

At this point we must call a halt to speculation, for there is one piece of evidence that seems to doom any attempt to identify the dark-haired odalisque with Mme Boucher. That is the drawing formerly in the Michel-Lévy collection and now in the Kimbell Art Museum, Fort Worth (fig. 150; AA 502; exh. cat. 1983, Atlanta, no. 75). The model in this drawing is in exactly the pose of the odalisque, save that she is not fingering a pearl necklace and that she is not fixing us with her gaze; her back is also completely bare. But the most significant thing about this drawing is that the features of the model are patently different from those of the odalisque, whereas they are entirely of the cast found in Boucher's other studies and paintings of nudes at this period. Yet the pose in this precise form is not found in any other painting: the presumption must be that it was a study for the present picture (and even if, as a beautifully finished study *aux trois crayons*, it was in fact made in its own right, it is impossible to conceive of it having been derived from the half-draped figure in the painting, rather than

6. 54 × 65 cm, illegible signature and date: Mme Besnard; [Marnier-Lapostolle] sale, Hôtel Drouot, Paris, 16 June 1923, ex catalogue; Cassel van Doorn sale, Paris, 9 Mar. 1954, lot 25.

7. Misc. sale, Paris, 16 June 1972, lot 4.

8. Dated 1749, 106 × 138 cm, private coll., Paris [?picture formerly in the collection of the comte de Lavalette; anon. sale, Hôtel Drouot, Paris, 27 Mar. 1965, lot 10].

9. Oval, 45.5 × 55.5 cm [in reverse], Palais des Congrès, Versailles, 3 Mar. 1968, lot 194.

10. With a different face, 73.5 × 126 cm, signed: formerly in the Bensa coll., Milan; exh. Dante di Zucca, Trieste, 1977–78, no. 56.

11. 54 × 65 cm: Ferdinand Houget coll., Belgium; Hôtel Drouot, Paris, 24 June 1981, lot 68; baronne de Thuret, sold Christie's, London, 15 Apr. 1983, lot 26.

12. With expanded background, 74 × 97 cm, Sotheby's Monaco, 9 Dec. 1984, lot 596.

13. Miniature by Jacques Charlier [with corner of a canapé substituted for screen], engraved by Janinet in 1784.

14. Miniature attributed to Charlier, 60 × 75 mm, Wallace Collection, London (*Wallace Collection Catalogues*, 1980, no. 76).

15. Miniature attributed to Charlier, 60 × 85 mm, anon. sale, Hôtel Drouot, Paris, 20 Dec. 1945, lot 59.

16. Gouache attributed to Charlier, 200 × 270 mm: anon. sale, Hôtel Drouot, Paris, 12 May 1905, lot ? ; G. Cognacq sale, ibid., 10 June 1932, lot 48.

17. Drawing in colored chalks, 360 × 430 mm, reputedly from the coll. of Jacques Aved; formerly coll. of M. and Mme Maurice Magnin, Paris [not in the Musée Magnin, Dijon].

18. Black and red chalk drawing heightened with pastel, 280 × 400 mm, signed *f. Boucher 174[?]*; Palais Galliera, Paris, 9 June 1964, lot 53; ibid., 11 June 1971, lot ? ; Hôtel Drouot, 16 June 1972, lot 4; ibid., 2 June 1981, lot 32.

the other way about). It is scarcely plausible that, with Mme Boucher to hand (whom he does not appear to have hesitated to use as a model for his mythological nudes, to judge by the comments of de Bachaumont and Le Bret), Boucher should have turned to one of his studio models in order to make a portrait of his wife in the nude. This, mutatis mutandis, is exactly what he would have had to do, however, if he was to paint a portrait of some other man's mistress (the legend of Apelles and Campaspe notwithstanding). What is more, it is only through assuming that the sitter was a courtesan—and no doubt the mistress of more than one man—that the existence of so many apparently autograph versions of this picture can be explained. One could at a pinch imagine (as Diderot did) Boucher's making a nude portrait of his wife for himself, but not his putting numerous versions of it into circulation. On the other hand, the existence of other versions with different heads could well be accounted for by other clients wanting a similar depiction of their own mistresses (when the heads are not simply spurious later alterations).

One further thing needs to be considered, and that is the question of the various versions of the composition and their dates. The date on the present picture is most plausibly to be read as 1745, with the "5" abbreviated in the way often found at this period. The version in Rheims, which is palpably inferior to this one, is dated 1743, but the "3" falls into the damaged margin of the picture and shows signs of abusive strengthening. Some other digit may well have been converted into a "3" to establish priority for the Rheims picture, taking its cue from the fact that 1743 is given as the date of the painting upon which Lévesque's engraving was based. Other versions carry dates that have been read as 1745 and 1755. Jean Cailleux (1966, p. v, n. 8) reports having seen "in a private collection in Paris a splendid example of this type which could well be the original of the whole series," but records no date for it. The fact that the prime version was most probably dated 1743 would make the present picture, which is strong, but perhaps slightly mechanical in its finish (and awry, for instance, in the perspective of the jewel box), just the best of the autograph replicas.

49 | *Nymphs Reposing from the Chase*

Oil on canvas
37 × 51½ in. (94 × 131 cm), after
enlargement to a rectangle in the nineteenth century
Signed bottom left: *f. Boucher 1745*
Musée Cognacq-Jay, Paris (inv. 10)
A & W 279

50 | *The Exchange of Confidences*

Oil on canvas
36¼ × 51½ in. (92 × 131 cm), returned
to original curvilinear shape
Signed on piece of wood at bottom right: *f. Boucher*
Los Angeles County Museum of Art (47.29.17)
A & W 280

PROVENANCE
Sale of Mme Chaillou of Châteaudun, Galerie Georges Petit, Paris, 2 Dec. 1911, lots 1, 2: *Nymphs Reposing* acquired by Ernest Cognacq, and bequeathed with the museum founded by him and his wife Louise Jay, opened in 1929; *The Exchange of Confidences* subsequently in the sale of prince Jacques de Broglie, Paris, 13 Mar. 1922, lot 15; acquired by Knoedler, London; Wildenstein & Co., Paris and New York; Marion Davies, Los Angeles; William Randolph Hearst, New York; donated with his collection to the Los Angeles County Museum in 1947.

ENGRAVINGS
As the *Retour de chasse de Diane* and *Les confidences pastorales*, in a set of four engraved and published by Claude Duflos *le jeune* (advertised in the *Mercure de France*, May and Feb. 1751 respectively; A & W fig. 826; J-R 919).

DRAWINGS
1. *Diana*, red, black, and white chalks, 387 × 323 mm, Sir Thomas Lawrence; C. J. Nieuwenhuys; J. P. Heseltine; Mary Benjamin Rogers; private coll., U.S.A. (exh. cat. 1973–74, Washington, no. 47).
2. *La toilette pastorale*, black chalk, 210 × 280 mm, attributed to Boucher, posthumous sale of baron L. [Roslin] d'Ivry, Paris, 7–9 May 1884, lot 80 (as *L'Eté*, paired with *L'Automne [Erigone vaincue]* as lot 81).
3. *Le Bain de Diane*, black chalk, 200 × 270 mm, A. Beurdeley sale, Paris, 13–15 Mar. 1905, lot 15 [in reverse, probably prepared by or for Duflos; reversed drawings *aux trois crayons* for *La toilette pastorale* and *Erigone vaincue*, from the coll. of Lord Duveen, were sold at Sotheby's, London, 6 July 1978, lot 11].

COPIES
1. Of both pictures, in a set of four reputedly from the Hôtel Bertin (the later Ministère des Affaires Etrangères), installed as overdoors in the *salon de la Pendule* at Versailles since 1896.
2. *Bad der Diana*, 140 × 140 cm, overdoor copied from the engraving, originally in the Residenz, Munich, transferred to Schloss Nymphenburg after World War II.
3. *L'Eté* (with nymph holding dead bird suppressed), shaped overdoor, 80 × 130 cm, Debacker sale, Paris, 1 June 1908.
4. *Retour de chasse de Diane*, Musée Baron Martin, Gray.
5. *Schäferszene*, reversed variant of *Les confidences pastorales* [after a pirated Augsburg engraving?], 128 × 175 cm, sale at Fischer, Lucerne, 23 Aug. 1928, lot 434; ibid., 2–5 May 1934, lot 1240.

Reunited here for the first time in well over a century are two of Boucher's overdoors, which show what he could rise to even in this essentially decorative genre. Their two fellows, with which they can regrettably never again be shown, are in the Wallace Collection in London (figs. 151, 152; inv. nos. P445 and P447; *Wallace Collection Catalogues*, 1968, pp. 35–36, as *Spring* and *Autumn*). All four were engraved by Duflos in rectangular form, evidently through the intermediary of drawings prepared by or for him, since the engravings are all inscribed *F. Boucher inv.* and differ from the paintings in several minor particulars. The engravings were published in 1751 under the titles *La toilette pastorale* (J-R 917–918, *Spring*), *Les confidences pastorales* (cat. 50; J-R 919; with a poem suggesting that the shepherdesses are showing one another their gifts from their rustic lovers), *Erigone vaincue* (J-R 920–922, *Autumn*), and *Retour de chasse de Diane* (cat. 49; A & W fig. 826).

Having been based on drawings rather than directly on the paintings, the engravings give no indication of the location of ownership of the latter. Ananoff and Wildenstein have suggested that the four paintings came from the Folie de Chartres, being those that featured with this provenance in a sale held in Paris on 28–29 November 1834. This provenance is open to objection on two counts. On the one hand, as Thérèse Burollet (1980, p. 49) has pointed out, the descriptions in the catalogue of the sale are too vague to make it certain that it is these pictures that were sold and not the set of overdoors from Harlaxton Manor (fig. 153; A & W 287–290). Indeed, the fact that the supposed Folie de Chartres pictures were sold as a set at the very time when Gregory Gregory was scouring Europe for furnishings for his astonishing house (see Girouard, 1979, pp. 92–93), whereas the present pair of pictures and the pair in the Wallace only came to light quite separately many years later, rather argues for it having been the Harlaxton pictures that were in the 1834 sale, especially since nothing was said in the catalogue of the pictures having been engraved. On the other hand, the provenance given in the 1834 sale was most probably spurious; the pavilion around which the object-stuffed gardens known as the Folie de Chartres (of which a portion survives as the Parc Monceau) were created was not built until 1769–73—far too late for such curvilinear overdoors as those here or from Harlaxton—and demolished between 1802 and 1806, at a time when such things were unlikely to have been rescued, or, if they were, for their provenance to be remembered a generation later (see exh. cat. 1981, Paris, esp. pp. 14–17, 60). What is more, were the provenance given in the 1834 sale to have been genuine, Louis-Philippe would surely have reclaimed what could only have been the confiscated or stolen property of his father, the duc de Chartres and later Philippe-Egalité. The other previous record of the pictures proposed by Ananoff and Wildenstein, the sale of four "dessus de portes, de forme chantournée, par *François Boucher;* differens sujets de Bergères & jeunes Filles, dans le genre Pastoral, & de son premier tems," on 21 vendémiaire, l'an VII (12 October ff. 1798), is entirely possible, but too slender to go on.

The titles and poems attached to the engravings after these pictures vest two of them with mythological significance—and the nymph undoing her buskin in the *Nymphs Reposing from the Chase* is even given a crescent moon in her hair, to strengthen her identification as Diana. What is interesting about these early pastorals, however, is precisely the ambiguous status of their protagonists. The two in the Wallace Collection include cupids or naked putti, suggesting—as does the loose, unwearable drapery in all four

49

50

222

Fig. 151. *La toilette pastorale*, signed and dated 1745. Wallace Collection, London.

Fig. 152. *Erigone vaincue*, signed and dated 1745. Wallace Collection, London.

Fig. 153. *Nymph Tickling Another with a Straw*, signed and dated 1745. Fine Arts Museums of San Francisco; Roscoe and Margaret Oakes Collection.

Fig. 154. *Shepherd Watching a Sleeping Shepherdess*, signed and dated 1743 or 1745. Wallace Collection, London.

pictures—that these are nymphs in the fabled vale of Tempe; while in the case of the chief figure in the Cognacq-Jay picture, the leopard skin and the subordination to her of the other nymphs would have suggested the identification as Diana, even without the crescent moon. The straw hat, basket of flowers, and sheep, however, already give the protagonists of *The Exchange of Confidences* more the air of shepherdesses in Arcadia, as implied by the poem composed subsequently for the engraving. They chime with Boucher's other pastorals from these years, e.g., the three painted in 1743 for the marquis de Beringhen (A & W 260–262), or the *Shepherd Watching a Sleeping Shepherdess*, dated 1743 or 1745, in the Wallace Collection (fig. 154; A & W 292), in which the protagonists still have either the partial nudity and the bare or buskined feet of figures from the classical repertoire, or the rich dress of ballets. The revolutionary step, Boucher's adoption of the more deliberately rustic protagonists introduced into the opéra comique by his friend Favart, was not to occur until a little later, around 1746–47 (see cat. 53). Yet perhaps even Favart was only feeling his way in 1745, since the first version of his immensely popular *Vallée de Montmorency* (1752), from which Boucher was to take the themes of so many of his paintings and his groups for Vincennes (see Zick, 1965), was called *Les vendanges de Tempé* when it was first performed in 1745. The change in title and location, from an ideal region of Greece to the rural environs of Paris, is in keeping with the change undergone by Boucher's pastorals in the same period.

The pose of the nymph identified as Diana is the most striking of the series. Thérèse Burollet (1980, pp. 49–50) has already drawn attention to its previous use by Boucher in the lost painting of *Le fleuve Scamandre*, the engraving of which by de Larmessin was exhibited in the Salon of 1743 (fig. 141; J-R 1254), and also to the fact that it is not so remote, albeit at a different angle and with different gestures, from the poses of the goddess in the *Diana at the Bath* in the Louvre (cat. 39) and of the young woman in *L'attention dangereuse* (J-R 866–868). It also appears, in different variations, in several engravings of bathing nymphs. At the same time, Burollet rightly points to precedents for the pose, in Watteau's *Diana at the Bath* and Louis de Boullongne's *Diana and Her Nymphs Resting from the Chase* (see exh. cat.

1984–85, Washington, no. 28). In view of the variations in viewpoint and angle of these essentially related poses, one is driven to wonder whether their ultimate inspiration may not have resided in a sculpture in the round, to which these painters had recourse as their starting point when posing their models. One such figure is the *Bather* attributed to Adrian de Vries, of which versions even appear to have been made in France in the eighteenth century (see National Gallery, 1973, no. 6378, p. 796). With the grace that Boucher gave his version of the pose, he conferred on it the timeless authority of a female equivalent of the *Spinario*.

# 51 | *The Milliner (Morning)*

Oil on canvas
25 × 21 in. (64 × 53 cm)
Signed on the bandbox: *f. Boucher 1746*
Nationalmuseum, Stockholm (NM 772)
S & M 1216      A & W 297

PROVENANCE
Commissioned by Crown Princess Lovisa Ulrica of Sweden in October 1745, delivered to the Swedish envoy in Paris in October 1746; Drottningholm until 1865, when transferred to the Nationalmuseum.

REPLICA
Salomon-Pierre de Prousteau, [58] rue de Tournelles; his sale, ibid. (Remy), 5 June ff. 1769, lot 53: "Une Dame à sa toilette, & une Marchande de rubans: Tableau peint d'après M. Boucher, sur toile de 23 pouces de haut, sur 19 pouces 6 lignes de large: on trouve une estampe gravé d'après ce morceau par Gaillard, sous le titre de la Marchande de mode" [bought by Basan for 45 livres]; sale of the comte de Morny, Phillips, London, 20–21 June 1848, lot 10; ?anon. sale, Paris, 19 Mar. 1852, lot 5 (S & M 1153); Richard, fourth marquess of Hertford; Sir Richard Wallace; Lady Wallace, by whom bequeathed with the rest of what was to be known as the Wallace Collection to the British Nation in 1897.

ENGRAVING
(After the Prousteau version) *La marchande de modes*, engraved and published by René Gaillard, advertised in May 1755 (J-R 1024).

COPY
Sale of Jaeger coll., Stockholm, date unknown, lot 1021.

This charming picture, which was to have been the first in a set of four showing women in the characteristic occupations of the Times of Day, was in the event Boucher's last treatment of such a genre interior subject. The pictures were commissioned by Count Tessin from Boucher on behalf of the Crown Princess Lovisa Ulrica in 1745, and we can follow almost the whole protracted saga of Boucher's procrastination, and ultimate failure to complete the commission, in the correspondence of the Swedish minister in Paris, Carl Fredrik Scheffer, with Tessin (Scheffer, 1982, passim). What these letters cannot tell us is Boucher's real reason for letting his client down. Whatever it was, it must surely have gone beyond the particular circumstances of the commission for him never to have taken his brush to such a subject again. The answer might shed much light on the apparent dissipation of Boucher's powers in his later years.

The saga begins with a letter from Tessin to Scheffer, dated 6 October 1745, saying that Lovisa Ulrica wanted to obtain from Boucher four pictures of Morning, Midday, Evening, and Night, slightly larger than his own picture of a *Woman Fastening Her Garter* (cat. 38), "showing fashionable figures, with the pretty little faces that he is so good at" (*"en figures de mode, avec les jolis minois qu'il sait peindre"* [Scheffer, 1982, p. 104, n. 9]). He told Scheffer to pretend that the pictures were for him, in order to obtain them cheaper—he estimated four hundred livres for each, or five hundred livres, including the frame.

This letter was answered on 17/27 October, not by Scheffer, but by the outgoing secretary to the legation, Carl Reinhold Berch, who had previously served Tessin in this capacity, and to whom Tessin appears to have written independently (Chennevières, 1856, pp. 56–57; reproduced by A & W doc. 249). He stated that Boucher had promised to deliver the four pictures by the end of the coming March, on condition that the price remained secret, since his official tariff for this kind of picture ("quand il y a du fini") was six

51

hundred livres. Berch reported him as happy to accept payment on delivery, provided that it was prompt. Berch also suggested ways of portraying the four Times of Day:

> Morning will be a woman who has finished with her hairdresser, but is still in her peignoir, enjoying examining knickknacks displayed by a milliner. Midday, an encounter in the Palais Royal between a lady and a wit reading her some dreadful poem calculated to bore her, so that she indicates the time by her watch; the sundial showing noon in the background. After dinner, or the Evening, gives us the most difficulty: either notes brought to arrange a rendezvous, or mantles, gloves, etc., being given by the lady's maid to her mistress wishing to pay calls. Night can be shown by some giddy things in ball gowns, making fun of someone who is already asleep. We will try and organize it, so that the Four Times of Day also yield the Four Seasons. . . . I hope in due course of time to have some sketches to send to Your Excellency. Mr. Boucher seems prepared to lend himself to this.

Not having been paid for the last of the six overdoors that he painted for the Royal Castle in Stockholm until April 1746, Boucher delayed setting to work in earnest on the Times of Day (Scheffer, 1982, pp. 120, 122, n. 5). In August he had still produced nothing, partly because of his work for the royal château at Choisy, and partly because of his "libertinage" (Scheffer, pp. 124–25, 132). It was not until October that he finally delivered the present picture, which he at least had the grace to do, in spite of being badgered by Crozat de Thiers to sell it to him instead for double the price (Scheffer, p. 144). What follows is a chapter of evasions and excuses, some of which are mutually contradictory, so that it is difficult to know what to believe. In October, for instance, Boucher was said to be busy completing *Le Soir,* yet in February 1747 nothing had been delivered, and it was said to be *Le Midi* that was six weeks from completion (Scheffer, p. 154). This same letter alleged a progressive enfeeblement of his eyesight, which, if it were true, would help to account both for Boucher's broader later manner and for his failure ever to tackle a genre subject again. In November there was still said to be two months' work on the painting, and Scheffer had to confess that Boucher had upped the price for each picture (having no doubt discovered their true destination) to six hundred livres without any frame (Scheffer, pp. 176–77). In December 1749 Boucher, "que je ne sais plus par quelle epitete designer," was now promising that it would "infallibly" be completed in time to catch the first sailing for Sweden in the spring (Scheffer, p. 200). Despite having delivered nothing by April 1750, Boucher then wrote to Scheffer to assure him of his good intentions (Scheffer, pp. 253–54), and was still begging to keep the commission for this one pendant, which would be "the prettiest and most unusual work yet to leave his hands"; but it now emerged that he had not even made a start on it, since he was asking for instructions from Tessin before doing so (Scheffer, p. 212). Very interestingly, however, he claimed to have had mannequins specially made in preparation for it (a practice that he was still adopting when Mannlich knew him, see Mannlich, 1805, I, p. 66). Most tantalizing of all, Scheffer enclosed with his next letter a hasty drawing of Boucher's new idea for the picture, which would indeed have been unusual. "A painter will be occupied in finishing a portrait, and this portrait will be of Madame Royale [Lovisa Ulrica]. A well-dressed lady will come to watch the work of the Painter from behind. The appurtenances of the picture will represent the chamber of Madame Royale." The annotations in pen on the sketch add the information that the lady would be wearing "a fine white satin dress in the manner of Mi[e]ris" (Scheffer, pp. 214–15).

The annotations are in Scheffer's hand—but is the rapid sketch? Jean Cailleux is reported as believing not; though summary, it conveys the whole scene with such assurance and economy that it is hard to believe it is from the hand of Scheffer. This kind of doodle, designed to convey a rapid idea of a composition to another person, is naturally not the kind of thing to have survived from Boucher's hands. Yet it could conceivably, as it would logically, be his, and a preliminary (though more developed) drawing such as that for *La quêteuse de grand chemin* in the Witt Collection in London (A & W fig. 766) does make it worth considering as such.

Most damning of Boucher's previous lies and evasions was the fact that he no longer even had the measurements of *The Milliner* in order to paint this pendant to it. It was no doubt this that finally cooked his goose, for we hear nothing more of the picture, or even of him, in the remaining two years of Scheffer's correspondence with Tessin. It was a sorry end to a fruitful relationship between painter and patron, all the more so in that Boucher was fertile in ideas to the last and might with application have produced a picture to rival the *Woman Fastening Her Garter* or *The Milliner*. Did failing eyesight really make this kind of detailed descriptive picture too demanding for him? Did he resent the attempt to get pictures from him on the cheap by playing on his old rapport with Tessin? Or was it simply a result of the pressures of his burgeoning practice for Mme de Pompadour, combined with the squandering of time in the pursuit of pleasure?

It comes as a considerable surprise after all the foregoing to discover that there is an autograph replica of *The Milliner* in the Wallace Collection in London (*Wallace Collection Catalogues*, 1968, P390, pp. 30–31). It is all but identical to the Stockholm picture, and almost its equal in quality (the official photographs of the Wallace picture, which come from an aged negative taken of the picture in its frame and cropped, do not do it justice). In certain respects, such as the placing of the lady's head (which in the Stockholm picture had visibly given Boucher trouble), and in the conversion of his signature on the bandbox into a florid form that suggests it is the name of the milliner's establishment, it even improves on the original. There is no doubting, however, that the Stockholm version is the prime one: not only are there the obvious pentimenti in the lady's head and foot, and in the positioning of the measuring rod, but it also has the fresher, more tentative quality noted by Voss as characteristic of Boucher's first versions (Voss, 1959).

It is commonly said that the Wallace version was prepared for the engraver. This can scarcely have been the case, since Gaillard's engraving of it, entitled *La marchande de modes*, was not published until May 1755, long after the original picture had gone to Sweden (J-R 1024). It is, however, the picture from which was made the engraving, which gives the owner as "Mr. Prousteau, Capitaine des Gardes de la Ville," in whose sale it was to feature fourteen years later. I owe to the kindness of Dr. Bruno Pons, in communicating to me the results of his researches in the Minutier Central, the closer identification of this intriguing figure. Salomon-Pierre Prousteau (d. 1781) followed his father as a *marchand de vins* of which he was accorded the *maîtrise* in 1730; he lived in [58] rue des Tournelles and was married twice, and his wine business appears to have been particularly flourishing around the time of the death of his first wife, in 1753.

It was presumably less flourishing in 1769, hence his extensive sale. This included four Bouchers, all painted between 1739 and 1747, and all engraved. They were *Le déjeuner* (cat. 33), the *Rape of Europa* (see cat. 54), the present picture, and *Vénus qui baigne l'Amour* (J-R 942–943; probably the picture from the Château de Coat an Noz sale at the Hôtel Drouot, Paris, 12–13 Dec. 1923, lot 52). Significantly, the *Rape of Europa* was also a second version from which the engraving was made, and was said by the cautious auctioneer, Pierre Remy, to have been "peinte dans l'Ecole de Boucher, que l'on croit rétouchée par ce Maître." The Wallace version of *The Milliner* was simply, and surely overscrupulously, said to be "peint d'après M. Boucher," no doubt because Remy was aware that the prime original had gone to Sweden. Yet all four pictures were included in the main body of the sale catalogue, and not in the section devoted to minor paintings and copies, while *The Milliner* fetched more than the wholly autograph *Vénus qui baigne l'Amour,* though a great deal less than *Le déjeuner.* Prousteau is also recorded as the owner of the two paintings of *The Education of Cupid* and *Venus Feeding Cupid with Nectar* engraved by Basan (and by Mme Dupont; J-R 262–263, 944–945), although they featured neither in his sale nor in his posthumous inventory.

There is more than a suggestion in all of this that Prousteau, in addition to being a *marchand de vins,* was also something of a *marchand-amateur* of paintings, with an entrepreneurial interest in engravings after them (his sale included several proofs of both *La marchande de modes* and *L'enlèvement d'Europe*). He would also appear to have had some personal connection with Boucher. On the one hand, there is the small but suggestive fact that Gravelot's *Le Lecteur* (probably the version now in Marble Hill House, Twickenham), of which Gaillard published an engraving in January 1756 as a pendant to *La marchande de modes,* is revealed by a note in the copy of the catalogue of Boucher's posthumous sale in the Bibliothèque d'Art et d'Archéologie in Paris to have been owned by the painter (lot 120). This fact suggests that Boucher would have taken some interest in the engraving of Prousteau's version of *The Milliner* (and that he would scarcely have encouraged it if he had not regarded his painting as essentially autograph)— unless, of course, he only acquired the Gravelot subsequent to its having been engraved. On the other hand, there is the presence in Prousteau's posthumous inventory of "une autre tableau représentant une décoration intérieure d'un sallon peint en esquisse par Boucher." This was surely not a design for interior decoration by Boucher, but a sketch for the setting of a picture. Neither the room in *Le déjeuner* nor that in *The Milliner* could properly be described as a salon. Could it possibly be that this sketch was made in preparation for *Le Soir,* on which Boucher had claimed he was working in October 1746, and that, having painted a replica for Prousteau of *The Milliner* before the first version went to Stockholm (a process that would itself have accounted for some of the delays in delivering the latter), he made over to him a sketch prepared for its intended pendant after he had abandoned any idea of painting it?

None of this explains why, when Tessin was pressing so insistently for the completion of the series and when Crozat de Thiers would apparently have paid great sums for such a picture, Boucher satisfied neither, but merely painted a replica for the obscure Prousteau (perhaps not wholly obscure, since his cabinet is referred to by Hébert, 1766, I, p. 135). Taken together, however, the evidence does suggest either that Boucher's eyesight was genuinely failing (we subsequently have his own reported admission that defects of color in his later paintings were ascribable to this cause; see *Galerie Françoise*, 1771, p. 5) or that success enabled him to renounce this demanding kind of subject for more facile compositions. When one thinks of the lovingly detailed, yet more broadly handled, appurtenances in the portrait of *Mme de Pompadour* (cat. 64), it is surely evident that Boucher continued to delight in such things. In which case, his later abstention from genre interior subjects probably does betoken problems in giving these kinds of picture the finish that potential collectors of them were conditioned by Dutch painting to expect; and his failure to produce any more of them would indicate the same awareness of his own limitations that led him to his virtual renunciation (save for Mme de Pompadour) of those other major branches of his art: religious painting and portraiture.

## 52 | *Portrait of Mme Bergeret(?)*

Oil on canvas
56 × 41½ in. (143 × 105 cm)
Signed far left, between backrest and topmost rose: *f Boucher / 1746*
National Gallery of Art, Washington, D.C.;
Samuel H. Kress Collection (1946. 7.3)
A & W 301

PROVENANCE
[As given in Eisler, 1977, p. 320, with minor amplifications]: Pierre-Jacques-Onésyme Bergeret, Paris; his posthumous inventory, 1785, p. 66, no. 22: "A l'égard du portrait de Madame Bergeret par Boucher, il n'en a été fait aucune prisée comme portrait de famille, pourquoy mémoire" (G. Wildenstein, 1961, p. 42); his son, Pierre-Jacques Bergeret (1744–1827), Paris or Cassan; his stepson (from the first marriage of his wife Catherine-Julie-Xavier Poisson de la Chabeaussière), Ange-Philibert Lyonard de la Girennerie; Barbe-Françoise-Victoire Poisson de la Chabeaussière, subsequently Mme Cotillon de Torcy; her daughter, Françoise-Julie Cotillon de Torcy, subsequently wife of contre-amiral Alexandre Le Bas de Sainte-Croix; their daughter, Angélique or Angelina Le Bas de Sainte-Croix, subsequently the comtesse Fontaine de Resbecq; sold by the Fontaine de Resbecq family to Wildenstein & Co., Paris and New York, before 1920; acquired from Wildenstein by the Kress Collection in 1942.

Boucher's difficulties in capturing a likeness were noted on more than one occasion. Mme de Pompadour herself alluded to the fact (Pompadour, 1878, p. 50); Boucher's failure to supply Le Bas with a passable likeness of Louis XV in his sketch for the frontispiece of the *Mémoires de l'Académie Royale de Chirurgie* (1743) must have been a contributory factor in the latter's lack of success in achieving one, and in the preference consequently given by the king to Cochin's design (see Jombert, 1770, p. 39; Cochin, 1880, pp. 80–81). The problem was obviously more acute with male sitters than female, since the vanity of the latter might rather be flattered by a depiction that approximated them to some ideal of beauty while devoting most attention to their dress and accessories. Thus, while Boucher is only known with certainty to have executed one male portrait, that of Mme de Pompadour's intimate, the maréchal de Lowendal (J-R 1256), he seems to have been in some demand as a painter of women, even if that demand was met only in the cases of his family and of the clients with whom he was most closely associated.

Despite the fact that the husband of the supposed sitter in the present portrait, Pierre-Jacques-Onésyme Bergeret (subsequently styled Bergeret de Grancourt; 1715–1785), was to become such a client in later life, and was to leave one of the three most important collections of paintings and drawings

Fig. 155. *Portrait of Mme de Pompadour*, signed and dated 1759. Wallace Collection, London.

by Boucher when he died, nothing in his collections or in the inventory drawn up on the death of his first wife in 1751 (see G. Wildenstein, 1961, p. 42) indicates that he had begun to form it at the period of the date on this portrait (even though he had ordered three of Boucher's chinoiserie tapestries from Beauvais in 1744 [Badin, 1909, p. 61; G. Wildenstein, 1961, p. 42, wrongly identified], he cannot yet have owned the sketches for them). It is even doubtful that there could have been a portrait of his first wife in his possession when she died, since none is listed. Georges Wildenstein is perfectly correct in saying that family portraits were exempt from posthumous valuations, but they were customarily mentioned *pour mémoire*, as in Bergeret's own posthumous inventory.

Perhaps one should look for possible links between the supposed sitter, or her husband, and Boucher for the explanation of this rare early essay in portraiture. Nothing is known of any friendships or relationships of Pierre-Jacques-Onésyme Bergeret that would connect him with Boucher or his circle at this date. His first wife, Marguérite Richard, whom he married in 1741, had slightly more promising connections. Her maternal grandfather was the former *premier Peintre*, Louis de Boullongne, and her brother was that dilettante artist, the abbé de Saint-Non. However, while Saint-Non was later certainly to execute a number of etchings and aquatints after Boucher, in 1746 he was only nineteen, and not yet interested in the art of engraving. Nor is there anything particularly to connect Boucher with that dynasty of painters turned financiers, the de Boullongne.

One is thus tempted to question the identity of the sitter, but not only is there the detailed family descent supplied by Wildenstein's to the museum, complete with the family tradition that it represented a Mme Bergeret, even if it was not known which (G. Wildenstein, 1961, p. 58, n. 11), but such a portrait is also supposed to be listed in Bergeret's posthumous inventory. It is here, however, that the web of evidence supporting the identification of the sitter as the first Mme Bergeret starts to unravel. For, contrary to what was asserted by Georges Wildenstein, the signs are that the Boucher portrait in the inventory was not of Bergeret's first wife, but of his third. There was a portrait of the first Mme Bergeret in the bedroom of Bergeret's widow, his third wife (item 12), but it was anonymous, and she was shown with her daughter. The assessors were careful to identify her as the first Mme Bergeret (which could have been relevant in any division of the property among the heirs from the various marriages) and her daughter as "fille aînée," just as they were to describe Bergeret himself as "feu" (the late) in the case of two portraits of him (item 30: the portrait *en pied* may have been the celebrated picture by Vincent now in Besançon), although they omitted to in the case of a miniature (item 40). Neither in the case of Boucher's original of the *Portrait de Mme Bergeret* (item 22) nor in the case of the copy (item 19) was she described either as the first wife or as "the late." Indeed, were we to accept Georges Wildenstein's identification of Bergeret's portraits (p. 64), there would have been no paintings of his third wife at all, only a miniature (item 40). This would be particularly surprising in view of the fact that this, of all his marriages, was one of inclination, in that Bergeret had married his mistress of several years' standing (although they only married in 1777, their liaison had begun several years before, since their daughter was born around 1770; see Darras, 1933, pp. 79–81. I thank Marie-Anne Dupuy for alerting me to this article).

The present portrait is, however, dated 1746, and was apparently identified in the family from which it came, that of the de Fontaine de Resbecq, as of Mme Bergeret, who at that date could only have been the first wife. There is something very curious about the purported descent of this picture. Tracing it back, we arrive at Barbe-Françoise-Victoire Poisson de la Chabeaussière, the younger sister of Catherine-Julie-Xavier Poisson de la Chabeaussière, whose second husband was Pierre-Jacques Bergeret (1744–1807), Pierre-Jacques-Onésyme's eldest son by his first wife. This second marriage of Catherine-Julie produced no children, contrary to what is asserted by the various editions of Saint Allais's *Nobiliaire Universel* (*sub voce* Poisson de la Chabeaussière) or by Georges Wildenstein (1961, p. 56). Their conflicting accounts arose because Pierre-Jacques Bergeret adopted his wife's daughter by her first marriage, who died a year later. Pierre-Jacques predeceased his wife, and since they had no offspring, his property appears to have passed to the Lyonard de la Girennerie, the children of his widow by her first husband. It was thus to the descendants of this first marriage that Pierre-Jacques-Onésyme Bergeret's château of Nègrepelisse, and such relics and memories as remained of his association with Fragonard, descended (see E. & J. de Goncourt, 1881, III, p. 341; Portalis, 1889, p. 185, n. 1; Tornezy, 1895, p. 54). With the continuance of the line of his stepchildren up until at least the end of the nineteenth century there seems no reason for any of Pierre-Jacques's property to have passed to the remote descendants of the younger sister of his wife.

There is a further curious feature about this portrait, and that is its pose. This is exactly the attitude struck in what—from the apparent age of the sitter—must be Boucher's earliest surviving portraits of Mme de Pompadour: the oil sketches in the Louvre (cat. 59) and in a private collection in England (A & W 520). In the latter, she even holds a hat in her right hand, as in the present picture. Now Boucher was notoriously adept at reemploying successful poses in his pictures and drawings (several instances are referred to in the present catalogue), but it is hard to imagine even him taking an old pose, even from what might have been his only full-length portrait to date, for a portrait that demanded the utmost of him, of the most powerful woman in the land. Even less so if the original sitter was the wife of a *fermier-général* —a man from the very class from which Mme de Pompadour had risen, and that she had put behind her.

The two oil sketches are patently experiments with the same pose, in the same interior setting, but with different accouterments. The present painting is a finished outdoor variant of the same scheme. There would appear to be two possible ways of accounting for this. Either it is a portrait of Mme de Pompadour (which is how the small-scale version of it formerly in the Rothschild collection in Paris was identified), in which the head has most probably been rejuvenated and an impossible date added (not only is the garden seat of almost the same model as that in the 1759 *Portrait of Mme de Pompadour* in the Wallace Collection [fig. 155], but the handling of paint—especially to form the roses—suggests a picture much nearer to that in date than to 1746); or, Mme de Pompadour having rejected the pose, the thrifty Boucher made use of it for another sitter. That sitter might have been a Mme de Bergeret, but, if it was, it is much more likely to have been Bergeret's third wife while she was still his mistress (with the date in the picture mishandled) than his first, because of the absence of any indication in his inventory that the Boucher portrait was of a wife who was deceased. If that argument ex silentio is invalid, the portrait is even so more likely to have been one of his second wife rather than his first, with the third digit of the date on the portrait falsified by restoration. For Bergeret married his second wife in 1766; not only would that date accord well with the style and pose of the picture, but the action of the sitter in plucking a rose carries suggestions of a marriage portrait.

The possibility that it is of none of Bergeret's wives, but the earliest known portrait of Mme de Pompadour by Boucher, is (in view of the date on it, and of the Rothschild version having been so identified) just as inviting. Since supposed portraits of Mme de Pompadour are legion, it is also the identification most subject to caution. One tantalizing possibility is that the Poisson de la Chabeaussière (who were, however, from Anjou) had some kinship with the Poisson de Malvoisin (who were from Champagne), the residuary legatees of Mme de Pompadour (née Poisson), and thus acquired a picture of the royal mistress by inheritance. There was a tradition in the Fontaine de Resbecq family that Mme de Pompadour had herself claimed such a connection and been rebuffed (Fontaine de Resbecq, 1906, p. 5)—perhaps the family was not always so averse to mementos of the would-be link.

## 53 | *Pensent-ils au raisin?*

Oil on canvas
Oval, 31½ × 27 in. (80 × 68.5 cm)
Signed bottom right: *f. Boucher 1747*
The Art Institute of Chicago
(S & M 1554)        A & W 310

PROVENANCE
?Exhibited as no. 33 bis: "Deux Pastorales, aussi en forme ovale"; ?Machault d'Arnouville; comte de Rohan-Chabot, Paris; from whom acquired in 1959 by Wildenstein; by whom sold to the Art Institute of Chicago in 1973.

VARIANT VERSION
?Baron Carl Hårleman; Queen Lovisa Ulrica of Sweden, Drottningholm; transferred to the Nationalmuseum in 1865.

ENGRAVING OF VARIANT VERSION
*Pensent-ils au raisin?* engraved and published by J.-P. Le Bas, dedicated to Baron Hårleman by D'Arcy (J-R 1344–1346).

DRAWINGS
1. Standing goat, on a sheet in the Mme [Blondel] d'Azaincourt coll., engraved by Demarteau (J-R 628).
2. Two foreground sheep, on a sheet in the Mme [Blondel] d'Azaincourt coll., engraved by Demarteau (J-R 629).

This picture is one of the first dated pastorals of Boucher's to show the protagonists in at least half-plausible rustic dress. Boucher had of course begun his career by depicting perfectly credible peasants (see cat. 9), but those pictures had taken their inspiration from Dutch painting rather than from the literary pastoral. When he began to turn to the latter for inspiration, his shepherds and shepherdesses—who, rather than undifferentiated peasants, were what the pastoral tradition required—were either in rich costumes (cat. 30, 31) or in loose draperies suggestive of Arcadia (cat. 50). The richly attired shepherdesses could reasonably have been castigated, as they were by Dufort de Cheverny (1909, I, p. 117), as "des bergères à pieds nus avec des paniers comme à l'Opéra." In his later pastorals, in which not only the shepherdesses but also the shepherds had bare feet—albeit of a scarcely credible cleanliness and delicacy—and in which the shepherdesses could no longer be accused of wearing hooped petticoats, the inspiration was still the stage, but from a quite different kind of theater.

As Gisela Zick (1965) has shown in a brilliant article to which too little attention has been paid outside the narrow circles of those interested in engravings and the transmission of models in the applied arts, Boucher derived his inspiration for a whole host of pictures, drawings, and designs for

233

*53*

porcelain groups for Vincennes and Sèvres from a piece called *Les vendanges de Tempé* by his friend Charles-Simon Favart. This began life as a pantomime put on for the first time at the Foire Saint-Laurent on 28 August 1745. When it was revived at the Théâtre Italien on 25 February 1752, it was as a more elaborate ballet-pantomime called *La Vallée de Montmorency,* with a setting among cherry orchards rather than vineyards (because of a successful ballet-pantomime by de Hesse called *Les Vendanges [troublées]* put on the year before), and with added characters and scenes. The text of neither version survives, but a plot summary based on the copy texts of the two was published by the brothers Parfaict in their *Dictionnaire des Théâtres de Paris* (1756, VI, pp. 69–84). Their attempts to distinguish the two versions are

TAPESTRY

Woven at Aubusson: examples in Rigaud coll., sold Paris, 3 Apr. 1933, lot 71 (A & W fig. 889); and in misc. sale, Nouveau Drouot, Paris, 21 June 1985.

COPIES

1. 76 × 90 cm, inscribed *F. B. 1749* [?]: ?anon. sale (exp. Vallée), Paris, 20–21 Feb. 1843, lot 1; ?anon. sale (comm.-priseur Déodor), Paris, 12–14 Apr. 1843, lot 57; Eugène Piot coll. (by 1874); his posthumous sale, 21–24 May 1890, lot 547; R. A. Trotti, Paris; Mr. and Mrs. Clarence Postley, Long Island, New York; by whom given to the M. H. de Young Memorial Museum, San Francisco, in 1972.

2. Painting, anon. sale, Paris (exp. Bloche), 20–21 Mar. 1891, lot 3.

3. Gouache, 15 × 19 in., Arthur Tooth & Son, London; sale of Senator Wm. A. Clarke, Plaza Hotel, New York, 11–12 Jan. 1926, lot 69.

4. 50 × 40 in., coll. of Archduke Franz Josef [*sic*]; private coll., New York, sold Parke-Bernet, New York, 28 Sept.–9 Oct. 1960.

5. Snuffbox, Schreiber Collection, Victoria and Albert Museum, London (1924, III, no. 13).

6. Gold box by Noël Hardivilliers, Wrightsman Collection, Metropolitan Museum, New York.

7. *En camaïeu rouge* in enamel jewel box, Sotheby's sale, London, 23 Nov. 1970, lot 118.

somewhat muddled, and it is possible that they did not in fact have access to the *Urtext*, since nothing in either of the versions as they present them justifies the classical setting implied in the original title by the Vale of Tempe, from which the name of one of the characters, Celadon, among others rustically French, suggests a survival.

If there ever was an original version with a classical setting, and the title was not simply an ironic play on the element of parody of traditional pastorals in the piece, it must rapidly have been supplanted by the version we know of. The revolution wrought by Favart in the opéra comique was to endow the lowlife characters of popular theater with the sensibilities of the protagonists of pastoral poetry: "The earliest Pieces of M. Favart already disclosed his taste for *Sentiment*, and it was really this that he introduced into a Spectacle where there was virtually no trace of it to be seen before" (Favart, 1763, I, p. ix). This elevation of the content of the pieces performed by the Opéra-Comique went hand in hand with the transformation wrought in the character and behavior of the audience by Jean Monnet, who took over the concession for it in 1743, and is supposed to have begun by clearing the parterre of the unruly rabble of liveried servants (Favart, 1763, I, p. xi; Monnet, 1909, pp. 78–84).

With these twin transformations of content and context, the Opéra-Comique had suddenly become *salonfähig*. Boucher, being closely associated with its promoters (see Monnet, 1909, pp. 85, 166–67, 175–76), was responsible for the actual introduction of their productions into salons, in the form of his own paintings and porcelain inspired by his designs. His indebtedness to Favart was perceived at the time, since the brothers Parfaict wrote: "Mr. *Boucher*, the Painter famous for his gracious compositions, took the idea of some of his pictures from here, and that is not the least of the honors paid to the *Pantomime* of the *Vendanges de Tempé*" ("*M. Boucher, Peintre fameux par ses compositions gracieuses, en emprunta l'idée de quelques-uns de ses tableaux, & ce n'est point le moindre honneur qu'ait reçu la* Pantomime *des* Vendanges du Tempé" [Parfaict, 1756, VI, p. 70]).

The brothers Parfaict had no reason to list every borrowing, but when summarizing the piece they found occasion to mention two, one of which was the subject of the present picture, whose title means "Are they thinking of the grape?" The simple plot of the pantomime concerns an unnamed "Little Shepherd" and a shepherdess called Lisette, whose burgeoning love for one another is thwarted by jealous rivals and parents, before ultimately winning the acceptance of the latter. The sixth scene opens with the Little Shepherd and Lisette giving one another grapes or cherries. The *Dictionnaire des Théâtres* (Parfaict, 1756, VI, pp. 78–79) says that, in the *Vallée de Montmorency*, they give one another both grapes *and* cherries, and that "this subject too has been seized upon by M. *Boucher*," but this is typical of its confusion of the two versions. Not only could grapes scarcely have been plucked in cherry orchards, but the transposition of the *Vendanges de Tempé* into the *Vallée de Montmorency* had yet to be devised when the present picture was painted. Not that the picture is a slavish depiction of the stage; for one thing the landscape setting is very different from that described in the pantomime (which approximates much closer to what is seen in the tapestry derivation of the picture woven at Aubusson; A & W fig. 889); for another— more crucially—the Little Shepherd was played *en travesti* by Mme Favart (who may also be intended in the Aubusson).

Fig. 156. *Le joueur de flageolet*, signed and dated 1746. Sold at the Palais Galliera, Paris, 17 June 1977.

Fig. 157. *Pensent-ils au raisin?* Nationalmuseum, Stockholm.

The present picture does not actually appear to have been the first to illustrate *Les vendanges de Tempé*. It seems to have been preceded by an oval picture, dated 1746, with a provenance from Machault d'Arnouville, that was sold at auction in Paris on 17 June 1977, under the title of *Le joueur de flageolet* (fig. 156). This shows the Little Shepherd playing the flute to Lisette, as at the beginning of scene 5 (before the later episode, also painted by Boucher and executed as a group by Vincennes, of him giving her a flute lesson). Although the dress of the protagonists of this oval picture retains slightly more of the richness of Opéra costumes, it appears nonetheless likely that the picture was originally a pendant of the present version of *Pensent-ils au raisin?*, and that the two pictures were exhibited together in the Salon of 1747. The provenance of *Le joueur de flageolet* (and thus by inference that of the present picture as its presumed pendant) from Machault d'Arnouville is particularly interesting, since his responsibilities as *contrôleur général* included the porcelain manufactory of Vincennes–Sèvres, where figures to Boucher's designs, taken from *La Vallée de Montmorency*, were to be made.

There is also a rectangular version of *Pensent-ils au raisin?* (fig. 157; Nationalmuseum, Stockholm; A & W 309) which has generally been regarded as the prime one, for no better reason than that it was (because of its destination) engraved. Now that it stands revealed as a compilation from the pair of ovals, this position can no longer be maintained. For while the figures and animals in the Stockholm picture are taken from the one in Chicago, the landscape background is borrowed from *Le joueur de flageolet*, which was painted the previous year. There is, however, a curious discrepancy between the characters of the Stockholm picture and those of the prime version in Chicago: the latter contains the additional figure of a small child, who is feeding one of the goats on the left. *Le joueur de flageolet* also contains a small child. Was he in the earliest version of *Les vendanges de Tempé*, and subsequently suppressed? Or did Boucher not originally set out to illustrate the pantomime so literally?

The Stockholm picture is generally said to have been acquired either by Tessin (Granberg, 1930, p. 164) or by Hårleman (exh. cat. 1984, Manchester, no. P6) for Crown Princess Lovisa Ulrica of Sweden, but no documentation appears to have been published about its purchase to justify either claim. The absence of any reference to it in the Swedish Royal Archives (in which the six overdoors painted by Boucher for the Royal Castle are recorded), or in Berch's correspondence with Tessin, indeed rather suggests that neither was the case. Carl Hårleman (1700–1753) was the architect in charge of the transformation of part of the Royal Castle of Drottningholm to house Lovisa Ulrica (see Stavenow, 1927, pp. 130–35). A cabinet picture such as this (unlike the overdoors) would have fallen not within his province, but within that of her artistic adviser, Count Tessin. How then to account for the fact that on the one hand the plate after the painting was dedicated to Hårleman, and that on the other hand the painting itself was catalogued in Queen Lovisa Ulrica's collection in 1760 (Sander, 1872, p. 79)? The answer, I believe, is simple: the picture was painted for Hårleman himself, and after his death it was acquired by the queen. Hence the absence of any mention of it in official files, and hence the fact that Boucher was ready to paint this picture when he was failing to complete the set promised to Lovisa Ulrica (see cat. 51).

Boucher was a friend of Hårleman's. They had known one another since the Swede had first gone to study in Paris in 1721–25 (Stavenow, 1927, p. 45).

He returned in 1732 to recruit French artists and craftsmen to work in Sweden, and again, to prepare himself for the task of modernizing Drottningholm and to acquire furnishings for the Royal Palace, from November 1744 to May 1745. He would have left Paris a little too soon to see *Les vendanges de Tempé*, but he, like Tessin, had a lively interest in whatever was new in France. Perhaps Boucher told him of the present picture when he was preparing it for the Salon, and he asked for something similar; or it might even have been a gesture of friendship on Boucher's part, and of gratitude for his role in procuring the commission for the Royal Palace. Some connection with that commission is suggested by the dedication of Le Bas's engraving after the picture, which is not only to *Monsieur le Baron de Horleman Sur-Intendant des Bâtimens de Sa Majesté le Roy de Suede*, but *Par son tres humble et tres obeissant Serviteur D'Arcy* (J-R 1346). Louis Darcy was not only himself an engraver, but also "Agent de sa Majesté Suedoise pour le commerce et les manufactures" (Scheffer, 1982, p. 211, n. 7), and the picture must somehow have passed through his hands for him to have had it engraved. It is in any case clear that it was because of the Swedish destination of the rectangular picture, and not because of any considered assessment of the merits of the two versions, that it—and not the present picture—was the one to have been engraved.

# 54 | *The Rape of Europa*

Oil on canvas
63 × 76 in. (160.5 × 193.5 cm)
Musée du Louvre, Paris (inv. 2714)
S & M 141, 142      A & W 350

PROVENANCE
Exhibited in the Salon of 1747, no. 8 of the *concours* entries; Château de la Muette, Paris (Dezallier, 1779, p. 19); intended for the Muséum in 1793 (*Archives de l'Art français* n.s. 3 [1909], p. 219); Château de Saint-Cloud, from which returned to the Louvre in 1870 or 1871.

REPLICA
63 × 76½ in., Prousteau sale, 5 June ff. 1769, lot 52: "belle & riche composition peinte dans l'Ecole de M. Boucher, que l'on croit ré-touchée par ce Maître. Cl. Duflos a gravé une estampe après ce tableau" [bought by Mr. *** for 150 livres]; Adolphe Warneck (sold privately); anon. sale, Paris (exp. Barré), 10 May 1867, unnumbered; M[ason] sale, Paris, 1 Feb. 1875, lot 6 [withdrawn]; [Mason] sale, Paris, 1 Mar. 1876, lot 1 [withdrawn]; Acquavella, New York; from which acquired in 1952 by the Museum of North Carolina, Raleigh.

In 1747 the new *directeur général des Bâtiments du Roi*, Mme de Pompadour's husband's uncle, Lenormant de Tournehem, decided to repeat the experiment of twenty years before, and to institute a competition among ten (ultimately eleven) selected artists from the Academy for the best picture (see esp. Locquin, 1912, p. 6). Although it was stated that each artist was to "work in the kind of painting for which he feels most inclination and inspiration" (A & W doc. 286), the real object was to encourage emulation in what was regarded as the highest branch of painting, and to provide economic support for it by guaranteeing the purchase of all the entries by the Crown for installation in the royal palaces. The completed pictures were all exhibited together at the Salon. By agreement among the artists themselves, to avoid jealousy and accusations of partiality, no prizes were in fact awarded, and the intended prize money was instead divided up among all the participants. It cannot be said that the competition had any direct effect in its intended object of reviving the practice and prestige of history painting; but it did so indirectly, in the further stimulus that it gave to the development of sustained art criticism inaugurated by La Font de Saint-Yenne, in the shape of the pamphlets by the abbé Le Blanc, Charles-Antoine Coypel, and the abbé Gougenot (qq.v.).

*54*

ENGRAVING

*L'Enlèvement d'Europe* [probably after the
replica now in Raleigh], engraved and published by Cl. Duflos, dedicated to the marquis
de Bonnac, Ambassador to Holland, advertised in Dec. 1752 (J-R 923–924).

DRAWINGS

1. *Europa*, sketch, Daniel Wildenstein coll.,
New York (A & W fig. 1024).

2. *Cupid* (between Europa and the bull),
red, black, and white chalks, 230 × 305 mm,
G. Mühlbacher sale, Paris, 15 May 1907, lot
63 (A & W fig. 1018).

3. *Three Cupids in the Air* (holding drapery
instead of flowers), red, black, and white
chalks, Albertina, Vienna (Schönbrunner &
Meder, 1896–1908, X, no. 1196; A & W fig.
1028).

Although the competition may have ended rather like that of the Caucus-
race in *Alice's Adventures in Wonderland*—"*Everybody* has won, and all must
have prizes"—the public was in no doubt as to the two preeminent works:
Natoire's *Triumph of Bacchus* and Boucher's *Rape of Europa* (see Le Blanc,
1747, p. 14; Gougenot, 1748, p. 59), a judgment seemingly confirmed by
posterity, in that, of the eleven entries, these two alone have remained in the
Louvre since 1870/72, when all the pictures were gathered in and redistrib-
uted (Jeaurat's *Diogenes Breaking His Bowl*, which is there now, was
originally left on deposit at Fontainebleau).

It is regrettable that we do not have for Boucher, as we have for Natoire
(Jouin, 1889), a correspondence showing how he approached the competition
and the subject he chose to tackle. Boucher's choice demonstrates, however,
that, like Natoire and most of the other competitors, he had no intention of
departing from his traditional subject matter to seek a novel theme. Rather
the reverse: it shows him, as with his reception piece for the Academy, eager

Fig. 158. *The Rape of Europa*, Beauvais tapestry. Los Angeles County Museum of Art; Gift of J. Paul Getty.

Fig. 159. *Head of a Girl Sniffing a Flower*. Reproduced from Soullié & Masson, plate facing page 8.

4. *Two Cupids with Drapery, One Brandishing a Torch*, 245 × 305 mm, G. Bourgarel sale, Paris, 15–16 June 1922, lot 17 (A & W fig. 1187).

5. *Girl Sniffing a Flower*, chalk heightened with pastel, 220 × 180 mm, [Vanbaal] sale, 9 Apr. ff. 1781, lot 127; de Sireul sale, 3 Dec. ff. 1781, lot 65; probably identifiable with the pastel drawing in Ch. Haviland's sale, Paris, 15–16 Dec. 1922, lot 3 (AA 346; A & W fig. 1027); cf. the pastel drawing from the Crozat de Thiers coll. now in the Hermitage (Stuffmann, 1968, p. 126 no. 110; Kamenskaya, 1960, pl. XXXII).

6. *Girl Holding Flowers in Her Drapery*, red-chalk counterproof, [used by another hand for study on recto for Sèvres statuette], private coll., Paris (A & W figs. 1021, 1022). A.D.L.

TAPESTRY

Woven at Beauvais as part of the series *Les Amours des Dieux*, with the right-hand side of the painting (the left of the tapestry) changed to show a river-god and some rocks and trees.

The first weaving was in a set of eight pieces made in 1750 for Don Felipe, Infante of Spain

to pit himself both against the great masters of the past, such as the Italians Titian and Albani, and against more recent artists of the French school, such as Noël-Nicolas Coypel (who painted this subject for the 1727 competition) or Natoire (who had painted it in 1731). Nor was he the only competitor to select it: the aging P-J. Cazes did so as well; but Cazes had not delivered his picture in time for the opening of the Salon, perhaps because he deliberately shunned the invidious comparisons that might be made, though when he did he found a defender in Lieudé de Sepmanville, if the latter was indeed the author of the *Réflexions nouvelles d'un amateur des beaux arts* (1747, pp. 19–20).

It was also a subject that Boucher had painted before, in the large picture for Derbais (see cat. 25); if that set out to impress, this has all the showy qualities of a competition piece. Whereas in his previous picture Boucher had set the scene entirely on dry land, here, though taking the same moment of the story when Europa, charmed by the bull's docility, sits upon his back, he manages to combine sea with land, and Europa's companions with tritons and a nereid; at the same time, cupids gambol in the sky with drapery and flowers, and Jupiter's eagle surveys his master's transformation. The woods to the left represent a rather improbable Phoenicia, with none of the palm trees that are supposed to have given it its name, while the distant rock must represent the island of Crete, to which Europa was borne. The weakest part of the picture is unfortunately the central figure of Europa, not so much on account of her pose, as because of the trivial expression on her face. One has the impression that this was derived from one of Boucher's pastel heads of young girls in the manner of Rosalba Carriera (see the pastel peeping over the screen in *Woman Fastening Her Garter*, cat. 38), just as the distracting figure of the handmaiden sniffing a flower at the left of the picture demonstrably derives from an earlier pastel once in the de Sireul collection (fig. 159; see AA 346; A & W fig. 1027). The foreground handmaiden is closely related to one of those in one of the overdoors of 1745 later at Harlaxton Manor (A & W 288).

Although Boucher emerged as one of the moral victors of the competition in terms of popular acclaim, it was over this picture that the first criticisms of him began to be voiced. Regrettably, none of these survive in printed form; but we can gain some idea of them from the defensive postures struck by the abbés Le Blanc and Gougenot (qq.v.). Both of them refer to the excessive use of pink, and Le Blanc to the hackneyed choice of subject; the latter criticism must have stemmed from amateurs such as Natoire's friend Antoine Duchesne, the *prévôt des Bâtiments du Roi*, whose intentions in promoting the competition (Jouin, 1889, pp. 140–42) had effectively been thwarted by most of the painters' refusal to experiment with new subject matter. Boucher's reaction to criticism was to design a frontispiece for Le Blanc's pamphlet, showing Painting sitting gagged before a picture on an easel, which a crowd of figures and animals symbolizing envy and stupidity (some of them curiously reminiscent of Carle Vanloo's entry, *The Drunkenness of Silenus*) make mock of (A & W fig. 77). One wonders whether he may not also have brought pressure to bear to have an ambiguity on page 59 removed from the second edition of Gougenot's pamphlet, which in the first (printed in A & W, doc. 349) might have been taken to mean that many people were astonished that it should have been the pictures of Natoire and Boucher that fought it out in popular esteem.

and son-in-law of Louis XV, who ruled Parma from 1748 to 1765, but it is not among the pieces of this set in the Quirinale Palace, Rome. The example in the set made in 1752 for Prince Esterházy was lost in World War II, but that in Frederick the Great's set of 1765 belongs to Prince Heinrich of Prussia and has been exhibited in the Charlottenburg Palace, Berlin. In 1754, Antoine de Crozat, baron de Thiers, took delivery of a set that had been made for Baron Johann Hartvig Ernest Bernstorff of Denmark, but the *Rape of Europa* in it has not been identified since 1929, when it was owned by the New York dealers French & Co. The Los Angeles County Museum has an example, and another was in the sale of works from Leningrad palaces held at the Rudolph Lepke auction house, Berlin, 6, 7 Nov. 1928, no. 221; it has been in the Pierre C. Cartier coll., Geneva. Other sales including examples of this tapestry are those of Charles Stein, Galerie Petit, Paris, 10–14 May 1886, no. 402 (A & W fig. 1020); Mme Dubernet Douine, Galerie Jean Charpentier, Paris, 11, 12, Apr. 1946, no. 154 (A & W 350/23); Palais Galliera, Paris, 3 Apr. 1968, no. 136; and the same auction house, 24 Nov. 1976, no. 135 (Standen, 1984–85).          E.A.S.

COPY
Central group, omitting standing handmaiden, 87 × 140 cm, Philippe Georges sale, Petit, Paris, 2 June 1891, lot 68.

Boucher's composition was given wider circulation, not only by being engraved by Duflos in 1752 (J-R 923–924), but also by serving as the source for a Beauvais tapestry cartoon in the series of the *Amours des Dieux*. The engraving was not actually made from the royal picture, but (as with *The Milliner*, see cat. 51) from a replica apparently painted for the *marchand de vins* Salomon-Pierre Prousteau.

Not only the picture but twenty proofs of the engraving (though no framed example) were in Prousteau's posthumous sale. Ananoff and Wildenstein are very probably correct in seeing this studio replica as the painting now in the North Carolina Museum at Raleigh. What is not evident is why Duflos should have dedicated his engraving to that great shell collector, the French ambassador in Holland, M. d'Usson, marquis de Bonnac. It would not appear to be an indication of ownership, although it is worth noting that de Bonnac sold his *hôtel* in the rue de Grenelle in 1768 (exh. cat. 1980, Paris, p. 30), the year before the picture appeared in Prousteau's sale, which might have induced him to dispose of both painting and proofs to the latter. When the *Rape of Europa* was adapted as a design for tapestry at Beauvais it was not only reversed but also altered and expanded on what was now the left-hand side (fig. 158). Instead of the marine deities of the painting, Boucher reverted to the idea of his picture for Derbais, and showed a river-god and -nymph beside a waterfall. It is an interesting illustration of Boucher's propensity to play with the same or similar forms over a short period, that he should have borrowed the figure of the naiad from the *Arion* that he painted in 1748 (cat. 55). The tapestry was woven thirteen times, from the first occasion in 1750 for the Infante Don Felipe of Spain, to the last in 1772 for M. Bertin (Badin, 1909, pp. 61–62).

## 55 | *Arion Rescued by the Dolphin (Water)*

Oil on canvas
34 × 53¼ in. (86 × 135.5 cm)
Signed in the water, lower left: *f. Boucher 1748*
The Art Museum, Princeton University, New Jersey (80.2)
(S & M 85)          (A & W 328)

## 56 | *Vertumnus and Pomona (Earth)*

Oil on canvas
34½ × 53½ in. (87 × 136 cm)
Signed on the vase, lower right: *f. Boucher 1749*
Columbus Museum of Art, Ohio (80.27)
(S & M 350)          (A & W 329)

PROVENANCE
Château de la Muette, Paris; posthumous sale of P-J-O. Bergeret de Grancourt, 24 Apr. ff. 1786, lot 49: "Ces deux Tableaux, dont le

These two pictures were intended as the first in a set of four depicting the *Four Elements* (Engerand, 1900, pp. 49–50). They were designed to be overdoors in the royal Château de la Muette, on the edge of the Bois de

premier est connu par l'Estampe qu'en a gravé *M. de Saint-Aubin*, réunissent au charme de la composition, une grande correction de dessin & la couleur la plus harmonieuse; il est rare de trouver d'aussi beaux Tableaux de ce Maître" [bought by Julliot for 320 livres]; Artemis, London (exh. cat. 1978, London, nos. 1, 2), from which bought by the two museums.

ENGRAVINGS

*Vertumne et Pomone,* by Augustin de Saint-Aubin, dated 1765, and dedicated to its publisher, Laurent Cars (J-R 1550–1554; F. L. Regnault, in the catalogue of Saint-Aubin's posthumous sale, 4 Apr. ff. 1808, says that he engraved the plate under the direction of Cars, who was prompted by it to propose him to the Academy in 1771).

*Arion,* etched by Augustin de Saint-Aubin in 1765 (J-R 1555), and completed with the burin by Jacques-Jean Pasquier in 1766, published by his master, Laurent Cars (J-R 1443–1446).

DRAWINGS

1. *Arion sur les flots échappé au naufrage,* pen and wash on blue paper, 222 × 295 mm, de Sireul sale, 3 Dec. ff. 1781, lot 88 [bought by M. Boulle for 45 livres 1 sol]; private coll., Paris (A & W fig. 953).

2. *Studies of legs, arms, and hands* (the legs for *Vertumnus and Pomona*), black chalk heightened with white, 237 × 325 mm, private coll., Geneva (A & W fig. 1122) [certain details suggest that these were in fact used in the adaptation to a cartoon for Beauvais (see Analogies, no. 1)].

REPLICAS AND COPIES

1. *Arion,* 45 × 52½ in., signed, reputedly commissioned by the comte de Toulouse for his château of Châteauneuf-sur-Loire [but not in the 1786 catalogue of the gallery there]; sale of the marquis de la Rocheb[ousseau; the *nom de guerre* of the dealer Léon Gauchez, according to Lugt], 5–8 May 1873, lot 112; given to the Metropolitan Museum, New York, by Léon Gauchez in 1875; deaccessioned, sold at Sotheby Parke Bernet, New York, 15 Feb. 1973, lot 71; Ira Spanierman, New York.

2. *Arion,* misc. sale, Palais des Congrès, Versailles, 24 Feb. 1974, lot 2.

3. *Arion,* 96 × 130 cm (reduced from a curvilinear overdoor), traces of signature bottom left, private coll., London (A & W 328, color pl. facing p. 100).

4. *Arion sur les eaux,* gouache, 9½ × 12½ pouces, posthumous sale of J-B-S. Chardin, 6 Mar. ff. 1780, lot 27.

5. *Arion on the waters* [in reverse and with the triton's head omitted, as in the engraving], drawing in red chalk, 330 × 493 mm, inscribed *retouché par gabrielle de St. aubin,* Kunstbibliothek, Berlin (Berckenhagen, 1970, pp. 306–07, *Hdz.* 2690).

Boulogne (A & W, II, p. 25, n. 1), which had just been extensively remodeled in 1746–48 (Tadgell, 1979, p. 162). Whether because Boucher never got down to executing the other two, or because the enlargement of the château determined upon by the king in 1753–54 (Tadgell, 1979, p. 162) did away with the room for which they had all been intended, the two that were painted never seem to have found employment there (they are never mentioned, for instance, in the fullish descriptions of the interiors by Dezallier d'Argenville or Dulaure). They are next heard of in the posthumous sale of Bergeret de Grancourt in 1786, after which they disappeared from view—during which time a replica of *Arion* was taken for the original (A & W 328)—until they were exhibited by Artemis in London in 1978 (exh. cat. 1978, London, nos. 1, 2).

The equation of the pictures in the Bergeret sale with those commissioned by the Crown has not met with universal acceptance. Despite the fact that there is no subsequent record of the pictures at La Muette or in the possession of the Crown or the State, it has been thought impossible that they should have been alienated. There is, in addition, a discrepancy between the painting of Arion presented here and the engraving of it by Saint-Aubin and Pasquier (fig. 160). The clue to the resolution of these difficulties resides in the history of La Muette. It is not simply that the château was constantly being transformed (Louis XV did so once again after the death of Mme de Pompadour in 1764 [Ginet, 1932, p. 14; Hillairet, 1963, I, p. 85]), or that Louis XVI put it up for sale in 1787 and that it was demolished in the Revolution, but that when Louis XV had it altered by Coustou the Younger after the death of Mme de Pompadour, it was so as to make it into a residence for the new Dauphin (the later Louis XVI) on the death of his father (1765). Louis XV had always used La Muette as a "demeure galante," in which he could live with successive mistresses in relative privacy, and from which he could hunt. Boucher's overdoors were no doubt disposed of, either by the Dauphin's moralizing preceptors, or by the upright Dauphin himself when he came to maturity, not simply because they were relics of an abandoned scheme, but also because the *Vertumnus and Pomona* at least was too reminiscent of the uses to which La Muette had formerly been put (the author of exh. cat. 1978, London, nos. 1, 2, even suggests that Pomona was a generalized portrait of Mme de Pompadour, which is perhaps going a little too far).

It is most likely that they were disposed of immediately, in 1765; for that is the date on Augustin de Saint-Aubin's engravings after the pictures. What is significant about these prints is that they carry no indication of ownership, and that the *Arion* bears no dedication, while the *Vertumnus and Pomona* bears one, not to any courtier or collector, but to Saint-Aubin's former teacher Laurent Cars. The implication is that at this stage they did not belong either to the king or to Bergeret but were on the market. The discrepancy between the engraving after the *Arion* and the picture itself can also be explained. It consists in the presence at the left of the painting of the head of a triton (a head also present in the copies of it) that is not to be found in the print. The engraving was evidently one that gave Saint-Aubin some trouble, since it was completed in 1766 by Jacques Pasquier. Perhaps because of this, or because the picture was snatched away before this detail could be put in, the triton's head was omitted. That it should be there is evident from the fact that the gaze of the nereid beside him has lost its motivation in the print.

55

56

Fig. 160. *Arion*, engraved by August de Saint-Aubin (1765) and J-J. Pasquier (1766) after Boucher.

Fig. 161. *Vertumnus and Pomona*. Fine Arts Museums of San Francisco.

6. *Vertumnus and Pomona*, 61 × 86 cm, Bayerische Staatsgemäldesammlungen, Munich (inv. 2863).

7. *Vertumnus and Pomona*, Bischoffsheim sale, Christie's, London, 7 May 1926, lot 12; M. et Mme L. C[otnaréanu] sale, Palais Galliera, Paris, 14 Dec. 1960, lot 2.

8. *Vertumnus and Pomona*, gouache, 185 × 205 mm, Hôtel Drouot, Paris, 4 Mar. 1931, lot 70 [as François Lemoyne, *Ceres et Pomone*].

ANALOGIES

1. *Arion*, sketch for an oval picture, apparently inserted by Boucher himself (see Fenaille, IV, 1907, p. 228) into a maquette by Maurice Jacques for one of the Gobelins tapestries with simulated paintings hung on a simulated damask ground (see cat. 92; A & W figs. 950, 1370).

2. *Vertumnus and Pomona* (fig. 161), cartoon for a Beauvais tapestry from the series of *Fragments d'Opéra*, first woven in 1758, adapted to an upright format, 123¼ × 72½ in., with minor changes in the figures and

There is a further reason for denying that the pictures are replicas of a lost pair painted for the Crown, and that is their divided dating. Not only does Boucher appear mostly to have avoided dating replicas at all, but were these to have been replicas, it is highly unlikely that they would have been completed or dated a year apart. What is more, the payment from the Crown assumed that both pictures had been painted in 1749; we know that in France commissions from the Crown took precedence over any others (see Scheffer, 1982, p. 132), and Boucher is hardly likely to have committed the lese majesty either of fobbing the Crown off with replicas, or of finishing a replica for another client before delivering the original to the Crown. Nor could the pictures have been painted for Bergeret. In 1748/49 he had not only not begun to patronize Boucher, he had not even started to take an interest in art (see cat. 52). He could, of course, have acquired the pictures from some other client of Boucher's, but we know of no such paintings in any sale or elsewhere, so that it is surely wiser to adopt Occam's rule of avoiding the unnecessary multiplication of entities. What one would like to know is where they were later concealed so long.

The unusual choice of Arion to symbolize Water, and of Vertumnus and Pomona to stand for Earth, derives from the ballet *Les Eléments*, written by Roy, with music by Lalande and Destouches. The first performance of this was mounted in the Tuileries in 1721, and the boy Louis XV himself danced in it (Parfaict, 1756, II, pp. 380–83). It was played at the Opéra in Paris in 1725, and revived in 1727, 1734, 1742, and 1754. If the role played by the king in his youth suggests an element of self-identification in the subject matter of the *Arion*, this is even more strongly implied by the *Vertumnus and Pomona*. For, as the writer of the entry in the Artemis catalogue pointed out, the role of Pomona was taken by Mme de Pompadour herself in two performances of *La Terre*, given as part of the *Fragmens* presented before the king in the Théâtre des Petits Appartements at Versailles on 15 January and 10 March 1749. The cataloguer presumed that Boucher had designed the sets for this, but while we have every reason to believe that he was later so employed at Bellevue, at Versailles there were others whose rights could not be overridden. The *Journal du Théâtre des petits Appartemens pendant l'Hiver de 1749 à 1750* (*Théâtre,* IV) indeed specifically says that "Messrs. Arnould and Tramblin continued to be responsible, in this as in previous years, for the execution of the stage sets and machinery."

Underlining the connection with the stage is the fact that Boucher only depicted Arion on this one occasion, and that in doing so, he followed the ballet. The story as told by Herodotus (1.24) tells of how Arion, having earned large amounts of money by a musical tour of Italy and Sicily, took ship to return home to Corinth. The crew, in order to seize his takings, forced him to jump overboard, but before doing so, allowed him a last song. The music charmed a dolphin, which carried him safely across the sea to Corinth, where he was able to convict the sailors of their attempted crime. In the ballet, however, Arion brought a storm and shipwreck on the crew—as can be seen to the left—and stayed to marry one of the sirens, Leucosia.

Vertumnus and Pomona were depicted by Boucher in a number of drawings, and again in a painting of 1763 in the Louvre. As related by Ovid in the *Metamorphoses* (14.621–770), the story is of the virginal nymph Pomona, who devoted herself exclusively to her securely fenced orchards. The orchard god Vertumnus, who was madly in love with her, managed to

major alterations in the setting (essentially a product of the studio); sold in strips by Beauvais in 1829; first recorded in 1902 (exh. cat. London, no. 39) as one of a set of four cartoons in the collection of Mme [Munroe] Ridgway, who lent them to her son-in-law, the marquis de Ganay, to adorn the dining room of his Paris *hôtel*; thence via the collections of Reginald Vaile, Sir Joseph Robinson, and Princess Ida Labia, to the California Palace of the Legion of Honor, San Francisco, in 1967.

3. *Vertumnus and Pomona*, red, black, and white chalks, 220 × 340 mm [more probably drawn autonomously, than as a first thought for this or any other painting], M[ayor] sale, 21–22 Nov. 1859, lot 27; [?Mühlbacher] sale, Paris, 17 Apr. 1899, lot 21; Trézel sale, Paris, 17 May 1935, lot 21.

4. *Le Repos de Vénus*, red, black, and white chalks, 292 × 440 mm [an autonomous later variant, using the same pose as Pomona]; M.E.M. Hodgkins sale, Paris, 30 Apr. 1914, lot 9 [bought by Lucien Kraemer]; private coll., New York (Slatkin, 1972, pl. 35; 1979, fig. 80); copied by Bonnet [?] (Slatkin, 1972, pl. 34; Christie's sale, London, 26 Nov. 1973, lot 353), and engraved by him in 1774 (J-R 384).

gain admittance to them in various disguises so as to enjoy the sight of her. Finally, he masked himself as an old woman so as to talk with Pomona and gain her confidence. Using various sophistries, he tried to convince her that it was wrong to deny her favors to a lover. Failing in this, he returned to his own shape, and lo!, where arguments had failed, his godlike beauty prevailed. Typically for the French stage, in Roy's version Pomona was already secretly in love with Vertumnus, which is surely what is suggested by her by no means rebarbative expression as she listens to his pleading here.

The theatrical themes of these two pictures were partly determined by their context, since they were originally intended as overdoors in a room that was to be hung with two tapestries, also designed by Boucher, whose subjects were likewise to be taken from the ballet. These were the two scenes from the *Fêtes Vénitiennes* and the *Fêtes de Thalie* of which Boucher was reported in 1748 as having shown sketches and begun the pictures but on which no further progress had been made by 1752 (Engerand, 1900, p. 56; A & W doc. 320). Uncertainty over their intended destination in La Muette could have led to the stagnation of the project, or it may have been Boucher's failure to complete the cartoons for the tapestries that resulted in a differently decorated room in which his overdoors of *Arion* and *Vertumnus and Pomona* were no longer appropriate.

# 57 | *La Lumière du Monde*

Oil on shaped canvas
69 × 51 in. (175 × 130 cm)
Signed bottom right: *f. Boucher/1750*
Musée des Beaux-Arts, Lyon
S & M 673       A & W 340

PROVENANCE
Exhibited in the Salon of 1750, no. 23, as "une Nativité, ou Adoration des Bergers, pour la Chapelle du Château de Belle-Vûë"; (until after 1762, when Dezallier d'Argenville, in the 2nd edition of his *Voyage pittoresque des environs de Paris*, not only retains, but expands, his mention of it from the 1755 edition); *garde-meuble* in the vestibule of the Hôtel de Pompadour [now the Elysée] in 1765 (Cordey, 1939, p. 91, inv. 1235/83); *Catalogue des Tableaux Originaux de différens Maîtres . . . &c de feue Madame de Pompadour*, grande rue du Faubourg S.-Honoré (Remy), 28 Apr. ff. 1766, lot 16: "Une Nativité. Ce beau Tableau, très-connu par l'exposition qui en a été faite au Sallon du Louvre, & dont on trouve l'Estampe gravée par E. Fessard . . ." [bought for 722 livres by "M. Dennery"]; *Catalogue des Tableaux des Trois Écoles . . . &c, du Cabinet de feu M. d'ENNERY, ÉCUYER*, rue Neuve-des-bons-Enfans, no. 10 (Remy & Miliotti), 11 Dec. ff. 1786, lot 26 [sold for 160 livres]; baron de Pontalba, Paris (exh. cat. 1860, Paris, no. 345);

Antoine Bret wrote in his measured obituary of Boucher that: "Among the devotional pictures that he did, the *Nativity* and the simple, graceful subject of *Holy Families* were most frequently the objects of his choice, because they did not distance him from either the graces or the beauty that he loved to paint, and which he effortlessly discovered in the shape of the Virgin and of the Child" ("*Dans le nombre de Tableaux de dévotion qu'il a faits, la* Nativité *& le sujet simple & gracieux des* Saintes Familles *font les objets qu'il a choisis le plus souvent, parce qu'ils ne l'éloignaient, ni des graces, ni de la beauté qu'il aimait à peindre, & qu'il retrouvait aisément dans la figure de la Vierge & dans celle de l'Enfant*" [Bret, 1771, p. 52]).

Normally, the painter of an altarpiece had no choice in the theme of what he was to paint—hence, indeed, the austerer subject matter of Boucher's other actual altarpieces (e.g., cat. 77), as opposed to his religious cabinet pictures, which do indeed center around the theme of the Holy Family. However, in the case of the present picture his tastes and, more importantly, those of his patron, had free rein. For this painting was the altarpiece in the private chapel of Mme de Pompadour in her Château de Bellevue. "Chapel" is perhaps to dignify its location too much, since it was really more of an antechamber, with the altar in a kind of cupboard, which, when closed, removed any

[Davillier] sale, Paris, 24 Mar. 1864, lot 35; coll. outside France until c. 1932; private[?] coll., Paris (cf. Jeannerat, 1932); M. Destrem, Château de Crespières; following World War II, recovered by the Offices des Biens Privés and allocated to the Louvre, by which deposited in the Musée de Lyon in 1948.

ENGRAVING

*La Lumière du Monde*, engraved by Etienne Fessard in 1761 (presented to the Academy to obtain protection of copyright on 4 Apr.) and published with the dedication: *A Madame de Pompadour Dame du Palais de la Reine* (A & W fig. 991).

REDUCTIONS

1. *En grisaille* on panel, c. 25.5 × 19 cm, *Catalogue Raisonné des Tableaux, Bronzes, Terres Cuites . . . &c, qui composent le Cabinet de feu M. CAYEUX, Sculpteur, Ancien Officier de l'Académie de S. Luc*, s.l. (Remy), 11 Dec. ff. 1769 (engravings and drawings), 8 Jan. ff. 1770 (paintings and sculpture), lot 49: "La Nativité de J. C., belle esquisse terminée, peinte en grisaille sur bois: hauteur 9 pouces 6 lignes, largeur 7 pouces, par le même *François Boucher*; c'est le petit tableau d'un grand, d'après lequel Etienne Fessard a gravé l'Estampe, où au bas on lit: *La Lumière du monde*" [bought by Menageot for 33 livres]; ?continuation of a forced sale of 28 Aug. ff. 1776, one of the rooms of MM. les Religieux de la Mercy, rue de Chaume, in the Marais (Hayot Delongpré & Joullain), 25 Feb. ff. 1777, under *Miniatures*, lot 140: "Une jolie Exquisse, par F. Boucher, qui représente la naissance de Jesus-Christ; projet d'un Tableau de la Chapelle de Bellevue."

2. With shaped top, c. 61 × 40.5 cm, ? *Catalogue des Tableaux . . . &c. après le décès de M. Nicolas, Doreur et Marchand d'Estampes*, rue des Bons-Enfans no. 30 (Regnault), 3 Nov. ff. 1806, lot 2: "La Nativité, bon tableau connu par l'Estampe qu'en a gravé *Eti. Fessard*, sous le titre de *la Lumiere du Monde*. Toile"; *Notice de Tableaux &c. du Cabinet de feu M. GUILLAUMOT, Directeur de la Manufacture impériale des Gobelins*, Hôtel de Bullion (Regnault), 15 Jan. 1808, lot 3.

3. "La Nativité, Sujet gracieux de composition et piquant d'effet, connu par l'Estampe de Fessard. 23 pouces sur 15 pouces. Toile, forme chantournée du haut."

COPIES

1. By the abbé Richard de Saint-Non [?], church of Pothières (see G. Wildenstein, 1959, p. 226, fig. 3), of which he was the *abbé commendataire*.

2. ?Drawing prepared for Fessard's engraving, black chalk heightened with white on bister paper, 400 × 290 mm (shaped top), Maurice Delacre sale, Gutekunst & Klipstein, Bern, 21 June 1949, part two (misc. properties), lot 545.

indication of the intermittent religious function of the room (see Biver, 1933, pp. 60–62, 170).

It is a conspicuous omission on the artist's part that, up until this time, he had painted no devotional pictures whatsoever, despite the welcome opportunity to work on a large scale that altarpieces would have afforded him (his early pictures of Old Testament subjects should be seen as following in the footsteps of old masters and the Italian School, rather than as any satisfaction of piety). Nor was Mme de Pompadour, who liked to surround herself with the more freethinking spirits of the day, conspicuous for religiosity. It is noteworthy that this altarpiece was commissioned before the death of her only daughter and the desire to make her position at Court unimpregnable, which impelled her toward manifestations of devotion from around 1754 onwards. Given its destination, the present altarpiece could not be on the large scale that Boucher might otherwise have welcomed, while Mme de Pompadour's reasons for commissioning it probably had more to do with the necessity of a private chapel to the status of Bellevue, than with any other consideration (but one should not overlook her commissioning of three pictures from Vien for the church at Crécy in 1752). Even so, in view of the other religious pictures that she was to obtain from Boucher (e.g., cat. 68), one must wonder whether, by allocating this commission to him rather than to, say, Carle Vanloo, she was not deliberately trying to extend her favorite painter's range. It should be remembered, however, that it appears to have been only in the year that he painted this that she started to employ Boucher on her own account.

Whatever the actual reasons behind the commissioning of this picture, it must be allowed that it represents a striking expansion of Boucher's range on the one hand, and a notable relaxation of the traditional austerity of the altarpiece on the other. One of the most conspicuous things about this picture is the difficulty of fitting its subject into any of the accepted categories of Christian iconography. It is not exactly a Nativity, in view of the extraneous characters present and the absence of the ass (though the presence of the latter is traditional rather than essential), nor does one shepherd constitute an Adoration. What is more, on closer analysis, the figure on the far right turns out not to be a shepherd at all, but—with his hat and water gourd—rather more of a pilgrim. This aperçu brings us closer to the true subject of the picture, and to the realization that, for once, the title of the engraving after it is truest to its content: *La Lumière du Monde*—The Light of the World.

What is being conveyed, both pictorially—by the radiance of light from the divine Child—and by the selection of the protagonists, is that Christ's birth has brought light to the whole of mankind. The witnesses of the newborn babe are essentially types of humanity, ranging from old men and women, through those in their prime, to children. Although the old man must be Joseph, the fact that he is consulting a scriptural-looking book, together with the presence of the old woman with her hands clasped in veneration, and that of the dove clasped by the small boy—all carry irresistible overtones of the iconography of the Purification, when Simeon and Anna were the first to acknowledge the divinity of Christ and to declare that he was to be: "A light to lighten the Gentiles, and the glory of thy people Israel" (Luke 2:32), a verse that is echoed by another at the beginning of the Gospel according to St. John (1:9), whence the engraving takes its title: "That was the true Light, which lighteth every man that cometh into the world." Not only is the ox the

Fig. 162. *Study of a Woman with Her Hands Together over an Urn*. Albertina, Vienna.

Fig. 163. *Study for the Head of an Old Woman*. Boymans–van Beuningen Museum, Rotterdam.

Fig. 164. *Study of a Half-Kneeling Peasant Girl Holding Child*. Staatliche Kunsthalle, Karlsruhe.

Fig. 165. *Standing Figure of a Peasant with Hands Clasped Over a Staff*. Sold Christie's, London, 29 March 1966.

Fig. 166. *Study for the Head of a Bearded Man in Profile*. British Museum, London.

Fig. 167. *Study of Six Cherubim*. Städelsches Kunstinstitut, Frankfurt.

symbolic beast of St. Luke, but in popular superstition, although the ox and the ass together are supposed (in the Gospel of Pseudo-Matthew) to have adored Christ and thus fulfilled the prophecy of Isaiah 1:3: "The ox knoweth his owner, and the ass his master's crib," the ass is sometimes taken to represent by his braying the refusal of the Jews to accept the revelation: "but Israel doth not know, my people doth not consider"—hence perhaps its omission from the scene. As for the trussed hen and the two eggs, it is hard to know whether they too are intended to carry their symbolic overtones of dawning light and resurrection, or whether they are simply Boucher's underscoring of the simple rusticity of the birth in a stable, like the milk churn on which the old woman supports her hands. In any event, the unorthodoxy of the depiction was surely only permissible in the seclusion of a private chapel.

Antoine Bret also seized the stylistic essence of the picture more justly in his obituary of Boucher than any of the critics at the time of its exhibition in

3. Painting after Fessard's engraving, 9 × 7 in., formerly J. R. Saunders coll., London (see H. Baily, 1912, p. 240 and fig. p. 234).

4. Copy sketch, camaïeu bistre clair, 45 × 32 cm, Mme Gustave Meunié coll. (exh. cat. 1932, Paris, no. 1); her sale, Galerie Charpentier, Paris, 14 Dec. 1935, lot 61 [carelessly described].

DRAWINGS

1. "Une femme vue à mi-corps, elle a les mains jointes au-dessus d'une Urne . . . à la sanguine & au crayon noir, rehaussé de blanc" (251 × 248 mm; study for the old woman), Huquier's posthumous sale, 9 Nov. ff. 1772, lot 386 [sold with other drawing in lot for 12 livres]; Herzog Albert von Sachsen-Teschen (d. 1822), Vienna; Albertina, Vienna (inv. 14.271) [Schönbrunner & Meder, I, p. 11; AA 128, fig. 24] (fig. 162).

2. Head of an Old Woman, red, black, and white chalks, 205 × 178 mm: engraved by Demarteau as no. 150 in 1767, when in the cabinet of Mme [Blondel] d'Azaincourt (J-R 721); posthumous sale of Prof. August Grahl of Dresden, Sotheby's, London, 27 April 1885, lot 34 [bought by Herbage for £4]; Property of a Gentleman living in Italy; Sotheby's, London, 7–10 Dec. 1920, lot 384; Boymans-van Beuningen Museum, Rotterdam (F.I. 34) [A & W fig. 983] (fig. 163).

3. Half-Kneeling Peasant Girl Holding Child (plausibly a first study for the girl in the picture), black chalk, stumped, heightened with white on beige paper, 470 × 296 mm, Wildenstein, Paris; Michael Grünwald, Munich, from whom acquired by the Staatliche Kunsthalle, Karlsruhe, in 1977 (A & W fig. 984; exh. cat. 1983, Karlsruhe, no. 26; here fig. 164).

4. Head of an Old Man, Looking Down (study for Joseph), red chalk, heightened with white, 240 × 194 mm, Herzog Albert von Sachsen-Teschen (d. 1822), Vienna; Albertina, Vienna (inv. 12.182; AA 429; A & W fig. 986).

5. Standing Figure of Peasant with Hands Clasped over a Staff, black chalk and gray wash highlighted with white on buff paper,

495 × 260 mm, Mrs. Maud Strauss coll., sold posthumously, Christie's, London, 29 Mar. 1966, lot 167 (here fig. 165).

6. Head of a Bearded Man in Profile Looking Left (study for the shepherd/pilgrim), red, black, and blue chalks touched with white, stumped, on buff paper, 185 × 144 mm: Colnaghi (1946); Sir Bruce Ingram coll; British Museum (inv. 1963. 12.14.4; A & W fig. 987; here fig. 166).

7. Six Cherubim, Städelsches Kunstinstitut, Frankfurt-am-Main (inv. 1160; A & W fig. 990; here fig. 167).

ANALOGIES

1. Head of a Bearded Man in Profile, Looking Right (?over an offset of a study for the shepherd/pilgrim), brown and ocher chalks with heightening in white, 181 × 146 mm, Ian Woodner coll. (exh. cat. 1973, New York, no. 100).

2. ?Head of a Nursling, drawing by Carle Vanloo, engraved by Demarteau no. 264 (exh. cat. 1977, Nice, no. 531). [Could Boucher possibly have borrowed this study, in the absence of one of his own? The resemblance is striking.]

the Salon of 1750, when, following Dezallier d'Argenville (1762, p. 32), he declared that Boucher in his Nativity and Holy Families emulated Carlo Maratta, "Carluccio delle Madon[n]e." There is the same approximation to ideal types of figures that profess to be observed from humble models, and there is the same unnatural clarity and unreal lighting, in a picture apparently dedicated to the correct observation of chiaroscuro. The latter phenomena are, of course, quite intentional, in that the main object of the picture is to convey the light divinely communicated from the heavens to the Christ Child, and thus radiated forth into the world.

The result was, however, clearly not sympathetic to all tastes. It was, no doubt, because of the associations of the picture with the person who commissioned it that it had been ejected from Bellevue some time between 1762 and Mme de Pompadour's death in 1764. This ejection tallies with the subsequent assertion of the by then royal status of Bellevue, in which Boucher's essentially rustic presentation of the Nativity (which Biver [1933, p. 174] saw as in keeping with the rural tone of much of Mme de Pompadour's decoration of the château) was replaced by an Adoration of the Kings by Doyen in 1769/70. What is more surprising is to find that the picture was not one of those that had belonged to his sister that Marigny attempted to retain, since he allowed it to be included in her posthumous sale (without the justification of difficulties over accommodating a picture of its size, such as may have compelled him to let the Lever and the Coucher du Soleil go). It fetched, however, a very respectable sum in that sale, while Fessard's engraving of it, which was one of his finest, continued to sustain its reputation even during the long periods when the painting itself was lost to view.

## 58 | Apollo Revealing His Divinity to Issé

Oil on canvas
50¾ × 62 in. (129 × 157.5 cm)
Signed bottom right: f. Boucher 1750
Musée des Beaux-Arts, Tours
(inv. 794–1–1)
S & M 82        A & W 355

58

?Direction des Bâtiments du Roi; gallery of the château of Châteauneuf-sur-Loire (Châteauneuf-sur-Loire, 1786, no. 8: "Un sujet allégorique représentant le lever du Soleil. Ce charmant Tableau est du meilleur tems de ce Maître, & fait honneur à l'École Françoise. Il est peint sur toile, & porte 3 pieds 8 pouces de haut, sur 4 pieds 10 pouces de large"); removed to the Château de Chanteloup in 1794 and sequestrated, appearing in the inventory of 25 thermidor, l'an II as *Apollon visitant Eglé sous la figure de feu[e] la dame Pompadour*; removed to the former Palais Archiépiscopal, to form the nucleus of the subsequent museum.

There is a mystery behind this picture, to which we regrettably do not have the key. On the one hand, it is evident from the picture itself that the face of Issé must be a portrait. On the other there is the problem that, though the painting was described in detail in the royal accounts when it was painted, it came to the museum in Tours not from one of the royal châteaux, but from Chanteloup, the château of the duc de Choiseul (but, from 1786, of the duc de Penthièvre). Somehow associated with this is the fact that Boucher's bill claiming that the picture was painted by order of Lenormant de Tournehem, the *directeur général des Bâtiments du Roi*, from whom all such commissions had to originate, was annotated by the *premier Peintre*, Charles-Antoine Coypel, the usual channel for such commands (see Locquin, 1912, p. 4, n. 1), with "*L'ordonnance n'est pas passée par mes mains*" ("the authorization did not pass through my hands"), although he ultimately sanctioned payment (A & W II, p. 57).

DRAWINGS

1. *Figure of Apollo*, formerly Delestre coll., Paris (A & W fig. 1046).

2. *Naiad Enlaced by Another's Arms*, red, black, and white chalks, 320 × 450 mm, David-Weill coll.; Georges Wildenstein; Barbara Hutton; John Goelet; Slatkin, New York; Art Institute of Chicago (exh. cat. 1976, Chicago, no. 43; here fig. 168).

3. *Two Cupids on the Ground*, black chalk, Metropolitan Museum of Art, New York (60.175.1; A & W fig. 1047; here fig. 169).

4. *Cupid on His Belly, Holding a Lyre*, sale, Paris, 23 Nov. 1953, lot 76 (A & W fig. 1048).

COPIES

1. Of central group only, entitled *Apollon enseignant Mme Deshoulières*, 97 × 129 cm, ex-coll. Dard, Musée des Beaux-Arts, Dijon.

2. Musée de Romarantin.

3. Bayerische Staatsgemäldesammlung (inv. 12 937).

4. Oil sketch of the two nymphs, executed in Tours in 1892 by Berthe Morisot, 64 × 79 cm (Bataille & Wildenstein, 1961, no. 320, p. 45, fig. 323; A & W fig. 1050).

Fig. 168. *Naiad Enlaced by Another's Arms.* Art Institute of Chicago.

Fig. 169. *Two Cupids on the Ground.* The Metropolitan Museum of Art, New York.

Three identifications of Issé have been proposed: de Nolhac (1925, pp. 123–25), the biographer of Mme de Pompadour, saw Issé as the royal mistress; "local tradition" in Tours saw her as the bride whom the comte de Stainville, the later duc de Choiseul, married on 12 December 1750, Mlle Crozat (Lossky, 1962, no. 5); while the copy of the central portion of the picture in the Musée des Beaux-Arts in Dijon used to be entitled *Apollon enseignant Mme Deshoulières*.

The last of the three can be dismissed immediately: Antoinette Deshoulières (1638–1694) was a bluestocking whose writings included the tragedy *Genséric* and some *Réflexions morales* written on her deathbed—scarcely of the right period or character for Boucher's melting nymph! (there is a genuine portrayal of her as a shepherdess, by Mignard, at Chantilly). The identification as Mlle Crozat has more to be said for it. This hypothesis would presuppose the picture having originally been painted by official command—even if this bypassed the usual channels—and then having been made over to de Stainville, who would have had his bride's features substituted for those of the original nymph. This has the merit of accounting for the distinctly awkward way in which Issé's head sits upon her shoulders (if Boucher were having to work from something like a miniature for Mlle Crozat's features, he would have had to conform to the angle at which it showed her face), and also for the discrepancy between the year in which Boucher claimed that he had painted the picture, and the year with which he dated it. The chief drawback to this hypothesis is that de Stainville's marriage to Mlle Crozat antedated by a couple of years his notorious rapprochement with Mme de Pompadour, through the betrayal to her of the letters of the king to his cousin Mme de Choiseul-Romanet (see Fleury, 1899, pp. 88–107). At the time the picture was painted he was still essentially only a military figure, on the fringes of the court, detested by Mme de Pompadour for his cruel epigrams at her expense, and consequently most unlikely to have secured for himself a picture painted by her favorite painter at the command of her husband's uncle. It is also far from certain that this picture ever even belonged to Choiseul. Although it came from Chanteloup, it is not (unlike the fixed overdoors by Houel) very likely to have been left there after his death in 1785 when the château was acquired by the king and made over to the duc de Penthièvre the next year.

The identification of Issé with Mme de Pompadour might find support from a hypothesis as to how this rare subject came to be painted. The rather obscure antique myth shown here was one that had been turned into a *pastorale héroïque* called *Issé* by Houdard de La Motte, with music by Destouches. It was given its first performance before Louis XIV at the Trianon in 1697. It was revived by the Opéra on several occasions, the last being the winter of 1741/42, when Boucher designed the opening set (see cat. 47). Over the winter of 1749/50 it was given three times in the private theater created by Mme de Pompadour at Versailles, on 26 November, 16 and 22 December (see *Théâtre*, IV). Mme de Pompadour took the title role, while Apollo was played by the vicomte de Rohan. The theme of the pastorale was surely congenial to her, in that it concerned Apollo casting aside his glory and disguising himself as a shepherd called Philemon in order to win the love of the shepherdess Issé for himself alone (so apposite was it that a ballet called *Aeglé*, with an almost identical theme, had been written by Laujon and put on at the Théâtre des Petits Appartements in January 1748):

*Je veux, sans le secours de ma grandeur suprême*
*Essayer de plaire en ce jour:*
*Qu'il est doux d'avoir ce qu'on aime*
*Par les seules mains de l'Amour!*

The present painting is certainly not a straightforward depiction of these performances; not only are its cavorting cupids clearly unstageable, but the setting for the moment depicted, when Apollo reveals himself in his true guise, shows no sign of the *solitude* giving way to the *palais magnifique* with the Horae on clouds, demanded by the transformation in the last act. Moreover, the painting would appear to have been commissioned before the piece was staged. Not necessarily, however, before it was planned.

Mme de Pompadour's self-identification with the subject seems evident; whether she is actually depicted in the present picture is less easy to affirm. We are hampered by the fact that all Boucher's finished portraits of her date from later in her life, when her health had been undermined and she had grown gaunt. Even so, it is hard to equate the puffy, rather featureless face of Issé with hers as it seems earlier to have been (see cat. 59). Possibly, since Apollo is certainly no portrait, only a generalized likeness to a lady of fashion was intended. If the picture were to have been painted for Pompadour, we would be handed the likeliest explanation of the irregular way in which it was commissioned. Mme de Pompadour would have used the authority of her uncle in commissioning it from Boucher; but, since he had not in fact ordered it, it was at first repudiated by Coypel.

This still supplies no explanation as to how the painting ever arrived at Chanteloup. The dévot duc de Penthièvre was not one of Mme de Pompadour's intimate circle, so that it is hard to imagine her having given it to him. Yet it does not feature in the very full posthumous inventory of her effects, or in her brother's sale. Perhaps, since he was after all to commission the four overdoors of *Sylvia and Amyntas* from Boucher only five years later (see cat. 62, 63), one should consider the possibility that it was also he who got Boucher to make this idealized portrayal of his wife in her lifetime. As a *prince du sang*, he might have been in a position to order it through irregular channels. In the absence of further evidence, the question must still remain open.

(Since writing the above I have been sent, thanks to the kindness of M. A. Bezançon of Châteauneuf-sur-Loire and Mlle Marie-Anne Dupuy respectively, transcripts from the exceptionally rare printed catalogue of the gallery of pictures in the duc de Penthièvre's château of Châteauneuf-sur-Loire [see Châteauneuf-sur-Loire, 1786], and from the inventory of pictures removed from there to de Penthièvre's other château of Chanteloup prior to the sequestration of all his collections, which was taken on 25 thermidor, l'an II [?August 1794; Archives Nationales F 17 1270B]. Between them, they establish beyond a doubt that the picture came to Chanteloup from Châteauneuf-sur-Loire, and thus it cannot have had anything to do with de Choiseul or his wife. Unfortunately, neither the ill-informed author of the Châteauneuf catalogue, nor the rather better-informed author of the inventory of sequestration was aware of the true subject of the picture [hence its presence in the two compilations having previously escaped notice], so what they say about it cannot be relied upon. It is, however, just possible that the title given to the picture by the inventory, *Apollon visitant Eglé sous la figure de feu[e] la dame Pompadour* [Apollo visiting Eglé (who is) in the guise of the late lady Pompadour] reflects a genuine tradition. The plots of *Aeglé* and *Issé* were virtually interchangeable, and Mme de Pompadour played in both [see above]. Yet if the picture does represent her, rather than the duchesse de Penthièvre, we still need to discover how the picture could have left her hands for those of the austere duc, who was certainly not one of her circle.)

## 59 | *Sketch for a Portrait of Mme de Pompadour*

Oil on paper laid down on canvas
23½ × 18 in. (60 × 45.5 cm)
Musée du Louvre, Paris (R.F. 2142)

PROVENANCE
Left to the Louvre in the bequest of baron Basile de Schlichting, 1914.

COPY
P. Romanelli coll. (Nolhac, 1925, pp. 113–14, color pl. facing p. 112, in lieu of the Schlichting picture discussed and illustrated in the 1907 edition, pp. 58–59 and color pl. facing p. 56).

Jeanne-Antoinette le Normant d'Etioles, née Poisson, and subsequently marquise de Pompadour (1721–1764), became Louis XV's mistress in the spring of 1745; Boucher began to work for her at Bellevue in 1750 (see cat. 57); his first portrait of her is dated 1756 (cat. 64). This delay, this absence of any portrait of her by her favorite artist while she was still in her prime, while she was still the king's mistress in deed as well as title (relations between them ceased some time in 1750), never seems to have occasioned surprise. Specialists have of course known of references to an earlier portrait on the one hand, and of the present sketch and its fellows on the other, but no attempt appears to have been made to ponder the possible relationship between the two. If comparisons have been made at all, they have been with much later portraits of Mme de Pompadour, and it has been assumed that the present sketch or one of its fellows is a preparation either for the seated portrait in a similar kind of setting dating from 1756, or for the standing portrait in a garden, dating from 1759 (A & W 522).

We know, however, that there was a portrait of Mme de Pompadour by Boucher that he was finishing in early 1750; for on 1 March that year she wrote to her brother, then only the marquis de Vandières, to say, "I shall take great care not to send you my portraits by Liotard, but I am going to send you the copy of one done by Boucher, which is charming, and which [the original, not the copy, as her subsequent letter of 15 June makes clear] he will finish from me" (Pompadour, 1878, p. 37). Her brother had left for his grand tour of Italy in December 1749, so presumably the portrait had not been begun then, or he would have been aware of it. Subsequent letters have her sending off the copy on 26 April: "it is very like the original, not much like me; but still quite pleasing" (Pompadour, 1878, p. 50); and then on 15 June sending him in Genoa "the first original by Boucher, which he has retouched from me, and which is better than the copy that I sent you in Rome" (Pompadour, 1878, p. 57).

None of this gives any indication of what the picture was like, but there are certain clues in the correspondence. In the first place, she calls it *"grand"* (large). This may simply have been in contrast to the portrait on a snuffbox that she was delaying having made, on the grounds that the need for the former was more pressing. However, she mostly talked of the copy of the

59

Fig. 170. *Sketch for a Portrait of Mme de Pompadour.* Private collection, England.

Boucher in the same breath as that of another, of Vanloo's portrait of the king. This is almost certainly the full-length state portrait that Carle Vanloo painted in 1750 (exh. cat. 1977, Nice, no. 299), after waiting almost a year for her copy of which (since the original itself had not been completed), she was prepared to settle for a head alone (Pompadour, 1878, p. 70). It is evident that both pictures were intended as a kind of reinforcement of de Vandières's status on his travels: the one a mark of his sovereign's favor, and the other a reminder of his kinship with the power behind the throne. That is at any rate the implication of Mme de Pompadour's statement that she was giving priority to Boucher's picture over the portrait box "in view of the fact that I believe the large portrait more urgent for the use that you want to make of it" (Pompadour, 1878, p. 37). Either her portrait would have been hung in state in his lodgings—for the proper effect of which a full-length would have been needed—or it would have been given away as a diplomatic gift for a similar function (hence her ultimately sending the original). Similarly, her readiness when the picture arrived back in France, as her brother was on the way home, to "have it placed wherever you tell me to" (Pompadour, 1878, p. 81), also suggests a picture of some consequence.

It would also appear that Mme de Pompadour had turned to Boucher, who was scarcely known for his portraits, because of her notorious difficulties with Maurice-Quentin de la Tour over the full-length pastel of her that he finally completed in 1755 (see Magnier, 1904); for on 28 May 1750 she wrote to her brother, "I am very glad that you are pleased with my portraits; they were found very pretty here, but little like. Still, since it is the best there is, I have sent it to you. There is absolutely nothing to be done with de Latour, his madness increases by the hour" (Pompadour, 1878, p. 55). Given the fact that the picture that de la Tour finally executed of her is not only full length, but shows her surrounded by evidence of her artistic tastes (Monnier, 1972, no. 74), one is tempted to speculate that what she obtained from Boucher was what—at this stage—she despaired of getting from de la Tour; and even whether de la Tour was to take his cue from Boucher's sketch.

This would very much suggest a picture with the character of the present portrait—the books, the music, the portfolios, the globe: all are in both. Many of these elements were of course to recur in the seated portrait of 1756 (cat. 64), but we can hardly conjecture that the 1750 portrait was simply a prime version of that, since the other was a completely new work, exhibited in the Salon. If one looks at the apparent age of Mme de Pompadour in this sketch (and there is no question that it is she, as not only the likeness to the later seated portrait but also the tower from her arms on the bookbinding make plain), nothing opposes a dating to 1750. If anything, she appears rather younger than twenty-eight; but that is possibly because the artist has succeeded in capturing the vivacity and mobility of her face, which—rather than a static beauty—were her distinguishing assets (see E. & J. de Goncourt, 1878, p. 13).

It is certainly hard to imagine two such sketches as the present one and the variant in oil on canvas in a private collection in England (fig. 170; A & W 520)—which shows her in the same setting but before a dressing table, with her hat in her hand, about to go out for a walk—having been made with no finished picture resulting. Yet the curious thing is that there appears to be no record of such a picture, either in her brother's posthumous sale or elsewhere, the possible references in her letters to her brother aside, and that no such portrait of her survives. The lack of contemporary references is not significant. We know virtually none of the portraits of Mme de Pompadour from either contemporary reports or engravings; they led a very private existence in the apartments of herself and her circle. That no such full-scale portrait survives could be ascribable to its greater vulnerability in the Revolution.

There is, however, one picture that sounds as if it could have been the final version for which this and the other oil sketch were preparations. This is a painting that belonged, as did the 1758 replica of the 1756 portrait, to Henri Didier, who exhibited it in the revelatory exhibition of 1860 (Paris, no. 76, 195 × 130 cm; it is possible that this was "le portrait en pied de Mme. de Pompadour, à vingt ans" that had previously been sold by de Cypierre to someone in London—see Thoré, 1844, p. 3). In the catalogue of this exhibition, Philippe Burty described the sitter thus: "Dressed in a yellow silk dress open to the corsage, with a bouquet on her breast; standing before an easel, and with her hand placed upon a drawings folder, she turns to look at a bust placed to her right, on a table." The pose sounds similar to that in the present picture, with yet a further variation in the artistic pastime depicted, and with the bust (which would presumably have been that of the king) to give point to her sideways gaze. However, it should be noted that, while Albert de la Fizelière (1860, p. 298) thought that the head in the picture had been the model for the posthumous mezzotint by Watson (J-R 1626), which would suggest that it was actually a later portrait than any other known, the Goncourt (1878, p. 426) doubted that it was by Boucher at all. The portrait was not in Didier's posthumous sale in 1868, and does not appear to have been recorded since—unless, of course, it has subsequently been quite differently identified. Most tantalizing of all is the fact that de la Fizelière (1860, p. 298), contradicting his other suggestion that the head was the model for Watson's mezzotint, quotes some unnamed memoirs to the effect that this portrait of Mme de Pompadour at an easel was exhibited *hors catalogue* in the Salon of 1763, despite the fact that it had actually been painted twelve to fifteen years before. I know of no corroboration of this, but it is hard to imagine that de la Fizelière would have invented this (decidedly unflattering) reference. The more one studies nineteenth-century accounts of Boucher, however, the more one sees that such spurious reference to supposed documents is entirely possible.

In the present sketch, Mme de Pompadour is touching a harpsichord. The effect is dilettantish; but in fact we know that she had been taught to play by no less than Jélyotte, and that when she did so before her marriage in the salon of Mme d'Angervilliers, the effect was such that the king's first mistress, Mme de Mailly, flung herself into her arms in tears—little imagining that her eventual successor could ever be this gifted little bourgeoise (Campardon, 1867, p. 5).

## 60 | *The Toilet of Venus*

Oil on canvas
43 × 33½ in. (108.5 × 85 cm)
Signed on the step, below right: *f. Boucher 1751*
The Metropolitan Museum of Art, New York;
Bequest of William K. Vanderbilt, 1920 (20.155.9)
S & M 283      A & W 376

PROVENANCE
Appartement des bains, Château de Bellevue [whence probably removed to an unknown location in 1757]; Hôtel de Pompadour (Palais de l'Elysée), 1764; marquis de Ménars; his posthumous sale, 18 Mar. ff. 1782, lot 19: "Cet Artiste, qui avec juste raison a été nommé le Peintre des Grâces, a developpé dans ce sujet tous ses talens & la fécondité de son génie . . ." [bought by Chereau for 587 livres]: *Catalogue des Tableaux . . . &c. après le décès de M. DE BOULLOGNE, Conseiller d'Etat, &c.*, son hôtel, rue S. Honoré (Folliot, Delalande & Julliot *fils*), 7 May ff., deferred to 19 Nov. ff. 1787, lot 6: "Rien n'est plus intéressant que ce Tableau, où l'on trouve

Georges Brunel, with a certain cruel aptness, has described this picture as "Second Empire Boucher." Contemporary critics in France might have described it as in the *goût financier* (see the 1706 edition of Brice's guide to Paris, *passim*) or *genre de fermier-général* (exh. cat. 1958, Bordeaux, p. 9), since it has all the array of rich stuffs and gilding, and is suggestive of the very idleness and superfluity that was condemned by opponents of the Rococo and of the newly and brazenly visible class that gave it encouragement (see esp. Sébastien Mercier, 1782–78, who, though writing after the Rococo was over, censured the attitudes and conditions that had sustained many of its manifestations in terms that would not have been possible at the time).

In the case of this picture, the criticisms would not have been so wide of the mark, since it was commissioned by the daughter of a financier, who was

60

married to the nephew of a *fermier-général*, and was mistress of the king, Mme de Pompadour (see Goncourt, 1878, pp. 1–5). What is more, this picture and its pendant, the *Bath of Venus*, now in the National Gallery in Washington (fig. 171; A & W 377), were both painted for the *salle de bain* of the retreat that she had created for herself and Louis XV, the Château de Bellevue (Dezallier, 1755, p. 29). She must have withdrawn the pictures from there when she made the château over to the king in 1757 (see Piganiol de la Force, 1765, IX, p. 46), so that they passed to her brother on her death in 1764 (they are listed in the posthumous inventory of her effects taken at the Hôtel de Pompadour [the present Palais de l'Elysée] as unframed and in a vestibule, indicating that they had been brought in from elsewhere [Cordey,

réunies à l'élégance des compositions de *F. Boucher les graces inimitables qu'il a répandues dans ses charmans Ouvrages*" [bought by Le Brun for either 460 livres or 640 livres]; *Catalogue d'une très-belle Collection de Tableaux d'Italie, de Flandre, de Hollande et de France. . . . &c, provenans du Cabinet de M\*\*\* [Calonne]*, rue de Cléry (Le Brun), 21 Apr. ff 1788, lot 156: "*Ce morceau, brillant de couleur, offre une des plus gracieuses compositions de ce Maître*" [bought by Marin for 390 livres]; *Catalogue d'une très-belle Collection de Tableaux d'Italie . . . &c., provenant du cabinet de feu M. Marin*, rue de Cléry (Le Brun & Saubert), 22 Mar. ff. 1790, lot 336: "*ce morceau, brillant de couleur est du meilleur temps de ce Maître*" [measurements inverted, sold for 316 livres to Le Brun *jeune*]; ? possibly *Notice de Bons Tableaux* [Mr. Streiffer], Hôtel des Fermes, Paris, 7 Oct. 1816, lot 6: "*Vénus à sa toilette. Tableau très-agréable*" [sold for 32.50]; and then some or all of the sales listed under S & M 279; sale of the comte de La Béraudière, Paris, 18–20 May 1885, lot 4 [sold for 133,000 francs to Lacroix]; William K. Vanderbilt coll., New York; by whom given to the museum in 1920.

ENGRAVING
*La toilette de Vénus*, colored aquatint by J. F. Janinent, published by Chereau, and dedicated to "Madame la Comtesse de Coaslin, née Mailly" (J-R 1225; A & W figs. 1105, 1106). In the final state of this, the cupid coiffing Venus's hair has been removed and her hair put into place.

Fig. 171. *The Bath of Venus*, signed and dated 1751. National Gallery of Art, Washington; Chester Dale Collection.

1939, p. 90, inv. 1230]; nevertheless, Bellevue having been stripped of its pictures when she relinquished it, it is improbable that they came directly from there). After her brother's posthumous sale (in which the paintings were separated) the *Toilet of Venus* was on the market for a while before passing to a member of another family of financiers, the de Boullongne. During that period, a dealer, the print publisher Chereau, had it engraved by Janinet, and with delicious (and even intended?) irony, dedicated to the comtesse de Coaslin (J-R 1225; A & W figs. 1105, 1106). For this dedicatee was none other than Mme de Coislin, who, pushed forward by the prince de Conti for political reasons in 1755–56, was the most serious rival for the position of mistress to the king that Mme de Pompadour had ever had to face (Fleury, 1899, pp. 145–55), and to whom she would have resigned her place but for the stiffening supplied by the abbé de Bernis (1980, pt. 3, chap. 2).

The irony of the dedication to Mme de Coislin was enhanced by the fact that there was (without any suggestion of portraiture) an element of self-identification in Mme de Pompadour's commissioning of these pictures. It is not simply that they were created for a room with erotic associations in her private retreat as mistress of the king; she had also played the title role in a piece called *La Toilette de Vénus*, or *Le Matin*, in a *ballet héroïque* called *La Journée Galante* by Laujon that had been put on at the Théâtre des Petits Appartements in Versailles on 25 February 1750. It was no doubt with his leading actress in mind that Laujon put into Mars's mouth:

*A-t-on des Rivales à craindre*
*Avec les attraits de Vénus?*
. . . . . . . . . . . . . . . . . . . . . . . . . . . . . . . .
*L'Amour, dont vous lancez les traits,*
*Pouroit seul à nos yeux vous rendre encore plus belle.*

Thoroughly Rococo though the composition may seem to us overall, there are interesting exceptions to this in the forms of the ewer and, particularly, the cassolette, or perfume burner. Not of any previously known form, this squat object bizarrely combines a classically inspired tripod base with *pieds de biche*, and *mosaïque* chasing with antique acanthus-leaf moldings and a pinecone finial. It is a heavy precursor of that graceful piece of neoclassical furniture par excellence, the *athénienne* devised by Ebert (see Eriksen & Watson, 1963). Even if there are reminiscences in it of the vanished perfume burners from Louis XIV's Versailles (as seen in, for instance, Noël Coypel's *Dejanira*), the intention was clearly to create something not so much Greek, in the sense of an archaeological reconstruction, as "à la grecque," in the sense employed by Mme Schneider, the wardrobe mistress of the Théâtre des Petits Appartements. The costume worn by Mme de Pompadour herself in the breeches and title role of *Le Prince de Noisy* in 1749–50, for instance, exemplifies the difference between the two (I leave this in the original French, both to convey its full flavor and to avoid false equivalents):

*Habit à la grecque en long de brillant d'argent peint en dessein courant, armures de gaze d'or bouillonnée garnie de plumes nuées, manches et pièce de dessous de moire d'Angleterre argent avec agrements d'or, mante de gaze d'or chamarée et bordée de rézeau d'argent, doublée de taffetas vert d'eau, écharpe en ceinture de même taffetas, garnie en rézeau d'argent et franges à graine d'épinard, chaussure et brodequins* (Campardon, 1867, p. 457).

Who knows, indeed, but what the four "grandes cassolettes de carton modelé et doré" listed as props in the same year (Campardon, 1867, p. 496) were not even of the form depicted here? The picture is in no sense an illustration of the stage, but it seems, like the latter, to revel in its own artifice. It is only to be regretted that it is deprived of its full "richesse de fermier-général" by having been divorced after the de la Bérandière sale from its original rocaille frame, which is now in the Musée des Arts Décoratifs in Paris (see *Cadres*, 1910, pl. 47, outer frame).

# 61 | *The Blonde Odalisque*

Oil on canvas
23¼ × 28¾ in. (59 × 73 cm)
Signed bottom left: *f. Boucher 1752*
Alte Pinakothek, Munich (1166)
(S & M 1175, 1193)      A & W 411
*Not in exhibition**

*Although the loan of this picture has ultimately been denied to us, the entry relating to it is retained here, both because of the painting's intrinsic importance, and because without it the discussion of the* Dark-Haired Odalisque *would have been incomplete.*

PROVENANCE
?Herzog Christian IV von Zweibrücken; Herzog Carl II August von Zweibrücken, ?Schloss Carlsberg; evacuated to Mannheim in 1793; Herzog Maximilian Joseph von Zweibrücken (succeeded 1795; later Elector [1799], and finally King [1806] of Bavaria); evacuated via Bamberg to Munich in 1799, and temporarily to Ansbach in 1800–01; Churpfalzbaierische Gemälde-Sammlungen (subsequently Königliche Gemälde-Galerie), Munich, until the opening of the Alte Pinakothek in 1836; Schloss Schleissheim; brought back to Munich in 1909.

OTHER VERSIONS
1. *Jeune femme couchée sur le ventre*, ?Hôtel de la Direction des Bâtiments, rue Saint-Thomas-du-Louvre, *cabinet particulier* of the marquis de Vandières (subsequently successively de Marigny, and de Ménars); *Catalogue des differens Objets de Curiosités dans les Sciences et Arts qui composoient le Cabinet de feu M. le Marquis DE MENARS . ∴. &c.*, son hôtel, Place des Victoires (Basan & Joullain), [18 Mar.–6 Apr.] 1782, lot 23: "Une femme nue & couchée sur un sopha avec de gros oreillers d'étoffe de soye. Ce sujet est connu par l'estampe qu'en a gravé Demarteau; sur toile, de 27 pouces sur 22 de haut" [bought

There is an irresistible temptation when two such representative figures of eighteenth-century eroticism as Boucher and Casanova live in the same city at the same time to bring them together. It is a product of that "romantic approach to the past, which regards history, not as an incomplete record of an unlimited number of lives and happenings, but rather as a well-ordered pageant, in which all the favorite highlights and episodes turn up at their cue" (Gombrich, 1972, p. 38). Significantly, it is not a temptation that Casanova—who muddled and embroidered, but did not invent—fell prey to when writing his memoirs. Yet it was only after the publication of the later, annotated editions of these that Boucher's two *Odalisques* came to be associated with a memorable episode in them, and were thus baptized with the name of Mlle O'Murphy, or "La Morphise."

Not that passages in other memoirs and journals relating to the O'Murphy sisters, some of which appeared to associate them with Boucher, were not known before, but they do not evoke a specific picture, while those paintings with which they have come to be linked subsequently had led a necessarily underground existence for most of the nineteenth century. It was only when the present picture was brought in from the gallery at Schleissheim to the Alte Pinakothek in 1909 that it became more widely known, and was connected by August Mayer in the eleventh edition of the catalogue of the latter gallery (Alte Pinakothek, 1911, p. 15) with Casanova's memoirs, and thus with Mlle Louise O'Murphy (Frankl, 1961, p. 139; albeit the draped version of the *Dark-Haired Odalisque* had already been called Mlle Victoire O'Murphy when exhibited in 1910 [exh. cat. 1910, Berlin, no. 146]).

Since nothing is known for certain about the origin of any of the versions of either *Odalisque*, it is necessary to glean what we can from the sources. To begin with Casanova, even though his account is among the least reliable because it is also the most specific about the picture involved, and thus the one that has done most to affix the name of Mlle O'Murphy to the

61

*Odalisques* (Casanova, 1960, III, pp. 197–201): As he tells the story, in 1751 he was introduced to two Flemish sisters living in Paris, the elder of whom (who was the mistress of his friend Patu) he calls "La Morfi," and the younger—who was only thirteen—"la petite Morfi," or "Hélène." Unwilling to pay six hundred francs for her virginity, he nonetheless disbursed half that sum to spend twenty-five nights with her, and also six louis to a German painter to depict her naked: "She was lying on her stomach, propping herself up with her arms and breast on a pillow, and holding her head as if she was lying on her back. The clever artist had depicted her legs and thighs in such a way that the eye could not desire to see more. I had someone inscribe below: *O-Morphi.* Not a Homeric word, but one that is nonetheless Greek. It signifies Beauty."

The confusing statement about her head aside, this sounds just like a description of a (maybe franker) version of Boucher's *Dark-Haired Odalisque* (cat. 48). Yet that, as we know, had been painted by 1743 at the latest. It emerges from what follows that the picture painted for Casanova was actually a miniature, so it is perfectly possible that the German was in fact a miniaturist (could he have been F. J. Kisling?), who simply borrowed the pose from Boucher. He made a copy of his original picture for Patu, which the latter took with a number of other portraits to Versailles, to show to Louis XV through the mediation of a certain M. de Saint-Quentin (really the *premier valet de chambre,* Quentin de Champcenetz, or the *premier valet de garde-robe,* Quentin de Champlost?). The king's curiosity was aroused by the

by Joullain for 579 livres 19 sous; Demarteau only made engravings of Boucher's drawings, not his paintings, so A & W are probably right in suggesting that the auctioneers were mistakenly thinking of his engraving no. 46 (J-R 615), after a drawing of 1761 of a girl and a cupid, belonging to Bergeret, in which the model's pose is virtually the same]; *Catalogue de Tableaux et Dessins de Maîtres distingués . . . &c. Une partie de ces Tableaux proviennent de la succession de M. du C[harteaux]*, 96 rue de Cléry (Remy & Le Brun), 2 May ff. 1791, lot 149: "Un autre tableau de Boucher [the preceding lot was *Le fleuve Scamandre*, also from de Ménars's collection], représentant un intérieur de Boudoir, ou l'on voit une jeune femme nue, groupée sur un sopha; des draperies ornent le fond. Hauteur 22 pouces; largeur 26 pouces. Toile."

2. *Catalogue des Tableaux . . . &c., qui composoient le Cabinet de feu M. de BILLY, Ecuyer, ancien Commissaire des guerres, & ancien premier Valet de Garde-Robe du Roi*, Hôtel de Bullion (Paillet & Boileau), 15 Nov. ff. 1784, lot 49: "Un Tableau très-agréable de ce Maître & de son meilleur tems; il représente une jeune femme nue, étendue sur un lit de repos, & des draperies de differentes couleurs; sa tête vue de profil porte le caractère de l'attention; le devant du Tableau est orné de quelques accessoires analogues à la composition; dont une cassolette, un coussin à parfums & une rose. . . . Hauteur 22 pouces, largeur 27 pouces. Toile" [bought by Hamon for 700 livres; there may have been an earlier attempt to sell part of this collection, as "la succession de M. P***, Ecuyer, ancien Contrôleur ordinaire des Guerres," on 25 May ff. 1784, which included as lot 26 *Une femme couchée* by Boucher].

3. Variant, heavily restored version, with open book on a footstool beside her, variations in the drapery, and the rose given two blooms and moved to the right, 59.5 × 73.5 cm, signed bottom right: *f. Boucher 1751*, Duke of Marlborough [not in the Blenheim Palace sales in 1886]; Charles Fairfax Murray sale, Paris, 15 June 1914, lot 5; Jean Charpentier coll., Paris; acquired in 1941 by the Wallraf-Richartz-Museum, Cologne [possibly the same as 1].

ENGRAVING
*Le lit de repos*, published by Basan, c. 1770 (Klesse, 1972, fig. 67) [after Cologne type, in reverse].

DRAWINGS
1. ?Barbier sale, 19 July ff. 1779, lot 28: "Académie de Femme couchée & vue par le dos, aux trois crayons."
2. ?[Le Brun] sale, 10 Dec. ff. 1778, lot 185: "Un dessin au crayon noir & blanc, sur papier bleu, représentant une femme couchée, nue & vue par le dos. Hauteur 12 pouces, largeur 15 pouces" [sold for 12 livres].

one of "la Grecque," so the painter was instructed to bring her to Versailles. She went with her sister to a rendezvous in a *cabinet de verdure* with the king, whose identity they did not know. There, while the king was taking the portrait of "la petite" out of his pocket and assuring himself that the painter had not lied about her appearance (or she about her virginity), her elder sister burst out laughing. When the king asked why, she replied, "I'm laughing because you're as like as two peas to an ecu of six francs" (a remark that, expressed more flatly, is put in most other accounts into the mouth of "la Morphise" herself). She was paid a thousand louis to surrender her sister, the painter got fifty louis and made another copy of his successful picture of her, and "la petite" herself was borne off to the Parc-aux-Cerfs. She had a son (or, according to some accounts, a daughter) by the king after one year, was disgraced for a disrespectful remark about Mme de Pompadour after three, but was still given a dowry of four hundred thousand francs to marry an impoverished officer from Brittany. Casanova claims to have met a son of the marriage at Fontainebleau in 1783.

The elements of this story all recur in most contemporary accounts and documents, albeit with small differences of detail. It is clear from these that Casanova mingled memories of his own experiences with those of rumors that were current in Paris when he was there and forged them into a consecutive, but slightly fanciful, narrative. When contemporary journals and police reports are compared, it can be seen that there is more than one amour of the king behind them.

The two most reliable witnesses are the former foreign minister, the marquis d'Argenson, and the *inspecteur de police* Meusnier—the one because he was in close touch with circles at court, so as to learn the course that the king's amours took, and the other because his network of informants gave him the best knowledge of the demimonde from which their objects were plucked (Soulavie, 1802, is utterly untrustworthy). D'Argenson's journals (which should be consulted in the edition edited by Rathery for the Société de l'Histoire de France rather than in the capricious edition produced by his namesake) have the additional advantage of allowing us to see him first becoming party to a rumor, and subsequently returning to it on a number of occasions, as he pieced the truth behind it together.

D'Argenson was actually the earliest to record the rumor that the king had started to have barely nubile mistresses procured for him by his *valet de chambre*, Lebel, in his journal entry for 6 March 1753 (VII, 1865, p. 420). On the 30th he felt able to say, "It is certain that the King's present concubine is a little girl of fourteen who used to serve the painter Boucher as a model; he saw her at Lebel's, his *valet de chambre;* he asked her if she recognized him; she said that she had seen his portrait on ecus" (Argenson, VII, 1865, p. 436). The next day he referred to her again, more generally, as "the little girl of fourteen who posed as a model for painters" (Argenson, VII, 1865, p. 439). The day after that he was able to amplify and refine the facts behind the rumor yet further, and put a name to the girl:

This winter [the king] enjoyed the favors of a little girl, who used to pose as a model for painters, for a fortnight. He now has a proper mistress of yet lower standing, if that were possible: she comes from the ranks of wh✳r✳s by birth and calling. The woman known as Morfi dealt in secondhand clothes, and had a small shop in the Palais Royal ten years ago; the mother of four daughters, she sold their m✳✳d✳nh✳✳ds,

3. Black chalk, with red and white high-lights, 220 × 360 mm, J. P. Heseltine coll., London; H. de W. coll. (AA 501, fig. 93) [apparently the original study from the life].

4. Red, black, and white chalks on cream paper, 317 × 467 mm, inscribed in ink bottom right *f. Boucher del. 1751,* art market, Paris (exh. cat. 1964, Paris, Cailleux, no. 55) [apparently a drawing worked up from the Cologne type].

5. Beits coll., Amsterdam, in 1932 (mentioned in exh. cat. Paris, 1964, no. 55).

PASTEL
*Right Foot,* rescued from destroyed pastel version of Cologne type, 313 × 305 mm, Musée Carnavalet, Paris (AA 538, fig. 100; here fig. 172).

COPIES
1. [None of the numerous *Femmes couchées* in 18th-century and early 19th-century sales are described, but Planchenault (1933, p. 23 n.) claims that the description of a copy painted by Mlle Lusurier for the marquis de Livois appears to have been of the so-called *Louise O'Murphy*]:

2. *Rêveuse,* oval, 50 × 95 cm, bearing signature, acquired by the Musée de Besançon in 1854, now in the Préfecture.

3. 60 × 74 cm, private coll., Vienna.

4. Miniature by Charlier, 9 *pouces* × 11 *pouces, Cabinet interessant, contenant 90 Tableaux en miniature . . . à vendre à l'aimable chez M. CHARLIER,* rue Thérèse, viewing 20 Oct. ff. 1778, no. 60.

5. ?Miniature by Charlier, without measurements, set in black tortoiseshell snuffbox, de Billy sale, 15 Nov. ff. 1784, lot 225.

6. Miniature by Charlier, 2 *pouces* × 3 *pouces,* baron [Baillet de Saint-Julien] sale, 14 Feb. ff. 1785, lot 140.

7. 19th-century French miniature, formerly attributed to Charlier, 51 × 73 mm, Wallace Collection (*Wallace Collection Catalogues,* 1980, no. 284).

one after another, as they reached puberty. . . . The youngest, who is now the favorite sultana, worked for a dressmaker called Mme Fleuret, who procures lovers for her seamstresses. . . . [The king] sent his first *valet de chambre,* Lebel, to Paris to shop for a new m⁙d⁙nh⁙d . . . he saw *la petite Morfi,* who is fourteen and a half, and he found her just right . . . (Argenson, VII, 1865, pp. 440–41).

And so the story of Louise O'Murphy (1737–1815), the daughter of a pair of Irish rogues, and the future mother of a regicide (see Fleury, 1899, pp. 111–44), rolls on, through this and subsequent entries in d'Argenson's journal (VII, pp. 447, 456–57, 459, 463, 466–67; VIII and IX, passim).

The crucial feature of d'Argenson's account is the distinction that he came to make between "la petite Morfi" and the painter's model, whose enjoyment of the king's favors preceded hers, and was of much shorter duration. This can be corroborated from the papers of the *inspecteur de police* Meusnier, from the archives of the Bastille, now preserved in the Bibliothèque de l'Arsenal. Though never published in extenso, they have been drawn on by the comte de Fleury (1899), by Charles Samaran (1914), and by Adhémar (1957). [I have not had the opportunity of consulting Gustave Capon's *Casanova à Paris* (1913).]

Meusnier, having given very much the same account as d'Argenson of how "la petite Louison," as he calls Louise O'Murphy, was procured by Lebel at Mlle Fleuret's for the king (since the marquis d'Argenson's father had been *lieutenant de police de Paris,* it is very possible that his son shared some of Meusnier's contacts), goes on deliberately to challenge the other version of the story that had at first misled d'Argenson too: "Although this event is reported differently, in that it is said that it was through the copy painted by Boucher for M. de Vandière[s, Mme de Pompadour's brother, the later marquis de Marigny] that the king became desirous of seeing the original, it is not possible to adopt this opinion, *or at least one would have to suppose a singular lack of judgment on M. de Vandière's part*" (Fleury, 1899, p. 116). His earlier detailing of the lives and occupations of the four O'Murphy sisters makes it clear that his skepticism was justified, in that the only one to have served as a model for painters was Brigitte, the second-born and ugliest, who for that reason chiefly modeled her hands (Fleury, 1899, pp. 112–13); none theless, her charms were sufficient to tempt the king for a moment after the disgrace of Louise—but then, as d'Argenson observed, "it is a quirk of our monarch's to pass from one sister to another" (Argenson, IX, p. 144; Fleury, 1899, p. 121). It is true that Vien, in a passage in his manuscript *Mémoires* (of which I am exceedingly grateful to Prof. Thomas Gaehtgens for sending me a photocopy), claims that "La Morphise" was the model for the head of the Virgin in the *Visitation* that he was commissioned to paint for the parish church of Crécy on behalf of Mme de Pompadour in July 1752; but he only supplies her name in a footnote, and may have been prompted by a faulty memory, or an old man's tendency to fabulism.

Meusnier's mention of a revealing painting of a young girl painted by Boucher for de Vandières/Marigny is nonetheless of great importance, since we know that the latter did possess just such a picture, painted at this very period. The source of our knowledge is a letter that de Vandières wrote to Natoire in Rome on 19 February 1753, asking him for a painting (*Correspondance des Directeurs,* X, 1900, p. 438–39):

I have a private cabinet that I have sought to enrich with four pieces by the four most skillful painters of our School. I have a *Vanloo*, a *Boucher*, and a *Pierre* already in place; you can well imagine that it is a *Natoire* that I lack. I am enclosing a piece of paper with this that is the exact size of the picture—that is to say that the canvas is 27 *pouces* long by 22½ high. I should add that, since this cabinet is very little and very warm, I have sought to have only nudities: *Carle's* picture shows *Antiope Asleep*; that of *Boucher*, a *Young Woman Lying on her Stomach*, and that of *Pierre*, an *Io*. Choose whatever subject you like, as long as it has no resemblance to any of those that I have cited, and as there is no—or at least, barely any—drapery.

Carle Vanloo had received the commission for, and begun working on, his picture by mid-October 1752 (Furcy-Raynaud, 1904, pp. 25–27), so we can presume that Boucher's dates from much the same epoch—unless it was only now that it sparked off the idea of a set in de Vandières's mind, and had in fact been painted a little time before. It cannot have been long before, since it was only in September 1751 that the latter had returned from his educational tour of Italy with Cochin, Soufflot, and the abbé Le Blanc, and not until March 1752 that the king gave him the former Hôtel de Lesdiguières as *directeur général des Bâtiments*. 1751 is the date on the Cologne version of the picture, which may thus have been de Vandières's.

What was probably another version of the picture was described in the posthumous sale of M. de Billy, with a cassolette, a scent cushion, and a single rose as accessories. All these occur in the present picture, which is dated 1752, though its provenance from the gallery in Zweibrücken must make it doubtful whether even this example once belonged to de Billy, rather than having been an autograph replica for Herzog Christian IV—alias Boucher's patron and Mme de Pompadour's friend, the duc de Deux-Ponts (it should be remembered that the posthumous sale of the latter's pictures in Paris in 1778 was only of those from the *galerie du petit château* in Zweibrücken, which fell to, and whose contents were disposed of by, the dowager duchess, see cat. 73, 74).

Nevertheless, the dates on these two surviving autograph versions of the *Blonde Odalisque* lend further support to the distinction made by d'Argenson and Meusnier between Boucher's model and Louise O'Murphy, for they both antedate the time at which she became the king's mistress. It is true that in April 1754 Meusnier estimated the affair to have been in existence for three years (Samaran, 1914, p. 65), but the duc de Croy only put it at eighteen months in January 1754 (Croy, I, 1906, p. 206), while it was probably even less than that, since both d'Argenson and Barbier (III, 1851, p. 453) only breathe the first word of it in March 1753, and—as Barbier remarked (III, 1851, p. 459)—no secret could be kept for long at court, whatever the precautions taken.

Taken together, the evidence does suggest that Louis XV enjoyed the favors of a nubile young girl who had posed for Boucher and other painters, but that this affair preceded the much more enduring one with Louise O'Murphy. What is more, the Odalisque has been plausibly identified in other pictures by Boucher, which suggests a professional model rather than "la Morphise"; the latter is described by Meusnier (p. 115) as being rather long in the face and "brune" (dark-haired) like her sisters, rather than round-faced and light-haired (by eighteenth-century standards) as the model appears to be here. One might be inclined to think that somebody had commissioned Boucher to paint this as a portrait of his mistress, as I have suggested for the *Dark-Haired Odalisque* (cat. 48). If the *Blonde Odalisque* is indeed the painters' model whose favors Louis XV enjoyed, it is unlikely that she had previously been anyone's mistress, since we know from d'Argenson (VII, 1865, p. 439) that what impelled the king to barely nubile virgins was his dread of venereal disease; a predecessor in her favors would not have been tolerated. What is possible is that the picture was indeed painted to whet the king's appetite.

The fact that M. de Billy owned not only a version of the present picture, but also a snuffbox apparently containing a miniature of it by Charlier (which was not in the posthumous sale of de Vandières/Ménars, making it unlikely that de Billy's was the same picture), suggests that his version was painted for him personally—all the more so in that, according to the introduction to the catalogue of his posthumous sale, his usual preference was for the Italian School (see *Almanach*, 1777, p. 181); his Bouchers (which included the *Pan and Syrinx* now in the National Gallery in London, and the sketch of *Mercury Confiding the Infant Bacchus* now on the art market in New York) were probably the result of some private connection with the artist. The other interesting thing about his sale catalogue is that it reveals him to have been "ancien premier Valet de Garde-Robe du Roi," a more exalted and gentlemanly post than that of the simple *valet de chambre*, Lebel, but enough to make one wonder whether he, like Casanova's M. de Saint-Quentin, was not also involved in the chain of procurement for Louis XV. Thus, if we no longer have a likeness of Louise O'Murphy, we may yet have a picture that was painted to pander to the king.

## 62 | *Sylvia Freed by Amyntas*

Oil on canvas
Oval, 41 × 55 in. (104 × 139 cm)
Signed on the ground to the left: *f. Boucher / 1755.*
Banque de France (Hôtel de Toulouse), Paris
S & M 1576        A & W 461

## 63 | *Amyntas Reviving in the Arms of Sylvia*

Oil on canvas
Oval, 48 × 55 in. (122.5 × 139 cm)
Signed on the ground, bottom right: *f. Boucher / 1756*
Musée des Beaux-Arts, Tours (794–1–3)
S & M 1381        A & W 463

PROVENANCE
Hôtel de Toulouse; *Amyntas Reviving* removed to the Château de Châteauneuf-sur-Loire by 1786, when included in the anonymous printed catalogue of the gallery as follows: "Renaud dans les bras d'Armide.

It is at first sight surprising to find Boucher departing from his usual subject matter to depict these episodes from Torquato Tasso's *Aminta* (1581); all the more so in that, unlike the same author's *Gerusalemme Liberata* (see cat. 26), this poem had generated no pictorial tradition. The particular circumstances

62

63

264

Minerve, sous la figure d'un vieillard, semble vouloir l'en tirer. Le Costume des habillemens est Asiatique . . . (Châteauneuf, 1786, no. 16; its pendant, *Sylvia Fleeing the Wounded Wolf,* was described under no. 20 as "Thysbé, poursuivie par une louve. . . ." I am indebted to M. A. Bezançon for transcripts of these entries from the exceptionally rare catalogue); removed to Chanteloup and confiscated in 1794; assigned to the new museum in 1802.

ENGRAVINGS

1. *L'Amour ranime Aminte dans les bras de Silvie,* engraved in reverse and published by L-S. Lempereur, along with *Silvie guérit Philis* and *Silvie fuit le loup,* and exhibited in the Salon of 1779, nos. 258, 257, 259 (J-R 1366–1367, 1369–1371, 1372).

2. *Le danger d'aimer,* reengraved in reverse and in rectangular format from Lempereur by [?Mme] Beauvarlet (A & W fig. 1299).

3. *Sylvie délivré par Aminte,* engraved in reverse and published by R. Gaillard (J-R 1036), advertised in the *Mercure de France,* October 1762.

DRAWINGS

1. *Silvie délivré par Aminte,* pen, india ink and wash, and bister, S[aint]-M[aurice] sale, 1 [postponed until 6] Feb. ff. 1786, lot 702.

2. *Naked Woman with Arms Outstretched,* black chalk heightened with white, anon. sale, Paris (exp. Gandouin), 23 Nov. 1899, lot 5; 17th auction of the Stuttgarter Kunstkabinett, 19–21 May 1953 (A & W figs. 445, 1293) [a more explicit version of this drawing was engraved or published by Le Rouge as *Femmes de Boucher No. 1,* signed: *f. Boucher 1763*].

3. *Study for the Figure of Nuncio/Ergaste,* ?black chalk (Fenaille, IV, p. 243, fig. p. 245).

4. *Study for the Head of Sylvia Cradling Amyntas,* formerly Cabinet de M. de la Haye, engraved by Demarteau no. 160 (J-R 729; according to whom there are two related drawings in the Hermitage).

TAPESTRIES

1. All four were used as upright oval medallions inset into surrounds designed by Jacques, in the last of the sets of wall hangings and furniture covers supplied by Neilson from the Gobelins, to the Duke of Portland in 1783 [originally for Bulstrode Park?], now at Welbeck Abbey (fig. 175; see Fenaille, IV, pp. 290–93). Fenaille recorded that he thought to be the original painting of *Sylvie Freed by Amyntas* at the Gobelins in 1907 (IV, p. 241, 130 × 145 cm) but subsequently realized that it was a copy (1923, p. 10). What is reputed to be a cartoon for the *Amyntas Reviving* belongs to the Louvre (inv. 2737) and has been deposited in the Mobilier National since 1960. Unlike the tapestry medallion, however, it is oblong (115 × 146 cm).

Fig. 173. *Sylvia Relieving Phyllis from a Beesting,* signed and dated 1755. Hôtel de Toulouse (Banque de France), Paris.

Fig. 174. *Sylvia Fleeing the Wounded Wolf,* signed and dated 1756. Musée des Beaux-Arts, Tours.

Fig. 175. Gobelins tapestry designed by Maurice Jacques, containing medallions after Boucher's paintings of *Sylvia and Amyntas* (Welbeck Abbey). Reproduced from Fenaille, IV, 1907, plate facing page 292.

of its commissioning by the duc de Penthièvre will be explored below. The point to be made immediately is that Boucher was the obvious choice as artist, because this *favola boschereccia* was, as the anonymous translator (actually Antoine Pecquet) of the bilingual edition published in Paris in 1734 said, the work to which Tasso owed his title of the "Father of the Italian Pastoral." He had thus revived in modern times the very literary tradition of which Boucher was the novel pictorial exponent in the eighteenth century.

Nor are these paintings the only manifestations of an interest in *Aminta* in France in the eighteenth century. Prault published a delightful duodecimo in Italian in Paris in 1745, with vignettes by Cochin *fils,* one of which is itself clearly inspired by Boucher's pastorals. And on 26 February 1749 a *pastorale héroïque* called *Silvie,* by Laujon, which took its characters—if little of its plot—from Tasso, was put on in the Théâtre des Petits Appartements at Versailles, with Mme de Pompadour in the title role (*Théâtre,* III).

The plot of this dramatic poem is very simple. The shepherd Amyntas pines hopelessly with love for the chaste nymph of Diana, Sylvia, all the more intensely after getting her to kiss his lips on the pretext of curing a beesting, as she had done for Phyllis. Even after he had rescued her from being tied up naked preparatory to rape by a satyr (act 3, scene 1), she had remained adamant, despite his touching reserve. When he thought that she had been torn to pieces by the wolves she had been hunting, he threw himself off a cliff in despair. Realizing only then that she loved him, and not knowing that his fall had been broken by a bush, she ran to cherish him in what she thought were his last moments (act 5), and thus her resistance was overcome.

2. The *Sylvia Freed by Amyntas* was also woven as an upright rectangular tapestry with an expanded landscape setting by Juliard (A & W fig. 1295). What appears to be the cartoon for this (Louvre, inv. 2717, 296 × 183 cm) was used to decorate the Château d'Eu under the July Monarchy; recovered from there, it has been on deposit since 1889 at Fontainebleau. There is also an upright rectangular cartoon of *Amyntas Reviving* on deposit from the Louvre (inv. 2735) at the Mobilier National (290 × 186 cm). It must be this that was seen by the Jury des Arts at the Gobelins in September 1794, just called *Aminte*, when they declared that the tapestry was superior in beauty of execution to the painting, which was to be "rejected on artistic grounds" (Guiffrey, 1897, p. 358).

COPIES

*Sylvia Freed by Amyntas*

1. *Catalogue d'une collection choisie*, Hôtel d'Espagne (Joullain *fils*), 18 June ff. 1770, lot 35: "Silvie délivré par Aminte, d'après F. Boucher, sans bordure; 2 pieds 6 pouces sur 3 pieds 6 pouces."

2. ?Reversed copy after Gaillard's engraving, posthumous sale of the marquis de la Chatai-gneraye, prince de Ponts, Hôtel Drouot, Paris, 5 May 1868, lot 7, as *Nymph delivrée (gravée)*, the pendant to lot 7 bis, after Gaillard's engraving of *Jupiter et Calisto*.

3. Misc. sale, A. Kende, Vienna, 1 Dec. 1919, lot 3, 92 × 74 cm [reversed].

4. Ex-Davidson coll., Sotheby's, London, 23 Feb. 1938, lot 79.

5. Ex-Oppenheim coll., Christie's, London, 26 May 1938, lot 79.

6. Palais Galliera, 7 June 1974, lot A, pastel (as *Roger délivrant Angélique*).

7. Fossati coll., 135 × 102 cm (A & W 461/10).

8. Glasgow Art Gallery, acquired in 1952, as pendant to *Amyntas Revived*, tondo, diam. 52¼ in.

9. Earl of Rosebery coll., Mentmore, sale, Sotheby's, 25 May 1977, lot 2450; Weston Gallery, Weston Longville; Christie's, 1 Dec. 1978, lot 53: 54½ × 60 in.

10. Höchst porcelain group, 1771 (example in Musée de Sèvres, inv. 11.184).

*Amyntas Reviving in the Arms of Sylvia*

1. Sale, Paris, 4 Dec. 1920 (fragment).

2. Earl of Rosebery coll., Dalmeny (attempted sale, Christie's, London, 5 May 1939, lot 24, bought in): 53½ × 60½ in.

3. Acquavella Galleries, New York (c. 1950): 35 × 39 in.

4. G. Campbell coll., presented to Glasgow Art Gallery in 1952, as pendant to *Amyntas Releasing Sylvia*, tondo, diam. 52¼ in.

5. X. G. coll. (exh. 1954, Geneva, Musée Rath, no. 35, as *Sylvie consolant Aminte de la piqure d'une abeille* [sic], paired with no. 34, *Sylvie et Philis*, 54 × 43 cm.

The two pictures shown here are from a set of four, the other two episodes being *Sylvia Relieving Phyllis from a Beesting* (fig. 173; Banque de France; A & W 460) and *Sylvia Fleeing the Wounded Wolf* (fig. 174; Musée des Beaux-Arts, Tours; A & W 462). All four were originally painted for the Hôtel de Toulouse. This was the *hôtel* originally built by François Mansart for the marquis de la Vrillière, which was acquired in 1713 by Louis XIV's illegitimate son, the comte de Toulouse, and sumptuously transformed by de Cotte. On the death of the comte de Toulouse in 1737, it passed to his serious-minded son, the duc de Penthièvre, who in turn had new apartments created for himself and his wife, Maria-Theresa d'Este, Princess of Modena, after their marriage in 1744 (see Dezallier, 1752, pp. 122–23; Blondel, III, 1754, pp. 26–32). It was doubtless for these apartments that the present pictures were painted as overdoors, though we know very little about them, since the rooms were never well recorded, and they have been swept away along with everything else but the celebrated *galerie dorée*, since the *hôtel* was taken over by the Banque de France in 1811.

There is clearly a discrepancy between the dates of the overdoors and those of the rooms for which they must have been painted. The reason for this sheds further light on the unusual subject of the pictures. In 1754 the duchess died in childbirth. The grief-stricken duke at first withdrew into total seclusion, with only his mother for company, and then traveled to his wife's country, Italy, to distract his grief, visiting Rome, Naples, and finally Modena, returning home in time for the anniversary of his wife's death, in April 1755 (see Lorin, 1907, pp. 197–98). It must have been in Italy that he had time to muse upon the works of Tasso, and to reflect that the latter had been the court poet of his wife's Este ancestors, before their transferral from Ferrara to Modena. Perhaps he also identified his love for her with that of Amyntas for Sylvia. In any event, after his return he commissioned these pictures from Boucher, and installed himself alone in their former joint apartment (Dezallier, 1752, p. 123; 1757, p. 199).

Around 1770 the *hôtel* was further transformed when the later tragic heroine, the princesse de Lamballe, came to live with her father-in-law, after the death of her husband, and the marriage of his only surviving daughter to the duc de Chartres in 1769. In the course of these alterations, two of the overdoors were reduced to a sleeker oval shape and reset in Louis XVI paneling in the apartment of the princess (Thiéry, 1787, I, p. 306), while the other two were dismounted, and were later sent in what are probably their original frames to the Château de Châteauneuf-sur-Loire, where they are recorded (under aberrant titles) in the catalogue published in 1786. A little before 1783, the duke must have allowed copies of all four to be taken for the Gobelins, in whose affairs he took a solicitous interest (Fenaille, IV, 1907, p. 292). Transported to the duke's other château of Chanteloup and seized in the Revolution, the pair from Châteauneuf became part of the nucleus of the new museum formed by Charles-Antoine Rougeot at Tours (see Fohr, 1982, p. 15).

The challenge of the novel subject matter appears to have acted as an inspiration to Boucher. For although the *Sylvia Relieving Phyllis of a Beesting* may be treated in a way that is all too suggestive of a cross between yet another *Diana and Calisto* and one of his *Pastorales* with a jealous rival lurking, the *Sylvia Freed by Amyntas* stimulated him to invent a striking pose for her, whose latent eroticism is made obvious by an anonymous print after it, while the *Amyntas Reviving in the Arms of Sylvia* has called forth a most unusual gamut of colors for Boucher—muted greens, mauves, and forget-me-not blues. His male characters (like the wolf in *Sylvia Fleeing*) may, as always, be somewhat lacking in virile character, but in this set of pictures this seems entirely appropriate to the pastoral poem they illustrate. As "Mme de Créquy" said of the duc de Penthièvre's protégé, the chevalier de Florian: "The innocence of his pastorals leaves nothing to be desired; there are no wolves in sheep's clothing in them" (*"L'innocence de ses pastorales ne laisse rien á desirer; il n'y a jamais de loups dans ses bergeries"* [Créquy, 1834–35, III, p. 150 n. 1]).

# 64 | *Portrait of Mme de Pompadour*

Oil on canvas
79 × 62 in. (201 × 157 cm)
Signed on lower shelf of writing table:
*f. Boucher 1756*
Bayerische Hypotheken- und Wechsel-Bank (no. 18), on deposit in the Alte Pinakothek, Munich
(S & M 1077)        A & W 475

As has already been remarked (cat. 59), it is a curious fact that we have no finished portrait of Mme de Pompadour by Boucher until this, painted eleven years after she had become Louis XV's mistress, and only eight before her death at the age of forty-two. It is also the only one of his portraits of her to have been given any public exposure in her lifetime, when it was exhibited in the Salon of 1757, on a special dais of its own (see Gaucherel's engraving of this Salon after Gabriel de Saint-Aubin, whose original drawing is at Waddesdon Manor, Blunt, 1973, pl. 5; for detailed discussions of the portrait, see Alte Pinakothek, 1972, pp. 20–22, and exh. cat. 1982, Tokyo, no. 51).

The reason for this new pictorial consecration of the favorite does not appear to have been noticed before: it is surely that, early in the year in which it was painted, on 7 February 1756, Mme de Pompadour was officially named a supernumerary *dame du palais* of Queen Marie Leczinska. With this, and with the admittance to the communion table that made it possible, her status at court, already enhanced by her promotion to the rank of duchess in 1752 (of which she enjoyed the privileges but not the title), was made unimpugnable. It set the seal of the transition that had begun in 1750 from the king's carnal to his purely titular mistress (see Gordon, 1968). Whether or not she had feigned a new piety in order to ingratiate herself with the queen (or in keeping with her aspiring role as a second Maintenon), once Mme de Pompadour had officially regularized her position in the eyes of the Church (although rigorists maintained that, to purge her fault, she should have withdrawn from court altogether, like Mme de Mailly), there was little that Marie Leczinska could do to oppose the will of her husband. Her reply to the king's request that she make this appointment (reputedly composed for

64

Fig. 176. *Table à écrire*, by Bernard II van Risenburgh. The Metropolitan Museum of Art, New York; Gift of Mr. and Mrs. Charles Wrightsman, 1984.

REDUCTION

Figure only, cut at knees, plain background, 14¼ × 17½ in., *Notice d'une Collection de jolis Tableaux des Trois Écoles . . . &c, provenant du Cabinet de M. B\*\*\*, et après son départ*, 3 Mar. 1817, lot 29: "Portrait de la Marquise du Pompadour, dans le riche costume du temps, et tenant un livre à la main. Ce tableau d'une exécution précieuse est fait à l'imitation des peintres hollandais" [presumably referring to its scale and finish; this, and the absence of any reference to a setting, strongly suggests that it was the Edinburgh version]; *Catalogue de Tableaux . . . &c, le tout faisant partie de la succession mobilière de feu M. LANEUVILLE, peintre, expert pour les objets d'art . . .*, his house, 15 rue Saint-Marc, 5–7 June 1826, lot 139: "Portrait de madame du Pompadour, asise sur un sopha, un livre à la main. T. h. 14 p., L. 16" [sold for 27 livres]; Gen. John Ramsay; his sale, Christie's, London, 19 June 1855, lot 278 [bought for £24 3s. od. by Nieuwenhuys, from whom presumably bought back by the general's sole heir, Lord Murray of Henderland]; bequeathed to the National Gallery of Scotland, Edinburgh, by his widow, Lady Murray of Henderland in 1861.

DRAWINGS

1. *Study of a Forearm and Hand*, red, black, and white chalks, 221 × 300 mm [for Mme de Pompadour's left arm, but with the bracelet carrying a medallion. This appears to have a man's head faintly indicated within it; if this was a cameo of the king, as in the portrait in the Fogg Art Museum (A & W 497), it was no doubt suppressed in the painting for reasons of *bienséance*], Metropolitan Museum of Art, New York (fig. 178; exh. cat. 1973–74, Washington, no. 72).

her by président Hénault) was: "Sire, I have a King in heaven who gives me the strength to suffer my woes, and a King on earth whom I shall always obey" (Argenson, IX, pp. 214–15).

The present picture appears to combine the private and public faces of the marquise. On the one hand, she is shown in the most elaborate dress of all her portraits (perhaps it is the very one in which she began her first week's duty with the queen, "parée comme un jour de fête," to the outrage of the already scandalized [Argenson, IX, p. 198]), which was particularly harshly criticized by Grimm when the picture was shown in the 1757 Salon: "surchargé d'ornemens, de pompons, et de toutes sortes de fanfreluches" (*Correspondance littéraire*, III, pp. 432–33). On the other hand, she is surrounded by the evidence of her artistic tastes, which met with special approbation from the anonymous critic in the *Mercure de France* (Oct. 1757, p. 159), but with no sympathy from Grimm, who found it simply "the same portrait" as that exhibited by de la Tour in the previous Salon (Louvre; see Monnier, 1972, no. 74); confusions between the two have indeed arisen since. As Boucher's sketches (see cat. 59) show, however, the idea of portraying Mme de Pompadour in this fashion was first tried out by him, though it no doubt originated with the sitter.

There is first of all the bookcase reflected in the mirror, complete with a clock, and adorned with the tower from the marquise's arms. It is not certain if this piece of furniture ever existed; its ornamentation is unusual, and it could just have been a fantasy of the artist's, particularly since it seems to be a free variation on the bookcase found in the earlier sketch portraits (see cat. 59). There are no titles to be read on the spines of the books; but for these we can turn to de la Tour's pastel—the latest volume of the *Encyclopédie*, Montesquieu's *Esprit des Lois*, Voltaire's *Henriade*, and Guarini's *Pastor fido*—testifying at once to her patronage of "advanced" thinkers and writers, and (the last of these) to her taste for one of the prime sources of the literary pastoral, the ultimate source of inspiration for Boucher's painted *bergeries*. The little *table à écrire* beside her is, by contract, of a known model, so precisely depicted down to the bronze mounts, that it can be attributed to B.V.R.B., Bernard II van Risenburgh (fig. 176; see Watson, 1966, p. 254). But rather than attempting to identify it with a particular table described in an

Fig. 177. *Le petit Savoyard*, etched by Mme de Pompadour after Boucher and with his guidance.

Fig. 178. *Study for the Left Hand and Forearm of Mme de Pompadour*. The Metropolitan Museum of Art, New York.

2. *Study of a Forearm and Hand Holding a Book*, black and white chalks, 220 × 290 mm [for Mme de Pompadour's right arm]: Carole Slatkin, New York (exh. cat. 1973–74, Washington, no. 73); Mr. and Mrs. Alvin Walker, Montreal.

COPIES

1. 28½ × 23 in., signed and dated 1756 [simplified, and omitting dog]: 12th Earl of Pembroke's posthumous sale, Paris, 30 June 1862, lot 26 [as *Madame du Barry*, after Boucher; but not only does the catalogue contain a slip explaining that it was drawn up in haste (the earl had only died on 25 April), Souillé's copy in the Bibliothèque d'Art et d'Archéologie in Paris corrects the name of the sitter, and says that the picture was a reduction of the Duclos (i.e., 1758) portrait; bought by Cournaré for 800 francs]; [Col. Milligan], Christie's, London, 13 July 1889, lot 101 [bought in at 225 guineas]; Christie's, London, 21 June 1890, lot 70 [sold to Zersh for £215 5s.]; "part of the collection of a gentleman," Puttick & Simpson, London, 31 May 1932, lot 125; Christie's, London, 23 Nov. 1962, lot 26; London antique trade, 1985.

2. Painting on porcelain formerly in coll. of Lord Pirbright (exh. cat. 1898, London, no. 61).

inventory, such as the one from the Château de Saint-Hubert, or seeking it among those supplied by Duvaux to the favorite, sometimes by the dozen (though these tended to be of plain mahogany; see Duvaux, 1873, II, nos. 1520, 1894; this is more like a singly supplied rosewood table, such as that in no. 1913), one might wonder whether it is not more likely to have been accessible as a model in Boucher's own household (since he too was a regular client of Duvaux's). The table is open to show its function, and supports a letter, sealing wax, candle, and seal, to allude to the sitter's acknowledged gifts as a correspondent (see not only the authentic letters, edited by Malassis [Pompadour, 1878], but also the spurious imitations published in London [Pompadour, 1772]). Books are scattered below the tabletop, to suggest that they were read rather than merely an adornment, and the marquise holds another open, as if meditating upon its contents (her brother, who evidently did not share her taste for belles lettres, made 41,940 livres from the sale of the 3,525 works in her library; see Campardon, 1867, pp. 308–09). Near her feet, a rolled-up map, music, and portfolios of drawings and engravings are in similar disorder. Allusion to her own activities as an engraver under Boucher's tuition (J-R 1478–1514; A & W figs. 100, 101) is underscored by her print after one of Guay's cameos and intaglios (de la Tour had included an engraving of hers from Mariette's *Traité des pierres gravées*), and another after Boucher's etching of *Le petit Savoyard* (fig. 177; J-R 10), signed *Boucher* and *Pompadour Sc.*, poking out of the papers at her feet. The King Charles spaniel beside this bohemian disorder may be Mimi, of which she was sufficiently fond to have her painted by Christophe Huet, in a picture engraved by Fessard in 1758 (A & W fig. 1318), a little while after another of the breed, called Inès (A & W fig. 1446), which appears in the outdoor portrait of her mistress in the Wallace Collection.

Evidence indicates that all of this must have been painted in the studio, on the basis of studies of no more than Mme de Pompadour's head and hands (fig. 178; but there is always the possibility that even the latter were done from Brigitte O'Murphy! see Fleury, 1899, p. 113). When the *Journal Encylopédique* for 1 October 1757 (vol. VII, pt. i, p. 102), while praising the accessories, found that "the figure is stiff, and suggests the mannequin," it implies that a lay figure was used, on which no doubt the fall of the sumptuous dress was studied. Lespinasse (1929, p. 9), without making it clear whether or not he is at this point relying on the unpublished memoir by Roslin's daughter, claims that Boucher was assisted in this by the recently arrived Swedish painter. If Boucher made a preliminary sketch from the sitter herself, it was probably nothing as elaborate as the oil sketch in the Louvre (cat. 59), but something more like the one in the de Sireul sale, which was in black and white chalk on canvas, a rather curious-sounding technique. Since the present portrait was the only one of Mme de Pompadour by Boucher to have been publicly exhibited, and the auctioneer felt no need to describe the chalk sketch in the de Sireul sale, it could well be that it was a preparation for the present picture. Duvaux's bill for the transport of a portrait to and from Versailles from Boucher's on 4 September and 1 October 1756 (Duvaux, 1873, II, nos. 2581, 2601), if it indeed refers to this picture, implies that it was being taken to the palace for the artist to "finish" the likeness from the sitter, as in the case of the lost portrait of 1750 (see Pompadour, 1878, pp. 37, 57), and then returned to him for the rest of the picture to be completed, or for its final retouching and varnish.

Of where the portrait hung in the sitter's lifetime, we know nothing. No such portrait was listed in the inventories taken after her death. It would seem surprising, in view of the existence of two full-scale versions of this picture, that she should not have owned at least one of them herself, and it is possible that it and other portraits were removed directly to her brother's after her death, since they would anyway not have been assessed for probate. We know that one of the two versions of this portrait must have hung at the Château de Ménars, which Marigny inherited from her and made his chief seat. It probably hung in his wife's bedchamber, where it would have been the one seen by Joseph Jekyll in 1775 (Jekyll, 1894, p. 60): "The bed was still in an interesting disorder; and . . . I was lost in the comparison of beauty which arose between the portraits of the Marchionesses of Pompadour and de Marigny, and the contemplation of a group of the most amiable pugs imaginable which belonged to the latter. . . ." One of the versions was certainly still at the château in the Revolution, since the commissioners who drew up an inventory of the works of art that were intended for removal to the new museum in Blois on 21 October 1792 (Dupré, 1860, p. 168) recorded: "Deux tableaux, de grandeur naturelle, peints l'un par Vanlos, l'autre par Boucher, représentant, le premier la Pompadour en grand costume, et le second, cette femme assise, et appuyée sur une table, avec une attitude et un costume voluptueux, son chien favori à ces pieds."

The museum at Blois was intended to demonstrate in the works of art shown "that if some of them reek of indolence and voluptuousness, and depict people who have become the scandal of their century because of their lives and the happy change wrought by the Revolution in the national spirit, they nonetheless exhibit an excellent taste, a beauty of form, admired by connoisseurs, which can serve as a model for budding artists . . ." ("*que si quelques-uns respirent la mollesse et la volupté, et représentent des personnages devenus l'opprobre de leur siècle par leur vies et par le changement heureux que la Révolution a produit dans l'esprit national, il y règne néanmoins un goût excellent, une beauté de forme, admirée des connaisseurs, et qui peut servir de modèle aux artistes dont le goût commence à se developper . . .*" [Dupré, 1860, p. 170]). This appears to have been overtaken by events (and by an equally drastic revolution in taste). There is, therefore, the intriguing possibility that the present version was rescued by an ancestor of its first-recorded owner after the Revolution, the dilettante artist-collector the marquis Casimir de Cypierre.

From 1760 until the Revolution the intendants of the nearby Orléans were Jean-Claude-François Perrin de Cypierre, who bought the Château d'Auvilliers from Mme de Pompadour, who had intended to use it as a place to break her journey between Paris and Ménars, and his son, Perrin de Cypierre de Chevilly (Dufort de Cheverny, 1909, I, pp. 28, 251–53, 332, 436, 473; a Nattier portrait presumed to be of the first intendant's wife is in the Linsky Collection in the Metropolitan Museum [Metropolitan Museum, 1984, no. 43]). The second intendant was the father of Casimir Perrin, marquis de Cypierre (*Annuaire de la Noblesse de France* 30 [1874], pp. 149–50), the first recorded owner of this portrait. Casimir de Cypierre was an amateur artist and the first substantial collector of Bouchers after the Revolution; it is nice to think that the present picture might have been his inspiration from his childhood.

## 65 | Venus at Vulcan's Forge

Oil sketch on canvas, *en grisaille*
13¾ × 16¾ in. (35 × 42.5 cm)
Musée des Arts Décoratifs, Paris
(inv. 36.231)
S & M 314     A & W 479 bis

## 66 | Venus at Vulcan's Forge

Oil sketch on canvas, in color
24 × 25 in. (61 × 63.5 cm)
Signed lower edge, right of center:
*f. Boucher, 1756*
Sterling and Francine Clark Art
Institute, Williamstown
A & W 479
*New York and Detroit*

## 67 | Venus at Vulcan's Forge

Oil on canvas
126 × 126 in. (320 × 320 cm)
Signed on rock below, right of center:
*f. Boucher 1757*
Musée du Louvre, Paris (inv. 2707 bis)
S & M 157, 352     A & W 478
*Paris*

PROVENANCE OF GRISAILLE
*Catalogue des differens Tableaux originaux des Trois Ecoles . . . &c. provenans du Cabinet de feu M. [Jean-Baptiste] LEMOYNE*, Hôtel d'Aligre (Le Brun), 10 Aug. ff. 1778, lot 22: "Une esquisse peinte à l'huile en grisaille, représentant Vénus qui demande des armes à Vulcain pour son fils Enée. Composition de 12 figures. Hauteur 13 pouces, largeur 15 pouces. Toile" [presumably bought in, like most of the other Bouchers in the sale, since next in the sale of his son]; *Catalogue de Tableaux, etc. du Cabinet de feu Pierre-Hippolyte Lemoyne, Architecte*, Hôtel Bullion (Duchesne *aîné*), 19 May ff. 1828, lot 68: "Vénus venant prier Vulcain de forger des armes pour Énée; esquisse peinte en camaïeu. Largeur 16 pouces, hauteur 14 pouces" [sold for 70 francs, together with a sketch of the *Triumph of Venus*]; sale of the architect Claret, Paris, 16–18 Dec. 1850, lot 89; posthumous sale of Eugène Tondu, 10 Apr. 1865, lot 18; E[tienne] A[rago] sale, Paris, 8 Feb. 1872, lot 6; Jules Ferry; Cailleux; Mlle Yznaga; by whom donated to the Musée des Arts Décoratifs in 1949.

Throughout his life, Boucher never tired of depicting *Venus at Vulcan's Forge*, above all on a large scale. When his pupil Johann Christian [von] Mannlich was asked by his patron and Boucher's friend, Duke Christian IV of Zweibrücken, to paint him a picture in 1765, with the choice of subject left up to the artist himself, he asked Boucher what he should depict. His master, like Natoire a believer in choosing subjects for the scope that they afforded artists rather than for the novelty that gratified literary-minded critics, recommended *Venus Coming to Vulcan to Ask for Arms for Her Son Aeneas*: "That will give you the fine figure of a woman surrounded by cupids, a muscular man, cyclops in the background, etc. . . ." (Mannlich, 1948, p. 264—disregarding Delage's reproduction of Boucher's 1732 picture in the Louvre as the one executed by Mannlich!). Among Boucher's criticisms of Mannlich's studies for the picture was precisely one regarding the figures of his women: "Your female models are too thin without being slender; others are too big, too masculine. One should hardly be able to imagine that a woman's body contains any bones; without being fat, they must be rounded, [yet] delicate and slim-waisted, without being skinny. Of the several hundreds that I have had undress for me, there is only one that I have found with this high degree of beauty" (Mannlich, 1948, p. 265). This was the wife of his gilder, who would not let her pose for anyone else. As told by Mannlich, the

65

66

67

PROVENANCE OF COLOR SKETCH
*Catalogue des différens Objets de Curiosités dans les Sciences et Arts qui composoient le Cabinet de feu M. le Marquis DE MENARS . . . &c.,* son hôtel, Place des Victoires (Basan & Joullain), (18 Mar.–6 Apr.) 1782, lot 24: "Vénus commande à Vulcain des armes pour Énée. Cette Déesse se voit sur un nuage accompagnée de Nymphes & d'Amours, dont plusieurs s'amusent avec un casque: dans le fond est l'antre des Cyclopes. Cette charmante Composition, pleine d'esprit et de feu, a été exécutée en tapisserie pour Madame de Pompadour [*sic*]. Tableau de 16 pouces en quarré" [sold with Pierre's similar sketch for the *Rape of Europa* to Remy for 199 livres 19 sous]; *Catalogue de Tableaux . . . &c. après le décès de M. BEAUJ[E]ON . . .,* Hôtel d'Evreux

story then goes on to relate how he himself succeeded in procuring her, not merely as a model, but as a mistress.

The details of the story are interesting, not merely in bearing out the evidence of Boucher's drawings, that he continued to make studies from life to the last and that he can only have been having the gullible Reynolds on when he claimed to have ceased to do so long before (Reynolds, 1959, p. 225), but also in showing the kind of alterations that he made to his pupil's intended composition. One of these, which he inserted against Mannlich's better judgment and with which the duke found fault, was to seat Venus on clouds, as in the present composition. His fidelity to this essentially Baroque device, and their distaste for it, are telling indicators of the way in which Boucher was overtaken by the revolution in taste that began to take shape toward the end of his life.

When he created the present composition in 1756, however, it was precisely

Fig. 179. *La cible d'Amour* (1758). Louvre.

[quondam de Pompadour, and now l'Elysée] (Remy & Julliot), 25 Apr. ff. 1787, lot 203 [among pictures removed from La Chartreuse, in the faubourg du Roule], same description [sold with the Pierre for 216 livres]; Dr. Schaffer, Berlin (1927); private coll., U.S.A.; Newhouse Galleries, from which bought by the Sterling and Francine Clark Art Institute in 1983.

PROVENANCE OF FINISHED PICTURE
Manufacture Royale des Tapisseries de la Couronne [Gobelins]; transferred to the Louvre between 1816 and 1824.

ENGRAVING
(After finished picture): *Vulcain présentant à Vénus des armes pour Enée*, engraved in reverse and published by Jacques Danzel, advertised in 1783 (J-R 532).

DRAWINGS
  1. ?*L'étude nue d'un Vulcain*, red, black, and white chalks, on gray paper, glazed, J-B. Lemoyne sale, 8 Dec. ff. 1778.
  2. *Two Cupids* at extreme left, Cabinet de M. de la Haye, engraved by Demarteau, no. 252 (A & W fig. 1335).

in response to the persistent clamor for his services. Although the terms of their petition suggest certain personal doubts as to Boucher's merits, the entrepreneurs of the Gobelins, Audran, Neilson, and Cozette, had already besought the *directeur des Bâtiments* in 1754 to woo Boucher away from Beauvais to their manufactory, in order to give them tapestry designs that would sell (Fenaille, IV, 1907, pp. 225–26). Their chance came the next year, when Oudry died, making it possible to appoint Boucher as *inspecteur* at the Gobelins in his place, with the promise not only to supply it with his productions, but to cease supplying them to the rival establishment at Beauvais (Fenaille, IV, pp. 226–27; A & W docs. 625, 627, 630, 632).

The first call for his services came when, in November 1755, Marigny pointed out to the king that his new apartment at Compiègne required seven new tapestries, four for the *cabinet du conseil* and three for the *cabinet du jeu* (Fenaille, IV, p. 228; A & W docs. 639–641). The suggestion was not acted upon, but Marigny must have continued to hope that some use would be found for a new set of tapestries, since the present color sketch (whose square format denotes it clearly as a tapestry design) is dated 1756, the year before the king finally gave his approval in May for a set of only four tapestries of *The Loves of the Gods*, with no specific destination, each to be designed by one of the leading artists of the day: Carle Vanloo, Boucher, Pierre, and Vien (Fenaille, IV, pp. 189–92; A & W doc. 670). The artists must immediately have been supplied with the exceptional-sized canvases for their full-scale pictures-cum-cartoons (A & W doc. 672), since these were all exhibited in the Salon, which opened as usual at the end of August, although Boucher's— despite his early start with his sketch—was late (*Journal Encyclopédique*, VII, pt. i, 1757, p. 100; curiously, this claimed that the actual pictures, like Carle Vanloo's *Iphigeneia*, were intended for the king of Prussia—no doubt through a confusion with the fact that the *Iphigeneia* was itself one of a set of four pictures by different artists). After the Salon was over, the pictures were transported to the Gobelins by the Academy's regular models, with outside help (A & W doc. 691). In 1758 all the artists were asked to supply cartoons for two additional narrower strips of tapestry, with cupids playing with attributes relative to the subjects of their earlier pictures. Boucher's picture— which interpreted the requirement rather freely—entitled *La cible d'Amour*, is in the Louvre (fig. 179; A & W 480).

Interestingly, Boucher's tapestry (like Vanloo's, see exh. cat. 1977, Nice, nos. 159–63) was never the success that the Gobelins hoped for: it was only woven four times (including a replacement for Marigny). The reason for this cannot entirely have been the fact complained of by the entrepreneurs at the Gobelins (Fenaille, IV, p. 163), that potential clients were put off by the set's lacking a unifying hand, since the compositions of Pierre and Vien were more frequently woven (admittedly mostly in the late weavings; Fenaille, IV, pp. 202–23). Was it that there was already a reaction against the obsolescent style of the two older masters (which seems unlikely in view of the comparative success of Boucher's other compositions)? Or was it that the weaving of these pieces was at first somehow jealously guarded by their original promoter, Marigny, for himself and his sister, as with the *Lever* and *Coucher du Soleil* (figs. 207, 208), the *Génies des Arts,* and the *Enfants Boucher* (nothing ever seems to have come, for instance, of the evident desire of the agent of the Infante Don Felipe of Parma to obtain tapestries of the *Lever* and *Coucher du Soleil* for his master after seeing them on the loom

Woven at the Gobelins manufactory as part of the series *Les Amours des Dieux*. The first example was in the set of four large hangings and a number of smaller pieces given by the king to the marquis de Marigny; it was made in the haute-lisse (upright loom) workshop of Michel Audran in 1758/59. It belongs to the Mobilier National and is in the Palazzo Farnese (French Embassy), Rome. In 1762 it was described as "passée" and replaced by another example, also by Audran, whose location is not known. Pierre François Cozette, head of the other haute-lisse shop, wove a set of three pieces for the comtesse du Barry in 1774/75, including a *Venus at Vulcan's Forge*, which is in the Mobilier National. Another example was in a set woven as a private commission before 1789, when it was confiscated (Fenaille, IV, pp. 202–04, 208–13, 220, 221). Another, from a set of four once owned by the princesse de Sagan, is in the Walters Art Gallery, Baltimore; it is signed by Audran.     E.A.S

COPIES

1. Red-chalk drawings after all four compositions by an unknown hand, 15 *pouces* square, were in the posthumous sale of the architect J. G. Soufflot, Marigny's intendant in the Gobelins, [20 Nov. ff.] 1780, [sold for 49 livres].

2. Oil sketch, 55 × 55 cm, Radischev Art Museum, Saratov.

3. Oil sketch, 46 × 36 cm, Yale University Art Gallery, New Haven, gift of Mr. and Mrs. André Blumenthal in 1959 (see exh. cat. 1956, New Haven, no. 17).

4. Oil painting, 59 × 47 cm, Sotheby's sale, London, 7 Oct. 1981, lot 110.

5. Oil painting, 108 × 132.5 cm, Hôtel Rampan, Versailles, 22 Dec. 1981, lot 73.

6. *Venus's Attendants*, free copy of this detail by Fantin-Latour, oil on board, 44 × 53 cm, Musée Magnin, Dijon (see Magnin, 1922, no. 650; *Musée Magnin*, 1938, no. 336).

7. *Two of Venus's Attendants*, copied by Berthe Morisot for an overmirror in her home in 1884, 114 × 138 cm (Bataille & Wildenstein, 1961, no. 143, pp. 17, 32, and fig. 175; A & W fig. 1337).     A.D.L.

[Fenaille, IV, p. 179], while Neilson was expressly forbidden to allow the seat tapestries of the *Enfants* to be woven for anyone but Mme du Pompadour).

Marigny's personal interest in the set is attested by his ownership of colored sketches of all four compositions. Their existence, and his possession of them, are less natural than they are generally taken to be. Such sketches for tapestries as we know of by Boucher (and these only exist in a minority of cases) are generally rapid productions *en grisaille* or *en camaïeu*, such as the one from the Musée des Arts Décoratifs shown here. If we have any early record of them, it is more likely to be in the collections of fellow artists (as in the case of the grisaille here) than in those of an administrator-collector, such as Marigny. Even where sketches of Boucher's are mentioned in connection with the Gobelins, as with those for the two unexecuted pictures for tapestries taken from the *Fêtes Vénitiennes* and the *Fêtes de Thalie*, the note states, "Il en a fait voir les Esquisses et travaille aux tableaux" (Engerand, 1900, p. 56; Fenaille, IV, p. 174), clearly implying that possession of the sketches stayed with the artist. Only in the case of the chinoiserie tapestries for Beauvais (cat. 41–44, 90, 91) do we otherwise know of a fully elaborated set of color sketches—and that is because the *tableaux en grand* were to be executed by someone else. What is more, even in this case the sketches did not remain the property of the manufactory or the *contrôleur général*, but are first recorded in the collection of an amateur and friend of Boucher's, Bergeret de Grancourt.

The ineluctable conclusion to all this is that the artists concerned agreed to make quite finished small colored pictures (which are not even described as sketches in the catalogue of Marigny's posthumous sale as the marquis de Ménars) as an especial favor to the *directeur général des Bâtiments*, not for their own or the manufactory's needs. In the case of Boucher, this is borne out by the fact that, while both sketches indeed differ from the completed picture, the Williamstown sketch is little more than a twopence-colored rendition of the penny-plain grisaille from the Musée des Arts Décoratifs. When the minimal differences of detail between one and the other are compared with the substantial changes registered in the finished composition, it is clear that the colored oil sketch—which was anyway not a habitual feature of Boucher's working practice—does not represent a genuine stage in the creative process. It is, for all that, or even because of that, a delightful object.

Although often called *Venus Requesting Vulcan for Arms for Aeneas*, even in some of the criticisms of the finished painting in the Salon and in early sales of the sketches, this composition should properly be called (as it was in the *livret* of the Salon) [*Venus at*] *Vulcan's Forge*, or *The Forge of Lemnos*. For it shows the moment in the eighth book of the *Aeneid*, not when the goddess ordered the arms, when she came alone in order to seduce her husband into acceding to her request, as in the 1732 painting also in the Louvre (cat. 17), but when she returned to collect them. Virgil does not describe this particular episode, which appears to have given Boucher the freedom to depict the scene in his own way, with Venus attended by cupids scattering roses, and by the Hours, or Graces. The significance of the rose-crowned nymph resting in Venus's lap is not clear—in the sketches she is less individualized—but her gesture of trying her finger on Cupid's dart is a clear allusion to the power of Love, through which Venus got her much-cuckolded husband to do her bidding.

# 68 | *The Rest on the Flight into Egypt*

Oil on canvas
55 × 58½ in. (139 × 149 cm)
Signed lower right: *f. Boucher / 1757*
The Hermitage Museum, Leningrad
(S & M 716)      A & W 477
*Paris*

PROVENANCE
Exhibited in the Salon of 1757; Mme de Pompadour (posthumous inv. 1764/65 no. 1234, valued at 1,000 livres, as in the vestibule of the Hôtel de Pompadour, which was serving as a *garde-meuble* for items brought in from her other residences); *Catalogue des Tableaux Originaux de différens Maîtres . . . &c., de feue Madame la Marquise de Pompadour,* grande rue du Fauxbourg S. Honoré (Pierre Remy), 28 Apr. ff. 1766, lot 15: "Le Repos en Egypte . . . La beauté et la sagesse, symbole de la Divinité, sont caractérisées dans la personne de la sainte Vierge qui est assise tenant un livre *[Sedes Sapientiae]* . . . un des plus estimables [Tableaux] de ce Maître, & qui a été trouvé tel dans l'exposition des Tableaux au Louvre" [sold for 405 livres]; acquired by the Czarina Catherine II of Russia by 1774; Imperial Palace of Gatchina, between 1838 and 1856; then transferred to the Hermitage Museum, Saint Petersburg (now Leningrad).

DRAWING
*Study of Six Cherubim* (A & W fig. 1325, details unspecified): [M. & Mme Arthur] Veil-Picard coll., Paris; ?M. & Mme Louis Chaubah, Paris [worked up from the painting, with one cherub added].

It was apparently this picture that provoked someone to say of Boucher that he "was not a painter, but painting itself" *("ce n'étoit point un peintre, mais la peinture elle-même"* [*Journal Encyclopédique*, 1757, p. 101]). Our anonymous informant about this remark himself singled out "the verve and passion of this genius, unconfined by rules . . . [he] has poured a portion of his soul into every part of it" (*"la fougue & l'importement de ce génie indépendant des règles . . . [il] a fait passer dans les parties de ce tableau une portion de son ame"*).

Strange words to hear concerning a religious picture by an artist whose name is generally regarded as a byword for insincerity, painted for a woman (Mme de Pompadour) condemned by her enemies as a monument of hypocrisy. Yet the *Journal Encyclopédique*, to avoid censorship, was published in the independent prince-bishopric of Liège, so one has no reason to suspect it of sycophancy toward the powers that be in the artistic or political world. What is more, the picture having been shown without being included in the Salon catalogue (possibly to keep the place of the *Venus at Vulcan's Forge* [cat. 67] until it was ready for exhibition), it may not have been generally known whom it had been painted for; in consequence it otherwise appears to have been noticed only by the likewise anonymous author of the "Lettre à l'auteur" in the *Observations Périodiques* (disclaimed by the editor, Toussaint, in an open letter to Carle Vanloo in the November *Mercure de France*, this review of the 1757 Salon was ascribed by the *Correspondance littéraire* to a young pupil of Vien's, who is identified as Antoine Renou in a handwritten note on the transcript in the Deloynes collection). Toadies already had quite enough to busy their pens in the shape of the *Portrait of Mme de Pompadour* (cat. 64).

Like *La Lumière du Monde* (cat. 57) the *Rest on the Flight* is far from orthodox in that it includes the infant St. John the Baptist, who did not accompany the Holy Family into Egypt (while both he and the Christ Child are portrayed too young for this to represent their meeting on the Return). He is seen paying precocious homage to the Christ Child, rather as in the small oval of this subject alone that was also painted for Mme de Pompadour in the same year (exh. cat. 1932, Paris, no. 3; replica dated a year later in the Uffizi, A & W 503). His presence serves as the convenient pretext for the introduction of a sheep, just as St. Joseph is almost subordinated to the colorfully caparisoned ass with the black hen trussed to its packsaddle. These are just a few of the wealth of elements with which Boucher has embellished the picture. Some of them—such as the remains of the classical temple in which the protagonists sit—have some symbolic or narrative connotation (in this particular instance perhaps both, as the replacement of the Old Order by the New, and as the ruins of

68

the temple of Hermopolis), others—such as the rich carpet or the overturned jar—are just part of the profusion that Boucher delighted in. In the case of the earlier of the two *Marches* from Bergeret's collection now at Boston (A & W 660) indeed, it would appear that the picture began life in 1761 as a similar *Rest on the Flight*, showing the Holy Family accompanied by Joseph's three sons by his first marriage, as in one of the apocryphal traditions; it may have been Boucher's proliferation of irrelevant detail as much as the by this date dubious orthodoxy of the legend that led to his labeling it merely as a *Pastorale* when he showed it in the Salon, and to his subsequently enlarging it into an unspecific *Marche*.

We know that the present *Rest on the Flight* belonged to Mme de

Pompadour from its presence in her posthumous inventory (Cordey, 1939, p. 90, no. 1234) and sale. The inventory enumerates it among the items brought from elsewhere and stored in the vestibule of the Hôtel de Pompadour (now l'Elysée) in Paris. We do not know where it came from, but its square format and even its subject make it unlikely that it was ever an altarpiece. It was rather a gallery picture, very possibly commissioned by Mme de Pompadour from Boucher to give him the opportunity of emulating such Italian painters as Albani, Pietro da Cortona, and Maratta, with whom he was so often compared. Why it should not have been retained by her brother but have been put by him into her posthumous sale is—as with all the contents of that sale—a mystery. Size (as with the *Lever* and the *Coucher du Soleil*) may have been a consideration, as may the religious subject matter, since the exiguous sale contained no less than three religious pictures by Boucher, including another masterpiece, *La Lumière du Monde* (cat. 57). But in that case it is hard to explain why he should apparently have owned an autograph replica of *The Infant Christ Blessing the Infant St. John the Baptist*—if he had not simply bought back the original version in his sister's sale.

Nor do we apparently know when or through whom Catherine the Great acquired the picture. One can well imagine her having acquired it directly at the sale through an agent, possibly even having been eager to own a celebrated picture that had belonged to Mme de Pompadour. She was certainly keen—despite what she must have read about him in Diderot's reviews of the Salons in the *Correspondance littéraire*—to have something from Boucher's hand; it is thus possible that she acquired the *Rest on the Flight* only once she had failed to obtain the picture that she had tried to commission from him through Prince Galitzin (Diderot, XVIII, 1876, p. 301).

Catherine the Great can hardly have wanted to own a painting such as this by Boucher because of any involvement with the subject. Primed by Diderot's criticisms, she may indeed have taken specific pleasure in the apparent discrepancy between the reputation of the painter and his theme. Had not Diderot written in the midst of his onslaught on Boucher in his review of the 1765 Salon: "Wasn't there a time when he was seized with a frenzy for doing Virgins? So! What were those Virgins?—Charming little minxes. And his angels? Lewd little satyrs" ("*N'a-t-il pas été un temps où il étoit pris de la fureur de faire des vierges? Eh bien! qu'étoit-ce que ses vierges? de gentilles petites caillettes. Et ses anges? de petits satyres libertins*" [Diderot, II, 1979, p. 76]). More specifically, when criticizing the *Nativity* from a set of eight miniatures of the *Life of the Virgin* exhibited by Baudouin in the Salon of 1767, he noted its complete dependence upon Boucher's picture of *Le Sommeil de Jésus*, including the "same coquettish Virgin, the same lewd angels" ("*même Vierge coquette, mêmes anges libertins*" [Diderot, III, 1983, p. 201–02]). The "frenzy for doing Virgins" noted by Diderot was evidently around this epoch, since the picture, which survives (A & W 498), is dated 1758. Curiously, this picture, too, is today in Russia (Pushkin Museum, Moscow), though we do not know how it got there, having no trace of it between its enumeration in Mme de Pompadour's posthumous inventory (Cordey, 1939, p. 91, no. 1242), and its reemergence in the Vorontsov-Dashkov collection at the beginning of this century.

When we look at *The Rest on the Flight into Egypt*, is it a little minx and lewd little satyrs counterfeiting piety that we see, or a picture into which the painter has poured his soul? There can be no certain answer, since we cannot avoid—like Diderot—interpreting the painting in the light of our preconceptions about Boucher. One thing we cannot deny, however, and that is that he has succeeded in rethinking the tired old theme of the *Rest on the Flight* completely afresh, in both human and artistic terms.

# 69 | *The Mill of Quiquengrogne at Charenton*

Oil on canvas
44½ × 57½ in. (113 × 146 cm)
Signed lower right, on the fence:
*f. Boucher / 1758*
The Toledo Museum of Art (54.18)
S & M 1763          A & W 505

The mill at Charenton was one of the earliest picturesque motifs in the environs of Paris to be seized on by French artists in the eighteenth century, when they began to look to local sites for inspiration for their landscapes. Unlike Arcueil, however, this was not simply the subject of an agreeable exercise for drawings and sketchbooks; the central motif was sufficiently striking to inspire paintings—above all in the case of Boucher, who focused at least three different compositions on it, and also used it as a setting for one of his series of Beauvais tapestries called *La Noble Pastorale*. What exactly was this mill, that it became such a favorite motif?

Charenton lies upriver and just to the east of Paris, at the confluence of the Seine and the Marne. The stretch of the river from Paris to here had been one of the preferred locations for excursions and for the suburban villas of rich Parisians since the Middle Ages. The Château de Conflans, which took its name from the confluence, had belonged since 1673 to the archbishops of Paris, the first of whom had had the grounds laid out by Le Nôtre. These were supplied with water by a "machine hydraulique" on the Seine, which is described by Piganiol (1765, IX, p. 170 ff.), and which Thiéry (1787, I, p. 629) even calls a "moulin." It is tempting to associate this description with the decidedly bizarre structure depicted by Boucher, but it does not quite seem to meet the case. The Seine also drove a number of watermills at this location, one of which, Quiquengrogne—whose alliterative name presumably derives from the groaning of its wheel (it was also the motto of the de Rupelmonde)—was evidently regarded as particularly picturesque. It is referred to by Hurtaut and Magny (1779, II, p. 538) in their entry on the Pont de Charenton: "Sous ce pont, il y a un très-beau moulin." Depictions of it vary somewhat, and it is not quite clear whether this is to be ascribed to artistic license, or to the existence of more than one mill of this unusual form.

69

Fig. 180. Nicolas Vleughels, *The Mill at Quiquengrogne(?)*, dated Ascension Day 1721. The Pierpont Morgan Library, New York.

The earliest depictions of the mill appear to be in two drawings made by Nicolas Vleughels before he left to become director of the French Academy in Rome, where he was to encourage his students to sketch from the motif in the Campagna. One, dated Ascension Day 1721, is in the Pierpont Morgan Library in New York (fig. 180; exh. cat. 1984, New York, PML, no. 34). The whereabouts of the other, dated St. Michael's Day 1723, is at present unknown (see Hercenberg, 1975, no. 324, fig. 174). Vleughels's use of the motif was followed by Lancret, who made a painting later engraved by Elisabeth Cousinet with the title *Le Moulin de Quiquengrogne*, and two others probably of the same mill (G. Wildenstein, 1924, fig. 27, nos. 41–43), and by Oudry, who made a drawing of it now in the Cabinet des Dessins of the Louvre (Opperman, 1977, D1111; Duclaux, 1975, no. 286).

Boucher's earliest depiction of the mill would also appear to have been his first painted landscape to take a French motif as its subject. This is the panel dated 1739 (A & W 167), which was engraved by J-P. Le Bas in 1747, with the title *Premiere veue de Charenton* (fig. 181; J-R 1342) and a dedication to

Portail, who, like Boucher, was a participant in the sketching parties at Arcueil. This first treatment of the subject is very sober, placing it parallel to the picture plane, as previous artists had done. Nonetheless—possibly because he is showing it from the other side—Boucher adds a penthouse on stilts, not found in other representations of the mill, and a three-arched stone bridge to the left. The half-timbering and thatch of the superstructure are already shown in a state of picturesque decay, with doves alighting on the roof. A very similar depiction, but on canvas and larger, and with different staffage, can be seen from the drawing by Saint-Aubin in his copy of the catalogue, now in the collection of Mr. and Mrs. Charles Wrightsman in New York, to have been in the supplement to the Sorbet sale, 1 April ff. 1776, lot 214, paired with another version of the *View of a Mill* in the Musée d'Orléans, with the claim that the owner had acquired them directly from Boucher himself.

A similar straight-on view, but showing the now four-arched bridge to the right rather than the left, and the mill itself of more solid construction, with two wheels (as in the Lancret) rather than one, is found in an undated ovoid picture that was in the Hearst sale in 1939 (A & W 318). This had a label on the back, with the ambitious claim that it was "painted by the artist for his friend, M. Portail, who gave it to Madame de Pompadour." The Pompadour owned no landscapes by Boucher, and the mention of Portail was no doubt inspired by Le Bas's engraving.

A more romantic portrayal of the mill is to be found in the background to the cartoon, dated 1748, for the Beauvais tapestry *La Fontaine d'Amour* (fig. 182; A & W 321). In this it is seen at a slight angle, under a sky with windswept clouds; it has reverted to a single broad opening, but the penthouse here overhangs to the right, while the now single-arched stone bridge reverts to the left.

All these depictions so far, despite the liberties that they must visibly have taken with the motif, at least pretend to be faithful transcriptions of reality. What sets the Toledo picture apart, and gives it its special quality, is that it is so obviously a fantasy, an impossible idyll of picturesque decay combined with the imagined contentment of rustic existence. Steps are added to the left of the mill, and a woman and child appear in the doorway at the top of them. A large glazed window (most improbable in such a humble dwelling in France at this date), out of which a woman leans, now pierces the half-timbering. Some of the stone arches of the bridge to the left have been replaced by a rickety wooden structure, which is echoed by the rudimentary fences to the right of the picture. In the foreground, a duck wings its way between a girl doing the washing with her idle companion, and a fisherman mooring a boat.

It is curious that this, one of the most spectacular of Boucher's landscapes, appears to have no history going back beyond the late nineteenth century. It is tempting to suggest that it may have been the *Vue d'un moulin de Charenton* that was recorded in 1792 on the first floor of the former royal château at Choisy, as one of the five Bouchers that were to be removed to the Petits-Augustins (Engerand, 1900, p. 44). Of the other contenders, the 1739 picture would presumably have had its pendant, while the Hearst picture is neither signed nor dated, nor even (from illustrations of it) self-evidently autograph. The chief objection to the identification is that all Boucher's pictures for Choisy—including the *Toilette de Vénus* and *L'Amour dans les bras de sa mère* inventoried in 1792—appear to have been painted between 1741 and 1750, when the chief campaign of decorating and furnishing the newly acquired château was undertaken (see Chamchine, 1910, pp. 159–63, 183). It is, however, always possible that it had been transported there from some other royal château. It is perhaps suggestive that the only known copy of it is paired with another royal picture, *Le pont rustique*, which belonged to the Dauphin (A & W 476; it is, however, too large to be identified with the undescribed pendant of this; see A & W doc. 987, and Engerand, 1900, p. 637). The unusual dimensions and splendor of this landscape do nothing to detract from the idea that it may have been painted for the king.

## 70 | *Jupiter in the Guise of Diana Seducing Callisto*

Oil on canvas
22 × 27 in. (56 × 74 cm)
Signed: *f. Boucher / 1759*
The Nelson-Atkins Museum of Art,
Kansas City (32–29)
S & M 180 [with extraneous
items]        A & W 518

PROVENANCE
*Catalogue d'une belle Collection de Tableaux . . . &c., provenant de la succession de M. DE MONTBLIN, Conseiller au Parlement,* rue de Verneuil, 25–26 Feb. 1777, lot 4: "Jupiter, sous la figure de Diane, surprend Calisto. Ce Tableau, peint par F. Boucher, est des plus agréables Tableaux de ce Maître. Il a été gravé par Gaillard; largeur vingt-cinq pouces, longueur [*sic*] vingt-un pouces"; *Catalogue de Tableaux précieux des Trois Ecoles . . . Le tout provenant du Cabinet de M. le Chevalier de C*** [?Mesnard de Clesle; possibly to be identified with M. le chevalier de Clere of the *Almanach,* 1777, p. 183], Hôtel de Bullion (Paillet), 4 Dec. ff. 1786, lot 65: "Jupiter métamorphosé sous la figure de Diane, séduisant la nimphe Callisto; ce grouppe intéressant est présenté avec tout le charme d'une composition flatteuse, & dans l'attitude la plus riante & la plus voluptueuse. . . . Nous croyons qu'il seroit difficile de présenter un morceau plus séduisant, d'une composition plus riche & plus soignée dans tous ses détails, la facilité de la touche & les graces du dessin indiquent un des momens brillans du génie de cet artiste . . ." [bought by Le Brun for 999 livres 19 sous]; sale of M. G[outte], préposé principal du Trésor aux Armées, Paris, 29 Mar.–3 Apr. 1841, lot 196; Edward Timson coll., sold Christie's, London, 18 July 1930, lot 61; Howard Young Galleries, London, from which acquired for the museum in 1932.

Of all mythological subjects, *Jupiter and Callisto* was—next to the *Birth and Triumph of Venus* and *Venus and Vulcan*—the one most frequently depicted by Boucher. It is not hard to see why. In addition to its erotic content, the episode required the depiction of the naked or half-naked bodies of women and putti alone, thus sparing Boucher his difficulties in creating convincing male protagonists. For some reason—probably because most of them were painted in the latter part of his career, when he favored this form—most of his finished depictions of the subject are oval. The two exceptions are his first known treatment of the subject, the painting of 1744 in the Pushkin Museum in Moscow (A & W 267), and the present picture.

The story comes from Boucher's favorite source, Ovid's *Metamorphoses* (book 2), and it was characteristic of him that he should choose the episode of the seduction, rather than of its consequences, as the preponderant pictorial tradition had done. Callisto was the favorite nymph of the virgin goddess and huntress, Diana. Discovering her in Arcadia, Jupiter took the form of Diana in order to win her confidence, before seducing her. This violation of her vows of chastity was only discovered some months later, when she stripped to bathe with the other nymphs, and resulted in her expulsion from their band. The jealous Juno then had her revenge by turning her smooth, delicate form into that of a lumbering, shaggy bear. Jupiter, however, converted her and his son by her into constellations—the Great and the Little Bear.

Although this and other versions of the theme are often hastily called *Diana and Callisto*, Boucher was always careful to include Jupiter's eagle, gripping his thunderbolts and keeping a vigilant eye on the event, to indicate that it is indeed the god and not the goddess. The crescent moon on his

70

Fig. 183. *Three Cupids in the Air.* The Nelson-Atkins Museum of Art, Kansas City.

forehead identifies his disguise as Diana, and he/she indicates the quiver and dead game to betoken the conversation about hunting, through which he lulled Callisto into a sense of false security. The cupids brandish darts and torches to signify the effects of love.

The earliest recorded appearance of this picture was in the posthumous sale of the lawyer M. de Montblin in February 1777. The coincidence of this sale with the engraving of the picture by Gaillard (which is already mentioned in the catalogue, though it was not advertised until August) makes one suspect, however, that it was an insertion by the auctioneer, particularly as the engraving carries no mention of ownership, but only a dedication to a M. d'Arbonne by the print dealer.

The Nelson-Atkins Museum has recently complemented its ownership of the painting by acquiring an associated drawing of three putti in clouds (fig. 183; A & W fig. 1433). Rather than seeing this as Ananoff and Wildenstein appear to do, and as Roger Ward does (1983), as a preparatory drawing for the picture, it should be regarded as a typical example of Boucher's taking elements from his paintings—or from the studies for these—and working

ENGRAVING
*Jupiter et Calisto*, engraved by R. Gaillard, and published by Buldet with a dedication to M. d'Arbonne, Grand Maître des Eaux et Forêts (J-R 1052–1054), in August 1760, as a pendant to Ryland's engraving of *Jupiter et Léda* (see cat. 40), published by him two years before.

DRAWING
Two putti from upper right, with a third added, red, black, and white chalks, 197 × 287 mm, François Renaud [framer], rue Feydeau, Paris; J. B. de Graaf, Amsterdam; ?Léon Decloux sale, Paris, 14–15 Feb. 1898, lot 75; Thos. Agnew & Sons, London; private coll.; Agnew's again, from whom acquired by the Nelson-Atkins Museum in 1983.

COPIES
1. ?Reversed copy after engraving by Gaillard, posthumous sale of the marquis de la Chataigneraye, prince de Ponts, Hôtel Drouot, Paris, 5 May 1868, lot 7 bis, as *Diane et Calisto (gravée)*, pendant to lot 7, *Nymphe délivrée (gravée)* [*Sylvie délivrée*, also engraved by Gaillard].

them up into drawings marketable in their own right (a point already made in an unpublished reply to Ward's note by William P. Miller, Jr.). The two putti in the painting are anyway, as Ward notes, already familiar in closely similar poses from other paintings, although the one that he cites itself looks merely like a pastiche, composed of one of the cupids from here and another from the *Chariot of Apollo* at Fontainebleau (A & W 417). The interesting thing, however, is that in none of the precedents that one can find is any of these cupids exactly repeated. It is this that enables one to put a plausible interpretation upon Sir Joshua Reynolds's observation (1959, p. 225), that Boucher appeared to work "without drawings or models of any kind." It was not that he had ceased to make drawings and studies, but that, having by means of them fixed a successful pose in his memory, he was capable of drawing it out and adapting it for whatever purpose he required it, without fresh recourse to the original study.

2. Upright variant, reversed, 39 × 32 cm, P. S. sale, Gudule, Brussels, May 1899.
3. Reversed variant on panel, 99 × 144 cm, anon. sale, Henrici, Berlin, 29 June 1920, lot 5.
4. Reversed variant lacking landscape, 56 × 86 cm, M. J. sale, Hôtel Drouot, Paris, 17 Apr. 1920, lot 14.

5. Painting, sale at Château de Maisons-Laffitte, 16 Nov. 1969, lot 18.
6. Pencil drawing for a miniature, strengthened in ink, Baudouin portfolio, Graphische Sammlung, Munich (inv. 10727).

## 71 | *The School of Love*

Oil on canvas
25½ × 32 in. (64.5 × 81 cm)
Signed on stone, bottom left: *f. Boucher / 1760*
Staatliche Kunsthalle, Karlsruhe (inv. 479)
A & W 542
*Paris*

## 72 | *The School of Friendship*

Oil on canvas
25¼ × 31¾ in. (64 × 80.5 cm)
Inscribed on stone, bottom right: *f. Boucher / 1790* [sic]
Staatliche Kunsthalle, Karlsruhe (inv. 480)
*Paris*

PROVENANCE
Acquired by Caroline Luise of Baden from the artist via J. H. Eberts; Schloss Karlsruhe; transferred to the Kunsthalle between 1833 and 1863.

DRAWING
Finished drawing of *The School of Friendship* prepared for the engraver, removing peeping tom, and substituting overturned vase for statue of putto, engraved by J-M. Delâtre and published by Daullé, as *L'Ecole de l'Amitié*.

Boucher's relationship with Caroline Luise, the Margravine of Baden, for whom this pair of pastorals was painted, is an attractive little episode that sheds interesting light upon how he was regarded by at least one creator of a deliberately planned *cabinet de peinture*.

Caroline Luise (1723–1783) was one of a number of remarkable women thrown up by the ruling houses of the Holy Roman Empire in the eighteenth century. Born a Landgravine of Hesse-Darmstadt, she was married in 1751—quite late in life for those days—to the Margrave Carl Friedrich of Baden-Durlach (with which Baden-Baden was to be reunited in 1771). Already

71

72

VARIANTS

*The School of Love:* oval, 77 × 65 cm, signed *f. Boucher 1761,* exhibited in the Salon of 1761, under no. 9; Randon de Boisset's posthumous sale, 27 Feb. ff. 1777, lot 191 [bought by Desmarest for 1180 livres]; intended posthumous sale of the marquis de Livois, Angers, 1791, no. 215; sequestered, but later reclaimed by his heirs, by whom sold to M. Gamba for 30 francs; sale of M. Gamba, 370 rue Saint-Honoré, Paris, 17 Dec. ff. 1811, lot 54 [bought by Le Brun for 54 francs]; probably acquired by Sir Richard Wallace, and thus to the Wallace Collection, London, P431 [only the figures retained, with variations in dress] (fig. 185).

*The School of Friendship:* c. 15 *pouces* × 13 *pouces,* Salon of 1765, no. 11, with pendant; engraved by Jacques Bonnefoy as *La Confidence* (fig. 186; J-R 313–314; A & W figs. 1602, 1603), with pendant as *Le Repos* (J-R 312; A & W figs. 1595, 1596); [upright composition, with considerable variations in setting and in the figure of the confidante].

COPIES

Red chalk, 410 × 510 mm, Kupferstichkabinett, Kunsthalle, Karlsruhe (inv. 691, 692) [by Caroline Luise, Margravine of Baden?].

Fig. 184. Caroline Luise of Baden(?), copy of Boucher's *The School of Friendship.* Staatliche Kunsthalle, Karlsruhe.

known as "the Hessian Minerva" when she married, and subsequently called the "Vielwisserin und Vielfragerin von Baden" ("the much-knowing and much-questioning lady of Baden") by Lavater, she was possessed of great intelligence, curiosity, and artistic aptitude. The first was recognized by her admittance into the academy of Arcadia in Rome in 1776, and the last by her reception into the Royal Danish Academy of Art in 1763. In the latter part of her life her interest in natural history came to predominate, but earlier it was art. As a girl she had been taught how to use pastel by Liotard, and until around 1770 she used pastel, oils, and red chalk to make careful copies of pictures by other artists and drawings of her intimate circle. Her most lasting achievement, however, was between 1759 and 1769 (and above all between 1759 and 1763, when prices were depressed by the Seven Years' War) to put together a choice collection of pictures, which still forms the core of the Karlsruher Kunsthalle (for her life and activities see esp. Lauts, 1980, and exh. cat. 1983, Karlsruhe, Schloss). Although she claimed that, "I regard my Cabinet as an educated person would his library, namely as a means of instruction" (Lauts, 1980, p. 157), she also said that, "I must confess that I am as mad for good pictures as books" (Lauts, 1980, p. 168).

Most of her pictures, whether from living artists or old masters from the art market, came from Paris, where her chief agent was the banker and artistic middleman from Strasbourg, J. H. Eberts (for this and what follows, see Obser, 1902, and Lauts, 1980, pp. 155–71). It was through him that she obtained her first two pictures by Boucher, a pair of pastel heads. She had only asked for one, in the summer of 1759 (and it is interesting that this was what she associated the artist with), but Boucher offered a pendant. When they arrived, she was delighted, describing them as "two admirable heads. . . . I find them every bit as beautiful as you had told me, my cabinet takes fresh luster from them." Encouraged by this, as Eberts wrote in December:

> Mr. Boucher has offered me to compose, paint, and give superior finish to two pastoral subjects, on canvases roughly two feet square. Ordinarily he is paid one hundred louis for two such pieces, but because of his respectful consideration for Your Highness, and his desire to enrich your fine cabinet with two pretty pieces, he would be content with fifty new louis. . . . The result will be a little compound of grace, tenderness, ingenuity, and taste—all the more precious because this charming artist is hardly going to do any more of these subjects.

The Margravine welcomed the proposal, only adding her wish that the artist might add one or two animals to his pictures, since, "I am told that he does them supremely well."

From this moment on, Eberts gave regular progress reports on the pictures, adding fire to the Margravine's expectations. Boucher had already made a start on one at the beginning of January 1760: "He has promised me two masterpieces, in which there will be a little of everything—figures, animals, flowers, and streams. . . ." So enthusiastic did he make the Margravine that she declared, "I foresee that I shall drop to my knees when I receive them." The first of the pair, *The School of Love,* was nearing completion by the end of March, inspiring Eberts to proclaim:

> The most beautiful nymph or shepherdess of the century of Astraea was never as beautiful as the one in this picture. The shepherd, whom she

Fig. 185. *A Shepherd and Shepherdess Gathering Roses,* signed and dated 1761. Wallace Collection, London.

Fig. 186. *La Confidence,* engraved by Jacques Bonnefoy after Boucher.

regards with a passionate glance, is also very choice; the lambs, sheep, streams, statues, flowers, etc., are like Nature herself, and prettily finished without being glacial.

When he sent the picture at the end of April, Eberts took the opportunity to extract two more heads in pastel from Boucher's studio. The Margravine expressed herself delighted with all three: the *Pastorale* had entirely lived up to her expectations, and the fresh color of one of the pastels, of a woman reading a letter, pleased her particularly. The second *Pastorale* followed at the beginning of June, and Caroline Luise continued to express her delight:

> I was highly contented with the first, but I am yet more so with this one, it is adorable, and of a really fine coloring. Thank Mr. Boucher for me, and tell him that he has really enriched my cabinet with his beautiful works. I am no less appreciative of the two fine prints that he had the goodness to send me; I have placed them among my best pictures, where—without color, and by their beautiful composition alone—they will always maintain the place that I have given them with distinction. The very calumny—or rather the envy—that is vented against Mr. Boucher seems to me to redound to his credit; his reputation is too solidly established for anything in the world to diminish it.

Even allowing for courtly exaggeration, it would appear that the Margravine was genuinely pleased with what she had obtained from Boucher—one has only to compare it with Marigny's tepid thanks to Natoire for the *Leda* that he painted to join Boucher's *Blonde Odalisque* (cat. 61) in the *petit cabinet chaud* to see this. Yet the fact that she felt compelled to allude to his critics, and the criticism of his coloring implicit in her hanging black-and-white prints of other pictures of his in her cabinet, suggest latent reservations. Even so, the deduction that has been made (see Lauts, 1980, p. 170) from the tone of her letters to Eberts and to J. F. von Reiffenstein (who, it should be remembered, was one of the pioneers of the reaction against the Rococo in Germany) and from the subsequent fate of the pictures, that she was disappointed in them, is overdrawn. It is true that the two *Pastorales* did not remain in her cabinet, but went to decorate the Schloss, so that her husband, in whose province this fell, had to reimburse her their purchase price (so tight was her budget!). But this was as much as anything a reflection of the carefully planned and balanced nature of her cabinet, which consisted essentially of small paintings by Dutch artists or by other artists employing similar types and *finish* (Lauts, 1980, p. 159)—even Italian pictures could scarcely find a toehold there (Lauts, 1980, pp. 203–05). Pictures she was really unenthusiastic about she gave away or sold (Lauts, 1980, pp. 167, 186, 189–91, 204). She was even sufficiently keen to obtain two more pastel heads from Boucher, one of Mme de Pompadour (in which it is no doubt true that the sitter interested her more than the artist), and the other of the dancer Mlle Bienvenue, or "Lindane."

Perhaps the most significant token of Caroline Luise's genuine interest in the *Pastorales* is that she used the head of the shepherdess in the *School of Love* for a red-chalk drawing of a *Woman Reading* (fig. 63; no doubt itself inspired by Boucher's pastel), which was one of the specimens of her work that she sent to Denmark to support her candidature for the Academy in 1763 (Lauts, 1980, pp. 198–99, fig. 33). What is more—unless they are actually preparations for never-executed engravings—it seems more plausible that the two copies of the *Pastorales* (see fig. 184) in red chalk in the Kupferstichkabinett of the Kunsthalle should be by Caroline Luise, who was a zealous copyist, than that they should be by the court artist, Boucher's former pupil Joseph Melling (exh. cat. 1983, Karlsruhe, Schloss, no. 91).

The sentimental subject matter and the painterly profusion of Boucher's two *Pastorales* do indeed strike a different note among the sober realism and high finish of the Margravine's predominantly Dutch pictures, but it is clear that he did exert himself particularly in painting them. Not only did he cram his whole pastoral repertoire into the small format of these two pictures, but he also strove to paint them more minutely. It may well have been true that, as he told Eberts, he intended these to be among his last pastorals, and that he had become a prisoner of his own success with the genre. Nevertheless, the *School of Friendship*, in particular, shows that he could still devise images within it that are replete with both naturalness and charm.

## 73 | *Landscape with a Distant Ruin*

Oil on canvas
19½ × 26 in. (49 × 66 cm)
Signed on stone bottom left: *f. Boucher / 1761*
Indianapolis Museum of Art; Gift of
Mr. and Mrs. Herman C. Krannert (60.248)
A & W 546

## 74 | *Landscape with a Weir*

Oil on canvas
18 × 26 in. (46 × 66 cm)
Signed bottom right: *f. Boucher / 1761*
Private collection, Bielefeld
A & W 547

PROVENANCE
*Catalogue des Tableaux Originaux des Grands Maîtres des Trois Ecoles, qui ornoient un des Palais de feu son Altesse Monseigneur Chris- tient, DUC DES DEUX PONTS*, Hôtel d'Al- igre (Remy), 6 Apr. ff. 1778, lot 79: "Deux paysages datés de 1761; dans l'un on voit un enfant près d'une femme qui pêche à la ligne: plus loin dans un chemin à gauche, un homme à cheval, & des moutons; dans l'autre un moulin à eau, un pont de bois, plusieurs figures, une vache & des moutons; ils sont sur toile, & portent chacun 17 pouces de haut, sur 24 pouces de large" [sold for 500 livres]; sale of Mme de Polès, Paris, 22–24 June 1927, lots 14, 13 [bought together by Mr. Lennie Davis for 450,000 francs, thereafter sold separately]:
*Landscape with a Distant Ruin*: Rosenberg & Stiebel, New York; Mr. and Mrs. Herman

These were the only two landscapes by Boucher in the posthumous sale of his great friend and patron Christian IV, Herzog von Zweibrücken ("le duc de Deux-Ponts"). Most of the Bouchers in this sale were mythological, though it also included a version of *The Surprise* (cat. 2), and the only other landscapes by a French artist were a *Landscape* paired with a *Seascape*, painted by Vernet in Rome in 1749 (lot 80). Not that it should be assumed that the duke had owned no others, since the statement of the catalogue that the pictures had "adorned *one* of the palaces of his late Highness" is confirmed by Mannlich (1948, p. 274), who says that it was the pictures in the gallery of the *petit château* (i.e., the so-called Kleines Palais or "Schlösschen" of the duke's morganatic wife, the Gräfin von Forbach) that were sold, since this pavilion passed to the dowager duchess after his death. The pictures were regarded by her as chattels and sent to Paris for sale despite the fact that many of them must have been let into the paneling (hence their being sold without

*73*

C. Krannert, New Augusta, by whom given to the Indianapolis Museum of Art in 1960.

*Landscape with a Weir:* The Hallsborough Gallery, London, from which acquired by the present owner in 1961.

frames). At least one Boucher appears to have been in either the Zweibrücker Residenz or Schloss Jägersburg, whence it ultimately came to reside in the Alte Pinakothek in Munich (cat. 61); while the portrait of Mme de Pompadour that was sent to the duke in 1764 was probably retained by Gräfin Forbach, since it, like Mannlich's conversation piece of the duke and his morganatic family in which her own pose was modeled on that of the Pompadour, appears to have been acquired by baron Edmond de Rothschild (with an erroneous provenance from the de Bernis family; see Mannlich, 1948, p. 121; Dahl & Lohmeyer, 1957, pp. 160–61, 169 n. 19, 309; A & W 170/2).

It is not clear whether these pictures were among those exhibited in the Salon of 1761. The *livret* simply lists an unspecified number of "Pastorales et Paysages, sous le même Numéro." Saint-Aubin only illustrates two landscapes (Dacier, III, no. 6, 1911, p. 54, facsimile), but two of the critics imply there were more (A & W docs. 796, 800). It could be that they were simply using "landscape" in the wider sense, to embrace the pastorals as well, but this is not self-evident. Saint-Aubin's two drawings are so fuzzy that it is hard to demonstrate anything more than a negative with them. They do not suggest either of the present pictures, nor is Ananoff and Wildenstein's proposal of the *Blanchisseuses dans un paysage* (A & W 532) very convincing:

74

not only does the drawing itself lack the vertical accents of the picture, but the pendant clearly represents a stone bridge rather than—as it should—*La passerelle* (A & W 531).

It is regrettable that we do not know for certain whether these landscapes were among those in the Salon, since one of the critics is particularly pertinent about them (A & W doc. 796). Having insisted upon the importance of constant expeditions to study nature on the spot (something one suspects that Boucher had long abandoned· he is never mentioned as taking part in the excursions of his friend Wille, for instance), he goes on to praise Boucher as the preeminent landscape painter of the day, but to "fear that with infinitely rare talents, too much artifice and too many pleasing colors are deployed in landscapes in which plain and simple nature should reign, and that the pretty and the affected usurp the place of the beautiful and the natural." ("*Mais n'est-il pas à craindre qu'avec des talens infiniment précieux, on ne mette dans des paysages ou doit regner la simple et naive nature, trop de manieres, trop de couleurs gracieuses, et que le joli et l'affecté ne prennent la place du beau et du naturel.*")

Boucher's misfortune with his critics was a double one. On the one hand, the definition of what was natural had shifted and become more rigorous since he had begun painting landscapes inspired by the picturesque motifs of the French countryside over twenty years before; on the other hand he had begun to fall back on formulae, putting all his skill into the cunning of his brushwork. As Diderot observed after talking about Boucher's landscapes in the same Salon:

> He is made to turn the heads of two types of people—society figures and artists . . . the latter, who see the degree to which this man has overcome the sheer difficulties of painting . . . bow their knee to him; he is their god. . . . He is to painting more or less what Ariosto is to poetry. . . . Boucher has a *faire* that is so perfectly his own that one could give him a figure to execute in any piece of painting whatsoever, and it would be instantly recognizable. *(Il est fait pour tourner la tête à deux sortes de personnes, les gens du monde, et les artistes . . . qui voient jusqu'à quel point cet homme a surmonté les difficultés de la peinture . . . [ils] fléchissent le genou devant lui; c'est leur dieu. . . . Ce peintre est à peu près en peinture ce que l'Arioste est en poésie. . . . Boucher a une faire qui lui appartient tellement, que dans quelque morceau de peinture qu'on lui donnât une figure à exécuter, on la reconnaîtrait sur-le-champ* [Diderot, 1975, p. 112].)

One is conscious in this passage, as so often, that Diderot was motivated by reactions to things extraneous to the paintings themselves—to society and to the old debate over the competence of non-artists to pass public judgment on works of art—but even so one must acknowledge the partial validity of his criticisms. The charm of these landscapes resides precisely in their handling and in their artifice: it is the painter that we are meant to address ourselves to, not the motif. As always, we are conscious of a splendid excess: effects intrinsically natural are piled upon one another in impossible and idyllic confusion. Taken alone, each detail—the creeper trailing over the weir, the gnarled willows, the crooked fences, the distant ruin (which is curiously reminiscent of the eroded tombs on the via Appia)—has verisimilitude, but the whole defies belief. Nor is it, as has been advanced (see exh. cat. 1983, Atlanta, no. 65), the artificiality of the stage set—of which neither picture has either the components or the composition; it is rather, as Diderot said, the subordination of everything to the demands of the brush, which proclaims "Boucher" in every stroke.

## 75 | *The Death of Socrates*

Oil on canvas, *en camaïeu brun*
16 × 22 in. (41 × 55 cm)
Musée de Tessé, Le Mans (inv. 1821)
A & W 536

PROVENANCE
Deposited by the Réunion des Musées Nationaux in 1957.

*The Death of Socrates* strikes a most unusual note in Boucher's oeuvre: a severe classical subject, taken from history rather than mythology, set in a prison, centered upon death, and requiring exclusively male protagonists. One's first reaction is that it cannot be by Boucher, but must be by his more artistically ambitious son-in-law, Jean-Baptiste Deshays.

75

DRAWING
*La mort de Socrate* (paired with *La mort de Callirhoé*), pen and bister wash heightened with white, 11 *pouces* × 14 *pouces*, Randon de Boisset's posthumous sale, 27 Feb. 1777 ff., lot 331: "D'un bon faire & très capitaux" [given to M. de Sireul (who had contributed the *Anecdotes* of the collector as a preface) by his nephews and heirs]; de Sireul's posthumous sale, 3 Dec. ff. 1781, lot 81 [bought by Paillet for 180 livres 1 sol and 80 livres 2 sous]; misc. sale (Paillet), 17 Dec. 1787 ff., lot 136 [bought by Bereyter for 146 livres 1 sol].

The idea is seductive, since this sketch has a vigor—almost a coarseness—that seems alien to Boucher, and more characteristic of Deshays. But the alternative attribution will not hold: the picture lacks the crude contour-defining black lines found in Deshays's sketches, and the paint has a liquidity alien to his abrupter hand. The often schematic faces of the protagonists can be paralleled elsewhere in Boucher's oeuvre: the face of the standing disciple holding a book at the left is a throwback to the type Boucher employed for elderly men early in his career (see cat. 7, 8), while the most summarily defined heads in the background relate to others in the backgrounds of the *St. Peter Attempting to Walk on the Waters* (cat. 77), and of the grisaille and camaïeu sketches for *St. John the Baptist Preaching* (A & W 558, 559; the third of the sketches they include, no. 560, now in the Art Institute of Chicago, is, however, most probably by Deshays). Seen in black-and-white illustration, there appear to be seductive similarities between the present sketch and that for Deshays's altarpiece of the *Marriage of the Virgin* in Saint-Pierre, Douai (Musée de la Chartreuse, Douai; see exh. cat. 1983–84, Rotterdam, no. 63; exh. cat. 1984, Langres, no. 8), but seen in the flesh, the harsh colors and coarse facture of the latter reveal a much more uncompromising hand at work. By comparison with his former teacher, indeed, Deshays made very little use of grisaille or camaïeu for his sketches, evidently preferring more pronounced accents. Nevertheless, just as in the—for him—unusually gentle scene of the Virgin's marriage, Deshays approached Boucher so closely that the picture was until recently ascribed to the latter, so, in the present sketch of an unwonted historical subject, Boucher appears to have responded to the influence of his former pupil.

There is no record of a finished picture to resolve the question of attribution. Nor does it help that both Boucher and Deshays are recorded as making wash drawings of the subject. Boucher's passed through the distinguished collections of Randon de Boisset and de Sireul, while Deshays made two of different sizes, one of which was in his own posthumous sale,

Fig. 187. J-P. de Saint-Quentin, *The Death of Socrates* (1762). Ecole des Beaux-Arts, Paris.

Fig. 188. *The Last Supper*. Albertina, Vienna.

and reappeared either in the shape of the drawing in the Ghendt sale in 1779 (15 Nov. ff., lot 254), or in that of the Le Brun sale of 29 April ff. 1782, lot 165.

Why the two artists should have taken this interest in a subject generally regarded as the epitome of neoclassicism is not immediately apparent. It had already been depicted by Dandré-Bardon in a painting exhibited in the Salon of 1753, when the episode was proposed as a moral exemplar by La Font de Saint-Yenne, in his *Sentiments sur quelques ouvrages de Peinture, Sculpture et gravure* in 1754 (see Rosenblum, 1970, pp. 56, 73–75). Yet it was not until 1761 that the suggestion was taken up, when it was adopted by Challe for his pioneering classicizing picture in the Salon of that year (see Diderot, 1975, pp. 89, 124–25, fig. 56). The following year it was both the subject of a picture by Sané (Locquin, 1912, pp. 249–50) and adopted as the first classical theme to be set in the Academy's annual competition for its pupils. Sané's picture was fulsomely praised by Cochin, and the latter was behind the choice of subject for the Grand Prix as well.

The present sketch is utterly remote in handling and spirit from the lost pictures by Challe and Sané, both of which aspired to the condition of bas-reliefs, and even from the declamatory Poussinism of the picture by the 1762 prizewinner, J-P. de Saint-Quentin (fig. 187; Ecole des Beaux-Arts, Paris), despite the fact that he was a pupil of Boucher's. It has much greater affinity with the busy vitality of some of Boucher's own drawings, especially the one of the *Last Supper* that belonged to Mariette (fig. 188; Albertina, Vienna, inv. 12.123; apparently executed over the offset of a drawing in the Art Institute of Chicago, of which there is a copy by J-B. Huet on the New York art market, exh. cat 1984, New York, no. 22), and it is also reminiscent of another scene set by him in a prison, the *Corps de Garde* engraved in aquatint by Floding in 1762 (J-R 1013).

It seems possible that Boucher was even inspired to produce this sketch by the competition of 1762. The competitors that year included not only one of his pupils, but also (among the architects) his son. The rules of the competition, which required the candidates to make their sketches in seclusion, and to adhere to these when painting their finished picture, would have precluded Boucher offering any guidance—even were it to have been welcome in such an event by this date—so that the sketch can only have been made for his own purposes. It must reflect his awareness of the new trends in painting, and his desire to meet their challenge—a desire that resulted in a number of drawings and sketches of classical subjects, but in no completed paintings, only in the failure to execute even those commissioned for the gallery at Choisy or for the Royal Castle in Warsaw. That the desire was present we know from a letter of Cochin's to Marigny of 16 October 1764 concerning the gallery at Choisy (Engerand, 1900, p. 225). In it, he proposed four artists to paint the elevating classical subjects that he had proposed: Carle Vanloo, Vien, Deshays, and Boucher, "who has for so long desired to treat a historical episode, and for whom the scale required by this gallery is an everyday thing." *("M. Boucher, qui désire si longtemps d'avoir enfin l'occasion de traitter un morceau d'histoire et pour qui la proportion, à laquelle cette galerie assujettit, est si ordinaire.")* In the event Boucher produced nothing—not even a sketch or a drawing—of the episode from the life of Titus or Trajan that he would have been required to paint; he was instead proposed by Cochin as the artist best fitted to provide the graceful and agreeable substitutes preferred by the king, at whose behest these sermonizing paintings had been taken down almost as soon as they were put up (Engerand, 1900, p. 401).

Perhaps Boucher had already been discouraged by the present sketch. Though it is a virtuoso piece of painting, as always, the stoic message of the episode is dissipated by the baroque agony of the chief protagonist, and Boucher's difficulty with his features makes it hard to identify him as an old man, let alone as Socrates. The identification of the subject of the picture has indeed been questioned, but the empty cup of hemlock beside the dying man, and the disciples recording his last words, leave little doubt about it. It is, however, precisely the ambiguity of the scene that demonstrates how far Boucher was from having grasped the pictorial correlative of the *exemplum virtutis.*

# 76 | *The Assumption of the Virgin*

Oil sketch on canvas
50¼ × 29¼ in. (127.5 × 74.5 cm)
National Galleries of Scotland,
Edinburgh (inv. 2179)

PROVENANCE
*Catalogue de Dessins, Tableaux et Estampes. Après le décès de M. DESHAYS, peintre du Roi,* dans l'appartement du Défunt, rue Neuve des Petits-Champs, à côté de la porte du Jardin du Palais Royal (Remy), 26 Mar. ff. 1765, in the section headed *Esquisses et Ebauches de M. Boucher, &c.,* either lot 123: "Une autre [i.e., esquisse de l'Assomption] colorée, de quatre pieds quatre pouces de haut, sur deux pieds trois pouces de large" [sold for 24 livres], or lot 124: "Autre Assomption colorée, de la même grandeur que la précédente" ["Néant," i.e., bought in]; then either *Catalogue des Tableaux . . . &c. après le décès de Mr. Baudouïn, Peintre de l'Académie Royale,* Hôtel d'Espagne (Remy), 15 Feb. ff. 1770, lot 5: "Une autre belle ébauche, représentant une Assomption, peinte sur toile. Hauteur 4 pieds 3 pouces; largeur 2 pieds 3 pouces" [bought by Monval for 40 livres], or *Catalogue Raisonné des Tableaux . . . &c. qui composent le Cabinet DE FEU M. BOUCHER, Premier Peintre du Roi,* Vieux Louvre, appartement du défunt sr. Boucher, 18 Feb. ff. 1771, lot 85 bis: "L'Assomption de la Vierge, ébauche peinte sur toile de 4 pieds 4 pouces, sur 2 pieds 3 pouces de large" [bought by Varanchamp for 36 livres]; then either *Cabinet d'un Artiste* (Le Brun & Boileau), 22 Jan. ff. 1787, lot 130: "Une belle esquisse en hauteur représentant l'Assomption de la Sainte Vierge. Hauteur 47 pouces, largeur 27 pouces. Toile" [sold for 3 livres], and *Catalogue d'une Collection . . .,* Hôtel de

The posthumous sales of Deshays, Baudouin, and their common father-in-law, Boucher, produced a clutch of sketches of the *Assumption* by the last of these. Evidently, some of these pictures were identical with one another. Since Deshays's sale in 1765 contained no less than three, all of the same dimensions, one in grisaille and two colored—one of which was bought in—while Baudouin's sale in 1770 and Boucher's in 1771 each contained one colored sketch of the same dimensions, it would appear that one of them had bought the colored sketch that was sold, and the other had acquired the picture that was bought in. The grisaille sketch had been bought by the architect de Wailly, yet in his sale in 1788 there was no such picture, but only two sketches of virtually the same dimensions by Boucher, representing the *Annunciation.* Since we have no other record of such a subject painted by Boucher (although there is a drawing for an altarpiece of the *Annunciation,* albeit of contested authorship, in the Musées d'Angers, cf. exh. cat. 1977–78, London, no. 12), it seems fairly clear that the auctioneer made a slip of the pen, and that both sketches were in fact of the *Assumption,* de Wailly having acquired one of the colored sketches in Baudouin's or in Boucher's posthumous sale, to add to the grisaille that he already owned.

What do these large oil sketches of an unwonted religious theme by Boucher, all in family ownership, signify? All three seem to be identifiable today (the grisaille—actually *en camaïeu brun*—in a private collection, A & W 526; and the other colored sketch, fig. 189, in the Musée des Beaux-Arts in Dijon, A & W 527, wrongly stated to be *en grisaille*); not only do they all relate to one another, but they also suggest a very late placing within the artist's output. They were evidently produced not at all long before Deshays's death, and the fact that they were all in his possession suggests that

76

Fig. 189. Colored sketch of *The Assumption*.
Musée des Beaux-Arts, Dijon.

Fig. 190. *The Assumption*. Albertina, Vienna.

they were somehow to have been exploited by him. The present picture has, indeed, been erroneously attributed to him in the past (see Sandoz, 1977, p. 74, no. 50C). Deshays, however, is known to have been commissioned to produce only one *Assumption,* in 1758 for the priory of Bellefonds, near his native Rouen, for which two sketches are known (Sandoz, 1977, pp. 73–74 and pl. v, nos. 50Ba, 50Bb). These bear no relation to the present picture or to the colored sketch in Dijon, although there is some thematic affinity with the painting *en camaïeu brun,* in that in this sketch alone the Virgin is ascending from the midst of the Apostles surrounding her tomb. It does not, however, seem possible to detach this sketch *en camaïeu brun* compositionally from the two colored sketches, and all three appear to date from later than 1758 on stylistic grounds.

The sequence of sketches would indeed rather appear to imply that it was instead Boucher who took Deshays's composition as his point of departure (if Deshays was not in turn taking his cue from the *Assumption* included in the eight drawings by Boucher inserted into Mme de Pompadour's *Office de la Sainte Vierge* [printed in 1757], A & W fig. 97, which were exploited by Baudouin in a set of miniatures for the same patron). In this sequence, the earliest sketch would be the one *en camaïeu brun,* which is the only one of the three that can strictly be called an *Assumption;* it shares with the second of Deshays's sketches the device of prominently featuring an Apostle cut off at the waist below, gazing up at the Virgin, so as to dramatize the fact of her ascent. The next sketch in the sequence would be the present one, in which the vacated tomb is still present, but in which a vigorously posed angel takes the place of the Apostle. This is just one of a number of changes that begin to convert this into a *Glorification of the Virgin* rather than strictly an *Assumption:* a putto-angel presents Mary with a lily from the right, a dove (symbolizing the Holy Ghost, and already present in the first sketch) is descending, and she is crowned with stars. The pose of the angel on the left is almost unaltered from the sketch *en camaïeu brun.* In the third and last sketch of the sequence, the picture in Dijon, which is also the most finished of the three—albeit regrettably disfigured by subsequent completion or repainting of the upper parts, including the face of the Virgin—the tomb has disappeared altogether. The only allusion to it is made by the putti-angels about to cast the roses that, in the legend, took the place of the Virgin's body. Boucher was in consequence forced to discard the pose of the bottommost angel used in the present sketch—despite the fact that it is the most powerful feature of the latter—and to bring him up into the clouds. He has also changed the position of the arms of the second angel, making him join them together across his breast, in the gesture of humility previously adopted by the Virgin. She, by contrast, now indicates herself with one arm, and flings the other wide, thus partially reverting to the attitude she has in Deshays's sketches. In this last sketch of Boucher's, however, she no longer ascends, but sits, while again looking downward as in the first sketch, thus further accentuating the iconography of the Glorification, as opposed to that of the Assumption. In a pen drawing in the Albertina (fig. 190; AA 654, fig. 114; AA 653, fig. 113 gives every sign of being merely a copy, and bears the quite impossible date of 1738)—which would appear to have been executed around the same time, without being part of the process of composition, since it plucks features at random from all the sketches, both those by Boucher himself and those by Deshays—the introduction of part of a crescent moon

297

Bullion (Constantin & Le Jeune), 6 Dec. ff. 1787, lot 43: "L'assomption de la Vierge. Esquisse terminée, agréablement composée. Hauteur 47 pouces, largeur 27 pouces"; or *Catalogue de Tableaux des Trois Ecoles . . . &c., appartenans à M. DE WAILLY, Architecte du Roi, &c.*, son logis, rue de la Pépinière, Faubourg Saint-Honoré (Paillet & Julliot *fils*), 24 Nov. ff. 1788, lot 50: "Deux Esquisses, toutes deux représentant l'Annonciation [*recte* l'Assomption?]. Sur T. 4 pieds de haut sur 2 de large" [sold with two other pictures in lot to Jolly for 30 livres 3 sous]; and then ?Marcille sale, 12–13 Jan. 1857, lot 4 or lot 9; R.T.G. Paterson bequest to the National Gallery of Scotland in 1955.

ANALOGIES

1. The second colored sketch, now measuring 112 × 61 cm, whose prior history is impossible to disentangle from that of the present one, and which was left by Anthelme and Edma Trimolet to the Musée des Beaux-Arts de Dijon in 1878 (fig. 189).

2. Sketch *en camaïeu brun*, now measuring 140 × 71 cm, Deshays's posthumous sale, 26 Mar. ff. 1765, lot 122: "L'Assomption de la Vierge, Esquisse en grisaille, sur toile, de quatre pieds quatre pouces de haut, sur deux pieds trois pouces de large" [bought by de Wailly for 15 livres 19 sous]; de Wailly sale, 24 Nov. ff. 1788, lot 50 [one of a pair of sketches carelessly identified as for an *Annunciation*, see above]; H. D. sale, Paris, 14 June 1946, lot 28.

3. Sketch with twelve figures [i.e., including all the Apostles?], [Baillet], baron de Saint-J[ulien] sale, 14 Feb. ff. 1785, lot 95: "L'Assomption de la Vierge, composition de douze figures; esquisse terminée. Hauteur 4 pieds et demi, largeur 30 pouces. Toile."

4. Colored sketch, 112 × 60 cm, [Hurault] sale, Paris (exp. Féral), 19 Feb. 1874, lot 1 [bought in by Eugène Féral]; by descent to Jules Féral (exh. cat. 1932, Paris, no. 5).

turns her into an *Immaculata*. The Madonna in the red-chalk "première pensée d'une *Assomption*" formerly in the collection of Henry Pannier (Nolhac, 1925, pl. facing p. 192), is also clearly an *Immaculata*, although it is just possible that this was the initial design in the series.

It seems very curious, not only that there should have been this wealth of activity, with sketches that are themselves almost the size of altarpieces for a domestic chapel, but also that no finished picture should have resulted from them. No other work by Boucher was prepared in this way. Yet the sketches are too richly painted to have been abandoned *ébauches*. One could almost imagine that the Dijon sketch was a half-completed picture—quite finished but very free in the lower half, and only sketched in (and crudely "completed" subsequently, thus accounting for its defects) in the upper half. It is much more probable, however, that all the sketches are studies for an altarpiece of notable dimensions. And there still remains the puzzle as to why all three sketches should have been in Deshays's possession when he died.

This mystery it does not seem possible to resolve, and it is only possible to put forward hypotheses as to the intended function of these sketches. One possibility would be that they were preparations for some further manifestation of piety on the part of Mme de Pompadour (see cat. 57); her death in 1764 would then have accounted for the sketches having been put up for sale a year later, without any use having been made of them. Another and more arguable possibility is suggested by de Wailly's apparent eagerness to own these sketches.

Charles de Wailly was the architect who was entrusted with the reconstruction of the Lady Chapel in Saint-Sulpice, which was finally carried out in 1774. This was necessitated, however, by something that had occurred much earlier—the damage caused to the chapel by the fire that destroyed the Foire Saint-Germain in 1762. Before the fire, the altar of the Lady Chapel had been occupied on special feast days by a life-size statue of the Virgin in silver, modeled by Bouchardon, popularly known as *Notre-Dame-de-la-vieille-vaisselle* because the silver was supposed to have been obtained from the dishes that the fund-raising curé, Languet de Gergy, had eaten from and subsequently made away with whenever he was asked to dine; and for the rest of the year by a painted substitute by Chevalier (Lemesle, 1931, p. 36). This simulacrum appears to have been destroyed in the fire. It was ultimately replaced by Pigalle's *Immaculata* (1754–74) in an altar redesigned by de Wailly, which took concealed lighting from the lantern built out over his remarkable *trompe*. It would seem eminently possible that, before arriving at this bold solution, de Wailly had considered a more conventional altar with a painted altarpiece. The fact that the chapel already contained four canvases of the *Life of the Virgin* by Carle Vanloo and that the vault was decorated with a fresco of the *Assumption* painted by Lemoine (itself damaged in the fire and subsequently restored by Callet) would naturally have suggested that the altarpiece should be a *Glorification of the Virgin* such as Boucher finally arrived at in his sketches, or an *Immaculata* such as Pigalle finally sculpted.

That this hypothesis is not pure speculation is suggested by a little-noticed passage in the correspondence between Cochin and Marigny (Furcy-Raynaud, 1903/04, II, p. 88). At the end of a very long letter thought to be datable to October 1766, in which Cochin recounted to Marigny how he had gotten Bachelier and de Loutherbourg to settle their differences over the former's accusation that the latter had attempted to wrest his studio from him, he added a note about how he had used the occasion to get Bachelier to make amends to Boucher for a fault that he had also inadvertently committed: "Mr. Boucher was under the impression that he [Bachelier] had made deliberate moves to rob him of the commission for a picture that he was to have made for Saint-Sulpice. Mr. Bachelier assured me that he had known nothing of this commission being promised to Mr. Boucher . . ." ("*M. Boucher avoit dans l'idée qu'il [Bachelier] avoit sciemment fait des démarches pour lui enlever un tableau qu'il devoit faire pour Saint-Sulpice. M. Bachelier m'assura qu'il n'avoit point sçu que ce tableau était promis à M. Boucher . . .*").

Cochin does not name the subject of the picture, and his wording rather implies that Bachelier's *démarches* had not been crowned with success. For this reason—and also because it would surely have been too long before for Boucher to have taken undeclared umbrage over it—this did not concern the vast experimental painting in encaustic of the *Resurrection* destined for Saint-Sulpice, which Bachelier exhibited in the Salon of 1759, and over which Diderot counseled him: "Go back to your tulips!" ("*M. Bachelier, mon ami; croyez-moi, revenez à vos tulippes*" [see Diderot, 1975, pp. 47, 67; it is not clear if, after the chorus of condemnation it aroused, it was ever actually installed despite certain indications that it was, see Malbois, 1926, pp. 115–19]). No other picture is known to have been painted by Bachelier or anyone else for Saint-Sulpice around 1766, so it seems most probable that the disputed commission did concern an early and unexecuted project for a new altarpiece for the Lady Chapel. Possibly Boucher had intended to pass the commission and his ideas on to his son-in-law Deshays, whose aptitude for this kind of painting was generally recognized. Only further research in the archives relating to Saint-Sulpice, or the researches into de Wailly currently being undertaken by Mlle Monique Mosser, might one day produce the answer as to why Boucher should have produced three large sketches of the *Assumption,* and why two of them appear to have been acquired by the architect.

# 77 | *St. Peter Attempting to Walk on the Waters*

Oil on canvas
92½ × 67 in. (235 × 170 cm)
Signed bottom left: *Boucher / 1764*
Cathédrale de Saint-Louis, Versailles
A & W 579

PROVENANCE
Sacristy of Saint-Louis, Versailles (by 1779); ?seized in 1793 and placed in the Muséum Central du département de Seine-et-Oise in the former palace of Versailles; returned to the church in 1802 (?); now hung in the Chapel of St. Peter in the north aisle.

It is one of the singular facts about Boucher's career that, despite his professed ambition to work on a large scale, and notwithstanding his production of a substantial number of drawings devoted to religious themes, he passed up one of the major opportunities for doing so—to wit, the production of altarpieces—until almost the end of his life.

After he had renounced any ambition (no doubt for want of clients) to paint large old-master-like compositions on Old Testament themes, such as

DRAWINGS

1. *Notre Seigneur* and *S. Pierre sur les eaux*, black chalk, two in a lot of four drawings in Boucher's posthumous sale, 18 Feb. ff. 1771, lot 376 [sold for 24 livres 1 sol].

2. *S. Pierre sur les eaux, composition différente du précédent*, Boucher's posthumous sale, 18 Feb. ff. 1771, lot 377, with five other drawings [bought by Chereau for 25 livres 1 sol].

3. *?Composition de deux figures principales qui paroissent des Etudes pour un Tableau de la Pêche miraculeuse* [John 21:1–14, frequently confused with Matthew 14:24–33, because in it St. Peter also casts himself into the water; conceivably identifiable with the drawing in lot 377 of Boucher's sale], black chalk heightened with white on blue paper, 10½ *pouces* by 12 *pouces*, posthumous sale of de Sireul, 3 Dec. ff. 1781, lot 176 [bought by Payant for 6 livres].

4. *?Une Etude en petit d'une figure de Saint Pierre*, black and white chalk on blue paper, 8 *pouces* by 6½ *pouces*, posthumous sale of de Sireul, 3 Dec. ff. 1781, lot 201 [conceivably identifiable with one of the two studies in lot 376 of Boucher's sale].

Fig. 191. *St. John the Baptist in the Wilderness.* The Minneapolis Institute of Arts.

the *Sacrifice of Gideon* (cat. 6) and *Moses before the Burning Bush* (cat. 14), his only large-scale religious compositions revolved around the essentially domestic motif of the Holy Family (see the remarks of Antoine Bret, 1771, pp. 52–53; A & W doc. 1082), together with a small altarpiece of *St. John the Baptist in the Wilderness* (fig. 191). The latter (see Slatkin, 1975) was for the funerary chapel acquired by Mme de Pompadour for her daughter and herself in the Eglise des Capucines, and many of Boucher's other sacred pictures were for her as well: the *Lumière du Monde* (cat. 57) for the chapel in Bellevue, the large *Rest on the Flight* now in the Hermitage (cat. 68), and the little *Infant Jesus Giving His Blessing to the Infant St. John* now in the Uffizi (A & W 503).

Then suddenly, in the last decade of his life, he painted a number of large sketches of the *Assumption* for an unknown destination (cat. 76), and the present *St. Peter Walking on the Waters* and an undated *St. John the Baptist Preaching* for the then parish church of old Versailles (A & W 562). His name is, however, conspicuously absent from among the six artists invited to contribute altarpieces to the recently completed church in 1761, despite the presence among them of his own pupil and son-in-law Deshays (see *L'Avant-Coureur*, 16 Feb. 1761, pp. 106–07, cited in A & W II, p. 222). Nor was his name added to the roll with that of Nöel Hallé (see *L'Avant-Coureur*, 25 May 1761, p. 328, cited in A & W II, p. 222). And despite the dating of the present picture to 1764, and the probably similar dating of the *St. John the Baptist Preaching*, they are not recorded in either Piganiol de la Force's *Description Historique de la Ville de Paris et ses environs* in 1765 or Hébert's *Dictionnaire Pittoresque et Historique* in 1766, nor even in the 1768 edition of Dezallier d'Argenville's *Voyage Pittoresque des Environs de Paris*, but only in the 1779 edition of the last (p. 140).

It is easiest to propose a sequence of events in the case of the *St. John the Baptist Preaching*. St. John was the name-saint of *Jeanne*-Antoinette, marquise de Pompadour (hence the painting of him in her chapel in the Capucines), and it therefore seems likely (since there was already a *St. John the Baptist Baptizing Christ* by Amedée Vanloo among the altarpieces commissioned in 1761) that this was her personal contribution to the church, in keeping with the newfound devoutness that she began to manifest after the death of her daughter in 1754, and prior to being named *dame du palais de la Reine* in 1756 (see Argenson, IX, pp. 195–203). The gift may well have been an embarrassment to the church authorities, but one from which they were soon released by her death. After a decent interval the picture could be put up, without any need to acknowledge the donor.

Can such an explanation be stretched to account for the *St. Peter Walking on the Waters* too? The date attached to the signature is the same as the year of Mme de Pompadour's death. There is, as has been said, no record of the picture's having been commissioned, and there is no sign of its having been installed until 1779. When it was, it was in the sacristy, which suggests that its originally intended location, surely as an altarpiece, was no longer available (that could not however have been in the chapel dedicated to St. Peter, since Deshays's *St. Peter Delivered from Prison*—opposite which it now hangs— had occupied this position since 1761). Yet there seems no particular reason for connecting a picture of this subject with Mme de Pompadour. An addition was built onto the church in 1764, Trouard's Chapelle des Catéchismes (see Gallet, 1976, pp. 205–06, fig. 3), but this was not intended

to have a painted altarpiece, and the subject would anyway have been inappropriate.

There is one institution with which this subject has a special connection, and that is the papacy. For St. Peter attempting to walk on the water is the subject of Giotto's mosaic known as the *Navicella,* which was regarded as sufficiently important to be transferred from the portico of Old St. Peter's in Rome to that of the New. The two main figures in this mosaic, Christ and St. Peter, inspired those of the Baroque reaffirmation of the theme in the heart of the basilica, Lanfranco's altarpiece (subsequently replaced by a copy in mosaic) on the northwest pier altar. It is therefore particularly striking that the composition of Boucher's picture should be indebted to Lanfranco's (which he would have known through the engraving of it by Gérard Audran). This may simply have been a case of the artist needing guidance for the iconography of the theme, which had gone almost undepicted in France, but it may have had greater significance than that. The reason for the scarcity of representations of it in France was that its message was ultramontane, a reinforcement of the claims of the popes as the successors to St. Peter.

It is hard to discover any political reason for such a picture having been commissioned from the chief court artist at this date, just as the expulsion of the Jesuits was reaching its conclusion (though it is true that the initiative in this was taken by the Parlements rather than the king). There may, however, be a reason connected with Saint-Louis itself. At this date it was only a parish church. According to information kindly supplied by Nicole de Blic of the Services d'Archives d'Yvelines, when Versailles was designated the seat of a constitutional bishop in 1790, popular opinion made Notre-Dame-de-Versailles his cathedral. After the restoration of the cult, however, a synod of diocesan clergy in 1796 chose Saint-Louis as the seat of the new bishop; following the Concordat, it was there that his successor was enthroned in 1802, and from thence forth it remained the cathedral.

It would require further research to determine when efforts to raise Versailles to the status of a see began, but if they already had in Louis XV's lifetime, one would expect the king to favor the church whose construction and decoration he had himself paid for. In which case, it might not be too speculative to suggest that Boucher's picture was intended to stand for the claims of the papacy, in anticipation of the pope's expected concession of the church's new cathedral status.

## 78 | *The Departure of the Pigeon Post*

Oil on canvas
Oval, 12¾ × 10½ in. (32 × 26.5 cm)
Signed on a stone, bottom right:
*f. Boucher / 1765*
The Metropolitan Museum of Art, New York; Gift of Mrs. Joseph Heine in memory of her husband, I. D. Levy, 1944 (44.141)
A & W 594

Exhibited in the Salon of 1765, under no. 11:
"Quatre Pastorales, dont deux sont ovales";
Mme Geoffrin, Paris; ?anon. sale, Paris (exp.
Laneuville), 29 Feb. 1856, lot 6, as "*La
Colombe messagère. Gravé*"; ?Eugène Tondu
sale Paris, 10 April 1865, lot 14, as "*Le Petit
Messager*. Delicieux tableau du Maître; sujet
gravé"; Sir Anthony de Rothschild, London
and Tring Park (until 1876); the Hon. Mrs.
Eliot Yorke [his daughter], London and Ham-
ble Cliff; her posthumous sale, by order of
Lady Battersea [her sister], Christie's, London,
6 May 1927, lot 26; Wildenstein & Co., Paris
(in 1928) and New York; Mrs. Isaac D. Levy,
New York (exh. cat. 1939, New York, no. 22);
Mrs. Rosetta Devis Heine, New York (exh.
cat. 1942, New York, no. 2); sale of Mrs.
Joseph Heine, Parke-Bernet, New York, 25
Nov. 1944, lot 251 [bought in]; given to the
museum by Mrs. Joseph Heine in 1944.

ENGRAVING
*Le départ du courier*, engraved and published
by J. F. Beauvarlet (J-R 298) with a dedication
to Mme la marquise de Montesquiou and the
following verse:

*Pars! Confident discret! Pars! mais dans le
voyage
Evite et le Chasseur et le cruel Vautour.
Souviens toi que ton sort est de servir l'Amour
Et qu'un baiser d'Agnès est le prix du message.*

Beauvarlet exhibited the drawings that he made
for this and its pendant, *L'arrivée du courier*,
in the Salon of 1769, no. 252, as simply *Deux
pastorales*. They are identifiable thanks to the
drawings made by Saint-Aubin in his copy of
the *livret* (Dacier, I, no. ii, 1909, exh. cat.
1984, Paris, La Monnaie, nos. 37, 147). The
drawings were in his posthumous sale, 13 Mar.
1798, lot 84.

78

Fig. 192. *L'arrivée du courier*, engraved by
J-F. Beauvarlet after Boucher.

It is distinctly surprising to find Diderot breaking off one of his customary
diatribes against Boucher's exhibits in the Salon of 1765, to praise this little
pastoral and its three fellows—all the more so in that he then returns to the
attack, on another picture of exactly the same character, with: "Shall I never
be rid of these damned pastorals?" ("*Ne me tirerai-je jamais de ces maudites
pastorales?*" [Diderot, 1979, pp. 80–82] ). The probable explanation emerges a
little later, when Grimm adds a note to Diderot's description of seven small
landscapes by Vernet, to say that they and the four pastorals were all intended
for a boudoir of Mme Geoffrin (Diderot, 1979, p. 123). Diderot was a
member of Mme Geoffrin's circle, and he would have known that she was the
correspondent of some of the same foreign sovereigns and dignitaries who
were recipients of Grimm's *Correspondance littéraire*, in which his reviews
were circulated. He would scarcely have wanted to run the risk that his
criticisms of works of art commissioned by her might filter back to her (for
equally laudatory praise of Boucher's technique in this set of pictures, see
under cat. 81).

But then it is equally surprising to find Mme Geoffrin commissioning four
such pictures from Boucher, when one considers that it was only a year later

that she was insisting to King Stanislas Augustus of Poland on taking over the supervision of Vien's and Boucher's pictures in the set of exalted classical compositions that he had commissioned for the Royal Castle in Warsaw (Moüy, 1875, pp. 208ff.), a commission that Boucher finally withdrew from, after making innumerable drawings of his allotted subject, *The Continence of Scipio,* because he could not tolerate her constant interference (see exh. cat. 1975, Brussels, no. 74). Not only was Boucher a friend of hers, however, but she also had a weakness for the pastoral, responding warmly to one of the more improbable literary essays in the genre, Marmontel's *La Bergère des Alpes,* and commissioning from Vernet a rather uncharacteristic picture illustrating an episode from it, which was shown in the previous Salon in 1763. On that occasion, Diderot made less attempt to disguise his distaste for the mode, but took care to refer to Mme Geoffrin herself as "femme célèbre à Paris" (see exh. cat. 1984, Paris, La Monnaie, no. 119). When it came to his tenderness toward her commissioning of Boucher's *Pastorales* in 1765, however, all his good work was undone by his editor, Grimm, who tore their little fantasy apart, and accused Diderot of having been so indulgent out of niceness of character, to avoid being entirely negative about Boucher (Diderot, 1979, p. 81).

According to Diderot, Mme Geoffrin's four *Pastorales* formed a sequence, despite the fact they could scarcely have been hung as such, since the first two were oval and the next two rectangular (though their overall dimensions were the same). In the first, shown here, the shepherd attaches his love letter to the neck of a pigeon and bids it fly to his shepherdess across a river. In the second (the picture is lost, but we know its composition from the engraving by Beauvarlet [fig. 192; J-R 300], while a slightly variant rectangular version has been given to the Musée de Versailles, subject to retention of a life interest), she is seen welcoming the bird. In the third (again lost, but its composition is known from an engraving by Bonnefoy [J-R 313]), a variant of the picture previously painted for Caroline Luise of Baden (cat. 72), she reads the letter with a female companion beside a watering trough. Finally, in the last picture (likewise lost, and its composition known only from the engraving by Bonnefoy [J-R 312]), the two lovers are united, and sit under a tree with a faithful dog and favorite sheep.

For the unusually indulgent Diderot (1979, p. 81):

> everything is subtle, delicate, prettily imagined; these are four little eclogues in the manner of Fontenelle. It is possible that the behavior found in Theocritus, or in *Daphnis and Chloé*—simpler, and more naive—would have appealed to me more. Everything that this shepherd couple are doing, mine would have done too; but the moment before they wouldn't have been intending to, whereas these ones knew in advance exactly what was going to happen, and I don't like that—at least, not unless it were much more candidly stated. *(le tout est fin, délicat, joliment pensé; ce sont quatre petites églogues à la Fontenelle. Peut-être les moeurs de Théocrite, ou celles de Daphnis et Chloé, plus simples, plus naïves, m'auroient intéressé davantage. Tout ce que font ces bergers-ci, les miens l'auroient fait; mais le moment auparavant ils ne s'en seroient pas douté; au lieu que ceux-ci savoient d'avance ce qui leur arriveroit, et cela me déplaît, à moins que cela ne soit bien franchement prononcé.)*

The severe Grimm, adopting the knowing man-of-the-world pose normally affected by Diderot himself, cannot refrain from bursting out in an annotation to this (Diderot, 1979, p. 81):

> My god, my dear philosopher, I fear lest all that may still be a trifle false in conception as it is in color. A shepherd and a shepherdess who have succeeded in turning a pigeon into a deliverer of the penny post are dreadfully corrupted—all the more so in that rustic love knows none of the shackles put upon that passion by civil society. . . . I believe that a shepherdess who had so corrupted the morals of a dove to accustom it to this servile and abject role, would have other things to do, when her lover is beside her, than to keep a lamb on her knees. This lot are straight out of French opera. . . . (*Ma foi, mon cher philosophe, je crains que tout cela ne soit encore un peu faux de pensée comme de couleur. Un berger et une bergère qui ont réussi à faire d'un pigeon un facteur de la petite poste sont prodigieusement corrompus, d'autant plus que l'amour champêtre ne connaît aucune des entraves que la vie civile a mises à cette passion. . . . Je pense aussi qu'une bergère qui aurait assez perverti les moeurs de la colombe pour l'accoutumer à cet emploi servile et abject, aurait autre choses à faire, quand son amant est à côté d'elle, qu'à tenir un agneau sur ses genoux. Tous ces gens-là sont de l'opéra français. . . .*)

That these are not real peasants, one does not need to have recourse to the statistics of adult literacy in France in the eighteenth century to ascertain. Nonetheless, it is probable that the theme of pigeons as messengers of love, which is one that occurs several times in Boucher's late works—including once more in this very Salon (no. 14), provoking Diderot to his final exasperated outburst about "ces maudites pastorales"—was one drawn from the sentimental literature of the period (though I am unable to identify a specific source) rather from the stage. A contributory element was no doubt the fact that pigeons/doves were the birds of Venus, the goddess of love.

## 79 | *The Shepherd's Idyll*

Oil on canvas
94½ × 93½ in. (240 × 237.5 cm)
Signed on the fence, bottom right: *f. Boucher 1768*
The Metropolitan Museum of Art, New York;
Gift of Julia A. Berwind, 1953 (53.225.1)
S & M 1463     A & W 654

## 80 | *The Washerwomen*

Oil on canvas
95 × 93 in. (241.5 × 236 cm)
Signed on the fence, bottom right: *f. Boucher 1768*
The Metropolitan Museum of Art, New York;
Gift of Julia A. Berwind, 1953 (53.225.2)
S & M 1751     A & W 655

79

Fig. 193. *The Exchange of Produce*, signed and dated 1768. Kenwood.

Toward the end of his life, as if to disguise the deterioration of his eyesight by the dexterity of his hand, Boucher painted a number of large decorative canvases. Besides the present pair, there is the pair of 1768 now at Kenwood (fig. 193; A & W 651, 652; though the difference of facture between these reveals that *La cueillette de cerises* was left to studio assistants to execute); there are the two *Marches* of 1765 and 1769, from Bergeret's collection, now in the Museum of Fine Arts in Boston (figs. 194, 195; A & W 660, 661; though—as Ananoff and Wildenstein have cleverly demonstrated—the first of these is the enlargement of a picture originally shown in the 1761 Salon); there are the six large mythological canvases of 1769 from the Hôtel Bergeret de Frouville (A & W 670, 671, 674–677), of which two are being shown in this exhibition (cat. 84, 85); and there are the three landscapes of 1769 on the art market in New York (A & W 681–683).

In painting these large decorative canvases, Boucher was in a way returning to the themes and character of the pictures he painted a little after his return from Italy, to the themes of the set of large *Pastorales* formerly in the collection of Edmond de Rothschild (see cat. 27 and figs. 118–20). But whereas

80

PROVENANCE
?Commissioned by the first Roslin d'Ivry for
the Château d'Hénonville, near Beauvais;
Hôtel d'Ivry, [5?] rue de la Baume, Paris; sale
of the baron L. [Roslin] d'Ivry, Galerie
Georges Petit, Paris, 7–9 May 1884, lots 3 and
4; duc de Montesquiou-Fezensac, [?5, rue de
la Baume, Paris]; Mr. Edward J. and Miss Julia
A. Berwind, New York; given by the latter to
the Metropolitan Museum in 1953.

ENGRAVINGS
Etched by E. Champollion, in the same
direction, for the sale of 1884.

COPIES
    1. *La fête du berger*, 156 × 120 cm, misc.
sale, Rouen, 10–11 Mar. 1975, lot 260.
    2. *Les Lavandières*, 72 × 91 cm, Auguste
Sichel sale, Hôtel Drouot, Paris, 1–5 Mar.
1886, lot 178; misc. sale, Paris, 20 Mar. 1959,
lot 6.

the protagonists of the earlier pastorals are primarily portrayed for their rough rusticity—and in one a crude sexual pass is made—in these later pastorals a strong sentimentalizing process has occurred. Greater importance is also given to the landscapes over the figures, which include such stock motifs from Boucher's repertoire as a putto-decorated fountain, a bridge, a distant tower, and crooked wooden fences.

Many of the figures appear to be adaptations from preexistent drawings or paintings. In the *Washerwomen*, the seated companion of the laundress with her child is adapted from a drawing now in the Forsyth Wickes Collection in the Museum of Fine Arts, Boston (fig. 196; A & W fig. 1711), and the standing women and child beside the donkey from a drawing of 1767 engraved by Demarteau as number 168 (J-R 736), which was itself an adaptation of a group in a landscape of 1760 (see A & W figs. 1472–1475).

In *The Shepherd's Idyll*, the standing woman's pose is adapted from one already employed in a painting of 1766 engraved as *La chasse* (A & W 632, whereabouts unstated; a drawing of 1768 derived from this in exh. cat. 1984, New York, Didier Aaron, no. 4), as well as in other instances (A & W figs.

Fig. 194. *The Rest on the Journey*, signed and dated 1765. Museum of Fine Arts, Boston; Gift of the Heirs of Peter Parker.

Fig. 195. *The Return from Market*, signed and dated 1769. Museum of Fine Arts, Boston; Gift of the Heirs of Peter Parker.

Fig. 196. *Seated Woman with Child*. Museum of Fine Arts, Boston; Forsyth Wickes Collection.

1286, 1612–1615); that of the seated woman at the right from a drawing now in the Johannesberg Art Gallery (A & W fig. 1708), which also appears to have been the prototype for a drawing engraved by Demarteau as number 137, *La dormeuse surprise* (J-R 713); while that of the woman seated below her is close (in reverse) to that of the woman exchanging an egg for a bunch of grapes in the picture of 1768 now at Kenwood (A & W 652), and also to that of the shepherdess in the lost picture engraved as *Le goûter de l'Automne* (A & W 394), which was probably of the same year (see cat. 81).

In no case is the correspondence exact. It is evident that Boucher was painting, as contemporary parlance had it, "de pratique"—from imagination and memory. There is indeed every chance that it was one of these two pictures that Sir Joshua Reynolds saw Boucher at work on when he visited him in 1768, when he recorded with dismay: "I found him at work on a very large Picture, without drawings or models of any kind. On my remarking this particular circumstance, he said, when he was young, studying his art, he found it necessary to use models; but he had left them off for many years" (Reynolds, 1959, p. 224). It is clear from Boucher's other late paintings, and from his continuing output as a draftsman, that Boucher was playing Old Father William with the younger artist, but in this particular case we can accept the evidence of Reynolds's own eyes. What is more, by this date the drawings that Boucher dashed off "de pratique" may even have been superior to those that he studied from a model (Diderot, XVIII, 1876, pp. 301–02).

We do not know whom he was painting these large canvases for, but their provenance is highly suggestive. They first appear in the posthumous sale of baron Roslin d'Ivry in 1884, with no indication of where they had come from. Thirion (1895, p. 332) tells us, however, that they came from his *hôtel* in the rue de la Baume—a location that is all the more probable in that the purchaser of the pictures, the duc de Montesquiou-Fezensac, was his son-in-law and succeeded him as owner of the *hôtel,* and may thus have needed to recover the pictures as an element of its decoration. The street was only created in 1858, however, so that the two pictures must have been brought there from elsewhere.

It is most probable that their original location was the Château d'Hénonville, the country estate of the *fermier-général* Roslin d'Ivry, the baron's ancestor. Roslin was the brother-in-law of the abbé de Saint-Non, and we have the evidence of one of the latter's etchings, of *La leçon de lecture à la ferme* (J-R 1576), that Roslin not only owned drawings by Boucher, but kept them at Hénonville, since this is signed: *Saint Non Sc. à Hénonville 1766 Boucher del.* Through the marriage of another of Saint-Non's sisters to P-J-O. Bergeret, as his first wife, Roslin was also a connection of this great patron of Boucher's; it could even be that his desire to have this exceptional-sized pair of canvases was inspired by emulation of the two huge *Marches* that Boucher painted for Bergeret. The spirit of the two pairs of paintings is entirely different—but that probably reflects the Italian-educated taste of Bergeret, as against the more conventional taste for pastorals of Roslin d'Ivry, who is otherwise not apparently recorded as a collector (it is possibly worth noting that the sister of Casimir de Cypierre [see cat. 64] was a baronne d'Ivry, and that one of his daughters was married to Eugène, marquis de Montesquiou-Fezensac). Moreover, these pictures were essentially intended as items of *grande décoration*, and in the very year that they were painted, Roslin d'Ivry was in the midst of great aggrandizement of Hénonville, using the architect J-B-V. Barré (Thirion, 1895, p. 332; Gallet, 1972, p. 141). It may well be, indeed, that they were intended for the salon—anachronistically located by Thirion in the Paris *hôtel*, but most plausibly originally in Hénonville—decorated with the superb set of furniture by L-C. Carpentier that was also sold in 1884 (lot 307): "en bois sculpté et peint en blanc, couvert de tapisseries des Gobelins à larges bouquets de fleurs se détachant en couleurs polychromes sur un fond bleu tendre rehaussé de branches de fleurs executées en bleu, ton sur ton." Somehow the combination seems just right.

# 81 | *L'obéissance récompensée*

Oil on canvas
20½ × 15½ in. (52 × 39 cm)
Signed bottom right: *f. Boucher 1768*
Inscribed in ink on the back of the
canvas: *M. De La Ferté*
Musée des Beaux-Arts, Nîmes
(S & M 1517)       A & W 656

PROVENANCE
First recorded in the Musée de Nîmes in 1840 (Perrot, 1840, I, p. 278, no. 6).

ENGRAVING
*L'obéissance récompensée*, engraved in reverse and published by René Gaillard, with *Le goûter de l'Automne* as pendant, both dedicated to Monsieur Papillon De La Ferté, and advertised in the *Mercure de France* in Dec. 1772 (J-R 1041, 1042).

DRAWING
The extended hand of the boy on a composite sheet of studies of hands, formerly in the collection of David Daniels, New York (A & W fig. 1396B); his sale, Sotheby's, London, 25 Apr. 1978, lot 66 (here fig. 197).

COPIES
1. *Le chien savant*, paper laid down on canvas, *en camaïeu bleu*, 23 × 33 cm, formerly with Cailleux (exh. cat. 1964, Paris, no. 77).
2. Pastel, 60.5 × 43.5 cm, misc. sale, Versailles, 8 June 1974, lot 44.
3. Drawing, signed *J. B. Huet 1768*, misc. sale, Galerie Georges Petit, 15 June 1928 (*Le Gaulois Artistique*, 26 May 1928, illus. p. 239).

Boucher's last years were almost entirely given over to the painting of pastorals and pastoral landscapes. These tend to be of two different kinds: the one, that of large, decorative paintings; the other, that of small-scale works appropriate to a *cabinet de peinture*. His skill with the latter was to avoid the possible consequences of his defective eyesight, and to paint with a breadth that suggests the sketch, but does not leave the impression of something merely unfinished or preparatory. As the review of the 1765 Salon in the *Mercure de France* (Oct. [I], p. 153) said of the pictures for Mme Geoffrin (see cat. 78): "It is hard to imagine what sorcery has been used by an Artist accustomed only to working on a large scale, to bring himself down to this quite different one, without forfeiting a jot of the breadth and freedom of his brushwork." ("*On a peine à concevoir par quelle sorte de magie de l'art, un Artiste, accoutumé a ne travailler que dans le grand, est parvenu à se réduire dans cet autre genre, sans que son pinceau en soit devenu ni moins large ni moins libre.*") Employing forms that he knew well, he could give full rein to the dexterity of his hand, creating the *fouilli[s]* (literally jumble, hodgepodge), that was—according to Watelet and Lévesque (1792, IV, p. 599)—not simply the delight of amateurs, but the very phenomenon responsible for this new piece of artistic jargon.

The present picture, which is one of the most successful of these later pastorals—possibly because it is for our tastes one of the least sentimentalized—may have been painted through the agency of just the kind of amateur whom Watelet and Lévesque blamed for perverting the development of—especially young—artists by their collections of *croquis* and *esquisses* [Watelet & Lévesque, 1792, *sub voces*].

It is hazardous to argue anything from the dedications of engravings, but the precedents of the dedication to the marquis de Marigny, *directeur général*

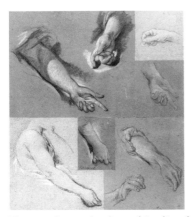

## 81

Fig. 197. Composite sheet of *Studies of Hands*. Formerly in the David Daniels collection, New York.

*des Bâtiments du Roi*, of the engraving after a picture that appears to have belonged to the Crown (J-R 571–572); to Baron Hårleman, *surintendant des Bâtiments* of the king of Sweden, of a picture that may have been destined for the Crown Princess (J-R 1344–1346; but see cat. 53); or to Portail, *garde des Tableaux du Roi*, of a picture that may also have belonged to the French Crown (J-R 1342; Engerand, 1900, p. 45)—all these are possible precedents for stating that the dedication of the engravings by Gaillard after this picture and its pendant, to Papillon de La Ferté, may not have been unconnected with his functions, as enumerated in them: *Intendant et Controleur Général de l'Argenterie, Menus Plaisirs et affaires de la chambre du Roi, et Trésorier Général de la Maison et Finances de Monseigneur le Comte de Provence*. It does not appear that the pictures were on the market, since they appear in no sale; nor is there any evidence that they belonged to Papillon de La Ferté himself (the early ink inscription *M. De La Ferté* on the back of the canvas probably had something to do with the engraving), not merely because ownership of the originals by dedicatees appears generally to have been mentioned, but also because they do not appear in either the inventory of sequestration drawn up by J-B-P. Le Brun after he had been guillotined, in frimaire, l'an III (Nov./Dec. 1794; generously communicated to me by Katie Scott), or in his posthumous sale on 20 February 1797. Nor, for that matter, do any of the landscapes engraved by de La Ferté, purportedly after Bouchers in his own collection (J-R 956–959, and A & W fig. 1150). If the two pictures were neither on the market nor in de La Ferté's own collection, the dedication (which generally presupposed some donation toward the capital cost of making an engraving) may indicate that they were in one of the two collections with which Papillon de La Ferté had some connection: that of the king, or that of his grandson, the comte de Provence (the future Louis XVIII). The king's collections are very well documented, but much less is known of those of his son or his grandson. Whether the comte de Provence would have so far shared the tastes of his grandfather and his treasurer as to own a pair of pictures by the aging Boucher requires further research to determine. There are, in any case, no Bouchers to be found in his manuscript *Catalogue de mes tableaux. 1781* in the Archives Nationales (R5 523; I am most grateful to Philip Mansell for alerting me to the existence of this, and to Marie-Anne Dupuy for consulting it on my behalf).

A peasant girl in an analogous pose, but for the position of her feet, is found in a black-chalk drawing of a *Fisherman and His Companion* in a sale at Paul Graupe, Berlin (17 April 1929, lot 53), and in an oval painting of a similar couple in a landscape, dated 1769, in the Walters Art Gallery in Baltimore (A & W 666).

# 82 | Landscape with a Fisherboy and His Companions

Oil on canvas
19½ × 25½ in. (49.5 × 64.5 cm)
Signed on a rock, bottom right:
*f. Boucher / 1768*, with *PDR* [*Peintre du Roi*] as if incised above
Manchester City Art Galleries (1981.60)
A & W 658 [as a copy]

## PROVENANCE

*Catalogue des Tableaux . . . etc. du Cabinet de M\*\*\** [reputedly the duc de Caylus], rue des Saints Peres, proche la rue Taranne (Remy), 19 Apr. ff. 1773, lot 1: "Deux paysages d'une fraîcheur de teintes agréable, par *François Boucher. . . . Le second tableau a pour objet un jeune pêcheur, une femme assise, et un enfant. Ils sont sur toile, et chacun porte 18 pouces 9 lignes de haut sur 24 pouces de large*" [sold together for 210 livres 19 sous]; sale of Mme X, Galerie Charpentier, 30 Mar. 1935, lot 87 [*not* one of the objects formerly in the collection of baron Carl Mayer de Rothschild], as pendant to lot 86, a landscape of 1765 (A & W 600), but sold separately; René Fribourg; comte Rivaud de La Raffinière, Paris; Mme de X sale, Palais Galliera, Paris, 28 Nov. 1972, lot C; David Carritt Ltd., London; from which bought by the Manchester City Art Galleries in 1981.

Fig. 198. *Landscape with a Watermill*, signed and dated 1768. Ostergotlands och Linköpings Stads Museum.

Many of Boucher's later landscapes are paired ovals, in which the primarily decorative function suggested by the shape (see exh. cat. 1975, Paris, pp. 1–13) seems to have elicited from him some of his less inspired essays in juggling stock motifs. The present picture is, by contrast, one of a pair (the other being in the Östergotlands och Linköpings Stads Museum, Sweden, fig. 198; A & W 657; see for both, exh. cat. 1984, Manchester, P8, 9) in which, while many familiar motifs recur—the round tower and the fisherboy and drover here, the boatsman and the mill in its former pendant—their combination and handling are fresh and delectable. They exemplify the marvelous prose poem on Boucher's landscapes by the Goncourt, which includes the more sober assessment that: "Nature, for him, is a jolly racket. . . . As a landscapist, Boucher's sole preoccupation seems to have been to relieve his age from the boredom of Nature" (*"La nature, pour lui, est un joli tapage. . . . Paysagiste, Boucher ne semble avoir d'autre préoccupation que celle de sauver à son temps l'ennui de la nature"* [E. & J. de Goncourt, 1881, pp. 214–15]).

Since this pair of pictures was in the reputed sale of the duc de Caylus on 19 April ff. 1773, and since the catalogue of the latter's collection drawn up in 1772 reveals him to have owned eight Bouchers (see A & W II, p. 326), it might be supposed that it was because Boucher was painting for a connoisseur of his works that he painted with particular delicacy. The equation is not so easily made, however. In the first place, not one of the pictures in the catalogue of the duc de Caylus's cabinet appears with certainty in his supposed sale (the closest correspondence is between the "Paysanne assise, l'air rêveuse, et tenant dans sa main droite un bouquet de roses" on page 225 of the catalogue of the cabinet, and the "paysanne assise et tenant dans sa main droite une rose," which was lot 3 of the sale catalogue. Quite apart from the discrepancy over the number of roses the peasant girl holds, however, there is also the awkward fact that the picture in the cabinet was apparently rectangular, measured 18 *pouces* by 16, and had no pendant, whereas the one in the sale was oval, measured 16½ *pouces* by 13 and had a pendant of *A Woman Sitting with Her Feet in the Water*). What is more, while the first lot in this sale, including this pair of landscapes, is stated to be by Boucher himself, the second lot, another landscape, is only attributed to him; and the third, the two ovals of women, carries no mention of an artist at all.

Further indications that the sale was not actually his are afforded by the facts that it was held by Remy at an address in the rue des Saints-Pères near the rue Taranne that is not known to have been inhabited by the duke, and

82

that the proprietor kept his anonymity, whereas the catalogues of the duc de
Caylus's collections of antiquities and natural history were published under
his own name by someone else that and the preceding year.

The riddle of these two landscapes' ownership may not be resolvable. More
disconcerting is the fact that two pictures with identical compositions
appeared in a bizarre anonymous sale held the next year, on 17 February ff.
1774. This we know, thanks to the drawings of them by Saint-Aubin in his
copy of the catalogue, now in the John G. Johnson Collection in the
Philadelphia Museum of Art (to the staff of which I am most grateful for a
photograph of the relevant page; fig. 199). The sale was one conducted by the
painter-dealer Paillet, and was prefaced with the surprisingly candid epigraph
from Martial's *Epigrams*: "There are bad ones, there are a certain number of
mediocre ones, and there are many good ones." (*"Sunt mala, sunt quadam
mediocria, sunt bona plura."*) This might have been designed to apply
specifically to the two landscapes, for whereas the first of them (lot 70)—the
description and the drawing of which by Saint-Aubin in the catalogue
correspond to the composition of the picture in Linköping—is described as
being by Boucher himself, the second (lot 71)—the drawing of which by

313

Saint-Aubin corresponds to the composition of the present picture—is merely described as "de l'école de ce Maître." Furthermore, the distinction is reflected in the difference between the prices that they fetched: the autograph work sold to Langlier for two hundred louis, and the school work to an unnamed buyer for seventy-two louis.

Could these pictures really be the same as those in the "Caylus" sale the year before, and could the second of them have been demoted so quickly? To anyone who saw the Linköping and Manchester pictures reunited two years ago, it would be impossible to believe that one was autograph and the other not—indeed, thanks to differences in preservation, the Manchester picture even seemed to have a slight edge over the other. There appear to be two possible explanations. The first, and less plausible, is that—since the height of the pictures in the 1774 sale was given as one-and-a-quarter *pouces* greater than that of those in the 1773 sale, the second pair simply consisted of an autograph and a nonautograph replica of the first. This difference was, however, probably ascribable to more approximate measurement in the second sale, while the coincidence of the two sales (and subsequent nonreappearance of the second pair of pictures) strains belief in such a solution. The other, and more plausible, hypothesis—and one that has the merit of likewise accounting for the divided existence of the "Caylus" pictures at that time and since—is that the buyer of them in the 1773 sale (who may well have been Paillet) had only resold the Manchester picture before the 1774 sale (possibly to a collector who already wanted a pendant for the picture with which it was sold in 1935), and commissioned a copy of it to re-create the pairing for the Linköping picture. In the event, the discrepancy between the two must have been too great to sell them as a pair, so that they were after all sold separately. But for the unusual honesty of Paillet, as suggested by his epigraph to the sale, it is a proceeding of which the sale catalogue would not normally have made us aware: *Caveat lector* is generally as necessary a warning now to the user of eighteenth-century sale catalogues, as *caveat emptor* was at the time.

## 83 | *The Abduction of Proserpine*

Oil on canvas, *en camaïeu brun*
23 × 19 in. (58 × 48 cm)
Signed bottom center: *f. Boucher / 1769*
Musée des Beaux-Arts, Quimper (inv. 873.1.385)
(S & M 220, as *Neptune et Amphitrite*)      A & W 669

PROVENANCE
?*Catalogue de Tableaux . . . &c. provenans du Cabinet de feu M. BARBIER, Peintre de l'Académie de Saint Luc*, Hôtel d'Aligre (Joullain & Graux), 19 July 1779, lot 6: "Neptune & Amphitrite; Esquisse grisaille de forme ovale, par *le même* [Boucher]. Hauteur

It is with considerable pleasure that one views this picture, revealing as it does that the fluency of Boucher's brush was unimpaired in the year before his death. Despite the fact that in this late sketch he produces something halfway between a drawing and a painting, with outlines quickly indicated in dark brown (something that is already observable in the *Venus Rescuing Paris from*

83

21 pouces, 6 lignes, largeur 17 pouces 6 lignes.
Toile"; ?sale of vicomte E. de Plinval, Paris,
14 Apr. 1846, lot 2 [still as *Neptune & Amphi-trite*]; comte de Silguy (1785–1864), Quimper,
by whom bequeathed to the museum [as
*Jupiter et une nymphe*].

*Menelaus* in the Worcester Art Museum, A & W 613), his painterliness is still
evident in the rich application of the chocolate brown medium and the trailed
white highlights over the gray-green ground. The forms of all the bodies and
of the women's faces are rendered with complete assurance, and they are
deftly manipulated into a grouping that sits naturally within the oval; it is
only in giving Pluto's face feature and expression that Boucher's touch
falters—as it always had when faced with the male physiognomy.

It was probably because of the demands of clarity within the restricting
oval that Boucher dispensed both with Pluto's chariot drawn by jet black
horses, and with Proserpine's flower-picking companions (all of which are
found in his Beauvais tapestry of the subject, A & W 345), in this depiction
of the abduction of Ceres's daughter by the god of the underworld. That he is
Pluto (the Hades of the Greeks) is made clear by his bident, or two-pronged
spear, and by the billowing smoke and flames, suggesting the open mouth of
the underworld. The girl resting on the urn represents one of the sea nymphs
known as the oceanids, with whom Proserpine (Persephone in Greek) was

playing when the god abducted her. It could even be that the abduction depicted is of one of the oceanids herself, Leuce, who was turned after her death into the white poplar, but this tale is improbably obscure for the context in which this sketch was in all likelihood created.

It is most plausible—in view of its oval shape—that this represents a first thought for one of a number of oval medallions that Boucher designed for incorporation in ornamental surrounds by Maurice Jacques for weaving by the Gobelins. These formed one of the most successful series to be woven there while Neilson was in charge of a workshop, albeit most of them, as seems always to have been the intention, went to foreign, and more particularly, English, clients (see Fenaille IV, 1907, pp. 263–64). The great advantage of the series for these clients (and for the Gobelins) was that they could order a set of hangings and coverings for a whole room, both walls and furniture, and that the wall hangings created the illusion of framed pictures hung over a damask ground—originally crimson.

Regrettably, the genesis of this series is inadequately documented, but it appears to have been first projected in 1758, when Boucher or his assistants inserted sketches of a rectangular *Triumph of Venus*, flanked by upright ovals of *Pan and Syrinx* and *Arion on the Dolphin*, into an ornamental surround painted by Jacques (cat. 92). Boucher appears to have gone on to execute a large variant oval sketch of the *Pan and Syrinx* for this project (Galerie Cailleux; exh. cat. 1964, Paris, no. 76), but otherwise there was a lull in proceedings, evidently because the Seven Years' War prevented contact with potential English customers. When the idea was taken up again after the Treaty of Paris in 1763, the layout of the tapestry designs was less cramped, with either a single large transverse oval, or a smaller upright one, in the center, or with two of the smaller upright ovals balancing one another at the sides.

The first pair of upright ovals that Boucher actually painted for the Gobelins, for which the canvases were delivered to him in 1763 (Fenaille, IV, p. 229), consisted of the *Vertumnus and Pomona* of 1763 and the *Aurora and Cephalus* of 1764 now in the Louvre (A & W 482, 481), although he did not claim payment for them until 1765, and they were not finally paid for until 1771 (Fenaille, IV, pp. 230–31; A & W docs. 925, 954). At the same time, Boucher supplied models for the large transverse ovals of *Neptune and Amymone* and *Venus and Vulcan* (A & W docs. 926, 950, and nos. 483, 484), although in the event he did not use the oval canvases supplied by the widow Flamant, and these were actually in the form of oblong paintings that were more employable in their own right, and also adaptable to a different form of tapestry, when occasion arose. These were followed by another upright oval, of *Venus on the Waters*, painted in 1766 (Engerand, 1900, p. 55; Fenaille, IV, pp. 231–32, 237; A & W docs. 960, 965, 1003, 1007, 1009, and no. 637/638), which was looted from the Gobelins in 1870 (and is almost certainly identifiable with the painting now in the North Carolina Museum of Art, Raleigh). Finally, two quite different paintings of pastoral themes, originally commissioned by Neilson on his own account, *La diseuse de bonne aventure* and *La pêche*, which were painted in 1767, were turned over to the manufactory for use as large transverse ovals in 1768 (Fenaille, IV, pp. 232, 237; A & W doc. 965, and nos. 640, 641).

These were all the pictures that were used in this Neilson series at the Gobelins in Boucher's lifetime, but more were evidently required, to provide sufficient variety. What appears to have happened first is that a reduced copy of a *Jupiter and Callisto* of 1769 in the collection of the duc de Caylus (now in the Wallace Collection, A & W 668. Could this originally have been painted for the prince de Condé? See Macon, 1903, pp. 128–29) was made to the same size as the *Venus on the Waters* (with which it was looted in 1870, and now hangs as its pendant in the North Carolina Museum of Art), very possibly by Boucher's studio and in his own lifetime. To this was added a *Psyche Examining the Sleeping Cupid* (first woven from in the 1770s) described as a copy in the inventories taken in 1792 and 1794 (Fenaille, IV, p. 239: the occasional ascription of the copy to Belle is probably attributable to the fact that he executed a painting of this subject and a copy of Charles-Antoine Coypel's *Psyche Abandoned* as additions to the latter's set of *Scènes d'opéra* for the Gobelins). This appears in fact to have been a picture worked up from a large colored oval sketch made by Boucher in his latter years (A & W 197: wrongly described as a grisaille and seriously misdated), and originally to have been made by Briard in 1771, for use in a set of four tapestries with Boucher medallions, which served as the *meuble d'hiver* in the *grande chambre* of the Palais Bourbon, that may well be identifiable with the set now in the Louvre (see Macon, 1903, p. 129, and Fenaille, IV, pp. 239, 299). Some years later, the duc de Penthièvre lent his four pictures of the story of *Sylvia and Amyntas* (see cat. 62, 63) to the Gobelins, from which copies were made, and a set of tapestries incorporating them was woven for the Duke of Portland in 1783 (Fenaille, IV, pp. 233, 300).

All this shows that the series continued to evolve for many years after Boucher's death. It is therefore highly probable that he continued to make designs with it in mind, beyond the seven pictures that were used as models for the medallions in his lifetime. It is possible that the reduction of the *Jupiter and Callisto* was prepared under his supervision—and even with his help—for this purpose, even though it was not in fact woven from until several years after his death. The series was variously referred to as *la tenture des Elemens* or *la tenture des Metamorphoses* when it was being prepared (Fenaille, IV, pp. 229–30). The *Jupiter and Callisto* would have fit very well into the latter concept, but the *Abduction of Proserpine* could easily have taken its place in the former, as the element of Fire. Just as the smaller upright oval of *Venus on the Waters* was apparently intended to replace the large transverse oval of *Neptune and Amymone* as the element of Water, when the space available for a tapestry was too small for the latter (Fenaille, IV, p. 236), so the *Abduction of Proserpine* could have taken the place of the *Venus in Vulcan's Forge*. If such was the idea, however, it was probably quickly abandoned, since in the very same year Boucher made use of the pose of Proserpine in the *Boreas Abducting Oreithyia* instead (see cat. 84, 85).

## 84 | *Juno Asking Aeolus to Release the Winds*

Oil on canvas
90 × 79 in. (228 × 201.5 cm)
Signed lower right: *f. Boucher / 1769*
Kimbell Art Museum, Fort Worth
A & W 674

## 85 | *Mercury Confiding the Infant Bacchus to the Nymphs of Nysa*

Oil on canvas
88 × 80 in. (222 × 203 cm)
Signed on rock, center left:
*f. Boucher / 1769*
Kimbell Art Museum, Fort Worth
A & W 676

PROVENANCE
Hôtel Bergeret de Frouville, [3] rue de Vendôme [from 1864 rue Béranger], Paris; this
*hôtel* passed successively through the hands of
Jean-François Bergeret de Frouville (d. 1783);
his daughter, Marie-Charlotte, whose second
husband, Antoine-Jean-Baptiste Hervé d'Arbonne, sold it in 1811 to Gabriel-Louis-Fran-
çois Périer (d. 1815); his son, Amédée-Gabriel
Périer (d. 1838); his cousin Pierre-Louis
Raffard de Marcilly; his widow [?], Eugénie-
Zoé de Marcilly, by whom the *hôtel* was
disposed of to the city of Paris for use as a
school in 1882, and the paintings removed and
sold to a M. Johnson; baron Edmond de
Rothschild, Hôtel de Pontalba, 41, rue du
Faubourg Saint-Honoré; baron Maurice de
Rothschild, 41, rue du Faubourg Saint-
Honoré; looted and taken to the German
Reich in the Second World War, and not
reinstalled after restitution; baron Edmond de
Rothschild from whom acquired via the
Hallsborough Gallery, London, by the Kim-
bell Art Foundation in 1972, with the two
similar-sized paintings from the same set.

DRAWINGS
*Mercury Confiding the Infant Bacchus to the
Nymphs of Nysa*
   1. *Head of Mercury,* engraved in reverse by
Demarteau, no. 412 (J-R 831), without indication of ownership, c. 1773; very possibly the
red-chalk drawing heightened with white in the
sale [of the duc de Rohan-Chabot], 21 July ff.
1777, lot 166; and in the supplement to the [de
Ghendt] sale, 15–22 Nov. 1779, lot 611 (where
described as "touchée avec esprit" and as
measuring 12 *pouces* × 9 *pouces*).

These are two paintings from a set of six of similar dimensions, which
together constitute a larger decorative scheme than Boucher had ever
previously undertaken (save, in some respects, in the ceiling of the *salle du
conseil* at Fontainebleau), despite the fact that he was in failing health and had
only one more year to live when he painted them. Yet there is no record of
them before the end of the nineteenth century, and we have no certain
evidence of by whom or for where they were commissioned.

   They are first mentioned by Alfred de Champeaux in 1891 (p. 412), as
having been removed from the Hôtel de Marcilly, in the street originally
known as the rue de Vendôme, and now called the rue Béranger, in the
Marais in Paris. According to him, they were sold by the last private owner
of the *hôtel,* the comtesse de Marcilly, to a certain M. Johnson (from whom
they must have soon been acquired by baron Edmond de Rothschild for his
*hôtel* in the Faubourg Saint-Honoré, see Dilke, 1899, p. 59), at the same time
as she removed the associated boiseries to her new *hôtel* in the avenue d'Iéna.
The *hôtel* in the rue de Vendôme had only been acquired by the de Marcilly
in the nineteenth century, but an investigation of its previous proprietors
brings to light an interconnecting kin group of patrons through which
Boucher very probably came to execute this exceptional commission (the
history of the house was examined, but these links were not pursued, by
Denys Sutton, in exh. cat. 1982, Tokyo, no. 71; more helpful than the sources
that he cites there is the thorough analysis of the building and its successive
proprietors contained in P. Jarry, 1930, pp. 9–11).

   The former Hôtel de Marcilly (no. 3, rue de Vendôme/Béranger) was
actually an agglomeration of three houses, extending from the rue de
Vendôme around the corner into the rue Charlot. The main building, with its
porte cochere in the rue de Vendôme, had been built about 1720 by the
financier Abraham Peirenc de Moras (who was, with increasing prosperity,
subsequently to build the *hôtel* that now houses the Musée Rodin, in the
more fashionable Faubourg Saint-Germain). This was sold by his son,

2. *Studies for Two Busts of Women*, for the two nymphs at the right, [?] black chalk heightened with white, c. 300 × 365 mm, formerly in coll. of Mme Hector Pétin (A & W fig. 1763).

3. Counterproof of 2, black chalk heightened with white on gray-blue paper, 300 × 365 mm, formerly coll. Georges Plach, Palais Galliera sale, Paris, 3 Dec. 1966, lot 2.

*Juno Asking Aeolus to Release the Winds*
1. Compositional sketch, pen and bister wash, Cayeux sale, 11 Dec. ff. 1769, lot 205 [bought by La Combe for 211 livres]; Collet sale, 14 May ff. 1787, lot 140 (8 *pouces* × 13 *pouces*) [bought by Constantin for 11 livres]; misc. sale (Le Brun & Constantin), 31 May ff. 1790, lot 145 (11 *pouces* × 15 *pouces*); MM. Cailleux, Paris (exh. cat. 1964, no. 53: 245 × 338 mm) [A & W fig. 1756].

2. *Aeolus Releasing the Winds*, black and white chalk on ochre paper, 292 × 200 mm, H. Shickman Gallery, New York (exh. cat. 1968, no. 91).

3. *Study of a Nude Woman Lying on Her Side, Seen from Behind* (used for the oceanid in the foreground), black and white chalk with touches of blue pastel, on orange paper, 280 × 350 mm, Goncourt coll. (engraved by Jules de Goncourt; Goncourt, 1881, I, p. 54), posthumous sale of Edmond de Goncourt, 15–17 Feb. 1897, lot 22; Cabinet des Dessins, Louvre (R.F. 3879) [AA 499, fig. 91; A & W fig. 1440] (fig. 204).

4. *Study of a Nude Woman Supported on Her Stomach and One Leg, with Her Arms Outstretched* (used for the nereid), black and white chalk with touches of red on grayish paper, 270 × 390 mm, Léon Michel-Lévy's posthumous sale, Galerie Georges Petit, Paris, lot 26 [bought by Schoeller]; M.A.G. sale, Paris, 8 May 1934, lot 84; Cotnareau, Paris; Cailleux, Paris; given by Robert H. and Clarice Smith to the National Gallery of Art, Washington, in 1980 [AA 500, fig. 92; exh. cat. 1982, Tokyo, no. 121].

5. *Two Studies of a Nereid*, black and white chalk on yellowed blue paper, 254 × 326 mm, G. W. Lundberg coll., Paris; acquired by the Cabinet des Dessins of the Louvre in 1982 (R.F. 38.983) [exh. cat. 1984, Paris, no. 79] (fig. 205).

6. *Nereid and Oceanid*, black and white chalk on buff paper, 210 × 363 mm, E. Desperet coll., Paris [not in his sale, 7 June 1865]; ?Fletcher Raincock; Sotheby's, London, 13 Dec. 1973, lot 49 [A & W fig. 1754; evidently derived from the painting].

7. ?"Un Dessin aux crayons noir & rouge sur papier gris, représentant une Nymphe de la mer. Elle a le bras droit appuyé sur une tête de Dauphin. Hauteur 11 pouces, largeur 14 pouces," de Sireul's posthumous sale, 3 Dec. ff. 1781, lot 148 [bought by Payane for 10 livres].

François-Marie Peirenc de Moras, to Jean-François Bergeret (later to become Bergeret de Frouville) on 18 April 1768. The remaining two buildings, one on the angle of the rue de Vendôme and the rue Charlot, and the other with a porte cochere on the rue Charlot, had been built by the sculptor Charles Poullain about 1750. These were bought by Bergeret from his son, Charles-Laurent Poullain, also a sculptor and director of the Académie de Saint-Luc, on 23 August 1768.

Jean-François Bergeret was the younger brother of one of Boucher's major patrons in his later years, Pierre-Jacques-Onésyme Bergeret (later to become Bergeret de Grancourt; see G. Wildenstein, 1961, esp. pp. 40, 59–60, no. 40; and in this exhibition, cat. 52). In 1749 he had married Elisabeth de la Haye Desfosses, the daughter of Salomon de la Haye Desfosses (brother of the immensely rich *fermier-général*, Marin de la Haye, who owned not only the Hôtel Lambert, but also paintings by Boucher, including cat. 34, 35 in this exhibition) and the sister both of Charles-Marin de la Haye—who was probably the M. de la Haye who owned so many of the drawings by Boucher that were engraved by Demarteau—and of the wife of that other great collector (and amateur engraver) of Boucher drawings, Blondel d'Azaincourt. In buying these three contiguous properties, J-Fr. Bergeret became the direct neighbor of his father-in-law, at what is now number 5, rue Béranger.

It can be seen from all this that, if J-Fr. Bergeret had not himself already been a client of Boucher's (for it is not clear from Georges Wildenstein's reference to his owning two overdoors by Boucher and several pictures of *paysages et architecture* jointly painted by Boucher and Hubert Robert, whether or not these were at Frouville, and so had been painted for his father from whom he only inherited the estate in 1771), he was at the center of a kin group of some of the artist's most supportive patrons. In view of this, and in view of the fact that he had just acquired the houses in the rue de Vendôme in 1768, it seems highly probable that this set of pictures was painted in 1769 for, and descended with, the Hôtel Bergeret de Frouville.

Less certain is the truth of de Champeaux's assertion that Mme de Marcilly had, when removing the fittings of the *hôtel* on its purchase by the city of Paris for use as a school in 1882, broken up the salon to keep the boiseries for herself, while selling the paintings. From his description of the boiseries and chimneypiece, and from Paul Jarry's illustrations of them (1930, pls. 36–37), it seems highly improbable that the Bouchers should ever have been inserted into so very Louis Seize a setting, whose remnants, furthermore, betray no sign of ever having made any provision for inset paintings. On the other hand, the curvilinear frames shown around the *Boreas Abducting Oreithyia* and the *Mercury Confiding the Infant Bacchus* in de Nolhac (1907, pls. facing pp. 90, 96) were evidently fitted to them in the Hôtel de Rothschild, since the illustration of *Mercury Confiding the Infant Bacchus* included by Lady Dilke (1899, pl. facing p. 60) shows the picture not only without the frame, but also without the additions to the top and bottom of the canvas that this necessitated. In view of the composite nature of the Hôtel Bergeret de Frouville, and of the fact that J-Fr. Bergeret did not die until 1783, there seems no reason why it should not have contained both a more Louis Quinze room incorporating the Bouchers, and another with the Louis Seize boiseries.

The earliest accounts of these pictures describe them as cartoons for tapestries, an error that is to be explained not only by their broad decorative

Fig. 200. *Venus at Vulcan's Forge*, signed and dated 1769. Kimbell Art Museum, Fort Worth.

Fig. 201. *Boreas Abducting Oreithyia*, signed and dated 1769. Kimbell Art Museum, Fort Worth.

Fig. 202. *Aurora and Cephalus*, signed and dated 1769. The J. Paul Getty Museum, Malibu.

Fig. 203. *Venus on the Waters*, signed and dated 1769. The J. Paul Getty Museum, Malibu.

handling, but also by the similarity of some of their subjects and compositions to tapestries for which Boucher had supplied pictures. The full set of paintings comprises, in addition to the pair shown here, another two of identical dimensions and in the same museum, representing *Venus at Vulcan's Forge* and *Boreas Abducting Oreithyia* (figs. 200, 201), and two narrower canvases of the same height, representing *Aurora and Cephalus* (described by Lady Dilke as "the inappropriate slumbers of *Un Berger endormi*") and *Venus on the Waters,* which appear to have been installed, not in baron Edmond de Rothschild's *hôtel* in the Faubourg Saint-Honoré, but in his château at Boulogne-sur-Seine, hence their having been sold separately at auction, to end up in the J. Paul Getty Museum in Malibu (figs. 202, 203; A & W 670, 671).

Fig. 204. *Study of a Nude Woman Lying on Her Side, Seen from Behind.* Cabinet des Dessins, Louvre.

Fig. 205. *Two Studies of a Nereid.* Cabinet des Dessins, Louvre.

*Venus at Vulcan's Forge* was one of Boucher's best-tried themes (see cat. 17, 67), as was *Venus on the Waters*, and their compositions are very similar to previous depictions of the subject by him. *Aurora and Cephalus* he had also portrayed on a number of occasions (cat. 18 in this exhibition; A & W 161, 481, but not 291, which is by another hand altogether), but *Boreas Abducting Oreithyia* only once before, as a tapestry for Beauvais (A & W 349). In this repetition of the theme, however, Boucher did not go back to his previous depiction of it for inspiration, but to his sketch of Pluto abducting Proserpine (cat. 83), from which he took the pose of Oreithyia.

In regard to the subjects of the two pictures shown here, Boucher had already depicted *Mercury Confiding the Infant Bacchus to the Nymphs of Nysa*, in the early picture painted for Derbais that is now in the Wallace Collection (fig. 39; A & W 106). Not surprisingly, with such a lapse in time, there is no compositional similarity between the two, despite the fact that as recently as 1767 Boucher had drawn on the Derbais composition when making a drawing to be engraved by Saint-Aubin for an edition of Ovid's *Metamorphoses* (J-R 1561). Again, Boucher would seem to have borrowed the essentials of the chief figure, the nymph holding the infant Bacchus, from what appears to have been a late picture of quite a different subject, *Cupid Teasing Venus at the Bath*, which (if it was ever executed) is known from a preparatory drawing by Boucher himself and a miniature by Charlier (A & W figs. 622, 623), as well as from a variant large-scale sketch in oil (A & W 198), which may be all that was ever produced.

The story behind the episode is that Bacchus had been fathered by Jupiter on Semele, and rescued from the flames that consumed the already pregnant princess when she had rashly asked the god to come to her in his full majesty. After completing his gestation sewn up in Jupiter's thigh, the infant Bacchus was taken by Mercury to the nymphs of Nysa, to be brought up out of the range of Juno's jealous rage. It was at Nysa, whose location is much disputed, that Bacchus discovered how to make wine—hence the cupid clutching grapes, and the other two bearing aloft the vine-entwined, pinecone-tipped staff, or thyrsus, with which he was to lead his wine-drunk following of satyrs and maenads. The goat stands for the fact that, in some accounts, Mercury was smuggled to the nymphs in this disguise.

*Juno Asking Aeolus to Release the Winds* was not a subject that Boucher had previously painted. He had, however, evidently contemplated it before—possibly for a tapestry in view of the format—since the two chalk drawings that have been associated with this composition ([1] black chalk, 226 × 293 mm, formerly A. Mos collection, sold R.W.P. de Vries, Amsterdam, 2 Nov. 1928, lot 117; Christie's, London, 6 July 1977, lot 93; [2] red chalk, 255 × 325 mm, Hôtel Drouot, Paris, 29 Oct. 1980, lot 67; Christie's, London, 3 Apr., 1984, lot 81 [the relationship between the two is somewhat baffling, and—without having seen either—impossible to pronounce on]) not only bear no relation to it, but are also manifestly earlier in date. It is even possible that they are studies for a horizontal painting with a slightly different subject, *Vénus implorant le secours d'Eole contre Télémaque*, an oil sketch for which was in Chardin's posthumous sale, 6 March ff. 1779, lot 12. On the other hand, the wealth of drawings that can be legitimately associated with the present composition is evidence of how thoroughly Boucher prepared this unfamiliar subject, and again belies the report given currency by Sir Joshua Reynolds (see cat. 79, 80) that he did not make studies from the life in his later years. The status of the drawings is not always straightforward, however, since some of them are clearly worked up from the painting, or from genuine studies for this, rather than the other way about.

The episode of Juno coming to Aeolus to ask that he release the winds stands at the beginning of the *Aeneid*. Pitiless in her detestation of the Trojans, even after their final defeat by the Greeks and the destruction of Troy (partly because she had never forgiven the Trojan prince Paris for giving Venus rather than her the prize for beauty), she was determined to prevent them from setting sail under the leadership of Aeneas to found a new kingdom in Italy. Aeolus, who was not a god, had been given charge of the Winds (which he kept locked in a cave on Lipara) and admitted by Jupiter to the feasts of the gods, at Juno's suggestion. Hence his readiness to do her bidding. Neptune, however, regarded the creation of storms at sea as his prerogative, and was to rescue Aeneas by threatening the Winds with his vengeance ("Quos ego . . ."), and calming the waves—here symbolized by the nereid and the oceanid. The young woman seated below Juno is the fairest of her attendant nymphs, Deiopea, whom the goddess offered Aeolus in marriage as an additional inducement to do her bidding.

# Boucher as a Tapestry Designer

EDITH A. STANDEN

The year 1734 was an important one for Jean-Baptiste Oudry; he became codirector of the tapestry manufactory at Beauvais, where he had been working as a designer since 1726. He was under contract to provide eight full-size cartoons every three years. But he had an even more demanding task at the time for the Gobelins manufactory, designing the huge tapestries of the *Chasses royales;* in July 1734, the original order of three scenes was enlarged to five. It is clear that he needed another artist to fulfill his obligation to Beauvais.

François Boucher, home from Italy, was at the meetings of the Académie Royale de Peinture et Sculpture on 24 November 1731 and 30 January 1734, when his reception picture was accepted. Oudry was not present on either occasion; he seldom attended meetings of the Académie. But both artists had exhibited at the "Exposition de la Fête-Dieu" in 1725, and Boucher had already begun to make a name for himself. Oudry was right when he decided that this young man was capable of designing on a very large scale; it was probably in 1734 that he chose Boucher as the person to supply the twenty-eight running ells *(aunes de cours)* of paintings that had to be provided for the Beauvais looms. The first Boucher-designed tapestries, three pieces of the series known as the *Fêtes Italiennes,* are recorded in the *régistres de fabrication* as woven in 1736.

For the next thirty-five years the manufactory produced primarily tapestries after Boucher; records of many years in the 1740s and almost all through the 1750s show no wall hangings made after any other artist. Without the six series Boucher designed between 1734 and 1755, the words "Beauvais tapestries" would have a very different connotation; the French Rococo, indeed, would be deprived of its grandest achievement. One could as well imagine Venetian eighteenth-century painting without the ceilings of Tiepolo.

The *régistres* give fourteen titles for the pieces that make up the *Fêtes Italiennes,* but a document of 1754 shows that Boucher provided two sets of four paintings.[1] The extant tapestries do, in fact, fall into two groups. In one, the four compositions of the *Opérateur* and the *Curiosité* (always woven together), the *Bohémienne* (also called the *Bergère*), the usually combined *Chasseurs* and *Filles aux raisins,* and the *Pêcheuse* were all woven at least once by 1739; the other four, the *Collation* (also called the *Cabaretier*), *Jardinier, Danse,* and *Musique,* were none of them woven before 1744. Two narrow pieces were only woven once, in 1762, long after Boucher had stopped working for Beauvais.[2]

The first four tapestries are full of reminiscences of Italy, as are Boucher's paintings of the early 1730s—umbrella pines, shattered columns, fragments of classical sculpture. The ruined temple and fountain of the Munich *Halte à la fontaine* (see cat. 27) are found again in the *Pêcheuse;* could Oudry have seen this painting and asked for four tapestry designs like it, only larger? The people, also like those in the paintings, are mostly only slightly idealized peasants. In the second group of four tapestries, the Italian ruins have almost

1. Weigert, 1933, p. 232.
2. Standen, 1977[b], pp. 110–13.

Fig. 206. *La toilette de Psyché*, Beauvais
tapestry. Palazzo Reale del Quirinale, Rome.

disappeared, the people have become young gentlefolk and are even waited
on by servants, like the picnickers of the *Collation*. All the scenes are well
designed for reproduction in wool and silk; there must be no large plain areas
in tapestries, which quickly become mere stretches of cloth to the viewer, and
the details, though lively, must not detract from the main figures nor be seen
purely as pattern.

The only set of more than five pieces of the *Fêtes Italiennes* that has
remained together is that in the Metropolitan Museum, eight panels made for
the Château de Gatellier in 1762 (see cat. 87–89). Photographs of the room in
which they hung show that they were set into boiseries and so had no
borders. The largest single piece known is in the Philadelphia Museum of
Art; it combines the *Opérateur, Curiosité, Filles aux raisins,* and *Chasseurs*; it
has the arms of Rohan-Soubise, like two more panels owned by the prince de
Ligne at Beloeil, Belgium. There is a set of five in the Palazzo Venezia, Rome,
perhaps the one made for Président Masson in 1739, and another in the
Huntington Library, San Marino, California. Many other tapestries of the
series are in public and private collections or have appeared in sales, so that a
fair proportion of the approximately 120 pieces in about thirty sets that are
listed in the *régistres* are known to exist.

The only weakness of the *Fêtes Italiennes* is some incoherence in the
compositions. Boucher apparently supplied paintings of groups of people
with suitable backgrounds; these could be woven separately or variously
juxtaposed according to the desired dimensions of each tapestry. The singers,
who are always on the far right of the *Opérateur,* seem to have come from
another setting, perhaps *Musique* or *Danse*. On wide versions of the latter are
a Savoyard, a pedlar, and some customers who would be much more suitably
placed in the country fair of the *Opérateur*. A painting, *The Little Pedlar* at
Gray (cat. 37), has been identified as a cartoon and may represent one of
Boucher's original groups.

Boucher's next series for Beauvais consists of five episodes in the story of
Psyche. Again the tapestries are of different sizes, but the figures added to the
wider versions are in keeping with the compositions. Two scenes, the *Arrivée*

and the *Richesses*, take place in the most stupendous baroque palace imaginable, and even the garden of the *Toilette* (fig. 206) has a largely architectural setting. In contrast to these are the rugged cave where Psyche takes refuge in the *Abandon* (an eighteenth-century Englishman would have called the scenery "horrid") and the untamed Nature surrounding the *Vannier*. Large pieces of the series can be some ten feet high and eighteen wide (3 × 5.50 meters); Boucher here shows how magnificently he could design on this scale. The details, so necessary to good tapestry design, are of unsurpassed sumptuosity, but they never compete with the lovely, clearly drawn figures. No tapestries have ever been better designed.

Three pieces of the Psyche series were woven in 1741 and a complete set in 1742, probably the five tapestries in the Philadelphia Museum of Art. The set made for the king of Sweden in 1745 is still in the Royal Palace in Stockholm; the room where it hangs was decorated in 1754 and is the finest place in the world in which to appreciate what Beauvais could do. Frederick the Great bought a set in 1764 that is now split between museums in East and West Berlin. There are other sets of four pieces and a number of single tapestries extant.

Strangely, the series did not do as well as the *Fêtes;* only some ten or twelve sets, less than fifty individual pieces, were made. It may have been very expensive to weave, because it contains so many figures and so few passages that could safely be left to apprentices. Or were prospective customers put off by such overwhelming exuberance, bursting with life and energy? The only purchaser after the king of Prussia was the king of France, whose taste presumably was not consulted. Also, once the neoclassic style had begun to dominate in the late 1760s, these Boucher tapestries probably looked overblown as well as old-fashioned.

At the Salon of 1742, Boucher exhibited "huit Esquisses de differens sujets Chinois pour être exécutez en Tapisseries à la Manufacture de Beauvais"; the entrancing sketches are now at Besançon (cat. 41–44). The full-scale cartoons are described in the manufactory records as made by "Dumont," always identified as Jean-Joseph Dumons, then a tapestry designer at Aubusson. A set of four pieces was woven in 1746. Only six of the designs were used for the tapestry series, and the only complete sets were made for Louis XV in 1758, 1759, and 1767. Otherwise, the sets were from two to five pieces; about fifty panels are recorded. The most famous set is the one that went to China in 1764; some pieces are said to be still in Peking, some went back to Europe after the Boxer Rebellion.[3]

A certain confusion exists in the present state of knowledge of this series. There are the titles in the *régistres de fabrication;* the sketches in Besançon; the Beauvais tapestries, widely scattered and poorly published; and, adding enormously to the general disarray, a vast number of copies and vaguely similar chinoiseries woven at Aubusson. Perhaps these are the work of Dumons, who had so much practice in this type of design. There is a set of six Beauvais pieces in the Palazzo Reale, Turin, and one of five is owned by the Earl of Rosebery (cat. 91); a sixth piece formerly in his collection was not from the same set and was sold in 1978. Individual tapestries are found in a number of collections and sales, including the piece in this exhibition from the Minneapolis Institute of Arts (cat. 90) and several in Copenhagen; these are from the set given by Louis XV to Count von Moltke, a high Danish official, in 1759.

3. Leroy, 1900, pp. 419–27.

A letter of Oudry's dated 12 August 1747 says that Boucher had then finished two tapestries of his next series, the *Amours des Dieux*.[4] The nine pieces of this series are not known to have been woven as a single set; the king took his set of six pieces several times for use as gifts, and customers bought many sets, usually of three or four pieces: at least eighty tapestries are recorded. The number of purchasers drops off, as usual, in the 1760s, though Frederick the Great bought a set in 1765, all but one of which are known to exist. Four of the eight made for Don Felipe, the Infante of Spain, in 1750, are in the Quirinale, Prince Esterházy's set of 1752 was lost in World War II, and two of Baron Bernstorff's order of 1754 are in the Metropolitan Museum. Many more have been identified.

Some of the subjects were never treated by Boucher elsewhere, but others are among the ones he repeated most frequently. The painting of the *Rape of Europa* (cat. 54) in the Louvre that was bought by the king in 1747 has the same main group as the corresponding tapestry, and the *Venus at Vulcan's Forge* is only one in a sequence of representations, from a 1732 painting in the Louvre to one of 1769 in Fort Worth, (see cat. 17, 67; fig. 200). Boucher was quoted as saying that the subject was "une tâche fort attrayante à remplir."[5] But the great Beauvais tapestries, sometimes five meters wide, are his most imposing presentations of the scene.

The *Fragments d'Opéra* is listed as a tapestry series first woven in 1752, but only five titles are named and one of them, the *Castagnettes,* was never woven and probably never existed. Few pieces were made and few have been located. It seems probable that the paintings were ordered primarily to supply extra subjects for *Amours des Dieux* sets when all the cartoons of this series were already in use on the looms. The painting of *Vertumnus and Pomona* (fig. 161) in the Fine Arts Museums of San Francisco consists of five vertical strips, with a horizontal section at the bottom joined together; thus it is presumably the cartoon, which was cut and placed under the warps of the horizontal looms used at Beauvais.

All the *Fragments d'Opéra* are full of echoes of earlier works by Boucher. This is even more true of his final Beauvais series, the *Noble Pastorale*, all five pieces of which were first woven in 1755; a sixth piece, the *Bergère*, woven once in 1769 (impossibly late for a new Boucher design), may have been the *Bohémienne* from the *Fêtes Italiennes*. Some closely related paintings are dated 1748 and may not have been made primarily as cartoons.[6] The scenes are like those of the *Fêtes Italiennes* twenty years earlier: groups of young people in landscapes full of classical temples, sculpture, fountains, and urns. The strange mill at Charenton, built like a bridge over the river, painted by Boucher in 1739 (see cat. 69), reappears in the *Fontaine d'Amour* tapestry, and its pendant, the *Vieux colombier,* in the *Joueur de flûte*. The compositions are incoherent, without rhyme or reason, the groups casually thrown together, and the vitality of the earlier series has disappeared. There are no more peasants and, though all the characters are in lustrous silks, they do not seem as fashionably dressed as the gentlefolk of the *Fêtes Italiennes*. Very little except placid lovemaking is going on; a sense of general languor prevails.

Beauvais had its troubles in the 1750s. Oudry's partner, Nicolas Besnier, retired at the end of 1753, and his successor, André-Charlemagne Charron, who took over early in 1754, was faced with the disaster of Oudry's death a year later. This meant the loss of Boucher as well. A note by Charron has survived that mentions Oudry's death as the moment when "M. Boucher

4. Böttiger, 1898, p. 96.
5. A & W doc. 920.
6. Townsend, 1940, pp. 84–86.

Fig. 207. *Le Lever du Soleil*. Wallace Collection, London.

Fig. 208. *Le Coucher du Soleil*. Wallace Collection, London.

refusoit des tableaux et ou la manufacture couroit le risque de le manquer."[7] Oudry had also been *surinspecteur*, cordially hated, at the Gobelins manufactory, and the post was immediately given to Boucher; the marquis de Marigny, *directeur des Bâtiments*, in charge of all the royal manufactories, wrote to him, "Vous sentés bien que je comte sur vos ouvrages pour cette manufacture."[8]

Two of Boucher's most radiant paintings, in fact, had already been made as cartoons for Gobelins tapestries, the *Lever* and *Coucher du Soleil* of 1752, now in the Wallace Collection, London, both over ten feet tall (3.21 meters and 3.24 meters; figs. 207, 208). Cartoons did not have to be cut into strips at this manufactory. The tapestries were made for Marigny's sister, Mme de Pompadour, and must have been among the finest ever woven at the Gobelins, but she soon returned them to the manufactory; in 1768, they were sold, probably to an Englishman, and have never been heard of since. The designs were not woven again.

Boucher made another large painting in 1757, one of four cartoons, the others being by other artists; this was the *Venus at Vulcan's Forge* in the Louvre (cat. 67), in a Gobelins *Amours des Dieux* series. There are tapestries after it in Rome and Baltimore; Vulcan and one of the nymphs are close to their counterparts in the Beauvais tapestry of the same scene. The Gobelins series was not a success; the workshop heads wrote to Marigny of their troubles in 1765, "personne ne voulant faire faire de Tapisserie pour un même salon, d'après plusieurs Maîtres."[9] Boucher also painted one of the large *tableaux d'Enfants*, also in the Louvre, that the artists made to go with the *Amours des Dieux;* it was only woven twice, for Marigny and for his sister.

7. A & W doc. 322.
8. Fenaille, IV, 1907, p. 227.
9. Fenaille, IV, 1907, p. 163.

Fig. 209. Croome Court Room, The Metropolitan Museum of Art, New York; Gift of the Samuel H. Kress Foundation, 1958.

Also considered to be part of this series was another of Boucher's finest works, the painting of the *Génies des Arts* in Angers, which was woven at Marigny's order for his sister in 1761.

These Boucher paintings for Gobelins tapestries were almost all made for two of the most important people in the kingdom and were of little use to the manufactory. There is an incident recorded when Boucher was ordered to perform a trivial task. Marigny wrote to Jean-Germain Soufflot, director of the royal manufactories, on 12 September 1757, about new borders that were needed for two of his sister's tapestries (the *Lever* and *Coucher du Soleil*); he added, "Ma soeur désire que le dessin de ces bordures soit fait par M. Boucher." One can imagine the dismay at the Gobelins. Soufflot was quick to express his zeal and answered that, not trusting the measurements given by Mme de Pompadour's upholsterer, he had been to her *hôtel* to verify them. Then he and Boucher had spent a morning at the Gobelins examining existing tapestry borders; then, "comme c'est affaire d'ornement et que le sieur Jacques [Maurice Jacques, a flower painter attached to the manufactory] le peint fort bien, M. Boucher lui a donné ses idées, et moi les mesures, pour qu'il en fasse une esquisse." Gilded wooden frames were brought to the Gobelins, so that Boucher could pick the most suitable for copying. On 15 July 1758, the borders were being woven and Soufflot wrote that the designs "ont occupé longtemps M. Jacques qui a suivi avec zèle les conseils de M. Boucher et fait avec plaisirs les changements qu'il a pu désirer dans le cours de l'ouvrage." It was also arranged that the king should pay the bill.[10] One senses the uneasiness of the great painter and the great architect when they had to report that the orders of the king's *maîtresse en titre* had not been precisely obeyed.

10. Mondain-Monval, 1918, pp. 61–63, 87.

Boucher had at this time many important commissions, so it is not surprising that his other paintings used at the Gobelins are small sketches and easel pictures. Four of the latter were made just before he was created *premier Peintre* in 1765 and relinquished his position at the Gobelins to Jean-Baptiste Pierre. They were used for the central medallions in the series called the *Tentures de Boucher*, the happiest of all Gobelins inventions, but an at least equal role is played in each large panel by the *alentour* or background; this is usually a brilliant crimson damask pattern, with the wealth of flowers, birds, animals, and trophies that make the series one of the great triumphs of the art of tapestry. Boucher's mythological scenes in the medallions are strong enough to stand out against the competition, playing the part of the saints and shepherds that dominate the millefleur backgrounds of tapestries woven nearly three hundred years before.

The first set of the *Tentures de Boucher*, made for Lord Coventry's house, Croome Court, between 1764 and 1771, is in the Metropolitan Museum (fig. 209). Several others are in the English country houses for which they were commissioned. By the time the second set was woven, another Boucher painting for a medallion was available and, by 1768, Jacques Neilson, a workshop head from 1749 to 1788, then working so hard to supply the milords, had himself bought two more. Long after Boucher's death, in 1783, four paintings of Tasso's story of Sylvia and Amyntas, dated 1755 and 1756, were borrowed by the manufactory to use as new subjects for the medallions (see cat. 62, 63). The *Tentures de Boucher* continued to be woven until long after the arrival of neoclassicism—though for Russia, Germany, England, and Spain, not for France. A panel with Neilson's name and the date of 1788 has the usual rococo *alentour*, but a purely classical border.[11]

Finally, there are the *Enfants Boucher*, a bewildering multitude of small tapestries, mostly upholstery panels, with many related paintings, drawings, prints, and porcelain figurines. No thorough study has been made of these often delightful little pieces. Many bear the name "Neilson," showing that they were woven at the Gobelins, and a 1792 inventory of the manufactory lists "31 petits tableaux représentant des *Jeux d'Enfants*, tant originaux que copies."[12] A large set is found on furniture in the Residenz Museum, Munich. It is sometimes said that the designs were also woven at Beauvais, but there is no convincing evidence for this. The only furniture coverings in the *régistres de fabrication* that can be identified as Boucher's are details from the *Noble Pastorale*.[13]

It is hard now to imagine what a room hung with a new set of *Psyche* or the *Amours des Dieux* must have looked like. Beauvais tapestries are often faded and were not meant to be displayed separately like pictures. But when one stands in the presence of even a few pieces in good condition, they conjure up a world of splendid shapes and colors, never petty, restless, or merely pretty, but always in harmony with the furnishings of the period and the costumes of the people who lived among them.

11. Exh. cat. 1980, New York, no. 21.
12. Fenaille, IV, 1907, p. 405.
13. Badin, 1909, pp. 68–70.

# Appendix

A partial list of public institutions owning tapestries designed by Boucher, not including furniture upholstery and other small pieces, follows herewith as an aid to further research.

Amsterdam, Rijksmuseum. *Foire chinoise*

Baltimore, Walters Art Gallery. *Collation* from *Fêtes Italiennes; Vénus et Vulcain* from Gobelins *Amours des Dieux*

Berlin, East, Schloss Köpenick. *Toilette de Psyché*

Berlin, West, Schloss Charlottenburg. Beauvais *Amours des Dieux*, 4 pieces; *Psyché et le vannier*

Boston, Museum of Fine Arts. *Déjeuner* from *Noble Pastorale*

Brussels, Musées Royaux d'Art et d'Histoire. *Mars et Vénus* from Beauvais *Amours des Dieux*

Cambridge, England, Fitzwilliam Museum. *Apollon et Clitie* from Beauvais *Amours des Dieux*

Chaâlis, Abbaye de. *Musique* from *Fêtes Italiennes*

Chantilly, Musée Condé. *Déjeuner* from *Noble Pastorale*

Chartres, Musée des Beaux-Arts. Beauvais *Amours des Dieux*, 3 pieces

Chicago, Art Institute. *Pipée aux oiseaux* from *Noble Pastorale*

Cleveland, Museum of Art. *Foire chinoise; Joueur de flûte* from *Noble Pastorale*

Compiègne, Palais. *Enlèvement d'Orythié* (fragment) from Beauvais *Amours des Dieux*

Copenhagen, Amalienborg. *Chasse chinoise* (fragment); *Foire chinoise*

Copenhagen, Kunstindustrimuseum. *Ariane et Bacchus* combined with *Jupiter et Antiopé* from Beauvais *Amours des Dieux*

Copenhagen, Rosenborg Palace. *Chasse chinoise* (fragment)

Detroit Institute of Arts. *Richesses* from *Histoire de Psyché*

Leningrad, Hermitage Museum. *Neptune et Amimone* from Beauvais *Amours des Dieux*

Lisbon, Gulbenkian Collection. *Jupiter et Antiopé* from Beauvais *Amours des Dieux*

London, Victoria and Albert Museum. *Bohémienne* from *Fêtes Italiennes*

Los Angeles County Museum of Art. Beauvais *Amours des Dieux*, 3 pieces

Ludwigsburg, Württemberg State Collection. *Tentures de Boucher*, 4 pieces

Malibu, J. Paul Getty Museum. *Jardinier* from *Fêtes Italiennes; Histoire de Psyché*, 4 pieces; *Bacchus et Ariane* combined with *Jupiter et Antiopé* from Beauvais *Amours des Dieux; Tentures de Boucher*, 4 pieces

Minneapolis Institute of Arts. *Foire chinoise; Apollon et Clitie* from Beauvais *Amours des Dieux*

New York, Metropolitan Museum of Art. *Fêtes Italiennes*, set of 8; *Opérateur et Curiosité, Danse* from *Fêtes Italiennes; Vénus et Vulcain, Ariane et Bacchus* from Beauvais *Amours des Dieux; Vertumne et Pomone* from *Fragments d'Opéra; Tentures de Boucher*, set

Osterley Park, England. *Tentures de Boucher*, set

Paris, City of. *Neptune et Amimone* from Beauvais *Amours des Dieux*

Paris, Grand Palais, Tuck Collection. *Richesses* combined with *Toilette de Psyché*

Paris, Musée Jacquemart-André. *Chasseurs* combined with *Filles aux raisins* from *Fêtes Italiennes*

Paris, Louvre. *Tentures de Boucher*, 4 pieces

Paris, Mobilier National. *Mars et Vénus, Vénus et Vulcain* from Beauvais *Amours des Dieux; Vénus et Vulcain* from Gobelins *Amours des Dieux; Tentures de Boucher*, 4 pieces

Paris, Musée Nissim de Camondo. *Pêcheuse* from *Fêtes Italiennes*

Philadelphia Museum of Art. *Opérateur, Curiosité, Filles aux raisins, Chasseurs* combined from *Fêtes Italiennes; Histoire de Psyché,* set; *Pêche chinoise*

Richmond, Virginia Museum of Fine Arts. *Opérateur* with *Curiosité* from *Fêtes Italiennes*

Rome, Palazzo Quirinale. *Histoire de Psyché,* 4 pieces; Beauvais *Amours des Dieux,* 4 pieces

Rome, Palazzo Venezia. *Fêtes Italiennes,* 5 pieces

San Francisco, Fine Arts Museums. *Bohémienne* from *Fêtes Italiennes*

San Marino, Huntington Art Gallery. *Fêtes Italiennes,* 5 pieces; *Noble Pastorale,* 5 pieces

Schwerin, Staatliches Museum. *Neptune et Amimone* from Beauvais *Amours des Dieux*

Stuttgart, Württembergisches Landesmuseum. *Ariane et Bacchus* with *Jupiter et Antiopé* from Beauvais *Amours des Dieux*

Turin, Palazzo Reale. *Tenture chinoise,* 6 pieces

Vienna, Austrian National Collection. *Tentures de Boucher,* set

Waddesdon Manor, England. *Noble Pastorale,* 3 pieces

Washington, Corcoran Gallery of Art. *Psyché conduite par Zéphir*

Washington, Hillwood Museum. *Opérateur* with *Curiosité* from *Fêtes Italiennes; Ariane et Bacchus, Jupiter et Antiopé* from Beauvais *Amours des Dieux*

Washington, National Gallery of Art. *Renaud endormi* from *Fragments d'Opéra*

## 86 | *The Charlatan and the Peep Show*

Wool and silk tapestry (Beauvais)
10 ft. 7½ in. × 13 ft. 8 in. (324 × 417 cm)
Inscribed on rock at left: BOUCHER 1736
The Metropolitan Museum of Art, New York;
The Jules Bache Collection, 1949 (49.7.119)
A & W 128/9

## 87 | *The Gypsy Fortune-Teller*

Wool and silk tapestry (Beauvais)
9 ft. 7 in. × 6 ft. 7½ in. (292 × 202 cm)
The Metropolitan Museum of Art, New York;
Gift of Mary Ann Robertson, 1964 (64.145.2)
A & W 129/6

## 88 | *The Collation*

Wool and silk tapestry (Beauvais)
10 ft. 10 in. × 8 ft. 6 in. (330 × 259 cm)
The Metropolitan Museum of Art, New York;
Gift of Mary Ann Robertson, 1964 (64.145.3)
A & W 135/5

## 89 | *The Gardener*

Wool and silk tapestry (Beauvais)
9 ft. 2½ in. × 6 ft. 1 in. (281 × 185 cm)
The Metropolitan Museum of Art, New York;
Gift of Mary Ann Robertson, 1964 (64.145.4)
A & W 137/2

PROVENANCE

The set is recorded as made for "M. Boulard de Gatillon," who also acquired tapestry upholstery for a sofa and six armchairs (Badin, 1909, pp. 60, 69). The furniture is now in the Louvre; the tapestry covers show figures after Boucher, but from the *Noble Pastorale*. The purchaser was actually Boulard de Gatellier and the set remained in the family château near the Loire until 1898, when it was purchased by the Duveen firm; borders were then added to the wall hangings, which were sold to R. W. Hudson, an English collector. After Hudson's death they came into the hands of the London dealer Frank Partridge and about 1928 they

The set of *Italian Village Scenes* to which three of these tapestries belong includes five other pieces, also in the Metropolitan Museum. It was woven in 1762 under the direction of André-Charlemagne Charron, the last in a number of weavings of the series that began in 1736. The French title for the series, *Fêtes Italiennes,* may be connected with the names of several popular operas, such as the *Fêtes Vénitiennes* by André Campra; the tapestries certainly show people amusing themselves rather than working, and "fêtes" or "holidays" is an appropriate description.

The *Charlatan and the Peep Show* (*L'opérateur* and *La curiosité,* always woven together) and the *Gypsy Fortune-Teller* (*La bohémienne*) belong to the first group of four compositions by Boucher, all woven by 1739; the

86

were bought by George and Florence
Blumenthal (Rubinstein-Bloch, VI, 1930, pls.
67–72). The set was given to the Metropolitan
Museum by Mary Ann Robertson in 1964.

The *Charlatan and the Peep Show* of the set
has been replaced in this exhibition by another
example.

ENGRAVINGS
A print, *Foire de Campagne*, by Charles-
Nicolas Cochin *fils* shows many of the same
figures as the *Charlatan and the Peep Show*
(A & W 127/1, fig. 457). The central boy in
the group of three around the box of *plaisirs*
was reproduced in a crayon-manner engraving
by Giles Demarteau (Slatkin, 1977, fig. 45),
and the drawing for the mother with a sleeping
child to the right of the peep show was
engraved in 1769 by Louis Bonnet (Slatkin,
1977, fig. 47). The woman with a music book
appears in a print by P. Aveline, *La Musique*
(A & W 144/1, fig. 486).

*Collation* and the *Gardener* (*Le jardinier*) are from the second four, not made
before 1742. They reveal the influence of Watteau and Bloemaert, characteristic of Boucher's early work (Slatkin, 1978, pp. 130–31).

Boucher was the mainstay of the Beauvais weavers for over twenty years,
from the *Italian Village Scenes* of 1736 to the *Noble Pastorale*. Even when in
1755 he abandoned Beauvais for the Gobelins, his designs remained on the
looms; no new cartoons by any other artist were woven until 1761. The
*Italian Village Scenes*, his first work for weavers, have the liveliness and
brilliance to be expected from a highly gifted young man facing his first large
commission and asked to design for a craft new to him. They show both the
artist and the weavers at their best.

The *Charlatan and the Peep Show* represents a country fair, presumably in
Italy, judging from the scattered fragments of Roman architecture; the ruined
round temple is like the Temple of Vesta at Tivoli. The charlatan, helped by a
pretty girl, a trumpeter, and a monkey, is peddling his nostrums from a raised
platform, while below him three eager small boys cluster around a box that
holds little wafers called "oublies" or "plaisirs." The box has a numbered disc

87

88

337

The couple on the left of the *Gypsy Fortune-Teller* are in prints by C. L. Duflos, *L'Hommage Champêtre,* and P. Aveline, *La bonne aventure* (A & W 81/1, fig. 462; 150/1, fig. 461). The young man reclining on the left of the *Collation* appears, with another companion, in *Les Amours Pastorales* by Duflos (A & W 135/3, fig. 476), and the woman with a parasol has been compared to the shepherdess with a distaff, *La Bergère Laborieuse,* by J. M. Liotard (Slatkin, 1977, fig. 53). The young man with the *gimblettes* is in a print by Daullé after Boucher's painting *Les charmes de la vie champêtre* (A & W 148/1, fig. 491).

DRAWINGS

The girl on the left in the *Charlatan and the Peep Show,* with a basket on her arm, and the child behind her are found on a drawing in the Nationalmuseum, Stockholm, and one of the girl selling *plaisirs* was formerly in the Heseltine collection (Slatkin, 1977, figs. 43, 44). A *Young Girl* in black chalk in the Boymans Museum, Rotterdam, is close to the head and hand of a figure watching the charlatan, and the boy working the peep show resembles a drawing sold at Sotheby's, London, 28 Nov. 1962, no. 33 (Slatkin, 1977, figs. 46, 48). A sheet with studies of hands sold at the same auction house on 25 Apr. 1978, no. 66, includes those of the seller of *plaisirs* and some of her customers. A drawing for the seated woman holding a music book in the Staatliches Museum, Schwerin, is considered a copy by Oudry after Boucher (exh. cat. 1982–83, Paris, p. 156, fig. 74b). In the *Gypsy Fortune-Teller* the young man with the *gimblettes* is after a drawing in the Louvre (Slatkin, 1977, fig. 51).

OTHER VERSIONS

*The Charlatan and the Peep Show*

The *Charlatan* appears in the manufactory records as woven twelve times between 1738 and 1762, the *Peep Show* only once, but all the published tapestries consist of the two subjects combined; it is, indeed, difficult to see how they could have been separated. Examples are in the Palazzo Venezia, Rome, possibly from a set made in 1737–40; the Virginia Museum of Fine Arts, Richmond, with the initials of A-C. Charron, director of the manufactory from 1753; the Huntington Collection, San Marino, Calif.; the Hillwood Museum, Washington, D.C.; and the Philadelphia Museum, with two other subjects and the arms of Rohan-Soubise, made in 1738. The Metropolitan Museum owns another version from the Boulard de Gatellier set besides the one in this exhibition. Sales with examples include those of Paul Dutasta, Galerie Georges Petit, Paris, 3, 4 June 1926, no. 193; François Coty, Galerie Jean Charpentier, Paris, 30 Nov.–1 Dec. 1936, no. 110; the Earl of Iveagh, Elveden Hall, sold by Christie's, 22 May 1984, no. 1766. The music-making trio as a separate subject is in the J. Paul Getty Museum, Malibu, Calif.

89

on top and a pointer that can be twirled; the digit at which it comes to rest indicates the number of wafers the purchaser will receive for his money. The large peep show, or "curiosité," is operated by a young man who pulls strings to change the pictures; a woman stoops to look through a viewing hole.

The characters in the *Gypsy Fortune-Teller* are, like those in the *Charlatan,* country people, though, except for the gypsy, somewhat fancifully dressed. But the picnickers in the *Collation* are gentlefolk, waited on by a man servant; the short-sleeved jackets worn by the reclining men and the straw hat that one of them has at his feet suggest that they are playing at being peasants. The pale rings held by one of them are a string of *gimblettes,* pretzel-shaped hard biscuits. Wider versions of this tapestry show that the building on the left may be an inn. The *Gardener* goes back to a classical setting; the statues are Hercules with his lion skin and club on the right and perhaps Bacchus on the left.

*The Gypsy Fortune-Teller*

This design is recorded under the name of *La bohémienne* as having been woven thirteen times between 1738 and 1762; it is probably identical with *La bergère*, woven four times. Examples are in the Huntington Collection; the Victoria and Albert Museum, London; the Palazzo Venezia; the Fine Arts Museums of San Francisco; and the collection of the Prince de Ligne, Beloeil, Belgium, with the Rohan-Soubise arms. Mme Barzin, Paris, owned one in 1967, and the dealers French & Co. lent one to the exhibition "Age of Elegance" at the Baltimore Museum of Art in 1959. Sales with examples include those of L. & A. Satori, Kende Gallery, Vienna, 24 Feb. 1926, no. 115; Gaston Menier, sold again at Christie's, London, 8 May 1973, no. 116, with the name of the manufactory director Besnier, who retired in 1753; Gustav Bader, sold several times, most recently at Christie's, Rome, 14 Oct. 1982, no. 25; baronne Eugène de Roth-schild, Sotheby's Monaco, 24 June 1976, no. 118. A small panel showing part of the shepherdess and the girl behind her was in the Georges Hoentschel sale, Galerie Georges Petit, Paris, 31 Mar.–2 Apr. 1919, no. 364. Nineteenth-century versions were in the Mrs. Grace T. Tobey sale, Parke-Bernet, New York, 21, 22 Nov. 1941, no. 446, and the Mrs. Jacob H. Schiff sale, American Art Association–Anderson Galleries, New York, 7–9 Dec. 1933, no. 593; the latter was made in the workshop of William Baumgarten, New York.

*The Collation*

The tapestry with this name was woven thirteen times between 1745 and 1762 and it is probably identical with *Le cabaretier*, recorded as woven twice. There are examples in the Huntington Collection and the Walters Art Gallery, Baltimore. Baron Guy de Rothschild has a wide piece, formerly at the Château de Ferrières, and one was sold at the Palais d'Orsay, Paris, 23 Feb. 1978, no. 119a. The Danesfield collection is said to have another (A & W 135/4), and there was one in the set at the Château de Balleroy, near Bayeux, which was sold in 1925 (Badin, 1909, p. 60 n.). The figures, except for the dog, are seen under the canopy and round temple of the *Charlatan* on a 19th-century tapestry from the William Baumgarten workshop that was in the Schiff sale, no. 592.

*The Gardener*

The design is recorded as woven eleven times between 1746 and 1762. There is an example in the J. Paul Getty Museum, and one combined with another subject was in the Château de Ferrières, owned by baron Guy de Rothschild. The same combination was used for a tapestry in the comte Greffulhe sale, Sotheby's, London, 23 July 1937, no. 62. A narrow example was sold at the Palais d'Orsay, Paris, 23 Feb. 1978, no. 119b.

# 90 | *La foire chinoise*

Wool and silk tapestry (Beauvais)
11 ft. 11 in. × 18 ft. 2½ in.
(357.5 × 546.25 cm)
The Minneapolis Institute of Arts

PROVENANCE
Edward T. Stotesbury coll., Philadelphia; sold at Parke-Bernet, New York, 18 Nov. 1944, no. 34, when it was described as from Duveen Brothers, Inc. It had belonged to M. Stettiner in 1921 (exh. cat. 1921, London, p. 7).

ANALOGIES
Like those of other pieces of the series, the figures of the *Foire* were adapted for use by the weavers of Aubusson (exh. cat. 1973, Berlin, p. 228, O. 5). An example showing the foreground group on the left with the tent, canopy, and palm trees, but no other figures, was sold at the Palais Galliera, Paris, 7 Apr. 1976, no. 98–99b; it had originally been joined to a version of the *Danse*.

OTHER VERSIONS
A tapestry in the Cleveland Museum of Art omits all the right side. It has the arms of Louis XV at the top and so has a claim to belong to the set that was taken to China (M. Jarry, 1972, p. 224, pl. II). But in the fullest account of this set (Leroy, 1900, p. 420), the *Marché chinois* of the Peking set was taken to Paris by a French officer, later owned by the Maison Braquenié, and bought by Pozzo di

The *Chinese Series (La tenture chinoise)* is the only one listed in the Beauvais manufactory records as after the cartoons of one artist working from sketches by another. There are two documents that make this statement. One, an inventory of 1754 in the Beauvais municipal archives, reads: "Six tableaux de *Desseins chinois*, dont un se partage en deux, peint par le sieur Aumont sur les esquisses du sieur Boucher et par lui retouché, fournis par ledit sieur Oudry, contenant vingt cinq aunes cinq seizes sans les bordures ny les rapports fournis depuis" (Weigert, 1933, p. 232). These are presumably *aunes de France*, 1.19 meters each; the usual measure used at the manufactory was the *aune de Flandre*, .7 meter, made up of sixteen *bâtons*, but sometimes a weaving is recorded in *aunes de France*, including the first set of the *Tenture chinoise* (Badin, 1909, pp. 55, 61; Delesalle, 1964, pp. 95–98).

The other document, in the Archives Nationales, Paris, also dated 1754, lists "Six tableaux dont un se partage en deux représentant des desseins de chinois peint par le S. Dumont sur les esquisses de S. Boucher et retouché par Oudry" (A & W doc. 581). The cartoon in two parts was perhaps *La pêche*; several tapestries are known that show the left or the right side of the design only.

If the man who made the cartoons and, presumably, the later additions ("rapports fournis depuis"), was, as is usually supposed, Jean-Joseph Dumons, he was living in Aubusson, far from either Paris or Beauvais, in

90

Borgo; he hung it in his Château de
Montretout, which was destroyed by fire in
1871.

An extremely wide example (20 ft. 9 in., 630
cm) was sold at Sotheby's, London, 3 Mar.
1978, no. 1; it had been at Mentmore, owned
by the Rosebery family, but it is not from the
same set as the five pieces now at Dalmeny
House (see cat. 91). It shows more plants and
trees on the left, but extends on the right
beyond the two palm trees to include a very
large, brass-bound chest (a tea chest?), more
vases, and some distant trees (M. Jarry, 1981,
pls. 12, 14, as in a private coll.). The chest is
partly seen on a tapestry of about the same
width (640 cm) from the Moltke set in the
Amalienborg Palace, Copenhagen, and on
another piece in the Rijksmuseum, Amsterdam
(*Bulletin Rijksmuseum*, 5, 1957, pp. 20, 21).
The *Marché* (presumably the *Foire*) of the
Turin set is less wide.

1743 when four pieces of the series were first woven. Whether Boucher
retouched the cartoons in Paris, or Oudry in Paris or at Beauvais, would be
hard to determine. Certainly the areas on the wider versions of the tapestries
that are not in the sketches are in Boucher's style, but Oudry is recorded on
another occasion as making additions to Boucher's designs; the *Psyche*
cartoons had "rapports fait depuis par ledit sieur Oudry" (Weigert, 1933,
p. 232).

Ten sets of the *Tenture chinoise* in from two to six pieces are recorded as
woven from 1743 to 1775, several of them for the king. Sets that have
remained together are one of six pieces in the Palazzo Reale, Turin (Chierici,
1969, p. x, pl. 10), signed by Besnier and Oudry and so certainly made before
1753 when their partnership came to an end, and one of five pieces, including
cat. 91, now at Dalmeny House, Scotland, owned by the Earl of Rosebery,
which has the same two names. One set of six pieces made in 1759 for the
king and given to Count Adam Gottlob von Moltke, court marshal and royal
favorite in Copenhagen, still exists in part in the Danish royal collection
(A & W 226/2, 228/10, 229/1, 229/2; M. Jarry, 1981, p. 26).

A set of six subjects was sent to the Affaires Etrangères in 1763, "livrée à
M. Bertin pour envoyer en Chine" (Badin, 1909, p. 84); it was probably the
one made in 1758, described as "pour le magazin," "avec armes du roi dans la
bordure" (Badin, 1909, p. 61). The history of this set is complicated (Leroy,
1900, pp. 413–30; Bernard-Maître, 1951, pp. 9, 10; see also cat. 41–44), but

another set, made in 1754 and 1755, is also listed as having the royal arms in the borders, so the presence of these arms on a tapestry does not necessarily mean that it was looted from the Summer Palace in Peking during the Boxer Rebellion.

No Beauvais upholstery with chinoiserie designs has been identified. A sofa and eight armchairs were delivered with six wall hangings to the Affaires Etrangères in 1769, but when M. de Croizilles acquired six armchair covers in 1745 to go with his two *chinois* pieces, they were described as "à fables," that is, ornamented with scenes from La Fontaine's *Fables* designed by Oudry. André-Charlemagne Charron, director of the manufactory, had a *Tenture chinoise* in 1763, but when his wife acquired furniture in 1768, the upholstery had figures from the *Noble Pastorale* (Badin, 1909, pp. 61, 67, 69, 85).

*La foire chinoise* appears in a set woven in 1743 and is listed again in 1744, 1750, 1754, 1758, 1763, and 1775. All those tapestries of which the dimensions are given were of comparable heights, ranging from 4¹⁄₁₆ to 5⁶⁄₁₆ *aunes*, but the widths varied greatly. The design of the example in this exhibition has been made slightly wider than Boucher's sketch (cat. 42). The blue-and-white Chinese vase on the right is now seen in its entirety, and the metal ewer beyond it is new; on the left, there is a different head behind the woman with her back turned, and the folded parasol carried by a boy is completely visible. But the greatest change was the most necessary one for a successful tapestry: the addition of the trees on the right. Boucher's great expanse of open sky would not have worked as well in the coarser medium of wool and silk as it does in oil paint. The daring layout of the sketch, with its diagonal of airy space extending to a vast distance, with dark foreground figures silhouetted against it, has been replaced by a more conventional, balanced composition, eminently proper for tapestry, a form of art in which pictorial innovations seldom succeed.

The actual event depicted, a lively fair, is much the same as that shown in the *Charlatan and the Peep Show* (cat. 86); the dignified gentleman under the canopy is the Chinese equivalent of the gesticulating quack of the earlier design. In the sketch his face is smooth and youthful, but in the tapestry he has long, drooping moustaches and, were it not for the prancing mountebank beside him, could be taken for a Confucian sage.

## 91 | *Le jardin chinois*

Wool and silk tapestry (Beauvais)
10 ft. 5 in. × 8 ft. (318 × 244 cm)
The Earl and Countess of Rosebery, Dalmeny House,
Scotland

PROVENANCE
Acquired by Baron Meyer Amschel de Rothschild (1818–1874) for his seat Mentmore in Buckinghamshire, built in 1854 (*Mentmore*, 1884, I, pp. vii, xvii). His only child, Hannah, married Archibald Philip Primrose, fifth Earl of Rosebery, in 1878.

The set of the *Tenture chinoise* at Dalmeny House consists of five pieces, *Le repas chinois, La danse, La pêche, La chasse,* and *La toilette* or *Le jardin chinois* (*Mentmore*, 1884, II, pp. 19–23, all illus.). Three of them have the names "Besnier et Oudry," showing that the set was woven while these two men were codirectors at Beauvais, between 1734 and 1753. One *Tenture*

91

ANALOGIES

Imitations made at Aubusson have appeared in a number of sales, including those of the princesse de X . . ., Galerie Charpentier, Paris, 2, 3 Dec. 1952, no. 213; Palais des Congrès, Versailles, 3 Mar. 1968, no. 168A (A & W 230/4); Palais Galliera, Paris, 29 Nov. 1974, no. 129.

OTHER VERSIONS

Palazzo Reale, Turin.

New York private coll. (A & W 230/2, fig. 695). Apparently the same as the piece sold at Drouot Rive Gauche, Paris, 26 June 1978, no. 195, though the reproduction seems to have been cut.

Private coll. (probably in France). Closer to the sketch than the other versions, showing more of the building, but without the pergola (M. Jarry, 1981, pl. 10).

American coll. or dealer, 1926 (Hunter, 1926[b], p. 88, illus.), with the royal arms; possibly the piece brought from Peking to England by Col. Greathed and owned by the Paris dealer Lowengard, in 1900 (Leroy, 1900, p. 420, no. 1).

*chinoise* of five pieces is recorded as woven in 1750 "pour l'Espagne" (Badin, 1909, p. 61), but it included a *Foire* and not a *Chasse*, so it could not have been the Rosebery set.

The *Jardin chinois* was first woven in 1743 and was included in the sets of 1744, 1754, 1763, and 1775; that of 1744, woven for M. Bergeret, the owner of the sketch (cat. 43), was wide, presumably reproducing Boucher's design in its entirety. Similar dimensions are recorded for the weavings of 1750 and 1754. The sets of six pieces made for the king presumably also included a *Jardin*. The example in a private collection in New York (A & W 230/2, fig. 695) is also taller than it is wide but shows the man leaning forward and carrying a long branch.

Boucher's design is eminently suited for reproduction in tapestry. It is full of attractive detail, but the figures of the women are clearly defined and pleasingly calm; there is no feeling of triviality or restlessness.

# 92 | *Sketch for a Gobelins tapestry*

Oil on canvas
19½ × 35 in. (50 × 90 cm)
Mobilier National,
Paris

PROVENANCE
The sketch is described by Jacques as "présenté
à M. le Directeur général comme utile à la
Manufacture" (Fenaille, IV, p. 229). Marigny
presumably turned it over to the Gobelins
immediately.

ANALOGIES
The scene in the medallion on the left, two
nymphs surprised by a satyr, has been connected with a painting of Pan and Syrinx
exhibited at the Salon of 1761 (A & W 549) and
the central medallion with a *Birth of Venus*
(A & W 577) and a *Triumph of Venus* (A & W
485); the last relationship seems slight. The
*Arion and the Dolphin* medallion on the right
is close to the central figures of the 1748
painting in Princeton (cat. 55).

For some later versions of the *Tentures de
Boucher*, another Boucher design with Venus, a
dolphin, and cupids was placed in one of the
medallions, but it is not closely related to the
similar subject in cat. 92 (Fenaille, IV, pl.
facing p. 294).

The first step in the creation of a tapestry is the *petit patron* or *modèle*, a careful sketch from which a full-scale cartoon can be made of the desired size of the finished product. At the Gobelins manufactory, these sketches were paid for by the king. A bill exists submitted by a flower painter employed there, Maurice Jacques, for work done in 1758. It includes several *esquisses*, one "peinte à l'huile composée d'une bordure d'ornemens, de trois médaillons en ornemens, avec des festons et groupes de fleurs épars dans toute l'étendue de l'esquisse, les sujets des milieux ont été faits chés M. Boucher" (i.e., in his workshop; Fenaille, IV, 1907, pp. 228, 256; A & W 456/5, fig. 1273). Another sketch listed in the bill was cat. 92, described as "dans le goût de celles susdites, dont les sujets des milieux sont faits par M. Boucher, lesquelles esquisses ont été faites sur l'idée de M. Soufflot" (Fenaille, IV, pp. 229, 255, illus. pl. facing p. 228; A & W fig. 1370). The director of the royal manufactories, Jean-Germain Soufflot, annotated the bill: "A remettre lors de l'exécution en grand," so Jacques could not have been paid for several years. He asked 150 livres for each of the two sketches.

What was Soufflot's contribution to these basically similar compositions? A clue is given in a letter that he wrote to his superior, the marquis de Marigny, on 23 September 1758. In it, he requested approval for a new design of a *Chancellerie*, the set of tapestries that the king gave to his chancellors, and

92

added: "on pouroit, je crois, Monsieur, faire un fond de mosaïques dans lesquelles seroient des fleurs de lys, enfermé dans une belle bordure à laquelle seroit attachée un tableau de moyenne grandeur qui feroit le milieu de la pièce." The design would be inexpensive to weave, "parcequ'elle peut occuper des ouvrieurs inférieurs, en exceptant la partie des figures" (Fenaille, III, 1904, p. 142). It was also eminently suitable for private commissions, as the tapestries based on it could easily be made larger or smaller to suit the customer.

The credit for substituting a silk damask pattern for the fleurs-de-lis appropriate for royal gifts has been assigned to the head of the basse lisse (horizontal loom) workshop, Jacques Neilson (Fenaille, III, p. 177), but it is clearly indicated on the two sketches, red in one and blue in the other. Neilson first used it on a set of *Don Quixote* tapestries in 1760, but the central medallions are not here so clearly defined as framed paintings, hung by ribbons with bows at the top from an apparent molding, as they are in the 1758 sketch and in the *Tentures de Boucher*.

The sketches of Jacques and Boucher were not used for making cartoons until a customer for hangings of this type appeared. He was the sixth earl of Coventry, who came to Paris to buy tapestry in August 1763. Substantial changes were then made in the design, with larger Boucher paintings of different subjects in the medallions; these paintings are now in the Louvre and at Versailles and are dated 1763 and 1765. But most of Jacques's original design, including the simulated frame and its garlands and the musical trophy with a bagpipe at the base, is to be seen on the walls of the Tapestry Room from Lord Coventry's seat, Croome Court, now in the Metropolitan Museum (fig. 209; Standen, 1964, pp. 18, 49, figs. 20, 22, 28).

# The Influence of Boucher's Art on the Production of the Vincennes–Sèvres Porcelain Manufactory

ANTOINETTE FAŸ-HALLÉ

To consider the relationship between the painter Boucher and the Vincennes–Sèvres porcelain manufactory is to consider in a classic fashion the relationship between a model and the work based upon it in another medium, and the relationship between the primary arts as the source of inspiration, and the minor arts that—or at least such was the case in the eighteenth century—often create fashion and sometimes direct the evolution of taste.

One thing should be clear from the outset: Boucher's models were of vital importance in the development of Vincennes–Sèvres porcelain, and particularly its sculpture. From 1752 to about 1766 almost all the freestanding Sèvres figures were derived from the work of this artist. During these years the same was true of painted figurative decoration, although this was less clear-cut because there were still large numbers of designs which included flowers, birds, and landscapes that were un-touched by Boucher's influence, and also because the painters as often adapted as simply copied the models from which they worked.[1]

As Boucher's influence was all-pervasive at Sèvres at a highly important period in its history—the time at which the greatest French porcelain manufactory was achieving its own coherent style, so his influence affected European ceramics as a whole. This was owing to the position achieved by Sèvres during 1755–60 when it overtook the dominance of Meissen.

We know the goal set by those who created the Sèvres manufactory, which had been set up at the Château de Vincennes in 1738 and moved to Sèvres in 1756: It was to compete with Meissen and Japanese porcelain.[2] To achieve this goal they had to solve the countless technical problems inherent in porcelain production. About 1745–47, this was accomplished, and it is then that we find the first team worthy of royal patronage being recruited in various capacities. Hendrik van Hulst was entrusted with "assuming direction over the ornament and painting,"[3] and with that responsibility in view he set out his production standards and goals:

> The diversity of tastes is the guardian angel of any manufactory revolving around objects of adornment: what does not please some will please others. With porcelain in particular, the most bizarre and fanciful designs will enjoy greater success than the most elegant and rational. Provided we eschew the heavy and the trivial, and turn to the light, the novel, and the varied, our success is assured.[4]

In the light of the success achieved, Boucher's style must at the time have seemed the perfect realization of Hulst's intentions!

1. In the exhibition catalogues *Porcelaines de Vincennes* (1977–78, Paris), out of 447 painted or gilded objects, 37 have painted decoration based on Boucher or in his style, that is to say almost all those decorated with figures.
2. Lechevallier-Chevignard, 1908, I, p. 10.
3. Lechevallier-Chevignard, 1908, I, p. 25.
4. Lechevallier-Chevignard, 1908, I, p. 28.

## WHITE-GLAZED PORCELAIN

In 1751 Jean-Jacques Bachelier was recruited, and it is to him that the principal role in the development of unglazed or biscuit porcelain can be attributed.[5] The Meissen porcelain factory in Saxony had launched the fashion for glazed and polychrome-enameled figures. To compete with Meissen, Vincennes also produced some glazed and painted models, for example *La source,* now in the Louvre.[6] However, now abandoning polychromy, Vincennes devoted itself to glazed but unpainted figures, which evoked the famous blanc de Chine. Bulidon, Chabry, Chanou, Depierreux, Louis Fournier, Laurent Hubert, Pierre Laurent, Patouillet, and Le Boiteux are some of the creators of these gods and goddesses, naiads, children, and animals—always delightful because of the quality and even sensuousness of the material from which they are formed and to which they are so well suited. Emile Bourgeois, indeed, criticized these sculptors: "they had no personality: like them, their figurines lack originality."[7] Nonetheless, from 1747 to 1751–52, their work laid the ground on which the work of the succeeding generation would flourish, a generation that no longer invented on its own but deferred, both in spirit and in form, to a single master—Boucher—and in so doing would ignore Hulst's injunctions.

There are several white-glazed figures and groups that suggest comparison with Boucher. Such is the case with the *Leda,* which the manufactory archives attribute to Depierreux in 1747,[8] if we connect that reference with a figure of which several examples exist, one lightly polychromed,[9] and if we compare the figure with Demarteau's engraving of the same subject.[10] The resemblance—if not the similarity—is striking: Leda's right arm is the sole element not in the same position in both examples. When Falconet turned to the same subject in 1764, this time inspired by Ryland's engraving,[11] he would alter the position of one of Leda's arms in the same manner: in porcelain, raised arms spell trouble. By and large, Depierreux's glazed figure is much closer to the "spirit" of Boucher; Falconet, idealizing the canon of female beauty, tended toward a neoclassicism of which his more naturalistic model betrays no trace.

We do not know the name of the modeler at Vincennes who created the group known as *Le berger galant* (cat. 97), mentioned in the Vincennes archives under 1752, but we can see that the work is a literal reproduction of an engraving by A. Laurent entitled *Le pasteur galant.*[12] It is most likely a porcelain from 1752: fidelity to an engraved source is characteristic of this period.

The case of *L'heure du berger*[13] is a bit more complex. It is possible, of course, to compare this white-glazed group to the *Repos de Diane,* engraved by Pelletier after Boucher,[14] for the pose of the female figure, but what the anonymous sculptor of this group retained above all is the essence of Boucher's style, his deft sensuality. Here there is a perfect equivalence between the spirit of a creative artist and the work inspired by him.

Among other works in white-glazed porcelain, mention should be made of the *Chinois soutenant une corbeille,*[15] known from three examples, one of which is in the British Royal Collection and another in the Musée National de Céramique de Sèvres. Boucher's name has been evoked in connection with this group, but without any evidence. As for the other

5. Biscuit porcelain has a matte appearance like marble, for which it was a sort of substitute, propitious to sculpture.
6. Exh. cat. 1977–78, Paris, no. 501, under its 18th-century name.
7. Bourgeois, 1909, I, p. 13.
8. Exh. cat. 1977–78, Paris, p. 171, no. 493.
9. Reproduced in *Les porcelainiers du XVIIIᵉ siècle français,* preface by S. Gauthier, Paris, 1964, p. 139; attributed to Mennecy. Another example in white enamel was acquired by the Musée National de Céramique de Sèvres in 1985, inv. MNC 25216.
10. J-R 834. Demarteau's engraving, published in 1773, is clearly posterior to the Vincennes group, and indeed to Boucher's own life, but must reflect a common, earlier, original composition.
11. Bourgeois, 1913, pl. 8, no. 386; J-R 1535–1539.
12. J-R 1313.
13. Exh. cat. 1977–78, Paris, no. 487; engraving, J-R 1454.
14. The group cannot derive directly from Pelletier's engraving as it was published in 1749 and Pelletier was only born c. 1736, but again one can imagine a source common to both engraving and porcelain.
15. Exh. cat. 1977–78, Paris, nos. 467, 468.

group published by Bourgeois under the title *Chinois à la corbeille*,[16] also attributed to Boucher and dated by Bourgeois to 1750, in all likelihood it is an 1891 cast based on a Pont-aux-Choux creamware porcelain group now in the Musée National de Céramique.[17]

## THE ENFANTS BOUCHER AND THE ENFANTS FALCONET

Beginning in 1752, a new team of modelers was being asked to take Boucher as their source: Blondeau, Suzanne, and de Fernex. A few fairly rare early works by them still bear traces of clumsiness, as can be seen in the white-glazed versions of *La petite fille à la cage* and the *Porteur d'oiseau*.[18] Thereafter these sculptors began to demonstrate real fidelity to an artist who was not their actual master, but who compelled obedience without being physically present: indeed, the manufactory either just purchased drawings from him or acquired engravings of his works.[19]

Today the Sèvres manufactory possesses only one of Boucher's drawings.[20] On the back is written *Le petit Jardinier: dessin de M. Boucher apartenant à la manufacture de Vincennes, le 29 aoust 1749*. In 1752 Blondeau used it as a model, but from it he made a *Jeune suppliant* in which the shovel has disappeared (cat. 99). Aside from that, Blondeau was entirely faithful, conveying admirably both the puppy fat of the boy and the ease of his pose. The sculptor's task was made easier because the painter had included with the child a small hillock on which a basket rests, a subsidiary motif indispensable for supporting the porcelain.

This figurine is only one of the first examples of what was to be a long series of little girls and boys engaged in eating gruel, reaping, carrying baskets of flowers or birds, laundering, patting dogs, mowing, etc. Under the skilled hands of Blondeau, Suzanne, and de Fernex, Boucher's drawn and painted models come to life in the terra-cottas, some of which still exist in the collections of the Musée National de Céramique de Sèvres. Molds were then taken from the terra-cottas in order to reproduce them in porcelain.[21] From 1752 on, the manufactory archives mention a large number of *Enfants Boucher* in the warehouse and workshops. One detail helps us distinguish them from the other children that were being turned out in increasing quantities at Vincennes during the same period: they are all clothed and engaged in identifiable pastimes, often in adult occupations. Such is not the case with the anonymous *Enfants saisons*,[22] which are barely clad; the *Enfants François*,[23] attributed by Emile Bourgeois to Louis Félix de la Rue after originals by François Flamant (i.e., Duquesnoy), which are nude and whose modeling is agonizingly weak; or the *Enfants La Rue*,[24] which were modeled by Louis Félix de La Rue after drawings by Boucher. The latter date from 1754: the factory has records of payments to de La Rue.[25] These children are nude and the quality of their modeling is unusually high. Grouped by threes on hillocks, playing with a fish, a bird, grapes, or a conch shell, they amuse themselves with all the seriousness of children, and we can only regret the rarity of surviving examples. De La Rue is the author of other groups of Sèvres children: *Bacchus à la panthère* of 1754 and some paperweights intended for the controller-general Machault d'Arnouville.[26] De La Rue's works have great charm, as, for that matter, do the majority of the works of Suzanne, Blondeau, and de Fernex—which have perhaps simply been too successful for their own good.

16. Bourgeois, 1913, pl. 3, no. 145.
17. Inv. MNC 23169.
18. Musée National de Céramique, Sèvres; exh. cat. 1977–78, Paris, nos. 508, 514.
19. Rosalind Savill (1982) makes an extremely precise, if not exhaustive, survey of the use of Boucher models at Vincennes and at Sèvres.
20. Savill, 1982, p. 162, fig. 1.
21. On the technique of biscuit manufacture, see Brunet & Préaud, 1978, p. 14.
22. Exh. cat. 1977–78, Paris, no. 477–80.
23. Bourgeois, 1909, I, pp. 36–37; and 1913, pls. 4 and 5, nos. 231–59.
24. Bourgeois, 1913, pl. 6, nos. 224, 262, 264, 266.
25. Exh. cat. 1977–78, Paris, p. 165.
26. Exh. cat. 1977–78, Paris, pp. 151, 180, nos. 515, 516.

The Sèvres manufactory, however, did not leave well enough alone. Carrying on with the creations of Vincennes in most spheres, it was in turn to produce immense quantities of "Boucher children," under the auspices of its new director of the sculpture workshops, Etienne-Maurice Falconet, who held the post from 1757 to 1766. With these so-called "Falconet children," we are confronted with a whole troop of children who seem downright restless;[27] some topple over into outright vulgarity—as in the two groups entitled *Le Maître* and *La Maîtresse d'école.* Yet in adapting Boucher's design[28] of *La Maîtresse d'école* Falconet was careful not to show the actual punishment (by beating on the naked bottom), but rather the moment immediately preceding it, as Rosalind Savill has noted.[29] As we have said, Hulst was wary of the "trivial": his fears were justified . . . and this is somewhat surprising, since Falconet's work as a whole did not tend toward naturalism. This series of works can only be explained by the response to the demand for a fashion vastly appreciated by both the manufactory's patrons and its clients. In forcing his talent in an uncongenial direction, Falconet could hardly have hoped for more.

### BISCUIT PORCELAINS AND THE THEATER

Boucher's reign was not limited to models of children. His painted works teem with shepherds and shepherdesses, pastoral figures with a certain air of the court about them. Indeed, the figures might better be described as "theatrical" than as "courtly." In the early 1750s, as Rosalind Savill has so rightly emphasized,[30] following Bourgeois,[31] Boucher and Falconet drew their inspiration for the majority of these figures or groups of young men and women (and some of the children we have just mentioned, i.e., *La petite fille à la cage, Le porteur d'oiseaux, La petite fille au tablier, Le moissonneur,* and *La moissonneuse*) from works performed at the Opéra-Comique. Here, there is not a trace of overt naturalism, notwithstanding the fact that the features of Mme Favart inspired those of *La Bergère assise* or that Mme Arimath's beauty underlies that of *Le Batelier de Saint-Cloud,* albeit a breeches part. Other works were originally designed by Boucher for translation into sculpture by Falconet himself, Allegrain, Vassé, and Coustou to decorate the dairy of Mme de Pompadour's Château de Crécy. Vincennes was not slow to seize upon the profit it could derive from the models, some depicting the most famous actors of the day inspired by fashionable plays *(Les amours de Bastien et Bastienne, La Vallée de Montmorency, La fête d'Amour, Le Batelier de Saint-Cloud),* and others first created as sculpture for the most prominent woman in the realm. Many of the groups or figures that were reproduced in biscuit, such as the famous *Mangeurs de raisins* (cat. 100) based on Boucher's painting *Pensent-ils au raisin?* (cat. 53), were among the prettiest of the Vincennes models, and it is easy to understand their popularity. Furthermore, while the basic composition of the biscuit is formed from molds that allow for a reproduction identical with the model, parts of the secondary decorative elements (bunches of grapes, flowers, etc.) were then modeled freehand by the *répareur* (assembler). Different versions thus included variants, which gave the client a wider range from which to choose.

For, despite their obvious charm, these pastoral biscuit sculptures are afflicted by the same defect as the various other children inspired by

27. Savill (1982) provides the list, pp. 169–70, n. 12.
28. J-R 1383.
29. Savill, 1982, p. 166.
30. Savill, 1982, p. 164.
31. Bourgeois, 1909, I, pp. 16 et seq.

Boucher: they relentlessly reiterate the same type of figure, the same aesthetic; the variety insisted on by Hulst is absent.

In this area, Falconet was unable to escape from Boucher's influence between 1757 and 1766, and even such groups as *Baiser donné* and *Baiser rendu* of 1765 are still faithful to the painter's spirit. Yet the reductions of his own sculpture, such as *La Baigneuse* and *Pygmalion*, presage a new era.

### BOUCHER AND SCENES PAINTED ON PORCELAIN

In her article entitled "François Boucher and the Porcelains of Vincennes and Sèvres" (Savill, 1982), Rosalind Savill has given a very precise evaluation of the influence of the painter on the porcelain manufactory, clearly demonstrating that the models were first reproduced in blue or pink camaïeu, with all the stylization that implies, and then, in the late 1750s, redone in polychrome against a landscape background: Vincennes can be said to have followed the spirit of the engravings after Boucher, Sèvres that of the paintings that had originally served as the models for the engravings.

In this sphere we find the same subjects as those treated in sculpture: the breakfast services in the Louvre and the Wadsworth Atheneum are famous for faithfully reproducing on the tray the same Le Prince engraving, *La chasse*,[32] whereas the cups, saucers, teapots, etc., reproduce in turn *La petite fille à la cage*, *La petite fille au tablier*, *Le jeune suppliant*, etc. The Vincennes painter of these two sets, André-Vincent Vielliard, was so prolific in this genre that Anne-Marie Belfort has devoted an entire article to the subject, "L'Oeuvre de Vielliard d'après Boucher."[33] From it we learn that the painter, although of relatively meager talent, did not slavishly follow his models, and he did not shrink from making modifications to suit himself, changing the positions of arms or legs, clothing children that Boucher had created nude, changing the activities in which they are engaged, etc., all of which make Vielliard's cupids into real puzzles. At their best such alterations, of course, become genuine originality. All of the cupids painted at Vincennes were not done by Vielliard, nor are they all based on Boucher; systematic investigation of the sources of inspiration for the various porcelain painters has not yielded any great results, which only underlines the truth of the statement in the introduction to Rosalind Savill's article: "By 1776, only six years after François Boucher's death, the term *'le goût de Boucher'* was an accepted description in sales catalogues of children painted on Sèvres porcelain."[34]

As for genre scenes derived from Boucher, in the vein of the *Mangeurs de raisins*, they were of course perfectly suited to Sèvres painted scenes.[35] Sometimes, they hew to masterpieces—for example, the depiction of *La musique* on a small milk jug (cat. 94). In other instances, their qualities or defects are simply those of the painter reproducing them on porcelain.

Some categories of models derived from Boucher deserve special attention: first, because of their rarity, are the landscapes. Indeed, we know of only one example of landscapes by Boucher reproduced on vases—the two *pots-pourris myrte* (from a set of three) in the Frick Collection, New York.[36]

Allegorical, mythological, or poetic scenes are equally rare. Rosalind Savill cites the famous Bernard Molitor *secrétaire* (Huntington Collection,

32. J-R 1384.
33. Belfort, 1976, pp. 6–35.
34. Savill, 1982, p. 162.
35. Savill, 1982, p. 166.
36. *Frick Collection*, VII, pp. 246–55, inv. 18–9–10 to 18–9–12. One vase reproduces the *Premiere veue de Charenton* (J-R 1342), another the *Seconde veue des environs de Charenton* (J-R 1343), both engraved by Le Bas.

San Marino) with a plaque painted by Charles-Nicolas Dodin in 1783, which depicts *Rinaldo and Armida* and is based on the painting done by Boucher upon his reception into the Academy in 1734 (see cat. 26).[37] In the sphere of history pictures there were plenty of models by other painters upon which the porcelain manufactory could draw. Boucher was not the painter who was particularly turned to for that kind of inspiration. Furthermore, this type of work is—in the majority of cases—contrary to what was generally done at Vincennes and at Sèvres on the basis of designs by Boucher: here, the copy is a literal one. We are dealing with a technical prowess that is remarkable for the porcelain's intact retention of the freshness of eighteenth-century polychromy, but it is not an original creation, nor even an adaptation.

The chinoiserie objects are more interesting. First, it should be noted that they are fairly few in number, both in the painter's work and in the production of the porcelain manufactory, but they are all the more pleasing for that. We are displaying three kinds of adaptation of Boucher's designs, and they are practically all that are known. The bottle coolers from the Musée National de Céramique (cat. 95) are painted in pink camaïeu, the glass cooler from the Musée des Arts Décoratifs in Paris (cat. 93) is polychrome; both pieces, however, are of equal quality, full of charm and imagination. The pots-pourris from the Detroit Institute of Arts (cat. 114), painted by Dodin, are quite different in character, but the porcelain painter, with all his skill, has retained all the savor of the originals.

A study of Boucher's influence on the porcelain of Vincennes–Sèvres thus demonstrates that it was vital and, in the sphere of biscuit sculpture, less consistently beneficial than is usually thought. Hulst, in his enthusiasm, declared his intention of achieving variety above anything else. In fact, such was the success of Boucher's models that their repetition represented good business for the manufactory, which simply gave its clientele what it wanted. It should not be reproached for doing so, nor should we be for preferring the white-glazed porcelain groups, whose scintillating character was abandoned by Bachelier in favor of the matte biscuit, to fidgety bambini engaged in adult pursuits. However, those are considerations that have more to do with the art of ceramics per se than with Boucher himself. Most important in the final analysis is the ability of the craftsman who seizes upon the work of a creative artist and makes it his own. In that context, Boucher was merely a vehicle!

37. Savill, 1982, p. 168, fig. 18.

## 93 | *Glass cooler (seau à verre)*

Soft-paste porcelain; polychrome and carmine red decoration
H. 4½ in (11.3 cm); diam. 7 in. (18.2 cm)
Vincennes, about 1745–50
Musée des Arts Décoratifs, Paris; Gould bequest (28693)

REFERENCE
Exh. cat. 1977–78, Paris, Grand Palais,
no. 271.

The decoration of this glass cooler is borrowed from a print with a chinoiserie subject by Gabriel Huquier, the *Chinois et Chinoise pêchant au bord d'un vivier* (J-R 1133). An ink drawing after the fishing scene, kept at the Sèvres manufactory (FS 5–1861–no. 24), was inscribed *F. Boucher* by a later hand. This drawing, like the one mentioned in cat. 95, may indicate that the painters at Vincennes worked mostly from simplified drawings done after original compositions or elaborate engravings.

*93*

*94*

## 94 | *Milk jug (pot à lait ordinaire)*

Soft-paste porcelain; polychrome decoration
H. 4¼ in. (11 cm)
Mark: interlaced L's
Vincennes, about 1745–50
Musée National de Céramique, Sèvres
(MNC 13214)

REFERENCE
Exh. cat. 1977–78, Paris, Grand Palais,
no. 168.

The artist who reproduced on this milk jug the engraving by Pierre Aveline, *La musique* (J-R 229), displayed his inventiveness by adapting the image to the shape of the vessel and by conferring on it a certain "Meissen" quality that was then sought after by the Vincennes artists. The miniaturization of the decorations—which in fact recalls Watteau more than Boucher—started indeed in the Saxon manufactory.

## 95 | *Pair of bottle coolers (seaux à bouteille ordinaires)*

Soft-paste porcelain; pink camaïeu and
gold decoration
H. 7¾ in. (19.7 cm);
W. with handles 10¼ in. (26.1 cm)
Marks: on one, interlaced L's, a dot; on
the other, interlaced L's, two dots
Vincennes, about 1750
Musée National de Céramique, Sèvres;
Gift of the heirs of Mme Poidatz
(MNC 16058)

REFERENCE
Exh. cat. 1977–78, Paris, Grand Palais,
nos. 246, 247.

The pink camaïeu admirably transcribes the spirit of the prints that served
as models for the decoration of these vases. Gabriel Huquier is once again
the engraver copied by the Vincennes painter. One recognizes here four of
his *Scènes de la vie chinoise*: *La pêche au cormoran, Le carillon, Flûtiste et
enfant timbalier,* and *Le thé* (J-R 1125–1128). It should be noted that the
manufactory at Sèvres owns a drawing of *La pêche au cormoran* bearing an
eighteenth-century registration mark and inscribed in a later hand with
Boucher's name.

95

96

## 96 | *Le joueur de musette*

Soft-paste biscuit porcelain
H. 9 in. (23 cm)
Mark: F incised under the base
Model attributed to Pierre Blondeau, 1752(?)
Vincennes
Musée National de Céramique, Sèvres (MNC 22449)

REFERENCE
Exh. cat. 1977–78, Paris, Grand Palais,
no. 492.

Although not attributed by Bourgeois to Pierre Blondeau, this model relates in both style and spirit to the *Jeune suppliant* (cat. 99), itself attributed by Bourgeois to that artist. Gisela Zick (1965) seems to have first established the attribution, which has since been widely accepted (exh. cat. 1977–78, Paris, Grand Palais). The date 1752 put forward by Bourgeois has also been generally accepted but lacks solid archival evidence, and cannot be established on the basis of firmly dated related works, although the composition was probably originally executed as upholstery for the seat furniture commissioned by Mme de Pompadour in 1751 (Fenaille, IV, 1907, pp. 384–88).

In any case the motif here adapted in porcelain is one that enjoyed considerable success; it was produced at Vincennes in both white-glazed soft-paste porcelain and biscuit. One will also note the presence of an incised F under the base of the example exhibited here, a mark which indicates that this earlier model was still being produced at the time of Falconet's direction of the manufactory.

A painting in the Boston Museum of Fine arts (A & W 437), although considered by Ananoff to be a copy, is the only painted version of the composition known to us. Boucher himself etched the composition (J-R 196, completed by F. A. Aveline) under the title *L'innocence,* and Gilles Demarteau engraved it as *L'enfant berger* in 1770.

One also finds the subject on a Gobelins tapestry panel, mounted as part of a screen in the Detroit Institute of Arts, and on a chair at the Musée du Petit Palais, Paris. A brocade satin panel at the Musée des Tissus, Lyon (inv. 1281), bears the same motif.

## 97 | *Le berger galant*

White-glazed soft-paste porcelain
H. 9 in. (23 cm)
Model of 1752
Vincennes, about 1752
Musée National de Céramique, Sèvres
(MNC 25135)

REFERENCE
Exh. cat. 1977–78, Paris, Grand Palais, p. 154 (not in exhibition).

The archives of the Sèvres manufactory do not identify the author of this group, which achieved particular popularity. Four examples were mentioned in 1752. They were sold in 1754 for 66 livres each. Besides the example at Sèvres, a second figure is now at the Boston Museum of Fine Arts (Forsyth Wickes Collection), a third appeared in the Mentmore sale (London, Sotheby's, 24 May 1977, lot 2010), and a fourth was on the London art market in 1984.

The model for the group is an engraving by André Laurent entitled *Le pasteur galant,* after the painting executed by Boucher around 1738 for the *salle d'audience* of the Hôtel de Soubise—now the Archives Nationales—in Paris (cat. 30; A & W 159). That the model was the engraving, executed by Laurent in 1742, rather than an original drawing, is confirmed by the fact that an engraving now kept at the manufactory at Sèvres bears a registration number indicating that it was at Vincennes before the manufactory transferred to Sèvres.

97

The motif of the *Berger galant* was, indeed, much favored by artists working with porcelain. It appeared on the painted decoration of a *pot à pommade* from Vincennes recently sold in Paris (Hôtel Drouot, 23 Nov. 1979, lot 79). It can also be seen on the center of the tray of a gueridon (J. Paul Getty Museum, Malibu) executed by Charles-Nicolas Dodin in 1761. A pink pot-pourri vase with the same scene, painted by Dodin in 1763, is at Waddesdon Manor (Eriksen, 1968, p. 156, no. 56, pl. on p. 158), and a *vase hollandois* of 1762 is in the Wallace Collection (Savill, 1982, p. 167 and fig. 12).

The fame of the motif reached other European porcelain centers, as exemplified, for instance, by a Meissen group modeled by J. J. Kändler about 1750–55, at the Victoria and Albert Museum (see Honey, 1934, pl. XLVIIb), made particularly exuberant by the addition of colorful garlands of flowers. A later (about 1762) and somewhat different Meissen group after the same subject is in the Hermitage (see exh. cat. 1970, Leningrad, no. 96).

# 98 | *Le flûteur*

Terra-cotta
H. 9¼ in. (24 cm)
Vincennes, about 1752
Musée National de Céramique, Sèvres
(MNC 7723)

REFERENCE
Exh. cat. 1977–78, Paris, Grand Palais,
no. 484.

The *marchand-mercier* Lazare Duvaux sold a Vincennes porcelain version of this celebrated group to the duchesse de Lauraguais in 1752 (Courajod, 1873, p. 132, no. 1181), thus allowing us to establish a terminus ante quem for the date of this terra-cotta model, whose author is still unknown. The skill of the artist, evidenced in the fine quality of the piece, lets one suppose that it could, indeed, be the work of one of the more gifted Vincennes artists (Pierre Blondeau, Suzanne, or de Fernex, for instance). The original inspiration for the group is a figure from a painting exhibited by Boucher at the Salons of 1748 and 1750, the *Berger montrant à sa bergère à jouer de la flûte* (National Gallery of Victoria; A & W 311) and engraved by René Gaillard as *L'agréable leçon*. Rosalind Savill (1982, p. 167) has pointed out that the engraving and the model face in opposite directions, thus questioning the dependence of one upon the other, and suggesting the convincing theory that the Vincennes group may ultimately

98

derive from another intermediary, such as a drawing by Boucher. As customary, the sculptor has rearranged the secondary elements of the composition (tree trunk, sheep, etc.) and notably has added a dog to it.

In order to execute a biscuit group, a mold must first be made from a terra-cotta. As many molds are used as necessary. An assembler then unmolds, assembles, and gives the finishing touches to all parts. His goal is to mask all joins and to enhance the plastic qualities of the group by reworking the modeling. Finally the assembler adds to the composition secondary elements of his choice.

Various examples of this group are known. The one at the Wadsworth Atheneum in Hartford is of white-glazed soft-paste porcelain. The sheep is standing up, and behind the shepherdess a basket rests on a pedestal. The version at the Musée des Arts Décoratifs, Paris, is of soft-paste biscuit porcelain, and in this, colorful flowers spring from the basket. Understanding the intervention of the assembler is essential to seeing the differences in quality among several examples of the same subject, and to grasping the distance that separates the final product from the original idea.

The popularity of the subject in its time is well indicated by its repetition at other factories. Polychrome versions, based either on Gaillard's engraving or on one in reverse by J. E. Nilson after Gaillard, were produced at Frankenthal about 1760, at Chelsea about 1765, and in Vienna about 1765–75 (see Zick, 1965, figs. 23, 24, 26).

## 99 | *Le jeune suppliant*

Soft-paste biscuit porcelain
H. 8 in. (20.5 cm)
Mark: F incised
Model attributed to Pierre Blondeau
Vincennes, about 1752
Musée National de Céramique, Sèvres (MNC 7755[3])

REFERENCE
Exh. cat. 1977–78, Paris, Grand Palais, no. 491.

This model is the only one for which an original preparatory drawing by Boucher has survived. Dated 1749, the drawing is still at the Sèvres manufactory. Its style is surprisingly coarse for the artist, but it is likely that, given its function, Boucher insisted above all on volumes and contour, which in turn were translated admirably into three dimensions by the modeler.

Boucher's original composition, ultimately altered probably by Blondeau himself, according to Emile Bourgeois (1913, no. 362), shows the artist's awareness of the need for support for small figures. Not only is the young boy firmly propped up by the basket of flowers beside him, but he is sturdily set upon a base which is clearly indicated in the drawing where he was also leaning on a shovel. Suppression of the shovel turned the resting gardener into a young suppliant.

The rare comparison allowed by this figurine and its preparatory drawing reveals both the faithfulness of the ceramicist to his model and his

*99*

freedom of expression. Particularly remarkable is the fact that, starting from a coarse drawing, Blondeau was able to create a work which transcends its model and captures, in fact, the spirit of Boucher's finest works. One can thus only regret the lack of information concerning Boucher's actual involvement in the daily work at Vincennes.

Like most *Enfants Boucher*, the *Jeune suppliant* was executed in both white-glazed porcelain and biscuit. Many examples have survived.

## 100 | *Les mangeurs de raisins*

Soft-paste biscuit porcelain
H. 8¾ in. (22.5 cm)
Mark incised on the front of the base: B
Model of 1752
Vincennes, about 1752
Musée National de Céramique, Sèvres; Gift of the children
of the comte de Chazelles-Chusclan (MNC 7755¹)

REFERENCE
Exh. cat. 1977–78, Paris, Grand Palais,
no. 496.

Thanks to the summaries of the otherwise unpublished early plays of Charles-Simon Favart for the Opéra-Comique by the brothers Parfaict, and their mention of Boucher's borrowing of the subject (Parfaict, 1756, VI, pp. 78–79), it is possible to trace the inspiration for this group to the beginning of the sixth scene of the pantomime of the *Vendanges de Tempé* (1745, an earlier version of the *Vallée de Montmorency*): the little shepherd is described as sharing grapes with his beloved Lisette (Zick, 1965, p. 26; see also cat. 53). Boucher exhibited an oval version of the painting at the Salon of 1747 (Art Institute of Chicago) and painted a rectangular one, apparently for the Swedish architect Carl Hårleman, which was engraved by Jacques-Philippe Le Bas under the title *Pensent-ils au raisin?*

The more prosaic title given at the Vincennes manufactory to this model, dated 1752 by Emile Bourgeois (1913, no. 398), did not prevent its success. It was repeated many times at Vincennes in both white-glazed and biscuit versions, each one displaying the inventiveness of the assembler in the various additions to the basic composition.

*100*

## 101 | Déjeuner Hébert

Soft-paste porcelain; yellow ground with blue camaïeu decoration
Tray, 11 × 9¾ in. (28 × 25 cm)
Teapot, H. 4¼ in. (11 cm)
Sugar bowl, H. 3¾ in. (9.5 cm)
Cup, H. 1¾ in. (4.5 cm)
Saucer, diam. 4 in. (10.5 cm)
Marks: in blue on each, interlaced L's, a dot beneath;
a heraldic label facing upward [Vielliard]
Decorator: André-Vincent Vielliard (working 1752–90)
Vincennes, about 1752–53
Wadsworth Atheneum, Hartford;
Gift of J. P. Morgan, 1917
*New York and Detroit*

REFERENCES
Belfort, 1976, pp. 22–24; Brunet & Préaud,
1978, pp. 32–33, pl. III.

This déjeuner, like the one at the Louvre (see cat. 102), is named after Thomas-Joachim Hébert, the famous dealer whose shop was on the rue Saint-Honoré. It also provides an "anthology" of Boucher themes used at Vincennes. On the tray, one finds *La chasse* after the engraving by Jean-Baptiste Le Prince (J-R 1384); on one side of the teapot, *L'innocence* after one by Francois Antoine Aveline (J-R 196), on the other side, the *Babet* or *Petite fille à la cage* (see cat. 104); on the saucer, the *Petit tailleur de pierre* which Jean-Baptiste de Fernex had modeled in biscuit in 1754.

*101*

102

## 102 | *Déjeuner Hébert*

Soft-paste porcelain; white ground with
colored flesh tone and blue camaïeu
Tray, 11¾ × 8¾ in. (30.1 × 22.5 cm)
Milk jug, H. 5¼ in. (13.3 cm)
Sugar bowl, H. 4 in. (10.1 cm)
Cup, H. 2½ in. (6.5 cm)
Saucer, diam. 5¼ in. (13.5 cm)
Marks on tray: in blue, interlaced L's; A [1753];
a heraldic label facing upward [Vielliard]; incised
Marks on all other pieces: in blue, interlaced L's, a dot;
A; Vielliard; no letter date on either cup or saucer
Decorator: André-Vincent Vielliard
Vincennes, 1753
Musée du Louvre, Paris (OA 4041)
*Paris*

REFERENCES
Belfort, 1976, no. 58, pp. 14–21, fig. 6; exh.
cat. 1977–78, Paris, Grand Palais, no. 75.

This déjeuner, like the one from the Wadsworth Atheneum (cat. 101),
presents a range of Boucher designs that were used at Vincennes around
1753; the same figures exist as white-glazed or biscuit models. The little
girl on the milk jug is *Babet* or *La petite fille à la cage* (see cat. 104). The
*Jeune suppliant* (see cat. 99) is on the sugar bowl. Anne-Marie Belfort has

recognized in the child blowing soap bubbles a disguised version of a flute player by Boucher. The tray displays a composition after the engraving by Jean-Baptiste Le Prince, *La chasse* (J-R 1384), that Vielliard used several times, as for instance on the decoration of a flowered basin now at Sèvres (MNC 23179).

*103*

## 103 | *Plateau Hébert*

Soft-paste porcelain; white ground with
blue camaïeu decoration
11 × 9 in. (28.3 × 23.2 cm)
Marks: interlaced L's, a dot beneath; a
heraldic lion facing upward [Vielliard]; A [1753]
Decorator: André-Vincent Vielliard
Vincennes, 1753
Musée du Louvre, Paris (TH 1231)

REFERENCE
Belfort, 1976, no. 58, p. 8, fig. 1.

At Vincennes, the painter André-Vincent Vielliard specialized in the figures of the *Enfants Boucher*, whether he faithfully copied them or interpreted them according to his whim. In this work, for instance, the putti are carefully reproduced; but instead of setting them on clouds, as Boucher had done (see La Rue's engraving *La Poésie* [J-R 1303], from the *Livre des Arts* published by Huquier), Vielliard set them on a grassy mound. This type of mound was used particularly in the painted decorations of the mid-eighteenth century, as its round shape helped fit the decoration into a circular piece.

# 104 | *Babet* or *La petite fille à la cage*

Soft-paste porcelain; polychrome
enamel and gilding
H. 8 in. (20.3 cm)
Model attributed to Pierre Blondeau,
1752
Vincennes, possibly 1753 (letter date
mostly effaced)
Musée National de Céramique, Sèvres;
Gift of A. Gerard (MNC 10446)

REFERENCE
Exh. cat. 1977–78, Paris, Grand Palais,
no. 509.

Like the *Petite fille au tablier* and the *Moissonneur* (see cat. 106, 107), this
figure illustrates one of the characters of the ballet-pantomime *La Vallée
de Montmorency* by Charles-Simon Favart, a later redaction of *Les*

*104*

*vendanges de Tempé.* Typical of the *Enfants Boucher* is the parody of the adult world by these children—a reduction *ad infantiam* that fascinated the eighteenth century in the same way that chinoiseries and other exotic subjects did.

The *Petite fille à la cage* clearly illustrates how a motif formulated by Boucher after any given mythological or, as in this case, theatrical subject could be used not only by ceramicists but also by craftsmen active in other fields. The exact model (drawing or engraving) used by Pierre Blondeau, according to Bourgeois (1913, no. 493), is not known, but a contemporary small painting (A & W 443, fig. 1254) was executed by Boucher (perhaps with some studio assistance) as a tapestry model for the Gobelins, where it was woven as an armchair back (such an armchair can be seen at Osterley Park).

The Sèvres manufactory still owns a model as well as some old molds for this figure, which enjoyed considerable success as proven by its multiple editions in porcelain as well as in biscuit and the copies by other European manufactories. It should be noted that besides the various editions made at Vincennes (see Zick, 1965, p. 8), at Sèvres André-Vincent Vielliard used the motif as *décor peint.* One finds versions of this model also among the productions of the manufactories of Wegely at Berlin and Hannong at Strasbourg, and a white faïence version of it was executed at Delft (Rijksmuseum, Amsterdam; see Zick, 1965, pls. 13, 15, 20).

## 105 | *Corydon* or *Le porteur d'oiseaux*

Terra-cotta
H. 8¼ in. (21.5 cm)
Model by Pierre Blondeau, 1753
Vincennes, about 1753
Musée National de Céramique, Sèvres
(MNC 7758)

REFERENCES
Exh. cat. 1977–78, Paris, Grand Palais, no. 514; Belfort, 1976, pp. 17, 18.

This figure, also from the *Vallée de Montmorency,* was often used as a pendant to the *Petite fille à la cage* (see cat. 104) and was equally repeated at Vincennes and other European manufactories, while a figure issued under Falconet at Sèvres, the *Floriste* (1760), may be an adaptation of the model (see exh. cat. 1977–78, Paris, Grand Palais, p. 181). It should also be noted that a smaller version (13.5 cm)—in white-glazed soft-paste porcelain—is at the Musée National de Céramique, Sèvres (MNC 1333), and could be an earlier version of the same subject.

In the terra-cotta, the basket that supports the figure is empty, while in the porcelain version it is filled with grapes. This is the kind of addition the assembler was allowed to make to complete the figurine.

105

## 106 | La petite fille au tablier

Soft-paste porcelain; white with blue enamel decoration
H. 8½ in. (21.6 cm)
Mark on underside: interlaced L's
enclosing A [1753] in blue enamel
Model attributed to Pierre Blondeau, 1752
Vincennes, 1753
The Metropolitan Museum of Art, New York;
Gift of R. Thornton Wilson, 1950, in memory of
Florence Ellsworth Wilson (50.211.167)

## 107 | Le moissonneur

Soft-paste porcelain; white with blue enamel decoration
H. 7¾ in. (19.7 cm)
Model attributed to Pierre Blondeau, 1752
Vincennes, probably 1753
The Metropolitan Museum of Art, New York;
Gift of R. Thornton Wilson, 1950, in memory of
Florence Ellsworth Wilson (50.211.166)

REFERENCE
Exh. cat. 1977–78, Paris, Grand Palais,
nos. 499, 510.

These two figures belong to a series based upon characters from a ballet-pantomime entitled *La Vallée de Montmorency*, first performed at the Paris Opéra-Comique in 1752. This ballet derived from another, the *Vendanges de Tempé*, first produced in 1745. Its author was Charles-Simon Favart, a friend of Boucher's (see discussion by Alastair Laing in "Boucher: The Search for an Idiom").

*106*
*107*

366

Although direct models, engravings or drawings, from which these figures were created are not known, they have traditionally been linked with Boucher's influence upon the Vincennes–Sèvres manufactory. More specifically, old inventories and sales registers refer to these figures as *Enfants Boucher* (Zick, 1965, p. 15). Their attribution to Blondeau was made, however, only in 1913 by Emile Bourgeois (1913, nos. 436, 494).

The variety of the models executed in glazed porcelain (with or without polychrome) and in biscuit, as well as the differences among them—due to the intervention and additions of the assembler—show the popularity of this type of figure. The quality of the soft-paste porcelain and the delicate highlights of color contribute to the success of these models.

*108*

# *108* | *Le grand jardinier*

Terra-cotta
H. 10¾ in. (27.3 cm)
Model attributed to Jean-Baptiste de Fernex
Vincennes, February 1754
Musée National de Céramique, Sèvres (MNC 7752)

REFERENCE
Exh. cat. 1977–78, Paris, Grand Palais, no. 485.

The attribution of this piece to de Fernex is based on the theory that it constitutes a pendant to the *Grande jardinière* executed by the same artist. The *Grande jardinière* is mentioned in the Sèvres archives among the works made in 1755 (*Jardinière de Fernex*) and is similar to the *Bergère tenant une corbeille de fleurs* produced in 1754.

De Fernex, if indeed the author of this sculpture, adapted a typical Boucher prototype. The child is shown engaged in an adult's activity. As always, the sculpture is made stable by the addition of a support, in this case a tree trunk. The details of the costume and of the flowered baskets allow the assemblers to display their virtuosity.

## 109 | *Le porteur de mouton*

Soft-paste biscuit porcelain
H. 8½ in. (21.7 cm)
Mark incised on tree trunk,
at the back: F
Model of 1754(?)
Vincennes, between 1754 and 1766
Musée National de Céramique, Sèvres;
Decle bequest (MNC 8826)

109

110

REFERENCE
Exh. cat. 1977 78, Paris, Grand Palais,
no. 513.

The date and authorship of this model are uncertain. While Emile Bourgeois attributed the model to J-B. de Fernex and dated it 1754, the F mark is presumed to indicate a model executed during Falconet's tenure at Sèvres (1757–66). Svend Eriksen has in fact assigned the date 1765 to a similarly marked example of the same model at the Pitti Palace, Florence (1968, cat. 29).

It is perhaps this mark which has prompted some authors, including Rosalind Savill (1982, p. 164), to see in this figure and its companion, the *Bergère assise*, porcelain reductions of the limestone *(pierre de Tonnerre)* sculptures created by Falconet (as well as by Coustou, Allegrain, and Vassé) for the dairy of Mme de Pompadour's château at Crécy in 1753. There is, however, no evidence of this, and Svend Eriksen, for instance, has prudently noted that the two compositions "are supposedly" part of the commission.

If, on the other hand, the model was indeed executed in 1754 and can be identified with the *Jardinier agenouillé* mentioned in the inventory of 1 January 1755, Emile Bourgeois's identification of the sitter with the actor Rochard de Bouillac, one of the performers in *Les amours de Bastien et Bastienne* (1753) of Mme Favart and Harny, could be correct (1909, I, p. 29).

Only biscuit porcelain versions of this model are known (see exh. cat. 1977–78, Paris, p. 180). By 1754, the fashion for white-glazed porcelain was fading, and indeed the model might simply be a later creation.

# 110 | *Le batelier de Saint-Cloud*

Soft-paste biscuit porcelain
H. 11½ in. (29.3 cm)
Model attributed to Suzanne, 1755
Vincennes, about 1755
Musée National de Céramique, Sèvres
(MNC 5269)

REFERENCE
Exh. cat. 1977–78, Paris, Grand Palais,
no. 458.

*La Vallée de Montmorency* was not the only play whose characters Boucher interpreted for the manufactory at Vincennes. The present figure derives from another production of Charles-Simon Favart, *Les bateliers de Saint-Cloud* (1741, revised in 1744), in which the famous actress Mlle Arimath appeared *en travesti*.

A drawing by Boucher in a private collection (see exh. cat. 1977–78, Paris, Grand Palais, p. 153) might be the primary source for this composition, of which the original terra-cotta is at the Musée National de Céramique at Sèvres (MNC 7994). Both the attribution of the model and its date were advanced by Emile Bourgeois (1909, I, p. 31; II, p. 6).

## 111 | *Le petit vendangeur*

Soft-paste biscuit porcelain
H. 5¾ in. (15 cm)
Model by Falconet, 1757
Sèvres, about 1757
Musée National de Céramique, Sèvres
(MNC 6566¹)

## 112 | *Le marchand de colifichets (ou de gimblettes)*

Soft-paste biscuit porcelain
H. 5¾ in. (14.8 cm)
Model by Falconet, 1757
Sèvres, about 1757
Musée National de Céramique, Sèvres
(MNC 15596)

## 113 | *Le petit pâtissier*

Soft-paste biscuit porcelain
H. 5¾ in. (15 cm)
Model by Falconet, 1757
Sèvres, about 1757
Musée National de Cèramique, Sèvres
(MNC 18702)

The success of the *Enfants Boucher* encouraged the manufactory after its transfer to Sèvres in 1756 to multiply this type of model. Etienne-Maurice Falconet, associated with the manufactory from 1757 until his departure for Russia in 1766, fostered this production (eighteen groups or single models were produced at Sèvres under him) while giving it a style distinctive from the earlier production at Vincennes.

The *Enfants Falconet* are somewhat more naturalistic than the *Enfants Boucher*. They go about their occupations without the kind of affectation that was the trademark of their predecessors. Yet they depend upon original designs by Boucher as much as the figures of the years 1752–55.

Both the *Petit vendangeur* and the *Marchand de colifichets* were engraved by Pierre-François Tardieu, author of a series of engravings after Sèvres figurines (J-R p. 386) done in 1763, which followed a *Premier Livre de Figures d'après les porcelaines de la Manufacture Royale de France, inventées en 1757, par Mr. Boucher*, published by François Joullain in 1761. To this first series for which the drawings were made by Falconet *fils* belongs the engraving after the *Petit pâtissier* (J-R 1233).

*III*

*II2*

*II3*

# 114 | *Pair of pots-pourris "triangle"*

Soft-paste porcelain; light blue ground
with polychrome and gold decoration
H. 11½ in. (29.2 cm); W. 7 in. (17.7 cm)
Marks: painted in blue on both, crossed
L's enclosing the letter I [1761]; lower-
case roman letter K [for Dodin]
Painted decoration by
Charles-Nicolas Dodin
(working 1754–1803)
Sèvres, 1761
The Detroit Institute of Arts;
Gift of Mrs. Horace E. Dodge
in memory of her husband
(71–246 and 247)

REFERENCE
Dauterman, to be published.

It is not possible to know if this pair of vases or a similarly shaped but differently decorated pair at the Metropolitan Museum, New York (58.75.118, 119), were the ones delivered to the king at Versailles in December 1762, their color not being mentioned (see Brunet & Préaud, 1978, p. 72, pl. XXVI).

Although the primary function of these vases is to serve as pots-pourris, the three other openings enable them also to be used as bulb vases. Both are decorated with chinoiseries, one of them directly taken from the engraving by Gabriel Huquier entitled *Soldat et montreuse de curiosité* (J-R 1131), the other after a sanguine drawing in the Louvre (see Guérin, 1911, pl. 69).

*114*

## 115 Pair of vases (vases cannelés à bandeau)

Soft-paste porcelain; turquoise blue
ground with polychrome and gold
decoration
On the front, pastoral scenes; on the
back, trophies of love and music
H. 14 in. (35.6 cm) and
14⅛ in. (35.9 cm)
Mark incised on (58.75.116): ℮⊃
Decorators: pastoral scenes
attributed to Charles-Nicolas Dodin
(active 1754–1803); trophies in the
manner of Charles Buteux the Elder
(active 1756–82)
Sèvres, about 1775
The Metropolitan Museum of Art,
New York; Samuel H. Kress Collection
(58.75.116ab,117ab)

REFERENCES
Dauterman, Parker & Standen, 1964, p. 230;
Brunet & Préaud, 1978, p. 180, no. 169.

Even after Boucher's death in 1770, the manufactory at Sèvres continued
to use his models for painted decorations on vases and plaques. Executed
about 1775, these fluted vases are already typical of the rising neoclassical
style, but their severe geometry is betrayed by the Rococo elegance of
Boucher's images.

The painter (evidently Charles-Nicolas Dodin) who decorated these
vases adapted two engravings after Boucher. One is *Les amants surpris*

(J-R 633) by Gilles Demarteau; the other *L'Ecole de l'Amitié* (J-R 588) by Jean-Marie Delâtre, after the painting executed by Boucher in 1760 for the Margravine of Baden (cat. 72; A & W 597/1a).

While the painters at Vincennes did not depart substantially from their engraved models, which they occasionally simplified but reproduced en camaïeu, thus truthfully respecting the spirit of the engravings, at Sèvres the artists carried out their works in polychrome, even when copying from engravings, giving the illusion of copies of paintings on porcelain.

## 116 | *Pair of vases (vases flacons à cordes)*

Soft-paste porcelain; apple-green ground with polychrome and gold decoration
On the front, pastoral scenes; on the back, trophies of gardening and love
H. 13⅜ in. (34 cm) and 13½ in. (34.3 cm)
Marks on both: interlaced L's enclosing T [1772] above lower case roman K [Dodin] in blue enamel; *c.p* incised
Decorators: pastoral scenes by Charles-Nicolas Dodin (active 1754–1803); trophies attributed to Charles Buteux the Elder (active 1756–82)
Sèvres, 1772
The Metropolitan Museum of Art, New York; Samuel H. Kress Collection (58.75.72ab, 73ab)

116

REFERENCE
Dauterman, Parker & Standen, 1964, p. 227,
illus. pp. 228–29.

Pierre Verlet believes that these two vases, formerly in the Hillingdon collection, are identical with those delivered to Mme Victoire, daughter of Louis XV, in 1772 (Archives Nationales, Manufacture Nationale de Sèvres, Registres de Ventes, vol. 3, p. 43). The shape of these vases was particularly suited to painted decoration, their relative simplicity enhancing it. Dodin was thus able to copy detailed engravings published in 1766 by Jacques-Firmin Beauvarlet (J-R 291, 294) after two paintings by François Boucher entitled *Les amusements de la jeunesse au village: La chasse* and *La pêche* (A & W 631, 632; whereabouts unknown). The painter at Sèvres only simplified certain motifs, deleting, for instance, the putti on the pedestal which can be seen in *La chasse*. He also slightly shifted the composition in order to center it better around the figures.

# References Cited

ADHEMAR, Jean. "Sirette, Casanova, et Boucher." *La revue française* 90 (June 1957): 37–40.

ALBERT, Maurice. *Les théâtres de la Foire (1660–1789)*. Paris, 1900.

*ALMANACH Historique et Raisonné des Architectes, Peintres, Sculpteurs, Graveurs et Cizeleurs . . . &c.*, [by J-B-P. Le Brun]. Paris, 1776; 1777. Facsimile edition of both years published in 1 vol., Geneva, 1972.

ALTE PINAKOTHEK, Munich. *Katalog der Kgl. Älteren Pinakothek*. 11th ed. Munich, 1911.

———. *Katalog*. Vol. IV, *Französische und spanische Malerei*. Munich, 1972.

AMIET, Henri. *Catalogue des dessins, tableaux, miniatures, estampes . . . &c., contenues Dans le Cabinet de S. E. Mr. le Comte VINCENT POTOCKI, Duc de Zbaraz . . . &c.* Warsaw, 1780.

ANANOFF, Alexandre. *L'oeuvre dessiné de François Boucher (1703–1770): Catalogue raisonné*. Vol. I. Paris, 1966. No more published.

ANANOFF, Alexandre, & WILDENSTEIN, Daniel. *François Boucher*. 2 vols. Lausanne and Paris, 1976.

———. *L'opera completa di Boucher*. Classici dell'arte, vol. 100. Milan, 1980.

ARGENSON, Maure-Charles-Marie-René, marquis d', ed. *Autour d'un ministre de Louis XV: Lettres intimes inédites*. Paris, 1923.

ARGENSON, René-Louis de Voyer, marquis d'. *Journal et Mémoires*. Edited by E.J.B. Rathery. 9 vols. Paris, 1859–67.

AVERY, Charles, & LAING, Alastair. *Fingerprints of the Artist: European Terra-Cotta Sculpture from the Arthur M. Sackler Collections*. Washington, D.C., and Cambridge, Mass., 1981.

BABAULT, [and others]. *Annales Dramatiques, ou Dictionnaire Général des Théâtres*. 9 vols. Paris, 1808–12.

BABELON, Jean-Pierre. *Histoire et description des bâtiments des Archives Nationales*. Paris, 1969.

BADIN, Jules. *La Manufacture de Tapisseries de Beauvais depuis ses origines jusqu'à nos jours*. Paris, 1909.

BAETJER, Katharine. *European Paintings in the Metropolitan Museum of Art by Artists Born in or before 1865: A Summary Catalogue*. 3 vols. New York, 1980.

BAILY, J. T. Herbert. "The Dickens Centenary Exhibition of Old Masters, New York." *The Connoisseur* 32 (Jan.–Apr. 1912): 220–40.

BALLOT DE SOVOT. *Eloge de M. Lancret, peintre du Roi*. Paris, 1743. Reprinted in *Nicolas Lancret, sa vie et son oeuvre*, by J-J. Guiffrey. Paris, [1873].

BARBIER, E.J.F. *Journal historique et anecdotique du règne de Louis XV*. Edited by A. de la Villegille. 4 vols. Paris, 1847–56.

BATAILLE, Marie-Louise, & WILDENSTEIN, Georges. *Berthe Morisot: Catalogue des peintures, pastels et aquarelles*. Paris, 1961.

BEAULIEU, M. "La fillette aux nattes de Saly: Note rectificative." *Bulletin de la Société de l'Histoire de l'Art français*, 1955: 62–66.

"A BEAUVAIS TAPESTRY by Boucher." *Bulletin of the Minneapolis Institute of Art* 2, 10 (Mar. 6, 1943): [31]–34.

BECKER, Wolfgang. *Paris und die deutsche Malerei: 1750–1840*. Munich, 1971.

BELFORT, Anne-Marie. "L'oeuvre de Vielliard d'après Boucher." *Cahiers de la céramique, du verre et des arts du feu* 58 (1976): 6–35.

BENISOVICH, Michel N. "A Bust of Alexandrine d'Etiolles by Saly." *Gazette des Beaux-Arts* 6th ser., 28 (July 1945): 31–42.

BENNETT, Anna G. *Five Centuries of Tapestry from the Fine Arts Museums of San Francisco*. San Francisco and Rutland, Vt., 1976.

BENOIS, Alexandre. "La Peinture Français, Italienne et Anglaise aux XVIIe et XVIIIe siècles." In *Les anciennes Ecoles de Peinture dans les Palais et Collections Privées Russes représentées à l'Exposition organisé à St.-Pétersbourg en 1909 par la revue d'art ancien "Staryé Gody"*: [105]–19. Brussels, 1910.

BERCKENHAGEN, Ekhart. *Die französische Zeichnungen der Kunstbibliothek Berlin*. Berlin, 1970.

BERNARD-MAITRE, Henri. *Tapisseries chinoises de F. Boucher au Palais Yuen-Min-Yuen de Pékin*. N.p., n.d.

———. "Les tapisseries chinoises de François Boucher à Pékin." *Bulletin de la Société de l'Histoire de l'Art français*, 1951: 9–10.

BERNIS, François-Joachim de Pierre, cardinal de. *Mémoires*. Edited by Ph. Bonnet. Paris, 1980. First published Paris, 1878.

BERNOULLI, Johann Jakob. *Reisen durch Brandenburg, Pommern und Pohlen in den Jahren 1777 und 1778*. Leipzig, 1780.

BIRYUKOVA, Nina. "Decoration and Diplomacy: Eighteenth-Century French Tapestries." *Apollo* 101 (June 1975): 458–65.

BIVER, Paul, le comte. *Histoire du Château de Bellevue*. Paris, 1933.

BJURSTROM, Per. *Drawings in Swedish Public Collections*. Vol. IV, *French Drawings: Eighteenth Century*. Stockholm: Nationalmuseum, 1982.

BLANC, Charles. *Histoire des Peintres: Ecole Française, François Boucher*. Paris, 1862. Originally published in parts on 1 Aug. 1851 as nos. 62–63 of *Histoire des Peintres*, and nos. 29–30 of *Ecole Française*.

BLAZY, Guy. *Musée de l'Hôtel Sandelin: Catalogue des Peintures*. Saint-Omer, 1981.

BLONDEL, Jacques-François. *De la distribution des Maisons de Plaisance et de la Décoration des Edifices en général*. 2 vols. Paris,

1737–38. Facsimile reprint, Farnborough, 1967.

———. *L'Architecture Françoise, ou recueil de plans, d'élévations, coupes et profils. . . .* 4 vols. Paris, 1752–56. Facsimile reprint, Paris, 1904–05.

BLUNT, Anthony. "Drawings at Waddesdon Manor." *Master Drawings* 11 (Winter 1973): 359–64, plates 1–21.

BOCCARA, Dario. *Les Belles Heures de la Tapisserie*. Paris, 1971.

BOFFRAND, Germain. *Livre d'Architecture*. Paris, 1745. Facsimile reprint, Farnborough, 1969.

BORDEAUX, Jean-Luc. "The Epitome of the Pastoral Genre in Boucher's Oeuvre: *The Fountain of Love* and *The Bird Catcher* from *The Noble Pastorale*." *The J. Paul Getty Museum Journal* 3 (1976): 75–101.

———. *François Le Moyne and His Generation, 1688–1737*. Paris, 1985.

BORSCH-SUPAN, H. "François Boucher." In *China und Europa: Chinaverständnis im 17. und 18. Jahrhundert*: 282–92. (Exh. cat. 1973, Berlin).

BOTTARI, Giovanni. *Raccolta di lettere sulla pittura, scultura et architettura. . . .* 6 vols. Rome, 1754–68. See especially vol. II (1757).

BOTTARI, Giovanni, & TICOZZI, Stefano. *Raccolta di lettere sulla pittura, scultura et architettura. . . .* pub. da Gio. Bottari e continuata fino ai nostri giorni da Stefano Ticozzi. 8 vols. Milan, 1822–25. See especially vol. II (1822).

BOTTIGER, Johan Fredrik. *La Collection des Tapisseries de l'Etat suédois*. Vol. IV. Stockholm, 1898.

BOURGEOIS, Emile. *Le biscuit de Sèvres au XVIIIe siècle*. 2 vols. Paris, 1909.

———. *Le biscuit de Sèvres, recueil des modèles de la manufacture de Sèvres au XVIIIe siècle*. Paris, [1913].

BOURNE, Jonathan. "Rothschild Furniture at Dalmeny." *Apollo* 119 (June 1984): 406–11.

[BOYER, marquis D'ARGENS, Jean-Baptiste de]. *Reflexions critiques sur les différentes écoles de peinture*. Paris, 1752. Published in a revised version entitled *Examen critique des différentes écoles de peinture*. Berlin, 1768.

B[RECK], J. "An Anonymous Gift." *Metropolitan Museum of Art Bulletin* 17, 3 (Mar. 1922): 51–55.

BRET, Antoine. "Eloge de M. Boucher." In *Le Nécrologe des Hommes Célèbres de France, par une Société de Gens de Lettres*, vol. IV: 47–70. Paris, 1771.

BRICE, Germain. *Description nouvelle de la ville de Paris*. [5th ed.]. 2 vols. Paris, 1706.

BRIGANTI, Chiara. *Curioso itinerario delle collezioni ducali parmensi*. Parma, 1969.

BRUHN, Thomas P. "The Loves of the Gods." *The Bulletin of the Walters Art Gallery* 21, 6 (Mar. 1969): [2]–[3].

BRUNET, Marcelle, & PREAUD, Tamara. *Sèvres: Des origines à nos jours.* Fribourg, 1978.

BUDZINSKA, Elżbieta. "Z wczesnej twórczości Franciszka Smuglewicza. Projekty obrazów do Sali Rycerskiej Zamku Warszawskiego." In *Biuletyn Historii Sztuki* 33, 2 (1971): 152–61.

BUROLLET, Thérèse. *Musée Cognacq-Jay: Peintures et dessins.* Paris, 1980.

*CADRES et Bordures de Tableaux de la fin du XVIᵉ siècle au Premier Empire.* Paris, [1910].

CAILLEUX, Jean. "Who Was Boucher's Best Beloved?" *The Burlington Magazine* 108 (Feb. 1966), advertisement supplement no. 15: i–vi.

CAMPARDON, Emile. *Madame de Pompadour et la cour de Louis XV au milieu du dix-huitième siècle.* Paris, 1867.

———. *Un artiste oublié, J. B. Massé, peintre de Louis XV. . . .* Paris, 1880.

CASANOVA, Jacques [de Seingalt]. *Histoire de ma vie.* 12 vols. in 6. Wiesbaden and Paris, 1960–62.

*CATALOGUE des sujets de theses formant le fonds général de feu M. Cars, graveur du Roi, acquis par Babuty, Libraire.* Paris, 1771.

*CATALOGUE HISTORIQUE du Cabinet de Peinture et Sculpture Française de M. de Lalive.* Paris, 1764.

CAVALLO, Adolph S. *Tapestries of Europe and of Colonial Peru in the Museum of Fine Arts, Boston.* 2 vols. Boston, 1967.

CAYLUS, Anne-Claude-Philippe de Tubières de Grimoard de Pestels de Levis, comte de. *La vie d'Antoine Watteau.* [Paris], 1748. See ROSENBERG, 1984[c].

———. *Vies d'artistes du XVIIIᵉ siècle.* Publié avec une introd. et des notes par André Fontaine. Paris, 1910.

CHAMCHINE, B. *Le Château de Choisy.* Paris, 1910.

CHAMPEAUX, Alfred de. "L'art décoratif dans le vieux Paris. 8ᵉ article, VI: Le Marais (fin)." *Gazette des Beaux-Arts* 3d ser., 6 (Nov. 1891): 404–26. One of a series of articles republished with revisions in book form under the same title in 1898.

CHARAVAY, Etienne. *Inventaire des Autographes et Documents Historiques réunis par M. Benjamin Fillon.* Vol. II. Paris, 1879.

———. *Lettres autographes composant la Collection de M. Alfred Bovet.* Paris, 1887.

CHATEAUNEUF-SUR-LOIRE. *Tableaux de la galerie du Château de Châteauneuf-Sur-Loire.* Paris, 1786.

CHENNEVIERES, Philippe de. "Chardin." *Portraits inédits d'artistes français* 3ᵉ livraison (April 1856): 56–57.

———. "Une lettre de M. de Tournehem (1746)." *Nouvelles Archives de l'Art français* 3d ser., 3 (1887): 361–62.

CHIERICI, Umberto. *Torino, il Palazzo Reale.* Turin, 1969.

"The CHINESE FAIR." *The Bulletin of the Minneapolis Institute of Arts* 35 (May 4, 1946): 85–92.

CHOMER, Gilles. "Le peintre Pierre-Charles Le Mettay (1726–1759)." *Bulletin de la Société de l'Histoire de l'Art français*, 1981: 81–102.

CHOUQUET, Gustave. *Histoire de la Musique Dramatique en France, depuis ses origines jusqu'à nos jours.* Paris, 1873.

CLARAC, Charles-Othon-Frédéric-Jean-Baptiste de, comte. *Musée de Sculpture antique et moderne.* 6 text vols., 6 plate vols. Paris, 1826–53.

COCHIN, Charles-Nicolas. *Mémoires inédits.* Edited by Ch. Henry. Paris, 1880.

COHEN, David H. "Four tables guéridons by Sèvres." *Antologia* 13–16 (Dec. 1980): 1–11.

CONISBEE, Philip. *Painting in Eighteenth-Century France.* Oxford, 1981.

CORCORAN GALLERY OF ART, Washington, D.C. *Illustrated Handbook of the W. A. Clark Collection.* Washington, D.C., 1932.

CORDEY, Jean. *Inventaire des biens de madame de Pompadour, rédigé après son décès.* Paris, 1939.

*CORRESPONDANCE des Directeurs de L'Académie de France à Rome avec les Surintendants de Bâtiments,* publiée d'après les manuscrits des Archives nationales par M. A. de Montaiglon & Jules Guiffrey. 18 vols., including an index vol. by Paul Cornu. Paris, 1887–1912.

*CORRESPONDANCE INEDITE du roi Stanislas-Auguste Poniatowski et de Madame Geoffrin (1764–1777).* Edited by Charles de Mouy. Paris, 1875.

*CORRESPONDANCE LITTERAIRE, philosophique et critique,* by Friedrich Grimm, Denis Diderot [and others]. 16 vols. Paris, 1877–82.

COURAJOD, Louis. *Livre-journal de Lazare Duvaux, marchand-bijoutier ordinaire du Roy 1748–1758, précédé d'une étude sur le goût et sur le commerce des objets d'art au milieu du 18ᵉ siècle. . . .* 2 vols. Paris, 1873.

COURAL, J. "La Manufacture royale de Beauvais." *Monuments historiques de la France* 6 (1977): 66–84.

COYPEL, Charles-Antoine. "Dialogue de M. Coypel, Premier peintre du Roi, sur l'exposition des Tableaux dans le Sallon du Louvre, en 1747." *Mercure de France,* Nov. 1751: 59–73.

CREQUY, Renée Caroline [de Froulay], marquise de. *Souvenirs de la marquise de Créquy,* by P-M-J. Cousin de Courchamps. 10 vols. 4th ed., n.d. First published Paris, 1834–35.

CRICK-KUNTZIGER, Marthe. *Catalogue des Tapisseries.* Brussels, 1966.

CROY, Emmanuel, duc de. *Journal inédit du duc de Croÿ, 1718–1784.* Edited by le vicomte de Grouchy and Paul Coffin. 4 vols. Paris, 1906–07.

DACIER, Emile. *Catalogues de Ventes et Livrets de Salons illustrés et annotés par Gabriel de Saint-Aubin.* 6 vols. Paris, 1909–21. Vol. I (1909), nos. 1 & 2; vol. II (1910), nos. 3 & 4; vol. III (1911), nos. 5 & 6; vol. IV (1913), nos. 7 & 8; vol. V (1919), nos. 9 & 10; vol. VI (1921), no. 11. See also DACIER 1953 and 1954.

———. "Le Sedaine du Musée Condé." *La revue de l'art ancien et moderne* 38 (1920): 5–18, 104.

———. "Catalogues de ventes et livrets de Salons illustrés et annotés par Gabriel de Saint-Aubin, 12: Catalogue de la vente Verrier (1776)." *Gazette des Beaux-Arts* 6th ser., 41 (May–June 1953): 297–334.

———. "Catalogues de ventes et livrets de Salons illustrés et annotés par Gabriel de Saint-Aubin, 13: Catalogue de la vente du Marquis de Calvière (1779)." *Gazette des Beaux-Arts* 6th ser., 44 (July–Aug. 1954): 5–46.

DACIER, Emile, & VUAFLART, Albert. *Jean de Jullienne et les graveurs de Watteau au XVIIIᵉ siècle.* 4 vols. Paris, 1921–29. See especially vol. I (1929), *Notices et documents biographiques* by Jacques HEROLD, & Albert VUAFLART; and vol. II (1922), *Historique.*

DAHL, Julius, & LOHMEYER, Karl. *Das barocke Zweibrücken und seine Meister.* Enlarged 2d ed. Waldfischbach, 1957.

DANDRE-BARDON, Michel-François. *Vie de Carle Vanloo.* Paris, 1765.

DANIELS, Jeffery. *Sebastiano Ricci.* Hove, 1976[a].

———. *L'opera completa di Sebastiano Ricci.* Milan, 1976[b].

DARRAS, Eugène. "La famille Bergeret de l'Isle-Adam et de Frouville (Seine-et-Oise)." *Mémoires de la Société historique et archéologique de l'arrondissement de Pontoise et du Vexin,* 1933: 65–92.

DAUTERMAN, Carl; PARKER, J.; & STANDEN, E. A. *Decorative Art from the Samuel H. Kress Collection at The Metropolitan Museum of Art.* [London], 1964.

DAUTERMAN, Carl, [and others]. *The Mr. and Mrs. Horace E. Dodge Memorial Collection: French and English Eighteenth-Century Decorative Arts, Paintings and Sculpture.* Detroit, [to be published].

DELESALLE, H. "Aunes de France et aunes de Flandre." *Revue de Métrologie,* March 1964.

DEMBOWSKI, L. *Moje wspomnienia.* Vol. I. St. Petersburg, 1898.

DEROY, Henri. *Les Hôtels du Crédit Foncier.* Paris, 1952.

DESBOULMIERS [Jean-Augustin Jullien des Boulmiers]. "Eloge de M. Boucher, premier peintre du Roi & directeur de l'Académie royale de peinture & sculpture, mort le 30 Mai 1770." *Mercure de France,* Sept. 1770: 181–89.

D[EZALLIER d'Argenville, Antoine-Nicolas]. *Voyage Pittoresque de Paris.* 1st ed., 1749; 2d ed., 1752; 3d ed., 1757; 4th ed., 1765; 5th ed., 1770; 6th ed., 1778. Paris.

———. *Voyage Pittoresque des Environs de Paris.* 1st ed., 1755; 2d ed., 1762; 3d ed., 1768; 4th ed., 1779. Paris.

———. *Vies des fameux architectes.* 2 vols. Paris, 1788.

DIDEROT, Denis. *Oeuvres complètes.* Edited by J. Assézat and Maurice Tourneux. 20 vols. Paris, 1875–77.

———. *Salons.* Vol. I, *1759. 1761. 1763.* 2d ed. Edited by Jean Seznec and Jean Adhémar. Oxford, 1975. Vol. II, *1765.* 2d ed. Edited by Jean Seznec. Oxford, 1979. Vol. III, *1767.* 2d ed. Edited by Jean Seznec. Oxford, 1983. Vol. IV, *1769. 1771. 1775. 1781.* Edited by Jean Seznec. Oxford, 1967.

DILKE, Lady. *French Painters of the XVIIIth Century.* London, 1899.

*Discours sur l'origine, les progrès, et l'état actuel de la peinture, contenant des notices sur les principaux artistes de l'Académie; pour servir d'introduction au Sallon.* Paris, 1785.

DOBSON, Austin. "The Story of Rosina: An Incident in the Life of François Boucher." In *Vignettes in Rhyme.* London, 1873.

DOWNS, Joseph. "A Beauvais Tapestry." *Pennsylvania Museum Bulletin* 24 (Mar. 1929): 3–5.

DUCLAUX, Lise. *Inventaire général des Dessins du Musée du Louvre: Ecole français.* Vol. XII, *Nadar–Ozanne.* Paris, 1975.

DUCLOS, [Charles Pinot, sieur]. *Oeuvres complètes.* Edited by L. S. Auger. 10 vols. Paris, 1806.

DUFORT DE CHEVERNY. *Mémoires du comte Dufort de Cheverny.* 2d ed. 2 vols. Edited by Robert de Crèvecoeur. Paris, 1909.

DULAURE, J-A. *Nouvelle Description des Environs de Paris.* 2 vols. Paris, 1786.

DUPRE, M. A. "Recherches Historiques sur le château, les seigneurs, et la paroisse de Ménars-lès-Blois." *Mémoires de la Société des Sciences et Lettres de la ville de Blois* 6 (1860): 99–177.

DUSSIEUX, Louis Etienne. *Les artistes français à l'étranger.* 3d ed. Paris and Lyon, 1876.

DUVAUX, Lazare. *Livre-Journal de Lazare Duvaux.* Edited by Louis Courajod. 2 vols. Paris, 1873. Facsimile edition, Paris, 1965.

EISLER, Colin. *Paintings from the Samuel H. Kress Collection: European Schools excluding Italian.* Oxford, 1977.

ENGERAND, Fernand. *Inventaire des Tableaux commandés et achetés par la Direction des Bâtiments du Roi (1709–1792).* Paris, 1900.

ERIKSEN, Svend. *Waddesdon Manor: The James A. de Rothschild Bequest to the National Trust.* [Aylesbury, Eng.], 1965.

———. *Sèvres Porcelain.* The James A. de Rothschild Collection, 2. Fribourg, 1968.

ERIKSEN, Svend, & WATSON, Francis. "The Athénienne and the Revival of the Classical Tripod." *The Burlington Magazine* 105 (Mar. 1963): 108–12.

ERMITAZH, Leningrad. *Musée de l'Ermitage. Peinture de l'Europe Occidentale, Catalogue I: Italie, Espagne, France, Suisse.* Leningrad, 1976.

FANTIN-DESODOARDS, A.E.N. *Louis Quinze.* 4 vols. Paris, [1796].

FAVART, Charles-Simon. *Théâtre de M. Favart.* 8 vols. Paris, 1763.

———. *Mémoires et correspondances littéraires, dramatiques et anecdotiques de C. S. Favart.* Edited by A.P.C. Favart. 3 vols. Paris, 1808.

FEINBLATT, Ebria. "Boucher and Van Loo: Two Drawings." *Los Angeles County Museum. Bulletin of the Art Division* 11, 1 (1959): 3–9, cover illus.

FENAILLE, Maurice. *Etat Général des Tapisseries de la Manufacture des Gobelins.* 6 vols. Paris, 1903–23. Especially vols. III (1904) & IV (1907), *Période du Dix-Huitième Siècle: Depuis la réouverture des ateliers en 1690 jusqu'à la mort du duc*

*d'Antin en 1739* and *Deuxième partie, 1737–1794*; vol. VI (1923), *Table.*

———. *François Boucher.* Paris, 1925.

FEULNER, Adolf. *Die Zick: Deutsche Maler des 18. Jahrhunderts.* Munich, 1920.

———. *Stiftung Sammlung Schloss Rohoncz.* Vol. 3, *Plastik und Kunsthandwerk.* Lugano-Castagnola, 1941.

FIORILLO, J. D. *Geschichte der zeichnenden Künste von ihrer Wiederauflebung bis auf die neuesten Zeiten.* 5 vols. Göttingen, 1798–1808. Especially vol. III (1805), *Die Geschichte der Mahlerey in Frankreich enthaltend.*

FITZWILLIAM MUSEUM, Friends of the. *Forty-First Annual Report.* Cambridge, 1949.

FIZELIERE, Albert de la. "Les portraits de Madame de Pompadour." *Gazette des Beaux-Arts* 8 (1860): 295–302.

FLEURY, Maurice, le comte. *Louis XV intime et les petites maîtresses.* 2d ed. Paris, 1899.

FOHR, Robert. *Tours, Musée des Beaux-Arts; Richelieu, Musée Municipal; Azay-le-Ferron, Château: Tableaux français et italiens du XVIIᵉ siècle.* Paris, 1982.

FONTAINE, André. *Les Collections de l'Académie Royale de Peinture et de Sculpture.* Paris, 1910.

FONTAINE DE RESBECQ, [Pierre], comte de. *Louis-Jean-Ange Poisson de la Chabeaussière.* Limoges, 1906.

FONTAINE-MALHERBE. "Eloge de Monsieur Carle Vanloo." In *Le Nécrologe des Hommes Célèbres de France.* Paris, 1768.

FONTENAI, [Louis-Abel de Bonafons], l'abbé de. *Dictionnaire des Artistes.* Paris, 1776.

FONTENELLE, Bernard le Bovier de. *Discours sur la Nature de l'Eglogue.* Paris, 1688. 4th ed., Amsterdam, 1716.

FRANKL, Paul. "Boucher's Girl on the Couch." In *Essays in Honor of Erwin Panofsky:* 138–52. New York, 1961.

FRENCH & Co., New York. *Royal Beauvais Tapestry, The Chinese Fair: One of a Series of Six Presented by Louis XV to the Emperor Kien-Lung.* New York, [1945?].

*The FRICK COLLECTION.* Vol. II, *Paintings: French, Italian and Spanish,* by B. F. Davidson [and others]. New York, 1968.

*The FRICK COLLECTION.* Vol. VII, *Porcelains: Oriental and French,* by J. A. Pope and Marcelle Brunet. New York, 1974.

FROTHINGHAM, Alice Wilson. *Capodimonte and Buen Retiro Porcelains: Period of Charles III.* New York: Hispanic Society of America, 1955.

FURCY-RAYNAUD, Marc. "Correspondance de M. de Marigny avec Coypel, Lépicié et Cochin." *Nouvelles Archives de l'Art français* 3d ser., 19 (1903); 20 (1904).

———. "Correspondance de M. d'Angiviller avec . . . Pierre." *Nouvelles Archives de l'Art français* 3d ser., 22 (1906[a]): 1–320.

———. "Correspondance de Lenormant de Tournehem . . . avec Charles Coypel . . . et N-B. Lépicié. . . ." *Nouvelles Archives de l'Art français* 3d ser., 22, Appendix (1906[b]): 321–59.

———. "Les tableaux et objets d'art saisis chez les émigrés et condamnés, et envoyés

au Muséum central." *Archives de l'Art français* n.s. 6 (1912): 245–343.

GALERIE FRANÇOISE, *ou Portraits des Hommes et des Femmes Célèbres qui ont paru en France, gravés en Taille-douce par les meilleurs Artistes, sous la conduite de M. Restout, Peintre ordinaire du Roi . . . &c. Avec un Abrégé de leur Vie par une Société de Gens de Lettres.* No. 5, BOUCHER. [Edited by J-B. Collet de Messine]. Paris, 1771.

GALLET, Michel. *Paris Domestic Architecture of the 18th Century.* London, 1972.

———. "Louis-François Trouard et l'architecture religieuse dans la région de Versailles au temps de Louis XVI." *Gazette des Beaux-Arts* 6th ser., 88 (Dec. 1976): 201–18.

GALLET, Michel, & BOTTINEAU, Yves, eds. *Les Gabriel.* Paris, 1982.

GAUTIER, Théophile. "Le Musée du Louvre." In the *Paris Guide, par les principaux écrivains et artistes de la France.* Paris, 1867.

GAUTIER [DAGOTY, Jacques]. "Observation IV. Sur l'Organe de la Vuë par rapport au sentiment de Monsieur de Buffon, & Reflexions à ce sujet sur les Tableaux exposés cette année 1753, dans le Salon du Louvre." *Observations sur l'Histoire Naturelle, sur la Physique et sur la Peinture* 8ᵉ partie (1753): 77–84.

GERSAINT, Edmé-François. *Catalogue Raisonné des diverses Curiosités du Cabinet de feu M. Quentin de Lorangère.* Paris, 1744. (Sale cat. of 2 March ff.).

GILLET, L. "Institut de France, Musée Jacquemart-André, Abbaye de Chaâlis." *Les Arts* 151 (July 1914): 1–32.

GINET, A. "Une résidence royale au XVIIIᵉ siècle, le château de la Muette." *Bulletin de la Société d'Etudes Historiques, Géographiques, et Scientifiques de la Région Parisienne* 6, 23 (Oct.–Dec. 1932): 12–18.

GIROUARD, Mark. *The Victorian Country House.* Revised and enlarged edition. New Haven and London, 1979.

GOBEL, Heinrich. *Wandteppiche.* Part I, *Die Niederlande.* 2 vols. Leipzig, 1923. Part II, *Die romanischen Länder.* 2 vols. Leipzig, 1928.

GOMBRICH, Ernst. *Symbolic Images.* London, 1972.

GONCOURT, Edmond de. *La maison d'un artiste.* 2 vols. Paris, 1881.

GONCOURT, Edmond, & Jules de. *Boucher: Etude contenant quatre dessins gravés à l'eau forte.* Paris, 1862. An amplified edition first appeared in *L'art du XVIII siècle,* in 4°, 1880, and in 8° (unillustrated) in 1881.

———. *Madame de Pompadour.* Revised edition. Paris, 1878.

———. *L'art du XVIII siècle.* Vol. I, part 3, *Boucher.* 3d ed. Paris, 1880.

———. *L'art du XVIII siècle.* 3 vols. Paris, 1881. Selected English translation, with plates added, by Robin Ironside, as *French XVIII Century Painters,* London, 1958.

GORDON, Katherine K. "Madame de Pompadour, Pigalle, and the Iconography of Friendship." *The Art Bulletin* 50, 3 (Sept. 1968): 249–62.

GOUGENOT, Louis, l'abbé. *Lettre sur la Peinture, Sculpture, et Architecture, à M\*\*\**. [Paris], 1748.

———. "Vie de Monsieur Oudry" (1761). In *Mémoires inédits sur la vie et les ouvrages des membres de l'Académie Royale de Peinture et de Sculpture*, edited by L. Dussieux [and others]. Vol. II: 365–403. Paris, 1854.

GRANBERG, Olof. *Inventaire Général des Trésors d'Art, Peintures & Sculptures, principalement des maîtres étrangers (non scandinaves) en Suède*. 3 vols. Stockholm, 1911–13. See especially vol. III (1913).

———. *Svenska Konstsamlingarnas Historia*. 3 vols. Stockholm, 1911–31. See especially vol. II (1930), *Karl X Gustav–Adolf Fredrik*.

GRONWOLDT, R. "Wandbehang: *Bacchus und Ariadne* und *Huldigung der Ariadne*." *Jahrbuch der Staatlichen Kunstsammlungen in Baden-Württemberg* 12 (1975): 379–81.

GUERIN, Jacques. *La chinoiserie en Europe au XVIII$^e$ siècle: Tapisseries, meubles, bronzes d'ameublement, céramiques, peintures et dessins exposés au Musée des Arts Décoratifs*. Paris, 1911.

GUERREIRO, Glória Nunes Riso. "Some European Tapestries in the Calouste Gulbenkian Collection in Lisbon." *The Connoisseur* 173 (April 1970): 229–37.

GUIFFREY, Jean, & MARCEL, Pierre. *Inventaire général des Dessins du Musée du Louvre et du Musée de Versailles: Ecole française*. Vols. II & III. Paris, 1908–09.

GUIFFREY, Jules. "Les modèles des Gobelins devant le Jury des Arts en Septembre 1794." *Nouvelles Archives de l'Art français* 3d ser., 13 (1897): 349–89.

HALLOPEAU, Marie-Laure. *Musée Bargoin: Beaux-Arts, Guide*. Clermont-Ferrand, [c. 1980].

HASKELL, Francis. *Patrons and Painters: A Study in the Relations between Italian Art and Society in the Age of Baroque*. New York, 1971.

HAUSSET, Madame du. *Mémoires de Madame du Hausset, Femme de Chambre de Madame de Pompadour*. Paris, 1824.

HAZLEHURST, F. Hamilton. "The Wild Beasts Pursued: The *Petite Galerie* of Louis XV at Versailles." *The Art Bulletin* 66, 2 (June 1984): 224–36.

HEBERT. *Dictionnaire Pittoresque et Historique*. 2 vols. Paris, 1766. Facsimile edition in 1 vol., Geneva, 1972.

HERCENBERG, Bernard. *Nicolas Vleughels*. Paris, 1975.

HERLUISON, H. *Actes d'état-civil d'artistes francais . . . extraits des registres de l'Hôtel-de-Ville de Paris, détruits dans l'incendie du 24 mai 1871*. Orléans, 1873.

HERMITAGE STATE MUSEUM, Leningrad. See ERMITAZH, Leningrad.

HEROLD, Jacques, & VUAFLART, Albert, 1929. See DACIER & VUAFLART, vol. I (1929).

HIESINGER, Kathryn B. "The Sources of François Boucher's *Psyche* Tapestries." *Bulletin of the Philadelphia Museum of Art* 72 (Nov. 1976): 7–23.

HILLAIRET, Jacques [Col. Auguste André Coussillan]. *Dictionnaire Historique des rues de Paris*. 2 vols. Paris, 1963; 7th ed., 1979.

HISTORISCHE ERKLAERUNGEN der Gemälde welche Herr Gottfried Winkler in Leipzig gesammlet. Leipzig, 1768.

HONEY, William Bowyer. *Dresden China: An Introduction to the Study of Meissen Porcelain*. London, 1934.

HONOUR, Hugh. *Chinoiserie: The Vision of Cathay*. London, 1961.

HOUSSAYE, Arsène. *Galerie de Portraits: Le Dix-Huitième Siècle*. Paris, 1845. Previous partial publication as *Le Dix-Huitième Siècle: Poètes, peintres, musiciens*. Paris, 1843.

HOWE, Thomas C. "*Vertumnus and Pomona* by François Boucher." *California Palace of the Legion of Honor Bulletin* n.s. 1, 5 (Mar.–Apr. 1968).

HUMBERT, Chantal. "L'exotisme dans les arts: La société française déguisée à la chinoise." *Gazette de l'Hôtel Drouot* 91 année, no.44 (Dec. 17, 1982): 28–30.

HUNTER, G. L. *The Practical Book of Tapestries*. Philadelphia and London, 1925.

———. "America's Beauvais-Boucher Tapestries." *International Studio* 85 (Oct. 1926[a]): 20–28.

———. "Beauvais-Boucher Tapestries." *Good Furniture* 26 (1926[b]): 82–89.

HURTAUT, Pierre-Thomas-Nicolas, & MAGNY. *Dictionnaire historique de la ville de Paris et de ses environs*. 4 vols. Paris, 1779.

HUSSMAN, Geraldine C. "Boucher's *Psyche* at the Basketmakers: A Closer Look." *The J. Paul Getty Museum Journal* 4 (1977): 45–50.

INGRAMS, Rosalind. "Bachaumont: A Parisian Connoisseur of the Eighteenth Century." *Gazette des Beaux-Arts* 6th ser., 75 (Jan. 1970): 11–28.

*ISOGRAPHIE des Hommes Célèbres, ou Collection de Fac-Simile de Lettres Autographes et de Signatures*. Edited by S. Berard [and others]. Vol. I. Paris, 1828–30.

JACOBY, Beverly Schreiber. "A Landscape Drawing by François Boucher after Domenico Campagnola." *Master Drawings* 17, 3 (Autumn 1979): 261–72, plate 34.

JAL, A. *Dictionnaire critique de Biographie et d'Histoire*. Paris, 1867.

JARRY, Madeleine. *World Tapestry*. New York, 1969.

———. "The Wealth of Boucher Tapestries in American Museums." *Antiques* 102 (1972): 222–31.

———. *Chinoiseries: Le rayonnement du goût chinois sur les arts décoratifs des XVII$^e$ et XVIII$^e$ siècles*. Fribourg, 1981. English translation, *Chinoiserie: Chinese Influence on European Decorative Art, 17th and 18th Centuries*, New York and London, 1981.

JARRY, Paul. *Les vieux hôtels de Paris: Le Temple et le Marais*. Vol. III. Paris, 1930.

JEAN-RICHARD, Pierrette. *Musée du Louvre, Cabinet des Dessins . . . Ecole française*. Vol. I, *L'oeuvre gravé de François Boucher dans la Collection Edmond de Rothschild*. Paris, 1978.

JEANNERAT, Carlo. "L'*Adoration des Bergers* de F. Boucher." *Bulletin de la Société de l'Histoire de l'Art français*, 1932: 75–83.

And, "Rectification d'attribution d'une toile présumé de F. Boucher." *BSHAF*, 1952: 94–95.

JEKYLL, Joseph. *Correspondence of Mr. Joseph Jekyll. . . .* Edited by Hon. Algernon Bourke. London, 1894.

JOMBERT, Charles-Antoine. *Catalogue de l'Oeuvre de Cochin fils*. Paris, 1770.

JONES, A. M. *A Handbook of the Decorative Arts in the J. Paul Getty Museum*. [Malibu], 1965.

JOUIN, Henry. "Charles Natoire et la peinture historique." *Nouvelles Archives de l'Art français* 3d ser., 5 (1889): 139–49.

*JOURNAL ENCYCLOPEDIQUE ou Universel*. [Early vols. have title *Journal Encyclopédique*.] 302 vols. Liège, 1756–59; and Bouillon, 1760–93. See especially vol. 7, pt. 1 (Oct. 1, 1757): 100–01, for review of 1757 Salon.

KALNEIN, Wend, Graf, & LEVEY, Michael. *Art and Architecture of the Eighteenth Century in France*. Harmondsworth, 1972.

KAMENSKAYA, T. D. *Pasteli Khudozhnikov Zapadnoevropeiskikh Shkol XVI–XIX Vekov*. Leningrad, 1960.

KETTERING, Alison McNeil. *The Dutch Arcadia: Pastoral Art and Its Audience in the Golden Age*. Montclair and Woodbridge, 1983.

KETTLEWELL, J. K. *The Hyde Collection Catalogue*. Glens Falls, 1981.

KLESSE, Brigitte. "Studien zu italienischen und französischen Gemälden des Wallraf-Richartz-Museums." *Wallraf-Richartz-Jahrbuch* 34 (1972): 175–262. See especially pp. 242–50 for Boucher.

———. *Katalog der italienischen, französischen, und spanischen Gemälde bis 1800 im Wallraf-Richartz-Museum*. Cologne, 1973.

KOPPLIN, Monika. *Das Fächerblatt von Manet bis Kokoschka*. Saulgau, 1981.

KROHN, Mario. *Frankrigs og Danmarks kunstneriske forbindelse i det 18 Aarhundrede*. Copenhagen, 1922.

KROL, Aleksander. *Zamek Królewski w Warszawie*. Cracow, 1926.

L.C.D.N. [?Neufville de Brunaubois-Montador]. *Description raisonnée des tableaux exposés au Louvre. Lettre à Mme. la marquise de SPR. . . .* 1738.

LACORDAIRE, K. L. *Notice historique sur les Manufactures Imperiale de Tapisseries des Gobelins*. Paris, 1855.

de LA CURNE DE SAINTE PALAYE. *Catalogue des Tableaux du Cabinet de M. Crozat, Baron de Thiers*. Paris, 1755.

[LA FONT DE SAINT-YENNE]. *Reflexions sur quelques causes de l'état présent de la peinture en France*. The Hague, 1747.

———. *Sentiments sur quelques ouvrages de peinture, sculpture, et gravure, écrits à un particulier en province*. N.p., 1754.

LAMI, Stanislas. *Dictionnaire des sculpteurs de l'Ecole française*. Vol. II, *Sous le règne de Louis XIV*. Paris, 1906.

———. *Dictionnaire des sculpteurs de l'Ecole française au dix-huitième siècle*. 2 vols. Paris, 1910–11.

LAPAUZE, Henry. *Histoire de l'Académie de France à Rome.* 2 vols. Paris, 1924.

LASZLO, E., & KIADO, C. *Flemish and French Tapestries in Hungary.* Budapest, 1981.

[LAUGIER, Marc-Antoine, le père]. *Jugement d'un amateur sur l'Exposition des tableaux. Lettre à M. le marquis de V\*\*\*.* Paris, 1753.

LAUJON, Pierre. *Oeuvres choisies.* 4 vols. Paris, 1811.

LAUTS, Jan. *Karoline Luise von Baden.* Karlsruhe, 1980.

LE BLANC, Jean-Bernard, l'abbé. *Lettre sur l'Exposition des Ouvrages de Peinture, Sculpture, & de l'Année 1747 . . . à Monsieur R.D.R.* Paris, 1747.

———. *Observations sur les Ouvrages de MM. de l'Académie de Peinture et de Sculpture, exposés au Sallon du Louvre, en l'Année 1753, et sur quelques Ecrits qui ont rapport à la Peinture. A Monsieur le Président de B\*\*\*.* [Paris], 1753.

LECHEVALLIER-CHEVIGNARD, Georges. *La Manufacture de porcelaine de Sèvres.* 2 vols. Paris, 1908.

LEIJONHUFVUD, Sigrid. *Carl Gustaf Tessin och hans Åkerökrets.* 2 vols. Stockholm, 1931–33.

LEMESLE, Gaston. *L'église Saint-Sulpice.* Paris, 1931.

LEMONNIER, Henry. "A propos des *Pastorales* de Boucher." In *L'art moderne (1500–1800): Essais et esquisses*: 215–31. Paris, 1912.

LEROY, Paul. "Notes sur les relations artistiques entre la France et la Chine aux XVIIe et XVIIIe siècles." *Réunion des Sociétés des Beaux-Arts des Départements en 1900*, 24th session: 413–30.

LESPINASSE, Pierre. "Les voyages d'Hårleman et de Tessin en France." *Bulletin de la Société de l'Histoire de l'Art français* 1910: 276–98.

———. *Le portraitiste Roslin et les artistes suédois en France pendant la seconde moitié du XVIIIe siècle.* Paris, 1929. Originally published in *BSHAF*, 1927: 234–97.

"LETTRE à l'auteur. Sur les Tableaux actuellement exposés au Louvre." *Observations Périodiques, sur la Physique, L'Histoire Naturelle, et les Beaux-Arts* 3 (1757): 161–79.

LEVEY, Michael. "A New Identity for Saly's *Bust of a Young Girl*." *The Burlington Magazine* 107 (Feb. 1965): 91.

———. "A Boucher Mythological Painting Interpreted." *The Burlington Magazine* 124 (July 1982): 442–46.

———. See also KALNEIN & LEVEY

[LIEUDE DE SEPMANVILLE]. *Réflexions nouvelles d'un amateur des beaux arts, adressés à Mme. de \*\*\*, pour servir de supplément à la Lettre sur L'Exposition . . . de l'année 1747.* [Paris, 1747].

"LIVING WITH ANTIQUES: Hillwood, the Home of Mr. and Mrs. Herbert A. May." *Antiques* 82, 3 (Sept. 1962): 262–69.

LOCHE, Renée, & ROETHLISBERGER, Marcel. *L'opera completa di Liotard.* Milan, 1978.

LOCQUIN, Jean. *La Peinture d'Histoire en France de 1747 à 1785.* Paris, 1912. Reprinted with many additional illustrations, Paris, 1978.

LORCK, Carl von. "Genius der Kunstlehre: Zwei Handzeichnungen von Benedetto Castiglione und François Boucher." In *Vom Geist des deutschen Ostens*: 94–101, figs. 41 and 42. Berlin, 1967.

LORENTZ, S. "Projets pour la Pologne de J. A. Meissonnier." *Biuletyn Historii Sztuki* 20, 2 (1958): 186–98.

———. "Projekty J. A. Meissonniers dla Pulaw." *Pulawy. Teka konserwatorska* 5 (1962): 42–46.

LORIN, F. *Rambouillet: La ville, le château, ses hôtes, 768–1906.* Paris, 1907.

LOSSKY, Boris. *Tours, Musée des Beaux-Arts: Peintures du XVIIIe siècle.* Paris, 1962.

LUGT, Frits. *Les marques de collections de dessins & d'estampes. . . .* Amsterdam, 1921. *Supplément.* The Hague, 1956.

———. *Répertoire des catalogues de ventes publiques intéressant l'art ou la curiosité.* Vol. I, *Première période: Vers 1600–1825* (1938); Vol. II (1953), *Deuxième période: 1826–1860*; Vol. III (1964), *Troisième période: 1861–1900.* The Hague.

LUNDBERG, Gunnar W. "Boucher och Carl Gustaf Tessin." In *Svenskt och Franskt 1700-tal*: 126–32. Malmö, 1972.

McCALL, George Henry. *The Joseph Widener Collection: Tapestries at Lynnewood Hall, Elkins Park, Pennsylvania.* Philadelphia, 1932.

MACON, Gustave. *Les Arts dans la maison de Condé.* Paris, 1903. Originally published as a series of articles in the *Revue de l'art* 1900–02.

MAGNIER, Charles. *Madame de Pompadour et La Tour.* Saint-Quentin, 1904.

MAGNIN, Jeanne. *La peinture et le dessin au Musée de Besançon.* Dijon, 1919.

———. *Un cabinet d'amateur parisien en 1922, Collection Maurice Magnin, II: Peintures et dessins de l'école française.* Dijon, 1922.

MAJEWSKA-MASZKOWSKA, B. *Mecenat artystyczny Izabelli z Czartoryskich Lubomirskiej, 1736–1816.* Warsaw, 1976.

MALBOIS, Emile. "Les anciens tableaux de l'église Saint Sulpice." *Bulletin de la Société de l'Histoire de l'Art français*, 1926: 113–33.

MANKOWSKI, Tadeusz. *Galerja Stanisława Augusta.* Lvov, 1932.

MANNLICH, Johann Christian von. *Beschreibung der Churpfalzbaierschen Gemälde-Sammlung zu München und zu Schleissheim.* 3 vols. Munich, 1805–10.

———. 1913. See STOLLREITHER 1913.

———. *Mémoires du chevalier Christian de Mannlich.* Edited by Joseph Delage. Paris, 1948. This is a complete edition of the early and Paris years; for abridged editions of the entire memoirs *see* STOLLREITHER, and MATTHAESIUS.

MANTZ, Paul. "Charles Natoire: Correspondance avec Antoine Duchesne." *Archives de l'Art français* 2 (1852–53): 246–304.

MANUSCRIT trouvé à la Bastille concernant les lettres de cachet lancées contre Mademoiselle de Chantilly et M. Favart par le Maréchal de Saxe. Brussels, 1868.

MARANDEL, J. Patrice. *French Oil Sketches from an English Collection.* Houston, 1975.

MARIETTE, Pierre-Jean. *Abecedario. . . .* Edited by Ph. de Chennevières & A. de Montaiglon. 6 vols. Paris, 1851–60. See especially vol. I (1851–53); and vol. II (1853–54).

MARMONTEL, [J-F.]. *Mémoires de Marmontel.* Edited by John Renwick. 2 vols. Clermont-Ferrand, 1972.

MATTHAESIUS, Friedrich. *Rokoko und Revolution: Lebenserinnerungen des Johann Christian von Mannlich.* Stuttgart, 1946.

MENTMORE. 2 vols. Edinburgh, 1884.

MERCIER, L. Sébastien. *Tableau de Paris.* 12 vols. Amsterdam, 1782–88.

MERE, Elisabeth Guénard, Mme. Brossin de. *Le Palais-Royal, ou Mémoires Secrets de la Duchesse d'Orléans, Mère de Philippe*, by M. D. F\*\*\* [Monsieur de Faverolles]. 2 vols. Hamburg, an. XIV [1806].

METROPOLITAN MUSEUM of Art, New York. *The Jack and Belle Linsky Collection.* New York, 1984.

MICHALOWSKI, Janusz M. "Deux toiles inconnues de J. P. Norblin de la Gourdaine à l'Ecole des Chevaliers dans la collection du salon d'antiquités Cailleux à Paris." *Biuletyn Historii Sztuki* 1 (1972): 74–80.

MICHEL, André. *François Boucher.* Les artistes célèbres, vol. 24. Paris, 1889.

———. *François Boucher.* Revised and enlarged edition with a catalogue raisonné added by Soullié & Masson. Paris, [1906].

MICHEL, Marianne Roland. "Observations on Madame Lancret's sale." *The Burlington Magazine* 111 (Oct. 1969), advertisement supplement no. 23: i–vi.

MIRIMONDE, A-P. de. "Un carton de tapisserie de Boucher." *La revue des arts* 5, 1 (1955): 124–27.

MONDAIN-MONVAL, Jean. *Correspondance de Soufflot avec les Directeurs des Bâtiments concernant la Manufacture des Gobelins (1756–1780).* Paris, 1918.

MONNET, Jean. *Supplément au roman comique, ou Mémoires pour servir à la vie de Jean Monnet.* 2 vols. "Londres" [Paris], 1772.

———. *Mémoires de Jean Monnet, Directeur du Théâtre de la Foire.* Paris, [1909].

MONNIER, Geneviève. *Musée du Louvre, Cabinet des Dessins: Pastels, XVIIème et XVIIIème siècles.* Paris, 1972.

MONTAIGLON, A. de. "François Boucher." *Archives de l'Art français* 6 (1858–60): 62–63.

MOUY, Charles de. *Correspondance inédite du Roi Stanislas Auguste Poniatowski et de Madame Geoffrin (1764–1777).* Paris, 1875.

MUSEE JACQUEMART-ANDRE, Paris. *Catalogue itinéraire.* Paris, n.d.

*MUSEE MAGNIN: Peintures et dessins de l'Ecole française.* Dijon, 1938.

*MUSEE NISSIM de Camondo.* Paris: Union Centrale des Arts Décoratifs, 1983.

NATIONAL GALLERY, London. *Illustrated General Catalogue.* London, 1973.

NICLAUSSE, Juliette. *Le Musée des Gobelins.* Paris, 1939.

———. *Tapisseries et Tapis de la Ville de Paris.* Paris, 1948.

NOLHAC, Pierre de. *François Boucher, premier peintre du Roi.* Paris, 1907. Includes a "Catalogue des oeuvres peintes de François Boucher, qui ont passé en vente publique depuis 1770 jusqu'en 1906," dressé par Georges Pannier.
———. *Boucher, premier peintre du Roi.* Revised ed. Paris, 1925. Lacks "Catalogue . . ."; different illustrations.
OBSER, Karl. "Zur Geschichte der Karlsruher Gemäldegalerie: François Boucher und Markgräfin Karoline Luise." *Zeitschrift für die Geschichte des Oberrheins* n.s. 17 (1902): 331–39.
*OBSERVATIONS PERIODIQUES, sur la Physique, l'Histoire Naturelle, et les Arts.* Edited by François Toussaint; illustrated by J.B.A. Gautier [Dagoty]. 3 vols. Paris, 1756–57. See especially vol. III (second half of 1757): 161–79, for review of 1757 Salon [by Antoine Renou?].
OESTERREICH, Matthias. *Description et explication des groupes, statues, bustes et demi-bustes, bas-reliefs, urnes et vases de marbre, de bronze et de plomb, antiques, aussi bien que des ouvrages modernes qui forment la collection de S. M. le Roi de Prusse.* Berlin, 1774.
OPPERMAN, Hal. "Observations on the Tapestry Designs of J-B. Oudry for Beauvais (1726–1736)." *Allen Memorial Art Museum Bulletin* 26 (1969): 49–71.
———. *Jean-Baptiste Oudry.* 2 vols. New York and London, 1977. *See also* exhib. cat. 1982–83, Paris.
PAIGNON DIJONVAL. *Cabinet de M. Paignon Dijonval.* Rédigé par M. Bénard. Paris, 1810.
P[APILLON] D[E] L[A] F[ERTE], [Denis-Pierre]. *Extrait des différens ouvrages publiés sur la vie des peintres.* 2 vols. Paris, 1776.
[PARFAICT, François & Claude]. *Dictionnaire des Théâtres de Paris.* 7 vols. Paris, 1756.
PARKER, James. "Eighteenth-Century France Recreated in the 'Cold, Barbarous Country': The Tapestry Room from the Bernstorff Palace, Copenhagen." *The Burlington Magazine* 115 (June 1973): 367–73.
PARKER, Karl. "A Drawing by Liotard." *Old Master Drawings* 5, 18 (1930): 36–37, plate 16.
*Le PAUSANIAS FRANÇAIS: Etat des Arts du Dessin en France à l'ouverture du XIXᵉ siècle,* publié par Un Observateur Impartial [Publicola Chaussard]. Paris, 1806.
PERROT, J.F.A. *Lettres sur Nismes et le Midi.* 2 vols. Nîmes, 1840.
PHILLIPS, John Goldsmith. "A Tapestry after Boucher." *Metropolitan Museum of Art Bulletin* n.s. 1 (Feb. 1943): 204–5.
PIGANIOL DE LA FORCE. *Description Historique de la Ville de Paris et de ses environs.* 2d ed. 10 vols. Paris, 1765. First edition, 1742.
PIGLER, Andor. *Barockthemen.* 1st ed. 2 vols. Budapest, 1956. 2d ed. 3 vols. Budapest, 1974.
PILES, Fortia de, & KERDU, Boisgelin de. *Voyage de deux Français en Allemagne, Danemark, Suède, Russie et Pologne (1790–1792).* Vol. V, *Pologne.* Paris, 1796.

PILON, Edmond. *Scènes galantes et libertines des artistes du XVIIIᵉ siècle.* Paris, 1909.
PIRON, Alexis. *Oeuvres complettes.* Edited by M. Rigoley de Juvigny. 9 vols. Paris, 1776.
PLANCHENAULT, René. "La collection du marquis de Livois." *Gazette des Beaux-Arts* 6th ser., 10 (July 1933): 14–30.
POMPADOUR, Jeanne-Antoinette Poisson, marquise de. *Lettres de Madame la Marquise de Pompadour.* ["Une production de jeunesse d'un magistrat."] London, 1772. Enlarged edition, 1776.
———. *Correspondance de Madame de Pompadour . . . &c.* Edited by A-P. Malassis. Paris, 1878.
POPHAM, Arthur E., & FENWICK, K. M. *European Drawings (and Two Asian Drawings) in the Collection of the National Gallery of Canada.* Toronto, 1965.
*Les PORCELAINIERS du XVIIIᵉ siècle français.* Preface by Serge Gauthier; edited by Claude Frégnac. Paris, 1964.
PORTALIS, Roger, baron. *Honoré Fragonard.* Paris, 1889.
*PROCES-VERBAUX de l'Académie Royale de Peinture et de Sculpture 1648–1793,* publiés . . . par M. Anatole de Montaiglon. Vol. IV, *1705–1725,* and vol. V, *1726–1744.* Paris, 1881–83.
PROSCHWITZ, Gunnar von. *Tableaux de Paris et de la cour de France 1739–1742: Lettres inédites de Carl Gustaf, comte de Tessin.* Göteborg and Paris, 1983.
RACINAIS, Henri. *Les Petits Appartements des Roys Louis XV et Louis XVI au Château de Versailles.* Paris, 1950.
REATH, Nancy Andrews. "The Stotesbury Collection: Tapestries and Carpets." *Pennsylvania Museum Bulletin* 28 (Dec. 1932): 29–31.
REAU, Louis. "Les artistes allemands en France au XVIIIème siècle." *Archives alsaciennes d'histoire de l'art* 3ᵉ ann. (1924[a]): 113–46.
———. *Histoire de l'expansion de l'art français moderne: Le monde slave et l'Orient.* Paris, 1924[b].
———. *Histoire de l'expansion de l'art français: Pays scandinaves, Angleterre.* Paris, 1931.
———. "Catalogue des oeuvres d'art français de la collection du Roi de Pologne Stanislas-August." In "L'art français dans les pays du Nord et de l'Est de l'Europe (XVIII–XIX siècles)." *Archives de l'Art français* n.s. 17 (1932): 225–48.
REYNOLDS, Sir Joshua. *Discourses on Art.* Edited by Robert R. Wark. San Marino, 1959.
RIEDER, William. "Eighteenth-Century Chairs in the Untermyer Collection." *Apollo* 107 (Mar. 1978): 181–85.
ROGERS, Meyric Reynold. "An Eighteenth-Century Masterpiece: Beauvais Tapestry of The Bird Snarers." *Bulletin of the Art Institute of Chicago* 38 (Jan. 1944): 2–5.
ROLAND, Berthold. *Die Malergruppe von Pfalz-Zweibrücken, Maler und Malerei eines kleinen Fürstenhofes im 18en. Jahrhundert.* Baden-Baden, 1959.
ROSENBERG, J.; SLIVE, S.; & TER KUILE, E. H. *Dutch Art and Architecture 1600–1800.* Rev. ed. Harmondsworth and New York, 1977.

ROSENBERG, Pierre. "Une esquisse de Carle Van Loo au musée de Hambourg." *Jahrbuch der Hamburger Kunstsammlungen* 14–15 (1970): 133–38.
———. "A propos de Lemoyne." *The Minneapolis Institute of Arts Bulletin* 1971–73: 53–59.
———. "Le Concours de 1727." *Revue de l'art* 37 (1977): 29–42.
———. [Catalog entries in] *Musée du Louvre. Nouvelles acquisitions du Département des Peintures (1980–1982).* Paris, 1983[a].
———. *Tout l'oeuvre peint de Chardin.* Paris, 1983[b].
———. *Musée du Louvre: Catalogue de la donation Othon Kaufmann et François Schlageter au Département des peintures.* Paris, 1984[a].
———. "Une correspondance de Julien de Parme (1736–1799)." *Archives de l'Art français* 26 (1984[b]): 197–245.
———. *Vie ancienne de Watteau.* Paris, 1984[c].
ROSENBLUM, Robert. *Transformations in Late Eighteenth Century Art.* 3d ed. Princeton, 1970.
ROTHSCHILD, Nathaniel, baron de. *Notizen über einige meiner Kunstgegenstände.* Vienna, 1903.
RUBINSTEIN-BLOCH, Stella. *Catalogue of the Collection of George and Florence Blumenthal, New York.* 6 vols. Paris, 1926–30. See especially vol. VI (1930), *Furniture and Works of Art, XVIII Century.*
RUCH, John E. "An Album of Early Drawings by François Boucher." *The Burlington Magazine* 106 (Nov. 1964): 496–500, figs. 16–24.
[SAINT-YVES, Charles Léoffroy de]. *Observations sur les Arts, et sur quelques morceaux de Peinture & de Sculpture, exposés au Louvre en 1748. Ou il est parlé de l'utilité des embellissemens dans les Villes.* Leyden, 1748.
SAINTE-MARIE, Jean-Pierre. "La Chapelle Godefroy: Orry et Natoire." *La Vie en Champagne* 263 (Feb. 1977), numéro spécial.
SAMARAN, Charles. *Jacques Casanova, vénitien.* Paris, 1914.
*SAMMLUNG THYSSEN-BORNEMISZA.* 2 vols. Castagnola: Villa Favorita, 1969–71.
SANDER, Frederik. *Nationalmuseum. Bidrag till Taflegalleriets Historia I: Riksrådet Grefve Carl Gustaf Tessins, Konung Adolf Fredriks och Drottning Lovisa Ulrikas Taflesamlingar.* Stockholm, 1872.
SANDOZ, Marc. *Jean-Baptiste Deshays, 1729–1765.* Paris, 1977.
SAURIN, Bernard-Joseph. *Oeuvres complettes.* 2 vols. Paris, 1783.
SAVILL, Rosalind. "François Boucher and the Porcelains of Vincennes and Sèvres." *Apollo* 115 (Mar. 1982): 162–70.
SCHEFFER, Carl Fredrik. *Lettres particulières à Carl Gustaf Tessin 1744–1752.* Edited by Jan Heidner. Stockholm, 1982.
SCHONBRUNNER, Joseph, & MEDER, Joseph. *Handzeichnungen alter Meister aus der Albertina und anderen Sammlungen.* 12 vols. Vienna, 1896–1908. See especially vol. II (1897).

SEDELMEYER GALLERY, Paris. *Illustrated Catalogue of 300 Pictures by Old Masters Which Have, at Various Times, Formed Part of the Sedelmeyer Gallery.* Paris, 1898.

SLATKIN, Regina Shoolman. Review of *L'oeuvre dessiné de Boucher,* by A. Ananoff. *Master Drawings* 5 (1967): 54–66, plates 44–49.

———. "Portraits of François Boucher." *Apollo* 94 (Oct. 1971[a]): 280–91.

———. "Two Early Drawings by François Boucher." *Master Drawings* 9 (1971[b]): 398–403, plates 41 and 42.

———. "Some Boucher Drawings and Related Prints." *Master Drawings* 10 (1972): 264–83, plates 30–41.

———. "François Boucher: St. John the Baptist, A Study in Religious Imagery." *The Minneapolis Institute of Arts Bulletin* 62 (1975): 4–27.

———. "Abraham Bloemaert and François Boucher: Affinity and Relationship." *Master Drawings* 14 (1976): 247–60, plates 1–15.

———. "The Fêtes Italiennes: Their Place in Boucher's Oeuvre." *Metropolitan Museum Journal* 12 (1977): 130–39.

———. "The New Boucher Catalogue." *The Burlington Magazine* 121 (Feb. 1979): 117–23, figs. 76–77, 80–88.

SOULAVIE, J. L., l'aîné. *Mémoires Historiques et Anecdotes de la Cour de France pendant la faveur de la Marquise de Pompadour . . . , ouvrage conservé dans les porte-feuilles de Madame la Maréchale D'[Estrees?].* Paris, 1802.

SOULLIE, L., & MASSON, Ch. "Catalogue raisonné de l'oeuvre peint et dessiné de François Boucher." In *François Boucher,* by André Michel. Paris, 1906.

SOYER, L. C. "François Boucher." In *Encyclopédie des Gens du Monde,* vol. III: 762. Paris, 1834.

STANDEN, Edith A. "The Croome Court Tapestries." In *Decorative Art from the Samuel H. Kress Collection,* by Dauterman, Parker & Standen: 7–21, 45–52. [London], 1964.

———. "The Story of the Emperor of China: A Beauvais Tapestry Series." *Metropolitan Museum Journal* 11 (1976): 103–17.

———. "Some Notes on the Cartoons Used at the Gobelins and Beauvais Tapestry Manufactories in the Eighteenth Century." *The J. Paul Getty Museum Journal* 4 (1977[a]): 25–28.

———. "Fêtes Italiennes: Beauvais Tapestries after Boucher in The Metropolitan Museum of Art." *Metropolitan Museum Journal* 12 (1977[b]): 107–30.

———. "Three Ladies in Tapestry." In *Studies in Textile History,* edited by Veronika Gervers: 335–37. Toronto: Royal Ontario Museum, 1977[c].

———. "The *Amours des Dieux*: A Series of Beauvais Tapestries after Boucher." *Metropolitan Museum Journal* 19/20 (1984–85): 63–84. To be published 1986.

STAVENOW, Åke. *Carl Hårleman.* Uppsala, 1927.

STERNBERG, V., & C. *Exhibition of Important Tapestries.* London, 1965.

STOLLREITHER, E., ed. *Ein deutscher Maler und Hofmann: Lebenserrinerungen des Johann Christian von Mannlich 1741–1822.* Berlin, 1910.

———. *Rokoko und Revolution.* Berlin, 1913. Second edition of *Ein deutscher Maler. . . .*

STUFFMANN, Margaret. "Les tableaux de la collection de Pierre Crozat." *Gazette des Beaux-Arts* 6th ser., 72 (July-Sept. 1968): 11–144. Especially the annex, "Tableaux acquis par Crozat de Thiers: Notices extraites de l'inventaire établi par François Tronchin en 1771, en vue de l'acquisition de l'ensemble de la collection par Catherine II," 115–35.

TADGELL, Christopher. *Ange-Jacques Gabriel.* London, 1978.

TENNER, Helmut. *Mannheimer Kunstsammler und Kunsthändler bis zur Mitte des 19en. Jahrhunderts.* Heidelberg, 1966.

*THEATRE DES PETITS APPARTEMENS* [à Versailles]. Vol. I, *Recueil des Comédies et Ballets representés sur le Théâtre des petits Appartemens pendant l'Hiver de 1747 à 1748*; vols. II & III, *Divertissemens du Théâtre des petits Appartemens pendant l'Hiver de 1748 à 1749*; vol. IV, . . . *pendant l'Hiver de 1749 à 1750.*

THIBAUDEAU, A. W. *Catalogue of the Collection of Autograph Letters and Historical Documents Formed between 1865 and 1882 by Alfred Morrison.* Compiled and annotated by A.W.T. Vol. I. N.p., 1883.

THIERY, [Luc-Vincent]. *Guide des Amateurs et des Etrangers Voyageurs à Paris. . . .* 2 vols. Paris, 1787.

———. *Guide des Amateurs et des Etrangers Voyageurs . . . aux Environs de Paris.* 2 vols. Paris, 1788.

THIRION, H. *La vie privée des financiers au XVIIIe siècle.* Paris, 1895.

THORE, Théophile. "Collection de M. de Cypierre." *Le Constitutionnel* [Paris], 1 Oct. 1844: 1–3.

TOLEDO MUSEUM OF ART. *European Paintings.* Toledo, Ohio, 1976.

TORNEZY, M-A. *Bergeret en Italie 1773–1774.* Paris, 1895.

TOURNEUX, Maurice. "Boucher, peintre de la vie intime." *Gazette des Beaux-Arts* 3d ser., 18 (Nov. 1897): 390–92.

TOWNSEND, Gertrude. "A Pastoral by François Boucher." *Bulletin of the Boston Museum of Fine Arts*: 38 (Dec. 1940): 81–86.

*Les TRESORS d'Art en Russie* (in Russian). 1901–07. Published annually by the Société Impériale d'Encouragement des Beaux-Arts.

TREVOR-ROPER, Patrick. *The World through Blunted Sight.* London, 1970.

UNDERHILL, Gertrude, & MAILEY, Jean. "Bequest of John L. Severance, 1936: Tapestries." *Bulletin of the Cleveland Museum of Art* 29 (Nov. 1942): 148–50.

VAUCAIRE, M. "Les tapisseries de Beauvais sur les cartons de F. Boucher." *Les Arts* 7 (Aug. 1902): 10–15.

VERLET, Pierre. "Un mobilier Delanois convert en tapisserie de Beauvais." *Bulletin des Musées de France* 11 (1946): 13–14.

———. "Furniture and Objets d'Art." In *The Joys of Collecting,* by J. Paul Getty: 139–67. New York, 1965.

———. *The Eighteenth Century in France.* Rutland, Vt. 1967.

VIATTE, Françoise. Review of *Caricatures d'Anton Maria Zanetti,* by A. Bettagno. [Exh. cat. 1969, Venice.] *Revue de l'art* 9 (1970): 92–93.

VICTORIA AND ALBERT MUSEUM, London. Department of Ceramics. *Catalogue of English Porcelain, Earthenware, Enamels and Glass collected by Charles Schreiber Esq. M. P. and the Lady Charlotte Elizabeth Schreiber and presented to the Museum in 1884,* by Bernard Rackham. Vol. III, *Enamels and Glass.* London, 1924.

VILAIN, Jacques. "Une esquisse de Jean-François de Troy au musée de Lille." *La Revue du Louvre . . . ,* 1971, no. 6: 353–56.

VIRCH, Claus. *Master Drawings in the Collection of Walter C. Baker.* [New York], 1962.

VIRGINIA MUSEUM OF FINE ARTS, Richmond. *European Art in the Virginia Museum of Fine Arts.* Richmond, 1966.

VOLTAIRE, François Marie Arouet de. *Oeuvres complètes.* Vol. XXXIX (June 1757). Paris, 1880.

VOSS, Hermann. "François Boucher's Early Development." *The Burlington Magazine* 95 (Mar. 1953): 81–93.

———. "François Boucher's Early Development—Addenda." *The Burlington Magazine* 96 (July 1954): 206–10.

———. "Repliken im Oeuvre von François Boucher." In *Studies in the History of Art Dedicated to William E. Suida*: 353–60. New York, 1959.

*WALLACE COLLECTION CATALOGUES: Pictures and Drawings.* 16th ed. London, 1968.

*WALLACE COLLECTION CATALOGUES: Catalogue of Miniatures,* by Graham Reynolds. London, 1980.

WARD, Roger. "A Drawing for Boucher's *Jupiter and Callisto* at Kansas City." *The Burlington Magazine* 125 (Dec. 1983): 753.

WARK, Robert Rodger. *Decorative Art in the Huntington Collection.* San Marino, Calif., 1961.

WATELET, [Claude-Henri], & LEVESQUE, [Pierre-Charles]. *Encyclopédie Méthodique: Beaux Arts.* Vol. I: Paris and Liège, 1788; vol. II: Paris, 1791; plate vol.: Paris, 1805. Subsequently republished in reduced format and without plates, as *Dictionnaire des Arts de Peinture, Sculpture et Gravure,* 5 vols., Paris, 1792.

WATSON, Francis. *The Wrightsman Collection.* Vol. I, *Furniture.* New York: Metropolitan Museum of Art, 1966. *See also* ERIKSEN.

WEBER, Wilhelm. *Johann Christian von Mannlich.* Zweibrücken, 1970.

WEIGERT, Roger-Armand. "La manufacture royale de tapisseries de Beauvais en 1754." *Bulletin de la Société de l'Histoire de l'Art français,* 1933: 226–42.

WILDENSTEIN, Daniel. *Documents inédits sur les artistes français du XVIIIe siècle.* Paris, 1966.

———. *Inventaires après décès d'artistes et de collectionneurs français du XVIIIe siècle.* Paris, 1967.

———. "Les tableaux italiens dans les catalogues de ventes parisiennes du XVIII<sup>e</sup> siècle." *Gazette des Beaux-Arts* 6th ser., 100 (July–Aug. 1982): 1–48.

WILDENSTEIN, Daniel, & ANANOFF, Alexandre. See ANANOFF & WILDENSTEIN.

WILDENSTEIN, Daniel, & MANDEL, Gabriele. *L'opera completa di Fragonard.* Milan, 1972.

WILDENSTEIN, Daniel, & Guy. *Documents complémentaires au Catalogue de l'oeuvre de Louis David.* Paris, 1973.

WILDENSTEIN, Georges. *Lancret.* Paris, 1924.

———. *Mélanges.* Paris, 1926.

———. *Chardin.* Paris, 1933.

———. "L'abbé de Saint-Non: Artiste et mécène." *Gazette des Beaux-Arts* 6th ser., 54 (Nov. 1959): 225–44.

———. *The Paintings of Fragonard.* London, 1960.

———. "Un amateur de Boucher et de Fragonard: Jacques-Onésyme Bergeret (1715–1785)." *Gazette des Beaux-Arts* 6th ser., 58 (July–Aug. 1961): 39–84.

WILLE, J[ohann] G[eorg]. *Mémoires et journal.* Edited by Georges Duplessis. 2 vols. Paris, 1857.

WILSON, Gillian. "New Information on French Furniture at the Henry E. Huntington Library and Art Gallery." *The J. Paul Getty Museum Journal* 4 (1977[a]): 29–31.

———. *Decorative Arts in the J. Paul Getty Museum.* [Malibu], 1977[b].

WINGFIELD DIGBY, G. F. "The Tapestries at Burlington House." *The Burlington Magazine* 92 (Feb. 1950): 46–50.

ZAHLE, E. "François Boucher's dobbelte billedvaevning." *Det Danske Kunstindustrimuseum Virksomhed,* 1959–64: 58–69.

ZAVA BOCCAZZI, Franca. *Pittoni.* Venice, 1977.

ZICK, Gisela. "D'après Boucher: Die *Vallée de Montmorency* und die europäische Porzellanplastik." *Keramos* 29 (July 1965): 3–47.

———. "Les Oies de Frère Philippe." *Keramos* 72 (May 1976): 17–28.

# EXHIBITION CATALOGUES

1860, PARIS, 26 boulevard des Italiens [Martinet]. *Catalogue de Tableaux et Dessins de l'Ecole Française, principalement du XVIII<sup>e</sup> Siècle, tirés des Collections d'Amateurs et exposés au profit de la Caisse de secours des Artistes Peintres, Sculpteurs, Architectes et Dessinateurs,* rédigé par M. Ph. Burty. 2d ed.

1874, PARIS, Palais de la Présidence du Corps Législatif. *Explication des Ouvrages de Peinture exposés au profit de la Colonisation de l'Algérie par les Alsaciens-Lorrains.* 23 avril ff. *Catalogue supplémentaire des Ouvrages de Peinture.* 22 juin ff.

1888, PARIS, [Hôtel de Chimay]. *Catalogue de l'Exposition de l'Art Français sous Louis XIV et sous Louis XV au profit de l'Oeuvre de l'Hospitalité de Nuit.*

1898, LONDON, Art Gallery of the Corporation of London [Guildhall]. *Catalogue of the Loan Collection of Pictures by Painters of the French School,* by A. G. Temple.

1901, PARIS, Palais des Beaux-Arts de la Ville de Paris [Petit Palais]. *Exposition de l'Enfance.*

1902, LONDON, Art Gallery of the Corporation of London [Guildhall]. *Catalogue of the Exhibition of a Selection of Works by French and English Painters of the Eighteenth Century,* by A. G. Temple.

1910, BERLIN, Königliche Akademie der Künste. *Ausstellung von Werken französischer Kunst des XVIII Jahrhunderts.*

1912, NEW YORK, The New Allom Galleries [New Burlington Galleries]. *Dickens Centenary Exhibition of Old Masters: Catalogue of Paintings.*

1921, LONDON, Victoria and Albert Museum. *The Franco-British Exhibition of Textiles, 1921.*

1926, NEW YORK, Wildenstein Galleries. *Paintings and Drawings of the French Eighteenth Century.*

1928, PARIS, Galerie d'Art Sambon. *Exposition des Paysagistes Vénitiens et Français des XVII<sup>e</sup> et XVIII<sup>e</sup> Siècles.*

1929, HARTFORD, Wadsworth Atheneum, Morgan Memorial. *Loan Exhibition of French Art of the XVIII Century.*

1932, PARIS, Fondation Foch, Hôtel de M. Jean Charpentier. *Exposition François Boucher.*

1935, LONDON, Frank T. Sabin. *A Descriptive Catalogue of a Collection of Paintings by French and Venetian XVIIIth Century Masters.*

1936, DALLAS, Museum of Fine Arts. *The Centennial Exposition, Department of Fine Arts: Catalogue of The Exhibition of Paintings, Sculptures, Graphic Arts.*

1939, NEW YORK, World's Fair. *Masterpieces of Art: Catalogue of European Paintings and Sculpture from 1300–1800.*

1942, NEW YORK, Parke-Bernet Galleries. *French and English Art Treasures of the XVIII Century.*

1945, BUENOS AIRES, Wildenstein & Co. *Obras maestras de la pintura francesa des siglo XVIII.*

1949, LONDON, Royal Academy. *Landscape in French Art.*

1951, GENEVA, Musée d'Art et d'Histoire. *De Watteau à Cezanne.*

1951, OBERLIN, Allen Memorial Art Museum. "Exhibition of *Master Drawings of the 18th Century in France and Italy.*" *Allen Memorial Art Museum Bulletin* 8, 2 (Winter, 1951): 50–79.

1952, LONDON, Frank T. Sabin. *Spring Exhibition.*

1954, GENEVA, Musée Rath. *Trésors des Collections romandes (Ecoles étrangères).*

1956, NEW HAVEN, Yale University Art Gallery. *Pictures Collected by Yale Alumni.*

1957, PARIS, Musée des Arts Décoratifs. *Besançon: Le plus ancien Musée de France.*

1958, BORDEAUX, Bibliothèque Municipal. *Victor Louis et Varsovie.*

1958, MUNICH, Residenz. *The Age of the Rococo: Art and Culture of the Eighteenth Century.*

1959, ROME, [Palazzo delle Esposizioni]. *Il Settecento a Roma.*

1964, BEAUVAIS, Hôtel de Ville. *Trois Siècles de Tapisseries de Beauvais.*

1964, PARIS, Galerie Cailleux. *François Boucher, Premier Peintre du Roi 1703–1770.*

1964, PARIS, Institut Néerlandais; Amsterdam, Rijksprentenkabinett. *Le dessin français de Claude à Cezanne dans les collections hollandaises, complété d'un choix d'autographes des artistes exposés.*

1965–66, PARIS, Ministère d'Etat Affaires Culturelles. *Chefs-d'oeuvre de la Peinture française dans les Musées de Leningrad et de Moscou.*

1968, LONDON, Royal Academy of Arts. *Winter Exhibition. France in the Eighteenth Century.*

1968, NEW YORK, H. Shickman Gallery. *Exhibition of Old Master Drawings.*

1969, HAMBURG, Kunsthalle. *Französische Zeichnungen aus dem Museum Besançon.*

1969, PARIS, Musée du Louvre. *Hommage à Louis La Caze.*

1969, VENICE, Fondazione Giorgio Cini. *Caricature di Anton Maria Zanetti,* by Alessandro Bettagno.

1970, LENINGRAD, Ermitazh. *François Boucher (1703–1770)* (in Russian).

1970, ROUEN, Musée des Beaux-Arts. *Jean Restout (1692–1768).*

1972, MINNEAPOLIS, Minneapolis Institute of Arts. *The J. Paul Getty Museum.*

1973, BERLIN, Schloss Charlottenburg. *China und Europa: Chinaverständnis und Chinamode im 17. und 18. Jahrhundert.*

1973, CHOLET, Musée. *Pierre-Charles Trémolières (Cholet, 1703–Paris, 1739).*

1973, NEW YORK, William H. Schab Gallery; Los Angeles County Museum of Art; Indianapolis, Museum of Art. *Woodner Collection II: Old Master Drawings from the XV to the XVIII Century.*

1973, POZNAN, Muzeum Narodowe. *Sztuka francuska w zbiorach polskich 1230–1830.* Catalogue by K. Secomska.

1973–74, WASHINGTON, D.C., National Gallery of Art; Chicago, The Art Institute. *François Boucher in North American Collections: 100 Drawings.*

1974, AMSTERDAM, Rijksprentenkabinett. *Franse tekenkunst van de 18de eeuw uit Nederlandse verzamelingen.*

1974, PARIS, Hôtel de la Monnaie. *Louis XV: Un moment de perfection de l'art français.*

1974–75, LONDON, Heim Gallery; Cambridge, Fitzwilliam Museum; Birmingham, City Museum and Art Gallery; Glasgow, Art Gallery and Museum. *From Poussin to Puvis de Chavannes: A Loan Exhibition of French Drawings from the Collections of the Musée des Beaux-Arts at Lille.*

1975, BRUSSELS, Palais des Beaux-Arts. *De Watteau à David: Peintures et Dessins des musées de province français.*

1975, PARIS, Galerie Cailleux. *Eloge de l'Ovale: Peintures et pastels du XVIII<sup>e</sup> siècle français.*

1975–76, TOLEDO, Museum of Art; Chicago, The Art Institute; Ottawa, National Gallery of Canada. *The Age of Louis XV: French Painting 1710–1774.*

1976, CHICAGO, The Art Institute. *Selected Works of 18th Century French Art in the Collections of The Art Institute of Chicago.*

1976, PARIS, Louvre. *Les dossiers du département des peintures 12: Technique de la peinture—l'atelier.*

1977, NICE, Musée Chéret; Clermont-Ferrand, Musée Bargoin; Nancy, Musée des Beaux-Arts. *Carle Vanloo,* by Marie-Catherine Sahut.

1977, TROYES, Musée des Beaux-Arts; Nîmes, Musée des Beaux-Arts; Rome, Villa Medici. *Charles-Joseph Natoire.*

1977–78, LONDON, Heim Gallery; Liverpool, Walker Art Gallery; Dublin, National Gallery of Ireland; Birmingham, City Museum & Art Gallery. *The Finest Drawings from the Museums of Angers.* French edition: Angers, Musée d'Angers. *Cent Dessins des Musées d'Angers.*

1977–78, PARIS, Grand Palais. *Porcelaines de Vincennes, les origines de Sèvres.*

1977–78, PARIS, Orangerie des Tuileries. *Collections de Louis XIV.*

1978, BRAUNSCHWEIG, Herzog Anton-Ulrich-Museum. *Die Sprache der Bilder.*

1978, LONDON, Artemis/David Carritt Ltd. *18th Century French Paintings, Drawings and Sculpture.*

1979, PARIS, Grand Palais; Cleveland, Museum of Art; Boston, Museum of Fine Arts. *Chardin.*

1979–81, WASHINGTON, D.C., National Gallery of Art [and eight other institutions in the U.S.A.]. *Old Master Paintings from the Collection of Baron Thyssen-Bornemisza.* Catalogue by Allen Rosenbaum.

1980, ALBUQUERQUE, University of New Mexico Art Museum. "French Eighteenth-Century Oil Sketches from an English Collection: Catalogue to an Exhibition . . .," by Peter Walch. *New Mexico Studies in the Fine Arts* 5 (1980).

1980, LONDON, Agnew's. *Old Master Paintings & Drawings.*

1980, LONDON, Heim Gallery. *100 of the Finest Drawings from Polish Collections.*

1980, MUNICH, Residenz. *Wittelsbach und Bayern.* II/2, *Um Glauben und Reich: Kurfürst Maximilian I.*

1980, NEW YORK, Wildenstein & Co. *François Boucher: A Loan Exhibition for the Benefit of the New York Botanical Garden.*

1980, NORD, Musées du Nord. *La Peinture française au XVIIe et XVIIIe siècles.* Trésors des Musées du Nord de la France, vol. IV.

1980, PARIS, Galerie de la Seita. *La rue de Grenelle.*

1981, COLOGNE, Wallraf-Richartz-Museum. *Johann Anton de Peters.*

1981, PARIS, Musée Cernuschi. *Grandes et petites heures du parc Monceau.*

1981–82, PARIS, Ecole Nationale Supérieure des Beaux-Arts; [Malibu], The J. Paul Getty Museum; Hamburg, Kunsthalle. *De Michel-Ange à Géricault: Dessins de la donation Armand-Valton.*

1982, NEW YORK, Maurice Segoura Gallery. *From Watteau to David: A Century of French Art.*

1982, TOKYO, Metropolitan Art Museum; Kumamoto, Prefectural Museum of Art. *François Boucher.*

1982–83, DIJON, Musée des Beaux-Arts. *La peinture dans la peinture.*

1982–83, PARIS, Galeries nationales du Grand Palais. *J-B. Oudry.* Modified version exhibited Fort Worth, Kimbell Art Museum, and Kansas City, The Nelson-Atkins Museum of Art, 1983.

1983, ATLANTA, High Museum of Art. *The Rococo Age.* Catalogue by Eric M. Zafran.

1983, KARLSRUHE, Schloss, Badisches Landesmuseum. *Caroline Luise: Markgräfin von Baden, 1723–1783.*

1983, KARLSRUHE, Staatliche Kunsthalle, Kupferstichkabinett. *Die französischen Zeichnungen 1570–1930.*

1983, LOS ANGELES, Los Angeles County Museum of Art. *An Elegant Art.*

1983, PARIS, Musée du Louvre, Cabinet des Dessins. *Les collections du comte d'Orsay: Dessins du Musée du Louvre.*

1983–84, ROTTERDAM, Museum Boymans-van Beuningen; Braunschweig, Herzog-Anton-Ulrich-Museum. *Schilderkunst mit de eerste hand: Olieverfschetsen von Tintoretto tot Goya/Malerei aus erster Hand: Ölskizzen von Tintoretto bis Goya.*

1984, LANGRES, Musée du Breuil de Saint-Germain. *Diderot et la Critique de Salon, 1759–1781.*

1984, LONDON, Kate Ganz Limited. *Old Master Drawings: Catalogue Number 4.*

1984, MANCHESTER, City Art Gallery. *François Boucher: Paintings, Drawings and Prints from the Nationalmuseum Stockholm.*

1984, NEW YORK, Didier Aaron, Inc. *French Master Drawings.*

1984, NEW YORK, Pierpont Morgan Library. *French Drawings, 1550–1825.*

1984, PARIS, Hôtel de la Monnaie. *Diderot & l'Art de Boucher à David. Les Salons: 1759–1781.*

1984, PARIS, Musée du Louvre, Cabinet des Dessins. *Acquisitions du Cabinet des Dessins 1973–1983.*

1984, PARIS, Musée Rodin. *La rue Saint-Dominique: Hôtels et Amateurs.*

1984, STUTTGART, Staatsgalerie, Graphische Sammlung; Zurich, Museum Bellerive. *Kompositionen im Halbrund: Fächer-blätter aus vier Jahrhunderten.* Catalogue by Monika Kopplin.

1984–85, BALTIMORE, Baltimore Museum of Art. *Regency to Empire: French Printmaking, 1715–1814.*

1984–85, WASHINGTON, National Gallery of Art; Paris, Galeries Nationales du Grand Palais; Berlin, Schloss Charlottenburg. *Watteau, 1684–1721.*

1985, NEW YORK, Stair Sainty Matthiesen. *The First Painters of the King: French Royal Taste from Louis XIV to the Revolution.*

1985, PARIS, Galerie Cailleux. *Oeuvres de jeunesse: De Watteau à Ingres.*